GCSE

modern
world
history
second
edition

Ben Walsh

Hodder Murray

A MEMBER OF THE HODDER HEADLINE GROUP

for Julia, Helen and Dan

FOCUS TASK

Support worksheets and extra help with the focus tasks and activities in this book can be found in the Teacher's Resource Book.

Note: Some written sources have been adapted or abbreviated to make them accessible to all students, while faithfully preserving the sense of the original.

Words in SMALL CAPITALS are defined in the glossary on page 424.

The main cover photo shows a young man staring through the Berlin wall as it is dismantled by German citizens in 1989.

First published in 1996
by Hodder Murray, a member of the Hodder Headline Group
338 Euston Road
London NW1 3BH

This second edition first published 2001

Reprinted 2001, 2002 (three times), 2003, 2004 (twice), 2005 , 2006 , 2007

Layouts by Fiona Webb
Illustrations by Karen Donnelly, Oxford Designers and Illustrators
Cover design by John Townson/Creation
Typeset in 11/13pt Garamond Light Condensed by Dorchester Typesetting, Dorchester
Colour separations by Colourscript, Mildenhall, Suffolk
Printed and bound in Dubai.

A CIP catalogue record for this book is available from the British Library.

Student's Book 978 0 719 577130
Teacher's Resource Book 0 719577714 4

Contents

Acknowledgements

The author and publishers would like to thank Craig Mair for permission to reproduce extracts from *Britain at War 1914–1919*. The lyrics to 'The Times They Are A-Changin'' on page 388 are reproduced by kind permission of Bob Dylan and ATV Music Publishing.

Photo credits

Cover *Main picture* Today/Rex Features, *remaining pictures* Popperfoto; **p.2** Time Pix/ Mansell Collection/Rex; **p.8** Imperial War Museum, London; **p.9** Hulton Getty; **p.14** Imperial War Museum, London; **p.15** *tl, tr & bl* Imperial War Museum, London; **p.16** © Punch Ltd; **p.19** Oberösterreichisches Landesmuseum, Linz (photo: B. Ecker) © DACS 2001; **p.20** Imperial War Museum, London; **p.21** *tl, tr & b* Imperial War Museum, London; **p.23** *t* Imperial War Museum, London, *b* Imperial War Museum, London/Bridgeman Art Library, London; **p.24** The Art Archive/Imperial War Museum; **p.25** Imperial War Museum, London; **p.26** *l* Illustrated London News Picture Library, *r* William Kimber Publishers, London; **p.27** Imperial War Museum, London/Bridgeman Art Library, London © ADAGP, Paris and DACS, London 2001; **p.28** *l & r* Imperial War Museum, London; **p.29** *l & r* Illustrated London News Picture Library; **p.33** *t* Source; *Drawing Support: Murals in the North of Ireland*, Belfast, Beyond the Pale Publications, 1992, p.12, (photo: W. J Rolston) *b* The Liddell Collection, University of Leeds Library; **p.34** *t* Hulton Getty, *b* Imperial War Museum, London; **p.35** Imperial War Museum, London; **p.39** Imperial War Museum, London; **p.46** *tl & tr* Imperial War Museum, London; **p.48** *both* Imperial War Museum, London; **p.49** *both* Imperial War Museum, London; **p.55** *both* Mary Evans Picture Library; **p.56** *tl & tr* Mary Evans Picture Library, *br* Hulton Getty; **p.57** Hulton Getty; **p.61** *l* © Punch Ltd; **p.62** *b* Mary Evans/Fawcett Library; **p.63** *tl* Mary Evans/Fawcett Library, *tr* Mary Evans Picture Library, *b* Popperfoto; **p.64** *l* Mary Evans Picture Library, *r* Popperfoto; **p.66** Imperial War Museum, London; **p.68** *l, c & r* Imperial War Museum, London; **p.69** *t* Mary Evans/Fawcett Library, *b* Reproduced with the permission of the Library Committee of the Religious Society of Friends; **p.70** Weidenfeld & Nicolson Archives; **p.71** *both* Imperial War Museum, London; **p.72** John Frost Historical Newspapers; **p.74** *t* The Robert Opie Collection, *b* Imperial War Museum, London; **p.76** *l* Imperial War Museum, London, *r* Falkirk Museums; **p.77** *both* Imperial War Museum, London; **p.78** Mary Evans/Fawcett Library; **p.80** Hulton Getty; **p.81** *both* Imperial War Museum, London; **p.82** Hulton Getty; **p.83** *both* Hulton Getty; **p.84** *all* © Punch Ltd; **p.88** Ullstein; **p.89** *l* Süddeutscher Verlag Bilderdienst, *r* © Punch Ltd; **p.90** Süddeutscher Verlag Bilderdienst; **p.91** News International Syndication; **p.94** Süddeutscher Verlag Bilderdienst; **p.97** Peter Newark's American Pictures; **p.98** David King; **p.99** David King; **p.100** *both* David King; **p.101** *both* David King; **p.103** David King; **p.104** *all* © Novosti (London); **p.105** David King; **p.107** *t* © Novosti (London), *b* David King; **p.112** *t* DOCTOR ZHIVAGO © 1965 Turner Entertainment Co. A Time Warner Company. All Rights Reserved (photo: BFI Stills, Posters and Designs), *b* David King; **p.114** David King; **p.115** David King; **p.116** David King; **p.119** The British Library; **p.120** *both* David King; **p.121** David King; **p.122** David King; **p.123** *l* David King, *r* Hulton Getty; **p.127** *both* David King; **p.130** *both* David King; **p.131** David King; **p.134** *l* David King; **p.135** *l* David King, *r* B.T. Batsford Ltd; **p.136** *both* David King; **p.137** Ullstein; **p.140** *t* Bildarchiv Preussischer Kulturbesitz, *b* Hulton Getty; **p.141** Bildarchiv Preussischer Kulturbesitz; **p.142** *l* Bildarchiv Preussischer Kulturbesitz, *r* © Punch Ltd; **p.143** *t* © Bettmann/Corbis, *b* Bildarchiv Preussischer Kulturbesitz; **p.144** Süddeutscher Verlag Bilderdienst; **p.146** *t* Ullstein, *b* AKG London; **p.147** *t* Staatliche Museen zu Berlin, Preussischer Kulturbesitz, Nationalgalerie, © DACS 2001 (photo: Bildarchiv Preussischer Kulturbesitz), *b* Ullstein; **p.148** *l* Ullstein, *r* AKG London; **p.151** Bildarchiv Preussischer Kulturbesitz; **p.152** Süddeutscher Verlag Bilderdienst; **p.153** *t & bl* AKG London; **p.154** AKG London; **p.156** Süddeutscher Verlag Bilderdienst; **p.157** Evening Standard; **p.158** *tl* © Punch Ltd, *bl* Bildarchiv Preussischer Kulturbesitz, *r* Bundesarchiv Koblenz; **p.160** *t* Süddeutscher Verlag Bilderdienst, *b* Hulton Getty; **p.161** *both* Ullstein; **p.163** Wiener Library; **p.164** *tl & bl* Hulton Getty, *r* Süddeutscher Verlag Bilderdienst; **p.165** *l* Stiftung Archiv der Akademie der Künste, Berlin, Kunstsammlung, Heartfield 2252 (photo: Roman März) © DACS 2001, *r* Robert Hunt Library; **p.166** *l* Bildarchiv Preussischer Kulturbesitz, *r* AKG London; **p.168** *t* Süddeutscher Verlag Bilderdienst; **p.169** Süddeutscher Verlag Bilderdienst; **p.170** *t* Bildarchiv Preussischer Kulturbesitz, *bl* AKG London, *br* Ullstein; **p.171** *both* Ullstein; **p.172** *l* Institut für Stadtgeschichte, Frankfurt am Main, *r* Ullstein; **p.175** Bundesarchiv Koblenz; **p.176** *t* Hulton Getty, *b* Ullstein; **p.177** Popperfoto; **p.178** *bl* Kunstbibliothek Preussischer Kulturbesitz, Berlin (photo: Bildarchiv Preussischer Kulturbesitz), *br* Bildarchiv Preussischer Kulturbesitz; **p.179** *l* Deutsches Historisches Museum, Berlin, *r* Ullstein; **p.181** *t* © Elek International Rights, NY (photo: Wiener Library), *b* AKG London; **p.184** *t* Courtesy George Eastman House, New York, *bl* Culver Pictures; **p.185** *tl & br* Peter Newark's American Pictures, *tr & bl* © Bettmann/Corbis; **p.188** Peter Newark's American Pictures; **p.189** © Bettmann/Corbis; **p.190** Ford Motor Company Limited; **p.191** Peter Newark's American Pictures; **p.192** © Bettmann/Corbis; **p.193** *l* © Bettmann/Corbis, *r* Peter Newark's American Pictures; **p.194** *t & b* Peter Newark's American Pictures; **p.195** Chicago Historical Society/ Chicago Daily News (DN-068755); **p.196** *both* © Bettmann/Corbis; **p.197** *t* Culver Pictures, *b* Topham Picturepoint; **p.198** Peter Newark's American Pictures; **p.199** © Reference Center for Marxist Studies, New York; **p.200** © Bettmann/Corbis; **p.201** Time Pix/Mansell Collection/ Rex; **p.202** *l* Hulton Getty, *r* © Bettmann/Corbis; **p.203** Brown Brothers; **p.204** *t* US National Archives, Rocky Mountains Division, *b* photo: BFI Films: Stills, Posters and Designs; **p.205** © Bettmann/Corbis; **p.206** *l* Peter Newark's American Pictures, *r* Culver Pictures; **p.207** *both* © Bettmann/Corbis; **p.208** *tl* © Bettmann/Corbis, *tr* Peter Newark's American Pictures,*b* Library of Congress (LC-USZ62-703124); **p.209** *t* Topham Picturepoint, *b* Peter Newark's American Pictures; **p.213** *l* Charles Deering McCormick Library of Special Collections, Northwestern University Library, © John T. McCutcheon Jr, *r* Popperfoto; **p.214** *both* Peter Newark's American Pictures; **p.215** *t* Topham Picturepoint, *b* Peter Newark's American Pictures; **p.216** Peter Newark's American Pictures; **p.217** Culver Pictures; **p.219** *b* Tennessee Valley Authority; **p.220** Tennessee Valley Authority; **p.221** *t* © Bettmann/Corbis, *c* National Archives and Records Administration, Washington, D.C., *b* Culver Pictures; **p.222** Peter Newark's American Pictures; **p.223** *t* Weidenfeld & Nicolson Archives, *bl* © Punch Ltd, *br* courtesy Franklin D. Roosevelt Library, Hyde Park, New York; **p.224** courtesy Franklin D. Roosevelt Library, Hyde Park, New York; **p.225** Peter Newark's American Pictures; **p.226** *t & c* Walter P. Reuther Library, Wayne State University, *b* Brown Brothers; **p.227** AKG London; **p.229** © Express Newspapers, London; **p.231** *t* © New York Times 1920, *br* © Punch Ltd; **p.232** *t* Hulton Getty; **p.234** *both* United Nations © DACS 2001; **p.235** United Nations © DACS 2001; **p.236** from Newman, *Danger Spots in Europe*, Right Book Club, 1939; **p.238** © Punch Ltd; **p.239** *r* From League of Nations: Greek Refugee Settlement, 1926 II 32; **p.241** *l* © Punch Ltd, *r* Evening Standard; **p.246** Hulton Getty; **p.247** *l* Evening Standard, *r* Topham Picturepoint; **p.249** *t* Evening Standard, *b* © Express Newspapers, London; **p.250** © Punch Ltd; **p.251** Evening Standard; **p.252** Bildarchiv Preussischer Kulturbesitz; **p.253** *both* © Punch Ltd; **p.255** *t* Ullstein, *b* AKG London; **p.258** Popperfoto; **p.259** AKG London; **p.260** *l* © Tribune Media Services, Inc. All Rights Reserved. Reprinted with permission, *r* The Art Archive; **p.261** © Punch Ltd; **p.262** Topham Picturepoint; **p.263** *l* © Punch Ltd; **p.265** *t & br* Evening Standard, *bl* © Punch Ltd; **p.267** *l* Popperfoto, *r* Topham Picturepoint; **p.268** *t* © Gabriel, *b* News of the World; **p.269** *t* Evening Standard, *b* John Frost Historical Newspapers (photo: John Townson/Creation); **p.270** Ullstein; **p.271** *l* Evening Standard; **p.272** Evening Standard; **p.275** The Art Archive; **p.276** *l* Topham Picturepoint, *r* Ullstein; **p.278** *l* Peter Newark's Military Pictures, *r* Ullstein; **p.281** *l & br* Imperial War Museum, London, *tr* The Art Archive/Imperial War Museum; **p.284** Imperial War Museum, London; **p.285** © Liverpool Daily Post & Echo Syndication Department; **p.288** David King; **p.290** Ullstein; **p.293** Imperial War Museum, London; **p.294** reproduced courtesy of SSVC; **p.296** © Bettmann/Corbis; **p.297** *l* The Art Archive, *r* Atlantic Syndication; **p.298** *l* Topham Picturepoint, *r* Popperfoto; **p.299** *tl* Ullstein/Chronos Dokumentarfilm GmbH, *tr* Hulton Getty, *bl* Topham Picturepoint, *br* Associated Press/Topham; **p.301** Imperial War Museum, London; **p.302** Imperial War Museum, London; **p.303** Imperial War Museum, London; **p.304** *t* Popperfoto, *b* Imperial War Museum, London; **p.305** Topham Picturepoint; **p.306** Imperial War Museum, London; **p.307** *tl* Public Record Office Image Library, *tr* Evening Standard, *b* John Frost Historical Newspapers (photo: John Townson/Creation); **p.308** *all* Imperial War Museum, London; **p.309** *t* Hulton Getty, *b* Imperial War Museum; **p.310** Imperial War Museum, London; **p.311** *t* Imperial War Museum, London, *b* Public Record Office Image Library; **p.313** *all* Popperfoto; **p.314** *t* Imperial War Museum, London, *b* Hulton Getty; **p.315** *t* Popperfoto, *b* Hulton Getty; **p.317** Associated Press/Topham; **p.319** The Art Archive; **p.322** Associated Press/Topham; **p.323** Evening Standard; **p.325** *t* Pravda 1947, *b* Atlantic Syndication; **p.327** Printed with permission of the Norman Rockwell Family Trust, © 1943 the Norman Rockwell Family Trust (photos: The Curtis Publishing Company); **p.330** *b* Evening Standard; **p.331** *l* photo: School of Slavonic and East European Studies, University of London, *r* Evening Standard; **p.332** Hulton Getty; **p.333** *t* Evening Standard, *b* Izvestia 1963; **p.334** Izvestia 1958; **p.339** Evening Standard; **p.340** Popperfoto; **p.341** *l* Associated Press/Topham, *r* Hulton Getty; **p.344** *t* Izvestia 1949, *b* Izvestia 1961; **p.345** photo: School of Slavonic and East European Studies, University of London; **p.346** © Bettmann/Corbis; **p.347** Pravda 1960; **p.348** Popperfoto; **p.354** Associated Press/Topham; **p.357** *l* David King, *r* Topham Picturepoint; **p.358** *t* Popperfoto, *b* Nguyen Kong (Nick) Ut/Associated Press; **p.359** Topham Picturepoint; **p.360** Topham Picturepoint; **p.361** Associated Press/Topham; **p.363** © Jules Feiffer; **p.366** © Bettmann/Corbis; **p.367** *t* Popperfoto, *b* Peter Newark's American Pictures; **p.368** *both* © Corbis; **p.371** *tl* © Bettmann/Corbis, *tr* © The Mariners' Museum/Corbis, *b* © Corbis; **p.374** *t* Weidenfeld & Nicolson Archives, *bl* © Bill Mauldin, *br* © Bettmann/Corbis; **p.375** Camera Press, London; **p.377** *both* © Bettmann/Corbis; **p.379** *l* Popperfoto, *r* Fred Blackwell/Associated Press; **p.380** Bill Hudson/Associated Press; **p.381** The Lyndon Baines Johnson Library; **p.382** © Bettmann/Corbis; **p.383** Associated Press/Topham; **p.386** 'Stop Era' 1975 by Paul Szep. Copyright 1975 by the Globe Newspaper Co. (MA). Reprinted by permission of the Globe Newspaper Co. (MA) via the Copyright Clearance Center (CCC); **p.387** *t* © Bettmann/Corbis, *b* Popperfoto/Reuters; **p.388** Hulton Getty; **p.389** *l* Hulton Getty, *r* Topham Picturepoint; **p.390** Topham Picturepoint; **p.391** 'Lincoln Mourns', 1963, by Bill Mauldin reprinted with special permission from the Chicago Sun-Times, Inc. © 2001; **p.392** *t & bl* Lyndon Baines Johnson Library (photo by Yoichi R. Okamoto), *br* © Robert Pryor; **p.393** 'Unity' 1968 by Paul Szep. © 1968 by the Globe Newspaper Co. (MA). Reprinted by permission of the Globe Newspaper Co. (MA) via the Copyright Clearance Center (CCC); **p.394** from *Herblock Special Report* (W.W. Norton, 1974); **p.395** *l* © 1973 by Herblock in *The Washington Post*, *r* © Tribune Media Services, Inc. All Rights Reserved. Reprinted with permission; **p.396** *t* Hulton Getty, *b* © Black Star/Colorific (photo: Werner Wolff); **p.397** Evening Standard; **p.399** Pravda 1949; **p.400** Pravda 1960; **p.401** David King; **p.403** *t & b* Hulton Getty; **p.405** *t* Topham, *b* © Josef Koudelka/Magnum Photos; **p.406** *both* The Open University; **p.407** *t* from *In the Name of Peace*, 1959, *c & b* Associated Press; **p.408** *t* Topham Picturepoint, *br* Popperfoto; **p.409** *t* Popperfoto, *b* Izvestia 1963; **p.412** Associated Press/Topham; **p.413** Hulton Getty; **p.418** *t* Popperfoto/Czech News Agency, *b* Topham Picturepoint; **p.419** DOONESBURY © 1988 G. B. Trudeau. Reprinted with permission of UNIVERSAL PRESS SYNDICATE. All rights reserved. **p.421** Popperfoto/Reuters; **p.422** AFP/Popperfoto; **p.423** Novosti/Topham.

t = top, *b* = bottom, *l* = left, *r* = right, *c* = centre

Every effort has been made to contact copyright holders, and the publishers apologise for any omissions which they will be pleased to rectify at the earliest opportunity.

SECTION 1

The First World War

The causes of the First World War

Who should bear the blame?

FOCUS

The First World War was a deadly war that killed millions of people. At the time, people in Britain and France had no doubt that Germany was to blame for starting the war. Nowadays, many historians ask whether other countries should share the blame.

In this chapter:

- **You will find out how Europe divided itself into two alliances in the years before the war.**
- **You will investigate how and why each country in Europe built up its armies and navies and made plans for war.**
- **Finally, you will make up your own mind about whether Germany caused the war or whether other countries should share the blame.**

Murder in Sarajevo

SOURCE 1

Sunday 28 June 1914 was a bright and sunny day in Sarajevo. Sarajevo in Bosnia was preparing for a royal visit from Archduke Franz Ferdinand of Austria [see Source 2]. Crowds lined the streets and waited for the procession of cars to appear. Hidden among the crowds, however, were six teenage [Bosnian Serb] terrorists sworn to kill the Archduke. They hated him and they hated Austria. They were stationed at intervals along the riverside route which the cars would follow on their way to the Town Hall. They all had bombs and pistols in their pockets, and phials of poison which they had promised to swallow if they were caught, so that they would not give the others away. It seemed as if the plan could not fail.

Finally, the cavalcade of four large cars came into sight. The Archduke was in a green open-topped car. He looked every inch a duke, wearing a pale blue uniform, a row of glittering medals and a military hat decorated with green ostrich feathers. Beside him sat his wife Sophie, looking beautiful in a white dress and a broad hat and waving politely to the crowd.

At 10.15 the cars passed Mehmedbasic, the first in line of the waiting killers. He took fright, did nothing, and then escaped. The next assassin, Cabriolvic, also lost his nerve and did nothing. But then as the cars passed the Cumurja Bridge, Cabrinovic threw his bomb, swallowed his poison, and jumped into the river. The Archduke saw the bomb coming and threw it off his car, but it exploded under the car behind, injuring several people. Now there was total confusion as the procession accelerated away, fearing more bombs. Meanwhile the police dragged Cabrinovic out of the river. His cyanide was old and had not worked.

The Archduke was driven to the Town Hall, where he demanded to be taken to visit the bomb victims in hospital. Fearing more terrorists, the officials decided to take a new route to avoid the crowds, but this was not properly explained to the driver of the Archduke's car. Moreover, no police guard went with the procession.

Meanwhile the other assassins, on hearing the bomb explode, assumed the Archduke was dead and left – all except Princip, who soon discovered the truth. Miserably he wandered across the street towards Schiller's delicatessen and café.

Princip was standing outside the café when, at 10.45, the Archduke's car suddenly appeared beside him and turned into Franz Josef Street. This was a mistake, for according to the new plan the procession should have continued straight along the Appel Quay. As the driver realised he had taken a wrong turn he stopped and started to reverse. Princip could hardly believe his luck. Pulling an automatic pistol from the right-hand pocket of his coat, he fired two shots at a range of just 3 or 4 metres. He could not miss. One bullet pierced the Archduke's neck and the other ricocheted off the car into Sophie's stomach. Fifteen minutes later she died and the Archduke followed soon after.

Princip was immediately seized. He managed to swallow his poison, but it did not work and he was taken off to prison. All the plotters except Mehmedbasic were eventually caught, but only the organiser, Ilic, was hanged, for the others were too young for the death penalty. Princip died in an Austrian jail, however, in April 1918, aged twenty-three.

Adapted from *Britain at War* by Craig Mair, 1982.

SOURCE 2

The Archduke Franz Ferdinand and his wife Sophie arrive in Sarajevo. The Archduke was heir to the throne of Austria, whose powerful empire covered much of central Europe (see page 4).

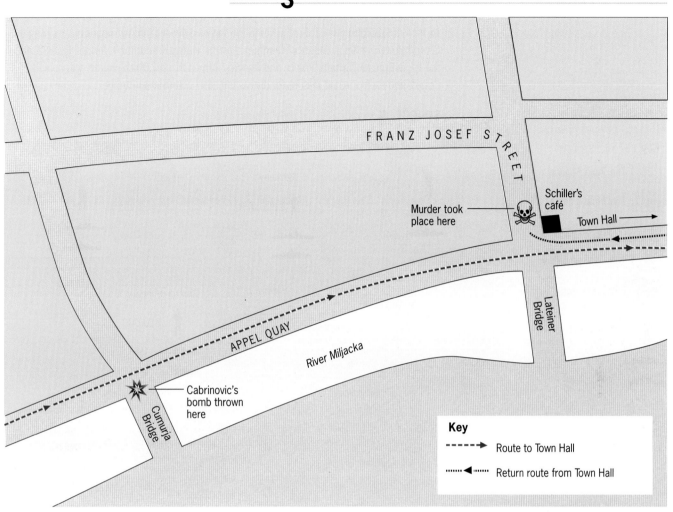

The route taken by Archduke Franz Ferdinand's car in Sarajevo, 28 June 1914.

At his trial, Princip said: 'I am not a criminal, for I destroyed a bad man. I thought I was right.' Two years later he said that if he had known what was to follow he would never have fired the two fatal shots – but his regret was too late. Within six weeks of the Archduke's assassination, almost all of Europe had been dragged into the bloodiest war in history.

On 23 July: Austria blamed Serbia for the death of Franz Ferdinand and sent it an ultimatum.

On 28 July: Austria declared war on Serbia and shelled its capital, Belgrade.

On 29 July: The Russian army got ready to help Serbia defend itself against the Austrian attack.

Germany warned Russia not to help the Serbs.

On 1 August: Germany declared war on Russia. It also began to move its army towards France and Belgium.

On 2 August: The French army was put on a war footing ready to fight any German invasion.

On 3 August: Germany declared war on France and invaded Belgium. Britain ordered Germany to withdraw from Belgium.

On 4 August: With the Germans still in Belgium, Britain declared war on Germany.

On 6 August: Austria declared war on Russia.

To understand **why** the murders in Sarajevo led so quickly to an all-out war involving all the main European powers, we need to find out more about what Europe was like in 1914.

1 There were many moments during 28 June 1914 when events could have turned out differently. Study the account of the murders in Source 1 and list any moments at which a different decision might have saved the lives of the Archduke and his wife.

2 Do you think that if the Archduke had not been shot, the war would not have started? Give your reasons. (These are only your first thoughts. You can revise your opinion later.)

The Alliances

In 1914 the six most powerful countries in Europe were divided into two opposing ALLIANCES: the Central Powers or Triple Alliance (Germany, Austria–Hungary and Italy), formed in 1882, and the Triple Entente (Britain, France and Russia), formed in 1907. Each country was heavily armed, and each one had reasons for distrusting other countries in Europe.

SOURCE 4

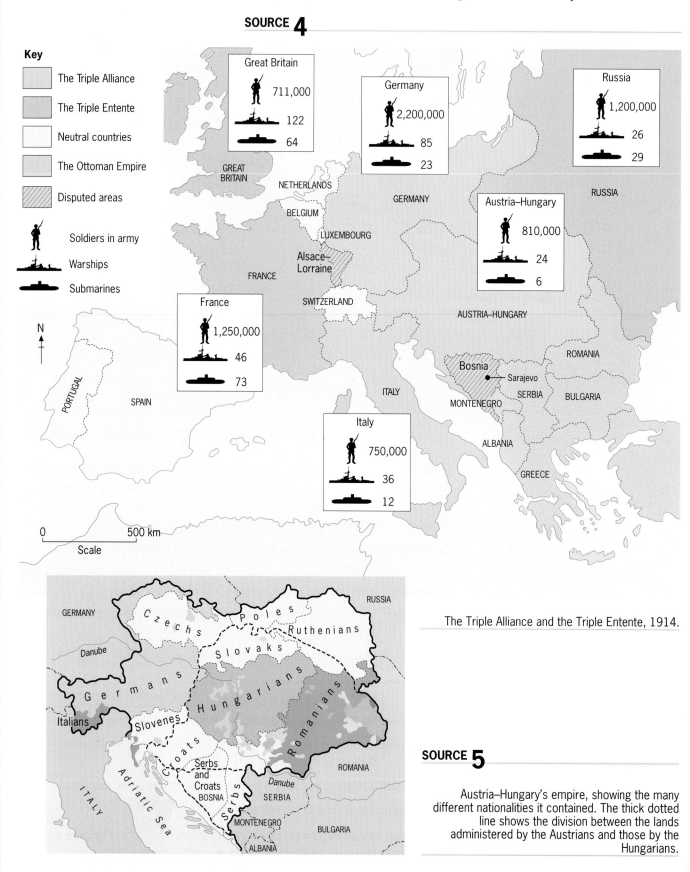

The Triple Alliance and the Triple Entente, 1914.

SOURCE 5

Austria–Hungary's empire, showing the many different nationalities it contained. The thick dotted line shows the division between the lands administered by the Austrians and those by the Hungarians.

The Central Powers or the Triple Alliance

Germany

Before 1870 Germany was a collection of small independent states of which Prussia was the most powerful. In 1870 the Prussian statesman Bismarck won a war against France, after which he united the many German states into a new and powerful German empire. Germany took from France the important industrial area of Alsace–Lorraine and, to guard against a revenge attack from the French, formed an alliance with Austria–Hungary and Italy.

The new Germany was especially successful in industry. By 1914 German industry had overtaken Britain's and was second in the world only to that of the USA.

However, Germany's leaders had greater ambitions, as well as concerns.

- The German Kaiser felt that Germany should be a world power and should have overseas COLONIES and an empire like France and Britain had (see Source 7). The Germans had established two colonies in Africa, but they wanted more.
- In the 1890s the Kaiser ordered the building of a large navy, which soon became the world's second most powerful fleet. Britain's was the largest and most powerful.
- German leaders were very worried by what they called 'encirclement'. Friendship between Russia to the east and France to the west was seen as an attempt to 'surround' and threaten Germany.
- Germany was also concerned by the huge build-up of arms, especially in Russia, and was itself building up a vast army.

Austria–Hungary

Austria–Hungary was a sprawling empire in central Europe. It was made up of people of different ethnic groups: Germans, Czechs, Slovaks, Serbs and many others. Each group had its own customs and language. Many of these groups wanted independence from Austria–Hungary.

- In the north the Czech people wanted to rule themselves.
- The Slav people in the south-west (especially the Croats) wanted their own state.
- The Serbs living in the south wanted to be joined to the neighbouring state of Serbia.

By 1914 the main concern of the Emperor of Austria–Hungary was how to keep this fragmented empire together.

Austria–Hungary also faced problems from neighbouring states:

- Its newly independent neighbour Serbia was becoming a powerful force in the Balkans. Austria was very anxious that it should not become any stronger.
- Another neighbour, Russia, supported the Serbs, and had a very strong army.

Italy

Like Germany, Italy was formed from a collection of smaller states. At first, its main concern was to get its government established, but by 1914 the country was settled and was looking to 'flex its muscles'.

Like some of the other European powers, Italy wanted to set up colonies and build up an overseas empire. With this aim in mind, Italy joined Germany and Austria in the Triple Alliance. However, there is some evidence that Germany and Austria did not entirely trust their ally. In any case, Italy was not a strong industrial or military power.

The Triple Entente

Britain

In the nineteenth century Britain had tried not to get involved in European politics. Its attitude became known as 'splendid isolation' as it concentrated on its huge overseas empire (see Source 7). For most of the nineteenth century, Britain had regarded France and Russia as its two most dangerous rivals. However, by the early 1900s the picture had begun to change.

European alliances in 1914.

1 Do you think that preserving peace was a priority for Germany, Austria–Hungary or Italy?

The three main reasons were that:

- France and Britain had reached a number of agreements about colonies in North Africa in 1904.
- Russia was defeated in a war against Japan in 1904. This weakened Russia so that Britain was less concerned about it.
- Above all, Britain was very worried about Germany. The German Kaiser had made it clear that he wanted Germany to have an empire and a strong navy, which Britain saw as a serious threat to its own empire and navy.

Britain began to co-operate more with France and signed an agreement with it in 1904. Britain signed another agreement with Russia in 1907.

SOURCE 7

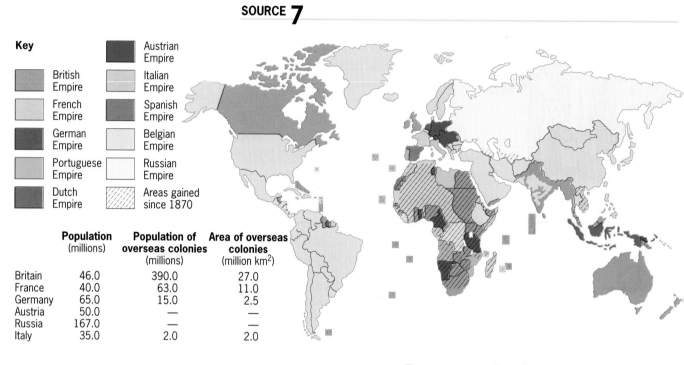

Key

	British Empire		Austrian Empire
	French Empire		Italian Empire
	German Empire		Spanish Empire
	Portuguese Empire		Belgian Empire
	Dutch Empire		Russian Empire
			Areas gained since 1870

	Population (millions)	Population of overseas colonies (millions)	Area of overseas colonies (million km²)
Britain	46.0	390.0	27.0
France	40.0	63.0	11.0
Germany	65.0	15.0	2.5
Austria	50.0	—	—
Russia	167.0	—	—
Italy	35.0	2.0	2.0

The overseas empires of the European powers in 1914.

France

France had been defeated by Germany in a short war in 1870. Since then, Germany had built up a powerful army and strong industries. It had an ambitious leader in Kaiser Wilhelm. France was worried about the growing power of Germany, so the French had also built up their industries and armies. France had also developed a strong and close friendship with Russia. The main concerns of France were:

- to protect itself against attack by Germany
- to get back the rich industrial region of Alsace–Lorraine which Germany had taken from it in 1870.

Russia

Russia was by far the largest of all the six powers, but was also the most backward. The country was almost entirely agricultural, although loans from France had helped Russia to develop some industries.

Russia shared France's worries about the growing power of Germany.

It also had a long history of rivalry with Austria–Hungary. This was one reason why Russia was so friendly with Serbia. Another reason was that both Russians and Serbs were Slavs. Many other Slavs lived in Austria–Hungary's empire. Russia felt it should have influence over them.

Russia lost a war with Japan in 1905. There was then a revolution against the ruler, Tsar Nicholas II. He survived, but he knew Russia could not afford to lose in any other conflict. The Russians began to build up a large army in case of emergencies in the future.

1 Do you think that preserving peace was a priority for Britain, France or Russia?

FOCUS TASK

1 Draw up a chart like this:

	Germany	Austria–Hungary	Italy
Britain			
France			
Russia			

2 Using the descriptions of the relationships between these countries on pages 5 and 6, complete the chart to show causes of tension between the countries. You may not be able to fill in all the spaces.

3 Which relationship is the greatest source of tension?

4 Explain how each of the following contributed to tensions between the European powers:
  a) colonies   **b)** people wanting independence   **c)** arms build-up.

2 Study the statistics in Source 8. Which country do you think is the strongest? Explain your choice.

3 Which alliance do you think is the strongest? Explain your choice.

SOURCE 8

		Britain	France	Russia	Germany	Austria–Hungary	Italy
Population (millions)		46	40	167	65	50	35
Steel production (millions of tons)		7.9	4	4	17	2.6	3.9
Merchant ships (millions of tons)		20	2	0.75	5	3	1.75
Foreign trade (£ million per year)		1	0.4	0.2	1	0.2	n/a
Number of soldiers available (in thousands), including reserve forces		711	1250	1200	2200	810	750
Warships (including under construction)		122	46	26	85	24	36
Submarines		64	73	29	23	6	12

Resources of the Great Powers in 1914.

The Balance of Power

Politicians at the time called this system of alliances the 'Balance of Power'. They believed that the size and power of the two alliances would prevent either side from starting a war.

SOURCE 9

4 Look at Source 9. Did the cartoonist think that the alliances helped to prevent war?

5 Do you think that the alliances made war more likely or less likely?

A modern redrawing of an American cartoon published in the *Brooklyn Eagle*, July 1914. The cartoon was called 'The Chain of Friendship'.

There is no comparison between the importance of the German navy to Germany, and the importance of our navy to us. Our navy is to us what their army is to them. To have a strong navy would increase Germany's prestige and influence, but it is not a matter of life and death to them as it is to us.

Sir Edward Grey, British Foreign Secretary, in a speech to Parliament in 1909.

You English are like mad bulls; you see red everywhere! What on earth has come over you, that you should heap on such suspicion? What can I do more? I have always stood up as a friend of England.

Kaiser Wilhelm, speaking in an interview with the *Daily Telegraph* in 1908. The Kaiser liked England and had friends there. He was a cousin of King George V of Britain.

The tension builds, 1900–1914

Anglo-German naval rivalry

One of the most significant causes of tension in Europe was the naval rivalry which developed after 1900. Ever since the Battle of Trafalgar in 1805, Britain had ruled the seas without any challenge. Its navy was the most powerful in the world. This situation began to change in 1898 when the new Kaiser, Wilhelm, announced his intention to build a powerful German navy.

Britain felt very threatened by this. Germany's navy was much smaller than Britain's but the British navy was spread all over the world, protecting the British Empire. Germany didn't have much of an empire. Why did it need a navy? What was Germany going to do with all of these warships concentrated in the North Sea?

Not surprisingly, Germany did not see things the same way. The Kaiser and his admirals felt that Germany needed a navy to protect its growing trade. They felt that the British were over-reacting to the German naval plans.

Britain was not convinced by what the Germans said. In fact, in 1906 Britain raised the stakes in the naval race by launching HMS *Dreadnought*, the first of a new class of warships. Germany responded by building its own 'Dreadnoughts'. The naval race was well and truly on and both Britain and Germany spent millions on their new ships.

Guns on rotating turrets can fire shells over 9 km in any direction

Fast modern turbine engines

Thick armour plating

A British 'Dreadnought', the HMS *Barham*, with the British fleet in Scapa Flow.

	Britain	Germany
1906	1	
1907	3	
1908	2	4
1909	2	3
1910	2	1
1911	5	3
1912	3	2
1913	7	3
1914	3	1

Britain	Total built by 1914: 29	Germany	Total built by 1914: 17

Number of 'Dreadnoughts' built by Britain and Germany, 1906–14.

1 Why was Britain concerned by Germany's naval plans?
2 How did Germany react to Britain's concerns?
3 Do you think that either country was acting unreasonably? Give your reasons.

Kaiser Wilhelm II

★ Born 1861, with a badly withered left arm. Historians also think he suffered slight brain damage at birth, which affected both his hearing and his attention span.
★ He did not have a loving family.
★ He became Kaiser at the age of 27 when German industry was growing fast and Germany was becoming a world power.
★ He was famous for his energy and enthusiasm, but he was also very unpredictable.
★ He was keen on military parades and liked to be photographed wearing his military uniform. He appointed military people to most of the important positions in his government.
★ He was very ambitious for Germany. He wanted Germany to be recognised as the greatest power in Europe by the older European states.
★ He liked physical exercise, and practical jokes.
★ He was very closely involved in Germany's plans for war.
★ When Germany was defeated in 1918 he fled into exile. He died in 1941.

The arms race on land

While Britain and Germany built up their navies, the major powers on mainland Europe were also building up their armies.

SOURCE 14

	1900	*1910*	*1914*
France	*0.7m*	*0.8m*	*0.9m*
Britain	*0.6m*	*0.55m*	*0.5m*
Russia	*1.1m*	*1.3m*	*0.8m*
Austria–Hungary	*0.25m*	*0.3m*	*0.35m*
Germany	*0.5m*	*0.7m*	*1.5m*
Italy	*0.25m*	*0.3m*	*0.35m*

The arms build-up. Military personnel of the powers, 1900–1914 (excluding reserves).

SOURCE 15

The arms race in which all the major powers were involved contributed to the sense that war was bound to come, and soon. Financing it caused serious financial difficulties for all the governments involved in the race; and yet they were convinced there was no way of stopping it.

Although publicly the arms race was justified to prevent war, no government had in fact been deterred from arming by the programmes of their rivals, but rather increased the pace of their own armament production.

James Joll, *Origins of the First World War*, 1992. Joll is a well-respected British historian with an expert knowledge of this topic.

In Germany, in particular, war and militarism were glorified. The Kaiser surrounded himself with military advisers. He staged military rallies and processions. He loved to be photographed in military uniforms. He involved himself closely in Germany's military planning.

Plans for war

Many countries felt so sure that war was 'bound to come' sooner or later that they began to make very detailed plans for what to do if and when it did.

Germany

Germany's army was not the biggest army in Europe but most people agreed it was the best trained and the most powerful.

The problem facing the German commanders was that if a war broke out they would probably have to fight against Russia and France at the same time.

The Germans came up with the Schlieffen Plan. Under this plan they would quickly attack and defeat France, then turn their forces on Russia which (the Germans were sure) would be slow to get its troops ready for war.

SOURCE 16

General von Moltke said: I believe war is unavoidable; war the sooner the better. But we ought to do more through the press to prepare the population for a war against Russia . . . the enemies are arming more strongly than we are.

From the diary of Admiral von Muller, head of the Kaiser's naval cabinet, December 1912.

SOURCE 17

In Moltke's opinion there was no alternative to making preventive war in order to defeat the enemy while we still had a chance of victory . . . I pointed out that the Kaiser . . . would only agree to fight if our enemies forced war upon us . . .

Written by Gottlieb von Jagow, the German Foreign Secretary, May 1914. He was writing this from memory, soon after the end of the war.

1 Read Source 17. What do you think the writer means by 'preventive war'?
2 Does either Source 16 or 17 suggest that people in Germany wanted a war?

SOURCE 18

The remark 'England and Germany are bound to fight' makes war a little more likely each time it is made, and is therefore made more often by the gutter press of each nation.

From *Howard's End*, a widely read novel by EM Forster, published in 1910.

3 Source 18 comes from a novel. In what ways is it useful as evidence about the mood in Britain before the First World War?

Austria–Hungary

Austria–Hungary knew it needed the help of Germany to hold back Russia. It too relied on the success of the Schlieffen Plan so that Germany could help it to defeat Russia.

Russia

The Russian army was badly equipped, but it was huge. Given enough time, Russia could eventually put millions of soldiers into the field. The Russian plan was to overwhelm Germany's and Austria's armies by sheer weight of numbers.

France

France had a large and well-equipped army. Its main plan of attack was known as Plan 17. French troops would charge across the frontier and attack deep into Germany, forcing surrender.

Britain

Britain's military planners had been closely but secretly involved in collaboration with French commanders. This led to Britain setting up the British Expeditionary Force (BEF), consisting of 150,000 highly trained and well-equipped professional soldiers. The BEF could go to France and fight alongside the French at short notice.

One thing that unites all of these plans was the assumption that a war, if and when it came, would be quick. These military plans were designed to achieve a quick victory. No one planned for what to do if the war dragged on. It was almost universally assumed that none of the powers would be able to keep up a long-drawn-out war. The sheer cost of a war would lead to economic collapse (of the enemy only, of course) and so the war would be over in a matter of weeks or months.

With so much talk of war and plans for war, you might think, as many at the time did, that war was inevitable.

Morocco, 1905 and 1911

In 1905 and 1911, two crises in Morocco raised the temperature in Europe.

In 1905 the Kaiser visited Morocco in North Africa. Germany was building up its own African empire and had colonies in central and southern Africa (see Source 7 on page 6). The Kaiser was now keen to show that Germany was an important power in North Africa as well. The French had plans to take control of Morocco so the Kaiser made a speech saying he supported independence for Morocco. The French were furious at his interfering in their affairs. An international conference was held in Algeciras in 1906. But the conference did not cool things down. In fact, it did the opposite: at the conference the Kaiser was humiliated. He had wanted to be seen as a major power in Africa. Instead his views were rejected. He was treated as if he had no right to speak on such matters. This made him bitter. He was also alarmed by the way that Britain and France stuck together at the conference to oppose him. These old rivals now seemed very close.

In 1907, in the wake of the Moroccan crisis, Britain and France formed an alliance with Russia, the Triple Entente. The Entente powers saw their alliance as security against German aggression. The Kaiser and his people saw a threatening policy of encirclement, with hostile powers surrounding Germany.

In 1911 Morocco saw another crisis. The French tried to take over Morocco again. They said they were prepared to compensate Germany if its trade suffered as a result. However, the Kaiser's response was to send a gunboat (the *Panther*) to Agadir. The British feared that the Kaiser wanted to set up a naval base in Agadir, and they did not want German ships in the Mediterranean. Another conference was called. The British and French again stood firm against Germany. France took control of Morocco. Germany was given land in central Africa as compensation. Behind the scenes, Britain and France reached an agreement that the French should patrol the Mediterranean and the Royal Navy should defend France's Atlantic and North Sea coasts.

SOURCE 19

The Balkans: the spark that lit the bonfire

The Balkans in 1908.

The Balkans were a very unstable area.

- Different nationalities were mixed together.
- The area had been ruled by Turkey for many centuries, but Turkish power was now in decline.
- The new governments which had been set up in place of Turkish rule were regularly in dispute with each other.
- Two great powers, Russia and Austria, bordered the countries in this region. Both wanted to control the area because it gave them access to the Mediterranean.

The first Balkan crisis came in 1908. Austria took over the provinces of Bosnia and Herzegovina. Russia and Serbia protested, but they backed down when Germany made it clear that it supported Austria. Neither Russia nor Serbia was prepared to risk war with Germany over this issue. However, there were some serious consequences. Austria now felt confident that Germany would back it in future disputes. Some historians think that this made Austria too confident, and encouraged it to make trouble with Serbia and Russia. Russia resented being faced down in 1909. It quickened its arms build-up. It was determined not to back down again.

From 1912 to 1913 there was a series of local wars. Serbia emerged from these as the most powerful country in the Balkans. This was very serious for Austria. Serbia had a strong army and it was a close ally of Russia. Austria decided that Serbia would have to be dealt with. By 1914 Austria was looking for a good excuse to crush Serbia.

Austria's opportunity came with the murder of Archduke Franz Ferdinand and his wife Sophie in Sarajevo (see pages 2–3). Although there was no hard evidence that Princip was acting under orders from the Serbian government, Austria blamed Serbia. Frantic diplomatic effort gave Austria a guarantee of German backing (see Witness 9 on page 13). With this support Austria now felt secure enough to deal with the Serbian problem once and for all. It gave Serbia a ten-point ultimatum that would effectively have made Serbia part of the Austrian Empire. The Serbs could not possibly accept it. When the Serbs asked for time to consider, Austria refused and declared war on 28 July 1914. The slide to all-out war had begun.

SOURCE 20

When I first heard of the assassination [murder] . . . I felt it was a grave matter . . . but my fears were soon calmed . . . the Kaiser left on his yachting holiday and . . . still more reassuring, the head of the German army left for his cure in a foreign spa [health resort] . . .

I remember that an influential Hungarian lady called on me and told me that we were taking the murder of the Grand Duke too quietly . . . it had provoked a storm in Austria . . . and might lead to war with Serbia . . . However, the official reports we had did not seem to justify this alarmist view.

David Lloyd George, *Memoirs*, 1938. David Lloyd George was a government minister in 1914 and became Prime Minister in 1916. His memoirs have a reputation for inconsistency.

4 Look back at your answer to question 2 on page 3. Would you like to change your answer now?

ACTIVITY

The atmosphere in Europe between 1900 and 1914 has been likened to a bonfire waiting to be lit.

1 Make your own copy of this bonfire diagram, and add labels to suggest factors that made war possible.
2 Put major factors on big sticks, less important factors on smaller sticks.
3 Add more sticks to the fire if you wish to show more factors.
4 Why do you think the Sarajevo murders 'lit the fire' when previous events such as the Moroccan crisis in 1905 had not? Mention these points in your answer:
   a) Austria's worries about Serbia
   b) the build-up of international problems
   c) the way the alliances worked.

Did Germany cause the war?

SOURCE 21

The Allied governments affirm, and Germany accepts, the responsibility of Germany and her allies for causing all the loss and damage to which the Allied governments and their peoples have been subjected as a result of the war.

The war guilt clause from the Treaty of Versailles, 1919.

After the war, the victorious Allies forced the defeated Germany to sign the 'war guilt' clause (Source 21). Germany had to accept that it was responsible both for starting the war and for all the damage caused by it. However, as the state 'on trial', Germany refused to accept the sole blame. Historians have argued about this issue ever since. Some have continued to blame Germany. Others have reached different verdicts.

FOCUS TASK

Was Germany to blame for the war?

What do you think? Was Germany to blame?
   Your task is to look over the evidence and hold your own retrial, looking back from today.
You will study evidence and hear from witnesses. You must then reach one of four verdicts:

Verdict 1: Germany was rightly blamed for starting the war.

Verdict 2: Germany was mainly responsible for starting the war, but the other powers should accept some of the blame.

Verdict 3: All of the major powers helped to start the war. They should share the blame.

Verdict 4: No one was to blame. The powers were swept along towards an inevitable war. It could not be stopped.

This is how to run the trial. You can work on your own, or in groups.

1 Draw up a table like the one below:

Witness	Which verdict does the witness support?	What evidence does the witness give to support the viewpoint?	Can I trust the witness?

2 Read all the witnesses' statements on page 13. Complete columns 1 and 2.
3 In column 3, note what evidence the witness gives to support his/her viewpoint.
4 In column 4, note what might make the witness reliable or unreliable.
   Think about:
   • the date and origin of each source
   • whether the witness was involved in the events of the time
   • the value and reliability of each witness.
5 Look through the other information in this chapter to see if there are other witnesses you should consider.
6 Choose your verdict from verdicts 1–4.
7 Once you have chosen a verdict, you should sum up the evidence for it in a short explanation.
   Remember to explain why you have chosen your verdict, but also explain why you have rejected the others.
8 Use your table and explanation for a class debate.

The witnesses

WITNESS 1

German militarism, which is the crime of the last fifty years, had been working for this for twenty-five years. It is the logical result of their doctrine. It had to come.

Walter Hines Page, US Ambassador in London, 1914. The USA was an ally of Britain and France during the war, and fought in it against Germany from 1917 to 1918.

WITNESS 2

Bethmann stood in the centre of the room . . . There was a look of anguish in his eyes . . . For an instant neither of us spoke. At last I said to him: 'Well, tell me, at least, how it all happened.' He raised his arms to heaven and answered, 'Oh – if only I knew!'

Prince von Bülow, speaking in 1918, remembers calling on the German Chancellor Bethmann-Hollweg in August 1914.

WITNESS 3

None of the rulers of the Great Powers really knew what they were fighting about in August 1914 . . . the crisis gathered pace and the calculations of statesmen were overwhelmed by the rapid succession of events, the tide of emotion in the various capitals, and the demands of military planning.

The Origins of the First World War by British historian LCF Turner, 1983.

WITNESS 4

The Schlieffen Plan must rank as one of the supreme idiocies of modern times . . . It restricted the actions of the German government disastrously. In July 1914 they had just two choices; either to abandon the only plan they had to win the next war, or to go to war immediately.

Historian DE Marshall in *The Great War: Myth and Reality*, 1988.

WITNESS 5

The World War was directly started by certain officials of the Russian General Staff. But their conduct was caused by the criminal activity of an Austrian Foreign Minister, and this in turn was aided by criminal negligence at Berlin . . .

But they would have been quite unable to start any war, had they not been equally with millions of common people . . . willing agents of forces moving the world towards war . . .

From the *Encyclopaedia Britannica*, 1926.

WITNESS 6

We are being forced to admit that we alone are to blame for the war: such an admission on my lips would be a lie. We are not seeking to absolve [pardon] Germany from all responsibility for this World War, and for the way in which it was fought. However, we do strongly deny that Germany, whose people felt they were fighting a war of defence, should be forced to accept sole responsibility.

Count Brockdorff-Rantzan, head of the German delegates at Versailles, 1919.

WITNESS 7

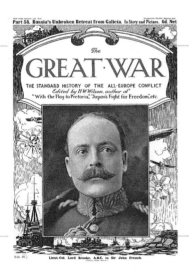

The greatest war of modern times, and perhaps in the whole history of the human race, was begun by Germany using the crime of a schoolboy as an excuse . . . Austria had regarded the growing power of Serbia with concern for many years . . . The situation in Europe seemed to encourage the German peoples in this adventure. England, it was thought, could do nothing . . . with the threats of civil war in Ireland. Russia was in the midst of the reorganisation of her army . . . As for France, Germany believed herself quite competent to deal with her, and sought an opportunity of doing so.

From *The Great War – The Standard History of the All-Europe Conflict*, 1914 (Vol IV). This was a patriotic weekly journal written and published in Britain, describing the war 'as it happened'.

WITNESS 8

German: *I wonder what history will make of all of this?*

Clemenceau: *History will not say that Belgium invaded Germany!*

From a conversation between French Prime Minister Clemenceau and a German representative at the peace conference after the war. Clemenceau was a hard-line anti-German.

WITNESS 9

. . . the Kaiser authorised me to inform our gracious majesty that we might, in this case as in all others, rely upon Germany's full support . . . it was the Kaiser's opinion that this action must not be delayed . . . Russia was in no way prepared for war and would think twice before it appealed to arms . . . If we had really recognised the necessity of warlike action against Serbia, the Kaiser would regret if we did not make use of the present moment which is all in our favour.

Count Szogyeny, the Austrian ambassador in Berlin, reporting a famous conversation with the Kaiser, July 1914. Historians are divided as to whether the Kaiser was making a planned policy statement or was simply giving reassurance on the spur of the moment.

2 Britain and the First World War: 1914–1918

Breaking the stalemate on the Western Front

The mood in 1914

When war broke out across Europe, it was greeted with enthusiasm. Everyone agreed it would all be over by Christmas (with a magnificent victory, of course). The populations of Europe were gripped by war fever. Newspapers and magazines filled their minds with images of brave young men charging on horseback or heroic soldiers putting the enemy to flight.

SOURCE 1

A German cavalryman ready for battle. Notice that he is wearing a gas mask. Each side expected cavalry charges to be a key part of winning the war.

SOURCE 2

Especially at small stations, the Russian leave-taking was an almost joyous affair, with the reservists dancing away to balalaika music and raising dust on the trampled earth . . .

From Alexander Solzhenitsyn's *August 1914*, a novel written in 1972. Solzhenitsyn is a Russian writer.

SOURCE 3

I discovered to my amazement that average men and women were delighted at the prospect of war.

Bertrand Russell, a British intellectual and writer, describing the mood in Britain in 1914.

There had not been a war in Europe involving the major powers since 1871. That had been a lightning German victory against France. Most civilians were untouched by that war and the young men joining up in 1914 had not even been born at the time.

There had been more recent wars overseas. The British had sustained heavy casualties in the Boer War in South Africa. Both soldiers and South African civilians had suffered greatly. Artillery bombardments in the Balkan wars of the previous year had resulted in heavy casualties. But if anyone did bring these wars to mind, they were not voicing their doubts publicly in 1914 as the young men of Europe flocked to join up. They had been persuaded that a modern war would be swift. A few lightning marches and a great battle would settle the matter.

SOURCE 4

Young Austrian soldiers setting out for the war in August 1914.

SOURCE 6

Britain's empire also contributed troops. Around 1.5 million Indians and 15,000 West Indians fought in the British army. Canadian, Australian and New Zealand troops also fought.

SOURCE 10

It is a heady atmosphere to move in, & it's infected me with a strong desire to do something more than stay in London & wait for a bunch of men to tell me what to do. I have heard of an ambulance corps which is going straight out to Belgium & shall apply to join it.

A young British woman writing in August 1914. She went on to serve through the whole of the war. Thousands of women served in the forces as nurses, drivers, clerks and in many other roles.

SOURCE 5

A group of British recruits who had just joined up in August 1914. Half a million young men signed up in the first four weeks. You can tell from the variety of hats and clothing that this group includes both middle-class and working-class people.

SOURCE 7

Such enthusiasm! – the whole battalion with helmets and tunics decked with flowers – handkerchiefs waving untiringly – cheers on every side – and over and over again the ever fresh and wonderful reassurance of the soldiers.

Letter from a young German who had been called up and was about to travel to the front.

SOURCE 8

Thirty years of life would not be worth all that we are going to accomplish within the next few weeks . . . I wish you could share in some measure the peace we experience here!

A letter from a young Frenchman. France had been defeated by Germany in a humiliating war in 1871. In France, there was a strong sense of settling old scores.

SOURCE 9

You must all keep cheerful for my sake and it will not be long before I am back again, at least the general view is that it will not be a long show.

Letter from a 30-year-old British officer to his parents, August 1914.

The soldiers who wrote Sources 7, 8 and 9 were all dead within a month. Others who went away to war so enthusiastically came back wounded and maimed. The reality of war was very different from what had been expected in August 1914. Instead of a swift victory, the troops got a bloody STALEMATE. Soldiers on the Western Front were bogged down in muddy trenches for most of the next four months.

ACTIVITY

It is August 1914. You are a reporter for a British newspaper. Write 100 words to describe the way in which the outbreak of war was greeted around Europe. Use Sources 1–10 in your article.

The war on the Western Front reaches stalemate

As soon as war was declared Germany's Schlieffen Plan went into operation. The Schlieffen Plan (see page 9) was simple but risky. The idea was to send German forces through Belgium and to quickly knock France out of the war. The theory was that Russia would take a long time to mobilise (get its forces ready for war). It was an all-or-nothing gamble. The Germans had to try to get to Paris and defeat France within six weeks, so that they could then send all their troops to fight against Russia. However, as Source 11 shows, neither the Belgians nor the Russians did what the Schlieffen Plan expected them to do.

1 Explain what Source 12 is saying about Belgium and Germany.

SOURCE 11

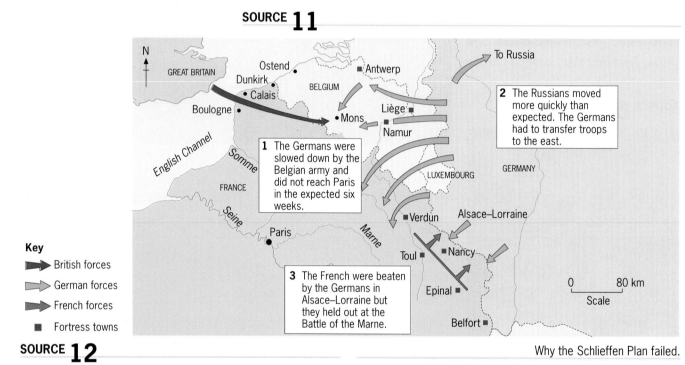

Key
- British forces
- German forces
- French forces
- ■ Fortress towns

1 The Germans were slowed down by the Belgian army and did not reach Paris in the expected six weeks.

2 The Russians moved more quickly than expected. The Germans had to transfer troops to the east.

3 The French were beaten by the Germans in Alsace–Lorraine but they held out at the Battle of the Marne.

0   80 km
Scale

Why the Schlieffen Plan failed.

SOURCE 12

NO THOROUGHFARE

A cartoon from *Punch*, August 1914.

At first, it looked as though the Germans could succeed. The German army invaded Belgium on 4 August. The Belgians put up a heroic resistance from their frontier forts but it did not stop the crushing German advance. Massive German artillery bombardments destroyed the Belgian forts and soon enormous numbers of well-equipped and well-trained German infantry and cavalry were moving ominously towards the French border. Even so, the Belgian resistance won them many friends and bought time for British and French troops to mobilise.

The British Expeditionary Force, led by Sir John French, landed in France and met the advancing Germans at Mons on 23 August. This small but well-trained force of professional soldiers gave the Germans a nasty shock. The troops at Mons were well led by Lieutenant-General Douglas Haig – remember that name, you'll find out a lot more about him later – and were using Lee Enfield .303 bolt action rifles which could fire quickly and accurately. German reports from the time showed that they thought they were up against machine-gun fire.

2 Read Source 13. What factors had influenced Walter Bloem's view of English soldiers?

3 Why was Bloem's first taste of action such a shock to him?

Sunday

Reports were coming back that the English were in front of us. English soldiers? We knew what they looked like from the comics; short scarlet tunics with small caps set at an angle on their heads, or bearskins with the chin-strap under the lip instead of under the chin. There was much joking about this, and also about a remark by Bismarck [the former German leader] about sending the police to arrest the English army.

(The Attack begins . . .)

We had no sooner left the edge of the wood than a volley of bullets whistled past our noses and cracked into the trees behind. Five or six cries near me, five or six of my grey lads collapsed on the grass. Damn it! This was serious . . . ! Forward again – at the double! We crossed the track, jumped the broad ditch full of water, and then on across the squelching meadow. More firing, closer now and tearing into our ranks, more lads falling . . . the 160 men that left the wood with me had shrunk to less than 100 . . .

From now on matters went from bad to worse. Wherever I looked, right or left, there were dead or wounded, quivering in convulsions, groaning terribly, blood oozing from flesh wounds . . .

We had to go back . . . A bad defeat, there could be no gainsaying it; in our first battle we had been badly beaten, and by the English – by the English we had so laughed at a few hours before.

Written by Walter Bloem, a German soldier, about the battle at Mons in Belgium. This was Walter Bloem's first experience of fighting.

Despite their early success, the British were hugely outnumbered. In fact, the best they could do was to organise an orderly retreat. They did slow the Germans down, but only the French had enough forces in the field to stop the German advance. However, the French were facing their own problems.

When war broke out, the French followed their Plan 17 (see page 10) and launched a direct attack on Germany through Alsace–Lorraine. On 20 August the German forces defending the frontier cut the attacking French troops to ribbons with artillery and machine-gun fire. The French lost over 200,000 men in 12 days. They now abandoned Plan 17, and regrouped their forces to defend Paris from the advancing Germans (see Source 14).

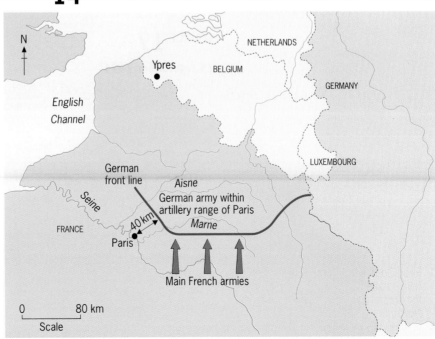

The threat to Paris. The situation in early September 1914.

SOURCE 15

That [French soldiers] who have retreated for ten days, sleeping on the ground and half dead with fatigue, should be able to take up their rifles when the bugle sounds is a thing which we never expected.

Written by General von Kluck, a German army commander, after the Battle of the Marne.

The Battle of the Marne

The French may have been on the defensive in September 1914, but by this stage things were not going entirely well for the Germans either. The German Supreme Commander Moltke had to pull 100,000 troops out of the army advancing on Paris because the Russians had mobilised far more quickly than expected and had already invaded Germany. This was to prove the break that the British and French needed. The German army also faced another problem. Their advance had been so fast that their supplies of food and ammunition could not keep up. The German soldiers were underfed and exhausted.

Von Kluck, the German commander, decided he could not swing round Paris according to the original plan, so he advanced straight towards it. While the Germans advanced on foot, the French diverted troops to Paris by rail, and then on to the front, transporting some of them there by taxi! The German army was weary and overstretched. The French were fighting to save their country.

SOURCE 16

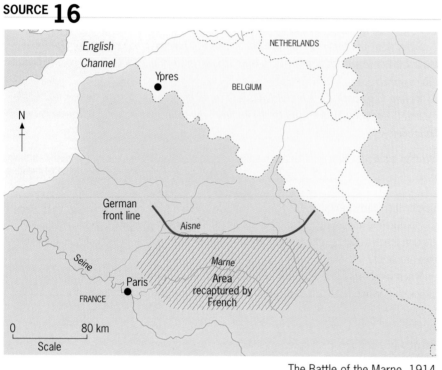

The combined British and French forces were able to stop the German advance along the line of the River Marne. They then counter-attacked and pushed the Germans back to the River Aisne. However, they could not drive them out of France entirely.

Neither side could make any progress and by 8 September troops on both sides were digging trenches to protect themselves from snipers and shell fire. Soon after, they added machine guns and barbed wire. Until now, it had been a war of movement, but these were the first signs of the stalemate that was to come.

The Battle of the Marne, 1914.

SOURCE 17

15 September 1914

We got here pretty beat at 11 pm last night . . . The last part was very tiring to the men and a good many fell out . . . We must have done twenty-five miles yesterday.

October 1914

We can apparently get no further because the Germans have brought up strong reinforcements, and also have a strongly prepared position which we are now up against, so it looks like another siege unless we are reinforced here.

25 October 1914

The last few days have been very busy. Our former forward line was too difficult to hold, we are too weak to shove ahead, so now we are back in a strong position which we dug before withdrawing. The end of our advance was shown by the almost complete loss of the Royal Irish in Le Pilly. Apparently they pushed on too far and were heavily attacked and surrounded. There are only about seventy survivors all told – a bad business.

From the diary of Billy Congreve, a young lieutenant from a soldiering family. He was widely respected and in two years rose to the rank of major. He kept a personal diary from 1914 until he was killed by a sniper at Ypres in 1916.

1 Read Source 17. What do the extracts tell you about how warfare changed on the Western Front between August and November 1914?
2 Is there any evidence that the mood of the soldiers had changed?

SOURCE 18

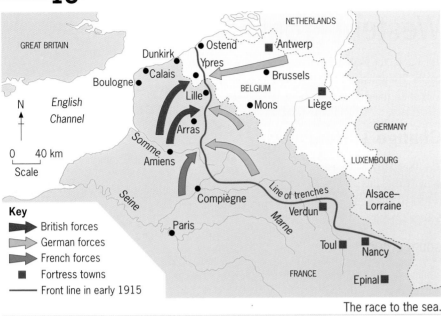

The race to the sea.

The race to the sea

The Battle of the Marne was a turning point. The Schlieffen Plan had failed. Germany was caught up in a two-front war. Worse still, the German generals realised that they could not break through the enemy lines. Moltke was replaced by a new commander, Falkenhayn, who decided to try to outflank (get round the end of) his enemy's lines. The charge began on 12 October. It became known as 'the race to the sea'.

As the Germans charged west towards the sea, the British and French moved troops to block them whenever it seemed that the Germans were about to break through. One observer at the time called these 'the Railway Battles of Northern France', because both sides moved their troops by rail.

The first Battle of Ypres in Belgium

The key battle in this race to the sea was the first Battle of Ypres (there were two more later in the war) from 12 October to 11 November 1914. The BEF lost around 50,000 men and the Germans probably 100,000, but the British (led by Lt-Gen. Haig in this area) held this important ground. They kept control of the English Channel ports, which meant they could be supplied with equipment and reinforcements.

By November 1914 it was a deadlock. The BEF had been decimated. The French had already suffered around 1 million dead or wounded in just ten weeks. Despite this, the French army tried to break through the German lines in Artois and Champagne in December, but they were beaten back with heavy losses. As 1914 ended, the fighting had reached a stalemate which was to last until 1918. Millions of troops were dug into a line of trenches that stretched from the sea in the west to the Alps in the east. It became known as the 'Western Front'. Over the next pages you will examine the war on the Western Front in detail.

SOURCE 19

A German painting from December 1914. The artist, Alfred Kubin, enthusiastically supported war earlier in 1914. By December, his work had changed to this style in which ghosts and demons often featured. The figure in this painting represents death. The houses represent ordinary life and people.

FOCUS TASK

Why was the war not over by Christmas?

It is Christmas 1914. People were told that the war would be over by Christmas. You have to explain why it isn't.

Work in pairs. You are going to write two reports about the progress of the war from August to December 1914. One of you should write for the British Prime Minister, explaining events as fully as you can. The other should write for the general public back in Britain, trying to give a positive and encouraging message about how the war is going.
   You may wish to mention these points:
• the successes and failures of the various plans
• the important battles that have taken place
• the new lessons being learnt about warfare
• the casualties
• the morale of the troops.

Conclude with:
• your explanation as to why the war is not over by Christmas
• your views on how the war will be fought through 1915.

When you have finished, compare your two reports. Discuss:
1 Are there differences in tone?
2 Have you included different details?
3 Is one more accurate than the other?

What was the fighting like on the Western Front?

The war on the Western Front was a new kind of warfare. No one had experienced war like it before. The generals' plans had not allowed for it. Everyone had to adapt. You are now going to look at the main changes in the techniques of warfare brought about by the First World War.

Change 1: trench warfare

The most obvious new feature of this kind of warfare was the system of trenches. Instead of a war of movement this war was static. Trenches began as simple shelters but by 1915 they had developed into complex defensive systems. Source 20 shows a cross-section of a trench. However, Source 22 probably gives a better idea of what the trenches were really like.

1 One of the biggest problems facing the army planners was supplying the army with food, weapons and other equipment. Use Sources 20–22 to compile a list of all the things they would need.
2 Sources 20–22 give you three different kinds of evidence about the trenches: a modern reconstruction drawing, an aerial photograph, and two ground-level photographs. Explain how each one is useful to a historian.
3 Write your own five-point definition of trench warfare. Your audience is a younger student in your school who has not yet studied this topic.
4 Explain why the two trenches shown in Source 22 are so different.

SOURCE 20

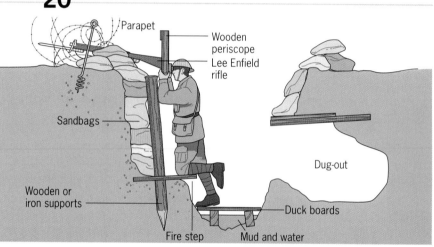

Cross-section of a front-line trench. These were supported by much stronger reserve trenches and linked by communication trenches. German trenches were generally stronger and better constructed than Allied trenches. The Germans generally held better ground and had established their trenches in the early stages of war. Many of their dug-outs and machine-gun posts were reinforced with concrete which provided a stronger defence against artillery bombardment.

SOURCE 21

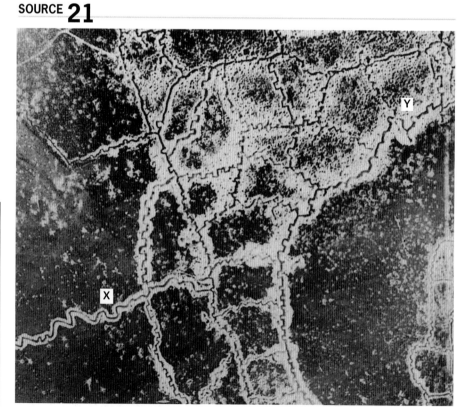

The trench system. This is an aerial photograph taken by British planes. The British trenches are on the right. The main trench area is German.

ACTIVITY

Study Source 21 carefully.

1 On your own copy of Source 21 label the following features:
 • front-line trenches
 • support trenches
 • no man's land (the area between front-line trenches).
2 Explain why you think the trenches are arranged as zig-zag lines, not straight lines.
3 If you had to get from your headquarters behind the lines (marked X) to the front-line position (marked Y), how would you get there?

SOURCE **22**

Trenches in **A** the Somme, July 1916, and **B** Guedecourt, December 1916.

Change 2: artillery became more powerful

For much of the war, all day, every day, artillery would pound the enemy's trenches with hundreds of shells. Artillery bombardments caused more casualties than any other weapon.

At the beginning of the war the guns were not very accurate. Firing from well behind their own lines, artillery often bombarded their own forward trenches before they got their range right.

By the end of the war, artillery was much bigger, and it was also more accurate. By 1918 artillery tactics were extremely sophisticated as well (see pages 30–32). Artillery was the key weapon of the Great War. Throughout the war a vast part of European industry was given over to making shells for the artillery.

Change 3: cavalry became less important

The First World War saw another major military change – the end of the cavalry as a weapon of the modern army. Before 1914, all sides thought the speed and mobility of the cavalry would be decisive. However, once trenches were dug cavalry became too vulnerable to artillery and machine guns. In one particular cavalry charge only three out of four hundred horses survived. Even so, horses and mules remained vital for transporting supplies and equipment in the swamp-like conditions of the Western Front.

SOURCE **23**

Horses at work for the British army near Ypres, 1917.

The spirit of the bayonet . . . must be inculcated into all ranks so that they may go forward with that aggressive determination and confidence of superiority born of continual practice . . . In an assault the enemy must be killed with the bayonet. Firing should be avoided for in the mix-up, a bullet, passing through an opponent's body, may kill a friend who happens to be in the line of fire.

From a government pamphlet on military training, published before the war.

Change 4: infantry became more important

The infantryman or foot soldier was the backbone of the army.

The standard equipment for an infantry soldier is shown in Source 25. Steel helmets giving some protection against shrapnel from enemy shelling only became standard equipment in 1916. Troops also improvised their own weapons for the conditions of trench warfare.

Before the war, the theory was that an attack on the enemy would be led by a cavalry charge. The infantry's job was to follow the cavalry and take charge of the captured positions. They then had to defend the position against counter-attack.

Trench warfare changed the role of the infantry dramatically. The cavalry charge was replaced by the 'infantry charge' which became the main tactic used in the war.

'Over the top'

A major assault would usually proceed like this:

1 The attacking side's artillery bombarded the front-line trenches of the enemy. This was called a 'barrage'.

2 As soon as the barrage stopped, attacking troops would go 'over the top' – that is, climb out of their trenches. It was now a race between them and the defenders, who had to emerge from their shelters and set up their machine guns before the attackers got over the barbed wire of no man's land.

3 The defenders usually had the advantage. They swept the advancing attackers with machine-gun fire, sometimes setting up a cross-fire.

4 If the attackers did capture forward positions, they then had to hold them. This generally proved impossible and they were usually forced back to their original position.

The machine gun was devastatingly effective against the infantry charge. It could fire eight bullets a second or more, and each trench would have a number of machine guns. During an infantry charge it could cut down a whole brigade in minutes. The machine gun made it inevitable that any charge on an enemy trench would cost many lives. However, the theory was that if enough soldiers charged then no matter how many were killed or wounded on the way there would still be enough men alive to capture the machine guns in the enemy trenches.

The infantry charge was the only attacking strategy the generals had. They thought that if they did it often enough, with enough men, eventually it would wear down the enemy, and they could break through. However, the idea that the generals simply threw away lives is not supported by the evidence. As the war continued, the generals tried new tactics, weapons and equipment. New camouflage techniques were used to protect troops and guns. Artillery and infantry attacks were better synchronised. Troops were given gas masks. One of the most promising developments came very late in the war: the tank (see page 25).

Day-to-day tasks

The soldiers did not spend all their time charging the enemy trenches. Far from it. Most of the infantry's work was more routine. Infantry soldiers spent much of their time digging new trenches or repairing old ones. They carted supplies and equipment up and down communications trenches. They spent long hours on sentry duty or in secret listening posts near to enemy trenches.

There were also specialist infantry called sappers. Sappers were usually ex-miners who dug tunnels below enemy trenches and placed huge mines there.

The infantry also made occasional raids in small numbers on enemy trenches – to capture prisoners or particular positions. Prisoners provided priceless information. If a new enemy unit was in your sector, you could soon be facing an attack.

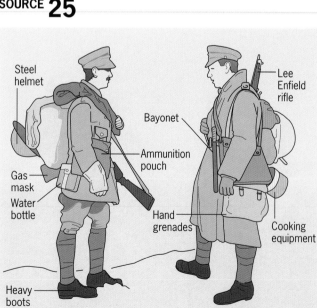

Steel helmet
Lee Enfield rifle
Bayonet
Ammunition pouch
Gas mask
Water bottle
Hand grenades
Cooking equipment
Heavy boots

An infantryman's weapons and equipment.

SOURCE 26

We see the attackers coming. Our machine guns rattle, rifles crack. We recognise the helmets of the attackers. They are French. They have already suffered heavily when they reach our barbed wire.

We retreat. We leave bombs behind us in the trench. We hurl explosives at the feet of the enemy before we run.

At last we reach one of our support trenches that is in somewhat better condition. It is manned and ready for the counter attack . . . Our guns open in full blast and stop the enemy attack . . . We counter attack. It does not come quite to hand to hand fighting; they are driven back. We arrive once again at our original shattered trench and pass on beyond it . . . Now we are so close on the heels of our retreating enemies that we reach their line almost at the same time as they do . . . But we cannot stay here long. We must retire under cover of our artillery to our own position . . . We get back pretty well. There is no further attack by the enemy.

Adapted from *All Quiet on the Western Front*, a novel by Erich Maria Remarque. He was a German who fought on the Western Front, and was twice badly wounded.

SOURCE 27

The miles of barbed wire that protected the German trenches from infantry charge.

SOURCE 28

1 Read Source 26. Draw a diagram to show what you think actually happened in this attack.
2 Why was it so easy for the Germans to win back their captured trench?
3 What was the role of the artillery in this attack?
4 Look at Source 27.
   a) If you were an attacking soldier how could you get through this barbed wire defence?
   b) How might the following factors affect your answer to a)?
      i) It is completely dark.
      ii) You are being fired on.
      iii) You are carrying heavy equipment.
      iv) You are wearing a gas mask.
5 Look at Source 28. One of the artist's aims was to show how vulnerable soldiers were when going over the top. Do you think he succeeded? Explain your answer.

Over the Top, a painting by John Nash. It is based on an attack that he took part in, in 1917, near Cambrai. The soldiers had to climb out of their own trench, charge towards the enemy trench and try to capture it. Of 80 men in his unit, 68 were killed in the first five minutes of the attack.

Change 5: poison gas

The first poison gas attack was made in April 1915. The Germans released chlorine which wafted on the wind across no man's land into the British trenches. There was panic there as the soldiers coughed, retched and struggled to breathe.

From that time gas attacks by both sides became a regular feature of the war. To start with, the aim of a gas attack was to disable enemy troops so that your own infantry charge would be successful. Later, scientists on both sides began to perfect new and more lethal gases such as mustard gas, which had a perfumed smell but which burned, blinded or slowly killed the victims over four to five weeks.

However, scientists also developed very effective gas masks. Soldiers in the trenches would carry their gas masks with them all the time. At the alert they would put them on. As a result only 3,000 British troops died from gas in the whole war. The main significance of gas was therefore its psychological impact. Soldiers who could bear a long bombardment by artillery often lived in fear of a gas attack.

1 According to Source 29 what were the effects of poison gas on the victim?
2 Why do you think gas attacks were regarded with such fear?
3 Do you think Wilfred Owen (Source 29) would have approved of Source 30? Explain your answer.

SOURCE 29

GAS! GAS! Quick, boys! – An ecstasy of fumbling.
Fitting the clumsy helmets just in time;
But someone still was yelling out and stumbling
And flound'ring like a man in fire or lime . . .
Dim, through the misty panes and thick green light,
As under a green sea, I saw him drowning.
In all my dreams, before my helpless sight,
He plunges at me, guttering, choking, drowning.
If in some smothering dreams you too could pace
Behind the wagon that we flung him in,
And watch the white eyes writhing in his face,
His hanging face, like a devil's sick of sin;
If you could hear, at every jolt, the blood
Come gargling from the froth-corrupted lungs,
Obscene as cancer, bitter as the cud
Of vile, incurable sores on innocent tongues, –
My friend, you would not tell with such high zest
To children ardent for some desperate glory,
The old Lie: Dulce et decorum est
Pro patria mori.
[How sweet and proper it is to die for your country]

From a poem by Wilfred Owen. Owen served on the Western Front through most of the war. He became the most celebrated of the poets of the First World War. He was killed just days before the final armistice in November 1918.

SOURCE 30

Gassed, a painting by John Singer Sargent. A famous portrait painter, Sargent was commissioned in 1918 to paint a memorial picture of the soldiers killed and injured in the war.

Change 6: tanks

The tank was a British invention. Early in the war inventors took the idea to the army leaders but it was rejected as impractical. However, Winston Churchill, head of the navy, thought that the idea had potential and his department funded its development.

Two years later, the tanks were used for the first time at the Battle of the Somme. They advanced ahead of the infantry, crushing barbed-wire defences and spraying the enemy with machine-gun fire. They caused alarm among the Germans and raised the morale of the British troops. Surely this was the weapon that could achieve a breakthrough!

However, these first machines only moved at walking pace. They were not very manoeuvrable and very unreliable – more than half of them broke down before they got to the German trenches. It was not until a year later, in November 1917 at Cambrai, that tanks actually achieved great success. Unfortunately they were too successful. They blasted through enemy lines so quickly that the infantry could not keep up.

By 1918, German forces were using armour-piercing machine-gun bullets to deadly effect. They had also learned how to adapt field guns to fire at tanks. Tanks were virtually impossible to miss because they were so large and slow. However, the tank offered a significant boost to morale.

SOURCE

A British tank crossing a trench on the Western Front, September 1916.

FOCUS TASK

How did the fighting on the Western Front change?

On pages 20–25 you have studied how the equipment and the tactics used on the Western Front were adapted to the realities of trench warfare.

1 Work in pairs. You each have to compile advice to be included in a 'Soldier's guide'. You should include advice on tactics and equipment. One of you should write the advice as it might be given in 1914 at the outbreak of war. The other should write your advice as if it was 1918, at the end of the war.
   Compare your ideas with your partner's.
2 Write three paragraphs to explain the changes in fighting during the war. You can use this structure:

   Paragraph 1: how the war was different from what people expected.
   Paragraph 2: ways in which techniques and equipment were adapted to trench warfare.
   Paragraph 3: what things did not change and why.

What was life like in the trenches?

Soldiers on the Western Front went through an enormous range of experiences, from extreme boredom to the appalling stress of an enemy bombardment or attack.

People often think that soldiers in the trenches spent all their time going over the top, attacking enemy trenches. In fact, such attacks were the exception rather than the rule. Soldiers spent much more time on guard, repairing trenches, or just trying to rest or sleep.

Nor did soldiers spend all their time in the front-line trenches. Sometimes it would be eight days in, four days out. Another arrangement was three days at the front line then three days in support trenches, followed by three more days in the front line then three days off behind the lines. However, during a major assault, such as the Battle of the Somme, soldiers could be in the front line for much longer.

Even in the front-line trenches soldiers could go for long periods without seeing an enemy soldier. As well as doing trench chores they would write letters or diaries. Many soldiers even took up correspondence courses to pass the hours.

SOURCE 32

We buried them behind the trench. One gets very callous I find. It was a poor sort of funeral, no service, nothing; just an old greatcoat over the face . . . Naturally one wishes to bury the body as far back from the trench as possible, but one doesn't much like leaving the shelter of the parapet, because of the risk of a stray bullet, so the graves are dug just about two yards behind the trench.

From the diary of Billy Congreve
(see Source 17).

SOURCE 33

The Eternal Question.
" When the 'ell is it goin' to be strawberry ? "

Illustration by British officer Bruce Bairnsfather. Soldiers complained about the quality of their tinned food, but rations were actually quite good.

SOURCE 34

Fourteen days ago we had to go up and relieve the front line. It was fairly quiet on our sector. But on the last day an astonishing number of English heavies opened up on us with high explosive, drumming ceaselessly on our position, so that we suffered severely and came back only eighty strong (out of 150).

From *All Quiet on the Western Front*, by
Erich Maria Remarque.

Millions of men and thousands of horses lived close together. Sanitation arrangements were makeshift. In the summer the smell of the trenches was appalling owing to a combination of rotting corpses, sewage and unwashed soldiers. The soldiers were also infested with lice, or 'chats' as they called them.

The weather had a marked effect on soldiers' lives. In summer the trenches were hot, dusty and smelly. In wet weather soldiers spent much time up to their ankles or knees in water. Many thousands suffered from 'trench foot', caused by standing in water for hours or days. In winter the trenches offered little protection from the cold. Many soldiers got frostbite.

To add to all of these unpleasant problems the trenches were infested by rats. Many soldiers on all sides described the huge, fat 'corpse rats' which thrived on the dead bodies and the rubbish created by the armies. Some accounts even speak of cats and dogs killed by rats in overwhelming numbers.

SOURCE 35

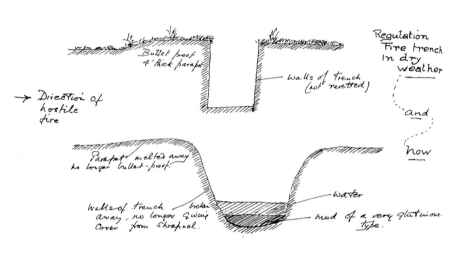

Sketch from Billy Congreve's diary showing a cross-section of a trench in dry and wet conditions.

All soldiers were aware that their daily lives could change at any time. Sometimes the soldiers' trenches could be subject to non-stop artillery bombardment for days on end. The majority of First World War casualties were caused by artillery. Death and injury could come almost without warning, as a shell buried soldiers under tons of earth, leaving smashed bodies and wrecked trenches, and the job of burying the dead.

Usually a long bombardment would be the prelude to an assault by the enemy; or a charge 'over the top' by your own side.

Despite all these hardships, it is worth remembering that discipline in all of the forces on the Western Front was good. There were relatively few desertions considering the huge scale of the armies. The only major mutiny among Allied forces was in 1917 when French soldiers refused to fight after appalling losses that year.

Historian Niall Ferguson's research suggests that a combination of factors kept discipline in the British army:

- A sense of comradeship and even achievement – many soldiers achieved more than they ever thought they could.
- Patriotism – most soldiers felt that they were fighting for their home and country.
- The quality and quantity of food rations for British troops were generally good, even if rather monotonous (mainly corned beef and jam). There were also regular luxuries such as tobacco, alcohol and parcels sent from home.
- Rest – most infantrymen spent about 60 per cent of their time behind the lines with comparatively light duties. Football matches were very popular.

Most surprisingly perhaps, soldiers had a respect for their leaders. There is a widespread modern myth that the generals wined and dined in the officers' mess while the men lived and died in the squalor of the trenches. But 78 officers above the rank of brigadier-general from Britain and the British Empire died on active service and 146 were wounded. This is evidence that British generals were often close enough to the front line to be in danger of losing their lives.

SOURCE 36

1 If you had to pair up Source 36 with one of the text sources on pages 17–28, which text source would you choose and why?

L'Enfer (Hell) by the French war artist Georges Leroux, 1916.

SOURCE 37

To live amongst men who would give their last fag, their last bite, even their last breath if need be for a pal – that is the comradeship of the trenches. The only clean thing to come out of this life of cruelty and filth.

A soldier quoted in J Ellis, *Eye Deep in Hell*, 1976.

FOCUS TASK

What was life like on the Western Front?

During the war, often the only chance a soldier had to be honest was when writing a diary. Using pages 20–27 to help you, write three diary entries which give a soldier's honest feelings about what life in the trenches was really like during a calm period, a bombardment and an assault.

SOURCE 38

I do not know why the various occasions on which battalions have fought till there were merely a few score survivors have not been properly chronicled . . . Certain platoons or companies fought shoulder to shoulder till the last man dropped . . . or . . . were shelled to nothingness, or getting over the top went forward till they all withered away under machine gun fire . . . . A fortnight after some exploit, a field-marshal or divisional general comes down to a battalion to thank it for its gallant conduct, and fancies for a moment, perchance, that he is looking at the men who did the deed of valour, and not a large draft that has just been brought up from England and the base to fill the gap. He should ask the services of the chaplain and make his congratulations in the graveyard or go to the hospital and make them there.

A private's view of warfare, 1916.

SOURCE 39

It was just as dangerous to go back as it was to go on. There were machine gun bullets spraying to and fro all the time . . . When I reached our trenches I missed my footing and fell on the floor, stunned. When I got up I saw an officer standing on the fire step looking through binoculars at No Man's Land. As I walked down the trench towards the dressing station he stood in my way with a pistol in his hand. He never said a word, but then he just stepped aside and let me pass. When I got to the dressing station I asked someone 'What's that officer doing back there with the gun in his hand?', and they said that his job was to shoot anyone who came back not wounded. I thought to myself, what kind of a job is that? Anyone could have lost his nerve that day.

Memories of the Somme. A British soldier interviewed by the *Sunday Times* for an article published in 1986 – the 70th anniversary of the Battle of the Somme.

SOURCE 40

It is all rot the stuff one reads in the papers about the inferiority of the German soldiers to ours. If anything, the German is the better, for though we are undoubtedly the more dogged and impossible to beat, they are the more highly disciplined.

From the diary of Billy Congreve.

1 Which of the illustrations in Sources 41 and 42 gives the more realistic impression of life for the soldiers?

The view from Britain

In the early stages of the war, it was difficult for people in Britain to get an accurate impression of what life in the trenches was really like. Letters from soldiers to their families were usually censored. No photographers were allowed in the trenches (except official photographers who had strict rules about what they could photograph). Even official war artists were forbidden from showing dead bodies in their paintings. Newspaper reports in Britain were heavily censored. People back home in Britain were therefore sheltered from the realities of trench warfare.

Sometimes this situation resulted in a gulf between a soldier and his family. No war like this had ever been fought. How could a soldier explain the horrors to a family who were still being fed a daily diet of glorious victories by the magazines and newspapers at home?

As the conflict continued, the realities of war began to sink in. War artists began to produce more sombre paintings. With huge casualties such as those at the Somme (see page 33), it was clear that this was not a glorious war, but a grim life or death struggle. Even so, the public in Britain had little idea of what trench warfare was like. The men in the trenches knew how inaccurate much of the reporting was, but they were caught between their knowledge of the truth and their reluctance to upset their families.

SOURCE 41

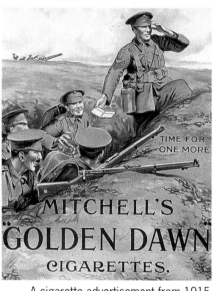

A cigarette advertisement from 1915.

SOURCE 42

The Kensingtons at Laventie by Eric Kennington. The artist painted this while recovering from his wounds in 1915. When it was put on display in 1916 it caused a sensation because there was no hint of glory or optimism in it, unlike all previous paintings.

SOURCE 43

We are the guns, and your masters!
Saw ye our flashes?
Heard ye the scream of our shells in the night, and the shuddering crashes?
Saw ye our work by the roadside, the shrouded things lying,
Moaning to God that he made them – the maimed and the dying?
Husbands or sons, fathers or lovers, we break them.
We are the guns!

From *The Guns* by Siegfried Sassoon.

2 Read Source 44. Choose one of the underlined phrases and write an explanation of what it means.

SOURCE 44

You love us when we're heroes, home on leave,
Or wounded in a mentionable place.
You worship decorations; you believe
That chivalry redeems the war's disgrace.
You make us shells. You listen with delight;
By tales of dirt and danger fondly thrilled
You crow our distant ardours while we fight,
And mourn our laurelled memories when we're killed.
You can't believe that troops retire
When hell's last horror breaks them and they run,
trampling the terrible corpses – blind with blood.
O German mother dreaming by the fire,
while you are knitting socks to send your son
His face is trodden deeper in the mud.

Written by Siegfried Sassoon, who volunteered for the war in 1914 and was wounded seriously enough to be sent home. He was so disgusted by the war that he wrote to his commanders that he was unwilling to fight any more (see page 75).

A

In and Out (I)

That last half-hour before "going in" to the same trenches for the 200th time

In and Out (II)

That first half-hour after "coming out" of those same trenches

B

'Well, if you knows of a Better 'ole, go to it!'

Cartoons by Bruce Bairnsfather, an officer serving on the Western Front. His light-hearted portrayal of trench life was immensely popular with soldiers, and his cartoons were regularly published in the British press. Yet even these were disapproved of by many officials in Britain.

3 Study Source 45. Why do you think officials in Britain might disapprove of these cartoons?

FOCUS TASK

How was the war portrayed?

1 a) Look back over pages 26–29 and find examples of each of the following kinds of source about the war:
- poem
- advertisement
- painting
- newspaper article
- cartoon
- diary
- novel
- any others you can think of.

b) Fill in a chart like this:

Kind of source	Example	How does it portray the war?

2 Choose the two sources which you think are most realistic. Explain your choice.
3 Choose two which are unrealistic. Explain your choice.
4 From what you now know about the war, explain why representations of it vary so greatly.

ACTIVITY

Look back at your diary entries from page 27.

Imagine you are going to show your diary to a family member at home. Edit your diary so that they will not be shocked by it.

Breaking the stalemate

Stalemate is a term borrowed from chess. It means that, however hard they try, neither player can make a winning move. It is a very good term to describe the situation on the Western Front from December 1914 right through to 1918. However hard they tried (and they did try – very hard indeed!), neither side could make a breakthrough. The reasons were simple. The techniques and the weapons were better suited to defence than to attack. It was much easier to defend a position than to attack one.

- Barbed wire, trenches and mud made cavalry charges ineffective.
- Machine guns could mow down charging infantry.
- The colossal new guns of the artillery could kill the enemy in their trenches, could wear down the troops and sap their morale and could disrupt enemy supplies, but they couldn't make a breakthrough.
- Artillery could also destroy enemy guns but the supply of weapons to both sides quickly became inexhaustible. Factories back home in each country were soon geared up to produce all the extra munitions needed.

In hindsight, it is easy to see how impossible it was to make a breakthrough. At the time, it must have been much harder, so on the Western Front the same basic pattern of barrage and infantry attack continued through 1915, 1916 and 1917.

1915: the stalemate continues

In 1915 the French, British and Germans all tried and failed to break the deadlock. Early in 1915 the French lost many thousands in an unsuccessful offensive in Champagne (arrow 1 in Source 46). The British gained some ground at Neuve Chapelle in March but at a heavy cost. The Germans were driven back from Ypres in April (arrow 2) with heavy losses and the British suffered a setback at Loos in September.

1916: the year of attrition – Verdun and the Somme

In February 1916 the Germans began a determined battle to capture strategic French forts surrounding Verdun (arrow 4). The Germans recognised that the French were leading the Allied effort at this stage of the war. The German commander, Falkenhayn, came up with a strategy of attrition. His tactic was to 'bleed France white'. The tactic failed, in that both sides suffered roughly equal losses. For six months both sides poured men and resources into this battle. Attacks were followed by counter-attacks and by July 1916 some 700,000 men had fallen. The French, led by General Pétain, held out, but by the summer of 1916 they were close to breaking. The huge losses had weakened both sides, but the Germans had greater resources. The French army was near breaking point.

To relieve the pressure, the British led by Field Marshal Douglas Haig launched their long-planned offensive at the Somme (arrow 5). After a week-long artillery bombardment of German trenches, British troops advanced. On the first day there were 57,000 British casualties. The fighting continued until November 1916 with the loss of 1.25 million men (see pages 33–36).

Back in Britain, politicians and public were horrified at the losses. But to the military leaders the nature of the exercise was clear. The war was a contest to see which side could last out the long and dreadful war of attrition. Douglas Haig briefed the government that 'the nation must be taught to bear losses'. The nation did accept them and in doing so played a key role in victory.

For British history, the Somme is one of the most important stories of the war. It tells you a lot about the war in general and reactions to it, so you will study the Battle of the Somme in detail on pages 33–36.

SOURCE **46**

Key

— Line of trenches

— Hindenburg Line

◯➤ Main Allied attacks

◯➣ Main German attacks

Major battles on the Western Front, 1915–17.

1917: USA in, Russia out

In 1917, the new French General, Nivelle, put forward a plan to break the deadlock. However, the Germans knew of his plans and retreated to their new, stronger positions, called the Hindenburg Line. Nivelle refused to change his plans. By previous standards the Nivelle Offensive (arrow 6) was quite successful, but again the casualties were huge. Nivelle had raised hopes which could not be met, and the French army mutinied. The crisis was resolved by Pétain. By a combination of ruthlessly punishing the leaders of the mutiny yet improving conditions for ordinary soldiers, he regained the confidence of the French troops.

The British and Canadians had some successes. The Canadians in particular enjoyed a spectacular victory, capturing the fortified Vimy Ridge in April 1917 (arrow 3).

In July the third battle of Ypres began. The British detonated huge mines at Messines which destroyed the German artillery positions, and killed 10,000 German soldiers at a stroke. However, the infantry advance which followed this became hopelessly bogged down. Heavy rain created nightmare conditions, particularly around the ruined village of Passchendaele (arrow 7).

Some successes came at Cambrai in November. The British used over 350 tanks to good effect, but were unable to hold the ground that they had captured. It was the same old story.

These were minor victories in the broader context. The decisive military breakthrough was still elusive. But elsewhere, away from the Western Front, other developments were taking place which might have a more decisive effect on the Western Front.

The British blockade

From the start of the war both sides tried to prevent the other from getting essential supplies to its soldiers. Maybe they could be starved into submission? The British had been blockading German ports since 1914. The blockade was supposed to strangle German industry so that it could not supply the German army. It reduced German trade from $5.9 billion in 1914 to just $0.8 billion in 1917. By 1917 civilians in Germany were experiencing severe shortages (see page 45).

The German U-boat campaign

The Germans tried something similar. They sank British ships supplying Britain. In 1917 they introduced a policy of unrestricted submarine warfare against all ships that they suspected were carrying goods to Britain (see page 44). This caused shortages in Britain but it also had another unintended effect. It helped to bring the USA into the war.

The USA joins the war

The USA was officially neutral but was supplying loans and equipment to the Allies. The Germans attacked and destroyed many American ships which they suspected of carrying supplies to the Allies. They also sank passenger ships, killing many American civilians. When the USA discovered that Germany hoped to ally with Mexico against them it was the final straw and the USA declared war on Germany on 1 April 1917.

The Russian Revolution

The Allies thought that the entry of the USA would turn the tide in their favour, but by late 1917 there was little cause for optimism. The Americans needed time to build up an army. Even worse, the most crushing blow of all, a revolution in Russia had brought in a Communist government and it had made peace with Germany. The Germans could now transfer hundreds of thousands of troops back to the Western Front. It looked as if 1918 could be decisive.

1 Look at Source 47. Explain what the German cartoonist is trying to say about the USA. Refer to details in the cartoon and the way the characters are drawn.

SOURCE 47

A German cartoon from February 1915 accusing the USA of double standards. The German text means: 'I am neutral'.

SOURCE 48

As the fog cleared a little, we saw the Germans for the first time, advancing in thousands. The whole area was darkened by their figures, a moving mass of grey . . . the ground favoured their advance; it was a maze of shell holes and they crawled from one to the other . . . All our Lewis guns, damaged earlier by shell fire, were out of action, and by now German bullets were whistling at us from all directions . . . it was only then that we realised that we were completely surrounded and hopelessly outnumbered. The first breakthrough had apparently come on our right when the enemy had captured our Company Headquarters.

G Wright, a soldier in the North Staffordshire Regiment, remembers the German attack in the Ludendorff Offensive.

ACTIVITY

Historians have disagreed as to what were the turning points of the war on the Western Front.

1 Work in groups of three. One of you take 1916, one take 1917, the other take 1918. Each of you write a paragraph explaining why your year saw the turning point in the war. Use the information on pages 30–32 to help you.
2 Show your paragraph to the other members of the group, then take a vote on which year saw the most important turning point.

FOCUS TASK

How was the stalemate broken?

1 Draw a chart like this:

Why the war reached stalemate	How and why the stalemate was broken

2 In each column write as many reasons as you can find on pages 30–32. Add any other reasons you can find on pages 20–29.
3 Draw lines to join up anything in column 1 with anything it matches in column 2.
4 Write your own brief account of the war in two parts: in Part 1 explain how and why the war reached stalemate; in Part 2 explain how and why the stalemate was broken.

1918: the Hundred Days – the stalemate is broken

Things may have looked bad for the Allies but the German situation was also desperate in early 1918. Despite the good news of the Russian surrender, the Allies' blockade of German ports had starved the economy of raw materials and the population (including the soldiers) of food. Worse still, the USA was moving troops to France at a rate of 50,000 per month. Above all, the German army was not the quality fighting machine it had been. Germany needed a quick victory and the surrender of Russia gave the Germans one last opportunity to achieve a military breakthrough and end the stalemate.

Through the early months of 1918 Germany transferred troops from the East to the Western Front. In March 1918 the German Commander Ludendorff launched the great gamble to win the war. It started with the typical huge bombardment and gas attacks. However, instead of the usual 'wave' of infantry, he followed up with attacks by smaller bands of specially trained and lightly equipped 'storm troops' (see Source 48) who struck during a heavy fog along the entire front line. The idea was to stop the Allies massing their defence in a single place. It was very effective. The Germans broke through the Allied lines in many places, advanced 64 kilometres and Paris was now in range of heavy gunfire.

The 'Ludendorff Offensive' had so far gone very well. However, the German army lost 400,000 men in making this breakthrough and they had no reserves to call on. The troops of 1918 did not compare well with those of 1914. Their discipline was poor and they were badly fed and supplied. Many of the planned German advances were held up as troops stopped to loot food and supplies from captured trenches or villages. They also came up against well-led and well-equipped Allied forces (see Source 49). The blockades had prevented the Germans from making similar technological improvements.

Between May and August the Germans made no further progress and it was clear that they had run out of time and resources. The Germans had ended trench warfare but it was the Allies who eventually gained the benefit. By now, they had large numbers of well-fed and well-equipped troops. These troops were supported by tanks, aircraft and improved artillery. By 1918 the big guns were capable of hitting targets with impressive accuracy as well as laying down smokescreens or giving covering fire for attackers.

On 8 August the Allies counter-attacked along much of the Western Front. It was now just a matter of time before the Allies defeated Germany. By late September they had reached the Hindenburg Line. By October the Germans were in full retreat. This period has become known as 'The Hundred Days'. Finally, on 11 November 1918 the Armistice (ceasefire) came into effect. The Great War was over.

SOURCE 49

The huge successes under Field Marshal Sir Douglas Haig between 8 August and 11 November 1918 are now largely forgotten by the British public. However, these were the greatest series of victories in the British Army's whole history . . .

Haig's armies took 188,700 prisoners and 2,840 guns – only 7,800 prisoners and 935 guns less than those taken by the French, Belgian and American armies combined. These successes were the result of the courage and endurance of the front-line soldiers. They were also the result of the commanders' tactical and technological improvements. By August 1918, Haig's forces were employing tanks; aircraft; armoured cars; motorised machine-gun units; wireless; and ammunition drops by parachute. They had an excellent communication and transport system that enabled Haig to switch attacks to another sector at short notice – so keeping the Germans off balance.

If we are to criticise Haig and his army commanders for their mistakes in 1916 and 1917, then it is perhaps only fair that, at the same time, they should receive due credit for their decisive, but forgotten victories.

Adapted from an article by Professor Peter Simpkin, senior historian at the Imperial War Museum, London.

Case study: General Haig and the Battle of the Somme

1 Look at Sources 50–52.
   a) Brainstorm a list of ten key words to define the Battle of the Somme that come to mind after looking at the sources.
   b) Compare your ten words with the person sitting next to you.
   c) Agree on the most appropriate five words.

SOURCE 50

A mural, painted in 1936, at Donegall Pass in Belfast. The 36th Ulster Division was one of the few units to achieve its objective on the first day of the Battle of the Somme. It suffered over 5000 casualties in the battle.

SOURCE 51

There was no lingering about when zero hour came. Our platoon officer blew his whistle and he was the first up the scaling ladder, with his revolver in one hand and cigarette in the other. 'Come on, boys,' he said, and up he went. We went up after him one at a time. I never saw the officer again. His name is on the memorial to the missing which they built after the war at Thiepval. He was only young but he was a very brave man.

The memories of Private George Morgan who took part in the attack on 1 July 1916 at the Battle of the Somme.

SOURCE 52

Reg. No.	Rank.	Name.	Date of Death.
12/288	Pte.	Bagshaw, William	1/7/16
12/289	,,	Bailey, Joseph	1/7/16
12/291	,,	Barlow, Wilfred	16/5/16
12/294	,,	Batley, Edward	1/7/16
12/296	,,	Baylis, Lawrence	1/7/16
12/307	Cpl.	Braham, George	1/7/16
12/310	Pte.	Bramham, George	13/10/18
12/314	C.S.M.	Bright, Arthur Willey	12/4/18
12/318	Pte.	Brookfield, Fredk. Harold	1/7/16
12/591	,,	Bedford, Norman	1/7/16
12/593	,,	Beniston, Aubrey	1/7/16
12/597	L/Cpl.	Blenkarn, William	10/9/16
12/600	Pte.	Bowes, Frank	1/7/16
12/604	,,	Bratley, Clifford William	11/4/18
12/606	,,	Brindley, Charles W.	14/3/17
12/607	,,	Brown, Arthur	1/7/16
12/608	,,	Brown, Samuel	6/12/17
12/611	,,	Busfield, Harry Craven	18/5/17
12/862	L/Cpl.	Barnsley, Frank	1/7/16
12/865	Pte.	Barrott, John Henry	1/7/16
12/867	,,	Barton, John Arthur	1/7/16
12/870	,,	Bennett, Joseph Arnold	1/7/16
12/871	L/Cpl.	Binder, Walter Bertram	1/7/16
12/874	,,	Bland, Ernest	1/7/16

Part of the list of dead and wounded from the Sheffield Pals Battalion on the first day of the Somme. Many soldiers were in 'pals' battalions. If you joined a pals battalion, you would be fighting with men from your local area. The Sheffield Pals suffered 548 casualties on the first day of the battle.

For British history, the Battle of the Somme is one of the most significant events in the war. Sources 50–52 give some idea of why. It was a massive battle. The casualties were horrific. Most casualties were young men in their late teens or early to mid twenties. Many pals battalions (see Source 52) were practically wiped out, and villages in Britain and around the empire lost an entire generation of young men at the Somme. For example, the 11th Cambridgeshire Battalion sent 750 men over the top on 1 July and 691 of them became casualties of war. The casualties alone would qualify this battle for a place in all history books.

But there is more. The Somme has become the focus of debate about leadership. The abiding impression of the war is that the volunteers who made up most of the army followed their orders with enormous courage, but were betrayed by their leaders. It is a popular view. It is also an easy view to support. But in this case study we want to look at the Battle of the Somme more objectively.

What actually went wrong? Was it all the fault of the British commander, General Haig? If it was Haig's fault, why are there military historians who argue that Haig was not a blundering incompetent and why are there also many military historians who believe that the Somme was not a military disaster?

General Sir Douglas Haig. He successfully commanded the British troops at Mons and Ypres in 1914. By the end of 1915 he was commanding all the British forces in France.

1 With hindsight, historians know of many of the planning errors made by Haig before the attack on the Somme.
  a) Make a list of the planning errors you think he made.
  b) Try to decide how many of these errors can only be seen with the benefit of hindsight.

ACTIVITY

Discuss this question as a class:

Is it morally acceptable to make the killing of enemy soldiers an objective for a military operation?

SOURCE **55**

Remembering the dissatisfaction displayed by ministers at the end of 1915 because the operations had not come up to their expectations, the General Staff took the precaution to make quite clear beforehand the nature of the success which the Somme campaign might yield. The necessity of relieving pressure on the French Army at Verdun remains, and is more urgent than ever. This is, therefore, the first objective to be obtained by the combined British and French offensive. The second objective is to inflict as heavy losses as possible upon the German armies.

Sir William Robertson, Chief of the Imperial General Staff, commenting on British plans at the Somme after the end of the war.

The plan

The battle was originally planned as an attack by the French army with British support. The British commander, General Haig, actually favoured an attack further north and west in Flanders. The German attack at Verdun altered these plans. By the summer of 1916 it was agreed that Haig would lead a mainly British offensive in the area around the River Somme. The objectives were to gain territory and to draw German troops away from Verdun. Another aim was to kill as many German soldiers as possible as part of the 'war of attrition'.

The tactics

Haig and his deputy, General Rawlinson, worked out the details.

- There would be a huge artillery bombardment, and mines would devastate German positions.
- The enemy's barbed wire would be cut and the German trenches and dug-outs smashed.
- The attacking British troops would be able to walk across no man's land rather than run.
- They would carry heavy packs and trench repair equipment so that they could rebuild and defend the German trenches and so stop the Germans retaking their lost territory.
- British cavalry forces were also kept in readiness to charge into gaps in the German line.

SOURCE **54**

A captured German dug-out, 1917.

Were these the right tactics?

Haig certainly knew about the German dug-outs and the masses of barbed wire in front of them. However, Haig overestimated the ability of the artillery to destroy the German defences.

- The defenders were on high ground with a good view of any attacking forces.
- The German defences had been in place since 1914 and the German soldiers had not been idle. Their dug-outs were deep underground and fortified with concrete.
- The Germans had stretched wire like a band more than 30 metres wide all along the front. It was almost impossible to penetrate.
- Many of the shells supplied to the Allied gunners were of poor quality. There was certainly a vast bombardment, but many shells were not powerful enough to destroy the defences or simply failed to go off.

SOURCE 56

Hundreds of dead were strung out like wreckage washed up to a high-water mark. Quite as many died on the enemy wire as on the ground, like fish caught in the net. They hung there in grotesque postures. Some looked as though they were praying; they had died on their knees and the wire had prevented their fall. From the way the dead were equally spread out, whether on the wire or lying in front of it, it was clear that there were no gaps in the wire at the time of the attack.

Concentrated machine gun fire from sufficient guns to command every inch of the wire had done its terrible work. The Germans must have been reinforcing the wire for months. It was so dense that daylight could barely be seen through it. Through the glasses it looked a black mass. The German faith in massed wire had paid off.

How did our planners imagine that Tommies, having survived all other hazards – and there were plenty in crossing No Man's Land – would get through the German wire? Had they studied the black density of it through their powerful binoculars? Who told them that artillery fire would pound such wire to pieces, making it possible to get through? Any Tommy could have told them that shell fire lifts wire up and drops it down, often in a worse tangle than before.

An extract from a book written by George Coppard after the war. Coppard was a machine-gunner in the British army and was at the Somme.

The battle

In the last week of June, the British pounded the German lines with 1.7 million shells.

SOURCE 57

French trenches used during the Battle of the Somme.

1 July 1916 . . .

The infantry attack began at 7.30 a.m. on 1 July. Attacks usually began at dawn, but the commanders were confident that there would be little resistance. Two huge mines placed under the German lines by sappers were detonated. The noise could be heard in London.

The assault began. Twenty-seven divisions (about 750,000 men) went over the top against the Germans' 16 divisions.

The French forces made some quick gains. They were more experienced than the British in such battles and they were moving quickly because they were not weighed down by packs. However, the French found themselves isolated and had to withdraw again because most of the British forces were advancing too slowly.

The slow pace of the British advance gave the Germans enough time to emerge from their dug-outs and to set up their machine guns. Some German gunners said that the sheer numbers of British forces would have overwhelmed them, if they had charged more quickly.

The wire was undamaged in many areas, so the British troops were funnelled into areas where there were gaps in the wire. They were sitting targets for German gunners. There were around 57,000 casualties on the first day, about a third of them killed.

At the time it was chaos. No one knew quite what was happening. But the picture soon emerged of a military disaster, the worst in the history of the British army. The ranks of the junior officers were devastated, leaving soldiers confused about what to do – there had been no orders to prepare them for the situation they found themselves in.

and thereafter . . .

Rawlinson was devastated by the events of the first day and expressed doubts about continuing, but Haig insisted that the attacks should continue through July and August – he had to relieve the French at Verdun and he also felt confident that he could win a great victory.

Some lessons were learnt after the initial disaster and some gains were made (for example, the village of Pozieres was captured on 23 July). Haig was bitterly criticised for simply throwing men at massed defences or being obsessed with out-of-date tactics like cavalry charges. This was not entirely fair. For example, on 15 September Haig varied his tactics when British forces attacked in a different part of the Somme area and used tanks for the first time in the war. There were no spectacular breakthroughs as Haig had hoped, but there was a steady grinding capture of territory and a destruction of enemy forces whenever weather conditions allowed.

Haig called off the attack with winter setting in and the battle ended on 18 November. A strip of land about 25 km long and 6 km wide had been taken. These small gains had cost the British casualties of around 420,000, the French around 200,000 and the Germans around 500,000.

---

2 'The key error was overconfidence in the artillery.' Read the section about the events of 1 July 1916 and decide whether you agree with this statement.

3 Read Source 56. Why would a British civilian have found this account shocking if they had seen it in 1916?

The aftermath

Haig was bitterly criticised after the battle by his own soldiers, by politicians and in the newspapers. He gained the unwanted title of 'The Butcher of the Somme'. Was this fair? Haig's interpretation was very different. He had warned the politicians in 1916 that the country needed to be prepared for heavy losses if the war was to be won. Haig believed that the key objectives of the Battle of the Somme were achieved. It saved Verdun – its main objective. And some of Germany's best troops were killed and injured in the battle – a fact that would come back to haunt them in 1918.

This was of little comfort to people in Britain. The Somme changed British attitudes to the war. Until the Somme, people believed that a victorious battle could lead to a breakthrough and thus end the war. The Somme brought home to many people that this would be a long, grim war of attrition.

The battle also damaged confidence in the leaders. In the chaos and confusion of the first days of the battle, many of the reports were misleading and over-optimistic. The high expectations and the confusion about what had happened made the press and public suspicious of their own commanders. Relations between Haig and the British Prime Minister David Lloyd George were particularly poor.

SOURCE 58

Should I have resigned rather than agree to this slaughter of brave men [at the Somme]? I have always felt there are solid grounds for criticism of me in that respect. My sole justification is that Haig promised not to press the attack if it became clear that he could not attain his objectives by continuing the offensive.

An extract from the war memoirs of David Lloyd George, the British Prime Minister during the war.

SOURCE 60

By 1918 the best of the old German army lay dead on the battlefields of Verdun and the Somme . . . As time passed, the picture gradually changed for the worse . . . as the number of old peacetime [1914] officers in a unit grew smaller and were replaced by young fellows of the very best will, but without sufficient knowledge.

A German opinion on the German army of 1918.

SOURCE 59

A *2nd Lieutenant G H Ball, C company, 1/5th South Staffordshires*
I . . . joined this battalion on 13 June 1916. Previous to this attack [1 July] I had only been in the trenches for two days – I am 18 years of age.

B *Captain John Kerr, 5th Sherwood Foresters, whose men in the fourth wave were supposed to carry supplies across to the men who had led the attack at 7.30 a.m.*
The smoke had at that time [approximately 8.10 a.m.] practically disappeared and the enemy's trenches were plainly visible – my men were shot down as soon as they showed themselves and I was unable to get forward beyond 70 or 80 yards.

Extracts from evidence given to the Inquiry into the 46th Division's performance on 1 July 1916.

FOCUS TASK

How should we remember the Battle of the Somme?

The Somme is remembered differently by many people. Historians disagree about whether it was a victory or a disaster. Ordinary people are unsure whether their grandfathers and great grandfathers died for a purpose.

Read the information and sources on pages 33–36 and do some research of your own, perhaps using the internet. Decide how you think people in Britain should remember the Battle of the Somme and prepare a presentation on the topic.
Here are some descriptions to start your thinking:
- a brutal campaign of attrition that achieved its main objectives
- a crucial battle that saved the French army
- a disaster
- a great victory at a terrible cost
- a shocking case of incompetent leadership on the part of General Haig
- one major step towards the defeat of Germany
- a tribute to the heroism of ordinary soldiers
- an example of cynical political leaders shifting the blame on to military leaders
- an example of society being shocked by the reality of war and looking for someone to blame.

You could present your conclusions as an ICT presentation. Alternatively, you could create a website about the battle.

1 Read Source 58. Is Lloyd George blaming himself or Haig for events at the Somme?
2 Do you regard Sources 59A and 59B as more or less shocking than Source 56? Explain your answer.
3 Source 60 seems to suggest that the tactics of attrition eventually worked. Does that mean it was morally justifiable? Give reasons.
4 How far does your work on this case study support or challenge your answer to the Focus Task on page 32?

2.2 The war on other fronts

SOURCE 1

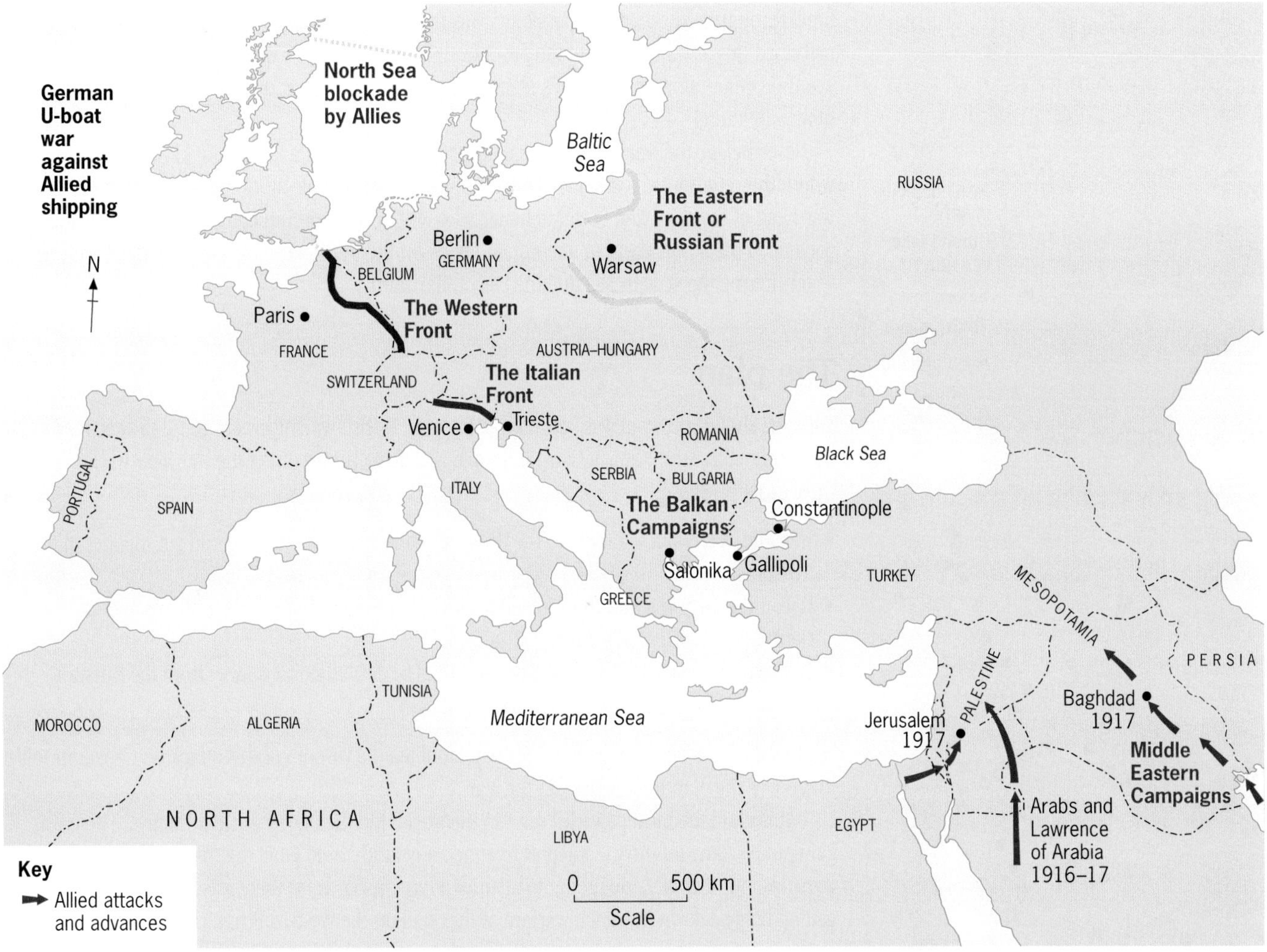

The main fronts of the First World War.

Source 1 shows you the scope of the fighting in the First World War. The Western Front was only part of a war that also caused suffering and destruction in eastern Europe, the Middle East and North Africa. There were spectacular battles in the mountains between Italian and Austrian troops. There were tremendous battles on the Eastern Front where Russians fought Germans and Austrians. In the Middle East, Turkish troops with German officers fought British Commonwealth and Empire troops, along with their Arab allies.

FOCUS TASK

1 Draw your own copy of the chart below.

Front	Similarities to the Western Front	Differences from the Western Front

2 Fill it out as you find out about each of the other fronts on pages 38–42.
3 Use your completed table to write an essay comparing the different fronts.

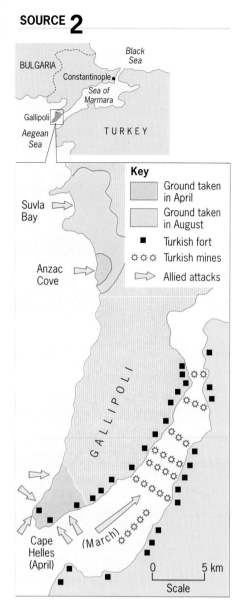

Key

- Ground taken in April
- Ground taken in August
- ■ Turkish fort
- ✿✿✿ Turkish mines
- ⇨ Allied attacks

The Dardanelles strait and the Gallipoli campaign.

Shells were moaning and whining all around us and the noise of gunfire was something terrible. The Fort was firing like Hell. It was one continual deafening roar caused by the firing of our ships and the moaning, hissing noise of the enemy's shells.

Then we saw the Bouvet *suddenly keel over and turn upside down. She sank in two and a half minutes taking the best part of her crew with her.*

Written by Able Seaman Kemm who was aboard the *Prince George* battleship.

Gallipoli

In 1915 casualties were mounting on the Western Front and government ministers in London could see no prospect of breaking the stalemate. They began to look for another way to gain a breakthrough in the war. One possibility was to attack one of Germany's allies. Lloyd George described this as 'knocking out the props from under Germany'. However, this was not a very accurate description of Germany's allies. Germany was propping up its allies rather than the other way round.

Nevertheless, the war planners were attracted to the idea of a knock-out blow against Turkey, whom they considered to be one of Germany's more vulnerable allies. Winston Churchill, who was head of the navy, and Lord Kitchener, who was in effect overall commander of the war effort, persuaded the government to attempt an attack on the Dardanelles strait, a narrow stretch of water linking the Aegean Sea and the Sea of Marmara.

The plan

Source 2 shows you what was supposed to happen. British warships were going to sweep through the Dardanelles strait, attack Constantinople and drive Turkey out of the war. This would have three other results:

- It would open up a sea route to the Russian Front so that the Allies could get supplies to the Russians.
- It would establish a new front. Allied troops could march through the Balkans and attack Germany's principal ally, Austria–Hungary.
- It would relieve pressure on the Russian forces by drawing troops away from the Russian Front.

Lord Kitchener even suggested to those who doubted the wisdom of this attack on Constantinople that it was the plan that would win the war.

Britain had the most powerful navy in the world and the plan seemed attractive. There was going to be some infantry in support to attack any land-based guns that might threaten the warships, but they were not going to attempt a land invasion, so there was no danger of troops getting bogged down in trench warfare as they had on the Western Front. Or so they thought!

What actually happened

In March 1915 the warships began their assault. They bombarded the strong forts that lined the strait, then made their advance. As the British and French ships entered the strait, a combination of mines and shell fire from the forts on the shore sank three battle cruisers and damaged others.

The heart of the British navy was thus threatened. The Allied commanders decided that this naval attack would not succeed, and that the risks of the navy's trying to continue towards Constantinople were too great. They decided that after all they would launch a land invasion to capture the peninsula. Once the Turks were driven off Gallipoli, the naval operation could restart.

In April a hastily assembled force of British, French and ANZAC (Australian and New Zealand) troops attacked Helles beach. However, the war commanders had severely underestimated the power of the defending army. The commanders had been refused aid from the Royal Flying Corps, which could have helped a lot in assessing the strength of the Turks.

The Turks had been well aware that an attack was coming. A new German commander Otto Liman von Sanders had doubled the defensive forces, and dug them into strong positions on the hills overlooking the beaches on which the Allies were likely to land. He had given the troops a crash course in defending trench positions – including training in the British speciality, the use of the bayonet.

At four o'clock in the morning on 25 April, in pitch dark, the first troops went ashore and charged up the steep hillsides under a hail of machine-gun fire which continued for most of the day.

SOURCE 4

1 And the band played Waltzing Matilda,
As we sailed away from the quay,
And amidst all the tears and the shouts
and the cheers,
We sailed off for Gallipoli.

2 How well I remember that terrible day
When the blood stained the sand and the
water
And how in that hell that they call Suvla
Bay
We were butchered like lambs at the
slaughter.
Johnny Turkey was ready,
He primed himself well,
He showered us with bullets and he
rained us with shells
and in five minutes flat he'd blown us
to hell
Nearly blew us right back to Australia.

3 And the band played Waltzing Matilda
As we stopped to bury our slain
And we buried ours
As they buried theirs
And started all over again.

An Australian folk song.

1 Use your knowledge of events at
   Gallipoli to write a verse-by-verse
   explanation of the song in Source 4.
2 Why is this source valuable to
   historians?

SOURCE 7

Disease dominated the whole situation. The
latrines were continually thronged with
men so that attempts at covering or
disinfecting excreta became a farce. Black
swarms of flies carried infection warm
from the very bowel to the food as it passed
the lips.

Written by the official historian of the
Australian Medical Services.

3 Would you agree that the Gallipoli
   campaign was a total failure? Explain
   your answer.
4 Why do you think the campaign was
   called off?
5 List the different kinds of source used
   on pages 38–39 to find out about
   Gallipoli. For each source explain why
   it is useful.

SOURCE 5

A model showing the landing on Helles beach, 25 April.

By mid-afternoon the beach was strewn with the dead and dying. Despite the massive odds against them, the troops fought very bravely and captured a number of Turkish trenches. However, by the following day it was already clear that the objective of clearing the Turks off the peninsula could not be achieved. Should they dig in or withdraw? The order came through to dig in. 'You have got through the difficult business,' said the commander, 'now you only have to dig, dig, dig, until you are safe.'

SOURCE 6

It seems that we have finished with general attack and are now reduced to the silly old game of trench warfare. Clearing the Dardanelles at this rate will mean some years' work.

Written by the commander of the naval forces at Gallipoli, Major-General Paris, 13 May.

Conditions for the troops were awful. In the blistering summer heat, and with decaying corpses strewn along the front line on both sides, disease was rampant. With so many unburied corpses lying in the no man's land between the trenches, on 20 May both sides agreed a one-day truce. They frantically buried the dead. Some Turks and Allied troops met and exchanged greetings. At sunset they returned to their trenches. And the next day the killing started again.

Neither side could break the deadlock and both poured more troops into the area. In August another landing was made at Suvla Bay, but again the troops could not break through the defences of the Turks.

One part of the Allies' campaign in the Dardanelles was successful. Submarines did get through the minefields of the strait to attack Constantinople harbour. Turkish warships, troopships and merchant vessels were sunk in such numbers that the Turkish war effort was seriously affected. But the main fleet never again attempted to get through.

In November the troops at Gallipoli were facing a new problem – frostbite. The hard Turkish winter had closed in. The troops were extremely ill-equipped. In one snowstorm there were 16,000 cases of frostbite and 300 deaths.

In December, eight months after the landing, there was no prospect of success. Tens of thousands of soldiers lay dead around the coasts of Gallipoli. The decision was taken to pull out. The withdrawal was supremely well organised and was a complete success. The campaign, however, was seen as a failure and Churchill was humiliated.

FOCUS TASK

Work in pairs. You are historical researchers who have been given two questions to investigate:
• Why was the Gallipoli campaign a failure?
• Why were the casualties so great?
Take one question each.
   As well as the information and sources on pages 38–39, you have Sources 8–14 on page 40 to help you. Taking each source in turn, decide whether it is relevant to your question. If it is, list the reasons it gives you.
   Now write a balanced answer to your question, using the sources to support your answer.

SOURCE 8

The expedition was plagued by inadequate resources. The question arose, if Britain lacked the resources to conduct such a campaign, was it wise to attempt it in the first place?

From *The Great War: Myth and Reality* by D Marshall, 1988.

SOURCE 9

The landing place was a difficult one. A narrow, sandy beach backed by a very high intricate mass of hills, those behind the beach being exceedingly steep. The moment the boats landed the men jumped out and rushed straight for the hills rising almost cliff-like only fifty yards or so beyond the beach.

I went ashore there yesterday, into their position, and it seemed almost incredible that any troops could have done it. It is a stiff climb even up the zig-zag path which the Engineers have now built! How they got up fully armed and equipped over the rough scrub-clad hillside one can hardly imagine!

From a letter by Captain Guy Downay.

SOURCE 10

A successful military operation against the Gallipoli peninsula must hinge upon the ability of the fleet . . . to dominate the Turkish defences with gunfire and to crush their field troops during that period of helplessness while an army is disembarking, but also to cover the advance of the troops once ashore . . .

From a pre-war report about the strength of the Gallipoli positions, which goes on to say that such an operation would not be possible. The report was not given to the commanders of the Gallipoli campaign.

SOURCE 11

General Hamilton informs me that the army is checked. The help which the navy has been able to give the army in its advance has not been as great as anticipated. Though effective in keeping down the fire of the enemy's batteries, when it is a question of trenches and machine guns the navy is of small assistance.

By the naval commander de Roebeck.

Why was Gallipoli a failure?

SOURCE 12

When I was there, in every case, attacks were ordered rather lightheartedly and carried out without method. The men on the spot were not listened to when they pointed out steps to be taken before entering on a special task.

The Turks had sited their trenches very cleverly and it was often useless to attack one set before another had been taken. The Turks dig like moles and prepare line after line for defence: seven or eight close behind the other. The great difficulty is in making attacks and supporting them. The trenches become congested: the telephone wires get cut by shrapnel: and the whole show gets out of control.

Almost always in Gallipoli the attacks were made by men in the trenches and not by fresh troops. The men are kept too long and too thick in the trenches: they become stupefied after five days.

Attacks seemed always to be ordered against very long strips of line at once without any weight anywhere. It all seemed very amateur. But I suppose it couldn't be helped, the idea was always to get through with a rush and to disregard losses.

Major H Mynors Farmar, Staff Captain, 86th Brigade, writing about fighting at Gallipoli.

SOURCE 13

At that time there was no centralized organization in Whitehall, and the Admiralty and War Office operated in water-tight compartments. Very little time had been given to combined planning. The navy would follow time-honoured drills for putting small expeditions ashore. Opposed landings on hostile beaches, under heavy close-range fire, do not seem to have entered the syllabuses at any of the service colleges.

It is clear that Kitchener had only a hazy idea of what was entailed, and that he was hoping Hamilton would pick up a multitude of loose ends and come up with a workable plan.

Considering the crucial importance of the operation, this was a hopeless briefing for a newly appointed commander-in-chief. Hamilton was at the outset the victim of gross dereliction of duty on the part of the General Staff.

Hamilton's only intelligence consisted of a 1912 manual on the Turkish army, some old (and inaccurate) maps, a tourist guide-book, and what little could be gleaned from the Turkish desk at the Foreign Office.

From *Gallipoli*, by Michael Hickey, 1995, describing the planning of the campaign in London. General Hamilton was appointed by Kitchener to lead the campaign.

SOURCE 14

[At Gallipoli], the casualties were appalling. Again and again, battalions were all but wiped out; the trauma inflicted on the survivors must have been terrible. Those who were unnerved had to work it out for themselves, helped when necessary by their officers, chaplains and more robust comrades. Those who failed – and there were some – could be court-martialled and shot; the sentence was frequently carried out down on Suvla beach, and in a sinister copse behind the lines at Helles. Gallipoli was not a friendly place.

They had made provision for about 10,000 casualties. However, planning was made on the assumption that there would be an immediate advance off the beaches, leaving room ashore for field ambulances followed rapidly by three stationary hospitals. It was dreadfully flawed.

Hamilton was deprived of the staff who should have been planning casualty evacuation and provision of essential stores. Most of the ships had been loaded so hurriedly that the equipment needed immediately by any force deposited on a hostile shore was buried under tons of less urgent stores.

From *Gallipoli*, as above, describing the arrangements made for the care of the wounded.

The Balkans and the Middle East

The Balkan Campaign

The Allied force at Salonika in Greece did not fare much better than that at Gallipoli. The aim was to land at Salonika, help Serbia to defeat Austria and Bulgaria and then march through what was described as the 'soft underbelly of Europe' to create a new front against Germany.

The whole scheme was beset by problems. Greece was neutral and wanted to stay out of the war. It was very lukewarm about the campaign. Russia was not particularly happy either about the Allies working with Greece. Greece and Russia were bitter rivals in the Balkans.

The Allied landing took place in October 1915 with a mixed force of British, French, Serb, Italian and Russian troops. They were immediately bogged down by Bulgarian resistance. Here again, as on the Western Front, a stalemate developed.

The main hazard facing the troops was not enemy action but disease – particularly malaria and dysentery. At any one time so many troops were ill that attempts to plan attacks were thwarted.

Leadership was poor. The commander of the French troops, General Maurice Sarrail, had been dismissed for incompetence on the Western Front, but had then been transferred to run the Balkan Campaign.

It was not until September 1918, under Sarrail's command, that the stalemate was broken. In the end, the Bulgarians were defeated in just two weeks. The whole campaign achieved little, apart from tying up the best part of one million British and French troops for much of the war.

SOURCE 15

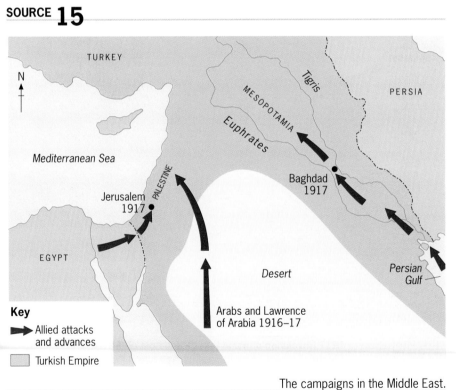

The campaigns in the Middle East.

Key

➡ Allied attacks and advances

▢ Turkish Empire

The Middle East

When Turkey entered the war it threatened Britain's oil supplies in Persia (now Iran) and its territory in Egypt. Turkish soldiers fought well and were ably led and supported by German officers and technical experts. They had such success in Mesopotamia that the Allies had to send 600,000 troops there. They sent a further half a million to Palestine.

Between 1916 and 1918 British, Australian, New Zealand and Indian troops gradually drove the Turks back through Palestine towards Turkey itself. The Turks, as well as facing superior forces, were harassed by guerrilla warfare from the many Arab tribes who wanted independence from Turkish rule. The Arabs were expert hit-and-run raiders and many followed the leadership of the Englishman TE Lawrence, the legendary Lawrence of Arabia.

Under the leadership of General Allenby, the British and Empire forces finally defeated the Turks at Megiddo in September 1918. As the Allies continued to advance, the Turks surrendered on 3 November.

The Eastern Front

Fighting took place across a vast area of land on the Eastern Front. There were some trenches, but warfare did not get bogged down in the same way as on the Western Front. Source 16 describes the course of the war on the Eastern Front.

SOURCE 16

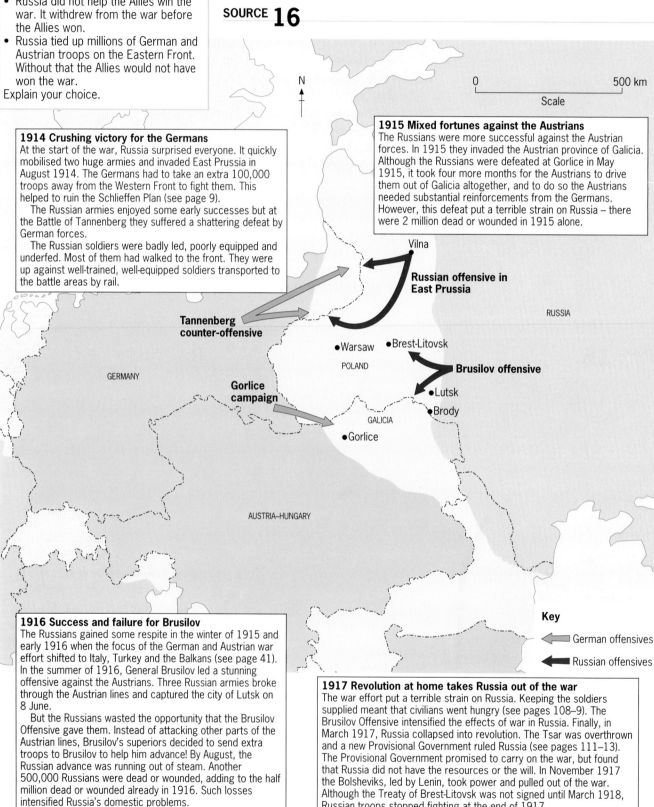

1914 Crushing victory for the Germans
At the start of the war, Russia surprised everyone. It quickly mobilised two huge armies and invaded East Prussia in August 1914. The Germans had to take an extra 100,000 troops away from the Western Front to fight them. This helped to ruin the Schlieffen Plan (see page 9).

The Russian armies enjoyed some early successes but at the Battle of Tannenberg they suffered a shattering defeat by German forces.

The Russian soldiers were badly led, poorly equipped and underfed. Most of them had walked to the front. They were up against well-trained, well-equipped soldiers transported to the battle areas by rail.

1915 Mixed fortunes against the Austrians
The Russians were more successful against the Austrian forces. In 1915 they invaded the Austrian province of Galicia. Although the Russians were defeated at Gorlice in May 1915, it took four more months for the Austrians to drive them out of Galicia altogether, and to do so the Austrians needed substantial reinforcements from the Germans. However, this defeat put a terrible strain on Russia – there were 2 million dead or wounded in 1915 alone.

1916 Success and failure for Brusilov
The Russians gained some respite in the winter of 1915 and early 1916 when the focus of the German and Austrian war effort shifted to Italy, Turkey and the Balkans (see page 41). In the summer of 1916, General Brusilov led a stunning offensive against the Austrians. Three Russian armies broke through the Austrian lines and captured the city of Lutsk on 8 June.

But the Russians wasted the opportunity that the Brusilov Offensive gave them. Instead of attacking other parts of the Austrian lines, Brusilov's superiors decided to send extra troops to Brusilov to help him advance! By August, the Russian advance was running out of steam. Another 500,000 Russians were dead or wounded, adding to the half million dead or wounded already in 1916. Such losses intensified Russia's domestic problems.

1917 Revolution at home takes Russia out of the war
The war effort put a terrible strain on Russia. Keeping the soldiers supplied meant that civilians went hungry (see pages 108–9). The Brusilov Offensive intensified the effects of war in Russia. Finally, in March 1917, Russia collapsed into revolution. The Tsar was overthrown and a new Provisional Government ruled Russia (see pages 111–13). The Provisional Government promised to carry on the war, but found that Russia did not have the resources or the will. In November 1917 the Bolsheviks, led by Lenin, took power and pulled out of the war. Although the Treaty of Brest-Litovsk was not signed until March 1918, Russian troops stopped fighting at the end of 1917.

The Eastern Front in the First World War.

SOURCE 17

Supplying a warship – an illustration from *The Standard History*. If this much was required for a warship with around 2000 men on board, try to imagine what the supplies needed for a city like London would look like.

The war at sea

The sea campaigns of the First World War were unusual in that, although they were vitally important, relatively little fighting took place between the warships. The key objective was to control the seas to stop supplies getting to the enemy. The British BLOCKADE of German ports which stopped supplies reaching Germany was a crucial factor in the Allied victory over Germany. It was just as important as any military victory on land.

Both sides knew how important it was to control the sea, and the war at sea became a cautious war. The British Commander Admiral Jellicoe said that he 'could lose the war in an afternoon' if he rashly allowed his fleet to be put out of action.

There were some battles at sea. In August 1914 the Royal Navy scored a clever (but small) tactical victory in the North Sea at Heligoland, but generally the German navy remained in its ports. Early in 1914 German battle cruisers shelled some British east coast towns (see page 67). In the Mediterranean, the German cruiser *Goeben* evaded the Royal Navy to reach Constantinople. This was an important event, since it influenced the Turks, who were pro-German, to make the decision to enter the war – otherwise they would have had to force the *Goeben* to leave.

The Germans had few ships in the Pacific, but a small squadron gained an early victory in November 1914 off the coast of Chile. The Royal Navy set out to remove this threat and the German ships were destroyed around the Falkland Islands in December 1914.

By 1915 only the ships in German ports remained. The Germans tried to enforce their own blockade of Britain by using submarines to sink merchant ships. This was highly effective. In May 1915 U-boats sank the liner *Lusitania*, with the loss of 1000 passengers.

FACTFILE

New weapons in the war at sea

★ When the war began, most people expected the war at sea to be a confrontation between the new Dreadnought battleships. In fact, submarines became a key feature of the war at sea.

★ Submarines were primitive and inefficient, but they were also very effective.

★ It was a new weapon – the torpedo – which made submarine warfare so effective. Even the mightiest battleship was vulnerable to a torpedo from the smallest submarine.

★ The mine also came into its own as a devastatingly effective weapon in the war at sea.

★ Several ships were lost in the Gallipoli campaign to mines. In the North Sea and the Baltic, minefields were used to protect harbours by both the French and the British.

★ Another tactic was for submarines to lay mines in harbours to catch enemy ships by surprise as they set out to sea.

SOURCE 18

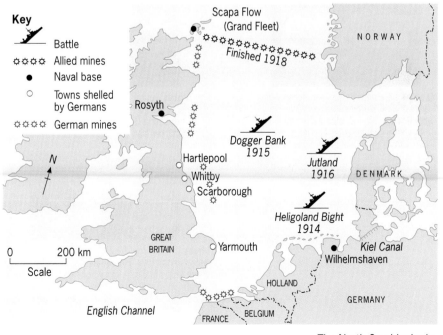

Key
- Battle
- ✪✪✪✪ Allied mines
- ● Naval base
- ○ Towns shelled by Germans
- ✪✪✪✪ German mines

Scapa Flow (Grand Fleet)

NORWAY

Finished 1918

Rosyth

Dogger Bank 1915

Hartlepool
Whitby
Scarborough

Jutland 1916

DENMARK

Heligoland Bight 1914

GREAT BRITAIN

Yarmouth

Kiel Canal
Wilhelmshaven

0   200 km
Scale

HOLLAND

GERMANY

English Channel

FRANCE   BELGIUM

The North Sea blockade.

The Battle of Jutland

The only major sea battle of the war was at Jutland in 1916. In the event, chaos and confusion reigned. The Germans had the best of the exchanges, but the British fleet was simply too large. The Germans sank 14 British ships and lost 11 themselves but never left their harbours again. Both sides claimed to have won the battle. On the one hand, the Germans caused more damage than they received. On the other, the Battle of Jutland certainly failed to achieve the most important objective for Germany which was to remove the blockade.

The U-boat campaign

In the early stages of the war, German U-boats concentrated their attacks on Allied warships. When the Allies learned to protect their warships the U-boats attacked Allied merchant ships instead.

To start with, the attackers would warn a merchant ship that it was about to be sunk and allow the crew to abandon ship. This 'convention' was abandoned in February 1915 when the Germans began a campaign of unrestricted submarine warfare. All Allied ships were targeted. They could be torpedoed without warning. A notable early casualty of the new campaign was the liner *Lusitania*. British propaganda painted this action as a criminal act, but there was some evidence that the ship was carrying explosives for the war effort.

Over 100 American citizens were killed on the *Lusitania*, causing great tension between the US and German governments. Two years later, in 1917, the USA cited the U-boat campaign as one of its reasons for declaring war on Germany.

After the sinking of the *Lusitania*, Germany called off unrestricted submarine warfare, but in 1916 started it again. The Germans' aim was to prevent essential supplies getting to Britain and they almost succeeded. By June 1917, Britain had lost 500,000 tons of shipping to the U-boats. At one point, it was estimated that London had only six weeks' supply of food remaining.

From 1916 the Allies improved their tactics for dealing with the U-boats (see Source 20). However, two other factors were significant in the fight against submarines: the dedication and heroism of the sailors of the merchant navy and the massive output of shipbuilders. By 1917 Britain and the USA were building so many ships that the U-boats could not possibly sink them all. The Germans simply did not have the resources to sustain their campaign and it was finally called off.

SOURCE 19

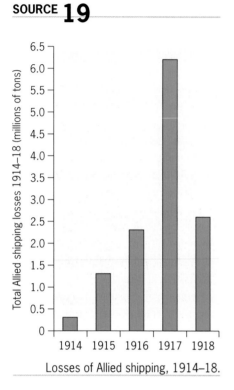

Losses of Allied shipping, 1914–18.

SOURCE 20

Q ships were decoy ships – merchant ships armed with disguised heavy guns. They were designed to fool U-boats into attacking well-defended targets. The immediate success of the Q ships was one reason why, in 1915, the U-boats stopped warning ships that they were about to be attacked.

Mines destroyed more U-boats than any other weapon. They were particularly effective in preventing U-boats from using the English Channel and sailing into British ports.

Depth charges (bombs set to go off underwater at certain depths) were introduced in 1916 and proved second only to mines as a weapon against the U-boats.

Convoys: From mid-1917 almost all merchant ships travelled in convoys. British and US warships escorted merchant ships in close formation. Allied shipping losses fell by about 20 per cent when the convoy system was introduced in mid-1917. Depth charges became even more effective when used together with the convoy system.

Long-range aircraft: By the end of the war, aircraft technology had developed so much that aircraft could protect convoys.

During the war, new tactics were developed to defend merchant ships against submarine attack.

The British blockade

The British blockade was a key factor in the defeat of Germany. Starved of supplies, the German army was weakened and the German people lost some of their will to support the war. The war at sea was therefore arguably as decisive as the war on land.

SOURCE 21

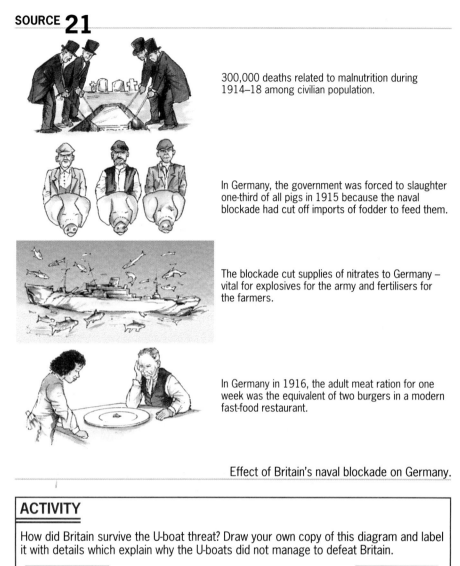

300,000 deaths related to malnutrition during 1914–18 among civilian population.

In Germany, the government was forced to slaughter one-third of all pigs in 1915 because the naval blockade had cut off imports of fodder to feed them.

The blockade cut supplies of nitrates to Germany – vital for explosives for the army and fertilisers for the farmers.

In Germany in 1916, the adult meat ration for one week was the equivalent of two burgers in a modern fast-food restaurant.

Effect of Britain's naval blockade on Germany.

ACTIVITY

How did Britain survive the U-boat threat? Draw your own copy of this diagram and label it with details which explain why the U-boats did not manage to defeat Britain.

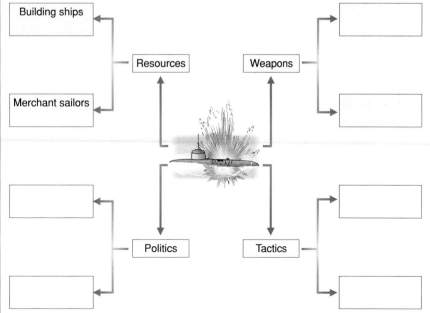

FOCUS TASK

'The war at sea was more important than the Western Front.'

Work in small groups. What evidence is there to support or contradict this view? You could consider the importance of
- the U-boat threat to Britain
- Britain's supply lines
- the British blockade
- the connections between the war at sea and the Western Front.

45

The war in the air

One aspect of the fighting which captured the public's imagination was the developing war in the air. This seemed to give people what they had been looking for in 1914, namely honourable one-to-one combat between gallant young men. The newspapers and journals began to pick up on the story of flying aces from an early stage in the war.

The Germans, French, Australians and other nations all had their own heroes. The most famous was probably the Baron von Richthofen (the Red Baron) and his squadron or 'flying circus'. He shot down 80 Allied planes. Not far behind this total was the Frenchman René Fonck with 75 kills.

SOURCE 22

A still of a 'dogfight' (aerial combat). Such battles were often shown in films.

SOURCE 23

The Red Baron with some of his men.

SOURCE 24

From The Standard History. There were two branches of the air service in 1914 – the Royal Flying Corps (RFC) and the Royal Naval Air Service (RNAS). They were merged in 1918 to form the Royal Air Force (RAF).

1 Use Source 22 to write an advertising slogan for a film.

In the 1920s, it was this aspect of the war, rather than the horrors of the trenches or the waiting games at sea, that was the most popular subject for the new film industry in Hollywood. It is easy to see why, but was the war in the air really as important as it is made out to be?

Airships

In the early stages of the war the most important aircraft were airships. Airships were essentially huge bags of lighter-than-air hydrogen gas. They were powered by engines carried in 'cars' in a keel-like structure underneath. The cars also carried the crew.

SOURCE 25

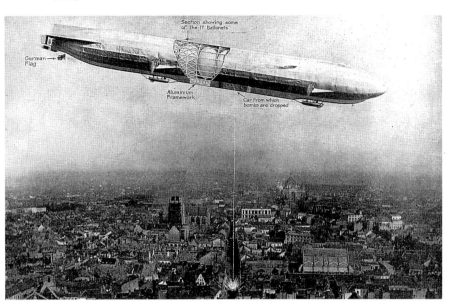

A typical First World War airship (above) with a bomb being dropped from its bullet-proof cage (left).

The British used airships mainly for escorting ships and for hunting U-boats. They could spot U-boats on the surface and warn the escort warships by radio.

German airships were much more advanced and more widely used. Known as ZEPPELINS (after the designer Count Zeppelin) they were a key weapon in the early war at sea. They were able to fly higher and faster than many early planes and were used as observation decks for the German fleet.

SOURCE 26

A Zeppelin with the German fleet.

It was not long before the Germans realised the potential of Zeppelins as bombers. The first raids hit British towns in early 1915. The Zeppelins could not carry enough bombs to do real damage, but what they did achieve was psychological damage – civilians in Britain no longer seemed safe.

The British government pulled back fighter planes to defend Britain from these attacks, but in fact such fears were exaggerated. Once air defences improved, it was clear that Zeppelins were very vulnerable. By 1918 speedy, powerful fighter planes and accurate anti-aircraft fire took a heavy toll of these giant aircraft, as these statistics show:

- 130 Zeppelins in service.
- 7 lost to bad weather.
- 38 lost in accidents.
- 39 lost in enemy action.

Bethnal Green Military Hospital, 9 September 1915

We had a pretty terrifying time with Zepps again last night. We were woken at 10.30 by a terrific noise of bombs, aircraft, guns etc. apparently all around us; we rushed on dressing gowns, said a prayer, and got downstairs as quickly as we could; the lights were put out just as we got to the bottom, and we were left in a herd of frightened females in pitch darkness.

There was a tremendous glare in the sky to the west of us, which came from a big fire in Wood Street . . . I believe most of the damage was done along Oxford Street, Holborn, Euston Road and Shoreditch . . . a lot of people were killed in a motorbus . . . it would have been terrifying to be out, as I believe there's a fearful panic in the streets. I am afraid there must have been a great many casualties.

3 September 1916

We had a most exciting time with Zepps last night . . . I went on to a bridge just by the ward and had a glorious view of a huge Zepp – apparently fairly close but not above us, so I wasn't frightened – with shells bursting all around it.

Quite suddenly the whole sky was lit up by an enormous glare and amid tremendous cheers from the hospital and from the people all round we saw her turn right on end and fall, apparently quite slowly, and with huge flames leaping upwards, to the ground. It must have been 8 or 10 miles away as we could hear very little, though there was great hush of listening for the expected explosion as she struck the earth with her bombs; but it never came.

Nurse Ursula Somervell describes her encounters with Zeppelins.

A Sopwith Camel (**A**) and a Fokker Triplane (**B**).

Aeroplanes

In 1914 aeroplanes were extremely primitive. They were also very unreliable and highly dangerous. Losses were very high indeed, especially among new pilots. At the start of the war planes did the same job as observation balloons.

Soon their speed and mobility meant that commanders used them for detailed reconnaissance work over enemy trenches. The photographs they took were very valuable. At the Battle of the Marne they spotted a potential break in the Allied lines that could have been fatal for the Allies.

Enemy aircraft would be sent to shoot down reconnaissance flights and soon the 'dogfight' had emerged. In the early dogfights the pilots used pistols and rifles. It was not until April 1915 that planes were successfully fitted with machine guns. These guns were synchronised so that they did not shoot through their own propeller. By 1918 spectacular dogfights were common over the Western Front. The rickety early planes had given way to sleek fighters such as the Sopwith Camel and the Fokker Triplane (Source 28).

Planes also played a part in slowing down the German advance in 1918 and in the Allied advances of the Hundred Days (see page 32).

Two machines jump up before me. A couple of shots. Gun jammed. I feel defenceless and in my rage I try to ram an enemy's machine. The guns begin to fire again. I see the observer and pilot lurch forward. Their plane crashes in a shellhole. The other Englishman vanishes.

A German airman describes a dogfight.

Pilots are always to be armed with a revolver or pistol . . . binoculars, some safety device, either waistcoat, patent lifebelt, or petrol can . . . At all times the pilot should carry out independent observations and note down what he sees (noting the times). Nail a pad of paper to the instrument panel for this purpose . . . Pilots and observers are to familiarize themselves with the photographs of Turkish men-of-war described in The World's Fighting Ships. *This book is in the office . . . Don't make wild statements; a small accurate report is worth pages of rhetoric giving no useful information. If an enemy aeroplane is sighted, attack it, reporting you are doing so. Don't try to do what is termed by some people as 'stunt flying'. This is not wanted for war and is not conduct required of an officer.*

Instructions given to early aerial reconnaissance pilots fighting against Turkey.

SOURCE 31

A British heavy bomber. Bombs came out through a sliding hatch in the base of the plane. From 1917, German heavy bombers attacked towns on the English coast, causing an estimated 1000 deaths as well as destroying property.

1 Why do you think the air war captured the imagination of the public more than the ground war?
2 Were airships more important than aeroplanes in the First World War?
3 'No one should underestimate the importance in war of the psychological impact of a new weapon, or of morale-boosting success.' Do you agree? Explain your answer by referring to the war in the air.

ACTIVITY

If you had signed up as a pilot for the RFC in 1914, what changes would you have seen by 1918 in:
a) your role
b) the machines you flew?
Describe these changes as two diary extracts or letters home: one for 1914, the other for 1918.

SOURCE 32

Really I am having too much luck for a boy. I will start straight away, and tell you all. On August 22 I went up. Met twelve Huns.

No. 1 fight. I attacked and fired two drums, bringing the machine down just outside the village. All crashed up.

No. 2 fight. I attacked and got under the machine, putting in two drums. Hun went down in flames.

No. 3 fight. I attacked and put in one drum. Machine went down and crashed on a housetop.

All these fights were seen and reported by other machines that saw them go down. I only got hit eleven times, so I returned and got more ammunition.

[Later Ball wrote:] I do not think anything bad about the Hun. Nothing makes me feel more rotten than seeing him go down . . . oh, I do get tired of always living to kill. I am beginning to feel like a murderer . . .

Lieutenant Ball, a British airman, was only nineteen when he wrote this letter, dated 25 August 1916. He became famous for his daredevil exploits. He was killed on a raid in 1917.

By the end of the war, aeroplanes had been designed that could drop bombs. Air raids took place as early as 1914 but they were notoriously ineffective and inaccurate. Zeppelin hangars were a favourite target. They were so huge they were hard to miss. As the war came to a close, the Germans had developed the Gotha heavy bomber which carried out a few raids on Britain. Similarly, the British developed the huge Handley Page which was capable of bombing Berlin but never got the chance to do so.

The war speeded up the development of air technology. In four years aircraft had changed from string bags to sophisticated machines. In four years the RAF had gone from having 37 aeroplanes to 23,000. Even so, aircraft were really only a side show to the land war. Air power was if anything more valuable at sea where the aircraft could observe and attack shipping.

SOURCE 33

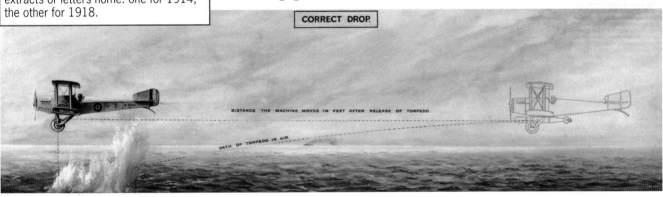

CORRECT DROP.

DISTANCE THE MACHINE MOVES IN FEET AFTER RELEASE OF TORPEDO.

PATH OF TORPEDO IN AIR

An aeroplane launches a torpedo.

FOCUS TASK

The land war, the air war and the war at sea were not separate. They interconnected with each other.

1 Draw up a table like this:

Developments	On land	At sea	In the air
The machine gun			
The torpedo			
Poison gas			
Fighter aircraft			

For each development, indicate how it was significant on land, at sea or in the air.

2 Make a copy of the table below. Fill it out to show how significant a role land forces, sea forces and air forces played in each event.

Events	Land	Sea	Air
The defeat of Germany in 1918			
The invasion of Gallipoli			
The blockade of Germany			

British depth study 1906–1918

How and why did the Liberals help the poor?

1 Look at Source 1. Do these sound very similar to or very different from the concerns of British politicians today?

Today we think of the Liberal Party (now the Liberal Democratic Party) as a 'third' party – it never gets enough votes to make a government. But at the beginning of the twentieth century it was the biggest party. In 1906 a new Liberal government was elected by a landslide.

Historians have looked carefully at the speeches made by Liberal MPs during the election campaign. Source 1 shows you what issues topped their agenda.

SOURCE 1

1	Attacks on the policy of the previous government
2	Keep free trade between Britain and other countries
3	Improve education
4	Sort out problems in Ireland
5	Change opening hours for public houses
6	End the enslavement of immigrant Chinese workers in South Africa
7	Reform of the Poor Law

0   10   20   30   40   50   60   70   80   90   100
Per cent

An analysis of the issues in the speeches of Liberal MPs before the 1906 election.

SOURCE 2

In Source 1 the problem of poverty comes seventh. However, some influential Liberal MPs put it much higher.

Source 2 may sound just like election-speak to you – politicians tend to say these idealistic things at election time then forget them once they are in power. That is probably how many people at the time saw Liberal promises to do something about poverty. However, to everyone's surprise (even some of their own supporters) the Liberals embarked on the most ambitious and expensive programme of welfare reforms ever undertaken in Britain. Why did they do this? Was it just the Liberals' far-sighted idealism, or were there other factors at work?

We will only be ousted from power if we fail to remove the national degradation of slums and widespread poverty in a land glittering with wealth.

David Lloyd George, October 1906.

Why did the Liberals introduce their welfare reforms?

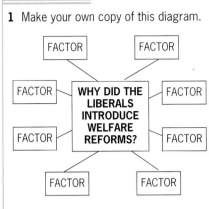
Self-help v. welfare state

In Britain today, we take it for granted that the state pays for health care, education, social services, unemployment benefit and many other services for whoever needs them. We call this the welfare state. We assume this is what governments do! This was not always the case. Before the early 1900s most politicians – including most Liberal politicians – would have said that the government should leave such matters to individuals or charities and that individuals should look after their own welfare by working hard and saving money carefully. This is known as 'self-help'. They would also have said that anyone could climb out of poverty if they tried hard enough, so it was their own fault if they stayed poor.

The Liberal reforms were based on quite different assumptions:

• It was not always the fault of the poor that they were poor.
• It was the role of government to support the poor when they needed it most.

There are many different reasons why they changed their views.

The social reformers

Leading Liberals were influenced by the work of researchers and social reformers such as Seebohm Rowntree. He was head of the famous confectionery company in York but he was also a committed social reformer.

In 1901 Rowntree published a book called *Poverty: A Study of Town Life*. This book was based on two years' research in his home town of York. It contained a huge amount of statistical and other kinds of evidence on wages, hours of work, diet, health and housing (see Sources 4–6). His main conclusions were:

• Poverty was generally caused by old age, illness or similar factors. It was not generally the result of the poor being lazy or careless with money.
• The poor often suffered from the ups and downs in Britain's trade cycle. Clearly, ordinary people could not be blamed for these changing circumstances putting them out of work and into poverty.
• In York, 27 per cent of the population lived below the poverty line (see Source 5).
• Poverty was not usually the result of the poor being careless with money (see Source 4).
• The state should introduce measures to protect and safeguard the very young, the old, the ill and the unemployed.

Because of his wealth and his connections, Rowntree had influence on the government. He had been a supporter of the Liberal Party all his life. He was a friend of the leading Liberal David Lloyd George, who became Chancellor of the Exchequer in 1908. Rowntree was asked by the Liberal government to carry out a study into rural poverty in 1913. He was an important influence behind the Old Age Pensions Act and the National Insurance Act (see pages 54–55).

SOURCE 3

What are the real causes of poverty among the industrial classes? Old age, bad health, the death of the breadwinner and unemployment due either to the running down of industries or to the depressions in trade. When Bismarck was strengthening the German Empire, one of his first tasks was to set up a scheme which insured German workers and their families against the worst evils arising from the accidents of life. And a superb scheme it is. It has saved a huge amount of human misery among thousands of people.

Lloyd George speaking in 1890.

SOURCE 4

Unemployment or partial unemployment: 5 per cent

Death of wage earner: 10 per cent

Illness or old age of wage earner: 5 per cent

Low wages: 22 per cent

Large family: 52 per cent

Other: 6 per cent

Rowntree's findings on the causes of poverty.

SOURCE 5

A family living on [the poverty line] must never spend a penny on railway fares or the omnibus. They must never go into the country unless they walk . . . They must never contribute anything to their church or chapel, or give any help to a neighbour which costs them money. They cannot save . . . The children must have no pocket money . . . The father must smoke no tobacco . . . The mother must never buy any pretty clothes . . . Should a child fall ill it must be attended by the parish doctor . . . Finally, the wage earner must never be absent from his work for a single day.

B. Seebohm Rowntree, *Poverty: A Study of Town Life*, 1901.

SOURCE 6

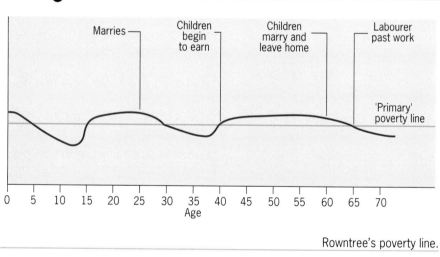

Rowntree's poverty line.

Political rivalry

The Liberals' main rivals were the Conservative Party. The Conservatives had introduced welfare measures of their own. In 1905 the Conservatives had introduced the Unemployed Workmen's Act to help fight the effects of high unemployment. This could be a vote-winner among the working classes.

I see little glory in an Empire which can rule the waves and is unable to flush its own sewers.

From a speech by Winston Churchill, 1899.

Key individuals: David Lloyd George and Winston Churchill

Without doubt, the Liberal politician David Lloyd George had great influence. Lloyd George's father, the head teacher in an elementary school in Manchester, died the year after his son was born. David and his poverty-stricken mother went to live in a Welsh village, where her brother, a shoemaker and Baptist minister, supported the family. With his uncle's help, Lloyd George became a solicitor. Lloyd George hated the way that the English upper classes dominated Welsh life and he sympathised with the ordinary people. He was also a very able politician, and by 1908 he had risen to the post of Chancellor of the Exchequer.

Another key figure was Winston Churchill. He had been a leading Conservative, but switched sides in 1906 when the Liberals started their welfare reforms, supposedly because he supported them, although his enemies said it was because he did not want to be in the party of opposition. In 1908, Churchill became President of the Board of Trade. These two and other leading Liberals had read the works of Seebohm Rowntree and other social reformers and felt that poverty needed to be tackled. They were aware of the contrast between Britain's vast wealth and its squalid urban slums.

The Boer War

Between 1899 and 1902, Britain was at war to defend its territory in southern Africa. Half of the recruits who volunteered to fight were found to be unfit for service because of ill health. In some poor areas of Britain, 69 per cent were unfit. The potential recruits were so badly fed that they had not grown properly. The army had to lower its minimum height for a soldier in order to find enough infantrymen.

This was alarming for a government that needed to be able to call up a strong army at short notice. The government set up the Committee on Physical Deterioration to investigate the issue, and its recommendations influenced the Liberal programme of reform.

Industrial decline

The country that spent £250 million to avenge an insult levelled at her pride by an old Dutch farmer [the Boer War] is not ashamed to see her children walking the streets hungry and in rags.

Lloyd George speaking in 1906.

Britain's military strength was not the only concern. From 1870 onwards, Britain's position as the world's leading industrial power was being challenged by the USA and Germany. By 1900, both countries had overtaken Britain. Lloyd George was extremely impressed with the welfare programme introduced by Bismarck, the German Chancellor (see Source 3 on page 51). Germany's rapid development appeared to be closely linked to its healthier, better-educated and therefore more efficient workforce. There was also a recognition that some unemployment was caused by foreign competition, not laziness. As a result, government help for the unemployed had widespread support.

The rise of Socialism

Finally, the Liberals saw welfare reforms as a way of fighting Socialism. If the working classes were healthier and happier, there would be less support for the type of revolutionary Socialist movements that were troubling France, Germany and Russia at this time. It was also hoped that reforms would undermine support for the new Labour Party. Most working-class men could vote in elections by 1906. The new Labour Party was calling for pensions, education and unemployment benefits. The party was only small in 1906, with 29 seats in Parliament. The Liberals hoped to keep it that way.

ACTIVITY

Write a short speech for either Winston Churchill or Lloyd George explaining why the Liberals need to introduce welfare reforms. You will be addressing a hostile audience who think that welfare reforms are expensive and who still believe in self-help. Choose three points from your diagram (page 51) that your audience may find important and use them to present your case. You can also include ideas from Sources 3–8.

How effective were the Liberal reforms?

1 Children

The Liberals began their programme of reforms almost as soon as they came to power. In 1906, an Act was passed that allowed (but did not force) local authorities to provide free school meals. The new law meant that children would eat at least one decent meal a day. In 1914, 14 million meals were served up, most of which were free. On the other hand, only half of Britain's local authorities actually set up a meals service.

In 1907, attention was turned to medical care. Many parents were not able to afford proper treatment. Now, every local education authority had to set up a school medical service. At first, the service provided only regular medical checks, but from 1912 this was extended to provide treatment in school clinics as well. But it was left to local authorities to make these measures work. As a result, medical care varied widely across the country.

In 1908, the Children and Young Persons Act was inspired by a terrible social evil. In the past, insurance companies had paid out money to parents on the death of their young children, even in suspicious circumstances, with predictable results. The Act gave children special status as protected persons, and their parents could now be prosecuted for neglect. It also made it illegal to insure a child's life.

The Act set up special courts to deal with child crime and also special homes or Borstals to house young offenders so that they did not need to be sent to adult prisons.

2 The old

In 1908, in his first budget as Chancellor of the Exchequer, Lloyd George introduced a government-funded old-age pension. A person over 70 with no other income would receive five shillings per week. Married couples would receive 7s 6d. Anyone who had an income of over £31 per year did not qualify for a state pension. Only British citizens who had been living in Britain for the last 20 years could receive a state pension. Pensions could be refused to people who had failed to work to their best abilities during their working life. Pensions were not new but poor people could not afford private pensions. Many old people had been dependent on poor relief or outdoor relief (handouts of food, clothing or small amounts of cash). Some still lived with the threat of the workhouse. Although the state pension was hardly a generous measure, the effect on the elderly poor was enormous. Their state pensions made them independent for the rest of their lives. In the first year, some 650,000 people collected their pensions. The number of people claiming outdoor relief fell by over 80,000.

As well as helping thousands of old people, the Act established new and important principles. First, it was non-contributory. In other words, people received it without having paid anything towards a pension fund. Second, poverty was being tackled by direct funding from the government, rather than from local rates. It was a small measure but a big step.

FOCUS TASK

Professor Change

These were totally new ideas – very radical – total change.

1 Make your own copy of this table. Fill it in using the information on pages 54–55.

Group	How helped before Liberal reforms	Measures taken by Liberals to tackle problem	Limitations of the reforms
Children	No real system – some charities helped poor families with children; orphans looked after in workhouses		
The old	Charities; family; the workhouse		
The sick	Charities; family; the workhouse		
The unemployed or underemployed	Outdoor relief; voluntary labour exchanges		

Professor Continuity

Ah, but look below the surface and the old ideas about poverty are still lurking.

2 The two professors want your help. Find them some evidence on pages 54–55 to back up their viewpoints.

3 The unemployed

Campaigners for social reform had shown how great a problem unemployment and underemployment (irregular work) could be. Labour exchanges run by volunteers had existed for some time. Here, workers could sign on to a register when they were unemployed, and they could find out about available work. In 1909 the government set up its own labour exchanges as part of its campaign against unemployment. By 1913 labour exchanges were putting 3000 people into jobs every working day.

SOURCE 9

Nothing wearies more than walking about hunting for employment which is not to be had. It is far harder than real work. The uncertainty, the despair, when you reach a place only to discover that the journey is fruitless. I've known a man to say: 'Which way shall I go today?' Having no earthly idea which way to take, he tosses up a button. If the button comes down on one side he treks east; if on the other, he treks west.

Written by William Crooks, a working man who later became a Labour MP.

SOURCE 10

A voluntary labour exchange in Chelsea, 1887.

SOURCE 11

The government labour exchange at Camberwell Green, February 1910.

4 Workers: the National Insurance Act

The National Insurance Act of 1911 was a really important measure. Insurance was not a new idea. It had been the basis of the friendly societies for two centuries or more. Indeed, the Liberals used the friendly societies to administer the national insurance scheme. But Lloyd George's scheme went far beyond any of these private schemes.

Sick pay

The first part of the Act dealt with health insurance. All men and women in lower-paid manual and clerical jobs earning under £160 per year had to join. They then had to pay 4*d* out of each week's wages. Each payment earned them a 'stamp' on their card. The employer added 3*d* worth of stamps and the government a further 2*d*. Liberal posters talked of workers getting 9*d* for 4*d*. The money was paid into a friendly society of the worker's choice.

In return, the worker received up to 26 weeks of sick pay at 10 shillings a week from the friendly society. There was also free medical care for the insured.

It was an important boost for low-paid workers, but it did not solve all their problems. The families of workers were not entitled to free treatment, and widows did not receive pensions.

Unemployment benefit

The second part of the Act dealt with unemployment and underemployment. In trades such as building, shipbuilding and engineering, occasional unemployment was common. To cover this, the Act required a further contribution of 2½*d* per week from the worker, supplemented by 2½*d* from the employer and 1¾*d* from the government. These sums paid for 'stamps' on the worker's card. During times of unemployment, a worker would receive seven shillings per week for up to 15 weeks. It was not much money, certainly not enough to support a working man and his family. This was deliberate, because the government wanted to encourage careful saving and did not want workers to 'sit back and enjoy' the benefits.

SOURCE INVESTIGATION

1 In what ways do Sources 12 and 13 give similar and different impressions of Lloyd George's attitude towards paying for welfare reforms?
2 What point is the cartoonist making in Source 14?
3 Would you agree that Source 15 is a balanced and reliable view of the effects of the 1911 National Insurance Act?
4 Which of Sources 16 or 19 is more useful to historians studying the effects of the Old Age Pensions Act of 1908?
5 Study Source 17. How far is Hopkins' view of the Liberal welfare reforms supported by Sources 18 and 20?

Reactions to the reforms

The reforms were controversial and were met with enormous opposition. Conservatives opposed the cost and the idea of the 'nanny state'. Doctors were not convinced about health insurance. The friendly societies and insurance companies prevented national insurance benefits being given to widows. Some workers resented the deductions from their wages. Some rich people resented paying for this too. Lloyd George said that the upper classes inherited much of their wealth and did little work to earn what they had, so they should pay for social reforms to help those who did work and suffered poverty. The House of Lords tried to stop the reforms going through. This was one cause of a major constitutional crisis which ended with the reduction of the power of the House of Lords.

The Labour Party criticised the fact that workers had to fund their own benefits. They felt it should come from taxation of the wealthy to help the poor.

Sources 12–20 give a range of viewpoints on the reforms.

SOURCE 12

RICH FARE.

THE GIANT LLOYD-GORGIBUSTER: "FEE, FI, FO, FAT, I SMELL THE BLOOD OF A PLUTOCRAT; BE HE ALIVE OR BE HE DEAD, I'LL GRIND HIS BONES TO MAKE MY BREAD."

Lloyd George is shown in this 1909 *Punch* cartoon as a giant preparing to force the rich to give some of their wealth to the less well-off.

SOURCE 13

THE PHILANTHROPIC HIGHWAYMAN.

Mr. LLOYD-GEORGE: "I'LL MAKE 'EM PITY THE AGED POOR!"

Lloyd George as a highwayman, in a 1909 *Punch* cartoon. Note the motor cars (a new symbol of wealth) approaching from the distance.

SOURCE 14

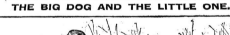

THE BIG DOG AND THE LITTLE ONE.

[From the Westminster Gazette.]

LORD HALSBURY: I don't think much of that paltry little thing—it's a mockery of a dog.

AGED PENSIONER: Well, my lord, 'tis only a little 'un, but 'tis a wunnerful comfort to me. Us bain't all blessed wi' big 'uns!

A cartoon from a Liberal Party leaflet, February 1909. Lord Halsbury had criticised the pension for being too small. As a former Conservative Lord Chancellor, his own was £5000.

SOURCE 15

THE DAWN OF HOPE.

Mr. LLOYD GEORGE'S National Health Insurance Bill provides for the insurance of the Worker in case of Sickness.

Support the Liberal Government in their policy of **SOCIAL REFORM.**

A 1911 Liberal election poster.

ACTIVITY

You are going to a public meeting in 1914 and Prime Minister Asquith, the Liberal leader since 1908, will be there. You are not a fan of the PM. Come up with five awkward questions relating to the Liberals' reforms in the period 1906–1914.

FOCUS TASK

How effectively did the Liberals help children, the old and the unemployed?

1 Add any extra ideas from Sources 12–20 to your chart from page 54.
2 You are now going to use your completed chart to help you to write a report answering the above question. You can organise your work in paragraphs:
 • introduction: for example, why help was needed
 • the Liberals' record on children
 • their record on the old
 • their record on the unemployed
 • your conclusion: which group was helped the most or the least; whether the group that most needed help received most help.

SOURCE 16

. . . now we want to go on living forever, because we give them [his son's family] the 10 shillings a week, and it pays them to have us along with them. I never thought we should be able to pay the boy back for all his goodness to me and the missus.

An old man talks about his pension, 1912.

SOURCE 17

There can be no doubt that taken as a whole the Liberal reforms constitute an impressive body of social legislation, the greatest ever passed by any one government up to that time . . . A radical new plan of campaign had been developed to meet the most urgent social needs of the working classes, and to do so outside the Poor Law System.

Eric Hopkins, *A Social History of the English Working Classes*, 1979.

SOURCE 18

. . . though the principle of social services according to need rather than ability to pay is commonplace today, in the very early 1900s it appeared revolutionary; fifty years earlier . . . such a proposal would have been unthinkable.

By the historian RN Rundle.

SOURCE 19

Elderly people collecting their pensions at a London post office on 1 January 1909.

SOURCE 20

National health insurance
• *To the industrialists it meant fitter workers returning faster to work.*
• *To the workers, despite the protests of some of their representatives, it meant, for the first time for many of them, professional medical treatment and an income during illness.*
• *To the medical profession it meant an expanded occupation at increased remuneration for the 'panel doctors'.*
• *To civil servants who operated the scheme it meant employment, prestige and as a civil servant in the Ministry of Health put it in 1913, 'We can make work at the Government Department the most marvellous means for true social reform that the world has ever seen.'*

Adapted from Harold Perkin, *The Rise of Professional Society: England since 1880*, published in 1990.

3.2 How and why did women try to win the right to vote?

How should citizens campaign for something they believe in?

A

B

Newspaper headlines from 18 June 1913.

Voting changes, 1800–1900

★ In 1800 very few people could vote. To vote was not seen as a 'human right' for all citizens. Only the rich were allowed to vote.

★ There was a property qualification for voting (that is, you had to own a certain amount of wealth or property before you were allowed to vote). It was thought that if you owned property then you were a respectable and responsible person who would use the vote properly.

★ There was also a gender qualification – only men could vote in general elections.

★ Electoral Reform Acts were passed in 1832, 1867 and 1884. Each of these reforms reduced the property qualification and so increased the number of men who could vote – as you can see from the graph below.

★ By 1900, most working men could vote in general elections if they had a permanent address.

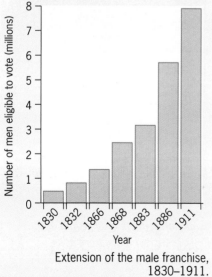

Extension of the male franchise, 1830–1911.

Compare Sources 1A and 1B. Both events happened on the same day. Both were part of the campaign to win the vote for women – or female suffrage (suffrage means the right to vote).

One protest was staged by the suffragists, who believed in peaceful, law-abiding protest, and the other by the suffragettes, who used violent methods to get their views across. Both groups had the same aim but different methods. Over the next eight pages you will be exploring the reasons for these protests and comparing the effectiveness of the two campaigns.

What were the arguments for and against female suffrage?

In the nineteenth century, new job opportunities emerged for women as teachers, as shop workers or as clerks and secretaries in offices. Many able girls from working-class backgrounds achieved better-paid jobs with higher status than those of their parents.

Women gained greater opportunities in education. A few middle-class women won the chance to go to university, to become doctors, for example.

A series of laws between 1839 and 1886 gave married women greater legal rights. However, they could not vote in general elections.

The number of men who could vote had gradually increased during the nineteenth century (see the Factfile). Some people thought that women should be allowed to vote too. Others disagreed. But the debate was not, as you might think, simply a case of men versus women. Any of the arguments that you see on page 59 might have been advanced by a woman or by a man.

What were the arguments for and against women's suffrage?

Use the information and sources on the opposite page to produce a leaflet presenting the arguments either for or against women's suffrage. Your audience should be MPs who are undecided about whether women should have the vote.

For votes for women

Parliament's decisions affect both men and women. So women should be able to vote for the MPs who pass those laws.

There are many single women and widows who bear the same responsibilities as men.

Women are the spiritual spine of the nation – they are the churchgoers. Give women the vote if you want MPs to show Christian leadership.

Women have increasing opportunities in education and work – the vote should come next.

SOURCE 2

LET THE WOMEN HELP!
Two heads are better than one.

A suffragette argues for female suffrage.

Women have special skills and expertise. They can help Parliament make better laws on issues such as education and the home where they are specialists.

Women pay taxes just like men.

Women should be able to influence MPs on how that money is spent.

Women can already vote in local elections. They serve on local government bodies, such as education committees and Poor Law boards. They have shown that they are able and can be trusted with a vote.

Many uneducated working men can vote while well-educated, 'respectable' women can't.

Against votes for women

Men and women have different interests and responsibilities. Women are home-makers and mothers. It is the role of men to debate and take difficult decisions.

It is mainly middle-class women campaigning for the vote. They will have little interest in laws to help ordinary working people.

Women are not rational. They are too emotional to be trusted with the vote.

Women are pure and should be protected from the grubby world of politics.

SOURCE 3

With the vote, women would become the most hateful, heartless and disgusting of human beings. Where would be the protection which man was intended to give to the weaker sex?

Queen Victoria commenting on female suffrage.

Giving respectable women the vote will also encourage them to develop their careers and neglect their family duties. Only the undesirable classes will have children.

Giving the vote to women will mean giving it to all men – including layabouts and riffraff.

Why worry about the vote? There are much more pressing concerns such as Ireland and the trade unions.

Women do not fight in wars for their country. So they should not have a say in whether the country should go to war.

How effective were the suffragist and suffragette campaigns?

Who were the suffragists?

The early campaigners for the vote were known as suffragists. They were mainly (though not all) middle-class women. When the MP John Stuart Mill had suggested giving votes to women in 1867, 73 MPs had supported the motion. After so many MPs voted in favour of women's suffrage in 1867, large numbers of local women's suffrage societies were formed. By the time they came together in 1897 to form the National Union of Women's Suffrage Societies (NUWSS), there were over 500 local branches. By 1902, the campaign had gained the support of working-class women as well. In 1901–1902, Eva Gore-Booth gathered the signatures of 67,000 textile workers in northern England for a petition to Parliament.

The leader of the movement was Mrs Millicent Fawcett. She believed in constitutional campaigning. She argued her case with MPs, issued leaflets, presented petitions and organised meetings. She thought that it was crucial to keep the issue in the public eye: at every election, suffragists questioned the candidates on their attitudes to women's suffrage. She talked of the suffragist movement as being like a glacier, slow but unstoppable. By 1900 they had achieved some success, gaining the support of many Liberal MPs and some leading Conservative MPs, as well as the new but rather small Labour Party.

However, there was a rather curious situation in Parliament with regard to women's suffrage. Many backbench Liberal MPs were supporters of votes for women, but the Liberal leaders were opposed to it. This was because they feared that, if only better-off, property-owning women got the vote, these women would vote for their arch rivals, the Conservative Party.

On the other hand, some Conservative leaders, liking the prospect of more Conservative voters, were quite keen on women's suffrage. But they took no action because their backbench MPs were completely opposed, on principle, to changing the role of women.

In addition, both parties had bigger worries than female suffrage. Neither party was prepared to adopt female suffrage as party policy, so it never got priority in Parliament. It was left up to individual MPs to introduce private bills, which were never allowed the time they needed to get through. In the years up to 1900, fifteen times Parliament received a bill to give women the vote; fifteen times the bill failed.

Who were the suffragettes?

This lack of success frustrated many suffragists. As a result, in 1903, Mrs Emmeline Pankhurst founded a new campaigning organisation, the Women's Social and Political Union (WSPU). Mrs Pankhurst thought that the movement had to become more radical and militant if it was to succeed. The *Daily Mail* called these new radicals 'suffragettes', and they soon made the headlines.

The suffragettes disrupted political meetings and harassed ministers. The Liberal Prime Minister, Asquith, who was firmly opposed to women's suffrage, came in for particularly heavy abuse.

1908: direct action begins

After the latest in a long line of women's suffrage bills ran out of time in 1908, the suffragette campaign intensified and became more vocal. The suffragette Edith New began making speeches in Downing Street; to stop the police from moving her on, she chained herself to the railings and so was arrested. In the same year, some suffragettes threw stones through the windows of 10 Downing Street (the Prime Minister's house). In October, Mrs Pankhurst, her daughter Christabel and 'General' Flora Drummond were sent to prison for inciting a crowd to 'rush' the House of Commons.

FACTFILE

Bills for female suffrage, 1906–1913

★ **January 1906** A Liberal government is elected with a massive majority. Four hundred out of 650 MPs are in favour of women's suffrage, including the Prime Minister, Henry Campbell-Bannerman.

★ **March 1907** A women's suffrage bill is introduced, but opponents delay it so long that it runs out of time.

★ **February 1908** A new women's suffrage bill is introduced and is passed on a second reading but it gets no further.

★ **March 1909** The Liberal government introduces a radical Suffrage Bill – giving votes to almost all adult men and women. It wins a majority of 34 on a second reading – but gets no further in Parliament.

★ **November 1909** A general election is called and the suffrage bill is temporarily dropped.

★ **June 1910** An all-party committee drafts a Conciliation Bill which gives women the vote and is acceptable to all parties. On a second reading, it is passed by a majority of 110.

★ **18 November 1910** Prime Minister Asquith calls another general election and so the bill is abandoned.

★ **May 1911** The Conciliation Bill is reintroduced. It gets a massive 167 majority. Asquith announces that the government will proceed with the bill in 1912.

★ **November 1911** The Liberal government will not support the Conciliation Bill. Instead, it wants a male suffrage bill that would widen the vote for men! The bill would not mention women, but Asquith says MPs can amend the bill to include women if they want.

★ **March 1912** Second reading of the Conciliation Bill. It is defeated by 14 votes.

★ **June 1912** Suffrage bill is introduced. Progress is postponed to the following year.

★ **1913** Attempts are made to include women in the Male Suffrage Bill, but the Speaker announces that the amendments would change the very nature of the bill. As a result, the women's vote amendments are withdrawn.

★ **May 1913** A new private member's bill to give women the vote is introduced but defeated by a majority of 48.

SOURCE 4

THE SHRIEKING SISTER.

The Sensible Woman. *"YOU HELP OUR CAUSE? WHY, YOU'RE ITS WORST ENEMY!"*

A 1906 cartoon from *Punch* magazine.

SOURCE 5

Hampstead Women's Social and Political Union,
178, FINCHLEY ROAD, N.W.

WINDOW BREAKING
AND
INCITEMENT
TO
MUTINY.

For Breaking Windows as a Political protest, Women are now in H.M. Gaols serving sentences of **Four and Six months imprisonment.**

For Inciting Soldiers to Disobey Orders, a much more serious crime, known to the law as a felony, and punishable by penal servitude, the Publishers of the "Syndicalist," were sentenced to nine months hard labour, and the Printers of the paper to six months hard labour.

The Government under the pressure of men with votes reduced this sentence on the Publishers to **Six months imprisonment without hard labour,**

and the sentence on the Printers to **One month without hard labour.**

IS THIS JUSTICE TO VOTELESS WOMEN ?

A suffragette handbill.

1 a) What is the attitude of the cartoonist in Source 4 to:
   i) the suffragists
   ii) the suffragettes?
 b) How can you tell?
2 Read Source 5 carefully. What point does it make?

SOURCE 6

Militancy is abhorred by me, and the majority of suffragists. None of the triumphs of the women's movement . . . have been won by physical force: they have been triumphs of moral and spiritual force. But militancy has been brought into existence by the blind blundering of politicians . . . If men had been treated by the House of Commons as women have been treated, there would have been bloody reprisals all over the country.

Millicent Fawcett on the events of 1908.

There was a logic to the suffragettes' actions. The suffragettes believed that the government did nothing about female suffrage because it did not think that it was a serious issue. The government had more pressing concerns. The suffragettes wanted to make women's suffrage a serious issue – one that the government could not ignore. That was the aim of their militancy: a woman getting arrested for her cause was news. It showed how important the vote was to her. Processions and petitions – however large – were easily ignored.

Reactions to direct action

The reaction of the public was mixed. Some people were sympathetic. Some were worried. Others were scornful. The reaction of the suffragists was also mixed. Many suffragists admired the heroism of the suffragettes – particularly their readiness to go to prison. When the first suffragettes were arrested and imprisoned for staging a protest in Parliament, Mrs Fawcett put on a banquet for them when they were released. However, as the suffragette campaign became more violent, relationships between the suffragists and suffragettes became very strained. The suffragists believed that you could not claim a democratic right (to vote) by undemocratic methods (such as smashing windows). They also believed that militancy would put off the moderate MPs who might otherwise back their cause.

So the two campaigns moved further apart. Both knew that rivalry between the two groups did not help the cause, and Christabel Pankhurst called for the two wings of the movement to join forces. However, Mrs Fawcett did not want her movement to be identified with militancy and so she refused. Even so, her sternest criticism was directed not at the suffragettes but at the inept politicians who had helped to create militancy.

Opposition intensifies

The suffrage campaigners had always faced opposition, but as suffragette militancy escalated, so did the campaign of their opponents.

SOURCE 7

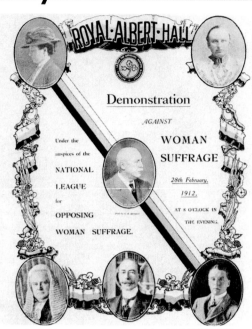

A poster advertising an anti-suffrage demonstration.

1 Do you regard Source 8 as effective propaganda? Explain your answer.
2 Why might a suffragette be more annoyed by Source 8 than Source 7?

SOURCE 8

An anti-suffragette poster, typical of the sort of attitude suffragettes faced.

SOURCE 9

VOTES FOR BABIES

Now that it is pretty well assured that women will vote, it is time to arouse public sentiment in favour of Votes for Babies. The awful state of our Government shouts aloud for the infant suffrage . . . Let the babies vote! For that matter let the cows vote.

From the *Gentleman's Journal*, 17 May 1913.

1911: a setback in Parliament

In 1911 the government promised a Conciliation Bill which won all-party support. The suffragettes suspended militant action. The suffragists held an incredible 4000 meetings (30 per day) to support the bill. It got a majority of 167 – the biggest ever. It looked as if success was just around the corner. Then Asquith dropped the bill! Instead, he announced that he planned to introduce votes for all men, and that an extra clause about women's votes could be tacked on to the bill if MPs wished to add it. Both suffragists and suffragettes were furious.

3 Which of these sources is the most effective piece of propaganda for or against women's suffrage? Explain your choice.

4 Some people say that 'all publicity is good publicity'. Would the Pankhursts agree? Would Mrs Fawcett agree?

The suffragist response

The suffragists' response was to lead a deputation to see the Prime Minister to persuade him to change his mind. They also decided to support the Labour Party at the next election, since it was the only party committed to female suffrage; they organised a peaceful pilgrimage from Carlisle to London involving thousands of suffragists (see Source 1A on page 58). They offered free membership to working women.

SOURCE 10

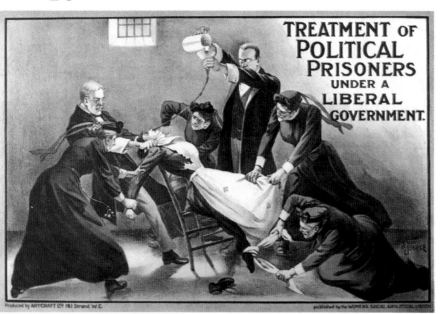

A suffragette poster from 1909, protesting about force feeding.

The suffragette response

By contrast, the suffragette response was to escalate their campaign of violence (although usually violence against property not people). They smashed windows, set fire to post boxes, bombed churches (see Source 1B on page 58) and damaged cricket pitches and golf courses. Bombs were placed in warehouses, and telephone wires were cut. Art galleries closed after suffragettes slashed valuable paintings. As a result, more and more suffragettes were sent to prison.

In prison, the suffragettes continued to protest by going on HUNGER STRIKE. The government responded by ordering the force feeding of protesters. The WPSU made the most of this, with posters such as Source 10, but posters were hardly necessary. Force feeding was brutal and degrading, and it won a good deal of public sympathy for the suffragettes.

In 1913, the government passed a new Act which allowed hunger strikers to leave prison, recover a little and then return to finish their sentence. Campaigners called this the Cat and Mouse Act (see Source 11).

Then in June 1913 came the most publicised protest of all: the death of Emily Davison. You can investigate the death of Emily Davison in the case study on pages 64–65.

SOURCE 11

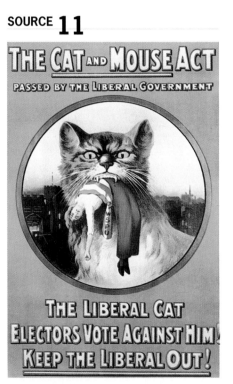

A suffragette postcard from 1913.

SOURCE 12

Police arresting a suffragette who has chained herself to the railings of Buckingham Palace, May 1914.

SOURCE 13

The woman rushed from the rails as the horses swept round Tattenham Corner. She did not interfere with the racing but she nearly killed the jockey as well as herself and she brought down a valuable horse. A deed of this kind is unlikely to increase the popularity of the women's cause.

The Times, 6 June 1913.

SOURCE 14

Millions of people, not only in our own country but in other countries too, had their attention riveted upon the race. It was an unsurpassable opportunity of proclaiming to a whole world, heedless, perhaps until then, that women claim citizenship and human rights. Miss Davison seized the opportunity, and with an amazing and incredible courage made a protest which has fired the imagination and touched the hearts of the people. Her act has proved to be an appeal infinitely more eloquent than all the words of all the speeches could be . . . She has taught the world that there are women who care so passionately for the vote and all it means that they are willing to die for it.

The Suffragette, 13 June 1913.

SOURCE 15

IN HONOUR AND IN LOVING, REVERENT MEMORY
OF
EMILY WILDING DAVISON.
SHE DIED FOR WOMEN.

The Suffragette, 13 June 1913.

Case study: the death of Emily Davison

It was 5 June 1913, the day of the world-famous horse race, the Derby, at Epsom race course. Tens of thousands of spectators were waiting for the big race. Among the crowds were members of the royal family, political leaders and many reporters and photographers. Anything that happened at the Derby was big news.

It was an ideal day for publicising the suffragette cause – or so Emily Davison thought. She was an experienced campaigner. She had been in prison nine times as part of the suffragette campaign. She had set fire to post boxes and even a post office. She had been on hunger strike while in prison.

As the horses rounded Tattenham Corner, Miss Davison rushed out and tried to catch hold of one of the horses. Source 16 shows you what happened next.

SOURCE 16

A newspaper photograph of the events that led to the death of Emily Davison on 5 June 1913. The *Daily Mail*'s headline in reporting the event was 'Day of Sensations at Epsom'.

Emily Davison was thrown to the ground, her skull fatally fractured by a blow from a horse's hoof. At the time, some people thought that Emily Davison had committed suicide, that she intended to kill herself in a most public arena to draw attention to the suffragette cause. The methods of the campaigners had been getting more and more extreme – a martyr might be very useful.

However, a different explanation later emerged. It appeared to be a publicity stunt that had gone terribly wrong. The King's horse, Anmer, was running in the race. Emily Davison thought it would be good publicity to attach a suffragette banner to it as it galloped by. It would enter the finishing straight literally flying the suffragette flag. She had been seen practising stopping horses in a lane near her home in Morpeth for some weeks previously. Sadly, when it came to the real event she misjudged the speed and power of the onrushing racehorses. She was hit and killed.

Was she brave or foolish? Her funeral, ten days later, was attended by thousands of suffragettes. It became a major celebration of her ultimate sacrifice.

SOURCE 17

In some respects it was the most remarkable funeral procession London has ever seen. It was a tribute of women to a woman who, in their eyes at least, had achieved martyrdom for the cause which they all represent . . . No one would grudge to the memory of Emily Wilding Davison any part of that tribute of honour and respect which her fellow women Suffragettes have desired to render at her obsequies [funeral rights] . . . She was herself the most unassuming and the gentlest of creatures, though she possessed a spirit capable of heroic deed and sacrifice.

Sunday Times, 15 June 1913, commenting on Emily Davison's funeral.

SOURCE 18

IMPRESSIVE LONDON PROCESSION
The procession, which was an impressive pageant, was watched by dense crowds . . . Nearly five thousand members from all parts of the country marched in undisturbed quiet and orderliness behind the coffin. Perhaps what impressed the London mind in it all was the note of colour. Among the women who walked there were hundreds dressed in black, but at the head was a young girl in yellow silk carrying a gilt cross.

Manchester Guardian, 16 June 1913, commenting on Davison's funeral.

SOURCE 19

The effect was gracious and dignified. Banners displayed the sentiments of those taking part in the procession who must have numbered some thousands.

Morning Post, 16 June 1913, also commenting on the funeral.

SOURCE INVESTIGATION

1 Explain the point that Source 18 is making.
2 Explain the contrast between Sources 13 and 14.
3 What are the strengths and weaknesses of Source 14 for historians investigating reactions to Emily Davison's death?
4 How far do Sources 17–19 agree with each other about Emily Davison's funeral?
5 Would you say there is a change in attitude towards the death of Emily Davison in these sources between 5 and 16 June? Explain your answer.

The impact of the suffragettes

There is little doubt that the suffragettes' increasing violence alienated support for the women's cause. By 1913, many suffragettes were in prison, and the Pankhursts were co-ordinating the campaign from exile in Paris. The suffragettes had certainly raised the profile of the issue, but they had also damaged their own cause, because they gave their opponents a reason for rejecting women's suffrage. If MPs gave in to violence on this matter, then what hope would they have when the Irish protested violently for HOME RULE, or the dockers or mine workers rioted for higher wages? Even more disturbing was that the suffragettes had lost the goodwill of many of their leading supporters (see Source 20). From 1911 onwards, each time the issue was raised in Parliament there was a bigger majority against women's suffrage.

SOURCE 20

Haven't the suffragettes the sense to see that the very worst kind of campaigning for the vote is to try to intimidate or blackmail a man into giving them what he would otherwise gladly give?

A comment by Lloyd George, 1913.

Suffragette leaders, of course, saw things differently. They pointed to the fact that the government had become more serious about passing a female suffrage bill only after militancy had started. They pointed to the fact that decades of suffragist campaigning had achieved nothing but empty promises from MPs.

However, the situation changed completely in August 1914 when the government declared war on Germany. Both suffragist and suffragette leaders called off their campaign and devoted all their energies to supporting the war effort. This war work would prove to have far-reaching consequences for women – which you can read about on pages 76–79.

FOCUS TASK

How effective were the suffragists and the suffragettes?

It is 1914. War has broken out and suffragist and suffragette leaders are looking back on their campaigns over the past nine years. You are going to help them to review their successes and failures.
   Write a paragraph to explain each of your answers to questions 1–4.

1 **a)** What do you think suffragists would look back on with most satisfaction?
   b) What do you think the suffragettes would look back on with most satisfaction?
2 **a)** What evidence is there to suggest that the suffragettes damaged the campaign for female suffrage?
   b) What evidence is there to suggest that suffragists' actions damaged the campaign?
3 What do you regard as the greatest achievement and the greatest failure of **a)** the suffragettes and **b)** the suffragists?
4 Do you think that suffragette or suffragist achievements most outweigh their failures? Explain your choice.
5 Give each of the campaigns a score out of 5 for effectiveness and write two paragraphs to explain your score. Keep a record of your scores as you will need them later.

The British Home Front during the First World War

The First World War was Britain's first total war. A total war involves or affects all of society – not just the armed forces. It was the first war to deeply affect most people back home in Britain. Previous wars had been remote from everyday life for most ordinary people. They were usually fought far away by small professional armies. All that ordinary people knew about the fighting was what they read in the newspapers or heard from soldiers who had taken part. This war was different. It touched almost everybody's life in one way or another, whether they were soldiers or civilians, men or women, adults or children. Some of this impact was unexpected. Some of it was planned. As you will see from pages 66–77, the government put an enormous effort into planning, organising and controlling life in Britain so that everybody would play their part. You are going to investigate how they did this and what impact it had on the life of ordinary people.

FOCUS TASK

How were civilians affected by the war?

Look carefully at Source 1. This poster shows some of the ways in which the government wanted the people of Britain to be involved in the war effort. Your aim over the next twelve pages is to prepare a short presentation based on this poster. The title of your presentation is: 'How were civilians affected by the war?' You will use this poster and other evidence on pages 66–77 to help you with your presentation.

1 Start by discussing this poster with the rest of the class. Make notes from the discussion.
• What impression of wartime Britain does this give?
• Who do you think the poster is aimed at?
• What is the purpose of the poster?
• Do you think it is effective?
• How might you have responded, if you had seen this poster in 1915?
2 Over the next few pages you will be prompted every now and then to take notes to help you with your presentation.

PROMPT 1
Read the Factfile on page 67. Make a list of all the ways in which the war affected civilian life.

SOURCE 1

Are YOU in this?

A government poster published in 1915. It was designed by Sir Robert Baden-Powell, founder of the Scout movement and a former British soldier.

FACTFILE

The 'Home Front' in the First World War

1914

★ *2 August* War declared on Germany. Britain needed an army quickly. The government launched a massive recruitment campaign. Half a million joined the army in one month.

★ *8 August* The Defence of the Realm Act (DORA) was introduced. It gave the government special powers such as the right to take over industries and land which were needed for the war effort, or to censor newspapers.

★ *Autumn* From August to September many different women's organisations were set up, including the Women's Hospital Corps and the Women's Police Volunteers.

★ *16 December* The first bombing of British civilians. German warships shelled the east coast of Britain. In Scarborough 119 people were killed.

1915

★ *19 January* First air raids by German Zeppelin airships, dropping bombs on East Anglian towns.

★ *May* It was recognised that the war needed much more careful organisation of all aspects of British life, so a coalition government with politicians from all parties was formed to handle the growing crisis in Britain.

★ *31 May* The first Zeppelin air raids on London. Air raids by Zeppelins and later by aircraft were a regular feature of the rest of the war.

★ *July* The MUNITIONS crisis: British troops were facing a severe shortage of shells and bullets. The government set up the Ministry of Munitions under David Lloyd George to reorganise Britain's munitions supply. Lloyd George and Mrs Pankhurst, a suffragette leader, organised a 'women's march for jobs' to recruit women to work in factories.

★ *Autumn* Many employers refused to take on women, and trade unions refused to allow women workers. The government had to come to an agreement with the trade unions that women would be paid the same as men and would only work 'until sufficient male labour should again be available'. The government also set up its own munitions factories, employing largely women.

1916

★ *25 January* First Military Service Bill introduced CONSCRIPTION of all single men aged 18–40.

★ *16 May* Second Military Service Bill extended conscription to married men.

★ *1 July* The Battle of the Somme began. More British soldiers were killed in this battle than in any previous battle.

★ *August* The British public flocked to cinemas to see the government's new feature film *The Battle of the Somme*, which the *Evening News* called 'the greatest moving picture in the world'.

★ *18 November* The Battle of the Somme was called off – with very little gain to show for the half a million British casualties.

★ *November* For the first time there was public criticism of the way the war was being run by the generals.

★ *7 December* Lloyd George, a critic of the army leadership, became Prime Minister in place of Herbert Asquith. He immediately reorganised the British government to focus all effort on the war. He set up the Ministry of Labour to deal with the labour supply in British industry. He set up the Ministry of Food to deal with the food supply.

1917

★ *February* Germany began its third and most devastating campaign of unrestricted submarine warfare against British merchant ships. The Women's Land Army was formed to recruit women as farm labourers.

★ *April* German U-boats sank one in four British merchant ships in the Atlantic. The food supply was running very low. Under DORA (see page 70) the government took over two and a half million acres of new farming land to help to feed Britain.

★ *November* A voluntary rationing scheme was introduced. It was a failure. Food prices continued to rise. Food queues got longer.

★ *December* Parliament agreed a law to give all women over 30 the right to vote in general elections.

1918

★ *25 February* Compulsory rationing scheme introduced in London and southern Britain with stiff penalties for offenders.

★ *April* Rationing of meat, butter and cheese extended to the entire country.

★ *11 November* At the eleventh hour of the eleventh day of the eleventh month of 1918 the Armistice was signed. The war was officially over.

★ *14 December* A general election was held in Britain. Women over 30 voted for the first time.

Recruitment and conscription

When war broke out Britain had only a small professional army. It needed a large one very quickly. The government began a massive recruitment drive, with posters, leaflets, recruitment offices in every town and stirring speeches by government ministers.

There was already a strong anti-German feeling in the country. The press strengthened it further with regular stories of German atrocities – babies butchered in Belgium, nurses murdered and, most famously of all, the German factory where they supposedly made soap out of boiled-up corpses.

The recruitment campaign was highly successful. Half a million signed up in the first month. By 1916 over two million had been enlisted (see Source 2).

SOURCE 2

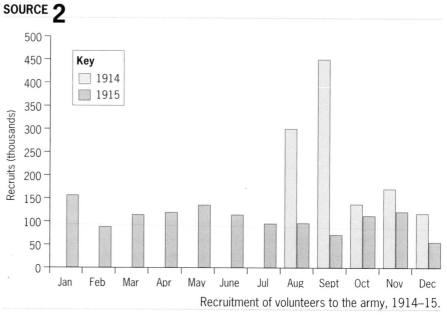

Recruitment of volunteers to the army, 1914–15.

1 Look at Sources 3–5. Describe the method each poster uses to encourage men to join up.
2 Draw up a list of arguments for and against this statement: 'Conscription was fairer than voluntary recruitment.'
3

> **PROMPT 2**
> Make notes about how recruitment to the army affected civilians.
> Include notes about:
> • voluntary recruitment
> • conscription
> • conchies
> • family life.

SOURCE 3

A 1914 recruitment poster. It features Lord Kitchener, a former successful general who became Secretary of State for War and the figurehead of the recruitment campaign.

SOURCE 4

A 1915 recruitment poster.

SOURCE 5

A 1915 recruitment poster.

SOURCE 6

COMPULSION BILL

"GOT HIM"

A cartoon published in the socialist newspaper *The Workers' Dreadnought* in 1916.

In 1916 the government decided to introduce conscription for the first time. All men aged between 18 and 40 had to register for active service. They could be called up at any time to fight.

The government did this for various reasons. The number of volunteers was falling. As you can see from Source 2, recruitment in December 1915 was the lowest for any month since the start of the war. But the demand for troops was increasing. The dead and wounded needed replacing. Another problem was that the volunteer system was damaging Britain's agriculture and industry. For example, so many miners joined up that there were reports of their having to be sent back to provide essential supplies of coal. The volunteer system was also seen as unfair. Not all parts of society took an equal share of the burden. There was a feeling that some groups avoided the war altogether. Some of the fittest and most able men were not volunteering at all. In the end, many welcomed the government's taking control of the situation and introducing conscription.

SOURCE 9

1 May 1915

William Milton, foreman of Lyons Hall Farm, does not approve of all the recruiting posters on the tree trunks and walls. 'If the government want more men let them take idlers not workmen. Unless the war is over before August there will not be enough men for the harvest.'

The men say 'We will go when we like, or when we are ordered.' Conscription, being just, would be welcome.

The Diary of Rev Andrew Clark, an Essex clergyman.

SOURCE 7

THE HARDEST QUESTION OF ALL

'Then you are willing to see your country defeated?'
That's the question that stops the mouths of many of us when we are trying to explain our position as 'conscientious objectors' . . . There is, I believe, hardly one of us who would, or could, say 'Yes'; but, if we say 'No', we are at once open to the crushing reply, 'Then you are willing to let other men fight and die for you, while you stay quietly and safely at home.'

From *The Friend*, published by the Quakers, a religious group who believed in non-violence, 21 January 1916.

Not everyone welcomed conscription, however. Fifty MPs, including leading Liberals, voted against it in Parliament. Another group who did not welcome it were those who were opposed to the war for religious or political reasons. It would be against their conscience to fight so they were called conscientious objectors or 'conchies'. Conchies had to appear before a TRIBUNAL and prove they had a genuine reason for objecting to war and were not just cowards. Some conchies were sent to prison, where they were often badly treated. Others actually went to the front and worked in field hospitals or as stretcher bearers.

SOURCE 10

Conscientious objectors, 1916. Four of these men, including Mr HHC Marten, second from left in the front row, had been sentenced to death as conchies, but had their sentence reduced to ten years' hard labour. This picture was taken at a granite quarry in Scotland where they were sent to serve their sentence.

SOURCE 8

Sir,
What right have 'conscientious objectors' to live in this country whose existence is only maintained by the fighting men of our Army and Navy?
G Moor, 3, Silverfields, Harrogate

From the *Daily Mail*, 10 January 1916.

DORA

In 1914 the government passed the Defence of the Realm Act which came to be known as DORA. It gave the government unprecedented and wide-ranging powers to control many aspects of people's daily lives. It allowed it to seize any land or buildings it needed, and to take over any industries which were important to the war effort. It allowed the government to control what the public knew about the war through censorship.

The government immediately took control of the coal industry so that the mines could be run to support the war effort rather than for the private profit of the owners.

The munitions crisis

In 1915 the first major problems began to emerge for the government. As the war became bogged down in a stalemate, it became increasingly obvious that planning for such a war was hopelessly inadequate. Most worryingly, there was a chronic shortage of shells, bullets and armaments on the Western Front. New soldiers had to train with wooden sticks instead of rifles as there were not enough rifles to go round. There were reports that soldiers in the front lines were rationed to three rounds of ammunition a day. The artillery were unable to keep up their barrage of enemy trenches because of the shortage of shells. The 'munitions crisis', as it was known, became a national scandal exposed by the *Daily Mail*, which was Britain's highest-circulation newspaper.

As a result of these problems, a coalition government was established – so all parties could work together to support the war effort. Lloyd George was made Minister of Munitions.

SOURCE 11

A postcard published by the government in 1915.

SOURCE 12

Details of munitions production, 1915–17.

1
PROMPT 3
Makes notes about the munitions crisis and how food shortages affected civilians.

2 What was the purpose of Source 11?
3 Source 11 shows Lloyd George 'delivering the goods'. Does Source 12 suggest he was successful or not?

ACTIVITY

Write a press release to go with Source 11 explaining how Lloyd George has dealt with the munitions crisis. Include reactions of:
a) the coalition government
b) women workers
c) trade unions.

Under DORA, Lloyd George introduced a range of measures to 'deliver the goods'. One problem was the shortage of skilled workers in key industries. Lloyd George tried to force skilled workers to stay where the government needed them instead of going to where they could get the best pay. The trade unions protested. Many of the bosses of the firms supplying the government were making huge profits out of the war, so the unions wondered why workers could not do so as well.

One other key element of Lloyd George's programme was to bring women into the workforce (see pages 76–77). Trade unions again resisted this. In 1915, 100,000 women registered for work in industry, yet to start with only 5000 were given jobs. The trade unions were worried about the effect of women workers on their members' wages. They argued that women worked for lower pay than men, so they 'diluted' men's wages. They refused to co-operate until the government gave a clear promise that women would be paid the same as men and would not be kept on when the men came back. Lloyd George gave them this undertaking. At the same time he also opened the government's own munitions factories, which employed a large number of women. By the end of 1915 the situation had improved. The British army was well supplied with munitions for the rest of the war, as you can see from Source 12.

A government poster issued in 1917.

Feeding the country

The government also needed to ensure that Britain was fed. Under DORA it was able to take over land and turn it over to farm production. In February 1917 it set up the Women's Land Army to recruit women as farm workers.

By then, however, the food supply in Britain had become quite desperate. In April 1917 German U-boats were sinking one in every four British merchant ships. Britain had only six weeks' supply of wheat left. As food supplies ran short, so prices rose. Wages had hardly risen during the war because people were mostly prepared to sacrifice better pay to support the war effort, but prices were now almost double what they had been in 1914. Richer people bought more than they needed and hoarded it. Poorer people could not afford even basic supplies such as bread. Shops closed early each afternoon as they had run out of goods to sell. In important industrial areas such as South Wales there were serious strikes over poverty-level wages.

The government again responded with a range of measures. Following strikes in 1917, it agreed to raise the wages of industrial workers. In May it started a system of voluntary rationing. The royal family led the way by announcing they were aiming to reduce their consumption of bread by one quarter, and 'to abstain from the use of flour in pastry and moreover carefully to restrict or wherever possible to abandon the use of flour in all articles other than bread'. They called on all people in Britain to do the same. In November the government introduced laws to control the price of bread – 'The Ninepenny Loaf'. It published many posters encouraging people to be economical with bread. It circulated recipe books with recipes which used less flour.

However, none of these measures was effective in reducing food shortages, so in early 1918 the government introduced compulsory rationing of sugar, butter, meat and beer. Every person had a book of coupons which had to be handed to the shopkeeper when rationed food was bought. There were stiff penalties facing anyone who broke the rationing rules.

On the whole, rationing was widely welcomed as a fairer system of sharing out the available food. By the end of the war, as a result of rationing, the diet and health of many poorer people had actually improved in comparison with pre-war days.

4 Why do you think the government was so concerned about flour and bread?

5 Why was the government reluctant to make rationing compulsory in 1917?

6 Look at Source 14. Why do you think the government published this leaflet?

DEFENCE OF THE REALM. E.P. 6.

MINISTRY OF FOOD.

BREACHES OF THE RATIONING ORDER

The undermentioned convictions have been recently obtained:—

Court	Date	Nature of Offence	Result
HENDON - -	29th Aug., 1918	Unlawfully obtaining and using ration books -	3 Months' Imprisonment
WEST HAM -	29th Aug., 1918	Being a retailer & failing to detach proper number of coupons	Fined £20
SMETHWICK -	22nd July, 1918	Obtaining meat in excess quantities - - -	Fined £50 & £5 5s. costs
OLD STREET -	4th Sept., 1918	Being a retailer selling to unregistered customer	Fined £72 & £5 5s. costs
OLD STREET -	4th Sept., 1918	Not detaching sufficient coupons for meat sold -	Fined £25 & £2 2s. costs
CHESTER-LE-STREET	4th Sept., 1918	Being a retailer returning number of registered customers in excess of counterfoils deposited - - - -	Fined £50 & £3 3s. costs
HIGH WYCOMBE	7th Sept., 1918	Making false statement on application for and using Ration Books unlawfully - - - - - - -	Fined £40 & £6 4s. costs

Enforcement Branch, Local Authorities Division,
MINISTRY OF FOOD.
September, 1918.

A leaflet produced by the government in 1918.

SOURCE **15**

'The Brown Family's Four War Christmases' – a cartoon from 1917.

ACTIVITY

Between 1914 and 1918 the war reached into every corner of people's lives. Family members were killed. Food was rationed. Freedom was restricted. Civilians faced danger. Source 15 shows one cartoonist's view of the impact of the war on a British family.

1 Write a detailed description of what each frame shows. Emphasise anything that has changed since the last frame.
2 From what you have found out about life on the Home Front, explain why these changes have taken place.

3 Write a phrase to sum up the family's attitude to the war in each year. You could choose from the following phrases or write your own: Grim determination, War enthusiasm, Let's get organised, Hard times.
4 Do you think this cartoon is an accurate representation of the attitudes of British people during the war? Explain your answer fully.
5 Based on what you have read on pages 66–72, write a description or draw a picture of what the cartoonist might have drawn at the end of 1918.

Propaganda and censorship

The government regarded it as essential that civilians should support the war effort. So DORA also gave the government the right to control the newspapers and other mass media that might influence people's opinions towards the war. On many occasions the government even kept Parliament in the dark about events on the front line.

Good news only

From the start of the war all news, especially bad news, was strictly controlled. Despite the problems of the first few months on the Western Front, the British people were told only of great British victories or heroic resistance. When the British battleship HMS *Audacious* was sunk in October 1914, it was simply not reported.

It was not until November 1916 that the government allowed journalists (and then only approved ones, of course) to be at the front. Reports focused on good news. The newspaper owners and editors themselves were the keenest supporters of the war effort. For example, Lord Beaverbrook, the *Daily Express* owner, was a cabinet minister from 1916, and became Minister for Information in 1918. He and other newspaper barons (as they are known) became an integral part of Britain's war effort. After the war, 12 leading members of the newspaper industry were given knighthoods in recognition of their wartime services.

The government also censored information from the soldiers at the front. The soldiers even censored themselves. There is much evidence that soldiers home on leave chose not to tell relatives the truth about what was going on at the front because they did not want to worry them.

Forced censorship

Some independent papers did publish more balanced news or even anti-war articles. Initially, they were tolerated. However, as the war dragged on papers like the pacifist newspaper *Tribunal* were closed down. Socialist newspapers such as the *Daily Herald* were monitored carefully by the censors.

The censors were also concerned with stopping sensitive information from leaking out to the enemy. In 1916 alone, the government Press Bureau and the Intelligence services examined 38,000 articles, 25,000 photographs and 300,000 private telegrams. Even magazines for railway enthusiasts found themselves in trouble for revealing too much about Britain's transport network.

Books and other publications

Leading authors – HG Wells, Arthur Conan Doyle, Thomas Hardy, Rudyard Kipling – all signed a Declaration by Authors in support of the war. Most of them produced patriotic publications for no fee. The history department at the University of Oxford produced a five-volume explanation of why Britain was justified in going to war (it became known as the Red Book because of its cover). The Red Book sold 50,000 copies.

Propaganda for children

Propaganda was aimed at children too. Toys were made that were intended to encourage support of the war effort, and there were many patriotic books and comics. Needless to say, the German enemy was always cowardly and treacherous and the British Tommy was always modest, brave and successful. We know that these books and magazines sold well because they were regularly reprinted. In fact, many of them were still being reprinted in the 1920s and 1930s and given as school prizes.

SOURCE 16

If the people really knew [the truth about the war] the war would be stopped tomorrow. But of course they don't – and can't – know. The correspondents don't write, and the censors would not pass, the truth.

Prime Minister Lloyd George in a private conversation with the editor of the *Manchester Guardian* in December 1917.

SOURCE 17

It is a domestic tragedy of the war that the country which went out to defend liberty is losing its own liberties one by one, and that the government which began by relying on public opinion as a great help has now come to fear and curtail it.

The Nation, May 1916. (This journal was later suppressed under DORA.)

---

1 Effective wartime propaganda aims to:
   a) keep up morale
   b) encourage civilians to support the war effort
   c) create hatred and suspicion of the enemy.
   Choose one example of each from pages 73–75.

2 **PROMPT 4**
   Make notes for your presentation about how propaganda was used to keep civilian support for the war.
   Mention:
   newspapers;
   censorship;
   films and books;
   patriotic organisations.

3 How do Sources 16 and 17 differ in their view of censorship and propaganda?

1 Most historians think that propaganda had more effect on children than any other group in society. Why do you think the toys in Source 18 might be effective?

SOURCE 18

A selection of toys and games from 1914 to 1918.

Films

The government did not even have to make its own propaganda films. British film makers produced 240 war films between 1915 and 1918, very few of which were actually commissioned by the War Department.

The British Topical Committee for War Films was a group of film companies who got together to make and sell films to the War Department. Their patriotic film *For the Empire* reached an estimated audience of 9 million by the end of 1916. The Committee made some of the most famous films of the war, including *The Battle of the Somme*.

The Battle of the Somme has generally been seen by historians as a propaganda triumph. It showed real scenes from the battle, including real casualties (13 per cent of its running time showed dead or wounded soldiers). It also included 'fake' scenes The film did not tell its audience which was which.

It was released in August 1916 and was a huge commercial success. Many people talked of it as their first chance to see what conditions were really like in the war – to get closer to the truth. By October 1916 it had been shown in over 2000 cinemas (out of 4500 in the country). Some anti-war campaigners approved of the film because it showed the horrors more truly than any previous film. But some people were shocked by its realism. The Dean of Durham Cathedral thought that it was wrong to exploit death and suffering to provide entertainment.

Did the propaganda work?

It is very hard to measure how effective the propaganda was. The ultimate test of the propaganda is whether it helped support for the war to stay firm (and, as you can see on page 75, it mostly did stay firm, despite immense casualties). However, it is almost impossible to judge how far the propaganda was responsible for this.

We can look at numbers: 9 million people saw the film *For the Empire*. Over half the population read a daily newspaper and newspaper circulation increased during the war. The circulation of the *Daily Express* went up from 295,000 in 1914 to 579,000 in 1918. The patriotic weekly journal *John Bull* was selling 2 million copies in 1918 and the *News of the World* was selling even more. These figures give the impression that the ordinary citizen was surrounded by what the government wanted them to hear and see.

In many ways the government did not have to resort to extreme propaganda measures. There is a lot of evidence to suggest that most people mobilised themselves to support the war of their own accord. Many ordinary citizens joined patriotic organisations such as the Fight for Right Movement, the Council of Loyal British Subjects or the Victoria League.

SOURCE 19

Some scenes from the film *The Battle of the Somme*. **A** and **B** were real. **C** was filmed at a training ground.

Did people support the war?

In the early years of the war the government faced very little opposition to the war. Some Socialists and pacifists protested against the war but they were drowned out by the surge of patriotic feeling. George Bernard Shaw's anti-war pamphlet 'Common Sense About the War' (1914) sold 25,000 copies, but he became the target of much criticism. Ramsay MacDonald had to resign as leader of the Labour Party because he did not support the war while his party did. The headmaster of Eton – an influential figure at the time – was hounded by the press because he simply called on Britain to fight a 'Christian and moral' war. He was eventually forced to take early retirement.

It was a similar story when conscription was introduced in 1916. Fifty MPs, including Liberal leaders, voted against it. The Socialist and pacifist critics of conscription found little sympathy among the general public. Conchies were mostly treated as cowards and shirkers by the press despite considerable evidence that many of them were brave individuals. Perhaps it is not surprising that there were not many conchies. Only 16,000 out of a possible 8 million affected by conscription actually refused to enlist.

From 1914 to 1916, then, the British people were remarkably consistent in their support for the war. However, many historians argue that the Battle of the Somme was a turning point. As the battle dragged on from July to November 1916, half a million soldiers died for just a few square kilometres of gained territory.

In the weeks after the end of the battle, the government faced some serious criticisms as politicians and soldiers questioned publicly for the first time the way the war was being fought. Source 20 is an extract from a letter that Lord Lansdowne, an ex-Cabinet minister, sent to the newspapers. It was debated in Parliament a few days later.

Many people in Britain echoed his feelings. The Battle of the Somme did seem to change the mood in Britain. If you had interviewed a British person about the war in late 1916, you would probably still have found a grim determination to finish the job that had been started, but very little sense of excitement about the war.

Criticism of the war effort left its mark on the government as well. In December the Prime Minister, Asquith, stood down in favour of Lloyd George, who was one of the critics of the army leadership and who was felt to be the only man with the energy and imagination to get Britain through the mounting crisis.

Even so, criticism of the war leadership continued into 1917, as you can see from Source 21 by Siegfried Sassoon. Sassoon was a celebrated war poet. He had been an officer on the Western Front for three years, twice wounded, and decorated for his bravery. In 1917 he wrote a number of poems which accused the generals of being out of touch and incompetent. In July 1917 he went further when he wrote his 'soldier's declaration', which was read out in the House of Commons and was published in the *Daily Mail* and *The Times*.

The government's response was to send Sassoon for psychiatric treatment in a hospital for victims of shell-shock. Sassoon later withdrew his criticism, putting it all down to a nervous breakdown. He returned to France to fight in 1918.

Sassoon was not a lone critic. Many Socialists had criticised the war from the very start. But he and they were in the minority. Even in 1917, when people were prepared to question the war leadership, there was still very little doubt in people's minds that the war against Germany should be pursued to a final victory.

The end of the war in November 1918 was greeted as much with relief as with a sense of triumph. People were all too well aware by then of the human and financial cost of the war in Britain and in other countries, and were desperate to rebuild their lives and their country.

SOURCE 20

We are slowly but surely killing off the best of the male population of these islands. Can we afford to go on paying the same price for the same sort of gain?

From Lord Lansdowne's letter to the press, 29 November 1917.

SOURCE 21

I believe that the war is being prolonged by those who have the power to end it. I believe that this war upon which I entered as a war of defence and liberation has now become a war of conquest and aggression. I have seen and endured the sufferings of the troops and I can no longer be a party to prolonging these sufferings for ends which I believe to be evil and unjust.

'A soldier's declaration' by Siegfried Sassoon, July 1917.

2 Read Source 21. How is this criticism of the war different from Lord Lansdowne's criticism in Source 20?
3 Which criticism would be most troubling to the government?

At this hour of England's grave peril and desperate need, I do hereby pledge myself most solemnly in the name of the King and Country to persuade every man I know to offer his services to the country, and I also pledge myself never to be seen in public with any man who, being in every way fit and free for service, has refused to respond to his country's call.

Part of the oath of the Active Service League.

How far did women contribute to the war effort?

As soon as the war broke out in 1914, both the suffragists and the suffragettes suspended their campaigns for the vote. The suffragists, with their formidable publicity machine, worked to persuade the men of Britain to join the army. Meanwhile, Mrs Pankhurst staged a huge demonstration demanding that women be allowed to work in munitions factories. Early in August, all suffragettes were released from prison. Other women's organisations also tried to boost recruitment. The Order of the White Feather encouraged women to give white feathers to young men not in the armed forces. The white feather was a symbol of a coward. The Mothers' Union published posters urging mothers to get their sons to join up. Women members of the Active Service League took an oath to promise to encourage young men to join up (see Source 22).

From an early stage in the war, British industry began to suffer a desperate shortage of labour. By early 1916, Britain had up to 2 million workers fewer than were necessary to keep the country going.

In offices the absence of men did not pose a particular problem. Women were soon employed in place of the male clerks who joined up, and by the end of the war half a million women had replaced men in office jobs. Government departments employed a further 200,000 female clerks.

In manufacturing, however, it was a different story, at least to start with. Employers were very reluctant to take on women to fill men's jobs. They thought that women would not learn the necessary skills, and also feared trouble from the unions. In fact, the unions did resist the employment of women workers, fearing that women would be paid less and that this would be a threat to men's wages. Most unions did not even accept female members.

By 1916, the shortage of engineering workers was desperate, especially as more and more munitions and supplies, and increasing numbers of men, were needed at the front. For practical reasons, employers were persuaded to take on women workers. The government set an example to private industry by employing women almost exclusively in its own munitions factories. By the end of the war, almost 800,000 women had taken up work in engineering industries. The evidence soon showed that even with very little training they were as skilled as men.

Munitions work was tiring and dangerous. As the war went on, shifts got longer and longer. There were disastrous accidents, such as the explosion at Silvertown in the East End of London, in January 1917. In August 1916, medical reports publicised the effects on women of handling TNT explosives. These included breathing difficulties, rashes and yellowing of the skin, digestion problems, blood poisoning and even brain damage.

SOURCE **23**

[The work women are doing] . . . is not of the repetitious type, demanding little or no manipulative ability . . . it taxes the intelligence of the operatives to a high degree. Yet the work turned out has reached a high pitch of excellence.

From the trade journal *The Engineer*, 20 August 1915.

SOURCE **24**

An official war painting of women at work in a munitions factory.

SOURCE **25**

A photograph taken in a munitions factory in 1917.

SOURCE 26

Women delivering coal in 1917.

As the war took its terrible toll on the male population, more and more women stepped in to fill the gaps. A kind of revolution was taking place. Women gained access to a whole range of jobs that had previously been the preserve of men. They worked as bus conductors, postal workers and farm labourers, and delivered coal. Some 1.6 million extra women workers took part in war work. They became grave diggers, road layers, welders, steel workers and bus drivers. There was a Women's Volunteer Police Service in most of the major cities. Some 260,000 women served in the Women's Land Army. In 1918, the first women's army unit (the Women's Army Auxiliary Corps, or WAAC) was founded, although members were never involved in front-line fighting. There were women nurses in medical stations near the front line. The Salvation Army sent female volunteers as nurses, cooks and helpers to aid soldiers and civilians in France. Women even kept the factory football teams going!

Women workers came from many different backgrounds. Some married women took on their husbands' jobs, but it was mostly unmarried women who took jobs in factories. The government called on middle-class families to do without their servants; with higher wages and preferable conditions in factories, many servants did not need much persuading.

SOURCE 27

Area of work	Women in 1914	Women in 1918	Women replacing men
Metals	170,000	594,000	195,000
Chemicals	40,000	104,000	35,000
Food and drink	196,000	235,000	60,000
Timber	44,000	79,000	23,000
Transport	18,000	117,000	42,000
Government	2,000	225,000	197,000

Women at work, 1914–18.

SOURCE 28

'Palmer's Munitionettes': a women's football team made up of workers from Palmer's Shipbuilding Company.

1

PROMPT 5

Make notes for your presentation on how the war affected women civilians. Mention:
- their role in recruitment
- job opportunities
- men's attitudes
- working conditions.

FOCUS TASK

How did women contribute to the war effort?

It is 1918. Use the information and sources on pages 76–77 to write a report for the Prime Minister. Your report is designed to convince him that the contribution of women to the war effort means they should get the vote. You should mention the role of women in:
- recruitment
- freeing men to fight
- munitions
- putting up with prejudice
- women's success at doing 'men's work'.

Why were some women given the vote in 1918?

SOURCE 29

The front cover of the magazine *Votes for Women*, 26 November 1915.

In 1915, the government began to consider changes to Britain's electoral system. Until then, citizens living outside Britain were not allowed to vote in elections. This was clearly unfair to soldiers who were serving abroad. They wanted to change the voting system to allow the 'hero' soldiers to vote. The campaigners jumped at this chance (see Source 29). Women had shown themselves to be capable and responsible under the strains of war. By 1916 women were even serving in the armed forces. There was no backlash against the women's movement now.

SOURCE 30

Former opponents are now declaring themselves on our side, or at any rate withdrawing their opposition. The change of tone in the press is most marked . . . The view has been widely expressed in a great variety of the organs of public opinion that the continued exclusion of women from representation will . . . be an impossibility after the war.

Millicent Fawcett writing in the magazine *Common Cause*, 1916.

The House of Commons passed the Representation of the People Act in 1917 by a massive majority of seven to one. It was given a rougher ride in the Lords, but even so was passed by 63 votes. It became law in 1918. As a result of the Act, all males aged over 21 gained the right to vote. Women over the age of 30, and women over 21 who were also householders or married to householders, also gained the vote – a total of about 9 million women.

However, you can see from this that the old fears about women having the vote had not entirely disappeared. Although all men now had the vote, MPs were prepared to support votes only for older married women, or women who owned property and were therefore considered more responsible. One leading historian has pointed out that the young, single working-class women who had done most of the war work were the ones who did not gain the vote. MPs were reluctant to enfranchise this new group, whose ideas might be a little too radical.

Women could now also stand for Parliament and in 1919 Nancy Astor became the first woman MP to take her seat in the Commons. (The first woman MP to be elected was Countess Makiewicz, but as an Irish nationalist she refused to sit at Westminster.)

Full voting rights for women were not granted until 1928. Even so, for Millicent Fawcett, the 1918 Act was the fulfilment of a lifetime's work.

SOURCE 31

The history of the women's movement for the last 50 years is the gradual removal of intolerable grievances. Sometimes the pace was fairly rapid; sometimes it was very slow; but it was always constant, and always in one direction. I have sometimes compared it . . . to the movement of a glacier. But like a glacier it was ceaseless and irresistible. You could not see it move, but if you compared it with a stationary object . . . you had proof positive that it had moved.

Written by Millicent Fawcett in 1918.

SOURCE 32

I'm against the extension of the franchise to women. I shall always be against the extension of the franchise to women . . . It was in the year 1918, after the war, that the disaster took place. Had it not been for the war, in my judgement we should have continued successfully to resist this measure for an indefinite period of time.

Lord Birkenhead, speaking just before all women gained the vote in 1928.

SOURCE 33

Some years ago I used the expression 'Let the women work out their own salvation.' Well, Sir, they had worked it out during the war. How could we have carried on the war without them?

Wherever we turn we see them doing work which three years ago we would have regarded as being exclusively 'men's work'. When the war is over the question will then arise about women's labour and their function in the new order of things. I would find it impossible to withhold from women the power and the right of making their voices directly heard.

From a speech by ex-Prime Minister Asquith in 1917.

ACTIVITY

Professor Change

The period 1906 to 1918 saw massive changes in life in Britain.

Professor Continuity

This might look like a period of great change in some ways – but for most people life carried on much as usual.

Professor Evolution

There were undoubtedly important changes in the years 1906 to 1918. However, most of them had already started well before and simply continued to develop during this period.

You have seen two of these professors before (on page 54). They have now been joined by a third.
   These three professors all interpret the events in Britain between 1906 and 1918 differently. There is good evidence to support all three views!

1   Using the information over pages 50–79, decide how each of the professors could support his or her view.
2   Then use your evidence to prepare for a class debate on 'Was 1906 to 1918 a time of change in Britain?'

FOCUS TASK

Why were some women given the vote in 1918?

SOURCE 34

There were three stages in the emancipation of women. The first was the long campaign of propaganda and organisation at the centre of which, patient, unwearying and always hopeful, stood Dame Millicent Fawcett. The second was the campaign of the militants. The third was war.

   Had there been no militancy and no war, the emancipation would have come, although more slowly. But without the faithful preparation of the ground over many years by Dame Millicent Fawcett and her colleagues, neither militancy nor the war could have produced the crop.

From the obituary to Millicent Fawcett in the *Manchester Guardian*, 6 August 1929.

Read Source 34. You are now going to consider how far you agree with this analysis.

1   Write each of the following labels on a separate card.
   • Peaceful suffragist campaigning
   • Militant suffragette campaigning
   • Women's support for the war effort
2   On each card, write your own explanation of how this factor helped to lead to women getting the vote.
3   Take one card (any card) away. Explain why women would not have got the vote with just the two remaining factors.
4   Is any one factor more important than the others? Explain your answer carefully.
5   Re-read Source 34, then explain in your own words how these factors are linked together.

4 The peace treaties after the First World War

Were they fair?

FOCUS

In 1919 the leaders of the victorious powers met in Paris to decide how to deal with the defeated powers. The leaders of Britain, France and the USA found it very hard to agree on what to do.

In this chapter you will:

- consider why the leaders had different aims at the Peace Conference, and why each could not get what they wanted
- find out how the Treaty of Versailles affected Germany
- investigate why the various treaties have been criticised, and make up your own mind about whether the peace treaties were fair.

FACTFILE

The Paris Peace Conference, 1919–1920

★ The Conference took place in the palace of Versailles (a short distance from Paris).

★ It lasted for 12 months.

★ Thirty-two nations were supposed to be represented, but no one from the defeated countries was invited.

★ Five treaties were drawn up at the Conference. The main one was the Treaty of Versailles which dealt with Germany. The other treaties dealt with Germany's allies.

★ All of the important decisions on the fate of Germany were taken by the 'Big Three': Clemenceau, Lloyd George and Wilson.

★ The Big Three were supported by many diplomats and expert advisers, but they often ignored their advice.

★ The Big Three got on badly from the start and relations between them got worse throughout the Conference, especially the relationship between Wilson and Clemenceau.

★ Wilson was very ill during parts of the Conference.

The Paris Peace Conference

SOURCE 1

Allied soldiers and officials watch the signing of the Treaty of Versailles.

Source 1 was taken at the signing of the Treaty of Versailles at the Paris Peace Conference. It was a spectacular occasion and a momentous event. Months of hard negotiation, argument and compromise ended when the two German representatives who had been summoned to sign the Treaty did so on 28 June 1919.

When the treaty terms were announced the Germans complained that it was unfair. Many historians have criticised it since. To understand this, we need to look at the mood in 1919.

The mood in 1919

When the leaders of Britain (Lloyd George), France (Clemenceau) and the USA (Wilson) arrived in Paris in January 1919 to draw up a treaty, they were already under pressure to deal severely with Germany. The people of the victorious countries, particularly in France and Britain, felt strongly that Germany was responsible for the war and should be punished.

There was also a strong feeling that Germany should pay for all the damage and destruction caused by the war. Apart from the USA, all of the countries that had fought in the war were exhausted. Their economies and their industries were in a bad state. Millions of young men had been killed or injured on both sides. Total British and French casualties, killed or injured, probably amounted to over 9 million. Ordinary civilians had faced shortages of food and medicine. Villages and towns in large areas of Belgium and France had been devastated.

1 You are a reporter for a Belgian newspaper. Write a caption to go with Source 2. Your caption should aim to persuade the Allied leaders to punish Germany.

SOURCE 2

An aerial photograph of Ypres in Belgium showing the almost complete destruction of the town by four years of heavy gun bombardment.

Although no fighting took place on British soil, the huge casualties left their mark on public opinion in Britain. Almost every family had lost a member in the fighting. In the British general election campaigns of 1918 politicians knew they could rely on the support of the British people if they demanded a harsh peace settlement with Germany.

SOURCE 4

If I am elected, Germany is going to pay . . . I have personally no doubt we will get everything that you can squeeze out of a lemon, and a bit more. I propose that every bit of [German-owned] property, movable and immovable, in Allied and neutral countries, whether State property or private property, should be surrendered by the Germans.

Sir Eric Geddes, a government minister, speaking to a rally in the general election campaign, December 1918.

The case for treating Germany harshly was strengthened when it became public how harshly Germany had treated Russia in the Treaty of Brest-Litovsk in 1918 (see page 118). The Treaty stripped Russia of huge amounts of land and 25 per cent of its population. From the point of view of the Allies this was further proof of the evil ambitions of the German regime. The Allies felt that this was what Germany would have done to Britain and France if it had won.

Although the war and the fighting had ended in November 1918, the bitterness, hatred and enmity between the warring countries was far from over.

SOURCE 5

To the Allied Powers the Treaty of Brest-Litovsk was almost as significant as to the Russians and Germans who signed it. The naked and brutal policy of annexation [take-over of land] as practised by a victorious Germany weakened the arguments of well-meaning but misguided pacifists in the countries of the Entente.

An extract from Purnell's *History of the War*, written in 1969.

SOURCE 3

British Empire Union cartoon, 1919. The BEU was a pressure group which campaigned for people to buy British Empire goods.

2 Explain in your own words what Source 3 is trying to say about 'the German'.
3 Read Source 5. What sort of treaty do you think the 'well-meaning but misguided pacifists' might have wanted?

ACTIVITY

Source 4 comes from a speech in the 1918 British general election campaign. Write an extra paragraph for the speech giving reasons for this harsh treatment of Germany.

At the end of the speech Geddes is holding a question time. What questions do you think might be asked, or what criticisms or comments might be made?

1 If you had been there to advise the Big Three, in what order of priority would you put the four aims described on the right?

The aims of the leaders at the Paris Peace Conference

As soon as the Paris Peace Conference began, there was disagreement about what the Conference was aiming to do.

- Some felt that the aim was to punish Germany.
- Others felt that the aim was to cripple Germany so that it could not start another war.
- Many felt that the point of the Conference was to reward the winning countries.
- Others believed that the aim of the Conference should be to establish a just and lasting peace.

PROFILE

Georges Clemenceau (Prime Minister of France)

Background
★ Born 1841 (he was aged 77 when the Paris Conference began).
★ First entered French politics in 1871.
★ Was Prime Minister from 1906 to 1909. From 1914 to 1917 he was very critical of the French war leaders. In November 1917 he was himself elected to lead France through the last years of the war.

Character
A hard, tough politician with a reputation for being uncompromising. He had seen his country invaded twice by the Germans, in 1870 and in 1914. He was determined not to allow such devastation ever again.

FOCUS TASK

What were the aims of the Big Three at the Paris Peace Conference?

Using the information and sources on pages 80–83, draw up a chart like the one below summarising the aims of the three leaders at the Paris Peace Conference.
  NB Leave the fifth column blank. You will need it for a later task.

Leader	Country	Attitude towards Germany	Main aim	

Georges Clemenceau (France)

France had suffered enormous damage to its land, industry, people – and self-confidence. Over two-thirds of the men who had served in the French army had been killed or injured. The war affected almost an entire generation. By comparison, Germany seemed to many French people as powerful and threatening as ever.

Ever since 1870, France had felt threatened by its increasingly powerful neighbour, Germany. The war increased this feeling. German land and industry had not been as badly damaged as France's. France's population was in decline compared to Germany's. Clemenceau and other French leaders saw the Treaty as an opportunity to cripple Germany so that it could not attack France again. The French President (Poincaré) even wanted Germany broken up into a collection of smaller states, but Clemenceau knew that the British and Americans would not agree to this. Clemenceau was a realist and knew he would probably be forced to compromise on some issues. However, he had to show he was aware of public opinion in France. He demanded a treaty that would weaken Germany as much as possible.

Woodrow Wilson (USA)

Wilson has often been seen as an idealist whose aim was to build a better and more peaceful world from the ruins of the Great War. This is partially true, but Wilson did believe that Germany should be punished. However, he also believed that the treaty with Germany should not be too harsh. His view was that if Germany was treated harshly, some day it would recover and want revenge. Wilson's main aim was to strengthen democracy in the defeated nation so that its people would not let its leaders cause another war.

He believed that nations should co-operate to achieve world peace. In January 1918 he published his Fourteen Points to help achieve this. The most important for Wilson was the fourteenth. In this he proposed the setting up of an international body called the League of Nations.

He also believed in self-determination (the idea that nations should rule themselves rather than be ruled by others). He wanted the different peoples of eastern Europe (for example, Poles, Czechs and Slovaks) to rule themselves rather than be part of Austria–Hungary's empire.

PROFILE

**Woodrow Wilson
(President of the USA)**

Background
★ Born 1856.
★ Became a university professor.
★ First entered politics in 1910.
★ Became President in 1912 and was re-elected in 1916.

Character
An idealist, and a reformer. As President, he had campaigned against corruption in politics and business. He concentrated on keeping the USA out of the war. Once the USA had joined the war, he drew up the Fourteen Points as the basis for ending the war fairly, so that future wars could be avoided.

PROFILE

**David Lloyd George
(Prime Minister of Britain)**

Background
★ Born 1863.
★ First entered politics in 1890. A very able politician who became Prime Minister in 1916 and remained in power until 1922.

Character
A realist. As an experienced politician, he knew there would have to be compromise. Thus he occupied the middle ground between the views of Wilson and those of Clemenceau.

THE FOURTEEN POINTS

1 No secret treaties.

2 Free access to the seas in peacetime or wartime.

3 Free trade between countries.

4 All countries to work towards disarmament.

5 Colonies to have a say in their own future.

6 German troops to leave Russia.

7 Independence for Belgium.

8 France to regain Alsace–Lorraine.

9 Frontier between Austria and Italy to be adjusted.

10 Self-determination for the peoples of eastern Europe (they should rule themselves).

11 Serbia to have access to the sea.

12 Self-determination for the people in the Turkish Empire.

13 Poland to become an independent state with access to the sea.

14 League of Nations to be set up.

Many people in France and Britain did not agree with the ideas contained in Wilson's Fourteen Points. They seemed impractical. Take self-determination, for example. It would be very difficult to give the peoples of eastern Europe the chance to rule themselves because they were scattered across many countries. For example, 25 per cent of the population of the new state of Czechoslovakia were neither Czechs nor Slovaks. Some people were bound to end up being ruled by people from another group with different customs and a different language. Some historians have pointed out that while Wilson talked a great deal about eastern and central Europe, he did not actually know very much about the area.

David Lloyd George (Great Britain)

At the peace talks Lloyd George was often in the middle ground between Clemenceau and Wilson. He wanted Germany to be justly punished but not too harshly. He wanted Germany to lose its navy and its colonies because Britain thought they threatened the British Empire. However, like Wilson, he did not want Germany to seek revenge in the future and possibly start another war. He was also keen for Britain and Germany to begin trading with each other again. Before the war, Germany had been Britain's second largest trading partner. British people might not like it, but the fact was that trade with Germany meant jobs for them.

SOURCE 6

We want a peace which will be just, but not vindictive. We want a stern peace because the occasion demands it, but the severity must be designed, not for vengeance, but for justice. Above all, we want to protect the future against a repetition of the horrors of this war.

Lloyd George speaking to the House of Commons, before the Peace Conference.

Like Clemenceau, Lloyd George had real problems with public pressures at home for a harsh treaty (see Sources 3 and 4 on page 81). Even his own MPs did not always agree with him and he had just won the 1918 election in Britain by promising to 'make Germany pay', even though he realised the dangers of this course of action.

1 Look at Sources 7–9. All the cartoons are commenting on the Peace Conference. Say which you think would most appeal to each of the Big Three.
2 All the cartoons come from the same magazine, *Punch*. Why do you think they take different viewpoints?

SOURCE 7

GIVING HIM ROPE?

GERMAN CRIMINAL (*to Allied Police*). "HERE, I SAY, STOP! YOU'RE HURTING ME! [*Aside*]
IF I ONLY WHINE ENOUGH I MAY BE ABLE TO WRIGGLE OUT OF THIS YET."

SOURCE 8

SOURCE 9

THE FINISHING TOUCH.

Disagreements and compromises

As the talks at Versailles went on, it became clear that the very different objectives of the three leaders could not all be met. Clemenceau clashed with Wilson over many issues. The USA had not suffered nearly as badly as France in the war. Clemenceau resented Wilson's more generous attitude to Germany. They disagreed over what to do about Germany's Rhineland and coalfields in the Saar. In the end, Wilson had to give way on these issues. In return, Clemenceau and Lloyd George did give Wilson what he wanted in eastern Europe, despite their reservations about his idea of self-determination. However, this mainly affected the other four treaties, not the Treaty of Versailles.

Clemenceau also clashed with Lloyd George, particularly over Lloyd George's desire not to treat Germany too harshly. For example, Clemenceau said: '. . . if the British are so anxious to appease Germany they should look overseas and make colonial, naval or commercial concessions.' Clemenceau felt that the British were quite happy to treat Germany fairly in Europe, where France rather than Britain was most under threat. However, they were less happy to allow Germany to keep its navy and colonies, which would be more of a threat to Britain.

Wilson and Lloyd George did not always agree either. Lloyd George was particularly unhappy with point 2 of the Fourteen Points, allowing all nations access to the seas. Similarly, Wilson's views on people ruling themselves were somewhat threatening to the British government, for the British Empire ruled millions of people all across the world from London.

ACTIVITY

1 Work in groups. Draw up a table to show what views:
   a) Clemenceau
   b) Lloyd George
   would have expressed on points 2, 4, 5, 8, 10 and 14 of President Wilson's Fourteen Points. You can find them on page 83.
2 On your own, write a letter from one of the two leaders to Wilson summarising your view of the Fourteen Points.
3 Copy the following diagram and use it to summarise the attitudes of the three leaders to each other.

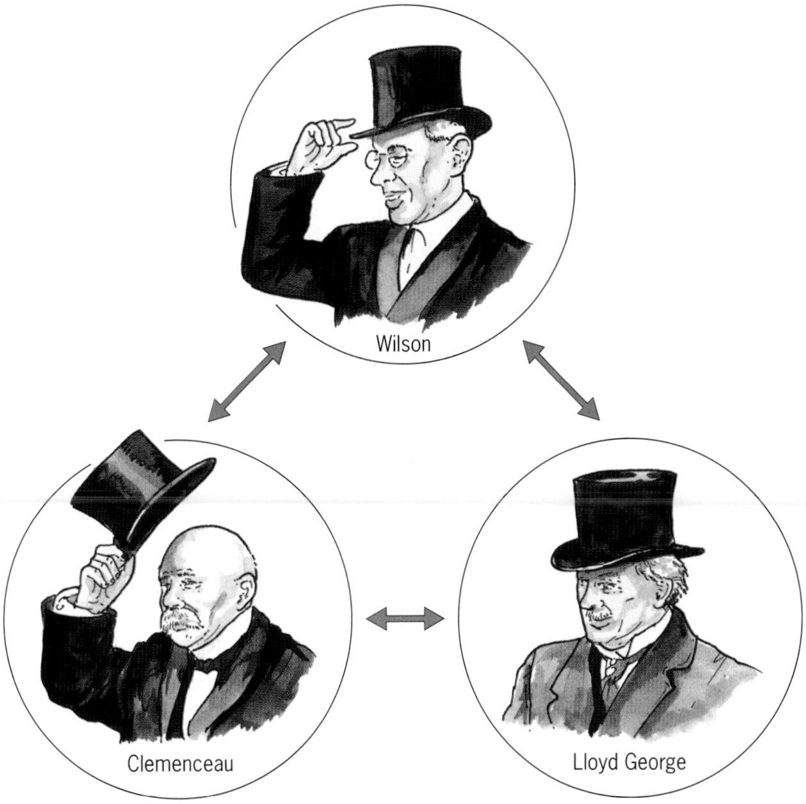

Wilson

Clemenceau

Lloyd George

The Treaty of Versailles

None of the Big Three was happy with the eventual terms of the Treaty. After months of negotiation, all of them had to compromise on some of their aims, otherwise there would never have been a treaty.

The main terms can be divided into five areas.

The terms of the treaty

1 War guilt

This clause was simple but was seen by the Germans as extremely harsh. Germany had to accept the blame for starting the war (see Source 21 on page 12).

2 Reparations

The major powers agreed, without consulting Germany, that Germany had to pay REPARATIONS to the Allies for the damage caused by the war. The exact figure was not agreed until 1921 when it was set at £6600 million – an enormous figure. If the terms of the payments had not later been changed under the Young Plan in 1929 (see page 146), Germany would not have finished paying this bill until 1984.

3 German territories and colonies

Germany's overseas empire was taken away (see Source 10). It had been one of the causes of bad relations between Britain and Germany before the war. Former German colonies became MANDATES controlled by the League of Nations, which effectively meant that France and Britain controlled them.

Germany's European borders were very extensive, and the section dealing with former German territories was a complicated part of the Treaty (see Source 11). In addition to these changes, the Treaty also forbade Germany to join together with its former ally Austria.

SOURCE 10

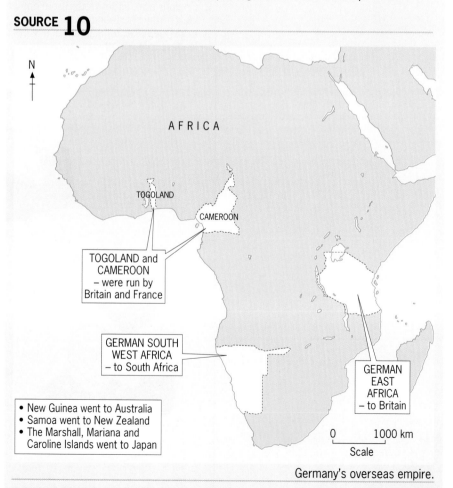

- New Guinea went to Australia
- Samoa went to New Zealand
- The Marshall, Mariana and Caroline Islands went to Japan

Germany's overseas empire.

4 Germany's armed forces

The size and power of the German army was a major concern of all the powers, especially France. The Treaty therefore restricted German armed forces to a level well below what they had been before the war.

- The army was limited to 100,000 men.
- Conscription was banned – soldiers had to be volunteers.
- Germany was not allowed armoured vehicles, submarines or aircraft.
- The navy could build only six battleships.
- The Rhineland became a demilitarised zone. This meant that no German troops were allowed into that area. The Rhineland was important because it was the border area between Germany and France (see Source 11).

SOURCE 11

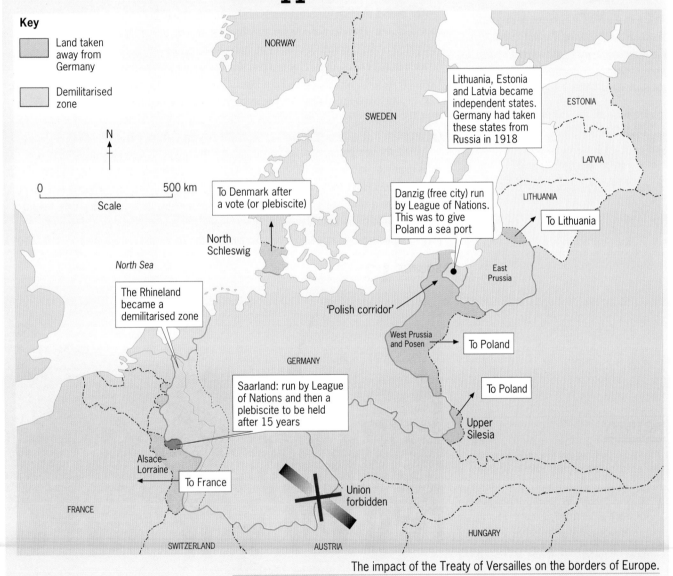

Key

Land taken away from Germany

Demilitarised zone

The impact of the Treaty of Versailles on the borders of Europe.

5 League of Nations

Previous methods of keeping peace had failed and so the League of Nations was set up as an international 'police force'. You will study the League in detail in Chapter 8. Germany was not invited to join the League until it had shown that it was a peace-loving country.

German reactions to the Treaty of Versailles

The terms of the Treaty were announced on 7 May to a horrified German nation. Germany was to lose:

- 10 per cent of its land
- all of its overseas colonies
- 12.5 per cent of its population
- 16 per cent of its coalfields and almost half of its iron and steel industry.

Its army was reduced to 100,000 men. It could have no air force, and only a tiny navy.

Worst of all, Germany had to accept the blame for starting the war and should therefore pay reparations.

The overall reaction of Germans was horror and outrage. They certainly did not feel they had started the war. They did not even feel they had lost the war. In 1919 many Germans did not really understand how bad Germany's military situation had been at the end of the war. They believed that the German government had simply agreed to a ceasefire, and that therefore Germany should have been at the Paris Peace Conference to negotiate peace. It should not have been treated as a defeated state. They were angry that their government was not represented at the talks and that they were being forced to accept a harsh treaty without any choice or even a comment.

At first, the new government refused to sign the Treaty and the German navy sank its own ships in protest. At one point, it looked as though war might break out again. But what could the German leader Ebert do? He consulted the army commander Hindenburg, who made it clear that Germany could not possibly win, but indicated that as a soldier he would prefer to die fighting.

Ebert was in an impossible position. How could he inflict war and certain defeat on his people? Reluctantly, he agreed to accept the terms of the Treaty and it was signed on 28 June 1919.

SOURCE 12

Today in the Hall of Mirrors the disgraceful Treaty is being signed. Do not forget it! The German people will, with unceasing labour, press forward to reconquer the place among the nations to which it is entitled.

From *Deutsche Zeitung* (German News), on the day the Treaty was signed.

SOURCE 13

Germans demonstrate against the Treaty, May 1919.

ACTIVITY

You have been asked to prepare some placards for the protest rally in Source 13.

1 Work in groups to write one placard for each of Germany's main complaints about the treaty.
2 Then decide which complaint is the most important. That one will be carried at the front of the march.

War guilt and reparations

The 'war guilt' clause was particularly hated. Germans felt at the very least that blame should be shared (see Witness 6, page 13). What made matters worse, however, was that because Germany was forced to accept blame for the war, it was also expected to pay for all the damage caused by it. The German economy was already in tatters. People had very little food. They feared that the reparations payments would cripple them.

SOURCE 14

A German cartoon published in 1919. The German mother is saying to her starving child: 'When we have paid one hundred billion marks then I can give you something to eat.'

SOURCE 15

THE RECKONING.

Pan-German. "MONSTROUS, I CALL IT. WHY, IT'S FULLY A QUARTER OF WHAT *WE* SHOULD HAVE MADE *THEM* PAY, IF *WE'D* WON."

A cartoon from *Punch* magazine, 1919.

SOURCE 16

The Allies could have done anything with the German people had they made the slightest move toward reconciliation. People were prepared to make reparations for the wrong done by their leaders . . . Over and over I hear the same refrain, 'We shall hate our conquerors with a hatred that will only cease when the day of our revenge comes.'

Princess Bleucher, writing in 1920. She was an Englishwoman married to a member of the German royal family.

Disarmament

The disarmament terms upset Germans. An army of 100,000 was very small for a country of Germany's size and the army was a symbol of German pride. Despite Wilson's Fourteen Points calling for disarmament, none of the Allies disarmed to the extent that Germany was disarmed in the 1920s. It is no great surprise that Adolf Hitler received widespread approval for his actions when he rebuilt Germany's armed forces in 1935.

German territories

Germany certainly lost a lot of territory. This was a major blow to German pride, and to its economy. Both the Saar and Upper Silesia were important industrial areas. Meanwhile, as Germany was losing land, the British and French were increasing their empires by taking control of German and Turkish territories in Africa and the Middle East.

The Fourteen Points and the League of Nations

To most Germans, the treatment of Germany was not in keeping with Wilson's Fourteen Points. For example, while self-determination was given to countries such as Estonia, Latvia and Lithuania, German-speaking peoples were being divided by the terms forbidding ANSCHLUSS with Austria or hived off into new countries such as Czechoslovakia to be ruled by non-Germans.

Germany felt further insulted by not being invited to join the League of Nations.

'Double standards'?

German complaints about the Treaty fell on deaf ears. In particular, many people felt that the Germans were themselves operating a double standard. Their call for fairer treatment did not square with the harsh way they had treated Russia in the Treaty of Brest-Litovsk in 1918 (see page 118). Versailles was much less harsh a treaty than Brest-Litovsk.

There was also the fact that Germany's economic problems, although real, were partly self-inflicted. Other states had raised taxes to pay for the war. The Kaiser's government planned to pay war debts by extracting reparations from the defeated states.

The impact of the Treaty on Germany

In 1919 Ebert's government was very fragile. When he agreed to the Treaty, it tipped Germany into chaos. You can read about this in detail on pages 140–41. Ebert's right-wing opponents could not bear the Treaty and they attempted a revolution against him.

This revolution, called the Kapp Putsch, was defeated by a general strike by Berlin workers. The strike paralysed essential services like power and transport. It saved Ebert's government but it added to the chaos in Germany – and the bitterness of Germans towards the treaty.

Worse was yet to come. Germany fell behind on its reparation payments in 1922, so in 1923 French and Belgian soldiers entered the Ruhr region and simply took what was owed to them in the form of raw materials and goods. This was quite legal under the Treaty of Versailles.

The German government ordered the workers to go on strike so that they were not producing anything for the French to take. The French reacted harshly, killing over 100 workers and expelling over 100,000 protesters from the region. More importantly, the strike meant that Germany had no goods to trade, and no money to buy things with.

The government solved this problem by simply printing extra money, but this caused a new problem – hyperinflation. The money was virtually worthless so prices shot up. The price of goods could rise between joining the back of a queue in a shop and reaching the front (see page 143)! Workers needed wheelbarrows to carry home their wages – billions of worthless marks. Wages began to be paid daily instead of weekly.

The Germans naturally blamed these problems on the Treaty. But the truth is more complex. Some say the French acted too harshly (even if the Treaty gave them the right). Others say that the Germans brought the problems on themselves by failing to pay reparations.

SOURCE 17

People coming from the bank with millions of paper marks in suitcases or wheelbarrows. People paying for seats at a theatre with eggs or pats of butter . . . Money that lost half its value in 12 hours. People who had been wealthy trying to sell watches or jewellery for food or articles instead of that hated money. A woman I knew had saved year by year, to assure her son's welfare. Her capital would have bought enough furniture for a decent house. Three months later it would not pay her tram fare.

An Englishman who before the war had lent £6000 in marks; when they were repaid, they were worth about 87p in English money. The middle class was wiped out in a matter of weeks.

A German woman describes her problems in 1923; from Vernon Bartlet, *Nazi Germany Explained*.

SOURCE 18

Hände weg vom Ruhrgebiet!

A German cartoon of 1923. The woman represents France. The text means 'Hands off the Ruhr!'

FOCUS TASK

What was the impact of the Treaty of Versailles on Germany?

It is New Year's Eve 1923. You are a German living in Berlin. As a civilian you survived the shortages and the starvation of the war. You are writing to a friend in America describing what your life has been like since the war ended.

In your letter, tell your friend about:
- the general strike in Berlin in 1920 (see page 141)
- the French and Belgians taking over the Ruhr in 1923
- the awful inflation of 1923.

Explain how each of these problems has been caused by the Treaty of Versailles and how each problem has affected your life. Sources 14–18 will help you. You can also find out a lot more about these events on pages 140–45.

Verdicts on the Treaty of Versailles

In 1919 the Treaty of Versailles was criticised not only by the Germans. As you saw on page 85, none of the Big Three who drew up the Treaty was satisfied with it.

Clemenceau's problem was that it was not harsh enough, and in 1920 he was voted out in a French general election.

Lloyd George received a hero's welcome when he returned to Britain. However, at a later date he described the treaty as 'a great pity' and indicated that he believed another war would happen because of it.

Wilson was very disappointed with the Treaty. He said that if he were a German he would not have signed it. The American Congress refused to approve the Treaty.

Sources 19–22 give you four views from Britain.

SOURCE 19

PEACE AND FUTURE CANNON FODDER

The Tiger: "Curious! I seem to hear a child weeping!"

A 1920 British cartoon. The '1940 class', presented as a weeping child, represents the children born in the 1920s who might die in a future war.

SOURCE 20

The historian, with every justification, will come to the conclusion that we were very stupid men . . . We arrived determined that a Peace of justice and wisdom should be negotiated; we left the conference conscious that the treaties imposed upon our enemies were neither just nor wise.

Harold Nicolson, British diplomat, 1919. He was one of the leading British officials at the Conference.

SOURCE 21

. . . a fair judgment upon the settlement, a simple explanation of how it arose, cannot leave the authors of the new map of Europe under serious reproach. To an overwhelming extent the wishes of the various populations prevailed.

Winston Churchill, speaking in 1919. He had been a member of the government and a serving officer during the war.

SOURCE 22

Severe as the Treaty seemed to many Germans, it should be remembered that Germany might easily have fared much worse. If Clemenceau had had his way . . . the Rhineland would have become an independent state, the Saar would have been annexed [joined] to France and Danzig would have become a part of Poland . . .

British historian W Carr, *A History of Germany*, 1972.

So . . . could it be justified?

History has shown how the Treaty helped to create a cruel regime in Germany and eventually a second world war. This will always affect modern attitudes to the Treaty. It has certainly affected historians' judgements. They have tended to side with critics of the Treaty. At the time, however, the majority of people outside Germany thought it was fair. Some indeed thought it was not harsh enough. A more generous treaty would have been totally unacceptable to public opinion in Britain or France. Today historians are more likely to point out how hard a task it was to agree the peace settlement. They suggest that the Treaty was the best that could be hoped for in the circumstances.

The other peace settlements

All these allies had to disarm and pay reparations. The four treaties that dealt with this (see below) were not negotiated by the Big Three but by officers and diplomats working with the foreign ministers of the Allied powers. The treaties were made in consultation with representatives of the nationalities in eastern and central Europe (except those of the defeated countries). Because the empire of Austria-Hungary collapsed in 1918, the treaties made eastern Europe a 'patchwork' of new states.

SOURCE 23

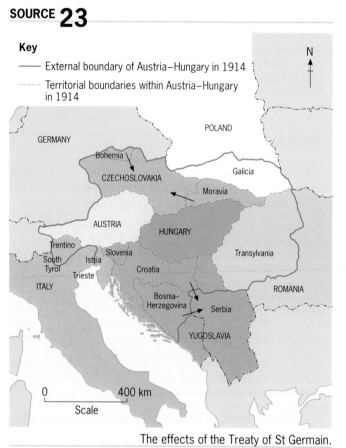

Key

—— External boundary of Austria–Hungary in 1914

----- Territorial boundaries within Austria–Hungary in 1914

The effects of the Treaty of St Germain.

Treaty of St Germain, 1919 – dealt with Austria

This treaty separated Austria from Hungary and confirmed that Austria was no longer a leading power. Under the treaty, Austrian territories were divided as follows:

Territory	From Austria to
Bohemia and Moravia	new state of Czechoslovakia
Bosnia and Herzegovina, Croatia	new state of Yugoslavia (which also included the former kingdom of Serbia)

Austria also lost Galicia to Poland and land to Italy. Its army was restricted to 30,000 and it was forbidden ever to unite with Germany.

The old Austrian Empire had already collapsed by 1918 and many new states had already been set up. The Treaty of St Germain was really about sorting out a chaotic jumble of territories into new states rather than punishing Austria. One state that was not entirely happy, however, was Italy, which felt it should have received more land. On the other hand, many millions in eastern Europe were given self-determination and freedom to rule themselves.

Austria suffered severe economic problems after the war, as much of its industry had gone to Czechoslovakia. Other areas also suffered, because they were suddenly part of foreign states. Whereas once their markets had been in one empire, now they were in different countries.

SOURCE 24

Key

▨ Territory lost by Bulgaria to Yugoslavia

▨ Territory lost by Bulgaria to Greece

☐ Territory lost by Turkey to Bulgaria

The effects of the Treaty of Neuilly.

Treaty of Neuilly, 1919 – dealt with Bulgaria

Bulgaria did well compared to Germany, Austria and Hungary. However, it lost lands to Greece, Romania and Yugoslavia and its access to the Mediterranean. It, too, had to limit its armed forced to 20,000 and pay £100 million in reparations. Bulgaria had played a relatively small part in the war and was treated less harshly than its allies. Nevertheless, many Bulgarians were governed by foreign powers by 1920.

SOURCE 25

Key
——— Frontier of Hungary before war
------- Frontier of Hungary after war

The effects of the Treaty of Trianon.

Treaty of Trianon, 1920 – dealt with Hungary

This treaty was not signed until 1920 but, like that of St Germain, its main terms involved the transfer of territories.

Territory	From Hungary to
Transylvania	Romania
Slovakia, Ruthenia	Czechoslovakia
Slovenia, Croatia	Yugoslavia

A number of other territories went to Romania.

Hungary lost a substantial amount of its territory and its population. (Three million Hungarians ended up in other states.) Its industries suffered from the loss of population and raw materials. It was due to pay reparations, but its economy was so weak it never did.

SOURCE 26

Key
Territory lost by Turkey:
- to Bulgaria
- to Italy
- to Greece
- British mandates
- French mandates
- French protectorates

The effects of the Treaty of Sèvres.

Treaty of Sèvres, 1920 – dealt with Turkey

The last of the treaties to be arranged was the Treaty of Sèvres with Turkey. Turkey was important because of its strategic position and the size of its empire. Its territorial losses are shown in the table below.

Territory	From Turkey to
Smyrna	Greece
Syria	Mandate under French control

Turkey also effectively lost control of the straits running into the Black Sea.

The Turks had formally to accept that many countries of their former empire, such as Egypt, Tunisia and Morocco, were now independent or were under British or French protection. In practice, this was already true, but under the treaty Turkey had to accept and agree to this.

It was not a successful treaty. Turks were outraged by it. Turkish nationalists led by Mustafa Kemal challenged the terms of the treaty by force when they drove the Greeks out of Smyrna. The result was the Treaty of Lausanne (1923) which returned Smyrna to Turkey.

There were other criticisms of the Treaty of Sèvres. The motives of Britain and France in taking control of former Turkish lands were suspect. The Arabs who had helped the British in the war gained little. Palestine was also a controversial area and remains a troubled region to the present day.

FOCUS TASK

In this chapter you have investigated a number of different treaties. Choose two treaties and give them a score on a scale of 1 to 5 for fairness: 1 is very fair, 5 is very unfair.
For each of the two treaties, write a paragraph to explain why you gave it the score you did.

The impact of the treaties on eastern and central Europe

The treaties you have studied in this chapter had a major impact on the map of eastern and central Europe. The most important consequence of the treaties was the creation or recreation of three countries: Czechoslovakia, Poland and Yugoslavia. The aim was to create states that were economically and politically stable, in an area of Europe that needed stability. In later chapters, you are going to see how successful the treaties were. For now, you are going to investigate the strengths and weaknesses of the new countries that they created.

Czechoslovakia

Czechoslovakia was possibly the key country in the plans of the Western Allies for the future security of Europe.
- Czechoslovakia was mostly carved out of the old Austrian Empire, with the addition of land taken from Germany.
- The Allies wanted it to be economically and politically strong, so they made sure that it included industrial areas from the former empire.
- It included a wide range of nationalities.

SOURCE 28

All the members of the Commission on Czechoslovak Claims – British, French, Italian and American alike . . . agreed that the border of Bohemia should be adopted as the frontier of the new state . . .

Economic reasons
The whole of the region occupied by the Germans of Bohemia is industrially and commercially dependent upon Bohemia rather than Germany. The Sudetenland Germans cannot exist without the economic co-operation of the Czechs, nor the Czechs without the economic co-operation of the Germans.

Security reasons
The chain of mountains which surrounds Bohemia constitutes a line of defence for the country. To take away this line of mountains would be to place Bohemia at the mercy of the Germans.

The Commission on Czechoslovak Claims explains how Czechoslovakia's western borders were decided. This was a League of Nations Commission set up to determine the exact borders of the new state.

SOURCE 27

Our firmest guarantee against German aggression is that behind Germany, in an excellent strategic position, stand Czechoslovakia and Poland.

Clemenceau, French Prime Minister, speaking in 1919.

FOCUS TASK A

What were the strengths and weaknesses of the new Czechoslovakia?

Look at Sources 28–33 and make a list of strengths and weaknesses under the following headings:
- Borders
- Industry
- Population

SOURCE 29

We all know that our ancestors did not come to this land as conquerors, but as pioneers in the swamp and wilderness . . . There is no right which can be stronger than ours . . . All the culture here was made by the Germans, the prospering farms and villages, the flourishing industry are all German labour. This has been the work of 600 years.

The German minority in the Sudetenland arguing against inclusion in the new state of Czechoslovakia.

SOURCE 30

The Skoda factory. Skoda was one of the most important exporters of machinery and arms in the new Czechoslovakia.

SOURCE 31

As far as is humanly possible the different races should be allocated to their motherlands . . . this should come before considerations of strategy or economics . . .

The Allied powers are creating a state inhabited by not only 6.5 million Czechs, but also some 3.5 million Germans, who will revolt from the very outset . . . also 2 million Slovaks who, in spite of their affinity with the Czech nation, have their own language and . . . have nothing in common with Bohemia and Moravia . . .

Lloyd George speaking in 1919 about plans for the formation of Czechoslovakia.

SOURCE 32

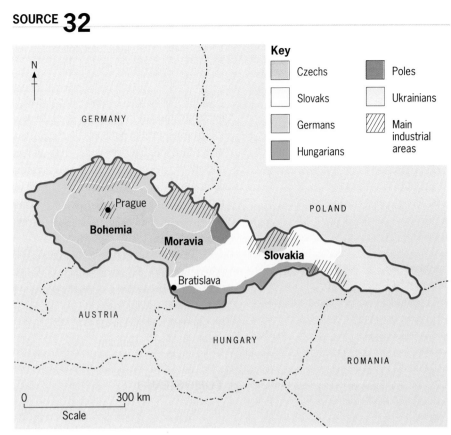

Czechoslovakia in the 1920s, showing regions, industry and nationalities.

SOURCE 33

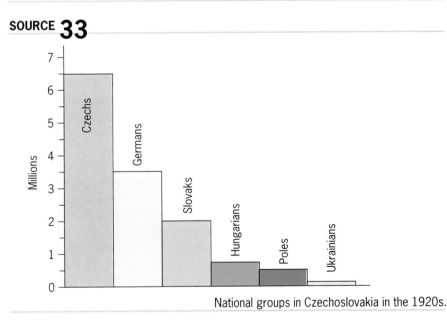

National groups in Czechoslovakia in the 1920s.

FOCUS TASK B

Why was Czechoslovakia important?

1 Write a note to yourself in your file or notebook:

   'Remember! Czechoslovakia comes back as a major issue in Hitler's foreign policy in 1938!'

2 Discuss with someone else in your class the following scenario (without cheating!).
   If Germany threatened Czechoslovakia in 1938:
   a) Would the new state be strong enough to stand up to Germany?
   b) What might be its major worries?
   c) Do you think the Western powers (for example, France and Britain) would support Czechoslovakia?

Poland

Poland had been an important state in the 1600s, but it had been swallowed up by Russia, Germany and Austria in the late 1700s.

The Western Allies were very keen on recreating the state of Poland. They wanted it to act as a potential watchdog on Germany in the years to come. They also hoped that Poland could form a barrier against any future threat from the new Communist government in Russia.

The peace treaties put it together again as an independent country. Poland's western frontiers were settled with Germany in the Treaty of Versailles. Poland's eastern frontiers were rather more difficult to agree on. Poland was a good example of the problems that arise when politicians sit down with a map and create new states that were not there before. Poland had no natural frontiers (rivers, mountains, etc.), and this made it vulnerable to attack. Also, around 30 per cent of the population of Poland were not ethnically Polish – it included Russians, Germans, Jews and many others.

Almost from its first day the new state was involved in fighting with Russia over the line of its eastern borders – this was eventually settled in 1921 with the help of the British diplomat Lord Curzon. The border was temporarily settled at the Curzon Line.

In order to have access to the sea, Poland was given a strip of German land around the city of Danzig. This became known as the 'Polish Corridor' (see Source 10 on page 86) and its loss was bitterly resented by Germany.

Yugoslavia

Yugoslavia was by far the most complicated of the new states created at the Paris Peace Conference. It was formed by merging Serbia with a number of its neighbours, most of whom had been part of the old Austria–Hungary Empire before the war (see Source 5 on page 4).

It began life as the Kingdom of the Serbs, Croats and Slovenes, but in 1929 it changed its name to Yugoslavia, which means 'land of the South Slavs'.

In a sense, Yugoslavia shows Wilson's idea of self-determination in action. It was partly the desire of the South Slav people to become independent from Austria–Hungary that had sparked off the First World War in the summer of 1914.

The Allies also hoped that a relatively large and powerful state could be a stabilising influence in the turbulent Balkans. Time would tell whether they succeeded . . .

SOURCE 34

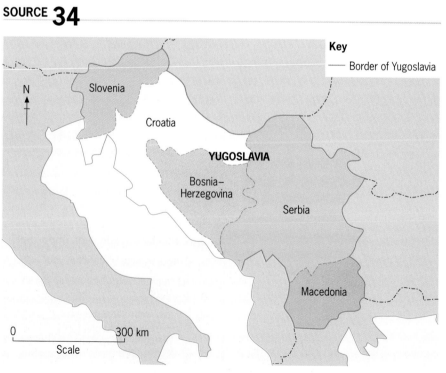

Yugoslavia – and the different ethnic groups that it contained.

SECTION 2

*The USSR,
Germany
and the USA
between the
Wars*

Russia and the USSR 1905–1941

How did the Bolsheviks take control?

FOCUS

In 1905 Russia was a vast but backward country. Its industry was under-developed. Its people were poor and uneducated. It was ruled by a Tsar who had complete power. Over the next 40 years it was transformed into a modern superpower.

In 5.1 you will investigate why the Tsar's regime finally collapsed in 1917.

In 5.2 you will explore how the Bolsheviks gained and held on to power.

In 5.3 you will consider:

■ how Stalin emerged as Lenin's successor
■ why Stalin tried to change Soviet industry and agriculture, and how those changes affected ordinary people in the Soviet Union
■ how successful Stalin was in modernising the Soviet Union.

Timeline

This timeline shows the period you will be covering in this chapter. Some of the key dates are filled in already.

To help you get a complete picture of the period, make your own copy and add other details to it as you work through the chapter.

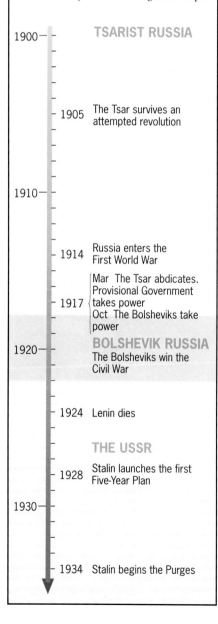

TSARIST RUSSIA

1900 —

1905 — The Tsar survives an attempted revolution

1910 —

1914 — Russia enters the First World War

1917 — Mar The Tsar abdicates. Provisional Government takes power
Oct The Bolsheviks take power

1920 — **BOLSHEVIK RUSSIA**
The Bolsheviks win the Civil War

1924 — Lenin dies

THE USSR

1928 — Stalin launches the first Five-Year Plan

1930 —

1934 — Stalin begins the Purges

The new Tsar

When Nicholas II was crowned Tsar of Russia in 1894, the crowds flocked to St Petersburg to cheer. There were so many people that a police report said 1200 people were crushed to death as the crowd surged forward to see the new Tsar, whom they called 'the Little Father of Russia'.

Twenty-three years later, he had been removed from power and he and his family were prisoners. They were held under armed guard in a lonely house at Ekaterinburg, far from the Tsar's luxurious palaces. Perhaps the Tsar might have asked himself how this had happened, but commentators were predicting collapse long before 1917.

SOURCE 1

The coronation of Nicholas II, Tsar of Russia

PROFILE

Tsar Nicholas II

★ Born 1868.
★ Crowned as Tsar in 1896.
★ Married to Alexandra of Hesse (a granddaughter of Queen Victoria).
★ Both the Tsar and his wife were totally committed to the idea of the Tsar as autocrat – absolute ruler of Russia.
★ Nicholas regularly rejected requests for reform.
★ He was interested in the Far East. This got him into a disastrous war with Japan in 1905.
★ He was not very effective as a ruler, unable to concentrate on the business of being Tsar.
★ He was a kind, loving family man but did not really understand the changes Russia was going through.
★ By 1917 he had lost control of Russia and abdicated.
★ In 1918 he and his family were shot by Bolsheviks during the Russian Civil War.

The Tsar's empire

Russia was a vast empire rather than a single country, and the Tsar was its supreme ruler. It was not an easy job.

Nationalities

The Tsar's empire included many different nationalities. Only 40 per cent of the Tsar's subjects spoke Russian as their first language. Some subjects, for example the Cossacks, were loyal to the Tsar. Others, for example the Poles and Finns, hated Russian rule. Jews often suffered racial prejudice and even vicious attacks, called pogroms, sponsored by the government.

ACTIVITY

Look at the profile of Tsar Nicholas II. Read through the information and sources on pages 100–102 and add four more points to the profile. You could work in pairs to draw up a list of points, then narrow them down to just four.

SOURCE 2

Population of the Russian Empire, according to a census in 1897

Russians	55,650,000	Letts	1,400,000
Ukrainians	22,400,000	Georgians	1,350,000
Poles	7,900,000	Armenians	1,150,000
Byelorussians	5,900,000	Romanians	1,110,000
Jews	5,000,000	Caucasians	1,000,000
Kirghiz	4,000,000	Estonians	1,000,000
Tartars	3,700,000	Iranians	1,000,000
Finns	2,500,000	Other Asiatic peoples	5,750,000
Germans	1,800,000	Mongols	500,000
Lithuanians	1,650,000	Others	200,000

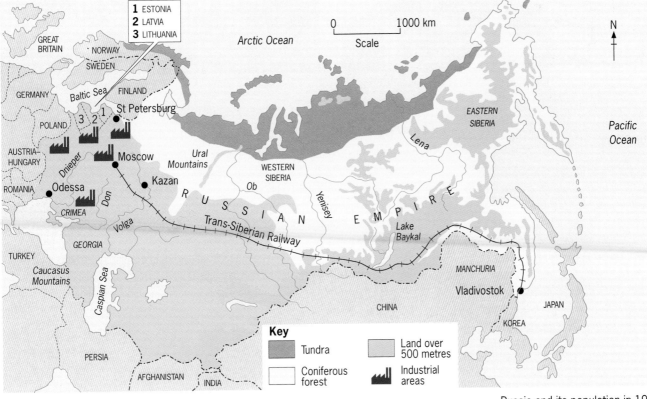

Russia and its population in 1900.

Peasants and the countryside

Around 80 per cent of Russia's population were peasants who lived in communes. There were some prosperous peasant farmers called kulaks, but living and working conditions for most peasants were dreadful. Famine and starvation were common and in some regions the life expectancy of a peasant farmer was only 40 years of age.

Much of Russia's land was unsuitable for farming. As a result, land was in very short supply because, by the early 1900s, the population was growing rapidly. (It increased by 50 per cent between 1860 and 1897.) Russian peasants were still using ancient farming techniques. In most villages, the land was divided into large fields. Each family was allotted a strip of land in one of the fields. This subdivision of the fields was organised by peasant councils called mir. When a peasant had sons, the family plot was subdivided and shared between them.

There was no basic education in Russia and very few peasants could read or write. But, despite all their hardships, many peasants were loyal to the Tsar. This was partly because they were also religious. Every week, they would hear the priest say how wonderful the Tsar was and how they, as peasants, should be loyal subjects. However, not all peasants were loyal or religious. Many supported the opposition, the Social Revolutionaries (see page 103). Their main discontent was over land – they resented the amount of land owned by the aristocracy, the Church and the Tsar.

1 Use Sources 3A and 3B to write a description of peasants' living conditions. Make sure you highlight the contrast with the conditions described in Source 4.

SOURCE 3A

The interior of a Russian peasant's cottage.

SOURCE 3B

A typical village in northern Russia.

SOURCE 4

In the big house the two women hardly manage to wash up all the crockery for the gentlefolk who have just had a meal; and two peasants in dress coats are running up or down stairs serving tea, coffee, wine and water. Upstairs the table is laid; they have just finished one meal and will soon start another that will go on till at least midnight. There are some fifteen healthy men and women here and some thirty able-bodied men and women servants working for them.

Count Leo Tolstoy, writer and improving landlord.

The aristocracy

The peasants' living conditions contrasted sharply with those of the ARISTOCRACY, who had vast estates, town and country houses and elegant lifestyles.

The aristocracy were about 1.5 per cent of society but owned about 25 per cent of the land. They were a key part of the Tsar's government, often acting as local officials. In the countryside they dominated the local assemblies or zemstva. Most were loyal to the Tsar and wanted to keep Russian society as it was.

Many of the richer aristocrats lived not on their estates but in the glamorous cities. Some landlords were in financial trouble and had to sell their lands, a piece at a time. Perhaps the greatest fear of the aristocracy was that the peasants would rise up and take their lands.

2 Look at Sources 3 and 5. Were workers in the town any better off than their cousins in the countryside? Explain your answer.

New industries, cities and the working class

From the later nineteenth century, the Tsars had been keen to see Russia become an industrial power. The senior minister Sergei Witte introduced policies that led to rapid industrial growth. Oil and coal production trebled, while iron production quadrupled (see Source 17 on page 106). Some peasants left the land to work in these newly developing industries. However, their living conditions hardly improved.

(see Source 17 on page 106)

SOURCE **5A**

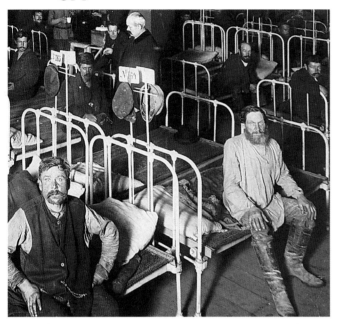

SOURCE **5B**

Workers' living conditions: **A** shows a dormitory and **B** shows a canteen in Moscow. Urban workers made up about 4 per cent of the population in 1900.

The greatest concentrations of these workers were in the capital, St Petersburg, and in Moscow. Here the population was growing fast as peasants arrived looking for a new way of life, or simply trying to earn some extra cash before returning for the harvest. Only a short walk away from the fabulous wealth of the Tsar's Winter Palace in St Petersburg, his subjects lived in filth and squalor. Overcrowding, terrible food, disease and alcoholism were everyday facts of life. The wretchedness of their living conditions was matched by the atrocious working conditions. Unlike every other European power, there were no government regulations on child labour, hours, safety or education. Trade unions were illegal. Low pay, 12 to 15-hour days, unguarded machinery and brutal discipline soon made the peasants realise that working in the factories was no better than working on the land.

The middle classes

As a result of industrialisation, a new class began to emerge in Russia – the CAPITALISTS. They were landowners, industrialists, bankers, traders and businessmen. Until this time, Russia had had only a small middle class which included people such as shopkeepers, lawyers and university lecturers. The capitalists increased the size of Russia's middle class, particularly in the towns. Their main concerns were the management of the economy, although the capitalists were also concerned about controlling their workforce. Clashes between workers and capitalists were to play an important role in Russia's history in the years up to 1917.

SOURCE **6**

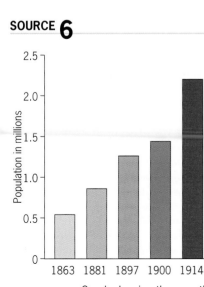

Graph showing the growth of St Petersburg.

I am informed that recently in some zemstva, voices have made themselves heard from people carried away by senseless dreams about participation by members of the zemstva in the affairs of internal government: let all know that I, devoting all my strength to the welfare of the people, will uphold the principle of autocracy as firmly and as unflinchingly as my late unforgettable father.

Part of Tsar Nicholas II's coronation speech in 1894. Zemstva were local assemblies dominated by the nobility in the countryside and professionals in the towns.

SOURCE **8**

We talked for two solid hours. He shook my hand. He wished me all the luck in the world. I went home beside myself with happiness and found a written order for dismissal lying on my desk.

Count Witte, Russian Prime Minister, 1906.

1 Draw up your own chart to summarise the Tsarist system of government.
2 Look at Sources 7 and 8. What do they suggest about
   a) the loyalty of the Tsar's ministers?
   b) the Tsar as a leader?
3 Describe and explain at least two ways in which Nicholas II made Russia's government weak.
4 Look carefully at Source 9. Would you interpret the contents of this source as:
   a) evidence of the strength of the Tsar's regime
   b) evidence of the weakness of the regime?
   Explain your answer and refer to the information in the text as well.

The Tsar and his government

The huge and diverse empire was ruled by an AUTOCRACY. One man, the Tsar, had absolute power to rule Russia. The Tsar believed that God had placed him in that position. The Russian Church supported him in this view. The Tsar could appoint or sack ministers or make any other decisions without consulting anyone else. By the early twentieth century most of the great powers had given their people at least some say in how they were run, but Nicholas was utterly committed to the idea of autocracy and seemed to be obsessed with the great past of his family, the Romanovs (see Source 7). He had many good qualities, such as his loyalty to his family, his willingness to work hard and his attention to detail. However, he was not an able, forceful and imaginative monarch like his predecessors.

Nicholas tended to avoid making important decisions. He did not delegate day-to-day tasks. In a country as vast as Russia, where tasks had to be delegated to officials, this was a major problem. He insisted on getting involved in the tiniest details of government. He personally answered letters from peasants and appointed provincial midwives. He even wrote out the instructions for the royal car to be brought round!

Nicholas also managed his officials poorly. He felt threatened by able and talented ministers, such as Count Witte and Peter Stolypin. He dismissed Witte (see Source 8) in 1906 and was about to sack Stolypin (see page 107) when Stolypin was murdered in 1911. Nicholas refused to chair the Council of Ministers because he disliked confrontation. He insisted on seeing ministers in one-to-one meetings. He encouraged rivalry between them. This caused chaos, as different government departments refused to co-operate with each other.

He also appointed family members and friends from the court to important positions. Many of them were incompetent or even corrupt, making huge fortunes from bribes.

Control

Despite everything you have read so far, it is important to remember that the Tsar's regime was very strong in some ways. Resistance was limited. At the local level, most peasants had their lives controlled by the mir. The mir could be overruled by land captains. Land captains were usually minor landlords appointed by the Tsar as his officials in local areas. The zemstva or local assemblies also helped to control Russia. They were dominated by the landlords in the countryside and by professional people in the towns. Then there were local governors, appointed by the Tsar from the ranks of the aristocracy. In some areas, Russia was a police state, controlled by local governors. There were special emergency laws that allowed the local governors to:

• order the police to arrest suspected opponents of the regime
• ban individuals from serving in the zemstva, courts or any government organisation
• make suspects pay heavy fines
• introduce censorship of books or leaflets or newspapers.

Local governors controlled the police. The police had a special force with 10,000 officers whose job was to concentrate on political opponents of the regime. There was also the Okhrana, the Tsar's secret police. Finally, if outright rebellion did erupt, there was the army, particularly the Tsar's loyal and terrifying Cossack regiments.

SOURCE **9**

A third of Russia lives under emergency legislation. The numbers of the regular police and of the secret police are continually growing. The prisons are overcrowded with convicts and political prisoners. At no time have religious persecutions [of Jews] been so cruel as they are today. In all cities and industrial centres soldiers are employed and equipped with live ammunition to be sent out against the people. Autocracy is an outdated form of government that may suit the needs of a central African tribe but not those of the Russian people who are increasingly aware of the culture of the rest of the world.

Part of a letter from the landowner and writer Leo Tolstoy to the Tsar in 1902. The letter was an open letter – it was published openly as well as being sent to the Tsar.

Opposition to the Tsar

The Tsarist government faced opposition from three particular groups. Many middle-class people wanted greater democracy in Russia and pointed out that Britain still had a king but also a powerful parliament. These people were called liberals or 'Cadets'.

Two other groups were more violently opposed to the Tsar. They believed that revolution was the answer to the people's troubles. The Socialist Revolutionaries (SRs) were a radical movement. Their main aim was to carve up the huge estates of the nobility and hand them over to the peasants. They believed in a violent struggle and were responsible for the assassination of two government officials, as well as the murder of a large number of Okhrana (police) agents and spies. They had wide support in the towns and the countryside.

The Social Democratic Party was a smaller but more disciplined party which followed the ideas of Karl Marx. In 1903 the party split itself into BOLSHEVIKS and MENSHEVIKS. The Bolsheviks (led by Lenin) believed it was the job of the party to create a revolution whereas the Mensheviks believed Russia was not ready for revolution. Both of these organisations were illegal and many of their members had been executed or sent in exile to SIBERIA. Many of the leading Social Democrat leaders were forced to live abroad.

By 1903 the activities of the opposition parties, added to the appalling conditions in the towns and the countryside, led to a wave of strikes, demonstrations and protests. The Tsar's ministers warned him that Russia was getting close to revolution.

SOURCE 10

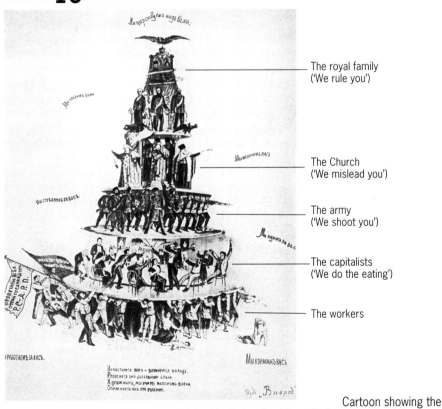

The royal family ('We rule you')

The Church ('We mislead you')

The army ('We shoot you')

The capitalists ('We do the eating')

The workers

Cartoon showing the Tsarist system. This was published in Switzerland by exiled opponents of the Tsar.

5 Read the section headed 'Opposition to the Tsar'. Is there anything the Cadets, the Socialist Revolutionaries, and the Social Democratic Party might agree on?

6 Look again at Source 7. Do you think the Tsar would listen to the ideas of the Cadets?

1 Read Source 11. Make two lists:
   a) the petitioners' complaints
   b) their demands.
2 Are these demands revolutionary demands? Explain your answer.
3 Choose two words to sum up the attitude of the petitioners to the Tsar.

SOURCE 11

Lord, we workers, our children, our wives and our old, helpless parents have come, Lord, to seek truth, justice and protection from you.

We are impoverished and oppressed, unbearable work is imposed on us, we are despised and not recognised as human beings. We are treated as slaves, who must bear their fate and be silent. We have suffered terrible things, but we are pressed ever deeper into the abyss of poverty, ignorance and lack of rights.

We ask but little: to reduce the working day to eight hours and to provide a minimum wage of a rouble a day.

Officials have taken the country into a shameful war. We working men have no say in how the taxes we pay are spent.

Do not refuse to help your people. Destroy the wall between yourself and your people.

From the Petition to the Tsar presented by Father Gapon, 1905.

4 a) Compare Sources 12–14. How do these scenes differ in their presentation of Bloody Sunday?
   b) How can you explain these differences?

The 1905 revolution

The government's attempts to deal with its problems failed dramatically. In 1903 it slightly relaxed censorship and other repressive measures. The result was an explosion of anti-government pamphlets, books and newspapers. It also tried to set up government-approved trade unions (free trade unions were illegal), but this simply led to strikes and demands for free unions. In 1904, hoping to unite the country behind him with spectacular victories, the Tsar embarked on a war against Japan. In fact, Russia suffered a series of humiliating defeats.

Bloody Sunday

These tensions all came together on Sunday, 22 January 1905, when a crowd of 200,000 protesters, led by the priest Father Gapon, came to the Winter Palace to give a petition to the Tsar. Many of the marchers carried pictures of the Tsar to show their respect for him.

The Tsar was not in the Winter Palace. He had left St Petersburg when the first signs of trouble appeared. The protesters were met by a regiment of soldiers and mounted Cossacks. Without warning, the soldiers opened fire and the Cossacks charged. It was a decisive day. The Tsar finally lost the respect of Father Gapon and the ordinary people of Russia.

SOURCE 12

Bloody Sunday – as painted in around 1910.

SOURCE 13

Bloody Sunday – as painted in around 1910.

SOURCE 14

Bloody Sunday, reconstructed for a film in the 1920s.

SOURCE 15

A clear, frosty day. There was much activity and many reports. Fredericks came to lunch. Went for a long walk. Since yesterday all the factories and workshops in St Petersburg have been on strike. Troops have been brought in to strengthen the garrison. The workers have conducted themselves calmly hitherto. At the head of the workers is some socialist priest: Gapon.

Sunday 22 January

A painful day. There have been serious disorders in St Petersburg because workmen wanted to come up to the Winter Palace. Troops had to open fire in several places in the city; there were many killed and wounded. God, how painful and sad! Mama arrived from town, straight to church. I lunched with all the others. Went for a walk with Misha. Mama stayed overnight.

From the Tsar's diary, recording the events of Bloody Sunday.

It might appear from Source 15 that the Tsar was out of touch with the seriousness of the situation. For the next ten months it seemed possible that he might lose control of Russia. His uncle was assassinated in Moscow, where striking workers put barricades in the streets. In June, the sailors aboard the battleship *Potemkin* mutinied (revolted). In September a GENERAL STRIKE began and paralysed Russian industry. Then revolutionaries, including Lenin and Trotsky, returned from exile to join the revolution. Workers' councils (or Soviets) were formed in the towns, while in the countryside peasants murdered landlords and their agents and took over their lands.

How did the Tsar survive?

It took the Tsar some time to respond. In his October Manifesto the Tsar offered the people a Duma (an elected parliament), the right to free speech and the right to form political parties. In November, he announced further concessions and financial help for peasants. This divided his opponents. The middle-class liberals were delighted, but the revolutionary groups were suspicious. In the end, they were proved right in not trusting the Tsar. While his opponents debated what to do next, the Tsar made peace with Japan and brought his best troops back to western Russia to crush the revolt. Rebellions in the countryside were ruthlessly put down (see Source 16).

In December 1905 leaders of the St Petersburg and Moscow soviets were arrested and exiled to Siberia. In Moscow this led to serious fighting in the streets, but the strikers were no match for the army. By March 1906 the revolution had been completely crushed and the revolutionary leaders were either dead, exiled or in hiding abroad. It was clear that no revolution would succeed as long as the army stayed loyal to the Tsar. In May 1906 the Tsar underlined his victory by introducing the Fundamental Laws. These Laws agreed to the existence of the Duma, but they put so many limitations on its powers that it could do virtually nothing.

SOURCE 16

Nightmare: the aftermath of a Cossack punishment expedition: cartoon from the Russian magazine Leshii, 1906.

5 Read Source 15. Do you agree that it suggests the Tsar was out of touch? Explain your answer.
6 Do you think 'Nightmare' is a good title for Source 16?

FOCUS TASK

How the Tsar crushed the revolution

How the Tsar kept control

THE TSAR SURVIVES

How did the Tsar survive the 1905 revolution?

1 Copy this diagram:
2 On the left-hand side, list the different steps the Tsar took to crush the revolution in 1905.
3 Explain how each step helped him.
4 As you read the next section of text, list on the right-hand side of your diagram the longer-term measures the Tsar took to keep control after the revolution.
5 Explain how each measure helped him.

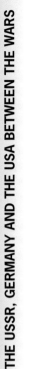

The troubled years, 1905–1914

The Tsar survived the 1905 revolution, but some serious questions remained. The most serious was the possibility of another revolution. If he was to prevent this, Nicholas needed to reform Russia and satisfy at least some of the discontented groups that had joined the revolution in 1905. The Duma deputies who gathered for its first meeting in 1906 were hopeful that they could help to steer Russia on a new course. They were soon disappointed (see Source 18). The Tsar continued to rule without taking any serious notice of them. The first and second Dumas were very critical of the Tsar. They lasted less than a year before Nicholas sent them home. In 1907 Tsar Nicholas changed the voting rules so that his opponents were not elected to the Duma. This third Duma lasted until 1912, mainly because it was much less critical of the Tsar than the previous two. But by 1912 even this 'loyal' Duma was becoming critical of the Tsar's ministers and policies. However, it had no power to change the Tsar's policies and criticism alone was not a serious threat to the regime so the Tsar's rule continued.

SOURCE 17

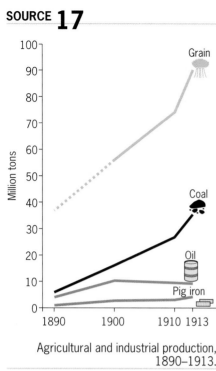

Agricultural and industrial production, 1890–1913.

1 What does Source 18 suggest about the attitude of the Tsar and the members of his court to the idea of the 'people' being more involved in running the country?
2 What does Source 19 suggest about working people's attitudes to the Tsar's regime?

SOURCE 19

Year	Strikes	Strikers
1905	13,995	2,863,173
1906	6,114	1,108,406
1907	3,573	740,074
1908	892	176,101
1909	340	64,166
1910	222	46,623
1911	466	105,110
1912	2,032	725,491
1913	2,404	887,096
1914	3,534	1,337,458

These figures were compiled by the Tsar's Ministry of Trade and Industry.

SOURCE 20

Let those in power make no mistake about the mood of the people . . . never were the Russian people . . . so profoundly revolutionised by the actions of the government, for day by day, faith in the government is steadily waning . . .

Guchkov, a Russian conservative in the Duma, 1913. By 1913, even staunch supporters of the Tsar were beginning to want change.

SOURCE 18

The two hostile sides stood confronting each other. The old and grey court dignitaries, keepers of etiquette and tradition, looked across in a haughty manner, though not without fear and confusion, at 'the people of the street', whom the revolution had swept into the palace, and quietly whispered to one another. The other side looked across at them with no less disdain or contempt.

The court side of the hall resounded with orchestrated cheers as the Tsar approached the throne. But the Duma deputies remained completely silent. It was a natural expression of our feelings towards the monarch, who in the twelve years of his reign had managed to destroy all the prestige of his predecessors. The feeling was mutual: not once did the Tsar glance towards the Duma side of the hall. Sitting on the throne he delivered a short, perfunctory speech in which he promised to uphold the principles of autocracy 'with unwavering firmness' and, in a tone of obvious insincerity, greeted the Duma deputies as 'the best people' of his Empire. With that he got up to leave.

As the royal procession filed out of the hall, tears could be seen on the face of the Tsar's mother, the Dowager Empress. It had been a 'terrible ceremony' she later confided to the Minister of Finance. For several days she had been unable to calm herself from the shock of seeing so many commoners inside the palace.

From the memoirs of Duma deputy Obolensky, published in 1925. He is describing the first session of the Duma in April 1906.

Stolypin

In 1906 the Tsar appointed a tough new Prime Minister – Peter Stolypin. Stolypin used a 'carrot and stick' approach to the problems of Russia.

The stick: He came down hard on strikers, protesters and revolutionaries. Over 20,000 were exiled and over 1000 hanged (the noose came to be known as 'Stolypin's necktie'). This brutal suppression effectively killed off opposition to the regime in the countryside until after 1914.

The carrot: Stolypin also tried to win over the peasants with the 'carrot' they had always wanted – land. He allowed wealthier peasants, the kulaks, to opt out of the *mir* communes and buy up land. These kulaks prospered and in the process created larger and more efficient farms. Production did increase significantly (see Source 17). On the other hand, 90 per cent of land in the fertile west of Russia was still run by inefficient communes in 1916. Farm sizes remained small even in Ukraine, Russia's best farmland. Most peasants still lived in the conditions you saw in the sources on page 100.

Stolypin also tried to boost Russia's industries. There was impressive economic growth between 1908 and 1911. But Russia was still far behind modern industrial powers such as Britain, Germany and the USA. Urban workers' wages stayed low and the cost of food and housing stayed high. Living and working conditions remained appalling (see page 101).

3 Make two lists:
  a) Stolypin's achievements
  b) Stolypin's failings.
4 If you were a senior adviser to the Tsar, which of Sources 17–21 would worry you most? Explain your answer.

The profits being made by industry were going to the capitalists, or they were being paid back to banks in France which had loaned the money to pay for much of Russia's industrial growth.

Stolypin was assassinated in 1911, but the Tsar was about to sack him anyway. He worried that Stolypin was trying to change Russia too much. Nicholas had already blocked some of Stolypin's plans for basic education for the people and regulations to protect factory workers. The Tsar was influenced by the landlords and members of the court. They saw Stolypin's reforms as a threat to the traditional Russian society in which everyone knew their place.

Relations between the Tsar and his people became steadily worse. The economy took a downturn in 1912, causing unemployment and hunger. The year 1913 saw huge celebrations for the three hundredth anniversary of the Romanovs' rule in Russia. The celebrations were meant to bring the country together, but enthusiasm was limited.

FOCUS TASK

How well was Russia governed in 1914?

1 Here are five characteristics that you might expect of a good government.
  • Trying to improve the lives of all its people
  • Building up its agriculture and industry
  • Listening to and responding to its population
  • Running the country efficiently
  • Defending the country from enemies (see pages 4–11).
  On a scale of 1–5, say how well you think the Tsarist government did on each one up to 1914. Explain your reason for giving that score. Your teacher can give you a worksheet to help you.
2 Now make a list of the successes and failures of the Tsarist government up to 1914.
3 Which of the following assessments do you most agree with? By 1913 the government was:
  • in crisis
  • strong but with some serious weaknesses
  • secure with only minor weaknesses.

SOURCE 22

A Russian cartoon. The caption reads: 'The Russian Tsars at home.'

5 Look at Source 22. How does the cartoonist suggest that Rasputin is an evil influence on the Tsar and Tsarina?

SOURCE 21

Tsar Nicholas at the 1913 celebrations of 300 years of Romanov rule. This was the first time since 1905 that the Tsar had appeared in public.

The government tried other measures to get the people behind them, such as discrimination and even violence against Jews, Muslims and other minorities. This had little effect, and discontent grew, especially among the growing industrial working class in the cities. Strikes were on the rise (see Source 19), including the highly publicised Lena gold field strike where troops opened fire on striking miners. However, the army and police dealt with these problems and so, to its opponents, the government must have seemed firmly in control.

Strangely, some of the government's supporters were less sure about the government (see Source 20). Industrialists were concerned by the way in which the Tsar preferred to appoint loyal but unimaginative ministers such as Goremykin.

Rasputin

Some of the Tsar's supporters were particularly alarmed about the influence of a strange and dangerous figure – Gregory Yefimovich, generally known as Rasputin. The Tsar's son Alexis was very ill with a blood disease called haemophilia. Through hypnosis, it appeared that Rasputin could control the disease. He was greeted as a miracle worker by the Tsarina (the Tsar's wife). Before long, Rasputin was also giving her and the Tsar advice on how to run the country. People in Russia were very suspicious of Rasputin. He was said to be a drinker and a womaniser. His name means 'disreputable'. The Tsar's opponents seized on Rasputin as a sign of the Tsar's weakness and unfitness to rule Russia. The fact that the Tsar either didn't notice their concern or, worse still, didn't care showed just how out of touch he was.

How did the First World War weaken the Tsar's government?

The First World War had a massive impact on Russia. Your task is to use the material on pages 108–110 to present an overview of how the war affected four different groups of people in Russian society. The groups are:
- the army
- the workers
- the middle classes
- the aristocracy.

1 As you read through pages 108–110 you will find out about the impact of the war on each group. Write a paragraph or series of notes summarising the impact of war on each group.
2 Organise your work as a presentation. You could use OHT acetates or computer presentation software. Do some research to locate pictures that support your presentation.

1 Was the Tsar's decision to take command of the army evidence that he was out of touch with the situation? Explain your answer.
2 Why were the Bolsheviks successful at gaining recruits in the army?

War and revolution

In August 1914 Russia entered the First World War. Tensions in the country seemed to disappear. The Tsar seemed genuinely popular with his people and there was an instant display of patriotism. The Tsar's action was applauded. Workers, peasants and aristocrats all joined in the patriotic enthusiasm. Anti-government strikes and demonstrations were abandoned. The good feeling, however, was very short-lived. As the war continued, the Tsar began to lose the support of key sectors of Russian society.

The army

The Russian army was a huge army of conscripts. At first, the soldiers were enthusiastic, as was the rest of society. Even so, many peasants felt that they were fighting to defend their country against the Germans rather than showing any loyalty to the Tsar. You can read about the Russian campaigns in the war on page 42. Russian soldiers fought bravely, but they stood little chance against the German army. They were badly led and treated appallingly by their aristocrat officers. They were also poorly supported by the industries at home. They were short of rifles, ammunition, artillery and shells. Many did not even have boots.

The Tsar took personal command of the armed forces in September 1915. This made little difference to the war, since Nicholas was not a particularly able commander. However, it did mean that people held Nicholas personally responsible for the defeats and the blunders. The defeats and huge losses continued throughout 1916. It is not surprising that by 1917 there was deep discontent in the army and that many soldiers were supporters of the revolutionary Bolshevik Party.

SOURCE 24

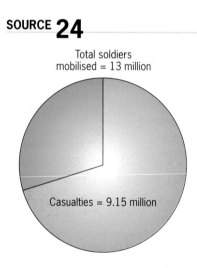

Total soldiers mobilised = 13 million

Casualties = 9.15 million

Russian casualties in the First World War.

SOURCE 25

Again that cursed question of shortage of artillery and rifle ammunition stands in the way of an energetic advance. If we should have three days of serious fighting, we might run out of ammunition altogether. Without new rifles, it is impossible to fill up the gaps.

Tsar Nicholas to his wife Alexandra, July 1915.

SOURCE 23

The army had neither wagons nor horses nor first aid supplies . . . We visited the Warsaw station where there were about 17,000 men wounded in battle. At the station we found a terrible scene: on the platform in dirt, filth and cold, on the ground, even without straw, wounded men, who filled the air with heart-rending cries, dolefully asked: 'For God's sake order them to dress our wounds. For five days we have not been attended to.'

From a report by Michael Rodzianko, President of the Duma.

Peasants, workers and the ethnic minorities

It did not take long for the strain of war to alienate the peasants and the workers. The huge casualty figures took their toll. In August 1916, the local governor of the village of Grushevka reported that the war had killed 13 per cent of the population of the village. This left many widows and orphans needing state war pensions which they did not always receive.

Despite the losses, food production remained high until 1916. By then, the government could not always be relied on to pay for the food produced. The government planned to take food by force but abandoned the idea because it feared it might spark a widespread revolt. There actually was a revolt in central Asian Russia when the Tsar tried to conscript Muslims into the army. It was brutally suppressed by the army.

By 1916 there was much discontent in the cities. War contracts created an extra 3.5 million industrial jobs between 1914 and 1916. The workers got little in the way of extra wages. They also had to cope with even worse overcrowding than before the war. There were fuel shortages. There were also food shortages. What made it worse was that there was enough food and fuel, but it could not be transported to the cities. The rail network could not cope with the needs of the army, industry and the populations of the cities. As 1916 turned into 1917, many working men and women stood and shivered in bread queues and cursed the Tsar.

SOURCE 26

The average worker's wage in 1917 was 5 roubles a day. This would buy you:

In 1914 — 2 bags of flour
In 1917 — ⅓ of a bag of flour

5 bags of potatoes
¾ of a bag of potatoes

5 kilograms of meat
0.8 kilograms of meat

Prices in Russia, 1914–17.

SOURCE 27

1914 (from July)
1915
1916
1917 (to June)
0 200 400 600 800 1000 1200 1400
Number of risings by peasants

1914 (from August)
1915
1916
1917 (Jan–Feb)
0 200 400 600 800 1000 1200 1400
Number of strikes by factory workers

Peasant risings and strikes, 1914–17.

SOURCE 28

Everybody was fed up with the Tsar because they felt he was weak. When he abdicated, there was great rejoicing. Everybody thought things would be much better.

Margot Tracey, the daughter of wealthy Russian capitalists, describing feelings towards the Tsar in 1917.

3 Imagine you are an adviser to the Tsar in 1916. Which of the sources on pages 108–109 would give you most concern? Explain your answer.

The middle classes

The middle classes did not suffer in the same way as the peasants and workers, but they too were unhappy with the Tsar by the end of 1916. Many middle-class activists in the *zemstva* were appalled by reports such as Source 23. They set up their own medical organisations along the lines of the modern Red Cross, or joined war committees to send other supplies to the troops. These organisations were generally far more effective than the government agencies. By 1916 many industrialists were complaining that they could not fulfil their war contracts because of a shortage of raw materials (especially metals) and fuel. In 1915 an alliance of Duma politicians, the Progressive Bloc, had urged the Tsar to work with them in a more representative style of government that would unite the people. The Tsar dismissed the Duma a month later.

The aristocracy

The situation was so bad by late 1916 that the Council of the United Nobility was calling for the Tsar to step down. The junior officers in the army had suffered devastating losses in the war. Many of these officers were the future of the aristocrat class. The conscription of 13 million peasants also threatened aristocrats' livelihoods, because they had no workers for their estates. Most of all, many of the leading aristocrats were appalled by the influence of Rasputin over the government of Russia. When the Tsar left Petrograd (the new Russian version of the Germanic name St Petersburg) to take charge of the army, he left his wife in control of the country. The fact that she was German started rumours flying in the capital. There were also rumours of an affair between her and Rasputin. Ministers were dismissed and then replaced. The concerns were so serious that a group of leading aristocrats murdered Rasputin in December 1916.

SOURCE 29

I asked for an audience and was received by him [the Tsar] on March 8th. 'I must tell Your Majesty that this cannot continue much longer. No one opens your eyes to the true role which this man is playing. His presence in Your Majesty's court undermines confidence in the Supreme Power and may have an evil effect on the fate of the dynasty and turn the hearts of the people from their Emperor' . . . My report did some good. On March 11th an order was issued sending Rasputin to Tobolsk; but a few days later, at the demand of the Empress, this order was cancelled.

M Rodzianko, President of the Duma, March 1916.

The March revolution

As 1917 dawned, few people had great hopes for the survival of the Tsar's regime. In January strikes broke out all over Russia. In February the strikes spread. They were supported and even joined by members of the army. The Tsar's best troops lay dead on the battlefields. These soldiers were recent conscripts and had more in common with the strikers than their officers. On 7 March workers at the Putilov steelworks in Petrograd went on strike. They joined with thousands of women – it was International Women's Day – and other discontented workers demanding that the government provide bread. From 7 to 10 March the number of striking workers rose to 250,000. Industry came to a standstill. The Duma set up a Provisional Committee to take over the government. The Tsar ordered them to disband. They refused. On 12 March the Tsar ordered his army to put down the revolt by force. They refused. This was the decisive moment. Some soldiers even shot their own officers and joined the demonstrators. They marched to the Duma demanding that they take over the government. Reluctantly, the Duma leaders accepted – they had always wanted reform rather than revolution, but now there seemed no choice.

On the same day, revolutionaries set up the Petrograd Soviet again, and began taking control of food supplies to the city. They set up soldiers' committees, undermining the authority of the officers. It was not clear who was in charge of Russia, but it was obvious that the Tsar was not! On 15 March he issued a statement that he was abdicating. There was an initial plan for his brother Michael to take over, but Michael refused: Russia had finished with Tsars.

FOCUS TASK A

How important was the war in the collapse of the Tsarist regime?

Historians have furiously debated this question since the revolution took place. There are two main views:

View 1

The Tsar's regime was basically stable up to 1914, even if it had some important problems to deal with. It was making steady progress towards becoming a modern state, but this progress was destroyed by the coming of war. Don't forget that this war was so severe that it also brought Germany, Austria-Hungary and Turkey to their knees as well.

View 2

The regime in Russia was cursed with a weak Tsar, a backward economy and a class of aristocrats who were not prepared to share their power and privileges with the millions of ordinary Russians. Revolution was only a matter of time. The war did not cause it, although it may have speeded up the process.

Divide the class into two groups.
One group has to find evidence and arguments to support View 1, the other for View 2.
You could compare notes in a class discussion or organise a formal debate. You may even be able to compare your views with students in other schools using email conferencing.

SOURCE 30

One company of the Pavlovsky Regiment's reserve battalion had declared on 26 February that it would not fire on people . . . We have just received a telegram from the Minister of War stating that the rebels have seized the most important buildings in all parts of the city. Due to fatigue and propaganda the troops have laid down their arms, passed to the side of the rebels or become neutral . . .

General Alekseyev, February 1917.

FOCUS TASK B

Why was the March 1917 revolution successful?

The Tsar faced a major revolution in 1905 but he survived. Why was 1917 different? Why was he not able to survive in 1917?

The Tsar's regime collapses

Failures in the war

The mutiny in the army

Duma setting up alternative government

Discontent in the countryside

Formation of soviets

The Tsarina and Rasputin

Strikes

Food shortages

Stage 1
1. Copy the headings in this diagram. They show eight reasons why the Tsar was forced to abdicate in March 1917.
2. For each of the factors, write one or two sentences explaining how it contributed to the fall of the Tsar.
3. Draw lines between any of the factors that seem to be connected. Label your line explaining what the link is.

Stage 2
4. In pairs or small groups, discuss the following points:
   a) Which factors were present in 1905?
   b) Were these same factors more or less serious than in 1905?
   c) Which factors were not present in 1905?
   d) Were the new factors decisive in making the March 1917 revolution successful?

1 Read Source 31. How popular do you think the Provisional Government's policies on
   a) the war
   b) land
   would be with the peasants and the soldiers?

The Provisional Government

Russia's problems were not solved by the abdication of the Tsar. The Duma's Provisional Committee took over government. It faced three overwhelmingly urgent decisions:

- to continue the war or make peace
- to distribute land to the peasants (who had already started taking it) or ask them to wait until elections had been held
- how best to get food to the starving workers in the cities.

The Provisional Government was a mixed group. While it included men such as the lawyer Alexander Kerensky – Justice Minister in the Provisional Government but also a respected member of the Petrograd Soviet – it also included angry revolutionaries who had no experience of government at all. The Provisional Government promised Russia's allies that it would continue the war, while trying to settle the situation in Russia. It also urged the peasants to be restrained and wait for elections before taking any land. The idea was that the Provisional Government could then stand down and allow free elections to take place to elect a new Constituent Assembly that would fairly and democratically represent the people of Russia. It was a very cautious message for a people who had just gone through a revolution.

However, the Provisional Government was not the only possible government. Most workers also paid close attention to the Petrograd Soviet. The Soviet had the support of workers in key industries such as coal mining and water, and the support of much of the army. During the crisis months of spring 1917, the Soviet and Provisional Government worked together.

One man was determined to push the revolution further. He was Lenin, leader of the Bolsheviks (see page 115). When he heard of the March revolution he immediately returned to Russia from exile in Europe. The Germans even provided him with a special train, hoping that he might cause more chaos in Russia!

When Lenin arrived at Petrograd station, he set out the Bolshevik programme in his APRIL THESES. He urged the people to support the Bolsheviks in a second revolution. Lenin's slogans 'Peace, Land and Bread' and 'All power to the soviets' contrasted sharply with the cautious message of the Provisional Government. Support for the Bolsheviks increased quickly (see Sources 32 and 33), particularly in the soviets and in the army.

SOURCE 31

The Provisional Government should do nothing now which would break our ties with the allies. The worst thing that could happen to us would be separate peace. It would be ruinous for the Russian revolution, ruinous for international democracy . . .

As to the land question, we regard it as our duty at the present to prepare the ground for a just solution of the problem by the Constituent Assembly.

A Provisional Government Minister explains why Russia should stay in the war, 1917.

SOURCE 32

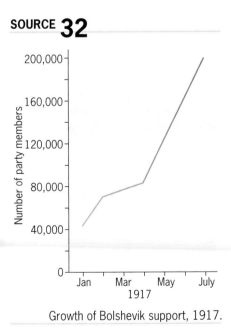

Growth of Bolshevik support, 1917.

SOURCE 33

The Bolshevik speaker would ask the crowd 'Do you need more land?'
   Do you have as much land as the landlords do?'
   'But will the Kerensky government give you land? No, never. It protects the interests of the landlords. Only our party, the Bolsheviks, will immediately give you land . . .'
   Several times I tried to take the floor and explain that the Bolsheviks make promises which they can never fulfil. I used figures from farming statistics to prove my point; but I saw that the crowded square was unsuitable for this kind of discussion.

A Menshevik writer, summer 1917.

In the second half of 1917, the Provisional Government's authority steadily collapsed.

- The war effort was failing. Soldiers had been deserting in thousands from the army. Kerensky became Minister for War and rallied the army for a great offensive in June. It was a disaster. The army began to fall apart in the face of a German counter-attack (see Source 34 on page 112). The deserters decided to come home.
- Desertions were made worse because another element of the Provisional Government's policy had failed. The peasants ignored the orders of the government to wait. They were simply taking control of the countryside. The soldiers, who were mostly peasants, did not want to miss their turn when the land was shared out.

SOURCE 34

The German offensive, which began on 6 July, is turning into an immense catastrophe which may threaten revolutionary Russia with ruin. A sudden and disastrous change has occurred in the attitude of the troops . . . Authority and obedience no longer exist . . . for hundreds of miles one can see deserters, armed and unarmed, in good health and in high spirits, certain they will not be punished.

A Russian officer reporting back to the Provisional Government, 1917.

SOURCE 36

The Provisional Government possesses no real power and its orders are executed only in so far as this is permitted by the Soviet of Workers' and Soldiers' Deputies, which holds in its hands the most important elements of actual power, such as troops, railroads, postal and telegraph service . . .

A letter from Guchkov, Minister for War in the Provisional Government, to General Alekseyev, 22 March 1917.

SOURCE 35

A still from the 1960s film *Doctor Zhivago* showing Russian deserters from the First World War. By the autumn of 1917 discipline among the Russian soldiers who had been fighting the Germans was beginning to collapse.

The Provisional Government's problems got worse in the summer. In July (the 'July Days'), Bolshevik-led protests against the war turned into a rebellion. However, when Kerensky produced evidence that Lenin had been helped by the Germans, support for the rebellion fell. Lenin, in disguise, fled to Finland. Kerensky used troops to crush the rebellion and took over the government.

SOURCE 37

Troops loyal to the Provisional Government fire on Bolshevik demonstrators during the July Days.

Kerensky was in a very difficult situation. The upper and middle classes expected him to restore order. By this time, however, real power lay with the soviets, especially the Petrograd Soviet. It had a Bolshevik majority and a Bolshevik chairman – Leon Trotsky. It also had the support of much of the army and all industrial workers.

Meanwhile, there was little reason for the ordinary people of Russia to be grateful to the Provisional Government (see Sources 38 and 39).

SOURCE 38

Cabs and horse-drawn carriages began to disappear. Street-car service was erratic. The railway stations filled with tramps and deserting soldiers, often drunk, sometimes threatening. The police force had vanished in the first days of the Revolution. Now 'revolutionary order' was over. Hold-ups and robberies became the order of the day. Politically, signs of chaos were everywhere.

HE Salisbury, *Russia in Revolution.*

SOURCE 39

Week by week food became scarcer . . . one had to queue for long hours in the chill rain . . . Think of the poorly clad people standing on the streets of Petrograd for whole days in the Russian winter! I have listened in the bread-lines, hearing the bitter discontent which from time to time burst through the miraculous good nature of the Russian crowd.

John Reed, an American writer who lived in Petrograd in 1917.

Others were also fed up with the Provisional Government. In September 1917, the army leader Kornilov marched his troops towards Moscow, intending to get rid of the Bolsheviks and the Provisional Government, and restore order. Kerensky was in an impossible situation. He had some troops who supported him but they were no match for Kornilov's. Kerensky turned to the only group which could save him: his Bolshevik opponents, who dominated the Petrograd Soviet. The Bolsheviks organised themselves into an army which they called the Red Guards. Kornilov's troops refused to fight members of the Soviet so Kornilov's plans collapsed.

But it was hardly a victory for Kerensky. In fact, by October Kerensky's government was doomed. It had tried to carry on the war and failed. It had therefore lost the army's support. It had tried to stop the peasants from taking over the land and so lost their support too. Without peasant support it had failed to bring food into the towns and food prices had spiralled upwards. This had lost the government any support it had from the urban workers.

In contrast, the Bolsheviks were promising what the people wanted most (bread, peace, land). It was the Bolsheviks who had removed the threat of Kornilov. By the end of September 1917, there were Bolshevik majorities in the Petrograd and Moscow soviets, and in most of Russia's other major towns and cities.

What do you think happened next?

FOCUS TASK

How effective was the Provisional Government?

1 Here is a list of some decisions that faced the Provisional Government when it took over in March 1917:
   a) what to do about the war
   b) what to do about land
   c) what to do about food.
   For each one, say how the government dealt with it, and what the result of the action was.
2 Based on your answers to question 1, how effective do you think the Provisional Government was? Give it a mark out of ten.
3 Read through pages 111–13 again. Look for evidence of how the actions of its opponents harmed the Provisional Government:
   • members of the soviets
   • Bolsheviks
   • General Kornilov.
4 Based on your answers to question 3, would you revise the score you gave the government in question 2?
5 Now reach an overview score. Out of 10, how effective was the Provisional Government? Write a paragraph to explain your score.

The Provisional Government has been overthrown. The cause for which the people have fought has been made safe: the immediate proposal of a democratic peace, the end of land owners' rights, workers' control over production, the creation of a Soviet government. Long live the revolution of workers, soldiers and peasants.

Proclamation of the Petrograd Soviet, 8 November 1917.

---

1 When the Bolsheviks stormed the Winter Palace, they actually faced very little resistance. Why do you think the artist who painted Source 41 suggests that they did?

Lenin, Trotsky and the Bolshevik Revolution

You have seen how Bolshevik support increased throughout 1917. By the end of October 1917, Lenin was convinced that the time was right for the Bolsheviks to seize power. Lenin convinced the other Bolsheviks to act swiftly. It was not easy – leading Bolsheviks like Bukharin felt that Russia was not ready, but neither he nor any other Bolshevik could match Lenin in an argument.

During the night of 6 November, the Red Guards led by Leon Trotsky took control of post offices, bridges and the State Bank. On 7 November, Kerensky awoke to find the Bolsheviks were in control of most of Petrograd. Through the day, with almost no opposition, the Red Guards continued to take over railway stations and other important targets. On the evening of 7 November, they stormed the Winter Palace (again, without much opposition) and arrested the ministers of the Provisional Government. Kerensky managed to escape and tried to rally loyal troops. When this failed, he fled into exile. On 8 November an announcement was made to the Russian people (see Source 40).

SOURCE **41**

The Bolsheviks storm the Winter Palace. A painting from 1937.

An analysis of the Bolshevik Revolution

Despite what they claimed, the Bolsheviks did not have the support of the majority of the Russian people. So how were they able to carry out their takeover in November 1917? The unpopularity of the Provisional Government was a critical factor – there were no massive demonstrations demanding the return of Kerensky!

A second factor was that the Bolsheviks were a disciplined party dedicated to revolution, even though not all the Bolshevik leaders believed this was the right way to change Russia. The Bolsheviks had some 800,000 members, and their supporters were also in the right places. At least half of the army supported them, as did the sailors at the important naval base at Kronstadt near Petrograd. (The Bolsheviks were still the only party demanding that Russia should pull out of the war.) The major industrial centres, and the Petrograd and Moscow soviets especially, were also pro-Bolshevik. The Bolsheviks also had some outstanding personalities in their ranks, particularly Trotsky and their leader Lenin.

ACTIVITY

Lenin and Trotsky

Work individually or in pairs, taking one personality each.

1 Using Sources 42–44, add extra details to the profile of Lenin:
   • why Lenin appealed to people
   • his personal qualities
   • his strengths as a leader.
2 Now do the same for Trotsky (see page 116).
3 Finally, write a short report on the contribution of each individual to the Bolsheviks' success in 1917.

PROFILE

Vladimir Ilich Lenin

★ Born 1870 into a respectable Russian family.
★ Brother hanged in 1887 for plotting against the Tsar.
★ Graduated from St Petersburg University after being thrown out of Kazan University for his political beliefs.
★ One of the largest Okhrana files was about him!
★ Exiled to Siberia 1897–1900.
★ 1900–1905 lived in various countries writing the revolutionary newspaper *Iskra* ('The Spark').
★ Took part in the 1905 revolution but was forced to flee.
★ Returned to Russia after the first revolution in 1917.
★ Led the Bolsheviks to power in November 1917.

SOURCE 42

This extraordinary figure was first and foremost a professional revolutionary. He had no other occupation. A man of iron will and inflexible ambition, he was absolutely ruthless and used human beings as mere material for his purpose. Short and sturdy with a bald head, small beard and deep set eyes, Lenin looked like a small tradesman. When he spoke at meetings his ill-fitting suit, his crooked tie, his ordinary appearance disposed the crowd in his favour. 'He is not one of the gentlefolk, he is one of us', they would say.

The Times, writing about Lenin after his death, 1924.

SOURCE 43

Lenin . . . was the overall planner of the revolution: he also dealt with internal divisions within the party and provided tight control, and a degree of discipline and unity which the other parties lacked.

SJ Lee, *The European Dictatorships*, 1987.

SOURCE 44

The struggle was headed by Lenin who guided the Party's Central Committee, the editorial board of Pravda, *and who kept in touch with the Party organisations in the provinces . . . He frequently addressed mass rallies and meetings. Lenin's appearance on the platform inevitably triggered off the cheers of the audience. Lenin's brilliant speeches inspired the workers and soldiers to a determined struggle.*

Soviet historian Y Kukushkin, *History of the USSR*, 1981.

Leon Trotsky

★ Born 1879 into a respectable and prosperous Jewish farming family.
★ Exceptionally bright at school and brilliant at university.
★ Politically active – arrested in 1900 and deported to Siberia.
★ Escaped to London in 1902 and met Lenin there.
★ Joined the Social Democratic Party, but supported the Menshevik wing rather than the Bolsheviks.
★ Played an important role in organising strikes in the 1905 revolution – imprisoned for his activities.
★ Escaped in 1907 and became a Bolshevik activist in the years before the First World War.
★ Published two Bolshevik newspapers, including *Pravda*.
★ In 1917 he returned to Russia and played a key role in the Bolshevik Revolution.
★ In 1918 he became the Commissar for War and led the Bolsheviks to victory in the Civil War which broke out in 1918.

SOURCE 45

The Bolshevik party was greatly strengthened by Trotsky's entry into the party. No one else in the leadership came anywhere near him as a public speaker, and for much of the revolutionary period it was this that made Trotsky, perhaps even more so than Lenin, the best known Bolshevik leader in the country. Whereas Lenin remained the master strategist of the party, working mainly behind the scenes, Trotsky became its principal source of public inspiration. During the weeks leading up to the seizure of power he spoke almost every night before a packed house . . .

He was careful always to use examples and comparisons from the real life of the audience. This gave his speeches a familiarity and earned Trotsky the popular reputation of being 'one of us'. It was this that gave him the power to master the crowd, even sometimes when it was extremely hostile.

Historian Orlando Figes, a leading international expert on the Russian Revolution, writing in 1996.

SOURCE 46

Now that the great revolution has come, one feels that however intelligent Lenin may be he begins to fade beside the genius of Trotsky.

Mikhail Uritsky, 1917. Uritsky was a Bolshevik activist and went on to play an important role in Bolshevik governments after 1917.

SOURCE 47

Under the influence of his tremendous activity and blinding success, certain people close to Trotsky were even inclined to see in him the real leader of the Russian revolution . . . It is true that during that period, after the thunderous success of his arrival in Russia and before the July days, Lenin did keep rather in the background, not speaking often, not writing much, but largely engaged in directing organisational work in the Bolshevik camp, whilst Trotsky thundered forth at meetings in Petrograd. Trotsky's most obvious gifts were his talents as an orator and as a writer. I regard Trotsky as probably the greatest orator of our age. In my time I have heard all the greatest parliamentarians and popular tribunes of socialism and very many famous orators of the bourgeois world and I would find it difficult to name any of them whom I could put in the same class as Trotsky.

From *Revolutionary Silhouettes*, by Anatoly Lunacharsky, published in 1918. The book was a series of portraits of leading revolutionaries. The author was a Bolshevik activist and knew Lenin and Trotsky well.

FOCUS TASK

Why were the Bolsheviks successful?

1 Read Source 48.

SOURCE 48

The [November] Revolution has often and widely been held to have been mainly Lenin's revolution. But was it? Certainly Lenin had a heavier impact on the course [of events] than anyone else. The point is, however, that great historical changes are brought about not only by individuals. There were other mighty factors at work as well in Russia in 1917 . . . Lenin simply could not have done or even co-ordinated everything.

Historian Robert Service, writing in 1990.

2 What do you think the writer had in mind when he said there were 'other mighty factors at work'? Make your own list of these factors.
3 Write two or more paragraphs to explain the importance of these factors.

5.2 Lenin's Russia

Lenin in power

Lenin and the Bolsheviks had promised the people bread, peace and land. Lenin knew that if he failed to deliver, he and the Bolsheviks would suffer the same fate as Kerensky and the Provisional Government.

Lenin immediately set up the Council of People's Commissars (the Sovnarkom). It issued its first decree on 8 November, announcing that Russia was asking for peace with Germany. There followed an enormous number of decrees from the new government that aimed to strengthen the Bolsheviks' hold on power (see Factfile). The peasants were given the Tsar's and the Church's lands. The factories and industries were put into the hands of the workers. The Bolsheviks were given power to deal ruthlessly with their opponents – and they did (see page 119).

The Bolshevik dictatorship

Lenin had also promised free elections to the new Constituent Assembly. Elections were held in late 1917. As Lenin had feared, the Bolsheviks did not gain a majority in the elections. Their rivals, the peasant-based Socialist Revolutionaries, were the biggest party when the Assembly opened on 18 January 1918.

SOURCE 1

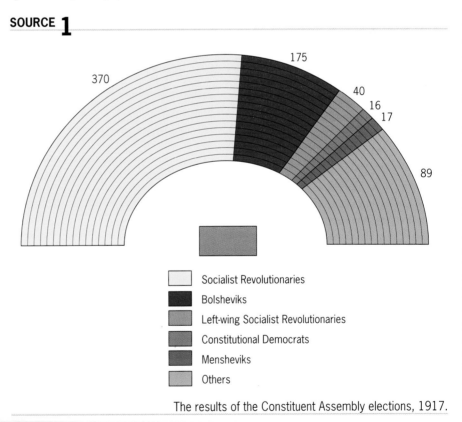

370   175   40   16   17   89

- Socialist Revolutionaries
- Bolsheviks
- Left-wing Socialist Revolutionaries
- Constitutional Democrats
- Mensheviks
- Others

The results of the Constituent Assembly elections, 1917.

Lenin solved this problem in his typically direct style. He sent the Red Guards to close down the Assembly. After brief protests (again put down by the Red Guards) the Assembly was forgotten. Lenin instead used the Congress of Soviets to pass his laws as it did contain a Bolshevik majority.

Russia's democratic experiment therefore lasted less than 24 hours, but this did not trouble Lenin's conscience. He believed he was establishing a dictatorship of the proletariat which in time would give way to true communism.

---

1 Study the Factfile. Which of the Bolshevik decrees would you say aimed to
  a) keep the peasants happy
  b) keep the workers happy
  c) increase Bolshevik control
  d) improve personal freedom in Russia?

SOURCE 2

The Treaty of Brest-Litovsk, 1918.

SOURCE 3

The bourgeoisie, landholders, and all wealthy classes are making desperate efforts to undermine the revolution which is aiming to safeguard the interests of the toiling and exploited masses . . . The partisans of the bourgeoisie, especially the higher officials, bank clerks, etc., are sabotaging and organising strikes in order to block the government's efforts to reconstruct the state on a socialistic basis. Sabotage has spread even to the food-supply organisations and millions of people are threatened with famine. Special measures must be taken to fight counter-revolution and sabotage.

From a letter written by Lenin in December 1917.

FACTFILE

The Whites

'Whites' was a very broad term and was applied to any anti-Bolshevik group(s). Whites were made up of:

★ Socialist Revolutionaries
★ Mensheviks
★ supporters of the Tsar
★ landlords and capitalists who had lost land or money in the revolution
★ the Czech Legion (former prisoners of war).

The Whites were also supported for part of the Civil War by foreign troops from the USA, Japan, France and Britain. They were sent by their governments to force Russia back into war against Germany.

Making peace

The next promise that Lenin had to make good was for peace. He put Trotsky in charge of negotiating a peace treaty. He told Trotsky to try to spin out the peace negotiations as long as possible. He hoped that very soon a socialist revolution would break out in Germany as it had in Russia. By February of 1918, however, there was no revolution and the Germans began to advance again. Lenin had to accept their terms in the Treaty of Brest-Litovsk in March 1918.

The Treaty was a severe blow to Russia. You can see how much land was lost in Source 2, but this was not the whole story. Russia's losses included 34 per cent of its population, 32 per cent of its agricultural land, 54 per cent of its industry, 26 per cent of its railways and 89 per cent of its coalmines. A final blow was the imposition of a fine of 300 million gold roubles. It was another example of Lenin's single-minded leadership. If this much had to be sacrificed to safeguard his revolution, then so be it. He may also have had the foresight to know that he would get it back when Germany lost.

Opposition and Civil War

Lenin's activities in 1917–1918 were bound to make him enemies. In fact, in August 1918 he was shot three times by a Social Revolutionary agent but had a miraculous escape. In December he set up a secret police force called the Cheka to crush his opponents.

By the end of 1918 an unlikely collection of anti-Bolshevik elements had united in an attempt to crush the Bolsheviks. They became known as the Whites (in contrast to the Bolshevik Reds) and consisted of enemies of the Bolsheviks from inside and outside Russia (see Factfile).

The Bolsheviks' stronghold was in western Russia. Much of the rest of the country was more sympathetic to the Social Revolutionary Party.

In March 1918 the Czech Legion seized control of a large section of the Trans-Siberian Railway.

Soon three separate White armies were marching on Bolshevik-controlled western Russia. Generals Yudenich and Denikin marched towards Petrograd and Moscow, while Admiral Kolchak marched on Moscow from central southern Russia.

SOURCE 4

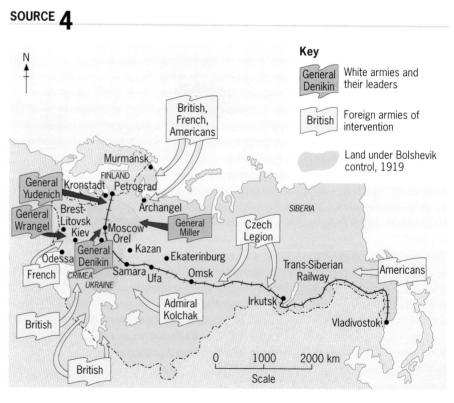

The main developments of the Civil War.

1 Read Source 3. What evidence does it provide of Lenin's
  a) political skill
  b) ruthlessness?

The reaction of the Bolsheviks was ruthless and determined. In an amazingly short time, Leon Trotsky created a new Red Army of over 300,000 men. They were led by former Tsarist officers. Trotsky made sure of their loyalty by holding their families hostage and by appointing political commissars to watch over them. The Cheka (secret police) made sure that nobody in Bolshevik territories co-operated with the Whites. There were many beatings, hangings and shootings of opponents or even suspects in what became known as the Red Terror.

Not even the Tsar escaped. In July 1918, White forces were approaching Ekaterinburg where the Tsar was being held. The Bolshevik commander ordered the execution of the Tsar and his family. Lenin could not risk the Tsar's being rescued and returned as leader of the Whites.

The fighting was savage with both sides committing terrible acts of cruelty. The people who suffered most were the ordinary workers and above all the peasants in the areas where the fighting took place.

SOURCE 5

In the villages the peasant will not give grain to the Bolsheviks because he hates them. Armed companies are sent to take grain from the peasant and every day, all over Russia, fights for grain are fought to a finish.

In the Red Army, for any military offence, there is only one punishment, death. If a regiment retreats against orders, machine guns are turned on them. The position of the bourgeoisie [middle class] defies all description. Payments by the banks have been stopped. It is forbidden to sell furniture. All owners and managers of works, offices and shops have been called up for compulsory labour. In Petrograd hundreds of people are dying from hunger. People are arrested daily and kept in prison for months without trial.

The Red Terror, observed by a British businessman in Russia in 1918.

SOURCE 6

Members of the Red Guard requisition grain from peasants during the Civil War.

SOURCE 7

Having surrounded the village [the Whites] fired a couple of volleys in the direction of the village and everyone took cover. Then the mounted soldiers entered the village, met the Bolshevik committee and put the members to death . . . After the execution the houses of the culprits were burned and the male population under forty-five whipped . . . Then the population was ordered to deliver without pay the best cattle, pigs, fowl, forage and bread for the soldiers as well as the best horses.

Diary of Colonel Drozdovsky, from his memoirs written in 1923. He was a White commander during the civil war.

2 Use Sources 5 and 6 to describe how the Civil War affected ordinary people.
3 Do you think Source 6 was painted by opponents or supporters of the Bolsheviks?

Through harsh discipline and brilliant leadership, Trotsky's Red Army began to turn back the White forces. Admiral Kolchak's forces were destroyed towards the end of 1919 and at the same time the foreign 'armies of intervention' withdrew. The Whites were not really a strong alliance, and their armies were unable to work together. Trotsky defeated them one by one. The last major White army was defeated in the Crimea in November 1920. Although scattered outbreaks of fighting continued, by 1921 the Bolsheviks were securely in control of Russia.

Why did the Bolsheviks win the Civil War?

The advantages of the Reds

The Red Army was no match for the armies that were still fighting on the Western Front in 1918. However, compared to the Whites, the Red Army was united and disciplined. It was also brilliantly led by Trotsky.

SOURCE 8

Trotsky's war train. For most of the campaign he travelled on an enormous train, giving orders, rallying the troops or transporting essential supplies.

SOURCE 9

An armoured train in the Civil War. The ability to move troops and supplies securely gave the Bolsheviks a huge advantage.

SOURCE 10

Arrests

	1918	1919
	47,348	80,662

Executions, 1918–19

counter-revolution	corruption	crime
7068	632	1024

The Red Terror.

SOURCE 11

We were constructing an army all over again and under fire at that . . . What was needed for this? It needed good commanders – a few dozen experienced fighters, a dozen or so Communists ready to make any sacrifice; boots for the bare-footed, a bath house, propaganda, food, underwear, tobacco, matches.

Trotsky writing about the making of the Red Army.

SOURCE 13

For the first time in history the working people have got control of their country. The workers of all countries are striving to achieve this objective. We in Russia have succeeded. We have thrown off the rule of the Tsar, of landlords and of capitalists. But we still have tremendous difficulties to overcome. We cannot build a new society in a day. We ask you, are you going to crush us? To help give Russia back to the landlords, the capitalists and the Tsar?

Red propaganda leaflet, *Why Have You Come to Murmansk?*

SOURCE 12

1 Every food requisition detachment is to consist of not less than 75 men and two or three machine guns.
2 The food requisition troop detachments shall be deployed in such a manner as to allow two or three detachments to link up quickly.

Instructions to Red Army units for requisitioning grain from the peasants.

The Bolsheviks also kept strict control over their heartlands in western Russia.

- They made sure that the towns and armies were fed, by forcing peasants to hand over food and by rationing supplies.
- They took over the factories of Moscow and Petrograd so that they were able to supply their armies with equipment and ammunition.
- The Red Terror made sure that the population was kept under strict control (see Source 10).
- The Bolsheviks raised fears about the intentions of the foreign armies in league with the Whites (Source 14). Effective propaganda also made good use of atrocities committed by the Whites and raised fears about the possible return of the Tsar and landlords (see Sources 13–16).

SOURCE 14

Bolshevik propaganda cartoon, 1919. The dogs represent the White generals Denikin, Kolchak and Yudenich.

1 Look at Source 14. Who is controlling the White forces?
2 Who do you think Source 13 is talking to?

Finally, the Reds had important territorial advantages. Their enemies were spread around the edge of Russia while they had internal lines of communication. This enabled them to move troops quickly and effectively by rail, while their enemies used less efficient methods.

A Red Army propaganda train in the early 1920s. This is the cinema carriage. The Red Army spread Communist ideas across Russia.

The disadvantages of the Whites

The Whites, in contrast with the Bolsheviks, were not united. They were made up of many different groups, all with different aims. They were also widely spread so they were unable to co-ordinate their campaigns against the Reds. Trotsky was able to defeat them one by one.

They had limited support from the Russian population. Russian peasants did not especially like the Bolsheviks, but they preferred them to the Whites. If the Whites won, the peasants knew the landlords would return.

Both sides were guilty of atrocities, but the Whites in general caused more suffering to the peasants than the Reds.

SOURCE **16**

The Civil War, 1918–1920, was a time of great chaos and estimates of Cheka executions vary from twelve to fifty thousands. But even the highest figure does not compare to the ferocity of the White Terror . . . for instance, in Finland alone, the number of workers executed by the Whites approaches 100,000.

R Appignanesi, *Lenin for Beginners*, 1977.

1 'Most Russians saw the Bolsheviks as the lesser of two evils.' With reference to Sources 5, 7, 13 and 16 explain whether you agree with this statement or not.

FOCUS TASK

Why did the Bolsheviks win the Civil War?

Imagine it is the end of the war and you have been asked to make a poster for the Bolsheviks celebrating the victory and showing the main reasons for success.

Design your poster using the information in the text, then write an explanation of your poster to send to Lenin.

The New Economic Policy

War Communism

War Communism was the name given to the harsh economic measures the Bolsheviks adopted during the Civil War, although the name is misleading in some ways (see Source 17). It had two main aims. The first aim was to put Communist theories into practice by redistributing (sharing out) wealth among the Russian people. The second aim was to help with the Civil War by keeping the towns and the Red Army supplied with food and weapons.

- All large factories were taken over by the government.
- Production was planned and organised by the government.
- Discipline for workers was strict and strikers could be shot.
- Peasants had to hand over surplus food to the government. If they didn't, they could be shot.
- Food was rationed.
- Free enterprise became illegal – all production and trade was controlled by the state.

War Communism achieved its aim of winning the war, but in doing so it caused terrible hardship. (Some historians believe that Lenin's ruthless determination to create a Communist society actually caused the war in the first place.) Peasants refused to co-operate in producing more food because the government simply took it away. This led to food shortages which, along with the bad weather in 1920 and 1921, caused a terrible famine. Some estimates suggest that 7 million Russian people died in this famine. There were even reports of cannibalism.

SOURCE 19

Children starving during the Russian famine of 1921.

In February 1921 Bolshevik policies sparked a mutiny at Kronstadt naval base.

SOURCE 20

After carrying out the October Revolution, the working classes hoped for freedom. But the result has been greater slavery. The bayonets, bullets and harsh commands of the Cheka – these are what the working man of Soviet Russia has won. The glorious emblem of the workers' state – the hammer and sickle – has been replaced by the Communist authorities with the bayonet and the barred window. Here in Kronstadt we are making a third revolution which will free the workers and the Soviets from the Communists.

Official statement from the Kronstadt sailors.

Trotsky's troops put down the uprising, but soon afterwards Lenin abandoned the emergency policies of War Communism. Considering the chaos of the Civil War years, it may seem strange that this particular revolt had such a startling effect on Lenin. It did so because the Kronstadt sailors had been among the strongest supporters of Lenin and Bolshevism.

SOURCE 17

The nature of the Bolsheviks' radical economic policies is a matter of controversy. The name usually given them, 'War Communism', is wrong on several counts . . . the term 'War Communism' was first used – in Lenin's notes – only in 1921. It suggests that the policy was a wartime stopgap . . . My view is that while the civil war deepened an existing crisis, the economic policies later called War Communism – food detachments, nationalisation of industry, restrictions of trade – had been developing . . . since the early winter of 1917–1918. There was no 'normal' period followed by a crisis.

Historian Evan Mawdsley's views on War Communism.

SOURCE 18

Bolshevik poster, 1920. The sailor is welcoming the dawn of the revolution. The Kronstadt sailors played a key role in the Bolsheviks' original success in 1917–20.

2 Read Source 20. What aspects of War Communism are the sailors most angry about?
3 Would you expect peasants in Russia to feel the same?
4 Why do you think Lenin was more worried about the revolt of the sailors than about starvation among the peasants?

The New Economic Policy

Many thousands of the Kronstadt sailors were killed. The mutiny was crushed. But Lenin recognised that changes were necessary. In March 1921, at the Party Congress, Lenin announced some startling new policies which he called the New Economic Policy (NEP). The NEP effectively brought back capitalism for some sections of Russian society. Peasants were allowed to sell surplus grain for profit and would pay tax on what they produced rather than giving some of it up to the government.

SOURCE 21

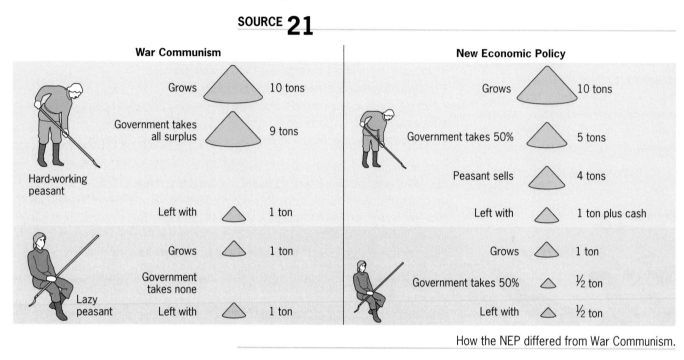

How the NEP differed from War Communism.

SOURCE 22

Our poverty and ruin are so great that we cannot at one stroke restore large-scale socialist production . . . we must try to satisfy the demands of the peasants who are dissatisfied, discontented and cannot be otherwise . . . there must be a certain amount of freedom to trade, freedom for the small private owner. We are now retreating, but we are doing this so as to then run and leap forward more vigorously.

Lenin, introducing the NEP at the Party Congress, 1921.

In the towns, small factories were handed back into private ownership and private trading of small goods was allowed.

Lenin made it clear that the NEP was temporary and that the vital heavy industries (coal, oil, iron and steel) would remain in state hands. Nevertheless, many Bolsheviks were horrified when the NEP was announced, seeing it as a betrayal of Communism. As always, Lenin won the argument and the NEP went into operation from 1921 onwards. By 1925 there seemed to be strong evidence that it was working, as food production in particular rose steeply. However, as Source 25 suggests, increases in production did not necessarily improve the situation of industrial workers.

SOURCE 23

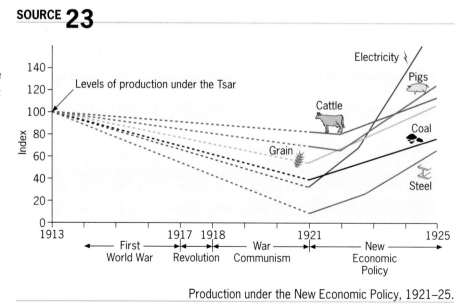

Production under the New Economic Policy, 1921–25.

1 Does the evidence of Source 23 prove that the NEP was a success? Explain your answer with reference to Sources 22, 24 and 25.
2 From all you have found out about Lenin, do you agree with Source 26?

SOURCE 24

Poor, starving old Russia, Russia of primitive lighting and the meal of a crust of black bread, is going to be covered by a network of electric power stations. The NEP will transform the Russian economy and rebuild a broken nation. The future is endless and beautiful.

Bukharin, speaking in 1922. He was a leading Bolshevik and a strong supporter of the NEP.

SOURCE 25

In 1925 the Soviet Commissar for Finance admitted that the pay of miners, metal workers and engine drivers was still lower than it had been before 1914. This in turn meant that workers' housing and food were poor. The factory committee of a cement works in Smolensk reported, for example, in 1929: 'Every day there are many complaints about apartments: many workers have families of six and seven people, and live in one room.'

Some problems identified by Soviet observers in the 1920s.

The death of Lenin and the creation of the USSR

Lenin did not live to see the recovery of the Russian economy. He suffered several strokes in 1922 and 1923 which left him paralysed and which led to his death in January 1924. He was a remarkable man by any standards. He led Russia through revolution and civil war and even in 1923 he supervised the drawing up of a new constitution that turned the Russian Empire into the Union of Soviet Socialist Republics. Source 26 gives the opinion of a British historian.

SOURCE 26

Lenin did more than any other political leader to change the face of the twentieth-century world. The creation of Soviet Russia and its survival were due to him. He was a very great man and even, despite his faults, a very good man.

The British historian AJP Taylor writing in the 1960s.

We will never know what policies Lenin would have pursued if he had lived longer – he certainly left no clear plans about how long he wanted the NEP to last. He also left another big unanswered question behind him: who was to be the next leader of the USSR?

FOCUS TASK

How did the Bolsheviks consolidate their rule?

It is January 1924. Lenin is dead. Your task is to look back at the measures he used to consolidate Bolshevik rule.

1 Draw a timeline from 1917 to 1924, and mark on it the events of that period mentioned in the text.
2 Mark on the timeline
   a) one moment at which you think Bolshevik rule was most threatened
   b) one moment at which you think it was most secure.
3 Write an explanation of how the Bolsheviks made their rule more secure. Mention the following:
   • the power of the Red Army
   • treatment of opposition
   • War Communism
   • the New Economic Policy
   • the Treaty of Brest-Litovsk
   • the victory in the Civil War
   • the promise of a new society
   • propaganda.
4 Is any one of these factors more important than any of the others? Explain your answer.

Stalin – success or failure?

Stalin or Trotsky?

When Lenin died in 1924 there were several leading Communists who were possible candidates to take his place. There would not be leadership elections. The Communist Party did not work that way. The leader would be the one who showed he had most power within the party. Among the contenders were Kamenev and Zinoviev, leading Bolsheviks who had played important parts in the Bolshevik Revolution of 1917. Bukharin was a more moderate member of the party who favoured the NEP and wanted to introduce Communism gradually to the USSR.

However, the real struggle to succeed Lenin was between two leading figures and bitter rivals in the Communist Party, Joseph Stalin and Leon Trotsky. The struggle between these two was long and hard and it was not until 1929 that Stalin made himself completely secure as the supreme leader of the USSR. Stalin achieved this through a combination of political scheming, the mistakes of his opponents and the clever way in which he built up his power base.

Why did Trotsky lose the leadership contest?

SOURCE 1

Comrade Stalin, having become Secretary General, has unlimited authority in his hands and I am not sure whether he will always be capable of using that authority with sufficient caution.

Comrade Trotsky, on the other hand, is distinguished not only by his outstanding ability. He is personally probably the most capable man in the present Central Committee, but he has displayed excessive self-assurance and preoccupation with the purely administrative side of the work.

Lenin's Testament. This is often used as evidence that Stalin was an outsider. However, the document contained many remarks critical of other leading Communists as well. It was never published in Russia, although, if it had been, it would certainly have damaged Stalin.

Source 1 shows Lenin's opinions of Trotsky and Stalin. As Lenin lay dying in late 1923 few people in the USSR had any doubts that Trotsky would win. Trotsky was a brilliant speaker and writer, as well as the party's best political thinker, after Lenin. He was also the man who had organised the Bolshevik Revolution and was the hero of the Civil War as leader of the Red Army (see page 119). Finally, he was the man who negotiated peace for Russia with the Treaty of Brest-Litovsk.

So how did Trotsky lose this contest? Much of the blame lies with Trotsky himself. He was brilliant, but also arrogant. He often offended other senior party members. More importantly, he failed to take the opposition seriously. He made little effort to build up any support in the ranks of the party. And he seriously underestimated Stalin.

SOURCE 2

Trotsky refrained from attacking Stalin because he felt secure. No contemporary, and he least of all, saw in the Stalin of 1923 the menacing and towering figure he was to become. It seemed to Trotsky almost a joke that Stalin, the wilful and sly but shabby and inarticulate man in the background, should be his rival.

Historian I Deutscher in *The Prophet Unarmed, Trotsky 1921–1929*, published in 1959.

Trotsky also frightened many people in the USSR. Trotsky argued that the future security of the USSR lay in trying to spread permanent revolution across the globe until the whole world was Communist. Many people were worried that Trotsky would involve the USSR in new conflicts.

1 Draw up a campaign poster or flier listing Trotsky's qualities for the leadership of the party. Make use of Lenin's Testament (Source 1).
2 Make a list of Trotsky's weaknesses.

FACTFILE

Stalin's steps to power

★ **1923** Stalin the outsider – Lenin calls for him to be replaced. Trotsky calls him 'the party's most eminent mediocrity'.
★ **1924** Lenin's death. Stalin attends funeral as chief mourner. Trotsky does not turn up (tricked by Stalin).
★ **1924** Stalin, Kamenev and Zinoviev form the triumvirate that dominates the Politburo, the policy-making committee of the Communist Party. Working together, these three cut off their opponents (Trotsky and Bukharin) because between them they control the important posts in the party.
★ **1925** Trotsky sacked as War Commissar. Stalin introduces his idea of Socialism in One Country.
★ **1926** Stalin turns against Kamenev and Zinoviev and allies himself with Bukharin.
★ **1927** Kamenev, Zinoviev and Trotsky all expelled from the Communist Party.
★ **1928** Trotsky exiled to Siberia. Stalin begins attacking Bukharin.
★ **1929** Trotsky expelled from USSR and Bukharin expelled from the Communist Party.

SOURCE 3

Lenin and Stalin. Stalin made the most of any opportunity to appear close to Lenin. This photograph is a suspected fake.

3 Draw up a campaign leaflet for Stalin. Remember to mention his strengths and the weaknesses of his opponent.

PROFILE

Stalin

★ Born 1879 in Georgia. His father was a shoemaker and an alcoholic. He abandoned the family while Stalin was still a young child.
★ Original name was Iosif Dzhugashvili but changed his name to Stalin (man of steel).
★ Twice exiled to Siberia by the Tsarist secret police, he escaped each time.
★ Made his name in violent bank raids to raise party funds.
★ He was slow and steady, but very hardworking.
★ He also held grudges and generally made his enemies suffer.
★ Became a leading Communist after playing an important role in defending the Bolshevik city of Tsaritsyn (later Stalingrad) during the Civil War.
★ Had become undisputed party leader by 1929.

As it often does in history, chance also played a part. Trotsky was unfortunate in falling ill late in 1923 with a malaria-like infection – just when Lenin was dying, and Trotsky needed to be at his most active.

He was also the victim of a trick by Stalin. Stalin cabled Trotsky to tell him that Lenin's funeral was to be on 26 January, when it was in fact going to be on the 27th. Trotsky was away in the south of Russia and would not have had time to get back for the 26th, although he could have got back for the 27th. As a result, Trotsky did not appear at the funeral whereas Stalin appeared as chief mourner and Lenin's closest friend.

How did Stalin win?

We have already seen that Stalin was a clever politician and he planned his bid for power carefully. He made great efforts to associate himself with Lenin wherever possible and got off to an excellent start at Lenin's funeral.

He was also extremely clever in using his power within the Communist Party. He took on many boring but important jobs such as Commissar for Nationalities and, of course, General Secretary. He used these positions to put his own supporters into important posts and even to transfer supporters of his opponents to remote postings. He was also absolutely ruthless in picking off his rivals one by one. For example he took Bukharin's side in the debate on the NEP in order to help get rid of Trotsky. Once he had got rid of Trotsky, he opposed Bukharin using exactly the same arguments as Trotsky had used before (see Factfile opposite).

Stalin's policies also met with greater favour than Trotsky's. Stalin proposed that in future the party should try to establish 'Socialism in One Country' rather than try to spread revolution worldwide. Finally, Stalin appeared to be a straightforward Georgian peasant – much more a man of the people than his intellectual rivals. To a Soviet people weary of years of war and revolution, Stalin seemed to be the man who understood their feelings.

ACTIVITY

In groups, look at the following statements and decide on a scale of 1–5 how far you agree with them.
• Stalin was a dull and unimaginative politician.
• Stalin appeared to be a dull and unimaginative politician.
• Trotsky lost the contest because of his mistakes.
• Stalin trusted to luck rather than careful planning.
• Stalin was ruthless and devious.
Try to find evidence to back up your judgements.

FOCUS TASK

Why did Stalin win?

Imagine you have to prepare a radio news feature on the reasons why Stalin, not Trotsky, became Lenin's successor.
Your feature should include:
• A brief introduction on Lenin's death.
• Profiles of the two main contenders. These could be done as descriptions by people who knew them.
• An interview with the contenders asking them to state what their aims would be as leader of the USSR. You could also summarise these aims as a slogan.
• A summary of the key events in their struggle (see Factfile).
• A conclusion on the reasons for Stalin's success.
You could work in groups of five and each be responsible for one part of the feature.

Modernising the USSR

Once in power Stalin was determined to modernise the USSR so that it could meet the challenges which were to come. He took over a country in which almost all the industry was concentrated in just a few cities and whose workers were unskilled and poorly educated. Many regions of the USSR were in the same backward state as they had been a hundred years earlier.

SOURCE 4

Throughout history Russia has been beaten again and again because she was backward . . . All have beaten her because of her military, industrial and agricultural backwardness. She was beaten because people have been able to get away with it. If you are backward and weak, then you are in the wrong and may be beaten and enslaved. But if you are powerful, people must beware of you.

It is sometimes asked whether it is not possible to slow down industrialisation a bit. No, comrades, it is not possible . . . To slacken would mean falling behind. And those who fall behind get beaten . . . That is why Lenin said during the October Revolution: 'Either perish, or overtake and outstrip the advanced capitalist countries.' We are 50 to 100 years behind the advanced countries. Either we make good the difference in ten years or they crush us.

Stalin speaking in 1931.

Industry and the Five-Year Plans

Stalin ended Lenin's NEP and set about achieving modernisation through a series of Five-Year Plans. These plans were drawn up by GOSPLAN, the state planning organisation that Lenin set up in 1921. They set ambitious targets for production in the vital heavy industries (coal, iron, oil, electricity). The plans were very complex but they were set out in such a way that by 1929 every worker knew what he or she had to achieve.

GOSPLAN set overall targets for an industry.

↓

Each region was told its targets.

↓

The region set targets for each mine, factory, etc.

↓

The manager of each mine, factory, etc. set targets for each foreman.

↓

The foremen set targets for each shift and even for individual workers.

The first Five-Year Plan focused on the major industries and although most targets were not met, the achievements were still staggering. The USSR increased production and created a foundation on which to build the next Five-Year Plans. The USSR was rich in natural resources, but many of them were in remote places such as Siberia. So whole cities were built from nothing and workers taken out to the new industrial centres. Foreign observers marvelled as huge new steel mills appeared at Magnitogorsk in the Urals and Sverdlovsk in central Siberia. New dams and hydro-electric power fed industry's energy requirements. Russian 'experts' flooded into the Muslim republics of central Asia such as Uzbekistan and Kazakhstan (see page 132), creating industry from scratch in previously undeveloped areas.

The second Five-Year Plan (1933–37) built on the achievements of the first. Heavy industry was still a priority, but other areas were also developed. Mining for lead, tin, zinc and other minerals intensified as Stalin further exploited Siberia's rich mineral resources. Transport and communications were also boosted, and new railways and canals were built. The most spectacular showpiece project was the Moscow underground railway.

Stalin also wanted industrialisation to help improve Russia's agriculture. The production of tractors and other farm machinery increased dramatically. In the third Five-Year Plan, which was begun in 1938, some factories were to switch to the production of consumer goods. However, this plan was disrupted by the Second World War.

SOURCE 5

Key
 New industry

0   500 km
Scale

The location of the new industrial centres.

FOCUS TASK

Why did Stalin introduce the Five-Year Plans?

Make a list of the objectives of the Five-Year Plans which could be hung up in Stalin's office.

SOURCE 6

What are the results of the Five-Year Plan in four years?

- *We did not have an iron and steel industry. Now we have one.*
- *We did not have a machine tool industry. Now we have one.*
- *We did not have a modern chemicals industry. Now we have one.*
- *We did not have a big industry for producing agricultural machinery. Now we have one.*

Stalin speaking about the first Five-Year Plan in 1932.

SOURCE 7

		1913	*1928*	*1940*
Gas	*(billion m³)*	*0.02*	*0.3*	*3.4*
Fertilisers	*(million tons)*	*0.07*	*0.1*	*3.2*
Plastics	*(million tons)*	*–*	*–*	*10.9*
Tractors	*(thousand)*	*–*	*1.3*	*31.6*

The growth in the output of the USSR, 1913–40.

SOURCE 8

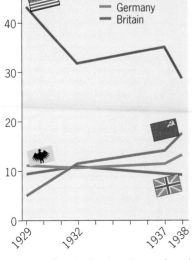

per cent share

- United States
- USSR
- Germany
- Britain

1929 1932 1937 1938

Graph showing share of world manufacturing output, 1929–38.

Were the Five-Year Plans a success?

There is much that could be and was criticised in the Five-Year Plans. Certainly there was a great deal of inefficiency, duplication of effort and waste, although the evidence shows that the Soviets did learn from their mistakes in the second and third Five-Year Plans. There was also an enormous human cost, as you will see on pages 131–33. But the fact remains that by 1937 the USSR was a modern state and it was this that saved it from defeat when Hitler invaded in 1941.

SOURCE 9

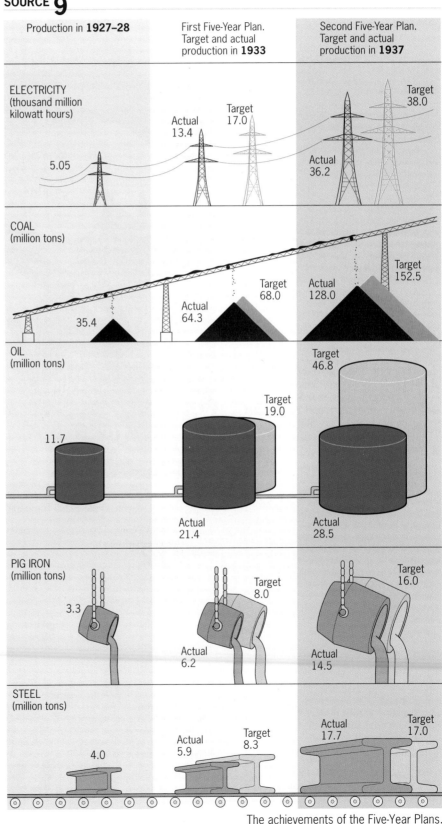

Production in **1927–28** | First Five-Year Plan. Target and actual production in **1933** | Second Five-Year Plan. Target and actual production in **1937**

ELECTRICITY (thousand million kilowatt hours)
5.05 | Actual 13.4 / Target 17.0 | Actual 36.2 / Target 38.0

COAL (million tons)
35.4 | Actual 64.3 / Target 68.0 | Actual 128.0 / Target 152.5

OIL (million tons)
11.7 | Actual 21.4 / Target 19.0 | Actual 28.5 / Target 46.8

PIG IRON (million tons)
3.3 | Actual 6.2 / Target 8.0 | Actual 14.5 / Target 16.0

STEEL (million tons)
4.0 | Actual 5.9 / Target 8.3 | Actual 17.7 / Target 17.0

The achievements of the Five-Year Plans.

SOURCE 10

There is evidence that he [Stalin] exaggerated Russia's industrial deficiency in 1929. The Tsars had developed a considerable industrial capacity . . . in a sense the spadework had already been done and it is not altogether surprising that Stalin should have achieved such rapid results.

Historian SJ Lee, *The European Dictatorships, 1918–1945*, published in 1987.

The Five-Year Plans were used very effectively for propaganda purposes. Stalin had wanted the Soviet Union to be a beacon of socialism and his publicity machine used the successes of industrialisation to further that objective.

SOURCE 11

Soviet propaganda poster, 1933. In the top half, the hand is holding the first Five-Year Plan. The capitalist is saying (in 1928), 'Fantasy, Lies, Utopia.' The bottom half shows 1933.

1 What is the message of Source 11?
2 How could Stalin use Sources 7 and 8 to support the claims of Source 11?
3 Compare Sources 6 and 10. Do they agree or disagree about the Five-Year Plans? Explain your answer.
4 Which of Sources 6 or 10 do Sources 7, 8 and 9 most support?

SOURCE 12

5 Look at Source 12. Stalin felt this project was not a good use of resources when it was begun in 1926. Why do you think he wanted to be shown alongside it?

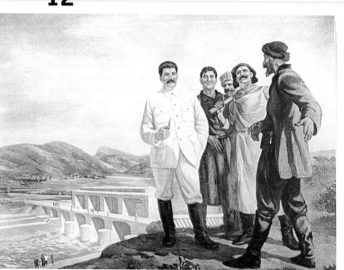

A propaganda painting showing Stalin at the Dnieprostroi Dam.

How was industrialisation achieved?

Any programme as extreme as Stalin's Five-Year Plans was bound to carry a cost. In the USSR this cost was paid by the workers. Many foreign experts and engineers were called in by Stalin to supervise the work and in their letters and reports they marvel at the toughness of the Russian people. The workers were constantly bombarded with propaganda, posters, slogans and radio broadcasts. They all had strict targets to meet and were fined if they did not meet them.

The most famous worker was Alexei Stakhanov. In 1935 with two helpers and an easy coal seam to work on, he managed to cut an amazing 102 tons of coal in one shift. This was 14 times the average for a shift. Stakhanov became a 'Hero of Socialist Labour' and the propaganda machine encouraged all Soviet workers to be Stakhanovites.

The first Five-Year Plan revealed a shortage of workers, so from 1930 the government concentrated on drafting more women into industry. It set up thousands of new crèches and day-care centres so that mothers could work. By 1937 women were 40 per cent of industrial workers (compared to 28 per cent in 1927), 21 per cent of building workers and 72 per cent of health workers. Four out of five new workers recruited between 1932 and 1937 were women.

SOURCE 14

We got so dirty and we were such young things, small, slender, fragile. But we had our orders to build the metro and we wanted to do it more than anything else. We wore our miners' overalls with such style. My feet were size four and the boots were elevens. But there was such enthusiasm.

Tatyana Fyodorova, interviewed as an old lady in 1990, remembers building the Moscow underground.

SOURCE 15

Nothing strikes the visitor to the Soviet Union more forcibly than the lack of fear. No fear of not having enough money at the birth of a child. No fear for doctor's fees, school fees or university fees. No fear of underwork, no fear of overwork. No fear of wage reduction in a land where none are unemployed.

Dr Hewlett Johnson, Dean of Canterbury Cathedral, visiting the USSR in 1939.

SOURCE 13

Propaganda poster showing Stalin as a comrade side by side with Soviet workers. The text means 'It is our workers who make our programme achievable.'

By the late 1930s many Soviet workers had improved their conditions by acquiring well-paid skilled jobs and earning bonuses for meeting targets. Unemployment was almost non-existent. In 1940 the USSR had more doctors per head of population than Britain. Education became free and compulsory for all and Stalin invested huge sums in training schemes based in colleges and in the work place.

But, on the other hand, life was very harsh under Stalin. Factory discipline was strict and punishments were severe. Lateness or absences were punished by sacking, and that often meant losing your flat or house as well. To escape the hard work and hard discipline, some workers tried to move to other jobs, so the secret police introduced internal passports which prevented free movement of workers inside the USSR.

On the great engineering projects, such as dams and canals, many of the workers were prisoners who had been sentenced to hard labour for being political opponents, or suspected opponents, of Stalin, or for being kulaks (rich peasants) or Jews. Many other prisoners were simply unfortunate workers who had had accidents or made mistakes in their work but had been found guilty of 'sabotage'.

6 Read Source 15. How can you tell that Dr Johnson was impressed by Stalin's USSR?

SOURCE 16

Half a billion cubic feet of excavation work . . . 25,000 tons of structural steel . . . without sufficient labour, without necessary quantities of the most rudimentary materials. Brigades of young enthusiasts arrived in the summer of 1930 and did the groundwork of railroad and dam . . . Later groups of peasants came . . . Many were completely unfamiliar with industrial tools and processes . . .

J Scott, *Behind the Urals*, 1943.

SOURCE 18

We were led down to the communal kitchen in the basement . . . 'My' section consisted of a packing case and two reeking kerosene stoves. On these I was expected to cook, boil up washing and heat water for an occasional bath taken in a basin in the room above . . . The room was good for Moscow we were assured. At least we would not have to share with another family.

Betty Rowland, *Caviar for Breakfast*. The novelist describes her experiences of Russia in the 1930s.

SOURCE 17

As usual, at five o'clock that first morning call was sounded by the blows of a hammer on a length of rail . . . the sound penetrated the window panes on which the frost lay two inches thick . . . [Sukhov] remembered that this morning his fate hung in the balance: they wanted to shift the 104th from the building shops to a new site, the 'Socialist Way of Life' settlement. It lay in open country covered with snowdrifts, and before anything else could be done there they would have to dig pits and put up posts and attach barbed wire to them. Wire themselves in, so they couldn't run away . . .

Alexander Solzhenitsyn, *One Day in the Life of Ivan Denisovich*, published in 1962. Solzhenitsyn was probably the most famous dissident in Stalin's USSR. He spent many years in labour camps. He was exiled in 1974. He lived for the next 20 years in the USA but in 1994 returned to Russia after the fall of Communism.

On these major projects conditions were appalling and there were many deaths and accidents. It is estimated that 100,000 workers died in the construction of the Belomor Canal.

At the same time, the concentration on heavy industry meant that there were few consumer goods (such as clothes or radios) which ordinary people wanted to buy. In the towns and cities, most housing was provided by the state, but overcrowding was a problem. Most families lived in flats and were crowded into two rooms which were used for living, sleeping and eating. What's more, wages actually fell between 1928 and 1937. In 1932 a husband and wife who both worked earned only as much as one man or woman had in 1928.

Stalin was also quite prepared to destroy the way of life of the Soviet people to help industrialisation. For example, in the republics of central Asia the influence of Islam was thought to hold back industrialisation, so between 1928 and 1932 it was repressed. Many Muslim leaders were imprisoned or deported, mosques were closed and pilgrimages to Mecca were forbidden.

SOURCE 19

What is the way out [of the food problem]? The way out is to turn the small and scattered peasant farms, gradually but surely, into large farms based on common, co-operative, collective cultivation of the land. There is no other way out.

Stalin in a speech in 1927.

ACTIVITY

'The Five-Year Plans brought glory to Stalin and misery to his people.' Is that a fair view of Stalin's industrialisation programme?

In pairs or small groups, discuss this question. Make sure you look at all the evidence and information before you make up your mind. You could then write up your conclusions in the form of a letter to Dr Hewlett Johnson, the writer of Source 15. The aim of your letter could be:
• to set him right.
• to agree with him.

FACTFILE

Collectivisation

★ Peasants were to put their lands together to form large joint farms (*kolkhoz*) but could keep small plots for personal use.
★ Animals and tools were to be pooled together.
★ Motor Tractor Stations (MTS), provided by the government, made tractors available.
★ Ninety per cent of *kolkhoz* produce would be sold to the state and the profits shared out.
★ The remaining 10 per cent of produce was to be used to feed the *kolkhoz*.

Modernising agriculture: collectivisation

For the enormous changes of the Five-Year Plan to be successful, Stalin needed to modernise the USSR's agriculture. This was vital because the population of the industrial centres was growing rapidly and yet as early as 1928 the country was already 2 million tons short of the grain it needed to feed its workers. Stalin also wanted to try to raise money for his industrialisation programme by selling exports of surplus food abroad.

The problem was that farming was not organised to do this. Under the NEP, most peasants were either agricultural labourers (with no land) or kulaks – prosperous peasants who owned small farms. These farms were too small to make efficient use of tractors, fertilisers and other modern methods. In addition, most peasants had enough to eat and could see little point in increasing production to feed the towns. To get round these problems, Stalin set out his ideas for collectivisation in 1929.

1 Explain why Stalin needed to change farming in the USSR.
2 Why did the peasants resist?

The government tried hard to sell these ideas to the peasants, offering free seed and other perks, but there were soon problems. The peasants, who had always been suspicious of government, whether it was the Tsar, Lenin or Stalin, were concerned about the speed of collectivisation. They disliked the fact that the farms were under the control of the local Communist leader. They were being asked to grow crops such as flax for Russia's industry rather than grain to feed themselves. In short, Stalin was asking the peasants to abandon a way of life that they and their ancestors had led for centuries.

Stalin had a difficult time convincing the peasants about collectivisation, but this was slight compared to the opposition of the kulaks who owned their own land. The kulaks simply refused outright to hand over their land and produce. Within a short time, collectivisation became a grim and bitter struggle. Soviet propaganda tried to turn the people against the kulaks. The war of words soon turned into violence. Requisition parties came and took the food required by the government, often leaving the peasants to starve. Kulaks were arrested and sent by the thousand to labour camps or were forced on to poor-quality land. In revenge, many kulaks burnt their crops and slaughtered their animals so that the Communists could not have them.

The countryside was in chaos. Even where collectivisation had been introduced successfully, peasants were unfamiliar with new ideas and methods. There was much bitterness as starving peasants watched Communist officials sending food for export.

Not surprisingly, food production fell under these conditions and there was a famine in 1932–1933. Millions died in Kazakhstan and the Ukraine, Russia's richest agricultural region. When the Germans invaded the Ukraine in 1941, they were at first made welcome for driving out the Communists.

SOURCE 20

In order to turn a peasant society into an industrialised country, countless material and human sacrifices were necessary. The people had to accept this, but it would not be achieved by enthusiasm alone . . . If a few million people had to perish in the process, history would forgive Comrade Stalin . . . The great aim demanded great energy that could be drawn from a backward people only by great harshness.

Anatoli Rybakov, *Children of the Arbat*, 1988. A Russian writer presents Stalin's viewpoint on the modernisation of Russia.

3 Read Source 21. Why do you think the only reports of the famine came from Western journalists?

SOURCE 21

'How are things with you?' I asked one old man. He looked around anxiously to see that no soldiers were about. 'We have nothing, absolutely nothing. They have taken everything away.' It was true. The famine is an organised one. Some of the food that has been taken away from them is being exported to foreign countries. It is literally true that whole villages have been exiled. I saw myself a group of some twenty peasants being marched off under escort. This is so common a sight that it no longer arouses even curiosity.

The *Manchester Guardian*, 1933.

Despite the famine, Stalin did not ease off. By 1934 there were no kulaks left. By 1941 almost all agricultural land was organised under the collective system. Stalin had achieved his aim of collectivisation.

SOURCE 22

Stalin, ignoring the great cost in human life and misery, claimed that collectivisation was a success; for, after the great famines caused at the time . . . no more famines came to haunt the Russian people. The collective farms, despite their inefficiencies, did grow more food than the tiny, privately owned holdings had done. For example, 30 to 40 million tons of grain were produced every year. Collectivisation also meant the introduction of machines into the countryside. Now 2 million previously backward peasants learned how to drive a tractor. New methods of farming were taught by agricultural experts. The countryside was transformed.

Historian E Roberts, *Stalin, Man of Steel*, published in 1986.

4 According to Source 22, what advantages did collectivisation bring?
5 Do you agree that these advantages outweighed the human cost?

FOCUS TASK

Stalin's economic policies: success or failure?

1 Draw up a chart like this:

	Industrialisation	Collectivisation
Reasons the policy was adopted		
Measures taken to enforce the policy		
Successes of the policy		
Failures of the policy		
The human cost of the policy		

2 Working with a partner, fill it out as fully as you can with details from pages 128–33.
3 Then use the chart to write an essay comparing the success of the two policies.

How powerful was Stalin?

It was not possible to make the huge changes which Stalin was carrying out without making enemies. However, one of Stalin's aims was to control his people to such an extent that they would be afraid even to think of opposing him. Throughout his time in power he used the secret police, at first called OGPU and then NKVD, to crush any opponents of his policies.

The Purges

The first signs of the terror which was to come appeared in 1928 when Stalin, without much evidence, accused a number of engineers of sabotage in the important Donbass mining region. In 1931 a number of former Mensheviks (see page 103) were put on trial on charges that were obviously made up.

However, the really terrifying period in Stalin's rule, known as the Purges, began in 1934 when Kirov, the leader of the Leningrad (the new name for Petrograd from 1924) Communist Party, was murdered. Stalin used this murder as an excuse to 'purge' or clear out his opponents in the party. Historians strongly suspect that Stalin arranged for Kirov's murder to give him this excuse. In great 'show trials' loyal Bolsheviks, such as Kamenev (1936), Bukharin (1938) and Zinoviev (1936), confessed to being traitors to the state. It was not only leading figures who were purged. Estimates suggest that around 500,000 party members were arrested on charges of anti-Soviet activities and either executed or sent to labour camps (gulags). In 1940, Trotsky, in exile in Mexico, was murdered by Stalin's agents.

After the trials, Stalin turned his attention to the army, particularly the officers. Approximately 25,000 officers were removed – around one in five – including the Supreme Commander of the Red Army, Marshal Tukhachevsky.

As the Purges were extended, university lecturers and teachers, miners and engineers, factory managers and ordinary workers all disappeared. It is said that every family in the USSR lost someone in the Purges. One of the most frightening aspects was the unpredictability. Arrests would take place in the middle of the night and victims were rarely told what they were accused of. Days of physical and psychological torture would gradually break the victims and they would confess to anything. If the torture failed, the NKVD would threaten the families of those arrested.

By 1937 an estimated 18 million people had been transported to labour camps. Ten million died. Stalin seriously weakened the USSR by removing so many able individuals. The army purges were nearly fatal to the USSR. When Hitler invaded the USSR in 1941, one of the key problems of the Red Army was a lack of good-quality, experienced officers. Stalin had also succeeded in destroying any sense of independent thinking. Everyone who was spared knew that their lives depended on thinking exactly as Stalin did. In the population as a whole, the long-term impact of living with terror and distrust haunted the USSR for a generation.

SOURCE 23

A tribute to Comrade Stalin was called for. Of course, everyone stood up . . . for three minutes, four minutes, the 'stormy applause, rising to an ovation' continued . . . Who would dare to be the first to stop? After all, NKVD men were standing in the hall waiting to see who quit first! After 11 minutes the director [of the factory] . . . sat down . . . To a man, everyone else stopped dead and sat down. They had been saved! . . . That, however, was how they discovered who the independent people were. And that was how they eliminated them. The same night the factory director was arrested.

Alexander Solzhenitsyn, *Gulag Archipelago*, published in 1973. Solzhenitsyn lost his Soviet citizenship as a result of this book.

---

1 According to Source 23, what sort of people did Stalin want in the USSR?

SOURCE 24

Stalin shown holding a young child, Gelya Markizova, in 1936. Stalin had both of her parents killed. This did not stop him using this image on propaganda leaflets to show him as a kind, fatherly figure.

SOURCE 25

Russian exiles in France made this mock travel poster in the late 1930s. The text says: 'Visit the USSR's pyramids!'

2 Look at Source 27. Summarise the message of the cartoon in your own words.

The new constitution

In 1936 Stalin created a new constitution for the USSR. It gave freedom of speech and free elections to the Russian people. This was, of course, a cosmetic measure. Only Communist Party candidates were allowed to stand in elections, and only approved newspapers and magazines could be published.

One of Stalin's opponents deleted from a photograph, 1935. Techniques of doctoring pictures became far more sophisticated in the 1930s. This allowed Stalin to create the impression that his enemies had never existed.

A cartoon published by Russian exiles in Paris in 1936. The title of the cartoon is 'The Stalinist Constitution' and the text at the bottom reads 'New seating arrangements in the Supreme Soviet'.

The cult of Stalin

Today, Stalin's rule is looked back on as a time of great terror and oppression. However, if you had visited the USSR in the 1930s, you would have found that the average Soviet citizen admired Stalin. Ask about the Purges and people would probably say that they were nothing to do with Stalin himself. For most Soviet citizens, Stalin was not a tyrant dominating an oppressed country. He and his style of government were popular. The Communist Party saw him as a winner and Soviet citizens saw him as a 'dictator of the people'. The Soviet people sincerely believed in Stalin and this belief was built up quite deliberately by Communist leaders and by Stalin himself. It developed into what is known as the Cult of the Personality. The history of the Soviet Union was rewritten so that Lenin and Stalin were the only real heroes of the Revolution.

These men lifted their villainous hands against Comrade Stalin. By lifting their hands against Comrade Stalin, they lifted them against all of us, against the working class . . . against the teaching of Marx, Engels, Lenin . . . Stalin is our hope, Stalin is the beacon which guides all progressive mankind. Stalin is our banner. Stalin is our will. Stalin is our victory.

From a speech made by Communist leader Nikita Khrushchev in 1937, at the height of the Purges. (Khrushchev later became leader of the USSR and in 1956 announced a 'de-Stalinisation' programme – see page 401).

The teacher showed us her school textbooks where the portraits of Party leaders had thick pieces of paper pasted over them as one by one they fell into disgrace – this the children had to do on instructions from their teacher . . . with every new arrest, people went through their books and burned the works of disgraced leaders in their stoves.

A Soviet writer describes how children in Soviet schools had to revise their school history books during the 1930s.

The Soviet education system was geared not to independent thinking but to Stalinist propaganda. Schoolchildren were also expected to join the Young Pioneers (see Source 30).

The Soviet people were deluged with portraits, photographs and statues of Stalin. Comrade Stalin appeared everywhere. Every Russian town had a Stalin Square or a Stalin Avenue and a large Stalin statue in the centre. Poets and playwrights praised Stalin either directly or indirectly. Composers wrote music praising him. All music and other arts in the USSR were carefully monitored by the NKVD. Regular processions were organised through the streets of Russian towns and cities praising Stalin and all he had achieved.

SOURCE 30

I, a Young Pioneer of the Soviet Union, in the presence of my comrades, solemnly promise to love my Soviet motherland passionately, and to live, learn and struggle as the great Lenin bade us and the Communist Party teaches us.

The promise made by each member of the Young Pioneers.

Religious worship of any kind was banned. Stalin did not want the people to have loyalty to anyone else but him. Instead, people were encouraged to worship Stalin. Belief in God and the words of priests had to be replaced by belief in Communism and the words of its leaders.

SOURCE 31

A

B

Posters of Stalin **A** pointing out the achievements of the USSR 'on the Leninist path' and **B** praising the strength of the Soviet army and people.

FOCUS TASK A

Stalin: success or failure?

Stalin died in 1953. There was deep distress at the loss of the successful and great leader. However, three years later, he was denounced as a failure by his successor, who paraded his faults before the nation. Join the debate – was Stalin a success or a failure?

Work in pairs to prepare for a class debate. One of you gather evidence and arguments from pages 126–36 that Stalin was a success as leader of the Soviet Union, the other gather evidence that he was a failure.

FOCUS TASK B

How did Stalin control the USSR?

Sources 29–31 show some methods Stalin used to control the USSR. Elsewhere in this chapter you have found out about other methods.

1 Draw up a table like the one here and fill it out as completely as you can. You may wish to add other subjects in the first column.
2 Use these subject headings to write a brief answer to the question 'How did Stalin control the USSR?' Mention whether he faced opposition and how he dealt with it.

Method of control	Example
Making people afraid	
Improving living conditions	
Propaganda	
Education	
Control of economy	
Control of mass media	
Cult of the personality	

Germany
1918–1945

The Weimar Republic and the rise of the Nazis

Timeline

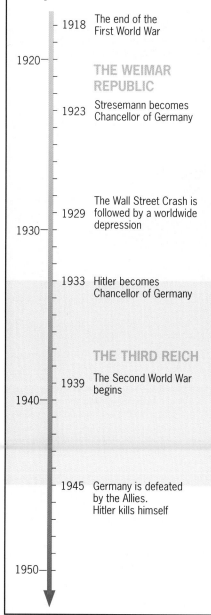

This timeline shows the period you will be covering in this chapter. Some of the key dates are filled in already.

To help you get a complete picture of the period, you can make your own copy and add other details to it as you work through the chapter.

1918	The end of the First World War
1920		
	THE WEIMAR REPUBLIC	
1923	Stresemann becomes Chancellor of Germany
1929	The Wall Street Crash is followed by a worldwide depression
1930		
1933	Hitler becomes Chancellor of Germany
	THE THIRD REICH	
1939	The Second World War begins
1940		
1945	Germany is defeated by the Allies. Hitler kills himself
1950		

FOCUS

The impact of the First World War on Germany was devastating. The Treaty of Versailles made the country's problems even worse. The Weimar government struggled from crisis to crisis. Out of this conflict Adolf Hitler and the Nazis emerged as the most powerful group in Germany.

In 6.1 you will investigate:

■ **the problems facing the Weimar government in the 1920s**
■ **how those problems helped Hitler and the Nazis to take power in 1933.**

In 6.2 you will investigate:

■ **how the Nazis controlled Germany**
■ **what it was like to live in Nazi Germany.**

The impact of the First World War

In 1914 the Germans were a proud people. Their Kaiser – virtually a dictator – was celebrated for his achievements. Their army was probably the finest in the world. A journey through the streets of Berlin in 1914 would have revealed prospering businesses and a well-educated and well-fed workforce. There was great optimism about the power and strength of Germany.

Four years later a similar journey would have revealed a very different picture. Although little fighting had taken place in Germany itself, the war had still destroyed much of the old Germany. The proud German army was defeated. The German people were surviving on turnips and bread, and even the flour for the bread was mixed with sawdust to make it go further. A flu epidemic was sweeping the country, killing thousands of people already weakened by rations.

This may not surprise you, given the suffering of the First World War. What might surprise you is that five years later the situation for many people in Germany was still very grim indeed.

Whatever had gone wrong in Germany? To find out, you are going to look back at the final stages of the First World War.

SOURCE 1

German women sell their possessions to buy food in 1922.

SOURCE **2**

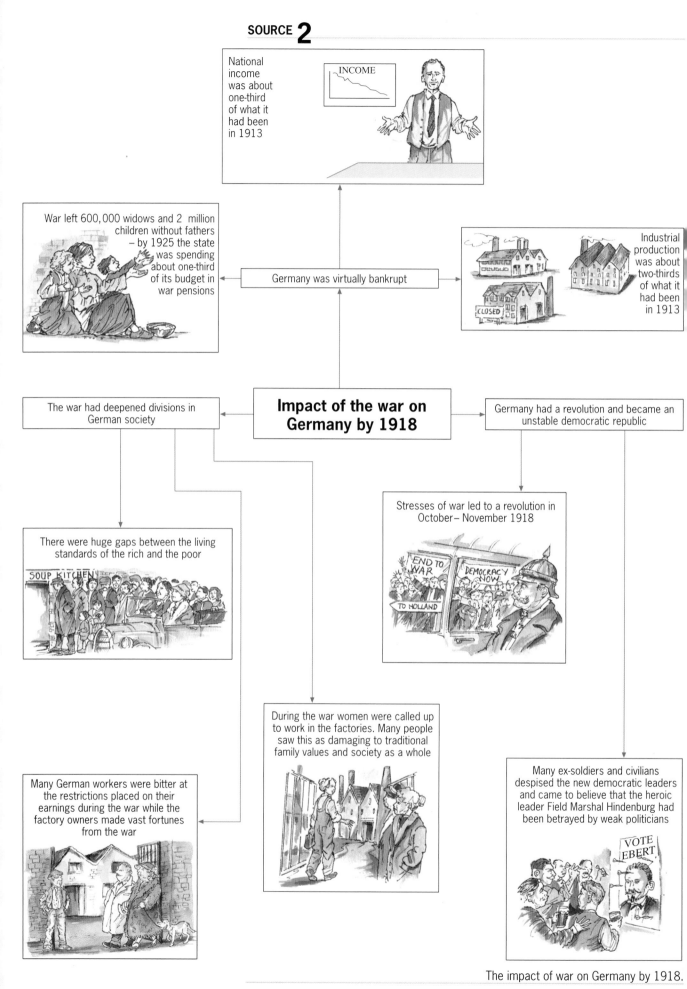

National income was about one-third of what it had been in 1913

INCOME

War left 600,000 widows and 2 million children without fathers – by 1925 the state was spending about one-third of its budget in war pensions

Germany was virtually bankrupt

Industrial production was about two-thirds of what it had been in 1913

CLOSED

The war had deepened divisions in German society

Impact of the war on Germany by 1918

Germany had a revolution and became an unstable democratic republic

Stresses of war led to a revolution in October–November 1918

END TO WAR
DEMOCRACY NOW
TO HOLLAND

There were huge gaps between the living standards of the rich and the poor

SOUP KITCHEN

During the war women were called up to work in the factories. Many people saw this as damaging to traditional family values and society as a whole

Many German workers were bitter at the restrictions placed on their earnings during the war while the factory owners made vast fortunes from the war

Many ex-soldiers and civilians despised the new democratic leaders and came to believe that the heroic leader Field Marshal Hindenburg had been betrayed by weak politicians

VOTE EBERT

The impact of war on Germany by 1918.

The birth of the Weimar Republic

In autumn 1918 the Allies had clearly won the war. Germany was in a state of chaos, as you can see from Source 2. The Allies offered Germany peace, but under strict conditions. One condition was that Germany should become more democratic. When the Kaiser refused, sailors in northern Germany mutinied and took over the town of Kiel. This triggered other revolts. The Kaiser's old enemies, the Socialists, led uprisings of workers and soldiers in other German ports. Soon, other German cities followed. In Bavaria an independent Socialist Republic was declared. On 9 November 1918 the Kaiser abdicated his throne and left Germany for the Netherlands.

The following day, the Socialist leader Friedrich Ebert became the new leader of the Republic of Germany. He immediately signed an armistice with the Allies. The war was over. He also announced to the German people that the new Republic was giving them freedom of speech, freedom of worship and better working conditions. A new constitution was drawn up (see Factfile).

The success of the new government depended on the German people accepting an almost instant change from the traditional, autocratic German system of government to this new democratic system. The prospects for this did not look good.

The reaction of politicians in Germany was unenthusiastic. Ebert had opposition from both right and left. On the right wing, nearly all the Kaiser's former advisers remained in their positions in the army, judiciary, civil service and industry. They restricted what the new government could do. Many still hoped for a return to rule by the Kaiser. A powerful myth developed that men such as Ebert had stabbed Germany in the back and caused the defeat in the war (see page 140). On the left wing there were many Communists who believed that at this stage what Germany actually needed was a Communist revolution just like Russia's in 1917.

Despite this opposition, in January 1919 free elections took place for the first time in Germany's history. Ebert's party won a majority and he became the President of the Weimar Republic. It was called this because, to start with, the new government met in the small town of Weimar (see Source 6) rather than in the German capital, Berlin. Even in February 1919, Berlin was thought to be too violent and unstable.

SOURCE 3

President → Appointed judges → Courts

President → Appointed → Chancellor

President → Controlled → Armed forces

Chancellor → Appointed → Government Ministers

Government sent laws to Reichstag for approval

17 local governments (*Lander*) for Bavaria, Prussia and all Germany's other regions. The Constitution limited their power as much as possible

Reichstag (Parliament)

Elected — Elected — Elected

German people

The Weimar Constitution.

SOURCE **4**

Spartacists – the Communists who felt that Germany was ready to follow Russia's example of Communist revolution.

SOURCE **5**

The Freikorps – ex-servicemen who were totally opposed to Communism.

SOURCE **6**

Problems for the Weimar Republic, 1919–24.

The Republic in danger, 1919–1924

From the start, Ebert's government faced violent opposition from both left-wing and right-wing opponents.

The threat from the Left

One left-wing group was a Communist party known as the SPARTACISTS. They were led by Karl Liebknecht and Rosa Luxemburg. Their party was much like Lenin's Bolsheviks, who had just taken power in Russia. They argued strongly against Ebert's plans for a democratic Germany (see Factfile). They wanted a Germany ruled by workers' councils or soviets.

Early in 1919 the Spartacists launched their bid for power. Joined by rebel soldiers and sailors, they set up soviets in many towns. Not all soldiers were on the side of the Spartacists, however. Some anti-Communist ex-soldiers had formed themselves into vigilante groups called FREIKORPS. Ebert made an agreement with the commanders of the army and the Freikorps to put down the rebellion. Bitter street fighting followed between the Spartacists and Freikorps. Both sides were heavily armed. Casualties were high. The Freikorps won. Liebknecht and Luxemburg were murdered and this Communist revolution had failed. However, another one was soon to follow.

It emerged in Bavaria in the south of Germany. Bavaria was still an independent Socialist state led by Kurt Eisner, who was Ebert's ally. In February 1919 he was murdered by political opponents. The Communists in Bavaria seized the opportunity to declare a soviet republic in Bavaria. Ebert used the same tactics as he had against the Spartacists. The Freikorps moved in to crush the revolt in May 1919. Around 600 Communists were killed.

In 1920 there was more Communist agitation in the Ruhr industrial area. Again police, army and Freikorps clashed with Communists. There were 2000 casualties.

Ebert's ruthless measures against the Communists created lasting bitterness between them and his Socialist Party. However, it gained approval from many in Germany. Ebert was terrified that Germany might go the same way as Russia (at that time rocked by bloody civil war). Many Germans shared his fears. Even so, despite these defeats, the Communists remained a powerful anti-government force in Germany throughout the 1920s.

The Treaty of Versailles

The next crisis to hit the new Republic came in May 1919 when the terms of the Treaty of Versailles were announced. You can read more about this on pages 86–96, but here is a summary. Germany lost:

- 10 per cent of its land
- all of its overseas colonies
- 12.5 per cent of its population
- 16 per cent of its coal and 48 per cent of its iron industry.

In addition:

- its army was reduced to 100,000; it was not allowed to have an air force; its navy was reduced
- Germany had to accept blame for starting the war and was forced to pay reparations.

Most Germans were appalled. Supporters of the Weimar government felt betrayed by the Allies. The Kaiser was gone – why should they be punished for his war and aggression? Opponents of the regime turned their fury on Ebert.

As you read on page 88, Ebert himself was very reluctant to sign the Treaty, but he had no choice. Germany could not go back to war. However, in the minds of many Germans, Ebert and his Weimar Republic were forever to blame for the Treaty. The injustice of the Treaty became a rallying point for all Ebert's opponents. They believed that the German army had been 'stabbed in the back' by the Socialist and Liberal politicians who agreed an armistice in November 1918. They believed not that Germany had been beaten on the battlefield, but that it had been betrayed by its civilian politicians who didn't dare continue the war. The Treaty was still a source of bitterness in Germany when Hitler came to power in 1933.

1 Why might the Right dislike the Weimar Constitution (see Factfile, page 139)?
2 For each aspect of the Treaty of Versailles, explain why it would anger Ebert's right-wing opponents.

The threat from the Right

Ebert's government faced violent opposition from the Right. His right-wing opponents were largely people who had grown up in the successful days of the Kaiser's Germany. They had liked the Kaiser's dictatorial style of government. They liked Germany having a strong army. They wanted Germany to expand its territory, and to have an empire. They had been proud of Germany's powerful industry.

In March 1920 Dr Wolfgang Kapp led 5000 FREIKORPS into Berlin in a rebellion known as the Kapp Putsch (Putsch means rebellion). The army refused to fire on the Freikorps and it looked as if Ebert's government was doomed. However, it was saved by the German people, especially the industrial workers of Berlin. They declared a general strike which brought the capital to a halt with no transport, power or water (see Source 7). After a few days Kapp realised he could not succeed and left the country. He was hunted down and died while awaiting trial. It seemed that Weimar had support and power after all. Even so, the rest of the rebels went unpunished by the courts and judges.

SOURCE 7

Berlin während des Verkehrsstreiks.
Kraftwagen nach Halensee.

Workers being bussed to work privately during the 1920 general strike.

Ebert's government struggled to deal with the political violence in Germany. Political assassinations were frequent. In the summer of 1922 Ebert's foreign minister Walther Rathenau was murdered by extremists. Then in November 1923 Adolf Hitler led an attempted rebellion in Munich, known as the Munich Putsch (see page 149). Both Hitler and the murderers of Rathenau received short prison sentences. Strangely, Hitler's judge at the trial was the same judge who had tried him two years earlier for disorder. Both times he got off very lightly. It seemed that Weimar's right-wing opponents had friends in high places.

3 From reading pages 140–41, what differences can you see between the treatment of left-wing and right-wing extremists? Can you explain this?

SOURCE 8

There was a lot of official harassment. There was widespread hunger, squalor and poverty and – what really affected us – there was humiliation. The French ruled with an iron hand. If they disliked you walking on the pavement, for instance, they'd come along with their riding crops and you'd have to walk in the road.

The memories of Jutta Rudiger, a German woman living in the Ruhr during the French occupation.

1 For each of Sources 9 and 10 write an explanation of its message.
2 Is it possible to answer the question 'Could Germany afford the reparations payments?' with a simple yes or no? Explain your answer.

Economic disaster

The Treaty of Versailles destabilised Germany politically, but Germans also blamed it for another problem – economic chaos. See if you agree that the Treaty of Versailles was responsible for economic problems in Germany.

The Treaty of Versailles forced Germany to pay reparations to the Allies. The reparations bill was announced in April 1921. It was set at £6600 million, to be paid in annual instalments. This was two per cent of Germany's annual output. The Germans protested that this was an intolerable strain on the economy which they were struggling to rebuild after the war, but their protests were ignored.

The Ruhr

The first instalment of £50 million was paid in 1921, but in 1922 nothing was paid. Ebert did his best to play for time and to negotiate concessions from the Allies, but the French in particular ran out of patience. They too had war debts to pay to the USA. So in January 1923 French and Belgian troops entered the Ruhr (quite legally under the Treaty of Versailles) and began to take what was owed to them in the form of raw materials and goods.

The results of the occupation of the Ruhr were disastrous for Germany. The government ordered the workers to carry out passive resistance, which meant to go on strike. That way, there would be nothing for the French to take away. The French reacted harshly, killing over 100 workers and expelling over 100,000 protesters from the region. More importantly, the halt in industrial production in Germany's most important region caused the collapse of the German currency.

SOURCE 9

A 1923 German poster discouraging people from buying French and Belgian goods, as long as Germany is under occupation.

SOURCE 10

A British cartoon from 1921.

SOURCE 11

A photograph taken in 1923 showing a woman using banknotes to start her fire.

Hyperinflation

Because it had no goods to trade, the government simply printed money. For the government this seemed an attractive solution. It paid off its debts in worthless marks, including war loans of over £2200 million. The great industrialists were able to pay off all their debts as well.

This set off a chain reaction. With so much money in circulation, prices and wages rocketed, but people soon realised that this money was worthless. Workers needed wheelbarrows to carry home their wages. Wages began to be paid daily instead of weekly. The price of goods could rise between joining the back of a queue in a shop and reaching the front!

Poor people suffered, but the greatest casualties were the richer Germans — those with savings. A prosperous middle-class family would find that their savings in the bank, which might have bought them a house in 1921, by 1923 would not even buy a loaf of bread. Pensioners found that their previously ample monthly pension would not even buy a cup of coffee.

SOURCE 12

	1918	0.63 marks
	1922	163 marks
January	1923	250 marks
July	1923	3465 marks
September	1923	1,512,000 marks
November	1923	201,000,000,000 marks

The rising cost of a loaf of bread in Berlin.

SOURCE 13

1921 £1 = 500 marks
Nov 1923 £1 = 14,000,000,000,000 marks

The exchange rate value of the mark in pounds.

SOURCE 14

A German banknote of 1923.

SOURCE 15

Billion mark notes were quickly handed on as though they burned one's fingers, for tomorrow one would no longer pay in notes but in bundles of notes . . . One afternoon I rang Aunt Louise's bell. The door was opened merely a crack. From the dark came an odd broken voice: 'I've used 60 billion marks' worth of gas. My milk bill is 1 million. But all I have left is 2000 marks. I don't understand any more.'

E Dobert, *Convert to Freedom*, 1941.

3 Look at Source 14. Use Source 12 to work out how much bread this banknote could buy in July 1923 and November 1923.
4 Use Sources 11–15 to describe in your own words how ordinary Germans were affected by the collapse of the mark.

FOCUS TASK

Was hyperinflation caused by the Treaty of Versailles?

Study Sources 16 and 17 carefully.

1 In what ways do they disagree about the causes of inflation?
2 How does Source 16 support the argument of Source 17?
3 In Source 15 Aunt Louise says 'I don't understand any more.' Imagine that the writer of Source 15 tries to explain the causes of inflation to Aunt Louise. What would they say? Who would they blame?
4 Whom, or what, would you blame for Germany's hyperinflation?

SOURCE 17

. . . the causes of hyperinflation were varied and complex, but the Germans did not see it that way. They blamed reparations and the Weimar Republic which had accepted them and had presided over the chaos of 1923. Many middle-class Germans never forgave the republic for the blow they believed it had dealt to them.

British historian Finlay McKichan, writing in 1992.

1 Read Source 18. Choose two of Sources 11–18 to illustrate a leaflet containing a published version of Hitler's speech. Explain your choice.
2 Explain why people might agree with Hitler that a dictatorship would solve Germany's problems.

SOURCE 18

Believe me, our misery will increase. The State itself has become the biggest swindler . . . Horrified people notice that they can starve on millions . . . we will no longer submit . . . we want a dictatorship!

Adolf Hitler attacks the Weimar government in a speech, 1924.

SOURCE 16

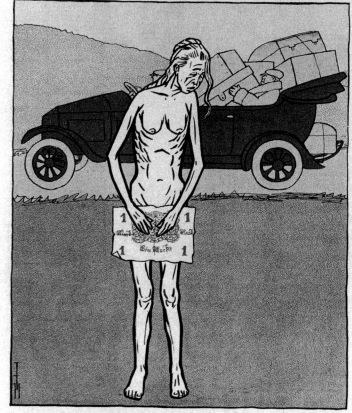

A 1920 German cartoon. Germany complains, 'My sons have taken everything away. All they have left me is a paper mark with which to cover my nakedness.'

It was clear to all, both inside and outside Germany, that the situation needed urgent action. In August 1923 a new government under Gustav Stresemann took over. He called off the passive resistance in the Ruhr. He called in the worthless marks and burned them, replacing them with a new currency called the Rentenmark. He negotiated to receive American loans under the Dawes Plan (see page 242). He even renegotiated the reparations payments (see page 146). The economic crisis was solved very quickly. Some historians suggest that this is evidence that Germany's problems were not as severe as its politicians had made out.

It was also increasingly clear, however, that the hyperinflation had done great political damage to the Weimar government. Their right-wing opponents had yet another problem to blame them for, and the government had lost the support of the middle classes.

144

FOCUS TASK

REVIEW: What was the state of the Weimar Republic in 1924?

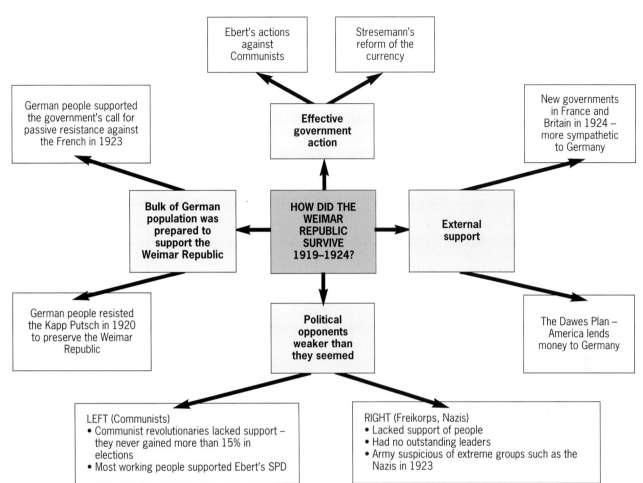

This diagram summarises how the Weimar Republic survived its problems between 1919 and 1924. On its own it presents quite a positive image of the Republic. Is it too positive, or is it about right?

Your task is to write a status report on the Weimar Republic in 1924. You could write your report as though you are advising Ebert or as a modern historian with the benefit of hindsight.

You could divide your report into sections:

a) Political opposition to Weimar

Explain whether you think <u>all</u> of the regime's political opponents had been <u>completely defeated</u> by 1924.

b) Economic problems

Explain whether you think <u>all</u> of the economic problems had been <u>completely solved</u> by 1924.

c) Popular support

Explain whether you think the regime had the <u>complete</u> support of <u>all</u> of the people of Germany.

d) Germany and the wider world

Explain
- whether you think Germany's relations with other countries had improved in 1924
- whether the problems created by the Treaty of Versailles had been resolved by 1924.

SOURCE 19

Gustav Stresemann, the most influential German politician from 1923 to 1929.

SOURCE 20

A wonderful ferment was working in Germany . . . Most Germans one met struck you as being democratic, liberal, even pacifist. One scarcely heard of Hitler or the Nazis except as jokes.

William Shirer, an American journalist, describing the mood during the Stresemann years.

SOURCE 21

A poster for one of Marlene Dietrich's films. In the 1930s she made most of her films in Hollywood.

The Weimar Republic under Stresemann

Achievements

The economy

Although Chancellor for only a few months, Stresemann was a leading member of every government from 1923 to 1929. He was a more skilful politician than Ebert, and, as a right-winger, he had wider support. He was also helped by the fact that through the 1920s the rest of Europe was gradually coming out of its post-war depression. Slowly but surely, he built up Germany's prosperity again. Under the Dawes Plan (see page 242), reparations payments were spread over a longer period, and 800 million marks in loans from the USA poured into German industry. By 1927 German industry seemed to have recovered very well. In 1928 Germany finally achieved the same levels of production as before the war. Reparations were being paid and exports were on the increase.

Culture

There was also a cultural revival in Germany. Writers and poets flourished, especially in Berlin. Artists produced powerful paintings such as Source 23. The famous Bauhaus style of architecture developed. The Bauhaus architects rejected traditional styles to create new and exciting buildings. They produced designs for anything from houses and shops to art galleries and factories. The first Bauhaus exhibition attracted 15,000 visitors.

The 1920s were a golden age for German cinema, producing one of its greatest ever international stars, Marlene Dietrich, and one of its most celebrated directors, Fritz Lang. Berlin was famous for its daring and liberated night life. Going to clubs was a major pastime. In 1927 there were 900 dance bands in Berlin alone. Under the Kaiser, there had been censorship in Germany; under the Weimar government it was removed. Cabaret artists performed songs criticising political leaders that would have been banned in the Kaiser's days. These included songs about sex that would have shocked an earlier generation of Germans.

Politics

Even politics became more stable. One politician who had been a leading opponent of Ebert in 1923 said that 'the Republic is beginning to settle and the German people are becoming reconciled to the way things are.' Source 22 shows that the parties that supported Weimar democracy did well in these years. Hitler's Nazis gained less than three per cent of the vote in the 1928 election.

SOURCE 22

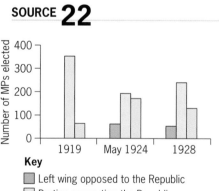

Number of MPs elected: 400, 300, 200, 100, 0

1919   May 1924   1928

Key
- Left wing opposed to the Republic
- Parties supporting the Republic
- Right wing opposed to the Republic

Support for the main political parties in Germany, 1919–28.

Foreign policy

Stresemann's greatest triumphs were in foreign policy. In 1925 he signed the Locarno Treaties (see page 240), guaranteeing not to try to change Germany's western borders with France and Belgium. As a result, in 1926 Germany was accepted into the League of Nations. Here Stresemann began to work, quietly but steadily, on reversing some of the terms of the Treaty of Versailles, particularly those concerning reparations and Germany's eastern frontiers. By the time he died in 1929, Stresemann had negotiated the Young Plan, which further lightened the reparations burden on Germany and led to the final removal of British, French and Belgian troops from the Rhineland.

The Pillars of Society, 1926, by George Grosz. His paintings criticised the old leaders of Germany.

FOCUS TASK

How far did the Weimar Republic recover after 1923?

Look back to the Focus Tasks on pages 139 and 145 which examined the state of the Weimar Republic in 1918 and 1924. You are now going to look at the state of the republic in 1928. You have to write or present another report. This time to discuss the view:

'How far has the Weimar Republic recovered?'

You could use the same headings as in 1924:
• Political opposition to Weimar
• Economic problems
• Popular support
• Germany and the wider world.
You could also add an additional section about the cultural achievements of the Weimar Republic.

Mention failings *and* achievements in your report. You could give each section a mark out of ten.

Finally, you need to decide on an overall judgement: in your opinion, how far *had* the Weimar Republic recovered?

In your answer, do remember that, in the view of many historians, it was probably a major achievement for the Weimar Republic just to have survived until 1928!

Problems

Economy

The economic boom in Weimar Germany was precarious. The US loans could be called in at short notice, which would cause ruin in Germany.

The main economic winners in Germany were big businesses (such as the steel and chemicals industries) which controlled about half of Germany's industrial production. Other winners were big landowners, particularly if they owned land in towns – the value of land in Berlin rose by 700 per cent in this period. The workers in the big industries gained as well. Most Weimar governments were sympathetic towards the unions, which led to improved pay and conditions.

The main losers were the peasant farmers and sections of the middle classes. The peasant farmers had increased production during the war. In peacetime, they found themselves overproducing. They had mortgages to pay but not enough demand for the food they produced. Many small business owners became disillusioned during this period. Small shopkeepers saw their businesses threatened by large department stores (many of which were owned by Jews). A university lecturer in 1913 earned ten times as much as a coal miner. In the 1920s he earned twice as much. These people began to feel that the Weimar government offered them little.

Culture

The Weimar culture was colourful and exciting to many. However, in many of Germany's villages and country towns, the culture of the cities seemed to represent a moral decline, made worse by American immigrants and Jewish artists and musicians. Organisations such as the Wandervogel movement were a reaction to Weimar's culture. The Wandervogel wanted a return to simple country values and wanted to see more help for the countryside and less decadence in the towns. It was a powerful feeling which the Nazis successfully harnessed in later years.

SOURCE **24**

A Wandervogel camp in the 1920s.

Politics

Despite the relative stability of Weimar politics in this period, both the Nazis and Communists were building up their party organisations. Even during these stable years there were four different chancellors and around 30 per cent of the vote regularly went to parties opposed to the Republic. Most serious of all, the German people elected Hindenburg as President in 1926. He was opposed to democracy and wrote to the Kaiser in exile for approval before he took up the post!

Foreign policy

There was also the question of international relations. Nationalists attacked Stresemann for joining the League of Nations and for signing the Locarno Pact, seeing it as an acceptance of the Treaty of Versailles. Communists also attacked Locarno, seeing it as part of a plot against the Communist government in the USSR. Germany was still a troubled place.

Hitler and the Nazis

Stresemann's government succeeded in stabilising Germany. However, as you have already seen, the extremist opponents of the Weimar government had not disappeared. Through the 1920s they were organising and regrouping, waiting for their chance to win power.

One of the most important of these extremist groups was the Nazi Party. You are now going to look back at what it had been doing since 1919.

The Nazis began as the German Workers' Party, led by Anton Drexler. In 1919 Adolf Hitler joined the party. Drexler soon realised that Hitler had great talent and within months he had put him in charge of propaganda and the political ideas of the party. In 1920 the party announced its Twenty-Five Point Programme (see Factfile), and renamed itself the National Socialist German Workers' Party, or Nazis for short.

SOURCE 25

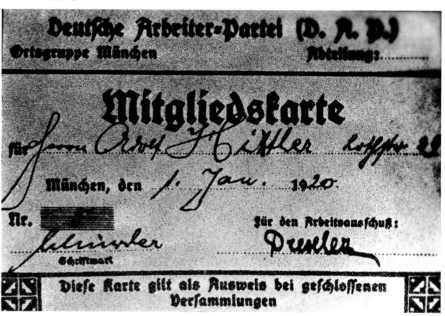

Hitler's renewed membership card of the German Worker's Party, issued 1 January 1920.

In 1921 Hitler removed Drexler as leader. Hitler's energy, commitment and above all his power as a speaker were soon attracting attention.

SOURCE 26

The most active political force in Bavaria at the present time is the National Socialist Party . . . It has recently acquired a political influence quite disproportionate to its actual numerical strength . . . Adolf Hitler from the very first has been the dominating force in the movement and the personality of this man has undoubtedly been one of the most important factors contributing to its success . . . His ability to influence a popular assembly is uncanny.

American intelligence report on political activities in Germany, 1922.

SOURCE 27

Hitler knew how to whip up those crowds jammed closely in a dense cloud of cigarette smoke – not by argument, but by his manner: the roaring and especially the power of his repetitions delivered in a certain infectious rhythm . . . He would draw up a list of existing evils and imaginary abuses and after listing them, in higher and higher crescendo, he screamed: 'And whose fault is it? It's all . . . the fault . . . of the Jews!'

A person who went to Nazi meetings describes the impact of Hitler's speeches. From *A Part of Myself: Portrait of an Epoch*, by C Zuckmayer.

'Power!' screamed Adolf. 'We must have power!' 'Before we gain it,' I replied firmly, 'let us decide what we propose to do with it.'

Hitler, who even then could hardly bear contradiction, thumped the table and barked: 'Power first – afterwards we can act as circumstances dictate.'

Leading Nazi Otto Strasser recalls a conversation with Hitler in the early 1920s.

Hitler had a clear and simple appeal. He stirred nationalist passions in his audiences. He gave them scapegoats to blame for Germany's problems: the Allies, the Versailles Treaty, the 'November Criminals' (the Socialist politicians who signed the Treaty), the Communists and the Jews.

His meetings were so successful that his opponents tried to disrupt them. To counter this, he set up the SA, also known as storm troopers or brownshirts, in 1921. These hired thugs protected Hitler's meetings but also disrupted those of other parties.

By 1923 the Nazis were still very much a minority party, but Hitler had given them a high profile.

It is 1923. Use the information and sources on pages 148–49 to write a newspaper article about the rise of Hitler and the Nazi Party. Your opening sentences could be:

'In recent months, a new force seems to be arising in German politics. Adolf Hitler and the Nazis have hit the headlines with their meetings, banners and radical ideas. What makes this man successful? . . .'

Your article should tell readers about:
• Hitler's background
• his qualities
• what he and the Nazis believe.

The Munich Putsch, 1923

By November 1923 Hitler believed that the moment had come for him to topple the Weimar government. The government was preoccupied with the economic crisis. Stresemann had just called off Germany's passive resistance in the Ruhr (see pages 142–44). On 8 November, Hitler hijacked a local government meeting and announced he was taking over the government of Bavaria. He was joined by the old war hero Ludendorff.

Nazi storm troopers began taking over official buildings. The next day, however, the Weimar government forces hit back. Police rounded up the storm troopers and in a brief exchange of shots 16 Nazis were killed by the police. The rebellion broke up in chaos. Hitler escaped in a car, while Ludendorff and others stayed to face the armed police.

Hitler had miscalculated the mood of the German people. In the short term, the Munich Putsch was a disaster for him. People did not rise up to support him. He and other leading Nazis were arrested and charged with treason. At the trial, however, Hitler gained enormous publicity for himself and his ideas, as his every word was reported in the newspapers.

In fact, Hitler so impressed the judges that he and his accomplices got off very lightly. Ludendorff was freed altogether and Hitler was given only five years in prison, even though the legal guidelines said that high treason should carry a life sentence. In the end, Hitler only served nine months of the sentence and did so in great comfort in Landsberg castle.

The Bavarian Ministry is removed. I propose that a Bavarian government be formed consisting of a Regent and a Prime Minister invested with dictatorial powers . . . The government of the November Criminals and the Reich president are declared to be removed . . . I propose that, until accounts have been finally settled with the November Criminals, the direction of policy in the National Government be taken over by me . . .

Hitler declares the revolution, 8 November 1923.

1 Read Source 29. What was Hitler trying to achieve through the Munich Putsch?

I alone bear the responsibility but I am not a criminal because of that . . . There is no such thing as high treason against the traitors of 1918 . . . I feel myself the best of Germans who wanted the best for the German people.

Hitler at his trial.

What did the Nazis stand for in the 1920s?

Imagine the judge at Hitler's trial has asked Hitler the question: 'What do the Nazis really stand for?' Write a reply that Hitler might have given to the judge.
Use Sources, the Profile and Factfile as well as the text. Mention:
• the Weimar Constitution
• the Treaty of Versailles
• the German people
and anything else that you think Hitler might consider important.

SOURCE 31

When I resume active work, it will be necessary to pursue a new policy. Instead of working to achieve power by armed conspiracy we shall have to take hold of our noses and enter the Reichstag against the Catholic and Marxist deputies. If out-voting them takes longer than out-shooting them, at least the results will be guaranteed by their own constitution. Any lawful process is slow. Sooner or later we shall have a majority and after that we shall have Germany.

Hitler, writing while in prison in 1923.

FACTFILE

Hitler's views

In *Mein Kampf* and his later writings, Hitler set out the main Nazi beliefs:

★ National Socialism: This stood for loyalty to Germany, racial purity, equality and state control of the economy.
★ Racism: The Aryans (white Europeans) were the Master Race. All other races and especially the Jews were inferior.
★ Armed force: Hitler believed that war and struggle were an essential part of the development of a healthy Aryan race.
★ Living space (*Lebensraum*): Germany needed to expand as its people were hemmed in. This expansion would be mainly at the expense of Russia and Poland.
★ The Führer: Debate and democratic discussion produced weakness. Strength lay in total loyalty to the leader (the Führer).

1 Read Source 32. List the five demands made by Goebbels.
2 Would you say this source appeals more to the hearts of German people than to their minds? Support your answer with evidence from the source.

The Nazis in the wilderness, 1924–1929

Hitler used his time in prison to write a book, *Mein Kampf* (My Struggle), which clarified and presented his ideas about Germany's future. It was also while in prison that he came to the conclusion that the Nazis would not be able to seize power by force. They would have to work within the democratic system to achieve power but, once in power, they could destroy that system.

As soon as he was released from prison, Hitler set about rebuilding the Nazi Party so that it could take power through democratic means. He saw the Communists building up their strength through youth organisations and recruitment drives. Soon the Nazis were doing the same.

They fought the Reichstag elections for the first time in May 1924 and won 32 seats. Encouraged by this, Hitler created a network of local Nazi parties which in turn set up the Hitler Youth, the Nazi Students' League and similar organisations.

SOURCE 32

The German people is an enslaved people. We have had all our sovereign rights taken from us. We are just good enough that international capital allows us to fill its money sacks with interest payments. That and only that is the result of a centuries-long history of heroism. Have we deserved it? No, and no again! Therefore we demand that a struggle against this condition of shame and misery begin, and that the men in whose hands we put our fate must use every means to break the chain of slavery.

Three million people lack work and sustenance. The officials, it is true, work to conceal the misery. They speak of measures and silver linings. Things are getting steadily better for them, and steadily worse for us. The illusion of freedom, peace and prosperity that we were promised when we wanted to take our fate in our own hands is vanishing. Only complete collapse of our people can follow from these irresponsible policies.

Thus we demand the right of work and a decent living for every working German.

While the front soldier was fighting in the trenches to defend his Fatherland, some Eastern Jewish profiteer robbed him of hearth and home. The Jew lives in palaces and the proletarian, the front soldier, lives in holes that do not deserve to be called 'homes'. That is neither necessary nor unavoidable, rather an injustice that cries out to the heavens. A government that does nothing is useless and must vanish, the sooner the better.

Therefore we demand homes for German soldiers and workers. If there is not enough money to build them, drive the foreigners out so that Germans can live on German soil.

Our people is growing, others diminishing. It will mean the end of our history if a cowardly and lazy policy takes from us the posterity that will one day be called upon to fulfil our historical mission.

Therefore we demand land on which to grow the grain that will feed our children.

While we dreamed and chased strange and unreachable fantasies, others stole our property. Today some say this was an act of God. Not so. Money was transferred from the pockets of the poor to the pockets of the rich. That is cheating, shameless, vile cheating!

A government presides over this misery that in the interests of peace and order one cannot really discuss. We leave it to others to judge whether it represents Germany's interests or those of our capitalist tormentors.

We, however, demand a government of national labour, statesmen who are men and whose aim is the creation of a German state.

These days anyone has the right to speak in Germany – the Jew, the Frenchman, the Englishman, the League of Nations, the conscience of the world and the Devil knows who else. Everyone but the German worker. He has to shut up and work. Every four years he elects a new set of torturers, and everything stays the same. That is unjust and treasonous. We need tolerate it no longer. We have the right to demand that only Germans who build this state may speak, those whose fate is bound to the fate of their Fatherland.

Therefore we demand the annihilation of the system of exploitation! Up with the German worker's state! Germany for the Germans!

A pamphlet called 'We demand', written in 1927 by Nazi propaganda expert Joseph Goebbels.

As you can see from Source 32, by 1927 the Nazis were still trying to appeal to German workers, as they had when the party was first founded. The results of the 1928 elections convinced the Nazis that they had to look elsewhere for support. The Nazis gained only 12 Reichstag seats and only a quarter of the Communist vote. Although their anti-semitic policies gained them some support, they had failed to win over the workers. Workers with radical political views were more likely to support the Communists. The great majority of workers supported the socialist Social Democratic Party (SPD), as they had done in every election since 1919. Indeed, despite the Nazis' arguments that workers were exploited, urban industrial workers actually felt that they were doing rather well in Weimar Germany in the years up to 1929.

Other groups in society were doing less well. The Nazis found that they gained more support from groups such as the peasant farmers in northern Germany and middle-class shopkeepers and small business people in country towns. Unlike Britain, Germany still had a large rural population who lived and worked on the land – probably about 35 per cent of the entire population. They were not sharing in Weimar Germany's economic prosperity. The Nazis highlighted the importance of the peasants in their plans for Germany, promising to help agriculture if they came to power. They praised the peasants as racially pure Germans. Nazi propaganda also contrasted the supposedly clean and simple life of the peasants with that of the allegedly corrupt, immoral crime-ridden cities (for which they blamed the Jews). The fact that the Nazis despised Weimar culture also gained them support among some conservative people in the towns, who saw Weimar's flourishing art, literature and film achievements as immoral.

SOURCE 33

At one of the early congresses I was sitting surrounded by thousands of SA men. As Hitler spoke I was most interested at the shouts and more often the muttered exclamations of the men around me, who were mainly workmen or lower-middle-class types. 'He speaks for me . . . Ach, Gott, he knows how I feel' . . . One man in particular struck me as he leant forward with his head in his hands, and with a sort of convulsive sob said: 'Gott sei Dank [God be thanked], he understands.'

E Amy Buller, *Darkness over Germany*, published in 1943. Buller was an anti-Nazi German teacher.

SOURCE 34

A Nazi election poster from 1928, saying 'Work, freedom and bread! Vote for the National Socialists.'

In 1925 Hitler enlarged the SA. About 55 per cent of the SA came from the ranks of the unemployed. Many were ex-servicemen from the war. He also set up a new group called the SS. The SS were similar to the SA but were fanatically loyal to Hitler personally. Membership of the party rose to over 100,000 by 1928.

Hitler appointed Joseph Goebbels to take charge of Nazi propaganda. Goebbels was highly efficient at spreading the Nazi message. He and Hitler believed that the best way to reach what they called 'the masses' was by appealing to their feelings rather than by rational argument. Goebbels produced posters, leaflets, films and radio broadcasts; he organised rallies; he set up 'photo opportunities'.

Despite these shifting policies and priorities, there was no electoral breakthrough for the Nazis. Even after all their hard work, in 1928 they were still a fringe minority party who had the support of less than three per cent of the population. They were the smallest party with fewer seats than the Communists. The prosperity of the Stresemann years and Stresemann's success in foreign policy made Germans uninterested in extreme politics.

FOCUS TASK

1 Look back at your answer to the Focus Task on page 149. If Hitler had been asked the same question, 'What do the Nazis really stand for?', in 1928, what would have changed?
2 Do you think Hitler would have liked your asking him this question? Explain your answer.

The Depression and the rise of the Nazis

In 1929 the American stock market crashed and sent the USA into a disastrous economic depression. In a very short time, countries around the world began to feel the effects of this depression. Germany was particularly badly affected. American bankers and businessmen lost huge amounts of money in the crash. To pay off their debts they asked German banks to repay the money they had borrowed. The result was economic collapse in Germany. Businesses went bankrupt, workers were laid off and unemployment rocketed.

SOURCE **35**

Upper Silesia in 1932: unemployed miners and their families moved into shacks in a shanty town because they had no money to pay their rent.

SOURCE **36**

No one knew how many there were of them. They completely filled the streets. They stood or lay about in the streets as if they had taken root there. They sat or lay on the pavements or in the roadway and gravely shared out scraps of newspapers among themselves.

An eyewitness describes the unemployed vagrants in Germany in 1932.

The Depression was a worldwide problem. It was not just Germany that suffered. Nor was the Weimar government the only government having difficulties in solving the problem of unemployment. However, because Germany had been so dependent on American loans, and because it still had to pay reparations to the Allies, the problems were most acute in Germany.

In addition, it seemed that the Weimar Constitution, with its careful balance of power, made firm and decisive action by the government very difficult indeed (see Factfile, page 139).

1 Draw a diagram to show how the Wall Street Crash in New York could lead to miners losing their jobs in Silesia.

SOURCE **37**

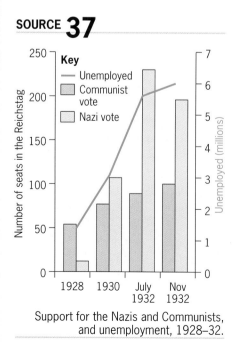

Key
— Unemployed
☐ Communist vote
☐ Nazi vote

Support for the Nazis and Communists, and unemployment, 1928–32.

Enter the Nazis!

Hitler's ideas now had a special relevance:

- Is the Weimar government indecisive? Then Germany needs a strong leader!
- Are reparations adding to Germany's problems? Then kick out the Treaty of Versailles!
- Is unemployment a problem? Let the unemployed join the army, build Germany's armaments and be used for public works like road building!

The Nazis' Twenty-Five Points (see page 148) were very attractive to those most vulnerable to the Depression: the unemployed, the elderly and the middle classes. Hitler offered them culprits to blame for Germany's troubles – the Allies, the 'November Criminals' and the Jews. None of these messages was new and they had not won support for the Nazis in the Stresemann years. The difference now was that the democratic parties simply could not get Germany back to work.

In the 1930 elections the Nazis got 107 seats. In November 1932 they got nearly 200. They did not yet have an overall majority, but they were the biggest single party.

Why did the Nazis succeed in elections?

When the Nazis were well established in power in Germany in the 1930s, their propaganda chief, Goebbels, created his own version of the events of 1929–33 that brought Hitler to power. In this version, it was Hitler's destiny to become Germany's leader, and the German people finally came to recognise this. How valid was this view? On pages 153–55 you are going to see if you agree with Goebbels.

SOURCE 38

My mother saw a storm trooper parade in the streets of Heidelberg. The sight of discipline in a time of chaos, the impression of energy in an atmosphere of universal hopelessness seems to have won her over.

Albert Speer, writing in 1931. Later, he was to become an important and powerful Nazi leader.

SOURCE 39

A poster for a 1931 midsummer festival organised by the Nazi Party. The poster proclaims 'Against Versailles'.

SOURCE 40

A Nazi Party rally in Frankfurt in 1932.

Nazi campaigning

There is no doubt that Nazi campaign methods were modern and effective. They relied on generalised slogans rather than detailed policies. They talked about uniting the people of Germany behind one leader. They also talked about going back to traditional values, though they were never very clear about what this meant in terms of policies. This made it hard to criticise them. When they *were* criticised for a specific policy, they were quite likely to drop it. (For example, when industrialists expressed concern about Nazi plans to nationalise industry, they simply dropped the policy.) The Nazis repeated at every opportunity that they believed Jews, Communists, Weimar politicians and the Treaty of Versailles were the causes of Germany's problems. They expressed contempt for Weimar's democratic system and said that it was unable to solve Germany's economic problems.

Their posters and pamphlets could be found everywhere. Their rallies impressed people with their energy, enthusiasm and sheer size.

At this time, there were frequent street battles between Communist gangs and the police. Everywhere large unruly groups of unemployed workers gathered on street corners. In contrast, the SA and SS gave an impression of discipline and order. Many people felt the country needed this kind of order. They welcomed the fact that the SA were prepared to fight the Communists (page 155). The SA were better organised and usually had the support of the police and army when they beat up opponents and disrupted meetings and rallies.

The Nazis also organised soup kitchens and provided shelter in hostels for the unemployed.

SOURCE 41

The Duties of German Communist Party volunteers

Unselfishly they help the farmers to dry the harvest.

Particular detachments are responsible for improving transport.

They work nights and overtime getting together useful equipment.

They increase their fitness for the fatherland with target practice.

An English translation of a 1931 Nazi election poster.

SOURCE 42

Our opponents accuse us National Socialists, and me in particular, of being intolerant and quarrelsome. They say that we don't want to work with other parties. They say the National Socialists are not German at all, because they refuse to work with other political parties. So is it typically German to have thirty political parties? I have to admit one thing – these gentlemen are quite right. We are intolerant. I have given myself this one goal – to sweep these thirty political parties out of Germany.

Hitler speaking at an election rally, July 1932.

ACTIVITY

On page 148 you wrote an article about Hitler and the Nazis in 1923. It is now late 1932, almost ten years on. Write a follow-up article explaining what has changed in that time.

SOURCE 44

*He began to speak and I immediately disliked him. I didn't know then what he would later become. I found him rather comical, with his funny moustache. He had a scratchy voice and a rather strange appearance, and he shouted so much. He was shouting in this small room, and what he was saying was very simplistic. I thought he wasn't quite normal.
I found him spooky.*

An eyewitness account of one of Hitler's meetings.

The Nazis' greatest campaigning asset was Hitler. He was a powerful speaker. He was years ahead of his time as a communicator. Hitler ran for president in 1932. He got 13 million votes to Hindenburg's 19 million. Despite Hitler's defeat, the campaign raised his profile hugely. Using films, radio and records he brought his message to millions. He travelled by plane on a hectic tour of rallies all over Germany. He appeared as a dynamic man of the moment, the leader of a modern party with modern ideas. At the same time, he was able to appear to be a man of the people, someone who knew and understood the people and their problems.

Nazi support rocketed. For example, in Neidenburg in East Prussia Nazi support rose from 2.3 per cent in 1928 to over 25 per cent in 1931, even though the town had no local Nazi Party and Hitler never went there.

SOURCE 43

A Nazi election poster from July 1932. The Nazis proclaim 'We build!' and promise to provide work, freedom and bread. They accuse the opposing parties of planning to use terror, corruption, lies and other strategies as the basis for their government.

'Negative cohesion'

As Source 44 shows, not everyone was taken in by Nazi campaigning methods and Hitler's magnetism. But even some of the sceptics supported the Nazis. The historian Gordon Craig (see Source 66 on page 181) believed that this was because of something he called 'negative cohesion'. This meant that people supported the Nazis not because they shared Nazi views (that would be positive cohesion) but because they shared Nazi fears and dislikes. They cohered (joined together) over negatives not positives: if you hate what I hate, then you can't be all bad!

Disillusionment with democracy

Perhaps the biggest negative factor was a shared dislike of democracy in Weimar Germany. Politicians seemed unable to tackle the problems of the Depression. When the Depression began to bite in 1930 the Chancellor, Heinrich Brüning, pursued a tough economic policy. He cut government spending and welfare benefits. He urged Germans to make sacrifices. Some historians think that he was deliberately making the situation worse in order to get the international community to cancel reparations payments. Other historians think that he was afraid of hyperinflation recurring as in 1923. In protest, the SPD (still the main party in the Reichstag) pulled out of the government. To get his measures passed, Brüning relied on President Hindenburg to use his powers under Article 48 (see Factfile, page 139) to bypass the Reichstag.

Brüning and Hindenburg decided to call new elections in 1930. This was a disastrous decision, as it gave the Nazis the opportunity to exploit the fear and discontent in Germany and make the gains you have seen in Source 37. The new elections resulted in another divided Reichstag, and the problems continued into 1931 and 1932. The impression was that democracy involved politicians squabbling over which job they would get in the Cabinet. Meanwhile, they did nothing about the real world, where unemployment was heading towards 6 million and the average German's income had fallen by 40 per cent since 1929. The Reichstag met fewer and fewer times (for only five days in 1932). Brüning had to continue to rely on Hindenburg's using his emergency powers, bypassing the democratic process altogether.

The Communist threat

As the crisis deepened, Communist support was rising too. The Nazis turned this to their advantage. 'Fear of Communism' was another shared negative. The Communist Red Fighting League broke up opposition party meetings, just like the SA. They fought street battles with police. So, out on the streets, the Nazi SA storm troopers met Communist violence with their own violence.

Many middle-class business owners had read about how the Communists in the USSR had discriminated against people like them. The owners of the big industries feared the Communists because of their plans to introduce state control of businesses. The industrialists were also concerned about the growing strength of Germany's trade unions. They felt the Nazis would combat these threats and some began to put money into Nazi campaign funds.

All farmers were alarmed by the Communists. They had read about Communist farming policies in the USSR where the Soviet government had taken over all of the land. Millions of peasants had been killed or imprisoned in the process. In contrast, the Nazis promised to help Germany's desperately struggling small farmers.

Decadence

As for modern decadent Weimar culture – the Nazis could count on all those who felt traditional German values were under threat. The Nazis talked about restoring these old-fashioned values.

The Social Democratic Party made a grave mistake in thinking that German people would not fall for these vague promises and accusations. They underestimated the fear and anger that German people felt towards the Weimar Republic.

SOURCE 45

The so-called race of poets and thinkers is hurrying with flags flying towards dictatorship . . . the radicalism of the Right [Nazis] has unleashed a strong radicalism on the Left [Communists]. The Communists have made gains almost everywhere. The situation is such that half the German people have declared themselves against the present state.

The Reich Interior Minister commenting on the rise of the Nazis and the Communists in 1932.

FOCUS TASK

How did the Depression help the Nazis?

Do you agree with Goebbels' view that people rallied to support Hitler for positive reasons – or do you think that Gordon Craig was right that people supported the Nazis out of fear and disillusionment?

Work through questions 1–4 to help you make up your mind.

1 Look carefully at Sources 37–41 and 43. For each source, write two sentences explaining whether you think it is evidence that:
   • supports the view of Goebbels
   • supports the view of Craig
   • could be used to support either interpretation.
2 Now work through the text and other sources on pages 152–55. Make a list of examples and evidence that seem to support either viewpoint.
3 Decide how far you agree with each of the following statements and give them a score on a scale of 1–5.
   • Very few people fully supported the Nazis.
   • The key factor was the economic depression. Without it, the Nazis would have remained a minority fringe party.
   • The politicians of the Weimar Republic were mainly responsible for the rise of the Nazis.
4 Write a short paragraph explaining your score for each statement.

How did Hitler become Chancellor in 1933?

After the Reichstag elections of July 1932 the Nazis were the largest single party (with 230 seats) but not a majority party. Hitler demanded the post of Chancellor from the President, the old war hero Hindenburg. However, Hindenburg was suspicious of Hitler and refused. He allowed the current Chancellor Franz von Papen (an old friend of Hindenburg) to carry on as Chancellor. He then used his emergency powers to pass the measures that von Papen had hoped would solve the unemployment problem.

However, von Papen was soon in trouble. He had virtually no support at all in the Reichstag and so called yet another election in November 1932. The Nazis again came out as the largest party, although their share of the vote fell.

Hitler regarded the election as a disaster for the Nazis. He had lost more than 2 million votes along with 38 seats in the Reichstag. The signs were that the Hitler flood tide had finally turned. The Nazis started to run out of funds. Hitler is said to have threatened suicide.

Hindenburg again refused to appoint Hitler as Chancellor. In December 1932 he chose Kurt von Schleicher, one of his own advisers and a bitter rival of von Papen. Von Papen remained as an adviser to Hindenburg.

Within a month, however, von Schleicher too was forced to resign. By this time it was clear that the Weimar system of government was not working. In one sense, Hindenburg had already overthrown the principles of democracy by running Germany with emergency powers. If he was to rescue the democratic system, he needed a Chancellor who actually had support in the Reichstag.

Through January 1933 Hindenburg and von Papen met secretly with industrialists, army leaders and politicians. And on 30 January, to everyone's great surprise, they offered Hitler the post of Chancellor. Why did they do this? With only a few Nazis in the Cabinet and von Papen as Vice Chancellor, they were confident that they could limit Hitler's influence and resist his extremist demands. The idea was that the policies would be made by the Cabinet, which was filled with conservatives like von Papen. Hitler would be there to get support in the Reichstag for those policies and to control the Communists. So Hitler ended up as Chancellor not because of the will of the German people, but through a behind-the-scenes deal by some German aristocrats. Both Hindenburg and von Papen were sure that they could control Hitler. Both were very wrong.

SOURCE 46

The majority of Germans never voted for the Nazis.

The Nazis made it clear they would destroy democracy and all who stood in their way. Why then didn't their enemies join together to stop Hitler? . . . Had the Communists and Socialists joined forces they would probably have been strong enough both in the Reichstag and on the streets to have blocked the Nazis. The fact was that by 1932–3 there were simply not enough Germans who believed in democracy and individual freedom to save the Weimar Republic.

S Williams, in *The Rise and Fall of Hitler's Germany*, published in 1986, assesses the reasons for Hitler's success.

SOURCE 47

The Nazis celebrate Hitler's appointment as Chancellor in 1933.

A British cartoonist comments on Hitler's ambitions.

1 Look at Source 48. Do you think Hitler would be pleased by this portrayal of him? Explain your answer.

FOCUS TASK

How did Hitler become Chancellor in 1933?

Here is a list of factors that helped Hitler come to power.

Nazi strengths
- Hitler's speaking skills
- Propaganda campaigns
- Violent treatment of their opponents
- Their criticisms of the Weimar system of government
- Nazi policies
- Support from big business

Opponents' weaknesses
- Failure to deal with the Depression
- Failure to co-operate with one another
- Attitudes of Germans to the democratic parties

Other factors
- Weaknesses of the Weimar Republic
- Scheming of Hindenburg and von Papen
- The impact of the Depression
- The Treaty of Versailles
- Memories of the problems of 1923

1 For each factor, write down one example of how it helped Hitler.
2 Give each factor a mark out of 10 for its importance in bringing Hitler to power.
3 Choose what you think are the five most important factors and write a short paragraph on each, explaining why you have chosen it.
4 If you took away any of those factors, would Hitler still have become Chancellor?
5 Were any of those five factors also present in the 1920s?
6 If so, explain why the Nazis were not successful in the 1920s.

6.2 **Hitler's Germany**

THE TEMPORARY TRIANGLE.

A British cartoon from early 1933. Hitler, as Chancellor, is being supported by Hindenburg and Von Papen. He needed their support and, although they were not happy with the idea, they needed his popularity with the masses.

The Reichstag in flames, 1933.

1 Some people suggest that the Nazis burnt down the Reichstag themselves. Explain why the Nazis might have wanted to do this.

Hitler's dictatorship

It is easy to forget, but when Hitler became Chancellor in January 1933 he was in a very precarious position (see Source 1). Few people thought he would hold on to power for long. Even fewer thought that by the summer of 1934 he would be the supreme dictator of Germany. He achieved this through a clever combination of methods – some legal, others dubious. He also managed to defeat or reach agreements with those who could have stopped him.

The Reichstag Fire

Once he was Chancellor, Hitler took steps to complete a Nazi takeover of Germany. He called another election for March 1933 to try to get an overall Nazi majority in the Reichstag. Germany's cities again witnessed speeches, rallies, processions and street fighting. Hitler was using the same tactics as in previous elections, but now he had the resources of state media and control of the streets. Even so, success was in the balance. Then on 27 February there was a dramatic development; the Reichstag building burnt down. Hitler blamed the Communists and declared that the fire was the beginning of a Communist uprising. He demanded special emergency powers to deal with the situation and was given them by President Hindenburg. The Nazis used these powers to arrest Communists, break up meetings and frighten voters.

There have been many theories about what caused the fire, including that it was an accident, the work of a madman, or a Communist plot. Many Germans at the time thought that the Nazis might have started the fire themselves.

Nazi storm troopers arrest suspected Communists, 1933.

The defeat in 1918 did not depress me as greatly as the present state of affairs. It is shocking how day after day naked acts of violence, breaches of the law, barbaric opinions appear quite undisguised as official decree. The Socialist papers are permanently banned. The 'Liberals' tremble. The Berliner Tageblatt *was recently banned for two days; that can't happen to the* Dresdener Neueste Nachrichten, *it is completely devoted to the government . . . I can no longer get rid of the feeling of disgust and shame. And no one stirs; everyone trembles, keeps out of sight.*

An extract for 17 March 1933 from the diary of Victor Klemperer, a Jew who lived in Dresden and recorded his experiences from 1933 to 1941.

FACTFILE

Hitler's consolidation of power

1933

★ **30 January** Hitler appointed Chancellor; Goering Minister of Interior.

★ **17 February** Goering ordered local police forces to co-operate with the SA and SS.

★ **27 February** Reichstag fire. Arrest of 4000 Communists and other Nazi opponents on the same night.

★ **28 February** Emergency Decree issued by Hindenburg at Hitler's request. The decree allowed
  – police to arrest suspects and hold them without trial
  – Hitler to take over regional governments (most were taken over by mid March).

★ **5 March** Reichstag elections: government used control of radio and police to intimidate opponents. Nazis attracted many new voters with election slogan 'The battle against Marxism'. Won 52 per cent of vote.

★ **13 March** Goebbels appointed head of new Ministry for Propaganda. Took control of all media.

★ **24 March** The Enabling Act
  – allowed Hitler to pass decrees without the President's involvement
  – made Hitler a legal dictator.

★ **7 April** Civil Service administration, courts, and education purged of 'alien elements', i.e. Jews and other opponents of the Nazis.

★ **1 May** Workers granted May Day holiday.

★ **2 May** Trade unions banned; all workers to belong to new German Labour Front (DAF).

★ **9 June** Employment Law: major programme of public works (e.g. road building) to create jobs.

★ **14 July** Law against the Formation of New Parties: Germany became a one-party state.

★ **20 July** Concordat (agreement) between the state and the Roman Catholic Church: government protected religious freedom; Church banned from political activity.

1934

★ **January** All state governments taken over.

★ **30 June** Night of the Long Knives.

★ **August** On death of Hindenburg, Hitler became Führer. German armed forces swore oath of loyalty to him.

2 Explain why the Enabling Act was so important to Hitler.

3 Why might Hitler have executed people such as von Schleicher who were nothing to do with the SA?

4 Why do you think Hitler chose the support of the army over the support of the SA?

SOURCE 5

Nazi Party	*288 seats*
Social Democrats (SPD)	*120 seats*
Communist Party	*81 seats*
Catholic Centre Party	*73 seats*
Others	*85 seats*

Election results, March 1933.

In the election, the Nazis won their largest-ever share of the votes and, with the support of the smaller Nationalist Party, Hitler had an overall majority. Using the SA and SS, he then intimidated the Reichstag into passing the Enabling Act which allowed him to make laws without consulting the Reichstag. Only the SPD voted against him. Following the election, the Communists had been banned. The Catholic Centre Party decided to co-operate with the Nazis rather than be treated like the Communists. In return, they retained control of Catholic schools. The Enabling Act made Hitler a virtual dictator. For the next four years if he wanted a new law he could just pass it. There was nothing President Hindenburg or anyone else could do.

Even now, Hitler was not secure. He had seen how the Civil Service, the judiciary, the army and other important groups had undermined the Weimar Republic. He was not yet strong enough to remove his opponents, so he set about a clever policy that mixed force, concessions and compromise (see Factfile).

The Night of the Long Knives

Hitler acted quickly. Within a year any opponents (or potential opponents) of the Nazis had either left Germany or been taken to special concentration camps run by the SS. Other political parties were banned.

Hitler was still not entirely secure, however. The leading officers in the army were not impressed by him and were particularly suspicious of Hitler's SA and its leader Ernst Röhm. The SA was a badly disciplined force and, what's more, Röhm talked of making the SA into a second German army. Hitler himself was also suspicious of Röhm. Hitler feared that Röhm's control over the 4 million SA men made him a potentially dangerous rival.

Hitler had to choose between the army and the SA. He made his choice and acted ruthlessly. On the weekend of 29–30 June squads of SS men broke into the homes of Röhm and other leading figures in the SA and arrested them. Hitler accused Röhm of plotting to overthrow and murder him. Over the weekend Röhm and possibly as many as 400 others were executed. These included the former Chancellor von Schleicher, a fierce critic of Hitler, and others who actually had no connection with Röhm. Although the killings took place over the whole weekend, this purge came to be known as the Night of the Long Knives.

Hindenburg thanked Hitler for his 'determined action which has nipped treason in the bud'. The army said it was well satisfied with the events of the weekend.

The SA was not disbanded afterwards. It remained as a Nazi paramilitary organisation, but was very much subordinate to the SS and never regained the influence of 1933. Many of its members were absorbed by the army and the SS.

Der Führer

Soon after the Night of the Long Knives, Hindenburg died and Hitler took over as Supreme Leader (Führer) of Germany. On 2 August 1934 the entire army swore an oath of personal loyalty to Adolf Hitler as Führer of Germany. The army agreed to stay out of politics and to serve Hitler. In return, Hitler spent vast sums on rearmament, brought back conscription and made plans to make Germany a great military power again.

Nazi control of Germany, 1933–1945

There was supposed to be no room for opposition of any kind in Nazi Germany. The aim was to create a totalitarian state. In a totalitarian state there can be no rival parties, no political debate. Ordinary citizens must divert their whole energy into serving the state and to doing what its leader wants.

The Nazis had a powerful range of organisations and weapons that they used to control Germany and terrorise Germans into submission.

The SS

SOURCE 6

SS guards after taking over the Berlin broadcasting station in 1933.

SOURCE 7

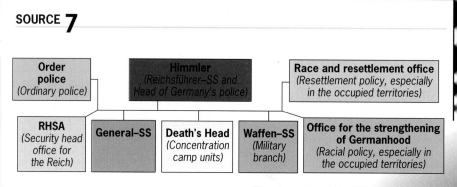

The elements of the SS during wartime.

The SS was formed in 1925 from fanatics loyal to Hitler. After virtually destroying the SA in 1934, it grew into a huge organisation with many different responsibilities. It was led by Heinrich Himmler. SS men were of course Aryans, very highly trained and totally loyal to Hitler. Under Himmler, the SS had primary responsibility for destroying opposition to Nazism and carrying out the racial policies of the Nazis.

Two important sub-divisions of the SS were the Death's Head units and the Waffen-SS. The Death's Head units were responsible for the concentration camps and the slaughter of the Jews. The Waffen-SS were special SS armoured regiments which fought alongside the regular army.

This chart gives the impression that Nazi Germany was run like a well-oiled machine: there to do the will of the Führer! Modern research suggests otherwise.

It was, in fact, somewhat chaotic and disorganised. Hitler was not hardworking. He disliked paperwork and decision making. He thought that most things sorted themselves out in time without his intervention. Officials competed with each other to get his approval for particular policies.

The result was often a jumble of different government departments competing with each other and getting in each other's way.

The Gestapo

SOURCE 8

The Gestapo, the German secret state police, in action.

The Gestapo (secret state police) was the force which was perhaps most feared by the ordinary German citizen. Under the command of Reinhard Heydrich, Gestapo agents had sweeping powers. They could arrest citizens on suspicion and send them to concentration camps without trial or even explanation.

Modern research has shown that Germans thought the Gestapo were much more powerful than they actually were. As a result, many ordinary Germans informed on each other because they thought the Gestapo would find out anyway.

The police and the courts

The police and courts also helped to prop up the Nazi dictatorship. Top jobs in local police forces were given to high-ranking Nazis reporting to Himmler. As a result, the police added political 'snooping' to their normal law and order role. They were, of course, under strict instructions to ignore crimes committed by Nazi agents. Similarly, the Nazis controlled magistrates, judges and the courts, which meant that opponents of Nazism rarely received a fair trial.

SOURCE **9**

German judges swearing their loyalty at the criminal courts in Berlin.

Concentration camps

SOURCE **10**

Political prisoners at the Oranienburg concentration camp near Berlin.

Concentration camps were the Nazis' ultimate sanction against their own people. They were set up almost as soon as Hitler took power. The first concentration camps in 1933 were simply makeshift prisons in disused factories and warehouses. Soon these were purpose-built. These camps were usually in isolated rural areas, and run by SS Death's Head units. Prisoners were forced to do hard labour. Food was very limited and prisoners suffered harsh discipline, beatings and random executions. By the late 1930s, deaths in the camps became increasingly common and very few people emerged alive from them. Jews, Socialists, Communists, trade unionists, churchmen and anyone else brave enough to criticise the Nazis ended up there.

FOCUS TASK

Summarise the information on these two pages in a table with the following headings:
• Method of control
• Controlled by
• Duties
• How it helped Hitler to make his position secure.

The average worker is primarily interested in work and not in democracy. People who previously enthusiastically supported democracy showed no interest at all in politics. One must be clear about the fact that in the first instance men are fathers of families and have jobs, and that for them politics takes second place and even then only when they expect to get something out of it.

A report by a Socialist activist in Germany, February 1936.

1 The writer of Source 11 was an opponent of the Nazi regime. Does that affect the value of this source as evidence? Explain your answer.

SOURCE **12**

November 1933

Millions of Germans are indeed won over by Hitler and the power and the glory are really his. I hear of some actions by the Communists . . . But what good do such pinpricks do? Less than none, because all Germany prefers Hitler to the Communists.

April 1935

Frau Wilbrandt told us that people complain in Munich when Hitler or Goebbels appear on film but even she (an economist close to the Social Democrats) says: 'Will there not be something even worse, if Hitler is overthrown, Bolshevism?' (That fear keeps Hitler where he is again and again.)

September 1937

On the festival of Yom Kippur the Jews did not attend class. Kufahl, the mathematician, had said to the reduced class: 'Today it's just us.' In my memory these words took on a quite horrible significance: to me it confirms the claim of the Nazis to express the true opinion of the German people. And I believe ever more strongly that Hitler really does embody the soul of the German people, that he really stands for Germany and that he will consequently keep his position. I have not only lost my Fatherland. Even if the government should change one day, my sense of belonging to Germany has gone.

Extracts from the diaries of Victor Klemperer, a Jewish university lecturer in Germany.

Why was there little opposition?

The Nazis faced relatively little open opposition during their 12 years in power. In private, Germans complained about the regime and its actions. Some might refuse to give the Nazi salute. They might pass on anti-Nazi jokes and rude stories about senior Nazis. However, serious criticism was always in private, never in public. Historians have debated why this was so. The main answer they have come up with may seem obvious to you if you've read pages 160–61. It was terror! All the Nazis' main opponents had been killed, exiled or put in prison. The rest had been scared into submission. However, it won't surprise you to learn that historians think the answer is not quite as simple as that. It takes more than just terror to explain why there was so little opposition to the Nazis.

'It's all for the good of Germany' – Nazi successes

Many Germans admired and trusted Hitler. They were prepared to tolerate rule by terror and to trade their rights in political freedom and free speech in return for work, foreign policy success and what they thought was strong government.

- Economic recovery was deeply appreciated.
- Many felt that the Nazis were bringing some much needed discipline back to Germany by restoring traditional values and clamping down on rowdy Communists.
- Between 1933 and 1938 Hitler's success in foreign affairs made Germans feel that their country was a great power again after the humiliations of the First World War and the Treaty of Versailles. For many Germans, the dubious methods of the Nazis may have been regrettable but necessary for the greater good of the country. You will read more about this on pages 172–75.

'I don't want to lose my job' – Economic fears

German workers feared losing their jobs if they did express opposition (see Source 11). Germany had been hit so hard by the Depression that many were terrified by the prospect of being out of work again. It was a similar situation for the bosses. Businesses that did not contribute to Nazi Party funds risked losing Nazi business and going bankrupt, and so in self-defence they conformed as well. If you asked no questions and kept your head down, life in Nazi Germany could be comfortable 'Keeping your head down' became a national obsession. The SS and its special security service the SD went to great lengths to find out what people were saying about the regime, often by listening in on conversations in cafés and bars. Your job could depend on silence.

'Have you heard the good news?' – Propaganda

Underlying the whole regime was the propaganda machine. This ensured that many Germans found out very little about the bad things that were happening, or if they did they only heard them with a positive, pro-Nazi slant. You'll study the Nazi use of propaganda in detail on pages 164–66. Propaganda was particularly important in maintaining the image of Hitler. The evidence suggests that personal support for Hitler remained high throughout the 1930s and he was still widely respected even as Germany was losing the war in 1944.

The July Bomb plot

In July 1944, some army officers came close to removing Hitler. By this stage of the war, many army officers were sure that the war was lost and that Hitler was leading Germany into ruin. One of these was a colonel in the army, Count von Stauffenberg. On 20 July he left a bomb in Hitler's conference room. The plan was to kill Hitler, close down the radio stations, round up the other leading Nazis and take over Germany. It failed on all counts, for the revolt was poorly planned and organised. Hitler survived and the Nazis took a terrible revenge, killing 5000 in reprisal.

How did the Nazis deal with the Churches?

The relationship between the Churches and the Nazis was complicated. In the early stages of the Nazi regime, there was some co-operation between the Nazis and the Churches. Hitler signed a Concordat with the Catholic Church in 1933. This meant that Hitler agreed to leave the Catholic Church alone and allowed it to keep control of its schools. In return, the Church agreed to stay out of politics.

Hitler tried to get all of the Protestant Churches to come together in one official Reich Church. The Reich Church was headed by the Protestant Bishop Ludwig Müller. However, many Germans still felt that their true loyalties lay with their original Churches in their local areas rather than with this state-approved Church.

Hitler even encouraged an alternative religion to the Churches, the pagan German Faith Movement (see Source 13).

Many churchgoers either supported the Nazis or did little to oppose them. However, there were some very important exceptions. The Catholic Bishop Galen criticised the Nazis throughout the 1930s. In 1941 he led a popular protest against the Nazi policies of killing mentally ill and physically disabled people, forcing the Nazis temporarily to stop. He had such strong support among his followers that the Nazis decided it was too risky to try to silence him because they did not want trouble while Germany was at war.

Protestant ministers also resisted the Nazis. Pastor Martin Niemöller was one of the most high-profile critics of the regime in the 1930s. Along with Dietrich Bonhoeffer, he formed an alternative Protestant Church to the official Reich Church. Niemöller spent the years 1938–45 in a concentration camp for resisting the Nazis. Dietrich Bonhoeffer preached against the Nazis until the Gestapo stopped him in 1937. He then became involved with members of the army's intelligence services who were secretly opposed to Hitler. He helped Jews to escape from Germany. Gradually he increased his activity. In 1942 he contacted the Allied commanders and asked what peace terms they would offer Germany if Hitler were overthrown. He was arrested in October 1942 and hanged shortly before the end of the war in April 1945.

SOURCE 13

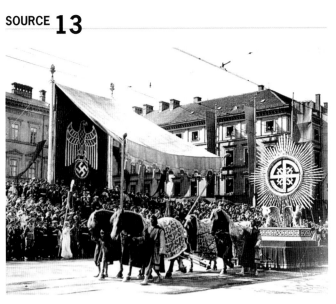

A parade organised by the German Faith Movement. This movement was a non-Christian movement based on worship of the sun.

SOURCE 14

Most postwar accounts have concentrated on the few German clerics who did behave bravely . . . But these were few. Most German church leaders were shamefully silent. As late as January 1945, the Catholic bishop of Würzburg was urging his flock to fight on for the Fatherland, saying that 'salvation lies in sacrifice'.

British historian and journalist Charles Wheeler, writing in 1996.

FOCUS TASK

How effectively did the Nazis deal with their opponents?

Work through pages 158–63. Use the information here to complete your own copy of this table.

Opponent	Reasons for opposing the Nazis	Actions	How the Nazis reacted to this opponent	Was the Nazi action effective?
Trade unionists				
Political opponents				
Church leaders				
Army officers				

Propaganda, culture and mass media in Nazi Germany

The Nazis gained 52 per cent of the vote in the March 1933 elections. This government will not be content with 52 per cent behind it and with terrorising the remaining 48 per cent, but will see its most immediate task as winning over that remaining 48 per cent . . . It is not enough for people to be more or less reconciled to the regime.

Goebbels at his first press conference on becoming Minister for Propaganda, March 1933.

1 Look at Source 16. How does the rally:
   a) make it clear who the leader is
   b) give people a sense of belonging
   c) provide colour and excitement
   d) show the power of the state
   e) show the Nazis' ability to create order out of chaos?

One reason why opposition to Hitler was so limited was the work of Dr Joseph Goebbels, Minister for Enlightenment and Propaganda. Goebbels passionately believed in Hitler as the saviour of Germany. His mission was to make sure that others believed this too. Throughout the 12 years of Nazi rule Goebbels constantly kept his finger on the pulse of public opinion and decided what the German public should and should not hear. He aimed to use every resource available to him to make people loyal to Hitler and the Nazis.

The Nuremberg rallies

Goebbels organised huge rallies, marches, torchlit processions and meetings. Probably the best example was the Nuremberg rally which took place in the summer each year. There were bands, marches, flying displays and Hitler's brilliant speeches. The rallies brought some colour and excitement into people's lives. They gave them a sense of belonging to a great movement. The rallies also showed the German people the power of the state and convinced them that 'every other German' fully supported the Nazis. Goebbels also recognised that one of the Nazis' main attractions was that they created order out of chaos and so the whole rally was organised to emphasise order.

A Hitler speaks to the assembled Germans.

B A parade through the streets.

C German youth marching with spades.

The annual rally at Nuremberg. The whole town was taken over and the rally dominated radio broadcasts and newsreels.

The 1936 Olympics

One of Goebbels' greatest challenges came with the 1936 Olympic Games in Berlin. Other Nazis were opposed to holding the Games in Berlin, but Goebbels convinced Hitler that this was a great propaganda opportunity both within Germany and internationally.

Goebbels and Hitler also thought that the Olympics could be a showcase for their doctrine that the Aryan race was superior to all other races. However, there was international pressure for nations such as the USA to boycott the Games in protest against the Nazis' repressive regime and anti-Jewish politics. In response the Nazis included one token Jew in their team!

Goebbels built a brand new stadium to hold 100,000 people. It was lit by the most modern electric lighting. He brought in television cameras for the first time. The most sophisticated German photo-electronic timing device was installed. The stadium had the largest stop clock ever built. With guests and competitors from 49 countries coming into the heart of Nazi Germany, it was going to take all Goebbels' talents to show that Germany was a modern, civilised and successful nation. No expense was spared. When the Games opened, the visitors were duly amazed at the scale of the stadium, the wonderful facilities, and the efficiency of the organisation. However, they were also struck, and in some cases appalled, by the almost fanatical devotion of the people to Hitler and by the overt presence of army and SS soldiers who were patrolling or standing guard everywhere.

To the delight of Hitler and Goebbels, Germany came top of the medal table, way ahead of all other countries. However, to their great dismay, a black athlete, Jesse Owens, became the star of the Games. He won four gold medals and broke 11 world records in the process. The ten black members of the American team won 13 medals between them. So much for Aryan superiority!

To the majority of German people, who had grown used to the Nazi propaganda machine, the Games appeared to present all the qualities they valued in the Nazis – a grand vision, efficiency, power, strength and achievement. However, to many foreign visitors who were not used to such blatant propaganda it backfired on the Nazi regime.

SOURCE 17

A poster about the 1936 Olympics. The figure on the right is Goebbels. The German text reads 'The purpose of the whole thing – Olympic guests, quick march!'

SOURCE 18

The stadium and swimming pool built for the 1936 Olympics.

2 Does Source 17 approve or disapprove of the Nazis' use of the Games for propaganda purposes?

3 In what ways was the Berlin Olympics a propaganda success for Goebbels?

4 In what ways was it a failure?

5 Why do you think Nazi propaganda was more successful within Germany than outside it?

6 You have already come across many examples of Nazi propaganda. Choose one example which you think is the clearest piece of propaganda. Explain your choice.

FOCUS TASK

How did the Nazis control Germany?

In groups, discuss which of the following statements you most agree with.

A Goebbels' work was more important to Nazi success than that of Himmler (head of the SS).
B Himmler's work was more important to Nazi success than Goebbels'.
C The techniques of repression and propaganda go hand in hand – neither would work without the other.

The media

Less spectacular than the rallies but possibly more important was Goebbels' control of the media. In contrast with the free expression of Weimar Germany, the Nazis controlled the media strictly. No books could be published without Goebbels' permission (not surprisingly the best seller in Nazi Germany was *Mein Kampf*). In 1933 he organised a high-profile 'book-burning'. Nazi students came together publicly to burn any books that included ideas unacceptable to the Nazis.

Artists suffered the same kinds of restriction as writers. Only Nazi-approved painters could show their works. These were usually paintings or sculptures of heroic-looking Aryans, military figures or images of the ideal Aryan family.

Goebbels also controlled the newspapers closely. They were not allowed to print anti-Nazi ideas. Within months of the Nazi takeover, Jewish editors and journalists found themselves out of work and anti-Nazi newspapers were closed down. The German newspapers became very dull reading and Germans bought fewer newspapers as a result – circulation fell by about 10 per cent.

The cinema was also closely controlled. All films – factual or fictional, thrillers or comedies – had to carry a pro-Nazi message. The newsreels which preceded feature films were full of the greatness of Hitler and the massive achievements of Nazi Germany. There is evidence that Germans avoided these productions by arriving late! Goebbels censored all foreign films coming into Germany.

Goebbels plastered Germany with posters proclaiming the successes of Hitler and the Nazis and attacking their opponents.

He banned jazz music, which had been popular in Germany as elsewhere around Europe. He banned it because it was 'Black' music and black people were considered an inferior race.

Goebbels loved new technology and quickly saw the potential of radio broadcasting for spreading the Nazi message. He made cheap radios available so, all Germans could buy one and that of course, he controlled all the radio stations. Listening to broadcasts from the BBC was punishable by death. Just in case people did not have a radio Goebbels placed loudspeakers in the streets and public bars. Hitler's speeches and those of other Nazi leaders were repeated on the radio over and over again until the ideas expressed in them – German expansion into eastern Europe, the inferiority of the Jews – came to be believed by the German people.

Throughout this period Goebbels was supported in his work by the SS and the Gestapo. When he wanted to close down an anti-Nazi newspaper, silence an anti-Nazi writer, or catch someone listening to a foreign radio station, they were there to do that work for him.

1 Look at Source 19 and explain why Goebbels wanted every German household to have a radio set.
2 Write your own ten-word definition of propaganda.
3 What does Source 20 tell you about the effectiveness of Nazi propaganda?

SOURCE 19

Poster advertising cheap Nazi-produced radios. The text reads 'All Germany hears the Führer on the People's Radio.' The radios had only a short range and were unable to pick up foreign stations.

SOURCE 20

There are cinema evenings to be caught up with, very enjoyable ones – if only there were not each time the bitterness of the Third Reich's self-adulation and triumphalism. The renewal of German art – recent German history as reflected in postage stamps, youth camp, enthusiastic welcome for the Führer in X or Y. Goebbels' speech on culture to the Germanised theatre people, the biggest lecture theatre in the world, the biggest autobahn in the world, etc. etc. – the biggest lie in the world, the biggest disgrace in the world. It can't be helped . . .

From the diary of Victor Klemperer for 8 August 1937.

SOURCE 21

Poster for an anti-Jewish exhibition, 1937. The caption reads 'The Eternal Jew'.

SOURCE 22

Our state is an educational state . . . It does not let a man go free from the cradle to the grave. We begin with the child when he is three years old. As soon as he begins to think, he is made to carry a little flag. Then follows school, the Hitler Youth, the storm troopers and military training. We don't let him go; and when all that is done, comes the Labour Front, which takes possession of him again, and does not let him go till he dies, even if he does not like it.

Dr Robert Ley, who was Chief of the Labour Front and in charge of making 'good citizens' out of the German people.

SOURCE 23

The Jews are aliens in Germany. In 1933 there were 66,060,000 inhabitants of the German Reich of whom 499,862 were Jews. What is the percentage of aliens in Germany?

A question from a Nazi maths textbook, 1933.

SOURCE 24

8.00	German (every day)
8.50	Geography, History or Singing (alternate days)
9.40	Race Studies and Ideology (every day)
10.25	Recess, Sports and Special Announcements (every day)
11.00	Domestic Science or Maths (alternate days)
12.10	Eugenics or Health Biology (alternate days)
1.00–6.00	Sport
Evenings	Sex education, Ideology or Domestic Science (one evening each)

The daily timetable for a girls' school in Nazi Germany.

4 Read Source 22. Do you think that the speaker is proud of what he is saying?
5 Do you think the real aim of the question in Source 23 is to improve mathematical skills?
6 Read Source 24. Eugenics is the study of how to produce perfect offspring by choosing ideal qualities in the parents. How would this help the Nazis?

How did the Nazis deal with young people?

It was Hitler's aim to control every aspect of life in Germany, including the daily life of ordinary people. If you had been a 16-year-old Aryan living in Nazi Germany you would probably have been a strong supporter of Adolf Hitler. The Nazis had reorganised every aspect of the school curriculum to make children loyal to them.

SOURCE 25

It is my great educative work I am beginning with the young. We older ones are used up . . . We are bearing the burden of a humiliating past . . . But my magnificent youngsters! Are there finer ones in the world? Look at these young men and boys! What material! With them I can make a new world.

Hitler, speaking in 1939.

At school you would have learned about the history of Germany. You would have been outraged to find out how the German army was 'stabbed in the back' by the weak politicians who had made peace. You might well remember the hardships of the 1920s for yourself, but at school you would have been told how these were caused by Jews squeezing profits out of honest Germans. By the time you were a senior pupil, your studies in history would have made you confident that loyalty to the Führer was right and good. Your biology lessons would have informed you that you were special, as one of the Aryan race which was so superior in intelligence and strength to the *Untermenschen* or sub-human Jews and Slavs of eastern Europe. In maths you would have been set questions like the one in Source 23.

SOURCE 26

All subjects – German language, History, Geography, Chemistry and Mathematics – must concentrate on military subjects, the glorification of military service and of German heroes and leaders and the strength of a rebuilt Germany. Chemistry will develop a knowledge of chemical warfare, explosives, etc, while Mathematics will help the young to understand artillery, calculations, ballistics.

A German newspaper, heavily controlled by the Nazis, approves of the curriculum in 1939.

As a member of the Hitler Youth or League of German Maidens, you would have marched in exciting parades with loud bands. You would probably be physically fit. Your leisure time would also be devoted to Hitler and the Nazis. You would be a strong cross-country runner, and confident at reading maps. After years of summer camps, you would be comfortable camping out of doors and if you were a boy you would know how to clean a rifle and keep it in good condition.

SOURCE 27

Typical day at a labour camp for 18- to 25-year-olds

6.00	Get up (5.00 in summer)	3.00–4.00	Rest
6.05–6.20	Exercises	4.00–5.00	Sport
6.20–6.40	Washing; bed making	5.00–6.00	Political studies
6.40–6.55	Breakfast	6.00–7.00	Allocation of jobs to be done the next day
7.00–7.30	Flag parade; speech by camp leader	7.00–8.00	Supper
7.30–2.30	March to work; six hours' farm work	8.00–9.00	Songs and dancing; speeches
2.30–3.00	Midday meal	10.00	Lights out

A young person's day in Nazi Germany.

SOURCE 28

Hitler looked over the stand, and I know he looked into my eyes, and he said: 'You my boys are the standard bearers, you will inherit what we have created.' From that moment there was not any doubt I was bound to Adolf Hitler until long after our defeat. Afterwards I told my friends how Hitler had looked into my eyes, but they all said: 'No! It was my eyes he was looking into.'

A young German describes his feelings after a Hitler Youth rally.

SOURCE 29

Children have been deliberately taken away from parents who refused to acknowledge their belief in National Socialism . . . The refusal of parents to allow their young children to join the youth organisation is regarded as an adequate reason for taking the children away.

A German teacher writing in 1938.

SOURCE 30

It was a great feeling. You felt you belonged to a great nation again. Germany was in safe hands and I was going to help to build a strong Germany. But my father of course felt differently about it. [He warned] 'Now Henrik, don't say to them what I am saying to you.' I always argued with my father as I was very much in favour of the Hitler regime which was against his background as a working man.

Henrik Metelmann describes what it was like being a member of the Hitler Youth in the 1930s.

1 Make a list of the main differences between your life and the life of a 16-year-old in Nazi Germany.
2 Totalitarian regimes through history have used children as a way of influencing parents. Why do you think they do this?
3 Read Source 30. Why do you think Henrik's father asks Henrik not to repeat what he says to him?

SOURCE 31

Members of the Hitler Youth in the 1930s. From a very early age children were encouraged to join the Nazi youth organisations. It was not compulsory, but most young people did join.

As a child in Nazi Germany, you might well feel slightly alienated (estranged) from your parents because they are not as keen on the Nazis as you are. They expect your first loyalty to be to your family, whereas your Hitler Youth leader makes it clear that your first loyalty is to Adolf Hitler. You find it hard to understand why your father grumbles about Nazi regulation of his working practices – surely the Führer (Hitler) is protecting him? Your parents find the idea of Nazi inspectors checking up on the teachers rather strange. For you it is normal.

SOURCE 32

Illustration from a Nazi children's book. The children are being taught to distrust Jews.

ACTIVITY

Draw up two posters summarising the aims and objectives of Nazi youth policy. One poster should be for the young people themselves. The other should be for the parents.

SOURCE 33

The formation of cliques, i.e. groupings of young people outside the Hitler Youth, has been on the increase before and particularly during the war to such a degree that one must speak of a serious risk of political, moral and criminal subversion of our youth.

From a report by the Nazi youth leadership, 1942.

Did all young people support the Nazis?

Many young people were attracted to the Nazi youth movements by the leisure opportunities they offered. There were really no alternatives. All other youth organisations had been either absorbed or made illegal. Even so, only half of all German boys were members in 1933 and only 15 per cent of girls.

In 1939 membership of a Nazi youth movement was made compulsory. But by this time the youth movements were going through a crisis. Many of the experienced leaders had been drafted into the German army. Others – particularly those who had been leaders in the pre-Nazi days – had been replaced by keener Nazis. Many of the movements were now run by older teenagers who rigidly enforced Nazi rules. They even forbade other teenagers to meet informally with their friends.

As the war progressed, the activities of the youth movements focused increasingly on the war effort and military drill. The popularity of the movements decreased and indeed an anti-Hitler Youth movement appeared. The Nazis identified two distinct groups of young people who they were worried about: the Swing movement and the Edelweiss Pirates.

SOURCE 34

The public hanging of twelve Edelweiss Pirates in Cologne in 1944.

The 'Swing' movement

This was made up mainly of middle-class teenagers. They went to parties where they listened to English and American music and sang English songs. They danced American dances such as the 'jitterbug' to banned jazz music. They accepted Jews at their clubs. They talked about and enjoyed sex. They were deliberately 'slovenly'. The Nazis issued a handbook helping the authorities to identify these degenerate types. Some were shown with unkempt, long hair; others with exaggeratedly English clothes.

The Edelweiss Pirates

The Edelweiss Pirates were working-class teenagers. They were not an organised movement, and groups in various cities took different names: 'The Roving Dudes' (Essen); the 'Kittelbach Pirates' (Düsseldorf); the 'Navajos' (Cologne). The Nazis, however, classified all the groups under the single name 'Edelweiss Pirates' and the groups did have a lot in common.

The Pirates were mainly aged between 14 and 17 (Germans could leave school at 14, but they did not have to sign on for military service until they were 17). At the weekends, the Pirates went camping. They sang songs, just like the Hitler Youth, but they changed the lyrics of songs to mock Germany and when they spotted bands of Hitler Youth they taunted and sometimes attacked them. In contrast with the Hitler Youth, the Pirates included boys and girls. The Pirates were also much freer in their attitude towards sex, which was officially frowned upon by the Hitler Youth.

The Pirates' activities caused serious worries to the Nazi authorities in some cities. In December 1942 the Gestapo broke up 28 groups containing 739 adolescents. The Nazi approach to the Pirates was different from their approach to other minorities. As long as they needed future workers for industry and future soldiers they could not simply exterminate all these teenagers or put them in concentration camps (although Himmler did suggest that). They therefore responded uncertainly – sometimes arresting the Pirates, sometimes ignoring them.

In 1944 in Cologne, Pirate activities escalated. They helped to shelter army deserters and escaped prisoners. They stole armaments and took part in an attack on the Gestapo during which its chief was killed. The Nazi response was to round up the so called 'ringleaders'. Twelve were publicly hanged in November 1944.

Neither of the groups described above had strong political views. They were not political opponents of the Nazis. But they resented and resisted Nazi control of their lives.

A painting showing the Nazis' view of an ideal German family.

Women in Nazi Germany

All the Nazi leaders were men. The Nazis were a very male-dominated organisation. Hitler had a very traditional view of the role of the German woman as wife and mother. It is worth remembering that many *women* agreed with him. In the traditional rural areas and small towns, many women felt that the proper role of a woman was to support her husband. There was also resentment towards working women in the early 1930s, since they were seen as keeping men out of jobs. It all created a lot of pressure on women to conform to what the Nazis called 'the traditional balance' between men and women. 'No true German woman wears trousers' said a Nazi newspaper headline when the film star Marlene Dietrich appeared wearing trousers in public.

Alarmed at the falling birth rate, Hitler offered tempting financial incentives for married couples to have at least four children. You got a 'Gold Cross' for having eight children, and were given a privileged seat at Nazi meetings. Posters, radio broadcasts and newsreels all celebrated the ideas of motherhood and homebuilding. The German Maidens' League reinforced these ideas, focusing on a combination of good physical health and housekeeping skills. This was reinforced at school (see Source 24).

With all these encouragements the birth rate did increase from 15 per thousand in 1933 to 20 per thousand in 1939. There was also an increase in pregnancies outside marriage. These girls were looked after in state maternity hostels.

Leni Riefenstahl directing the shooting of her film of the 1936 Olympics.

Girls from the German Maidens' League camping. The League offered excitement and escape from boring duties in the home.

SOURCE 38

Gertrude Scholz-Klink, head of the Nazi Women's Bureau.

SOURCE 39

A German woman and her Jewish boyfriend being publicly humiliated by the SA in 1933.

There were some prominent women in Nazi Germany. Leni Riefenstahl was a high-profile film producer. Gertrude Scholz-Klink was head of the Nazi Women's Bureau, although she was excluded from any important discussions (such as the one to conscript female labour in 1942). Many working-class girls and women gained the chance to travel and meet new people through the Nazi women's organisation. Overall, however, opportunities for women were limited. Married professional women were forced to give up their jobs and stay at home with their families, which many resented as a restriction on their freedom. Discrimination against women applicants for jobs was actually encouraged.

In the late 1930s the Nazis had to do an about-turn as they suddenly needed more women workers because the supply of unemployed men was drying up. Many women had to struggle with both family and work responsibilities. However, even during the crisis years of 1942–1945 when German industry was struggling to cope with the demand for war supplies, Nazi policy on women was still torn between their traditional stereotype of the mother, and the actual needs of the workplace. For example, there was no chance for German women to serve in the armed forces, as there was in Allied countries.

SOURCE 40

I went to Sauckel [the Nazi minister in charge of labour] with the proposition that we should recruit our labour from the ranks of German women. He replied brusquely that where to obtain which workers was his business. Moreover, he said, as Gauleiter [a regional governor] he was Hitler's subordinate and responsible to the Führer alone . . . Sauckel offered to put the question to Goering as Commissioner of the Four-Year Plan . . . but I was scarcely allowed to advance my arguments. Sauckel and Goering continually interrupted me. Sauckel laid great weight on the danger that factory work might inflict moral harm on German womanhood; not only might their 'psychic and emotional life' be affected but also their ability to bear children.

Goering totally concurred. But just to be absolutely sure, Sauckel went immediately to Hitler and had him confirm the decision. All my good arguments were therefore blown to the winds.

Albert Speer, *Inside The Third Reich*, 1970. Speer was Minister of Armaments and War Production.

FOCUS TASK

How successful were the Nazi policies for women?

Read these two statements:
• 'Nazi policy for women was confused.'
• 'Nazi policy for women was a failure.'

For each statement explain whether you agree or disagree with it and use examples from the text to support your explanation.

171

Did Germans gain from Nazi rule?

Economic recovery and rearmament

Hitler and the Nazis came to power because they promised to use radical methods to solve the country's two main problems – desperate unemployment and a crisis in German farming. In return for work and other benefits, the majority of the German people gave up their political freedom. Was it worth it?

At first, many Germans felt it was, particularly the 5 million who were unemployed in 1933. Hitler was fortunate in that by 1933 the worst of the Depression was over. Even so, there is no doubt that the Nazis acted with energy and commitment to solve some of the main problems. The brilliant economist **Dr Hjalmar Schacht** organised Germany's finances to fund a huge programme of work creation. The National Labour Service sent men on **public works projects** and conservation programmes, in particular to build a network of motorways or **autobahns**. Railways were extended or built from scratch. There were major house-building programmes and grandiose new public building projects such as the Reich Chancellery in Berlin.

Other measures brought increasing prosperity. One of Hitler's most cherished plans was **rearmament**. In 1935 he reintroduced **conscription** for the German army. In 1936 he announced a **Four-Year Plan** under the control of **Goering** to get the German economy ready for war (it was one of the very few clear policy documents that Hitler ever wrote).

ACTIVITY

As you read through pages 172–75, you will come across a number of individuals, organisations and terms in bold type in the text, **like this**. You could add more of your own if you wish. Draw up a table containing definitions of the words, or explanations of their importance to the Nazi's economic policies. The completed table will help you with your revision. You could organise your table like this:

Key word/term/person	Definition/explanation

SOURCE 42

A completed autobahn.

SOURCE 41

Previously unemployed men assemble for the building of the first autobahn, September 1933.

Conscription reduced unemployment. The need for weapons, equipment and uniforms created jobs in the coal mines, steel and textile mills. Engineers and designers gained new opportunities, particularly when Hitler decreed that Germany would have a world-class air force (the Luftwaffe). As well as bringing economic recovery, these measures boosted Hitler's popularity because they boosted **national pride**. Germans began to feel that their country was finally emerging from the humiliation of the Great War and the Treaty of Versailles, and putting itself on an equal footing with the other great powers.

SOURCE 43

Unemployment and government expenditure in Germany, 1932–1938. Economic recovery was almost entirely funded by the state rather than from Germans investing their own savings. Despite this, unemployment fell steadily and Germany was actually running short of workers by 1939.

SOURCE 44

Early one morning, a neighbour of ours, a trade-union secretary, was taken away in a car by the SS and police. His wife had great difficulty finding out what had happened to him. My mother was too scared to be seen talking to her and Father became very quiet and alarmed and begged me not to repeat what he had said within our four walls about the whole Nazi set-up . . .

I loved it when we went on our frequent marches, feeling important when the police had to stop the traffic to give us right of way and passing pedestrians had to raise their arm in the Nazi salute. Whenever we were led out on a march, it was always into the working-class quarters. We were told that this was to remind the workers, but I sometimes wondered what we wanted to remind them of, after all most of our fathers were workers . . .

When war broke out and I was about to be called up, Father fell ill and never recovered. Just before he died, he made one final effort to bring me to my senses. Now that his life was coming to an end, he was no longer frightened of the 'brown pest'. He had been a soldier in the 1914–18 war and like so many of the working people of his generation in Hamburg he hated the Nazis like poison.

From *Through Hell for Hitler*, the memoirs of Henrik Metelmann, published in 1970. Metelmann came from a working-class family in Hamburg but was an enthusiastic member of the Hitler Youth and served in the German army in the Second World War.

The Nazis and the workers

Hitler promised (and delivered) lower unemployment which helped to ensure popularity among **industrial workers**. These workers were important to the Nazis: Hitler needed good workers to create the industries that would help to make Germany great and establish a new German empire in eastern Europe. He won the loyalty of industrial workers by a variety of initiatives.

- Propaganda praised the workers and tried to associate them with Hitler.
- Schemes such as **Strength Through Joy (KDF)** gave them cheap theatre and cinema tickets, and organised courses and trips and sports events. Workers were offered cut-price cruises on the latest luxury liners.
- Many thousands of workers saved five marks a week in the state scheme to buy the **Volkswagen Beetle**, the 'people's car'. It was designed by Ferdinand Porsche and became a symbol of the prosperous new Germany, even though no workers ever received a car because all car production was halted by the war in 1939.
- Another important scheme was the **Beauty of Labour** movement. This improved working conditions in factories. It introduced features not seen in many workplaces before, such as washing facilities and low-cost canteens.

What was the price of these advances? Workers lost their main political party, the SDP. They lost their trade unions and for many workers this remained a source of bitter resentment. All workers had to join the **DAF (General Labour Front)** run by **Dr Robert Ley**. This organisation kept strict control of workers. They could not strike for better pay and conditions. In some areas, they were prevented from moving to better-paid jobs. Wages remained comparatively low, although prices were also strictly controlled. Even so, by the late 1930s, many workers were grumbling that their standard of living was still lower than it had been before the Depression (see Source 43).

The Nazis and the farming communities

The **farmers** had been an important factor in the Nazis' rise to power. Hitler did not forget this and introduced a series of measures to help them. In September 1933 he introduced the **Reich Food Estate** under **Richard Darre**. This set up central boards to buy agricultural produce from the farmers and distribute it to markets across Germany. It gave the peasant farmers a guaranteed market for their goods at guaranteed prices. The second main measure was the **Reich Entailed Farm Law**. It gave peasants state protection for their farms: banks could not seize their land if they could not pay loans or mortgages. This ensured that peasants' farms stayed in their hands.

The Reich Entailed Farm Law also had a racial aim. Part of the Nazi philosophy was **'Blood and Soil'**, the belief that the peasant farmers were the basis of Germany's master race. They would be the backbone of the new German empire in the east. As a result, their way of life had to be protected. As Source 46 shows, the measures were widely appreciated.

However, rather like the industrial workers, some peasants were not thrilled with the regime's measures. The Reich Food Estate meant that efficient, go-ahead farmers were held back by having to work through the same processes as less efficient farmers. Because of the Reich Entailed Farm Law, banks were unwilling to lend money to farmers. It also meant that only the eldest child inherited the farm. As a result, many children of farmers left the land to work for better pay in Germany's industries. **Rural depopulation** ran at about three per cent per year in the 1930s – the exact opposite of the Nazis' aims!

SOURCE 45

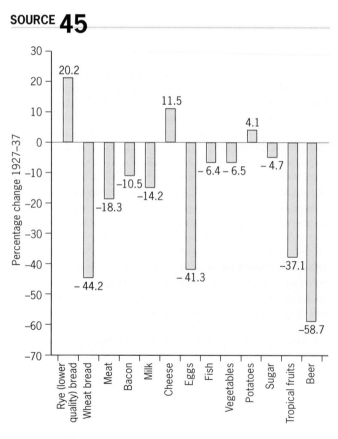

Annual food consumption in working class families, 1927–37 (% change).

SOURCE 46

Thousands of people came from all over Germany to the Harvest Festival celebrations . . . We all felt the same happiness and joy. Harvest festival was the thank you for us farmers having a future again. I believe no statesman has ever been as well loved as Adolf Hitler was at that time. Those were happy times.

Lusse Essig's memories of harvest festivals in the 1930s. Lusse was a farm worker who went on to work for the Agriculture Ministry between 1937 and 1945.

Big business and the middle classes

The record of the Nazis with the **middle classes** was also mixed. Certainly many middle-class business people were grateful to the Nazis for eliminating the Communist threat to their businesses and properties. They also liked the way in which the Nazis seemed to be bringing order to Germany. For the owners of small businesses it was a mixed picture. If you owned a small engineering firm, you were likely to do well from government orders as rearmament spending grew in the 1930s. However, if you produced consumer goods or ran a small shop, you might well struggle. Despite Hitler's promises, the large department stores which were taking business away from local shops were not closed.

It was **big business** that really benefited from Nazi rule. The big companies no longer had to worry about troublesome trade unions and strikes. Companies such as the chemicals giant IG Farben gained huge government contracts to make explosives, fertilisers and even artificial oil from coal. Other household names today, such as Mercedes and Volkswagen, prospered from Nazi policies.

1 On your own copy of Source 47 label the features that are attempting to comment on life in Nazi Germany.

DIE
NSDAP
SICHERT DIE
VOLKS-
GEMEINSCHAFT

VOLKSGENOSSEN
BRAUCHT IHR RAT UND HILFE
SO WENDET EUCH AN DIE
ORTSGRUPPE

A Nazi propaganda poster from the 1930s encouraging people to turn to Nazi–led community groups for help and advice.

Did most people in Germany benefit from Nazi rule?

Here are some claims that the Nazi propaganda machine made about how life in Germany had been changed for the better:

- 'Germans now have economic security.'
- 'Germans no longer need to feel inferior to other states. They can be proud of their country.'
- 'The Nazi state looks after its workers very well indeed.'
- 'The Nazis are on the side of the farmers and have rescued Germany's farmers from disaster.'
- 'The Nazis have ensured that Germany is racially pure.'
- 'The Nazis have made Germany safe from communism.'

You are now going to decide how truthful these claims actually are.

1 Look back over pages 158–75. Gather evidence that supports or opposes each claim. You could work in groups taking one claim each.
2 For each claim, decide whether, overall, it is totally untrue; a little bit true; mostly true; or totally true.
3 Discuss:
  a) Who do you think benefited most from Nazi rule: the workers, the farmers, big business or the middle classes?
  b) Who did not benefit from Nazi rule?

The 'national community' – *Volksgemeinschaft*

We have divided this section by social group, but the Nazis would not want Germans to see their society that v   Hitler wanted all Germans to think of themselves as part of a **national community**, or *Volksgemeinschaft*. Under Nazi rule, workers, farmers, and so on, would no longer see themselves primarily as workers or farmers; they would see themselves as Germans. Their first loyalty would not be to their own social group but to Germany and the Fuhrer. They would be so proud to belong to a great nation that was racially and culturally superior to other nations that they would put the interests of Germany before their own. Hitler's policies towards each group were designed to help win this kind of loyalty to the Nazi state.

The evidence suggests that the Nazis never quite succeeded in this: Germans in the 1930s certainly did not lose their self-interest, nor did they embrace the national community wholeheartedly. However, the Nazis did not totally fail either! In the 1930s Germans did have a strong sense of national pride and loyalty towards Hitler. For the majority of Germans, the benefits of Nazi rule made them willing – on the surface at least – to accept some central control in the interests of making Germany great again.

The impact of the Second World War on Germany

In Chapters 8 and 9 of this book you can find out how, through the 1930s, Hitler fulfilled his promises to the German people that he would:

- reverse the Treaty of Versailles
- rebuild Germany's armed forces
- unite Germany and Austria
- extend German territory into eastern Europe.

He fulfilled each of these aims, but started the Second World War in the process.

Germans had no great enthusiasm for war. People still had memories of the First World War. But in war, as in peace time, the Nazis used all methods available to make the German people support the regime.

Food rationing was introduced soon after war began in September 1939. Clothes rationing followed in November 1939. Even so, from 1939 to 1941 it was not difficult to keep up civilian morale because the war went spectacularly well for Germany. Hitler was in control of much of western and eastern Europe and supplies of luxury goods flowed into Germany from captured territories.

However, in 1941 Hitler took the massive gamble of invading the Soviet Union, and for the next three years his troops were engaged in an increasingly expensive war with Russian forces who 'tore the heart out of the German army', as the British war leader, Winston Churchill, put it. As the tide turned against the German armies, civilians found their lives increasingly disrupted. They had to cut back on heating, work longer hours and recycle their rubbish. Goebbels redoubled his censorship efforts. He tried to maintain people's support for the war by involving them in it through asking them to make sacrifices. They donated an estimated 1.5 million fur coats to help to clothe the German army in Russia.

At this stage in the war, the German people began to see and hear less of Hitler. His old speeches were broadcast by Goebbels, but Hitler was increasingly preoccupied with the detail of the war. In 1942 the 'Final Solution' began (see pages 179–82), which was to kill millions of Jewish civilians in German-occupied countries.

Heinrich Himmler, leader of the SS.

From 1942, Albert Speer began to direct Germany's war economy. All effort focused on the armament industries. Postal services were suspended and letter boxes were closed. All places of entertainment were closed, except cinemas – Goebbels needed these to show propaganda films. Women were drafted into the labour force in increasing numbers. Country areas had to take evacuees from the cities and refugees from eastern Europe.

These measures were increasingly carried out by the SS. In fact, the SS became virtually a state within the German state. This SS empire had its own armed forces, armaments industries and labour camps. It developed a business empire that was worth a fortune (see Source 49). However, even the SS could not win the war, or even keep up German morale.

With defeat looming, support for the Nazis weakened. Germans stopped declaring food they had. They stayed away from Nazi rallies. They refused to give the 'Heil Hitler' salute when asked to do so. Himmler even contacted the Allies to ask about possible peace terms.

A disused mineshaft at Merkers where, in 1945, US forces found a stash of valuables hidden by the SS. The sacks mainly contained gold.

Goebbels does not always tell you the truth. When he tells you that England is powerless do you believe that? Have you forgotten that our bombers fly over Germany at will? The bombs that fell with these leaflets tell you . . . The war lasts as long as Hitler's regime.

Translation of a leaflet dropped by the Allies on Berlin.

SOURCE 51

The greatest effect on [civilian] morale will be produced if a new blow of catastrophic force can be struck at a time when the situation already appears desperate.

From a secret report to the British government, 1944.

1 What do Sources 50–53 tell you about
a) the aims of the bombing
b) the success of the bombing?

The bombing of Dresden

It was the bombing of Germany which had the most dramatic effect on the lives of German civilians. In 1942 the Allies decided on a new policy towards the bombing of Germany. Under Arthur 'Bomber' Harris the British began an all-out assault on both industrial and residential areas of all the major German cities. One of the objectives was to cripple German industry, the other was to lower the morale of civilians and to terrorise them into submission.

The bombing escalated through the next three years, culminating in the bombing of Dresden in February 1945 which killed between 35,000 and 150,000 people in two days. Sources 51–53 tell you more about that bombing.

SOURCE 52

The centre of Dresden after the bombing in February 1945.

SOURCE 53

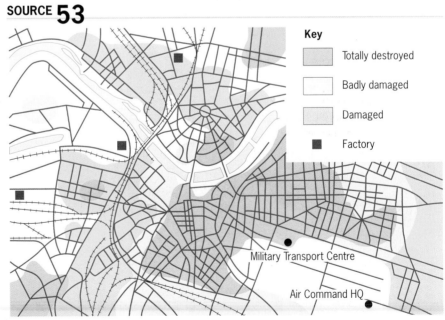

Key

Totally destroyed

Badly damaged

Damaged

■ Factory

Military Transport Centre

Air Command HQ

A map showing the destruction of Dresden. Dresden was an industrial city, but the major damage was to civilian areas.

By 1945 the German people were in a desperate state. Food supplies were dwindling. Already 3.5 million German civilians had died. Refugees were fleeing the advancing Russian armies in the east.

Three months after the massive destruction of Dresden, Germany's war was over. Hitler, Goebbels and other Nazi war leaders committed suicide. Germany surrendered. It was now a shattered country. The Nazi promises lay in tatters and the long, painful process of rebuilding Germany had to begin again.

FOCUS TASK

How did the war change life in Germany?

1 Draw a timeline from 1939 to 1945 down the middle of a page.
2 On the left, make notes to show how the war was going for Germany's army.
3 On the right, make notes to show how the war affected Germans at home in Germany.
4 Choose one change from the right-hand column that you think had the greatest impact on ordinary Germans and explain your choice.

ACTIVITY

Wartime propaganda

In 1939 Germany went to war. The first two years were an unprecedented success for Hitler. By 1941 his armies controlled much of western, central and eastern Europe. However, in 1943 the tide turned. German forces were being beaten, bombing of civilian targets in Germany was increasing and life for many Germans was severely disrupted by shortages of food, fuel and other essentials. Goebbels' propaganda machine tried to rise to this challenge.

From your knowledge of Nazi Germany in peacetime and wartime, describe and explain Sources 54–56 as fully as you can. Include an analysis of:
• the objectives of the propaganda
• the methods used.

SOURCE 54

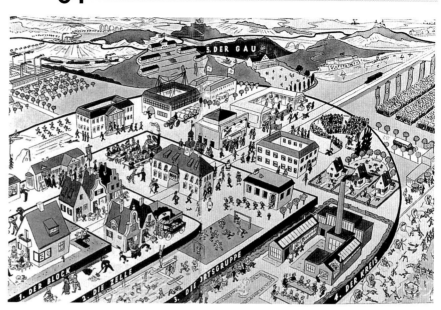

From the Nazi propaganda magazine *Signal*, 1941, showing life in Germany continuing as normal despite the war.

SOURCE 55

The text on this poster reads 'Hard times, hard tasks, hard hearts'.

SOURCE 56

A 1943 poster telling people to black out their windows: 'The enemy sees your light!'

The persecution of minorities

The Nazis believed in the superiority of the Aryan race. Through their 12 years in power they persecuted members of other races, and many minority groups such as gypsies, homosexuals and mentally handicapped people. They persecuted any group that they thought challenged Nazi ideas. Homosexuals were a threat to Nazi ideas about family life; the mentally handicapped were a threat to Nazi ideas about Germans being a perfect master race; gypsies were thought to be an inferior people.

The persecution of such minorities varied. In families where there were hereditary illnesses, sterilisation was enforced. Over 300,000 men and women were compulsorily sterilised between 1934 and 1945. A so-called 'euthanasia programme' was begun in 1939. At least 5000 severely mentally handicapped babies and children were killed between 1939 and 1945 either by injection or by starvation. Between 1939 and 1941, 72,000 mentally ill patients were gassed before a public outcry in Germany itself ended the extermination. The extermination of the gypsies, on the other hand, did not cause an outcry. Five out of six gypsies living in Germany in 1939 were killed by the Nazis. Similarly, there was little or no complaint about the treatment of so-called 'asocials' – homosexuals, alcoholics, the homeless, prostitutes, habitual criminals and beggars – who were rounded up off the streets and sent to concentration camps.

You are going to investigate this most disturbing aspect of Nazi Germany by tracing the story of Nazi treatment of the Jewish population in which anti-semitism culminated in the dreadful slaughter of the 'Final Solution'.

SOURCE 57

A poster published in 1920, directed at 'All German mothers'. It explains that over 12,000 German Jews were killed fighting for their country in the First World War.

SOURCE 58

SA and SS men enforcing the boycott of Jewish shops, April 1933.

SOURCE 59

To read the pages [of Hitler's Mein Kampf] is to enter a world of the insane, a world peopled by hideous and distorted shadows. The Jew is no longer a human being, he has become a mythical figure, a grimacing leering devil invested with infernal powers, the incarnation of evil.

A Bullock, *Hitler: A Study in Tyranny,* published in 1990.

1 What does Source 57 suggest about attitudes to Jews in 1920?
2 Why did Hitler hate the Jews?

Hitler and the Jews

Anti-semitism means hatred of Jews. Throughout Europe, Jews had experienced discrimination for hundreds of years. They were often treated unjustly in courts or forced to live in GHETTOS. One reason for this persecution was religious, in that Jews were blamed for the death of Jesus Christ! Another reason was that they tended to be well educated and therefore held well-paid professional jobs or ran successful stores and businesses.

Hitler hated Jews insanely. In his years of poverty in Vienna, he became obsessed by the fact that Jews ran many of the most successful businesses, particularly the large department stores. This offended his idea of the superiority of Aryans. Hitler also blamed Jewish businessmen and bankers for Germany's defeat in the First World War. He thought they had forced the surrender of the German army.

As soon as Hitler took power in 1933 he began to mobilise the full powers of the state against the Jews. They were immediately banned from the Civil Service and a variety of public services such as broadcasting and teaching. At the same time, SA and later SS troopers organised boycotts of Jewish shops and businesses, which were marked with a star of David.

SOURCE 60

A cartoon from the Nazi newspaper *Der Stürmer*, 1935. Jews owned many shops and businesses. These were a constant target for Nazi attacks.

SOURCE 61

[The day after Kristallnacht*] the teachers told us: don't worry about what you see, even if you see some nasty things which you may not understand. Hitler wants a better Germany, a clean Germany. Don't worry, everything will work out fine in the end.*

Henrik Metelmann, member of the Hitler Youth, in 1938.

SOURCE 62

Until Kristallnacht, *many Germans believed Hitler was not engaged in mass murder. [The treatment of the Jews] seemed to be a minor form of harassment of a disliked minority. But after* Kristallnacht *no German could any longer be under any illusion. I believe it was the day that we lost our innocence. But it would be fair to point out that I myself never met even the most fanatic Nazi who wanted the extermination [mass murder] of the Jews. Certainly we wanted the Jews out of Germany, but we did not want them to be killed.*

Alfons Heck, member of the Hitler Youth in 1938, interviewed for a television programme in 1989.

1 Read Sources 61–64. How useful is each source to a historian looking at the German reaction to *Kristallnacht*?
2 Taken together, do they provide a clear picture of how Germans felt about *Kristallnacht*?
3 Could Germans have protested effectively about *Kristallnacht*? Explain your answer with reference to pages 160–66.

In 1935 the Nuremberg Laws took away German citizenship from Jews. Jews were also forbidden to marry or have sex with pure-blooded Germans. Goebbels' propaganda experts bombarded German children and families with anti-Jewish messages. Jews were often refused jobs, and people in shops refused to serve them. In schools, Jewish children were humiliated and then segregated.

Kristallnacht

In November 1938 a young Jew killed a German diplomat in Paris. The Nazis used this as an excuse to launch a violent revenge on Jews. Plain-clothes SS troopers were issued with pickaxes and hammers and the addresses of Jewish businesses. They ran riot, smashing up Jewish shops and workplaces. Ninety-one Jews were murdered. Hundreds of synagogues were burned. Twenty thousand Jews were taken to concentration camps. Thousands more left the country. This event became known as *Kristallnacht* or 'The Night of Broken Glass'. Many Germans watched the events of *Kristallnacht* with alarm and concern. The Nazi-controlled press presented *Kristallnacht* as the spontaneous reaction of ordinary Germans against the Jews. Most Germans did not believe this. However, hardly anyone protested. The few who did were brutally murdered.

SOURCE 63

I hate the treatment of the Jews. I think it is a bad side of the movement and I will have nothing to do with it. I did not join the party to do that sort of thing. I joined the party because I thought and still think that Hitler did the greatest Christian work for twenty-five years. I saw seven million men rotting in the streets, often I was there too, and no one . . . seemed to care . . . Then Hitler came and he took all those men off the streets and gave them health and security and work . . .

H Schmidt, Labour Corps leader, in an interview in 1938.

SOURCE 64

I feel the urge to present to you a true report of the recent riots, plundering and destruction of Jewish property. Despite what the official Nazi account says, the German people have nothing whatever to do with these riots and burnings. The police supplied SS men with axes, house-breaking tools and ladders. A list of the addresses of all Jewish shops and flats was provided and the mob worked under the leadership of the SS men. The police had strict orders to remain neutral.

Anonymous letter from a German civil servant to the British consul, 1938.

The ghettos

The persecution developed in intensity after the outbreak of war in 1939. After defeating Poland in 1939, the Nazis set about 'Germanising' western Poland. This meant transporting Poles from their homes and replacing them with German settlers. Almost one in five Poles died in the fighting and as a result of racial policies of 1939–45. Polish Jews were rounded up and transported to the major cities. Here they were herded into sealed areas, called ghettos. The able-bodied Jews were used for slave labour but the young, the old and the sick were simply left to die from hunger and disease.

Mass murder

In 1941 Germany invaded the USSR. The invasion was a great success at first. However, within weeks the Nazis found themselves in control of 3 million Russian Jews in addition to the Jews in all of the other countries they had invaded. German forces had orders to round up and shoot Communist Party activists and their Jewish supporters. The shooting was carried out by special SS units called *Einsatzgruppen*. By the autumn of 1941, mass shootings were taking place all over occupied eastern Europe. In Germany, all Jews were ordered to wear the star of David on their clothing to mark them out.

SOURCE 65

KNEE BENDS
A FEW PUSH UPS WILL PROVE
IF MAN CAN STAY ON DUTY
OR HAS TO BE SENT TO THE GAS CHAMBER.
PRISONERS' NUMBERS ARE BEING TAKEN —
AND CALLED OUT AT THE NEXT ROLL CALL 104

A drawing by a prisoner in Auschwitz concentration camp. The prisoners are being made to do knee bends to see if they are fit enough to work. If not they will be killed in the gas chambers.

SOURCE 66

The extermination of the Jews is the most dreadful chapter in German history, doubly so because the men who did it closed their senses to the reality of what they were doing by taking pride in the technical efficiency of their actions and, at moments when their conscience threatened to break in, telling themselves that they were doing their duty . . . others took refuge in the enormity of the operation, which lent it a convenient depersonalisation. When they ordered a hundred Jews to get on a train in Paris or Amsterdam, they considered their job accomplished and carefully closed their minds to the thought that eventually those passengers would arrive in front of the ovens of Treblinka.

American historian Gordon Craig, 1978.

4 The systematic killing of the Jews by the Nazis is generally known today as the Holocaust, which means 'sacrifice'. Many people prefer the Jewish term Sho'ah, which means 'destruction'. Why do you think this is?

5 You can see many web sites, TV programmes and books about the mass murders. Many of these resources contain terrible scenes showing dead bodies, gas chambers, cremation ovens and other horrors. We have chosen Source 67. Why do you think we did this?

The 'death camps'

In January 1942, senior Nazis met at Wannsee, a suburb of Berlin, for a conference to discuss what they called the 'Final Solution' to the 'Jewish Question'. At the Wannsee Conference, Himmler, head of the SS and Gestapo, was put in charge of the systematic killing of all Jews within Germany and German-occupied territory. Slave labour and death camps were built at Auschwitz, Treblinka, Chelmo and other places. The old, the sick and young children were killed immediately. The able-bodied were first used as slave labour. Some were used for appalling medical experiments. Six million Jews, 500,000 European gypsies and countless political prisoners, Jehovah's Witnesses, homosexuals and Russian and Polish prisoners of war were sent to these camps to be worked to death, gassed or shot.

Was the 'Final Solution' planned from the start?

Historians have debated intensely as to whether or not the 'Final Solution' was the result of a long-term plan of Hitler. Some historians (intentionalists) believe the whole dreadful process was planned. Other historians (structuralists) argue that there was no clear plan and that the policy of mass murder evolved during the war years. Part of the problem is the lack of evidence. Hitler made speeches in which he talked of the annihilation of the Jews, but he never signed any documents or made any recorded orders directly relating to the extermination of the Jews. The Nazis kept the killing programme as secret as they could, so there are relatively few documents.

Although historians disagree about whether there was a plan, they do generally agree that Hitler was ultimately responsible. However, they also point to others who bear some of the responsibility as well. The genocide would not have been possible without:

- The Civil Service bureaucracy – they collected and stored information about Jews.
- Police forces in Germany and the occupied lands – many victims of the Nazis, such as Anne Frank, were actually taken by the police rather than the Gestapo or SS.
- The SS – Adolf Eichmann devised a system of transporting Jews to collection points and then on to the death camps. He was also in charge of looting the possessions of the Jews. The SS Death's Head battalions and *Einsatzgruppen* also carried out many of the killings.
- The Wehrmacht (German armed forces) – the army leaders were fully aware of events.
- Industry – companies such as Volkswagen and Mercedes had their own slave labour camps. The chemicals giant IG Farben competed with other companies for the contract to make the Cyclon B gas which was used in the gas chambers.
- The German people – there was widespread support for anti-semitism, even if these feelings did not include support for mass murder. Many Germans took part in some aspect of the Holocaust, but closed their eyes to the full reality of what was happening (see Source 66).

SOURCE 67

Wedding rings taken from people killed at Buchenwald concentration camp.

SOURCE 68

Dear Teacher,
I am a survivor of a concentration camp.
My eyes saw what no man should witness:
Gas chambers built by learned engineers;
Children poisoned by educated physicians;
Infants killed by trained nurses;
Women and babies shot and burned by
*   high school and college graduates.*
So, I am suspicious of education.
My request is: help your students become
*   human.*
Your efforts must never produce learned
*   monsters, skilled psychopaths, educated*
*   Eichmanns.*
Reading, writing, arithmetic and history
*   are important only if they serve to make*
*   our children more human.*

A letter written by a Holocaust survivor to the United Nations explaining the importance of students studying history.

Resistance

Many Jews escaped from Germany before the killing started. Other Jews managed to live under cover in Germany and the occupied territories. Gad Beck, for instance, led the Jewish resistance to the Nazis in Berlin. He was finally captured in April 1945. On the day he was due to be executed, he was rescued by a detachment of troops from the Jewish regiment of the Red Army who had heard of his capture and had been sent to rescue him. There were 28 known groups of Jewish fighters, and there may have been more. Many Jews fought in the resistance movements in the Nazi-occupied lands. In 1945 the Jews in the Warsaw ghetto rose up against the Nazis and held out against them for four weeks. Five concentration camps saw armed uprisings and Greek Jews managed to blow up the gas ovens at Auschwitz.

We know that many Germans and other non-Jews helped Jews by hiding them and smuggling them out of German-held territory. The industrialist Oskar Schindler protected and saved many by getting them on to his 'list' of workers. The Swedish diplomat Raoul Wallenberg worked with other resisters to provide Jews with Swedish and US passports to get them out of the reach of the Nazis in Hungary. He disappeared in mysterious circumstances in 1945. Of course, high-profile individuals such as these were rare. Most of the successful resisters were successful because they kept an extremely low profile and were discovered neither by the Nazis then, nor by historians today.

SOURCE 69

Hitler's dictatorship differed in one fundamental point from all its predecessors in history. It was the first dictatorship in the present period of modern technical development which made complete use of all technical means for the domination of its own country.

Through technical devices like the radio and loud-speaker, eighty million people were deprived of independent thought. It was thereby possible to subject them to the will of one man . . . The nightmare of many a man that one day nations could be ruled by technical means was realised in Hitler's totalitarian system.

Albert Speer, a leading Nazi, speaking at the Nuremberg war trials.

SOURCE 70

We didn't know much about Nazi ideals. Nevertheless, we were politically programmed: to obey orders, to cultivate the soldierly virtue of standing to attention and saying 'Yes, Sir' and to stop thinking when the word Fatherland was uttered and Germany's honour and greatness were mentioned.

A former member of the Hitler Youth looks back after the war.

FOCUS TASK

What are the dangers of totalitarianism?

For many people, the awful horrors of the Holocaust show most clearly the evils of a totalitarian state. If there is no effective opposition, eventually the leaders can do what they want.

1 Write your own definition of totalitarianism.
2 Explain how the Nazis attempted to achieve a totalitarian state. You could refer to Sources 69 and 70.
3 Using the example of the Holocaust, explain the dangers of totalitarianism. Explain:
   • why the Nazis started persecuting the Jews
   • how the persecution was made acceptable to ordinary German people
   • why the Nazis were able to proceed with their 'Final Solution'.
4 At the trials for war crimes after the war, many former guards at concentration camps said in their defence that they were simply obeying orders. Explain how you would respond to this defence of their actions.

The USA 1919–1941

7.1 What was the USA like in the 1920s?

FOCUS

In the 1920s the USA was the richest and most powerful country in the world. Its industry was booming. Then in 1929 disaster struck. The Wall Street Crash plunged the United States into a deep economic depression – and the rest of the world followed it.

In 7.1 you will study American society in the 1920s. You will investigate:

■ whether the economic boom in the 1920s was as widespread as it is sometimes made out to be
■ how and why American society was changing in the 1920s.

In 7.2 you will explore:

■ the causes and consequences of the Wall Street Crash.

In 7.3 you will examine:

■ how successfully Roosevelt's New Deal dealt with the problems facing the USA in the 1930s.

Timeline

This timeline shows the period you will be covering in this chapter. Some of the key dates are filled in already.

To help you get a complete picture of the period, you can make your own copy and add other details to it as you work through the chapter.

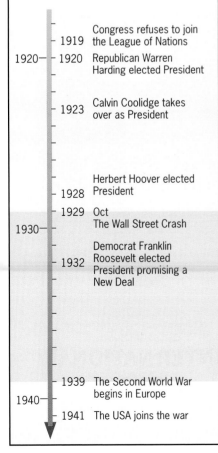

1920	1919	Congress refuses to join the League of Nations
	1920	Republican Warren Harding elected President
	1923	Calvin Coolidge takes over as President
	1928	Herbert Hoover elected President
1930	1929	Oct The Wall Street Crash
	1932	Democrat Franklin Roosevelt elected President promising a New Deal
1940	1939	The Second World War begins in Europe
	1941	The USA joins the war

Isolationist USA

As you have seen in Chapter 2, President Wilson took the USA into the First World War in 1917. It was a controversial decision. For decades, the USA had deliberately isolated itself from the squabbles of Europe and most Americans thought that was the right policy. But despite their opposition, Wilson took the USA into war. It was German submarine warfare against US ships that finally forced the USA into the conflict, but Wilson presented the war to the American people as a struggle to preserve freedom and democracy.

When the war ended in 1918, the divisions in the USA about what its role in the world should be resurfaced. Wilson got hopelessly bogged down in the squabbles of the European states after the war. Some Americans believed, as Wilson did, that the time had come for the USA to take a leading role in world affairs – that there was more chance of peace, if they were involved than if they stayed out. Others felt that Wilson had gone too far already. Thousands of American soldiers had been killed or wounded in a war that they felt was not their concern. US troops were even now involved in a civil war in Russia (see page 118). Now Wilson wanted the USA to take the lead in a League of Nations. Would this mean the USA supplying the troops and resources for this new international police force?

President Wilson travelled the country in 1919 to get the American people – and Congress – to accept the Treaty of Versailles and the League of Nations. The President needed to have the support of Congress (see the Factfile on page 187 to see how the US system of government works). Wilson had many political enemies and eventually they brought him down. In the end, the ISOLATIONISTS in the USA won the debate. You can read more about this on pages 229–31.

The USA then turned its back on Europe for much of the next 20 years. A new Republican President, Warren Harding, was elected in 1920 promising a return to 'normalcy' – normal life as it had been before the war. Americans turned their energies to what they did best – making money! Over the next ten years the USA, already the richest country in the world, became richer as its economy boomed. The next two pages will give you an idea of what this economic boom was like.

What was the 'boom'?

SOURCE 1

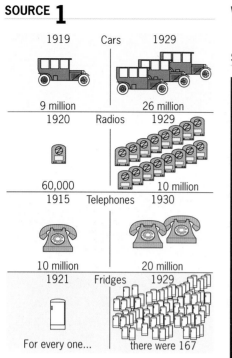

1919	Cars	1929
9 million		26 million
1920	Radios	1929
60,000		10 million
1915	Telephones	1930
10 million		20 million
1921	Fridges	1929
For every one...		there were 167

Sales of consumer goods, 1915–30. Overall, the output of American industry doubled in the 1920s.

SOURCE 2

Skyscrapers being built in New York City. There was more building being done in the boom years of the 1920s than at any time in the history of the USA.

SOURCE 3

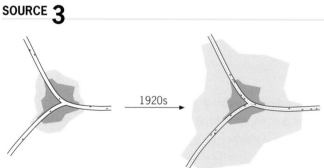

1920s

The car made it possible for more Americans to live in their own houses in the suburbs on the edge of towns. For example, Queens outside New York doubled in size in the 1920s. Grosse Point Park outside Detroit grew by 700 per cent.

SOURCE 4

Workers on the government's road-building programme. The Federal Road Act of 1916 began a period of intense road building all over the country. Road building employed more people than any other industry in the USA for the next ten years. During the 1920s the total extent of roads in the USA doubled.

SOURCE 5

 the most complete line of 4 and 6-cylinder Speed Trucks

For 1927

THE HARVESTER organization announces a complete line of improved Speed Trucks of six distinct chassis designs to meet every requirement for loads up to 1½ tons.

MODEL S is built to carry a 1½ ton load. It comes equipped with a 4 or 6-cylinder power plant and with any type of body for hauling and delivery.

MODEL SL—safe and low and easy to work with—is a 1½ ton chassis with either 6-cylinder engine and has wheelbase of 160 inches. Total of the frame is only 20 inches from the ground.

MODEL SD is a handy, specially-built 1½-ton chassis with a wheelbase of 110 inches, de-

signed for dump or tractor work. It is ideal for general contracting, road building and trailer hauling.

Every International Speed Truck is truck from the ground up—not a rebuilt passenger car. Engine, clutch transmission, axles, springs, frame and all the other essentials are the result of 22 years of truck building experience.

Whether your load run to bulk or weight whether your business calls for style and distinction plain utility in its hauling equipment—there is a 6-cylinder Speed Truck in either a 1½ or ¾ ton chassis made to meet your needs exactly

The International line also includes Heavy-Duty Trucks up to tons capacity, Motor Coaches, and the McCormick-Deering Industrial Tractor

INTERNATIONAL HARVESTER COMPANY
OF AMERICA
606 SO. MICHIGAN AVE. (INCORPORATED) CHICAGO, ILL
124 Company-owned Branches in the United States

INTERNATIONAL TRUCKS

The new roads gave rise to a new truck industry. In 1919 there were 1 million trucks in the USA. By 1929 there were 3.5 million.

SOURCE 6

"Onyx" Silk Hosiery

Lord & Taylor   New York

Silk stockings had once been a luxury item reserved for the rich. In 1900 only 12,000 pairs had been sold. In the 1920s rayon was invented which was a cheaper substitute for silk. In 1930, 300 million pairs of stockings were sold to a female population of around 100 million.

SOURCE 7

A passenger aircraft in 1927. There were virtually no civilian airlines in 1918. By 1930 the new aircraft companies flew 162,000 flights a year.

SOURCE 8

Workers erecting electricity pylons. In 1918 only a few homes had electricity. By 1929 almost all urban homes had it, although not many farms were on the electricity supply grid.

1 Use Sources 1–9 to make a list of features of the economic boom of the 1920s under the following headings:
  - Industry
  - Transport
  - Home life
  - Cities
2 Draw a chart to show connections between any of the features shown in the sources.
3 Using these sources, write a 20-word definition of 'the economic boom of the 1920s'.

SOURCE 9

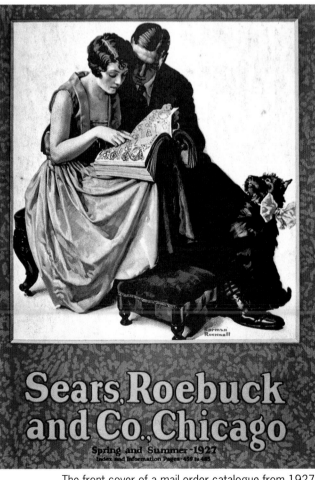

Sears, Roebuck and Co., Chicago

Spring and Summer-1927
Index and Information Pages 459 to 465

The front cover of a mail order catalogue from 1927.

Why was there an economic boom in the 1920s?

As you can see from Sources 1–9, it seemed that everything in the USA was booming in the 1920s. You are now going to investigate the various reasons for that boom.

Industrial strength

The USA was a vast country, rich in natural resources (see Source 10 below), with a growing population. It didn't need to import many raw materials, and it didn't need to export all its goods. The home market was large and was growing.

SOURCE 10

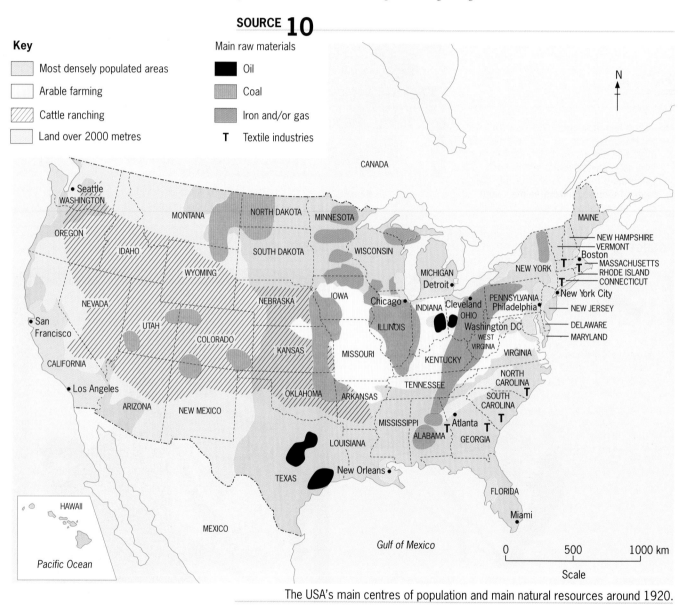

Key

Most densely populated areas
Arable farming
Cattle ranching
Land over 2000 metres

Main raw materials

■ Oil
Coal
Iron and/or gas
T Textile industries

The USA's main centres of population and main natural resources around 1920.

Ever since the 1860s and 1870s, American industry had been growing vigorously. By the time of the First World War, the USA led the world in most areas of industry. It had massive steel, coal and textile industries. It was the leading oil producer. It was foremost in developing new technology such as motor cars, telephones and electric lighting. Its newer industries such as chemicals were growing fast. Its new film industry already led the world.

The managers of these industries were increasingly skilled and professional, and they were selling more and more of their products not just in the USA but in Europe, Latin America and the Far East.

American agriculture had become the most efficient and productive in the world. In fact, farmers had become so successful that they were producing more than they could sell, which was a very serious problem (see page 191). In 1914, however, most Americans would have confidently stated that American agriculture and industry were going from strength to strength.

The First World War

The Americans tried hard to stay out of the fighting in the First World War. But throughout the war they lent money to the Allies, and sold arms and munitions to Britain and France. They sold massive amounts of foodstuffs as well. This one-way trade gave American industry a real boost. In addition, while the European powers slugged it out in France, the Americans were able to take over Europe's trade around the world. American exports to the areas controlled by European colonial powers increased during the war.

There were other benefits as well. Before the war Germany had had one of the world's most successful chemicals industries. The war stopped it in its tracks. By the end of the war the USA had far outstripped Germany in the supply of chemical products. Explosives manufacture during the war also stimulated a range of by-products which became new American industries in their own right. Plastics and other new materials were produced.

Historians have called the growth and change at this time the USA's second industrial revolution. The war actually helped rather than hindered the 'revolution'.

When the USA joined the fighting it was not in the war long enough for the war to drain American resources in the way it drained Europe's. There was a downturn in the USA when war industries readjusted to peacetime, but it was only a blip. By 1922 the American economy was growing fast once again.

Republican policies

A third factor behind the boom was the policies of the Republican Party. From 1920 to 1932 all the US presidents were Republican, and Republicans also dominated Congress. Here are some of their beliefs.

1 Laissez-faire

Republicans believed that government should interfere as little as possible in the everyday lives of the people. This attitude is called 'laissez-faire'. In their view, the job of the President was to leave the businessman alone – to do his job. That was where prosperity came from.

2 Tariffs

The Republicans believed in import TARIFFS which made it expensive to import foreign goods. For example, in 1922 Harding introduce the Fordney–McCumber tariff which made imported food expensive in the USA. These tariffs protected businesses against foreign competition and allowed American companies to grow even more rapidly. The USA also began closing its borders to foreign immigrants (see page 200).

3 Low taxation

The Republicans kept taxation as low as possible. This brought some benefits to ordinary working people, but it brought even more to the very wealthy. The Republican thinking was that if people kept their own money, they would spend it on American goods and wealthy people would reinvest their money in industries.

4 Trusts

The Republicans also allowed the development of trusts. These were huge super-corporations, which dominated industry. Woodrow Wilson and the Democrats had fought against trusts because they believed it was unhealthy for men such as Carnegie (steel) and Rockefeller (oil) to have almost complete control of one vital sector of industry. The Republicans allowed the trusts to do what they wanted, believing that the 'captains of industry' knew better than politicians did what was good for the USA.

---

1 List the benefits that the First World War brought to the US economy.

FACTFILE

US system of government

★ **The federal system:** The USA's federal system means that all the individual states look after their own internal affairs (such as education). Questions that concern all of the states (such as making treaties with other countries) are dealt with by Congress.

★ **The Constitution:** The Constitution lays out how the government is supposed to operate and what it is allowed to do.

★ **The President:** He is the single most important politician in the USA. He is elected every four years. However, the Constitution of the USA is designed to stop one individual from becoming too powerful. Congress and the Supreme Court both act as 'watchdogs' checking how the President behaves.

★ **Congress:** Congress is made up of the Senate and the House of Representatives. Congress and the President run the country.

★ **The Supreme Court:** This is made up of judges, who are usually very experienced lawyers. Their main task is to make sure that American governments do not misuse their power or pass unfair laws. They have the power to say that a law is unconstitutional (against the Constitution), which usually means that they feel the law would harm American citizens.

★ **Parties:** There are two main political parties, the Republicans and the Democrats. In the 1920s and 1930s, the Republicans were stronger in the industrial north of the USA while the Democrats had more support in the south. On the whole, Republicans in the 1920s and 1930s preferred government to stay out of people's lives if possible. The Democrats were more prepared to intervene in everyday life.

Average annual industrial wages	1919:	$1,158
	1927:	$1,304
Number of millionaires	1914:	7,000
	1928:	35,000

Wealth in the USA.

A pre-war anti-trust cartoon. Although there was opposition to trusts, they were so successful and influential that it was difficult to limit their power.

1 How could the Republicans use Sources 11 and 13 to justify their policies?
2 How could critics of Republican policies use Sources 11 and 13 to attack the Republicans?

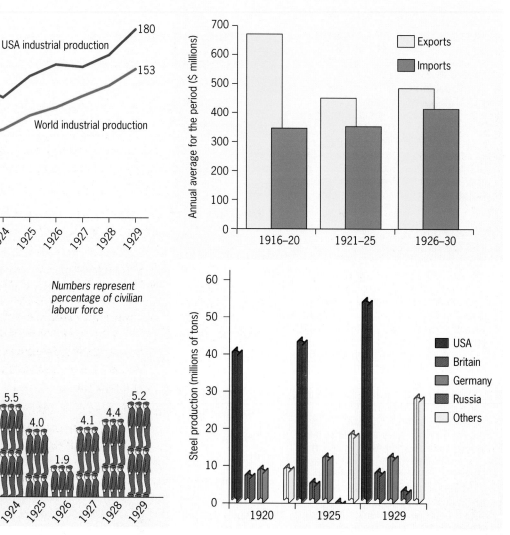

The growth of the US economy in the 1920s.

New industries, new methods

Through the 1920s new industries and new methods of production were developed in the USA. The country was able to exploit its vast resources of raw materials to produce steel, chemicals, glass and machinery.

These products became the foundation of an enormous boom in consumer goods. Telephones, radios, vacuum cleaners and washing machines were mass-produced on a vast scale, making them cheaper so more people could buy them. New electrical companies such as Hoover became household names. They used the latest, most efficient techniques proposed by the 'Industrial Efficiency Movement'.

At the same time, the big industries used sophisticated sales and marketing techniques to get people to buy their goods. Mass nationwide advertising had been used for the first time in the USA during the war to get Americans to support the war effort. Many of the advertisers who had learned their skills in wartime propaganda now set up agencies to sell cars, cigarettes, clothing and other consumer items. Poster advertisements, radio advertisements and travelling salesmen encouraged Americans to spend. Even if they did not have the money, people could borrow it easily. Or they could take advantage of the new 'Buy now, pay later' hire purchase schemes. Eight out of ten radios and six out of ten cars were bought on credit.

The most important of these new booming industries was the motor-car industry. The motor car had only been developed in the 1890s. The first cars were built by blacksmiths and other skilled craftsmen. They took a long time to make and were very expensive. In 1900 only 4000 cars were made. Car production was revolutionised by Henry Ford. In 1913 he set up the first moving production line in the world, in a giant shed in Detroit. Each worker on the line had one or two small jobs to do as the skeleton of the car moved past him. At the beginning of the line, a skeleton car went in; at the end of the line was a new car. The most famous of these was the Model T. More than 15 million were produced between 1908 and 1925. In 1927 they came off the production line at a rate of one every ten seconds. In 1929, 4.8 million cars were made.

SOURCE 14

We are quick to adopt the latest time and labour saving devices in business. The modern woman has an equal right to employ in her home the most popular electric cleaner: The Frantz Premier. Over 250,000 are in use. We have branches and dealers everywhere. Our price is modest — time payments if desired.

Advertisement for the Frantz Premier vacuum cleaner.

SOURCE 15

Ford's production line in 1913.

Model Ts in an American high street. In 1925 a Model T cost $290.
This was almost three months' wages for an American factory worker.

By the end of the 1920s the motor industry was the USA's biggest industry. As well as employing hundreds of thousands of workers directly, it also kept workers in other industries in employment. Glass, leather, steel and rubber were all required to build the new vehicles. Automobiles used up 75 per cent of US glass production in the 1920s! Petrol was needed to run them. And a massive army of labourers was busily building roads throughout the country for these cars to drive on. In fact, road construction was the biggest single employer in the 1920s.

Owning a car was not just a rich person's privilege, as it was in Europe. There was one car to five people in the USA compared with one to 43 in Britain, and one to 7000 in Russia. The car made it possible for people to buy a house in the suburbs, which further boosted house building. It also stimulated the growth of hundreds of other smaller businesses, ranging from hot dog stands and advertising bill boards to petrol stations and holiday resorts.

A state of mind

One thing that runs through all the factors you have looked at so far is an attitude or a state of mind. Most Americans believed that they had a right to 'prosperity'. For many it was a main aim in life to have a nice house, a good job and plenty to eat, and for their home to be filled with the latest consumer goods. Consuming more and more was seen as part of being American.

In earlier decades, thrift (being careful with money and saving 'for a rainy day') had been seen as a good quality. In the 1920s this was replaced by a belief that spending money was a better quality.

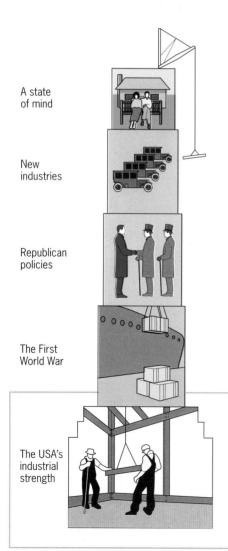

A state of mind

New industries

Republican policies

The First World War

The USA's industrial strength

FOCUS TASK

What factors caused the economic boom?

1 Make a copy of this diagram. Complete it by adding notes at the right-hand side for each heading. You will need to refer to the information and sources on pages 186–90.
2 One historian has said: 'Without the new automobile industry, the prosperity of the 1920s would scarcely have been possible.'
   Explain whether you agree or disagree with this statement. Support your explanation by referring to the sources and information on pages 186–90.

A cartoon showing the situation faced by American farmers in the 1920s.

1 Explain the message of Source 17.

Problems in the farming industry

While so many Americans were enjoying the boom, farmers most definitely were not. Total US farm income dropped from $22 billion in 1919 to just $13 billion in 1928. There were a number of reasons why farming had such problems.

After the war, Europe imported far less food from the USA. This was partly because Europe was poor, and it was partly a response to US tariffs which stopped Europe from exporting to the USA (see page 187).

Farmers were also struggling against competition from the highly efficient Canadian wheat producers. All of this came at a time when the population of the USA was actually falling and there were fewer mouths to feed.

Underlying all these problems was overproduction. From 1900 to 1920, while farming was doing well, more and more land was being farmed. Improved machinery, especially the combine harvester, and improved fertilisers made US agriculture extremely efficient. The result was that by 1920 it was producing surpluses of wheat which nobody wanted.

In the 1920s the average US farmer was each year growing enough to feed his family and 14 others. Prices plummeted as desperate farmers tried to sell their produce. In 1921 alone, most farm prices fell by 50 per cent (see Source 18). Hundreds of rural banks collapsed in the 1920s and there were five times as many farm bankruptcies as there had been in the 1900s and 1910s.

Not all farmers were affected by these problems. Rich Americans wanted fresh vegetables and fruit throughout the year. Shipments of lettuce to the cities, for example, rose from 14,000 crates in 1920 to 52,000 in 1928. But for most farmers the 1920s were a time of hardship.

This was a serious issue. About half of all Americans lived in rural areas, mostly working on farms or in businesses that sold goods to farmers. Problems in farming therefore directly affected more than 60 million Americans.

Six million rural Americans, mainly farm labourers, were forced off the land in the 1920s. Many of these were unskilled workers who migrated to the cities, where there was little demand for their labour. America's black population was particularly badly hit. They had always done the least skilled jobs in the rural areas. As they lost their jobs on the farms, three-quarters of a million of them became unemployed.

FOCUS TASK

Why did agriculture not share in the prosperity?

Farmers became the fiercest critics of the policies of the Republican Party.

Write a letter from the farmer in Source 17 to the Republican President, Calvin Coolidge, to complain about Republican policies.

Explain to the President why farming is in the state it's in and why his government should do something about it.

SOURCE **18**

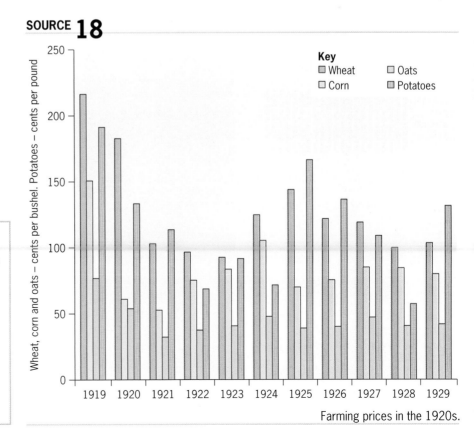

Key
Wheat   Oats
Corn   Potatoes

Farming prices in the 1920s.

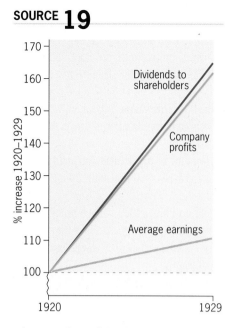

A comparison of the growth of profits and the growth of average earnings.

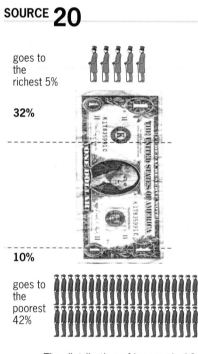

goes to the richest 5%

32%

10%

goes to the poorest 42%

The distribution of income in 1925.

Did all Americans benefit from the boom?

You have already seen how the farmers – a very large group in American society – did not share in the prosperity of the 1920s. But they were not alone. Workers in many older industries, such as coal, leather and textiles, did not benefit much either. Coal suffered from competition from new industries such as oil and electricity. Leather and textiles were protected from foreign competition, but not from domestic competition. They suffered from the development of new man-made materials. They also struggled to compete with cheap labour in the southern states. Even if workers in these industries did get a pay rise, their wages did not increase on the same scale as company profits or dividends paid to shareholders (see Source 19).

In 1928 there was a strike in the coal industry in North Carolina, where the male workers were paid only $18 and women $9 for a 70-hour week, at a time when $48 per week was considered to be the minimum required for a decent life. In fact, for the majority of Americans wages remained well below that figure. It has been estimated that 42 per cent of Americans lived below the poverty line – they did not have the money needed to pay for essentials such as food, clothing, housing and heating for their families.

What's more, throughout this period unemployment remained a problem. The growth in industry in the 1920s did not create many new jobs. Industries were growing by electrifying or mechanising production. The same number of people (around five per cent) were unemployed at the peak of the boom in 1929 as in 1920. Yet the amount of goods produced had doubled. These millions of unemployed Americans were not sharing in the boom. They included many poor whites, but an even greater proportion of black and Hispanic people and other members of the USA's large immigrant communities.

The plight of the poor was desperate for the individuals concerned. But it was also damaging to American industry. The boom of the 1920s was a consumer-led boom, which means that it was led by ordinary families buying things for their home. But with so many families too poor to buy such goods, the demand for them was likely to begin to tail off. However, Republican policy remained not to interfere, and this included doing nothing about unemployment or poverty.

A hunger march staged by workers in Washington in the 1920s.

1 Use the text and sources on this page to explain:
   a) why the government should have been concerned about poverty
   b) why, in the event, it did very little to help the poor.

SOURCE 22

The 1922 coal strike.

SOURCE 23

A doctor visiting a poor American family in the 1920s. Doctors' fees were very expensive. They would only be called out if someone was seriously ill.

Chicago in the 1920s

You can find out more about a period by looking at particular places or people. Historians have found out a lot about Chicago in the 1920s. Chicago was one of America's biggest cities. It was the centre of the steel, meat and clothing industries, which employed many unskilled workers. Such industries had busy and slack periods. In slack periods the workers would be 'seasonally unemployed'. Many of these workers were Polish or Italian immigrants, or black migrants from the southern United States. How far did they share in the prosperity of the 1920s?

Only three per cent of semi-skilled workers owned a car. Compare that with richer areas where 29 per cent owned a car. It was the middle classes, not the workers in industry, who bought cars. On the whole, workers in Chicago didn't like to buy large items on credit. They preferred to save for when they might not have a job. Many of them bought smaller items on credit, such as phonographs (record players) and radios. Chicago became the centre of a growing record industry specialising in Polish and Italian records for the immigrant communities.

The poor whites did not benefit much from the new chain stores which had revolutionised shopping in the 1920s. These stores sold the same standard goods all across the country but they mostly served the middle classes. Nearly all of them were in middle-class districts. Poorer white industrial workers preferred to shop at the local grocer's where the owner was more flexible and gave them credit, even though they could have saved money by going to the chain stores.

However, the poor did join the movie craze. There were hundreds of cinemas in Chicago with four performances a day. Working people in Chicago spent more than half of their leisure budget on movies. Even those who were so poor that they were getting Mothers' Aid Assistance went often. It only cost 10 or 20 cents to see a movie. Yet even in cinema-going the poor were separated from the rich. They went to the local cinema because they couldn't afford the $1 admission, plus the bus fare, to the more luxurious town-centre cinemas.

By 1930 there was one radio for every two to three households in the poorer districts of Chicago. Those who didn't own a radio set went to shops or to neighbours to listen. It was a communal activity – most families listened to the radio together.

SOURCE 25

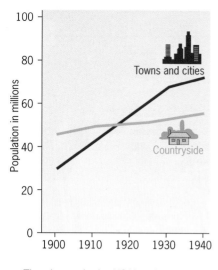

The change in the USA's urban and rural populations, 1900–1940.

SOURCE 26

The Builder, painted by Gerrit A. Beneker in the 1920s.

1 Write an advertising slogan to go with Source 26, inviting workers to come to New York City.

SOURCE 27

King Oliver's Creole Jazz Band, 1920. Louis Armstrong is kneeling at the front.

The USA in the Roaring Twenties

The 1920s are often called the Roaring Twenties. The name suggests a time of riotous fun, loud music and wild enjoyment when everyone was having a good time.

You have already found out enough about the USA in the period to know that this is probably not how everyone saw this decade. For example, how do you think the poor farmers described on page 191 would react to the suggestion that the 1920s were one long party?

What is in no doubt is that this was a time of turmoil for many Americans. For those who joined in 'the party', it was a time of liberation and rebellion against traditional values. For those who did not, it was a time of anxiety and worry. For them, the changes taking place were proof that the USA was going down the drain and needed rescuing.

All this combined to make the 1920s a decade of contrasts.

Growing cities

In 1920, for the first time in American history, more Americans lived in towns and cities than in the country. As you can see from Source 25, throughout the 1920s cities were growing fast. People flocked to them from all over the USA. The growing city with its imposing skyline of skyscrapers was one of the most powerful symbols of 1920s USA. In New York, the skyscrapers were built because there was no more land available. But even small cities, where land was not in short supply, wanted skyscrapers to announce to the country that they were sharing in the boom.

Throughout the 1920s there was tension between rural USA and urban USA. Many people in the country thought that their traditional values, which emphasised religion and family life, were under threat from the growing cities, which they thought were full of atheists, drunks and criminals. Certain rural states, particularly in the south, fought a rearguard action against the 'evil' effects of the city throughout the 1920s, as you will see on page 205.

Entertainment

During the 1920s the entertainment industry blossomed. The average working week dropped from 47.4 to 44.2 hours so people had more leisure time. Average wages rose by 11 per cent (in real terms) so workers also had more disposable income. A lot of this spare time and money was channelled into entertainment.

Radio

Almost everyone in the USA listened to the radio. Most households had their own set. People who could not afford to buy one outright, could purchase one in instalments. The choice of programmes grew quickly. In August 1921 there was only one licensed radio station in America. By the end of 1922 there were 508 of them. By 1929 the new network NBC was making $150 million a year.

Jazz

The radio gave much greater access to new music. Jazz music became an obsession among young people. Black people who moved from the country to the cities had brought jazz and blues music with them. Blues music was particularly popular among the black population, while jazz captured the imagination of both white and black young Americans.

Such was the power of jazz music that the 1920s became known as the Jazz Age. Along with jazz went new dances such as the Charleston, and new styles of behaviour which were summed up in the image of the flapper, a woman who wore short dresses and make-up and who smoked in public. One writer said that the ideal flapper was 'expensive and about nineteen'.

The older generation saw jazz and everything associated with it as a corrupting influence on the young people of the USA. The newspapers and magazines printed articles analysing the influence of jazz (see Source 28).

SOURCE 28

(i) Jazz employs primitive rhythms which excite the baser human instincts.

(ii) Jazz music causes drunkenness. Reason and reflection are lost and the actions of the persons are directed by the stronger animal passions.

Comments on jazz music in articles in the 1920s.

2 What do you think the writers in Source 28 mean by 'the baser human instincts' and 'the stronger animal passions'?

SOURCE 29

Crowds queuing for cinema tickets in Chicago. In 1920, 40 million tickets were sold per week and in 1929, 100 million.

SOURCE 30

There was never a time in American history when youth had such a special sense of importance as in the years after the First World War. There was a gulf between the generations like a geological fault. Young men who had fought in the trenches felt that they knew a reality their elders could not even imagine. Young girls no longer consciously modelled themselves on their mothers, whose experience seemed unusable in the 1920s.

William E Leuchtenberg, *The Perils of Prosperity*, 1958.

Sport

Sport was another boom area. Baseball became a big money sport with legendary teams like the New York Yankees and Boston Red Sox. Prominent figures such as Al Capone (see pages 209–10) were baseball fans. Boxing was also a very popular sport, with heroes like world heavyweight champion Jack Dempsey.

Cinema

In a small suburb outside Los Angeles, called Hollywood, a major film industry was developing. All-year-round sunshine meant that the studios could produce large numbers of films or 'movies'. New stars like Charlie Chaplin and Buster Keaton made audiences roar with laughter, while Douglas Fairbanks thrilled them in daring adventure films. Until 1927 all movies were silent. In 1927 the first 'talkie' was made.

During the 1920s movies became a multi-billion dollar business and it was estimated that, by the end of the decade, a hundred million cinema tickets were being sold each week. That's as many as are sold in a year in Britain today.

Morals

Source 30 is one historian's description of this period. He refers to new attitudes among young women (see pages 196–97). The gulf he mentions was most obvious in sexual morals. In the generation before the war, sex had still been a taboo subject. After the war it became a major concern of tabloid newspapers, Hollywood films, and everyday conversation. Scott Fitzgerald, one of a celebrated new group of young American writers who had served in the First World War, said: 'None of the mothers had any idea how casually their daughters were accustomed to be kissed.'

The cinema quickly discovered the selling power of sex. The first cinema star to be sold on sex appeal was Theda Bara who, without any acting talent, made a string of wildly successful films with titles like *Forbidden Path* and *When a Woman Sins*. Clara Bow was sold as the 'It' girl. Everybody knew that 'It' meant 'sex'. Hollywood turned out dozens of films a month about 'It', such as *Up in Mabel's Room, Her Purchase Price* and *A Shocking Night*. Male stars too, such as Rudolph Valentino, were presented as sex symbols. Women were said to faint at the very sight of him as a half-naked Arab prince in *The Sheik* (1921).

Today these films would be considered very tame indeed, but at the time they were considered very daring. The more conservative rural states were worried by the deluge of sex-obsessed films, and 36 states threatened to introduce censorship legislation. Hollywood responded with its own censorship code which ensured that, while films might still be full of sex, at least the sinful characters were not allowed to get away with it!

Meanwhile, in the real world, contraceptive advice was openly available for the first time. Sex outside marriage was much more common than in the past, although probably more people talked about it and went to films about it than actually did it!

The car

The motor car was one factor that tended to make all the other features of the 1920s mentioned above more possible. Cars helped the cities to grow by opening up the suburbs. They carried their owners to and from their entertainments. Cars carried boyfriends and girlfriends beyond the moral gaze of their parents and they took Americans to an increasing range of sporting events, beach holidays, shopping trips, picnics in the country, or simply on visits to their family and friends.

FOCUS TASK

The Roaring Twenties

Draw a diagram to summarise the features of the Roaring Twenties. You can get lots of ideas from the text on these two pages, but remember that other factors may also be relevant: for example, material on the economy (pages 184–90) or on women (pages 196–97). You could also use the internet.

A school teacher in 1905.

Women in 1920s USA

Women formed half of the population of the USA and their lives were as varied as those of men. It is therefore difficult to generalise. However, before the First World War middle-class women in the USA, like those in Britain, were expected to lead restricted lives. They had to wear very restrictive clothes and behave politely. They were expected not to wear make-up. Their relationships with men were strictly controlled. They had to have a chaperone with them when they went out with a boyfriend. They were expected not to take part in sport or to smoke in public. In most states they could not vote. Most women were expected to be housewives. Very few paid jobs were open to women. Most working women were in lower-paid jobs such as cleaning, dressmaking and secretarial work.

In rural USA there were particularly tight restrictions owing to the Churches' traditional attitude to the role of women. In the 1920s, many of these things began to change, especially for urban women and middle-class women. When the USA joined the war in 1917, some women were taken into the war industries, giving them experience of skilled factory work for the first time. In 1920 they got the vote in all states. Through the 1920s they shared the liberating effects of the car, and their domestic work was made easier (in theory) by new electrical goods such as vacuum cleaners and washing machines.

For younger urban women many of the traditional rules of behaviour were eased as well. Women wore more daring clothes. They smoked in public and drank with men, in public. They went out with men, in cars, without a chaperone. They kissed in public.

In urban areas more women took on jobs – particularly middle-class women. They typically took on jobs created by the new industries. There were 10 million women in jobs in 1929, 24 per cent more than in 1920. With money of their own, working women became the particular target of advertising. Even women who did not earn their own money were increasingly seen as the ones who took decisions about whether to buy new items for the home. There is evidence that women's role in choosing cars triggered Ford, in 1925, to make them available in colours other than black.

Women were less likely to stay in unhappy marriages. In 1914 there were 100,000 divorces; in 1929 there were twice as many.

Films and novels also exposed women to a much wider range of role models. Millions of women a week saw films with sexy or daring heroines as well as other films that showed women in a more traditional role. The newspaper, magazine and film industries found that sex sold much better than anything else.

Limitations

It might seem to you as if everything was changing, and for young, middle-class women living in cities a lot was changing in the 1920s. However, this is only part of the story. Take work, for example. Women were still paid less than men, even when they did the same job. One of the reasons women's employment increased when men's did not was that women were cheaper employees. In politics as well, women in no way achieved equality with men. They may have been given the vote but it did not give them access to political power. Political parties wanted women's votes, but they didn't particularly want women as political candidates as they considered them 'unelectable'. Although many women, such as Eleanor Roosevelt (see Profile), had a high public standing, there was only a handful of women elected by 1929.

Young flappers in the 1920s.

1 Compare the clothes of the women in Sources 31 and 32. Write a detailed description of the differences between them.
2 Flappers were controversial figures in the 1920s. List as many reasons as possible for this.

SOURCE 33

Gloria Swanson in *The Trespasser* (1929). Gloria Swanson was one of the most successful film stars of the 1920s and *The Trespasser* was her first 'talkie'.

PROFILE

Eleanor Roosevelt

★ Born 1884 into a wealthy family.
★ Married Franklin D Roosevelt in 1905.
★ Heavily involved in:
  – League of Women Voters
  – Women's Trade Union League
  – Women's City Club (New York)
  – New York State Democratic Party (Women's Division).
★ Work concentrated on:
  – bringing New York Democrats together
  – public housing for low-income workers
  – birth control information
  – better conditions for women workers.

3 How does Source 35 contrast with the image of women given by Sources 32 and 33?

Were the lives of American women changing?

From films such as Source 33 you would think that all American women were living passionate lives full of steamy romance. However, novels and films of the period can be misleading.

Women certainly did watch such films, in great numbers. But there is no evidence that the majority of women began to copy what they saw in the 1920s. In fact the evidence suggests that the reaction of many women was one of opposition and outrage. There was a strong conservative element in American society. A combination of traditional religion and old country values kept most American women in a much more restricted role than young urban women enjoyed.

SOURCE 34

It is wholly confusing to read the advertisements in the magazines that feature the enticing qualities of vacuum cleaners, mechanical refrigerators and hundreds of other devices which should lighten the chores of women in the home. On the whole these large middle classes do their own housework with few of the mechanical aids . . .

Women who live on farms – and they form the largest group in the United States – do a great deal of work besides the labour of caring for their children, washing the clothes, caring for the home and cooking . . . thousands still labour in the fields . . . help milk the cows . . .

The other largest group of American women comprise the families of the labourers . . . of the miners, the steel workers . . . the vast army of unskilled, semi-skilled and skilled workers. The wages of these men are on the whole so small [that] wives must do double duty – that is, caring for the children and the home and toil on the outside as wage earners.

Doris E Fleischman, *America as Americans See It*, F J Ringel (ed.), 1932.

SOURCE 35

Though a few young upper middle-class women in the cities talked about throwing off the older conventions – they were the flappers – most women stuck to more traditional attitudes concerning 'their place' . . . most middle-class women concentrated on managing the home . . . Their daughters, far from taking to the streets against sexual discrimination, were more likely to prepare for careers as mothers and housewives. Millions of immigrant women and their daughters . . . also clung to traditions that placed men firmly in control of the family . . . Most American women concentrated on making ends meet or setting aside money to purchase the new gadgets that offered some release from household drudgery.

J T Patterson, *America in the Twentieth Century*, 1999.

FOCUS TASK

Did the role of women change in the 1920s?

Work in pairs. Write a script for a story strip to complete this conversation. You will need at least seven more scenes with speech bubbles.

SOURCE 36

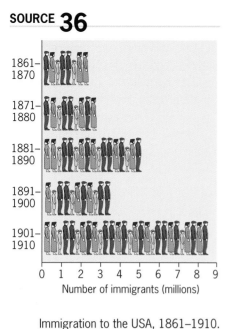

| 1861–1870 |
| 1871–1880 |
| 1881–1890 |
| 1891–1900 |
| 1901–1910 |

Number of immigrants (millions)

Immigration to the USA, 1861–1910.

Prejudice and intolerance

At the same time as some young Americans were experiencing liberation, others were facing intolerance and racism.

The vast majority of Americans were either immigrants or descendants of recent immigrants. Source 37 shows you the ethnic background of the main groups.

As you can see from Source 36, immigration to the USA was at an all-time high from 1901 to 1910. Immigrants were flooding in, particularly Jews from eastern Europe and Russia who were fleeing persecution, and people from Italy who were fleeing poverty. Many Italian immigrants did not intend to settle in the USA, but hoped to make money to take back to their families in Italy.

The United States had always prided itself on being a 'melting pot'. In theory, individual groups lost their ethnic identity and blended together with other groups to become just 'Americans'. In practice, however, this wasn't always the case. In the USA's big cities the more established immigrant groups – Irish Americans, French Canadians and German Americans – competed for the best jobs and the best available housing. These groups tended to look down on the more recent eastern European and Italian immigrants. These in turn had nothing but contempt for black Americans and Mexicans, who were almost at the bottom of the scale.

SOURCE 37

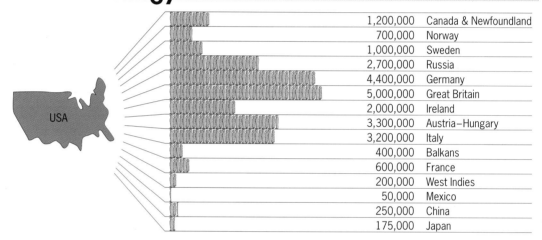

1,200,000	Canada & Newfoundland
700,000	Norway
1,000,000	Sweden
2,700,000	Russia
4,400,000	Germany
5,000,000	Great Britain
2,000,000	Ireland
3,300,000	Austria–Hungary
3,200,000	Italy
400,000	Balkans
600,000	France
200,000	West Indies
50,000	Mexico
250,000	China
175,000	Japan

The ethnic background of Americans.

SOURCE 38

Italians were reluctant to live alongside people with darker skins and tended to class Mexicans with Negroes. A social worker noted, however, that newly arrived Italians got on well with Mexicans; only after they had been in the United States for some time did they refuse to associate with them. 'In Italy', he said to one Italian, 'you would not be prejudiced against the Mexicans because of their colour.' The reply was 'No, but we are becoming Americanised.'

Maldwyn Jones argues in *Destination America* (published in 1985) that in many ways racist attitudes were more firmly entrenched in America than they had been in Europe.

SOURCE 39

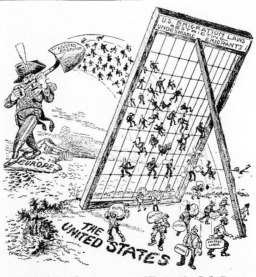

A FINER SCREEN NEEDED.

By permission of] [The Brooklyn Daily Eagle.

A cartoon from 1904.

The Red Scare

In the 1920s these racist attitudes towards immigrants were made worse by an increased fear of Bolshevism or Communism. The USA watched with alarm as Russia became Communist after the Russian Revolution of 1917 (see pages 114–16). It feared that many of the more recent immigrants from eastern Europe and Russia were bringing similar radical ideas with them to the USA. This reaction was called the Red Scare.

In 1919 Americans saw evidence all around them to confirm their fears. There was a wave of disturbances. Some 400,000 American workers went on strike. Even the police in Boston went on strike and looters and thieves roamed the city. There were race riots in 25 towns.

Today, most historians argue that the strikes were caused by economic hardship. High levels of wartime production were being scaled down – so fewer workers were needed. Most strikers were poorly paid labourers in heavy industry who had been taken on for wartime contracts and then laid off. Many were immigrant workers, since they were usually the first to lose their jobs. Other workers were simply striking for improvements in low pay and appalling working conditions.

However, many prominent Americans in the 1920s saw the strikes as the dangerous signs of Communist interference. Communism meant state control of agriculture and industry, taking it away from its owners, which alarmed Americans. Fear of Communism combined with prejudice against immigrants was a powerful mix.

SOURCE 40

The blaze of revolution is eating its way into the homes of the American workman, licking at the altars of the churches, leaping into the belfry of the school house, crawling into the sacred corners of American homes, seeking to replace the marriage vows with libertine laws, burning up the foundations of society.

Mitchell Palmer, US Attorney General, speaking in 1920.

SOURCE 41

A 1924 cartoon showing attitudes to Communism in the USA.

SOURCE 42

The steamship companies haul them over to America and as soon as they step off the ships the problem of the steamship companies is settled, but our problem has only begun – Bolshevism, red anarchy, black-handers and kidnappers, challenging the authority and integrity of our flag . . . Thousands come here who will never take the oath to support our constitution and become citizens of the USA. They pay allegiance to some other country while they live upon the substance of our own. They fill places that belong to the wage earning citizens of America . . . They are of no service whatever to our people . . . They constitute a menace and a danger to us every day.

Republican Senator Heflin speaking in 1921 in a debate over whether to limit immigration.

The fears were not totally unjustified. Many immigrants in the USA did hold radical political beliefs. Anarchists published pamphlets and distributed them widely in American cities, calling for the overthrow of the government. In April 1919 a bomb planted in a church in Milwaukee killed ten people. In May, bombs were posted to 36 prominent Americans. In June more bombs went off in seven US cities, and one almost succeeded in killing Mitchell Palmer, the US Attorney General. All those known to have radical political beliefs were rounded up. They were generally immigrants and the evidence against them was often flimsy. The person responsible for this purge was J Edgar Hoover, a young clerk appointed by Palmer. Hoover was to become an immensely important and deeply sinister figure in US history (see page 216). He built up files on 60,000 suspects and in 1919–20 around 10,000 individuals were informed that they were to be deported from the USA.

As Palmer discovered that these purges were popular, he tried to use the fear of revolution to build up his own political support and run for president. Trade unionists, black people, Jews, Catholics and almost all minority groups found themselves accused of being Communists. In the end, however, Palmer caused his own downfall. He predicted that a Red Revolution would begin in May 1920. When nothing happened, the papers began to make fun of him and officials in the Justice Department who were sickened by Palmer's actions undermined him. Secretary of Labor Louis Post examined all of the case files prepared by Hoover and found that only 556 out of the thousands of cases brought had any basis in fact.

ACTIVITY

Work in pairs.

1 One of you collect evidence to show that the Red Scare was the result of fear of Communism.
2 The other collect evidence to show that the Red Scare was the result of prejudice and intolerance.
3 Now try to come up with a definition of the Red Scare that combines both of your views.

1 Look at Sources 40–42. Do they tell historians more about Communists or the enemies of Communism? Explain your answer.

1 Look again at Sources 38 and 42 on pages 198–99. What problems are associated with immigration?
2 How do you think a supporter of Sacco and Vanzetti would reply to Source 42?
3 Do you think that the US immigration policy was racist? Explain your answer.

Sacco and Vanzetti

Two high-profile victims of the Red Scare were Italian Americans Nicola Sacco and Bartolomeo Vanzetti. They were arrested in 1920 on suspicion of armed robbery and murder. It quickly emerged that they were self-confessed anarchists. Anarchists hated the American system of government and believed in destroying it by creating social disorder. Their trial became less a trial for murder, more a trial of their radical ideas. The case against them was very shaky. The prosecution relied heavily on racist slurs about their Italian origins, and on stirring up fears about their radical beliefs. The judge at the trial said that although Vanzetti 'may not actually have committed the crime attributed to him he is nevertheless morally culpable [to blame] because he is the enemy of our existing institutions'. After the trial, the judge referred to the two as 'those anarchist bastards'.

Sacco and Vanzetti were convicted on flimsy evidence. Explaining the verdict, a leading lawyer of the time said: 'Judge Thayer is narrow minded . . . unintelligent . . . full of prejudice. He has been carried away by fear of Reds which has captured about 90 per cent of the American people.' After six years of legal appeals, Sacco and Vanzetti were eventually executed in 1927, to a storm of protest around the world from both radicals and moderates who saw how unjustly the trial had been conducted.

SOURCE 43

Therefore, I, Michael S Dukakis, Governor of the Commonwealth of Massachusetts . . . hereby proclaim Tuesday, August 23, 1977, Nicola Sacco and Bartolomeo Vanzetti Memorial Day and declare, further, that any stigma and disgrace should be forever removed from the names of Nicola Sacco and Bartolomeo Vanzetti, from the names of their families and descendants, and so . . . call upon all the people of Massachusetts to pause in their daily endeavours to reflect upon these tragic events, and draw from their historic lessons the resolve to prevent the forces of intolerance, fear, and hatred from ever again uniting to overcome the rationality, wisdom, and fairness to which our legal system aspires.

Part of a proclamation by the Governor of Massachusetts, Michael Dukakis, 50 years after the execution of Sacco and Vanzetti.

SOURCE 44

A protest against the execution of Sacco and Vanzetti in 1927.

ACTIVITY

Make or design a poster to be displayed in the immigrant reception area on Ellis Island, New York. It should either:
a) warn immigrants of the problems they might face in the USA, or
b) encourage them to see the opportunities that America offers to immigrants.

Immigration quotas

In 1924, in direct response to its fear of radicals, the government took action. It restricted immigration. It introduced a system that ensured that the largest proportion of immigrants was from north-west Europe (mainly British, Irish and German) and that limited immigration from southern and eastern Europe. From a high point of more than a million immigrants a year between 1901 and 1910, by 1929 the number arriving in the USA had fallen to 150,000 per year.

200

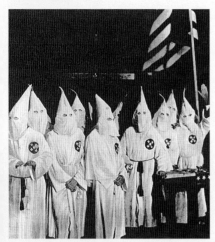
4 What does Source 45 tell you about the motives of Klan violence?
5 Explain why the Klan became so powerful.

The experience of black Americans

Black people had long been part of America's history. The first black people had been brought to the USA as slaves by white settlers in the seventeenth century. By the time slavery was ended in the nineteenth century, there were more black people than white in the southern United States. White governments, fearing the power of black Americans, introduced many laws to control their freedom. They could not vote. They were denied access to good jobs and to worthwhile education, and well into the twentieth century they suffered great poverty.

The Ku Klux Klan

The Ku Klux Klan was a white supremacy movement. It used violence to intimidate black Americans. It had been in decline, but was revived after the release of the film *The Birth of a Nation* in 1915. The film was set in the 1860s, just after the Civil War. It glorified the Klan as defenders of decent American values against renegade black people and corrupt white businessmen. President Wilson had it shown in the White House. He said: 'It is like writing history with lightning. And my only regret is that it is all so terribly true.' With such support from prominent figures, the Klan became a powerful political force in the early 1920s.

SOURCE 45

A lad whipped with branches until his back was ribboned flesh . . . a white girl, divorcee, beaten into unconsciousness in her home; a naturalised foreigner flogged until his back was pulp because he married an American woman; a negro lashed until he sold his land to a white man for a fraction of its value.

> RA Patton, writing in *Current History* in 1929, describes the victims of Klan violence in Alabama.

Black Americans throughout the south faced fierce racism. Source 46 gives you one example. In 1930 James Cameron, aged 16, had been arrested, with two other black men, on suspicion of the murder of a white man, and the rape of a white woman. The writer survived this attempt to lynch him (hang him without a trial: see Source 47). In his book he vividly describes the fury of the white racists.

SOURCE 46

Little did I dream that one night I would fall into the hands of such a merciless mob of fanatics, that they would attempt to execute me because of the color of my skin. This whole way of life was – and is – a heritage of black slavery in America.

A huge and angry mob were demanding from the sheriff 'those three niggers'. They had gathered from all over the state of Indiana. Ten to fifteen thousand of them at least, against three. Many in the crowd wore the headdress of the Ku Klux Klan.

[The mob broke down the door of the jail, and beat and then hanged his two friends. Source 47 shows you the scene that greeted Cameron as he was dragged out of the jail for his turn.]

The cruel hands that held me were vicelike. Fists, clubs, bricks and rocks found their marks on my body. The weaker ones had to be content with spitting. Little boys and little girls not yet in their teens, but being taught how to treat black people, somehow managed to work their way in close enough to bite and scratch me on the legs.

And over the thunderous din rose the shout of 'Nigger! Nigger! Nigger!'

[Cameron did not know what saved him. The crowd had the rope round his neck before they suddenly stopped and let him limp back to the door of the jail. He called it 'a miraculous intervention'.]

> James Cameron, *A Time of Terror*, 1982.

The scene outside the jail in Marion, Indiana. Abram Smith and Thomas Shipp have already been lynched.

Cameron's experience was not unusual. Thousands of black Americans were murdered by lynching in this period. Many reports describe appalling atrocities at which whole families, including young children, clapped and cheered. It is one of the most shameful aspects of the USA at this time.

Faced by such intimidation, discrimination and poverty, many black people left the rural south and moved to the cities of the northern USA. Through the 1920s the black population of both Chicago and New York doubled: New York's from 150,000 to 330,000 and Chicago's from 110,000 to 230,000.

Improvements

In the north, black Americans had a better chance of getting good jobs and a good education. For example, Howard University was an exclusively black institution for higher education.

In both Chicago and New York, there was a small but growing black middle class. There was a successful 'black capitalist' movement, encouraging black people to set up businesses. In Chicago they ran a successful boycott of the city's chain stores, protesting that they would not shop there unless black staff were employed. By 1930 almost all the shops in the South Side belt where blacks lived had black employees.

There were internationally famous black Americans, such as the singer and actor Paul Robeson (see Profile). The popularity of jazz made many black musicians into high-profile media figures. The black neighbourhood of Harlem in New York became the centre of the Harlem Renaissance. Here musicians and singers made Harlem a centre of creativity and a magnet for white customers in the bars and clubs. Black artists flourished in this atmosphere, as did black writers. The poet Langston Hughes wrote about the lives of ordinary working-class black Americans and the poverty and problems they suffered. Countee Cullen was another prominent poet who tried to tackle racism and poverty. In one famous poem ('For A Lady I Know') he tried to sum up attitudes of wealthy white employees to their black servants:

> She even thinks that up in heaven
> Her class lies late and snores
> While poor black cherubs rise at seven
> To do celestial chores.

PROFILE

Paul Robeson

★ Born 1898, son of a church minister who had been a former slave.
★ Went to Columbia University and passed his law exams with honours in 1923.
★ As a black lawyer, it was almost impossible for him to find work, so he became an actor – his big break was in the hit musical *Showboat*.
★ Visited Moscow in 1934 on a world tour and declared his approval of Communism saying 'Here, for the first time in my life, I walk in dignity.'
★ As a Communist sympathiser, Robeson suffered in the USA – he was banned from performing, suffered death threats and had his passport confiscated.
★ He left the USA in 1958 to live in Europe, but returned in 1963.

ACTIVITY

Read the profile of Paul Robeson. Imagine you are interviewing him on the radio. Write three questions you'd like to ask him.

Black Americans also entered politics. WEB DuBois founded the National Association for the Advancement of Colored People (NAACP). In 1919 it had 300 branches and around 90,000 members. It campaigned to end racial segregation laws and to get laws passed against lynching. It did not make much headway at the time, but the numbers of lynchings did fall.

Another important figure was Marcus Garvey. He founded the Universal Negro Improvement Association (UNIA). Garvey urged black Americans to be proud of their race and colour. He instituted an honours system for black Americans (like the British Empire's honours system of knighthoods). The UNIA helped black people to set up their own businesses. By the mid 1920s there were UNIA grocery stores, laundries, restaurants and even a printing workshop.

Garvey set up a shipping line to support both the UNIA businesses and also his scheme of helping black Americans to emigrate to Africa away from white racism. Eventually, his businesses collapsed, partly because he was prosecuted for exaggerating the value of his shares. He was one of very few businessmen to be charged for this offence, and some historians believe that J Edgar Hoover was behind the prosecution. Garvey's movement attracted over 1 million members at its height in 1921. One of these was the Reverend Earl Little. He was beaten to death by Klan thugs in the late 1920s, but his son went on to be the black rights leader Malcolm X (see page 382).

Problems

Although important, these movements failed to change the USA dramatically. Life expectancy for blacks increased from 45 to 48 between 1900 and 1930, but they were still a long way behind the whites, whose life expectancy increased from 54 to 59 over the same period. Many black people in the northern cities lived in great poverty. In Harlem in New York they lived in poorer housing than whites, yet paid higher rents. They had poorer education and health services than whites.

In Chicago blacks suffered great prejudice from longer-established white residents. If they attempted to move out of the black belt to adjacent neighbourhoods, they got a hostile reception (see Source 50).

SOURCE 48

If I die in Atlanta my work shall only then begin . . . Look for me in the whirlwind or the storm, look for me all around you, for, with God's grace, I shall come and bring with me countless millions of black slaves who have died in America and the West Indies and the millions in Africa to aid you in the fight for Liberty, Freedom and Life.

Marcus Garvey's last word's before going to jail in 1925.

SOURCE 49

Marcus Garvey after his arrest.

SOURCE 50

There is nothing in the make up of a negro, physically or mentally, that should induce anyone to welcome him as a neighbour. The best of them are unsanitary . . . ruin follows in their path. They are as proud as peacocks, but have nothing of the peacock's beauty . . . Niggers are undesirable neighbours and entirely irresponsible and vicious.

From the *Chicago Property Owners' Journal*, 1920.

They got a similarly hostile reception from poor whites. In Chicago when blacks attempted to use parks, playgrounds and beaches in the Irish and Polish districts, they were set upon by gangs of whites calling themselves 'athletic clubs'. The result was that black communities in northern areas often became isolated ghettos.

Within the black communities prejudice was also evident. Middle-class blacks who were restless in the ghettos tended to blame newly arrived migrants from the south for intensifying white racism. In Harlem, the presence of some 50,000 West Indians was a source of inter-racial tension. Many of them were better educated, more militant and prouder of their colour than the newly arrived black Americans from the south.

ACTIVITY

James Cameron, who wrote Source 46 on page 201, went on to found America's Black Holocaust Museum, which records the suffering of black people through American history.

Write a 100-word summary for the museum handbook of the ways in which the 1920s were a time of change for black people.

'The vanishing Americans'

The native Americans were the original settlers of the North American continent. They almost disappeared as an ethnic group during the rapid expansion of the USA during the nineteenth century – declining from 1.5 million to around 250,000 in 1920. Those who survived or who chose not to leave their traditional way of life were forced to move to reservations in the mid-west.

SOURCE 51

1 Make two lists:
   a) evidence of prejudice and discrimination towards native Americans
   b) evidence that the treatment of native Americans was improving in the 1920s.

Photograph of a native American, Charlie Guardipee, and his family taken for a US government report of 1921. According to the report Charlie Guardipee had twenty horses, ten cattle, no chickens, no wheat, oats or garden, and no sickness in the family.

SOURCE 52

A scene from the 1925 film *The Vanishing American*. This film was made by Paramount, a big Hollywood studio. It was extremely unusual for its time in having a native American hero – Nophaie, a Navajo warrior who tried to adapt his people's traditional ways to live in peace with the white man. The drama in the film came from an evil and corrupt government agent who managed to stir up a native American revolt which the warrior tried to prevent.

In the 1920s the government became concerned about the treatment of native Americans. Twelve thousand had served in the armed forces in the First World War, which helped to change white attitudes to them. The government did a census in the 1920s and a major survey in the late 1920s which revealed that most lived in extreme poverty, with much lower life expectancy than whites, that they were in worse health and had poorer education and poorly paid jobs (if they were able to get a job at all). They suffered extreme discrimination. They were quickly losing their land. Mining companies were legally able to seize large areas of Indian land. Many Indians who owned land were giving up the struggle to survive in their traditional way and selling up.

They were also losing their culture. Their children were sent to special boarding schools. The aim of the schools was to 'assimilate' them into white American culture. This involved trying to destroy the native Americans' beliefs, traditions, dances and languages. In the 1920s the native Americans were referred to as 'the vanishing Americans'.

However, the 1920s were in some ways a turning point. In 1924 native Americans were granted US citizenship and allowed to vote for the first time. In 1928 the Merriam Report proposed widespread improvement to the laws relating to native Americans, and these reforms were finally introduced under Roosevelt's New Deal in 1934.

The Monkey Trial

While the Sacco and Vanzetti trial became a public demonstration of anti-immigrant feelings, another trial in the 1920s – the Monkey Trial – became the focus of ill-feeling between rural and urban USA.

Most urban people in the 1920s would have believed in Charles Darwin's theory of evolution. This said that over millions of years human beings evolved from ape-like ancestors.

Many rural Americans, however, disagreed. They were very religious people. They were mostly Protestants. They went to church regularly and believed in the Bible. When the Bible told them that God made the world in six days, and that on the sixth day He created human beings to be like Him, they took the teachings literally. People with these views were known as Fundamentalists. They were particularly strong in the 'Bible Belt' states such as Tennessee.

At school, however, even in these states, most children were taught evolution. Fundamentalists felt that this was undermining their own religion. It seemed to be yet another example of the USA's abandoning traditional values in the headlong rush to modernise in the 1920s. They decided to roll back the modern ideas and so, in six states, the Fundamentalists led by William Jennings Bryan managed to pass a law banning the teaching of 'evolution'.

A biology teacher called John Scopes deliberately broke the law so that he could be arrested and put his case against Fundamentalism in the courts. The best lawyers were brought in for both sides and in July 1925, in the stifling heat of a Tennessee courtroom, the USA's traditionalists joined battle with its modernists.

The trial captured public imagination and the arguments on both sides were widely reported in the press. Scopes was convicted of breaking the law, but it was really American Fundamentalism itself which was on trial – and it lost! At the trial the anti-evolutionists were subjected to great mockery. Their arguments were publicly ridiculed and their spokesman Bryan, who claimed to be an expert on religion and science, was shown to be ignorant and confused. After the trial, the anti-evolution lobby never recovered.

SOURCE 53

. . . for nearly two hours . . . Mr Darrow [lawyer for the defendant] goaded his opponent. [He] asked Mr Bryan if he really believed that the serpent had always crawled on its belly because it tempted Eve, and if he believed Eve was made from Adam's rib . . .

[Bryan's] face flushed under Mr Darrow's searching words, and . . . when one [question] stumped him he took refuge in his faith and either refused to answer directly or said in effect: 'The Bible states it; it must be so.'

From the report of the Monkey Trial in the *Baltimore Evening Sun*, July 1925.

---

2 Why do you think the trial became known as the Monkey Trial?

3 In what ways did the trial show American intolerance of other points of view?

ACTIVITY

The Monkey Trial attracted considerable media attention.

Draw up an anti-evolution leaflet, to be handed out to journalists at the trial, explaining the views of Fundamentalists. Make your leaflet as convincing as possible. Explain:
a) why you think the theory of evolution is wrong
b) why you think its teaching should be banned.

FOCUS TASK A

How far was American society changing in the 1920s?

At the end of the First World War, one young man said of his war experience: 'The lad from the north was the pal of the lad from the south. Acquaintance meant friendship and what will this friendship mean to America when we return? New bonds will draw us together . . . and the fabric of the nation will be strengthened.'

As this man looked back in 1929, what comments do you think he might have made about the USA in the 1920s? In your answer you should refer to:
- the economic successes of the USA
- the economic divisions within the USA
- the cultural and social changes of the 1920s
- the darker side of the USA in the 1920s.

SOURCE 54

John Scopes (seated second from the right) surrounded by his lawyers.

FOCUS TASK B

How widespread was intolerance in the 1920s?

You have looked at various examples of intolerance and prejudice in the 1920s. Draw up a chart like this, and fill it in to summarise the various examples.

Group	How did prejudice or intolerance affect them?	How did they react?

Prohibition – did the Americans make a mistake?

Why was prohibition introduced?

In the nineteenth century, in rural areas of the USA there was a very strong 'temperance' movement. Members of temperance movements agreed not to drink alcohol and also campaigned to get others to give up alcohol. Most members of these movements were devout Christians who saw what damage alcohol did to family life. They wanted to stop that damage.

In the nineteenth century the two main movements were the Anti-Saloon League and the Women's Christian Temperance Union (see Sources 55 and 56).

SOURCE 55

Daddy's in There---

And Our Shoes and Stockings and Clothes and Food Are in There, Too, and They'll Never Come Out.

A poster issued by the Anti-Saloon League in 1915.

SOURCE 56

A poster issued by the Women's Christian Temperance Union.

SOURCE 57

Our nation can only be saved by turning the pure stream of country sentiment and township morals to flush out the cesspools of cities and so save civilisation from pollution.

A temperance campaigner speaking in 1917.

1 Look at Sources 55 and 56. What do you think the aim of each one is?
2 What is wrong with alcohol according to these sources?
3 Prohibition did not actually make it illegal to drink alcohol. Why not?
4 List all the reasons why prohibition was introduced.
5 Do you think prohibition sounds like a good idea?

The temperance movements were so strong in some of the rural areas that they persuaded their state governments to prohibit the sale of alcohol within the state. Through the early twentieth century the campaign gathered pace. It became a national campaign to prohibit (ban) alcohol throughout the country. It acquired some very powerful supporters. Leading industrialists backed the movement, believing that workers would be more reliable if they did not drink. Politicians backed it because it got them votes in rural areas. By 1916, 21 states had banned saloons.

Supporters of PROHIBITION became known as 'dries'. The dries brought some powerful arguments to their case. They claimed that '3000 infants are smothered yearly in bed, by drunken parents.' The USA's entry into the First World War in 1917 boosted the dries. Drinkers were accused of being unpatriotic cowards. Most of the big breweries were run by German immigrants who were portrayed as the enemy. Drink was linked to other evils as well. After the Russian Revolution, the dries claimed that Bolshevism thrived on drink and that alcohol led to lawlessness in the cities, particularly in immigrant communities. Saloons were seen as dens of vice that destroyed family life. The campaign became one of country values against city values.

In 1917 the movement had enough states on its side to propose the Eighteenth Amendment to the Constitution. This 'prohibited the manufacture, sale or transportation of intoxicating liquors'. It became law in January 1920 and is known as the Volstead Act.

SOURCE 58

Gallons of alcohol

Key
— Beer
— Spirits

Period of prohibition

Average alcohol consumption (in US gallons) per year of Americans, 1905–40.

How was prohibition enforced?

SOURCE 59

	1921	**1925**	**1929**
Illegal distilleries seized	*9,746*	*12,023*	*15,794*
Gallons (US) of spirit seized	*414,000*	*11,030,000*	*11,860,000*
Arrests	*34,175*	*62,747*	*66,878*

Activities of federal prohibition agents.

Prohibition lasted from 1920 until 1933. It is often said that prohibition was a total failure. This is not entirely correct. Levels of alcohol consumption fell by about 30 per cent in the early 1920s (see Source 58). Prohibition gained widespread approval in some states, particularly the rural areas in the mid-west, although in urban states it was not popular (Maryland never even introduced prohibition). The government ran information campaigns and prohibition agents arrested offenders (see Source 59). Two of the most famous agents were Isadore Einstein and his deputy Moe Smith. They made 4392 arrests. Their raids were always low key. They would enter speakeasies (illegal bars) and simply order a drink. Einstein had a special flask hidden inside his waistcoat with a funnel attached. He preserved the evidence by pouring his drink down the funnel and the criminals were caught!

SOURCE 60

Alcohol being tipped down the drain. Vast quantities of bootleg (illegal) liquor were seized, but were only a fraction of the total.

SOURCE 61

Prohibition agents Isadore Einstein and Moe Smith (usually known as Izzy and Moe). They were so successful that speakeasies actually put up posters warning people to watch out for these men.

Supply and demand

Despite the work of the agents, prohibition proved impossible to enforce effectively in the cities. Enforcement was underfinanced. There were not enough agents – each agent was poorly paid and was responsible for a huge area. By far the biggest drawback was that millions of Americans, particularly in urban areas, were simply not prepared to obey this law. So bootleggers (suppliers of illegal alcohol) made vast fortunes. Al Capone (see page 209) made around $60 million a year from his speakeasies. His view was that 'Prohibition is a business. All I do is supply a public demand.' And the demand was huge. By 1925 there were more speakeasies in American cities than there had been saloons in 1919. Izzy Einstein filed a report to his superiors on how easy it was to find alcohol after arriving in a new city. Here are the results:

- Chicago: 21 minutes
- Atlanta: 17 minutes
- Pittsburg: 11 minutes
- New Orleans: 35 seconds (he was offered a bottle of whisky by his taxi driver when he asked where he could get a drink!)

6 Which of Sources 58–61 is the most useful to the historian, or are they more useful when taken together? Explain your answer.

7 Is it possible to enforce any law when the population refuses to obey it? Try to think of laws that affect you today.

SOURCE **62**

A visit to a speakeasy.

SOURCE **64**

Statistics in the Detroit police court of 1924 show 7391 arrests for violations of the prohibition law, but only 458 convictions. Ten years ago a dishonest policeman was a rarity . . . Now the honest ones are pointed out as rarities . . . Their relationship with the bootleggers is perfectly friendly. They have to pinch two out of five once in a while, but they choose the ones who are least willing to pay bribes.

E Mandeville, in *Outlook* magazine, 1925.

1 Read Source 64. How has prohibition affected the police in Detroit?

SOURCE **65**

'The National Gesture': a cartoon from the prohibition era.

SOURCE **63**

An illegal still.

Illegal stills (short for distilleries) sprang up all over the USA as people made their own illegal whisky – moonshine. The stills were a major fire hazard and the alcohol they produced was frequently poisonous. Agents seized over 280,000 of these stills, but we have no clear way of knowing how many were not seized. Most Americans had no need for their own still. They simply went to their favourite speakeasy. The speakeasies were well supplied by bootleggers. About two-thirds of the illegal alcohol came from Canada. The vast border between the USA and Canada was virtually impossible to patrol. Other bootleggers brought in alcohol by sea. They would simply wait in the waters outside US control until an opportunity to land their cargo presented itself. One of the most famous was Captain McCoy, who specialised in the finest Scotch whisky. This is where the phrase 'the real McCoy' comes from.

Corruption

Prohibition led to massive corruption. Many of the law enforcement officers were themselves involved with the liquor trade. Big breweries stayed in business throughout the prohibition era. This is not an easy business to hide! But the breweries stayed in operation by bribing local government officials, prohibition agents and the police to leave them alone.

In some cities, police officers were quite prepared to direct people to speakeasies. Even when arrests were made, it was difficult to get convictions because more senior officers or even judges were in the pay of the criminals. One in 12 prohibition agents was dismissed for corruption. The New York FBI boss, Don Chaplin, once ordered his 200 agents: 'Put your hands on the table, both of them. Every son of a bitch wearing a diamond is fired.'

SOURCE 66

Al Capone in 1930. Everyone knew of his activities, but it was impossible to convict him because of his control of the police.

2 Write a definition of the term 'gangster' for an encyclopaedia of American history.

Chicago and the gangsters

The most common image people have of the prohibition era is the gangster. Estimates suggest that organised gangs made about $2 billion out of the sale of illegal alcohol. The bootlegger George Remus certainly did well from the trade. He had a huge network of paid officials that allowed him to escape charge after charge against him. At one party he gave a car to each of the women guests, while all the men received diamond cuff links worth $25,000.

The rise of the gangsters tells us a lot about American society at this time. The gangsters generally came from immigrant backgrounds. In the early 1920s the main gangs were Jewish, Polish, Irish and Italian. Gangsters generally came from poorer backgrounds within these communities. They were often poorly educated, but they were also clever and ruthless. Dan O'Banion (Irish gang leader murdered by Capone), Pete and Vince Guizenberg (hired killers who worked for Bugsy Moran and died in the St Valentine's Day Massacre), and Lucky Luciano (Italian killer who spent ten years in prison) were some of the most powerful gangsters. The gangs fought viciously with each other to control the liquor trade and also the prostitution, gambling and protection rackets that were centred on the speakeasies. They made use of new technology, especially automobiles and the Thompson sub-machine gun, which was devastatingly powerful but could be carried around and hidden under an overcoat. In Chicago alone, there were 130 gangland murders in 1926 and 1927 and not one arrest. By the late 1920s fear and bribery made law enforcement ineffective.

The gangsters operated all over the USA, but they were most closely associated with Chicago. Perhaps the best example of the power of the gangsters is Chicago gangster boss Al Capone. He arrived in Chicago in 1919, on the run from a murder investigation in New York. He ran a drinking club for his boss Johnny Torio. In 1925 Torio retired after an assassination attempt by one of his rivals, Bugsy Moran. Capone took over and proved to be a formidable gangland boss. He built up a huge network of corrupt officials among Chicago's police, local government workers, judges, lawyers and prohibition agents. He even controlled Chicago's mayor, William Hale Thompson. Surprisingly, he was a high-profile and even popular figure in the city. He was a regular at baseball and American football games and was cheered by the crowd when he took his seat. He was well known for giving generous tips (over $100) to waiters and shop girls and spent $30,000 on a soup kitchen for the unemployed.

Capone was supported by a ruthless gang, hand picked for their loyalty to him. He killed two of his own men whom he suspected of plotting against him by beating their brains out with a baseball bat. By 1929 he had destroyed the power of the other Chicago gangs, committing at least 300 murders in the process. The peak of his violent reign came with the St Valentine's Day Massacre in 1929. Capone's men murdered seven of his rival Bugsy Moran's gang, using a false police car and two gangsters in police uniform to put Moran's men off their guard.

SOURCE 67

THREE CENTS | THE CHICAGO DAILY NEWS | BLUE STREAK

MASSACRE 7 OF MORAN GANG

HAFFA CHANGES HIS MIND; WILL FIGHT PRISON

KILLING SCENE TOO GRUESOME FOR ONLOOKERS

VICTIMS ARE LINED AGAINST WALL; ONE VOLLEY KILLS ALL

Newspaper headlines reporting the St Valentine's Day Massacre, 1929.

1 Why do you think the public were so distressed by the St Valentine's Day Massacre?

Why was prohibition ended?

The St Valentine's Day Massacre was a turning point. The papers screamed that the gangsters had graduated from murder to massacre. It seemed that prohibition, often called 'The Noble Experiment', had failed. It had made the USA lawless, the police corrupt and the gangsters rich and powerful. When the Wall Street Crash was followed by the Depression in the early 1930s, there were sound economic arguments for getting rid of it. Legalising alcohol would create jobs, raise tax revenue and free up resources tied up in the impossible task of enforcing prohibition. The Democrat President Franklin D Roosevelt was elected in 1932 and prohibition was repealed in December 1933.

ACTIVITY

Why did prohibition fail?

In the end prohibition failed. Here are four groups who could be blamed for the failure of prohibition.

a) the American people who carried on going to illegal speakeasies

b) the law enforcers who were corrupt and ignored the law breakers

c) the bootleggers who continued supplying and selling alcohol

d) the gangsters who controlled the trade through violence

1 For each of the above groups find evidence on pages 206–209 to show that it contributed to the failure of prohibition.
2 Say which group you think played the most important role in the failure. Explain your choice.
3 Draw a diagram to show links between the groups.

FOCUS TASK A

Why was prohibition introduced in 1920 and then abolished in 1933?

Many people who were convinced of the case for prohibition before 1920 were equally convinced that it should be abolished in 1933.

Write two letters.
  The first should be from a supporter of prohibition to his or her Congressman in 1919 explaining why the Congressman should vote for prohibition. In your letter, explain how prohibition could help to solve problems in America.
  The second should be from the same person to the Congressman in 1933 explaining why the Congressman should vote against prohibition. In your letter, explain why prohibition has failed.

FOCUS TASK B

Review of the 1920s

In many democracies today, governments use focus groups to help them work out policies and also to help them keep an eye on how people feel about their policies. The idea of a focus group is that the group represents a broad cross-section of society. It is 1928. President Hoover wants to create a focus group.

1 Your first task is to select for him the members of a focus group to represent American society. The group should contain a minimum of six and a maximum of 12 members. You have to draw up a list of possible members. They can be actual individuals (e.g. Louis Armstrong) or representative types (e.g. a Detroit car worker). You must be able to explain why you have chosen each member of the group.
2 Your second task is to think of some positive and negative issues for the group to discuss.
   a) Brainstorm the events in 1920s USA that you think a US President would be proud of.
   b) Brainstorm anything that a US President in the 1920s would prefer to keep quiet.
3 Turn these issues into a maximum of four questions for the focus group to discuss.
4 Finally, choose two contrasting members of the group and summarise how they might answer some of the questions.

7.2

FACTFILE

Investment and the stock market

★ To set up a company you need money to pay staff, rent premises, buy equipment, etc.
★ Most companies raise this money from investors. In return, these investors own a share in the company. They become 'shareholders'.
★ These shareholders can get a return on their money in two ways:
  a) by receiving a dividend – a share of the profits made by the company;
  b) by selling their shares.
★ If the company is successful, the value of the shares is usually higher than the price originally paid for them.
★ Investors buy and sell their shares on the stock market. The American stock market was known as Wall Street.
★ The price of shares varies from day to day. If more people are buying than selling, then the price goes up. If more are selling than buying, the price goes down.
★ For much of the 1920s the price of shares on the Wall Street stock market went steadily upwards.

The Wall Street Crash

In 1928 there was a presidential election. Herbert Hoover was the Republican candidate. Nobody doubted that the Republicans would win again. The US economy was still booming. After so much success, how could they lose? His opponent Al Smith was an Irish Catholic and a 'wet' – an opponent of prohibition – although he was a highly successful governor of New York.

Hoover did win, by a landslide, and all seemed well. One of his earliest statements as President was: 'We in America today are nearer to the final triumph over poverty than ever before … The poor man is vanishing from among us.' (See Source 24 on page 193.) When Hoover formally moved into the White House in March 1929 the mood of confidence was still there. He pointed out that Americans had more bathtubs, oil furnaces, silk stockings and bank accounts than any other country.

Six months later it was a very different picture. In October 1929 the Wall Street stock market crashed, the American economy collapsed, and the USA entered a long depression that destroyed much of the prosperity of the 1920s.

You are going to investigate what went wrong. Some say that Hoover and the Republicans should have seen what was coming and done something about it. (You have studied some of the USA's economic weaknesses in 7.1.) Others say that at the time no one could really have known how great the problem was or what to do about it. See what you think.

What caused the Wall Street Crash?

To understand the Wall Street Crash you first need to understand how the stock market is supposed to work (see Factfile).

Speculation

You can see that investment on the stock market would be quite attractive during an economic boom. The American economy was doing well throughout the 1920s. Because the economy kept doing well, there were more share buyers than sellers and the value of shares rose (see Source 1).

It seemed to many Americans that the stock market was an easy and quick way to get rich. Anyone could buy shares, watch their value rise and then sell the shares later at a higher price. Many Americans decided to join the stock market. In 1920 there had been only 4 million share owners in America. By 1929 there were 20 million, out of a population of 120 million (although only about 1.5 million were big investors).

Around 600,000 new investors were speculators. Speculation is a form of gambling. Speculators don't intend to keep their shares for long. They borrow money to buy some shares, then sell them again as soon as the price has risen. They pay off their loan and still have a quick profit to show for it. In the 1920s speculators didn't even have to pay the full value of the shares. They could buy 'on margin', which meant they only had to put down 10 per cent of the cash needed to buy shares and could borrow the rest. Women became heavily involved in speculation. Women speculators owned over 50 per cent of the Pennsylvania Railroad, which became known as the 'petticoat line'. It was not only individuals who speculated. Banks themselves got involved in speculation. And certainly they did nothing to hold it back. American banks lent $9 billion for speculating in 1929.

Through most of the 1920s the rise in share prices was quite steady. There were even some downturns. But in 1928 speculation really took hold. Demand for shares was at an all-time high, and prices were rising at an unheard-of rate. In March, Union Carbide shares stood at $145. By September 1928 they had risen to $413.

One vital ingredient in all this is confidence. If people are confident that prices will keep rising, there will be more buyers than sellers. However, if they think prices might stop rising, all of a sudden there will be more sellers and … crash, the whole structure will come down. This is exactly what happened in 1929.

SOURCE 1

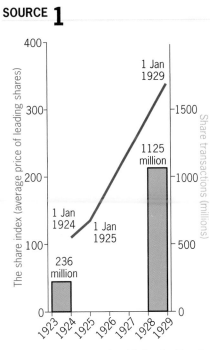

The average price (dollars) of leading shares, and share transactions, 1923–29.

SOURCE 2

The stock market hysteria reached its apex that year [1929] . . . Everyone was playing the market . . . On my last day in New York, I went down to the barber. As he removed the sheet he said softly, 'Buy Standard Gas. I've doubled . . . It's good for another double.' As I walked upstairs, I reflected that if the hysteria had reached the barber level, something must soon happen.

Cecil Roberts, *The Bright Twenties*, 1938.

SOURCE 3

Selected share prices, 1928–29.

Weaknesses in the US economy

The construction industry (one of the leading signs of health in any economy) had actually started its downturn as far back as 1926. You have already seen how farming was in trouble in the 1920s. You have also seen the decline in coal, textile and other traditional trades. There were other concerns, such as the unequal distribution of wealth and the precarious state of some banks. In the decade before the Crash, over 500 banks had failed each year. These were mainly small banks who lent too much.

By 1929 other sectors of the economy were showing signs of strain after the boom years of the 1920s. The boom was based on the increased sale of consumer goods such as cars and electrical appliances. There were signs that American industries were producing more of these goods than they could sell. The market for these goods was largely the rich and the middle classes. By 1929 those who could afford consumer goods had already bought them. The majority of Americans who were poor could not afford to buy them, even on the generous hire purchase and credit schemes on offer.

Companies tried high-pressure advertising. In 1929 American industry spent a staggering $3 billion on magazine advertising. But with workers' wages not rising and prices not falling, demand decreased.

In the past, American industry would have tried to export its surplus goods. But people in Europe could not afford American goods either. In addition, after nine years of American tariffs, Europe had put up its own tariffs to protect its industries.

By the summer of 1929 these weaknesses were beginning to show. Even car sales were slowing, and in June 1929 the official figures for industrial output showed a fall for the first time for four years. Speculators on the American stock exchange became nervous about the value of their shares and began to sell.

As you can see from the Factfile, the slide in share values started slowly. But throughout September and October it gathered pace. Many investors had borrowed money to buy their shares and could not afford to be stuck with shares worth less than the value of their loan. Soon other investors sold their shares and within days panic set in. On Tuesday 29 October 1929 it became clear to the speculators that the banks were not going to intervene to support the price of shares, and so Wall Street had its busiest and its worst day in history as speculators desperately tried to dump 13 million shares at a fraction of the price they had paid for them.

FACTFILE

The Wall Street Crash, 1929

★ **June** Factory output starts declining. Steel production starts declining.
★ **3 Sept** The hottest day of the year. The last day of rising prices.
★ **5 Sept** 'The Babson Break': Roger Babson, economic forecaster, says 'Sooner or later a crash is coming and it may be terrific.' The index of share prices drops ten points.
★ **6 Sept** Market recovers.
★ **Mon 21 Oct** Busy trading. Much selling. So much trading that the 'ticker' which tells people of changes in price falls behind by 1½ hours. Some people don't know they are ruined until after the exchange closes. By then it is too late to do anything about it.
★ **Thu 24 Oct** Busiest trading yet. Big falls. Banks intervene to buy stock. Confidence returns. Prices stabilise.
★ **Mon 28 Oct** Massive fall. Index loses 43 points. It is clear that the banks have stopped supporting share prices.
★ **Tue 29 Oct** Massive fall. People sell for whatever they can get.

FOCUS TASK

How far was speculation responsible for the Wall Street Crash?

Work in groups.

1 Here are five factors that led to the Wall Street Crash. For each one explain how it helped to cause the crash:
   • poor distribution of income between rich and poor
   • overproduction by American industries
   • the actions of speculators
   • no export market for US goods
   • decision by the banks not to support share prices.
2 If you think other factors are also important, add them to your list and explain why they helped to cause the crash.
3 Decide whether there is one factor that is more important than any of the others. Explain your choice.

The consequences of the Wall Street Crash

At first, it was not clear what the impact of the Crash would be. In the short term, the large speculators were ruined. The rich lost most because they had invested most (see Source 4). They had always been the main buyers of American goods, so there was an immediate downturn in spending. Many others had borrowed money in order to buy shares that were now worthless. They were unable to pay back their loans to the banks and insurance companies, so they went bankrupt. Some banks themselves also went bankrupt.

At first, however, these seemed like tragic but isolated incidents. President Hoover reassured the nation that prosperity was 'just around the corner'. He cut taxes to help to stimulate people to buy more goods and by mid 1931 production was rising again slightly and there was hope that the situation was more settled.

SOURCE 4

- The Vanderbilt family lost $40 million.
- Rockefeller lost 80 per cent of his wealth – but he still had $40 million left.
- The British politician Winston Churchill lost $500,000.
- The singer Fanny Brice lost $500,000.
- Groucho and Harpo Marx (two of the Marx Brothers comedy team) lost $240,000 each.

Major losers in the crash.

1 Look at Source 5. Do you think the cartoonist is sympathetic or critical of the man on the bench? Explain your opinion.

SOURCE 5

A cartoon by American cartoonist John McCutcheon, 1932. The man on the bench has lost all his savings because of a bank failure.

FOCUS TASK

What impact did the crash have on the American economy?

1 Draw a diagram to show how the following were connected to each other:
- the Wall Street Crash
- the banking crisis
- reduced spending
- unemployment.

Research Task
2 On page 195 you investigated various features of the boom. Try to find out from your own research what happened between 1929 and 1933 to at least two of the industries or activities covered on pages 189–90 and 194–95.

SOURCE 6

An attempt to make some cash after the Wall Street Crash, 1929.

In fact, it was the worst of the Depression that was 'just around the corner', because the Crash had destroyed the one thing that was crucial to the prosperity of the 1920s: confidence.

This was most marked in the banking crisis. In 1929, 659 banks failed. As banks failed people stopped trusting them and many withdrew their savings. In 1930 another 1352 went bankrupt. The biggest of these was the Bank of the United States in New York, which went bankrupt in December 1930. It had 400,000 depositors – many of them recent immigrants. Almost one-third of New Yorkers saved with it. This was the worst failure in American history. To make matters worse, 1931 saw escalating problems in European banks, which had a knock-on effect in the USA. Panic set in. Around the country a billion dollars was withdrawn from banks and put in safe deposit boxes, or stored at home. People felt that hard currency was the only security. Another 2294 banks went under in 1931.

So while Hoover talked optimistically about the return of prosperity, Americans were showing their true feelings. They now kept their money instead of buying new goods or shares. The downward spiral was firmly established. Businesses cut production further and laid off more workers. They reduced the wages of those who still worked for them. Between 1928 and 1933 both industrial and farm production fell by 40 per cent, and average wages by 60 per cent.

As workers were laid off or were paid less, they bought even less. By 1932 the USA was in the grip of the most serious economic depression the world had ever seen. By 1933 there were 14 million unemployed, and 5000 banks had gone bankrupt. Farm prices had fallen so low that the cost of transporting animals to market was higher than the price of the animals themselves. Total farm income had slipped to just $5 billion. The USA's international trade had also been drastically reduced, falling from $10 billion in 1929 to $3 billion in 1932.

SOURCE 7

During the last three months I have visited . . . some 20 states of this wonderfully rich and beautiful country. A number of Montana citizens told me of thousands of bushels of wheat left in the fields uncut on account of its low price that hardly paid for the harvesting. In Oregon I saw thousands of bushels of apples rotting in the orchards. At the same time there are millions of children who, on account of the poverty of their parents, will not eat one apple this winter.

. . . I saw men picking for meat scraps in the garbage cans of the cities of New York and Chicago. One man said that he had killed 3,000 sheep this fall and thrown them down the canyon because it cost $1.10 to ship a sheep and then he would get less than a dollar for it.

The farmers are being pauperised [made poor] by the poverty of industrial populations and the industrial populations are being pauperised by the poverty of the farmers. Neither has the money to buy the product of the other; hence we have overproduction and under-consumption at the same time.

Evidence of Oscar Ameringer to a US government committee in 1932.

SOURCE 8

Unemployed workers queuing for a cheap meal. For Americans used to prosperity and believing in self-help, needing charity was a hard blow to their pride.

The human cost of the Depression

People in agricultural areas were hardest hit by the Depression, because the 1920s had not been kind to them anyway. Huge numbers of farmers were unable to pay their mortgages. Some farmers organised themselves to resist banks seizing their homes. When sheriffs came to seize their property, bands of farmers holding pitch forks and hangman's nooses persuaded the sheriffs to retreat. Others barricaded highways. Most farmers, however, had no choice but to pack their belongings into their trucks and live on the road. They picked up work where they could.

To make matters worse for farmers, overfarming and drought in the central southern states turned millions of acres into a dust bowl and drove farmers off their land. Many of these ruined farmers headed to California looking for labouring work.

SOURCE 9

A dust bowl farm. Overfarming, drought and poor conservation turned farmland into desert.

In the towns, the story was not much better. For example, in 1932 in the steel city of Cleveland, 50 per cent of workers were now unemployed and in Toledo 80 per cent. At night the parks were full of the homeless and unemployed. In every city, workers who had contributed to the prosperity of the 1920s now queued for bread and soup dished out by charity workers. Every town had a so-called Hooverville. This was a shanty town of ramshackle huts where the migrants lived, while they searched for work. The rubbish tips were crowded with families hoping to scrape a meal from the leftovers of more fortunate people. Through 1931, 238 people were admitted to hospital in New York suffering from malnutrition or starvation. Forty-five of them died.

SOURCE 10

Last summer, in the hot weather, when the smell was sickening and the flies were thick, there were a hundred people a day coming to the dumps . . . a widow who used to do housework and laundry, but now had no work at all, fed herself and her fourteen-year-old son on garbage. Before she picked up the meat she would always take off her glasses so that she couldn't see the maggots.

From *New Republic* magazine, February 1933.

SOURCE 11

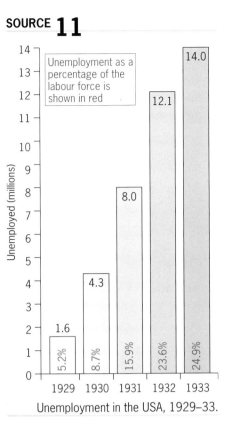

Unemployment in the USA, 1929–33.

SOURCE 12

A Hooverville shanty town on wasteland in Seattle, Washington.

SOURCE 14

A migrant family.

SOURCE 13

There is not an unemployed man in the country that hasn't contributed to the wealth of every millionaire in America. The working classes didn't bring this on, it was the big boys . . . We've got more wheat, more corn, more food, more cotton, more money in the banks, more everything in the world than any nation that ever lived ever had, yet we are starving to death. We are the first nation in the history of the world to go to the poorhouse in an automobile.

Will Rogers, an American writer, 1931. Rogers had a regular humorous column in an American magazine which was popular with ordinary people.

1   Read Source 13. What do you think Will Rogers means by 'the big boys?'
2   Explain how a writer such as Rogers can be useful to a historian studying the impact of the Depression in the 1930s.

FOCUS TASK

What were the human consequences of the Crash?

You have been asked to prepare an exhibition of photos which compares the life of Americans during the boom times of the 1920s with the depressed years of the 1930s. Choose two pictures from the 1920s and two from the 1930s which you think present the greatest contrast.

Explain your choice.

Do you think everyone suffered equally from the Depression? Explain your answer by referring to Sources 7–14.

The 1932 presidential election

In the 1932 election President Hoover paid the price for being unable to solve the problems of the Depression. It was partly his own fault. Until 1932 he refused to accept that there was a major problem. He insisted that 'prosperity is just around the corner'. This left him open to bitter criticisms such as Source 17. A famous banner carried in a demonstration of Iowa farmers said: 'In Hoover we trusted and now we are busted.'

SOURCE 15

Smile away the Depression!

Smile us into Prosperity!
wear a
SMILETTE!

This wonderful little gadget will solve the problems of the Nation!

APPLY NOW AT YOUR CHAMBER OF COMMERCE OR THE REPUBLICAN NATIONAL COMMITTEE

WARNING—Do not risk Federal arrest by looking glum!

A 1932 Democrat election poster.

SOURCE 16

Never before in this country has a government fallen to so low a place in popular estimation or been so universally an object of cynical contempt. Never before has [a President] given his name so freely to latrines and offal dumps, or had his face banished from the [cinema] screen to avoid the hoots and jeers of children.

Written by a political commentator after the event.

SOURCE 17

Farmers are just ready to do anything to get even with the situation. I almost hate to express it, but I honestly believe that if some of them could buy airplanes they would come down here to Washington to blow you fellows up . . . The farmer is a naturally conservative individual, but you cannot find a conservative farmer today. Any economic system that has in its power to set me and my wife in the streets, at my age what can I see but red?

President of the Farmers' Union of Wisconsin, AN Young, speaking to a Senate committee in 1932.

SOURCE 18

When I think of what has been happening in this country since unemployment began, and when I see the futility of the leaders, I wish we might double the number of Communists in this country, to put the fear, if not of God, then the fear of something else, into the hearts of our leaders.

Written by a Catholic priest, Father J Ryan.

1 Source 15 had a very powerful effect on Americans. Explain why.
2 From Sources 16–18 make a list of criticisms of Hoover and his government.

Hoover was regarded as a 'do nothing' President. This was not entirely fair on Hoover. He tried to restart the economy in 1930 and 1931 by tax cuts. He tried to persuade business leaders not to cut wages. He set up the Reconstruction Finance Company, which propped up banks to stop them going bankrupt. He tried to protect US industries by introducing tariffs, but this simply strangled international trade and made the Depression worse.

To most observers these measures looked like mere tinkering. Hoover and most Republicans were very reluctant to change their basic policies. They believed that the main cause of the Depression had been economic problems in Europe, not weaknesses in the USA's economy. They said that business should be left alone to bring back prosperity. Government help was not needed. They argued that business went in cycles of boom and bust, and therefore prosperity would soon return. In 1932 Hoover blocked the Garner–Wagner Relief Bill, which would have allowed Congress to provide $2.1 billion to create jobs.

Even more damaging to Hoover's personal reputation, however, was how little he tried to help people who were suffering because of the Depression. He believed that social security was not the responsibility of the government. Relief should be provided by local government or charities. The Republicans were afraid that if the government helped individuals, they would become less independent and less willing to work.

PROFILE

Franklin D Roosevelt

★ Born in 1882, son of a rich New York family.
★ He went to university and became a successful lawyer.
★ In 1910 he entered politics as a Democratic senator for New York.
★ In 1921 he was paralysed by polio and he spent much of the rest of his life in a wheelchair. He fought bravely against his illness.
★ He became President in 1933, in the middle of the USA's economic crisis.
★ Roosevelt was an excellent public speaker, an optimist and a firm believer in the 'American dream' – that anyone who worked hard enough could become rich.
★ His policies of providing benefit for the unemployed, and employing men to work on massive state building projects (known as the 'New Deal' – see pages 218–26), made him extremely popular.
★ He was elected President four times.
★ He was determined to defeat Fascism – during the war he placed trade sanctions on Japan and supplied Britain with arms and food, and in 1941 he entered the war on the side of the Western Allies.
★ He died in 1945.

Hoover's reputation was particularly damaged by an event in June 1932. Thousands of servicemen who had fought in the First World War marched on Washington asking for their war bonuses (a kind of pension) to be paid early. The marchers camped peacefully outside the White House and sang patriotic songs. Hoover refused to meet them. He appointed General Douglas MacArthur to handle the situation. MacArthur convinced himself (with little or no evidence) that they were Communist agitators. He ignored Hoover's instructions to treat the marchers with respect. Troops and police used tear gas and burned the marchers' camps. Hoover would not admit he had failed to control MacArthur. He publicly thanked God that the USA still knew how to deal with a mob.

SOURCE 19

Police attacking the war bonus marchers.

There could be no greater contrast to Hoover than his opponent in the 1932 election, the Democrat candidate, Franklin D Roosevelt. Roosevelt's main characteristics as a politician were:

- He believed strongly in 'active government' to improve the lives of ordinary people.
- He had plans to spend public money on getting people back to work. As Governor of New York, he had already started doing this in his own state.
- He was not afraid to ask for advice on important issues from a wide range of experts, such as factory owners, union leaders and economists.

The campaign

With such ill-feeling towards Hoover being expressed throughout the country, Roosevelt was confident of victory, but he took no chances. He went on a grand train tour of the USA in the weeks before the election and mercilessly attacked the attitude of Hoover and the Republicans.

Roosevelt's own plans were rather vague and general. But he realised people wanted action, whatever that action was. In a 20,800 km campaign trip he made 16 major speeches and another 60 from the back of his train. He promised the American people a 'New Deal'.

The election was a landslide victory for Roosevelt. He won by 7 million votes and the Democrats won a majority of seats in Congress. It was the worst defeat the Republicans had ever suffered.

SOURCE 20

Millions of our citizens cherish the hope that their old standards of living have not gone forever. Those millions shall not hope in vain. I pledge you, I pledge myself, to a New Deal for the American people. This is more than a political campaign; it is a call to arms. Give me your help, not to win votes alone, but to win this crusade to restore America . . . I am waging a war against Destruction, Delay, Deceit and Despair . . .

Roosevelt's pre-election speech, 1932.

FOCUS TASK

Why did Roosevelt win the 1932 election?

In many ways Roosevelt's victory needs no explanation. Indeed, it would have been very surprising if any President could have been re-elected after the sufferings of 1929–32. But it is important to recognise the range of factors that helped Roosevelt and damaged Hoover.

Write your own account of Roosevelt's success under the following headings:
- The experiences of ordinary people, 1929–32
- The policies of the Republicans
- Actions taken by the Republicans
- Roosevelt's election campaign.

3 Make a list of the differences between the views of Hoover and Roosevelt.
4 Explain why Hoover disliked Roosevelt's ideas.

Franklin D Roosevelt and the New Deal

During his election campaign Roosevelt had promised the American people a New Deal. It was not entirely clear what measures that might include. What was clear was that Franklin D Roosevelt planned to use the full power of the government to get the US out of depression. He set out his priorities as follows:

- getting Americans back to work
- protecting their savings and property
- providing relief for the sick, old and unemployed
- getting American industry and agriculture back on their feet.

The Hundred Days

In the first hundred days of his presidency, Roosevelt worked round the clock with his advisers (who became known as the 'Brains Trust') to produce an enormous range of sweeping measures.

From his first day, Roosevelt went straight into action. One of the many problems affecting the USA was its loss of confidence in the banks. He immediately tackled this banking crisis.

The day after his inauguration Roosevelt ordered all of the banks to close and to remain closed until government officials had checked them over. A few days later 5000 trustworthy banks were allowed to reopen. They were even supported by government money if necessary. At the same time, Roosevelt's advisers had come up with a set of rules and regulations which would prevent the reckless speculation that had contributed to the Wall Street Crash.

These two measures, the **Emergency Banking Act** and the **Securities Exchange Commission**, gave the American people a taste of what the New Deal was to look like, but there was a lot more to come. One of Roosevelt's advisers at this time said, 'During the whole Hundred Days Congress, people didn't know what was going on, but they knew something was happening, something good for them.' In the Hundred Days, Roosevelt sent 15 proposals to Congress and all 15 were adopted. Just as importantly, he took time to explain to the American people what he was doing and why he was doing it. Every Sunday he would broadcast on radio to the nation. An estimated 60 million Americans tuned in to these **'fireside chats'**. Nowadays, we are used to politicians doing this. At that time it was a new development.

The **Federal Emergency Relief Administration** set about meeting the urgent needs of the poor. A sum of $500 million was spent on soup kitchens, blankets, employment schemes and nursery schools.

The **Civilian Conservation Corps** (CCC) was aimed at unemployed young men in particular. They could sign on for periods of six months, which could be renewed if they could still not find work. Most of the work done by the CCC was on environmental projects in national parks. The money earned generally went back to the men's families. Around 2.5 million young men were helped by this scheme.

The **Agricultural Adjustment Administration** (AAA) tried to take a long-term view of the problems facing farmers. It set quotas to reduce farm production in order to force prices gradually upwards. At the same time, the AAA helped farmers to modernise and to use farming methods that would conserve and protect the soil. In cases of extreme hardship, farmers could also receive help with their mortgages. The AAA certainly helped farmers, although modernisation had the unfortunate effect of putting more farm labourers out of work.

The **National Industrial Recovery Act** (NIRA) set up two important organisations:

- The **Public Works Administration** (PWA), which used government money to build schools, roads, dams, bridges and airports. These would be vital once the USA had recovered, and in the short term they created millions of jobs.
- The **National Recovery Administration** (NRA), which improved working conditions in industry and outlawed child labour. It also set out fair wages and sensible levels of production. The idea was to stimulate the economy by giving workers money to spend, without overproducing and causing a slump. It was voluntary, but firms which joined used the blue eagle as a symbol of presidential approval. Over two million employers joined the scheme.

SOURCE 1

This is the time to speak the truth frankly and boldly . . . So let me assert my firm belief that the only thing we have to fear is fear itself – nameless, unreasoning, unjustified terror which paralyses efforts to convert retreat into advance . . . This nation calls for action and action now . . . Our greatest primary task is to put people to work . . . We must act and act quickly.

Roosevelt's inauguration speech, 1933.

1 Read Source 1. What do you think Roosevelt means by 'the only thing we have to fear is fear itself'?

SOURCE 2

The bank rescue of 1933 was probably the turning point of the Depression. When people were able to survive the shock of having all the banks closed, and then see the banks open up again, with their money protected, there began to be confidence. Good times were coming. It marked the revival of hope.

Raymond Moley, one of Roosevelt's advisers during the Hundred Days Congress session.

FACTFILE

The Hundred Days

- ★ **4 March** Roosevelt inaugurated.
- ★ **5 March** Closed banks.
- ★ **9 March** Selected banks reopened.
- ★ **12 March** Roosevelt's first radio 'fireside chat'. Encouraged Americans to put their money back into the banks. Many did so.
- ★ **31 March** The Civilian Conservation Corps set up.
- ★ **12 May** The Agricultural Adjustment Act passed.
- ★ **18 May** The Tennessee Valley Authority created.
- ★ **18 June** The National Industrial Recovery Act passed.

SOURCE 3

A

B

Two 1933 American cartoons.

2 Look carefully at Source 3. Put the message of each cartoon into your own words.

The Tennessee Valley Authority

As you can see from Source 4, the Tennessee Valley was a huge area that cut across seven states. The area had great physical problems. In the wet season, the Tennessee river would flood. In the dry it would reduce to a trickle. The farming land around the river was a dust bowl. The soil was eroding and turning the land into desert. The area also had great social problems. Within the valley people lived in poverty. The majority of households had no electricity. The problems of the Tennessee Valley were far too large for one state to deal with and it was very difficult for states to co-operate.

SOURCE 4

Key
◗ Dams   ▨ Area covered by TVA

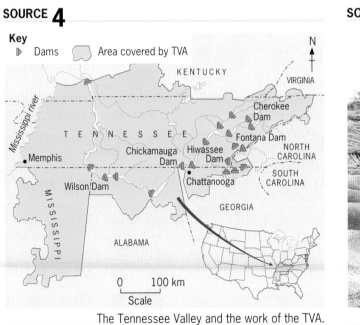

The Tennessee Valley and the work of the TVA.

SOURCE 5

Effects of erosion in the Tennessee Valley.

Roosevelt therefore set up an independent organisation called the **Tennessee Valley Authority** (TVA), which cut across the powers of the local state governments. The main focus of the TVA's work was to build a series of dams on the Tennessee river. They transformed the region. The dams made it possible to irrigate the dried-out lands. They also provided electricity for this underdeveloped area. Above all, building the dams created thousands of jobs in an area badly hit by the Depression.

FACTFILE

Achievements of the Hundred Days

★ Above all, it restored confidence and stopped investors pulling money out of the banks.
★ Banking measures saved 20 per cent of home owners and farmers from repossession.
★ Farmers were 50 per cent better off under AAA by 1936.
★ TVA brought electrical power to underdeveloped areas.
★ Public Works Administration created 600,000 jobs and built landmarks like San Francisco's Golden Gate Bridge.

1 After reading pages 218–20, add three more bullet points to this Factfile.

The Fontana Dam, one of the TVA's later projects. Dams such as these revitalised farmland, provided jobs and brought electric power to the area.

The measures introduced during the Hundred Days had an immediate effect. They restored confidence in government. Reporters who travelled the country brought back reports of the new spirit to be seen around the USA.

Historians too agree that Roosevelt's bold and decisive action did have a marked effect on the American people.

SOURCE 7

Wandering around the country with one of New York's baseball teams, I find that [what was] the national road to ruin is now a thriving thoroughfare. It has been redecorated. People have come out of the shell holes. They are working and playing and seem content to let a tribe of professional worriers do their worrying for them.

Rudd Rennie, an American journalist, describes what he saw around the USA in the early days of the New Deal. From *Changing the Tune from Gloom to Cheer*, 1934.

SOURCE 8

The CCC, the PWA, and similar government bodies (the alphabet agencies as Americans called them) made work for millions of people. The money they earned began to bring back life to the nation's trade and businesses. More customers appeared in the shops . . . As people started to buy again, shopkeepers, farmers and manufacturers began to benefit from the money the government was spending on work for the unemployed. This process was described by Roosevelt as 'priming the pump'. By this he meant that the money the Federal Government was spending was like a fuel, flowing into the nation's economic machinery and starting it moving again.

DB O'Callaghan, *Roosevelt and the USA*, published in 1966.

SOURCE 9

As Roosevelt described it, the 'New Deal' meant that the forgotten man, the little man, the man nobody knew much about, was going to be dealt better cards to play with . . . He understood that the suffering of the Depression had fallen with terrific impact upon the people least able to bear it. He knew that the rich had been hit hard too, but at least they had something left. But the little merchant, the small householder and home owner, the farmer, the man who worked for himself – these people were desperate. And Roosevelt saw them as principal citizens of the United States, numerically and in their importance to the maintenance of the ideals of American democracy.

Frances Perkins, *The Roosevelt I Knew*, 1947. Perkins was Labour Secretary under Roosevelt from 1933.

FOCUS TASK

What was the New Deal of 1933?

Look back over pages 218–20 and complete your own copy of this table.

New Deal measure/agency	Issue/problem it aimed to tackle	Action taken/ powers of agency	Evidence it was/was not effective

Workers widening a road under the Works Progress Administration.

Migrant Mother (number 6) by Dorothea Lange, taken in Nipomo, California, March 1936. Many farmers migrated to California where farming had been less badly hit by the Depression.

2 What impression of the New Deal does Source 12 attempt to convey?
3 Why do you think Roosevelt wanted artists and photographers to be employed under the New Deal?

The Second New Deal

Despite his achievements, by May 1935 Roosevelt was facing a barrage of criticism Some critics (like Senator Huey Long, see page 222) complained that he was doing too little, others (mainly the wealthy business sector) too much. The USA was recovering less quickly than Europe from Depression. Business was losing its enthusiasm for the NRA (for example Henry Ford had cut wages). Roosevelt was unsure what to do. He had hoped to transform the USA, but it didn't seem to be working.

Tuesday, 14 May, 1935 turned out to be a key date. Roosevelt met with a group of senators and close advisers who shared his views and aims. They persuaded him to take radical steps to achieve his vision and make the USA a fairer place for all Americans (see Source 9). One month later, on 14 June, he summoned the leaders of Congress and presented them with a huge range of laws that he wanted passed. This became known as the Second New Deal. The most significant aspects were:

- The **Wagner Act** which forced all employers to allow trade unions to operate in their companies and to let them negotiate with employers for better pay and conditions. The new Act made it illegal to sack workers for being in a union.
- The **Social Security Act** which provided state pensions for the elderly and for widows. It also allowed state governments to work with the federal government to provide help for the sick and the disabled. Most importantly, the Act set up a scheme for unemployment insurance. This meant that employers and workers made a small contribution to a special fund each week. If workers became unemployed, they would receive a small amount of benefit to help them out until they could find work.
- The **Works Progress Administration (WPA),** later renamed the Works Projct Administration, which brought together all the organisations whose aim was to create jobs. It also extended this work beyond building projects to create jobs for office workers and even unemployed actors, artists and photographers. The photograph in Source 11 was taken by a photographer working for the New Deal's Farm Security Administration Photographic Project. This project took 80,000 photos of farming areas during the New Deal. Source 12 was produced by an artist working for the Federal Arts Project. The government paid artists to paint pictures to be displayed in the city or town they featured.
- The **Resettlement Administration (RA)** which helped smallholders and tenant farmers who had not been helped by the AAA. This organisation moved over 500,000 families to better-quality land and housing. The **Farm Security Administration (FSA)** replaced the RA in 1937. It gave special loans to small farmers to help them buy their land. It also built camps to provide decent living conditions and work for migrant workers.

Steel Industry by Howard Cook, painted for the steel-making town of Pittsburgh, Pennsylvania.

FOCUS TASK

Draw up two spider diagrams to compare the objectives and measures of the New Deal and the Second New Deal.

Opposition to the New Deal

A programme such as Roosevelt's New Deal was unheard of in American history. It was bound to attract opposition and it did.

The New Deal isn't doing enough!

A number of high-profile figures raised the complaint that the New Deal was not doing enough to help the poor. Despite the New Deal measures, many Americans remained desperately poor. The hardest hit were black Americans and the poor in farming areas.

A key figure in arguing on behalf of these people was Huey Long. Long was a remarkable character. He became Governor of Louisiana in 1928 and a senator in 1932. His methods of gaining power were unusual and sometimes illegal (they included intimidation and bribery). However, once he had power he used it to help the poor. He relentlessly taxed big corporations and businesses in Louisiana and used the money to build roads, schools and hospitals. He employed black people on the same terms as whites and clashed with the Ku Klux Klan. He supported the New Deal at first, but by 1934 he was criticising it for being too complicated and not doing enough. He put forward a scheme called Share Our Wealth. All personal fortunes would be reduced to $3 million maximum, and maximum income would be $1 million a year. Government taxes would be shared between all Americans. He also proposed pensions for everyone over 60, and free washing machines and radios. Long was an aggressive and forceful character with many friends and many enemies. Roosevelt regarded him as one of the two most dangerous men in the USA until Long was assassinated in 1935.

Others also criticised the New Deal for not doing enough. Dr Francis Townsend founded a number of Townsend Clubs to campaign for a pension of $200 per month for people over 60, providing that they spent it that month, stimulating the economy in the process. A Catholic priest, Father Coughlin, used his own radio programme to attack Roosevelt. He set up the National Union for Social Justice and it had a large membership. However, by the early 1940s the movement had faded in importance.

The New Deal is doing too much!

The New Deal soon came under fire from sections of the business community and from Republicans for doing too much. There was a long list of criticisms:

- The New Deal was complicated and there were too many codes and regulations.
- Government should not support trade unions and it should not support calls for higher wages – the market should deal with these issues.
- Schemes such as the TVA created unfair competition for private companies.
- The New Deal schemes were like the economic plans being carried out in the Communist USSR and unsuitable for the democratic, free-market USA.
- Roosevelt was behaving like a dictator.
- The wealthy were wealthy because they had worked hard and used their abilities. High taxes discouraged people from working hard and gave money to people for doing nothing or doing unnecessary jobs (see Source 14).

Roosevelt was upset by the criticisms, but also by the tactics used against him by big business and the Republicans. They used a smear campaign against him and all connected to him. They said that he was disabled because of a sexually transmitted disease rather than polio. Employers put messages into their workers' pay packets saying that New Deal Schemes would never happen. Roosevelt turned on these enemies bitterly (see Source 16). And it seemed the American people were with him. In the 1936 election, he won 27 million votes – with the highest margin of victory ever achieved by a US president. He was then able to joke triumphantly, 'Everyone is against the New Deal except the voters.'

1 Make a list of the main complaints and suggestions of those who felt the New Deal did not do enough.

SOURCE **13**

I HOPE THIS WILL MAKE 'ER WORK

THE NEW DEAL PUMP

7 THOUSAND MILLIONS MORE

THE TAXPAYER

16 BILLIONS SPENT

A cartoon attacking the New Deal in the mid 1930s. Most newspaper owners were hostile to Roosevelt.

SOURCE **14**

The New Deal is nothing more or less than an effort to take away from the thrifty what the thrifty and their ancestors have accumulated, or may accumulate, and give it to others who have not earned it and never will earn it, and thus indirectly to destroy the incentive for all future accumulation. Such a purpose is in defiance of all the ideas upon which our civilisation has been founded.

A Republican opponent of the New Deal speaking in 1935.

2 Look at the criticisms of the New Deal (right). Roosevelt's opponents were often accused of being selfish. How far do the criticisms support or contradict that view?
3 What do Sources 13 and 14 suggest about Roosevelt's New Deal?

SOURCE 15

A 1930s cartoon attacking critics of the New Deal.

SOURCE 16

For twelve years this nation was afflicted with hear-nothing, see-nothing, do-nothing government. The nation looked to government but government looked away. Nine crazy years at the stock market and three long years in the bread-lines! Nine mad years of mirage and three long years of despair! Powerful influences strive today to restore that kind of government with its doctrine that government is best which is most indifferent . . . We know now that government by organised money is just as dangerous as government by organised mob. Never before in all our history have these forces been so united against one candidate – me – as they stand today. They are unanimous in their hate of me – and I welcome their hatred.

A speech by Roosevelt in the 1936 presidential election campaign.

4 What do Sources 15 and 16 suggest about the critics of the New Deal?

Opposition from the Supreme Court

Roosevelt's problems were not over with the 1936 election. In fact, he now faced the most powerful opponent of the New Deal – the American Supreme Court. This Court was dominated by Republicans who were opposed to the New Deal. It could overturn laws if those laws were against the terms of the Constitution. In May 1935 a strange case had come before the US Supreme Court. The Schechter Poultry Corporation had been found guilty of breaking NRA regulations because it had:

- sold diseased chickens for human consumption
- filed false sales claims (to make the company worth more)
- exploited workers
- threatened government inspectors.

It appealed to the Supreme Court. The Court ruled that the government had no right to prosecute the company. This was because the NRA was unconstitutional. It undermined too much of the power of the local states.

Roosevelt was angry that this group of old Republicans should deny democracy by throwing out laws that he had been elected to pass. He asked Congress to give him the power to appoint six more Supreme Court judges who were more sympathetic to the New Deal. But Roosevelt misjudged the mood of the American public. They were alarmed at what they saw as Roosevelt's attacking the American system of government. Roosevelt had to back down and his plan was rejected. Even so his actions were not completely pointless. The Supreme Court had been shaken by Roosevelt's actions and was less obstructive in the future. Most of the main measures in Roosevelt's Second New Deal were approved by the Court from 1937 onwards.

SOURCE 17

THE ILLEGAL ACT.

PRESIDENT ROOSEVELT. "I'M SORRY, BUT THE SUPREME COURT SAYS I MUST CHUCK YOU BACK AGAIN."

A *Punch* cartoon, June 1935, attacking the decisions of the Supreme Court.

SOURCE 18

A cartoon from the *Brooklyn Daily Eagle*, February 1937, attacking Roosevelt's attempts to 'pack' the Supreme Court.

FOCUS TASK

What were the motives of the opponents of the New Deal?

The thought bubbles below show some of the reasons why people opposed the New Deal. Use the text and sources on these two pages to find examples of individuals who held each belief. Try to find two more reasons why people opposed the New Deal.

It won't work.

It'll harm me.

It'll harm the USA.

Was the New Deal a success?

The events of 1936 took their toll on Roosevelt and he became more cautious after that. Early in 1937 prosperity seemed to be returning and Roosevelt did what all conservatives had wanted: he cut the New Deal budget. He laid off many workers who had been employed by the New Deal's own organisations and the cut in spending triggered other cuts throughout the economy. This meant that unemployment spiralled upwards once more.

The 1937 recession damaged Roosevelt badly. Middle-class voters lost some confidence in him. As a result, in 1938 the Republicans once again did well in the congressional elections. Now it was much harder for Roosevelt to push his reforms through Congress. However, he was still enormously popular with most ordinary Americans (he was elected again with a big majority in 1940). The problem was that the USA was no longer as united behind his New Deal as it had been in 1933. Indeed, by 1940 Roosevelt and most Americans were focusing more on the outbreak of war in Europe and on Japan's exploits in the Far East (see Chapter 8).

So, was the New Deal a success? Only one other President had faced the problems confronting Roosevelt – Herbert Hoover. No one doubts that Roosevelt tackled the problems better than Hoover. But the question remains as to whether the New Deal did actually succeed. Historians have had many decades to judge the successes and failures of Roosevelt's policies. You are now going to study some of the evidence they have assembled and the conclusions they have reached.

Aspect 1: Attitudes

SOURCE 19

A 1937 cartoon from the *Portland Press Herald* showing Harold Ickes in conflict with big business.

- The New Deal restored the faith of the American people in their government.
- The New Deal was a huge social and economic programme. Government help on this scale would never have been possible before Roosevelt's time. It set the tone for future policies for government to help people.
- The New Deal handled billions of dollars of public money, but there were no corruption scandals. For example, the head of the Civil Works Administration, Harold Hopkins, distributed $10 billion in schemes and programmes, but never earned more than his salary of $15,000. The Secretary of the Interior, Harold Ickes, actually tapped the phones of his own employees to ensure there was no corruption. He also employed black Americans, campaigned against anti-semitism and supported the cause of native Americans.
- The New Deal divided the USA. Roosevelt and his officials were often accused of being Communists and of undermining American values. Ickes and Hopkins were both accused of being anti-business because they supported trade unions.
- The New Deal undermined local government.

Aspect 2: Industrial workers

- The NRA and Second New Deal measures strengthened the position of labour unions against the large American industrial giants.
- Roosevelt's government generally tried to support unions and make large corporations negotiate with them.
- Some labour unions combined forces to form the Committee for Industrial Organisation (CIO) in 1935. This union was large enough to be able to bargain with big corporations.
- The Union of Automobile Workers (UAW) was recognised by the two most anti-union corporations: General Motors (after a major sit-in strike in 1936) and Ford (after a ballot in 1941).
- Big business remained immensely powerful in the USA despite being challenged by the government.
- Unions were treated with suspicion by employers.
- Many strikes were broken up with brutal violence in the 1930s (see Source 22 on page 226).
- Companies such as Ford, Republic Steel and Chrysler employed their own thugs or controlled local police forces.

Aspect 3: Unemployment and the economy

SOURCE 20

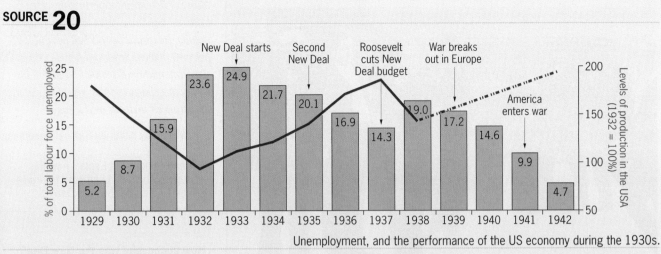

Unemployment, and the performance of the US economy during the 1930s.

(Annotations on chart: New Deal starts; Second New Deal; Roosevelt cuts New Deal budget; War breaks out in Europe; America enters war)

Left axis: % of total labour force unemployed (0–25)
Right axis: Levels of production in the USA (1932 = 100%) (50–200)

Unemployment percentages by year:
1929: 5.2; 1930: 8.7; 1931: 15.9; 1932: 23.6; 1933: 24.9; 1934: 21.7; 1935: 20.1; 1936: 16.9; 1937: 14.3; 1938: 19.0; 1939: 17.2; 1940: 14.6; 1941: 9.9; 1942: 4.7

- The New Deal created millions of jobs.
- It stabilised the American banking system.
- It cut the number of business failures.
- Projects such as the TVA brought work and an improved standard of living to deprived parts of the USA.
- New Deal projects provided the USA with valuable resources such as schools, roads and power stations.
- The New Deal never solved the underlying economic problems.
- The US economy took longer to recover than that of most European countries.

- Confidence remained low – throughout the 1930s Americans only spent and invested about 75 per cent of what they had before 1929.
- When Roosevelt cut the New Deal budget in 1937, the country went back into recession.
- There were six million unemployed in 1941.
- Only the USA's entry into the war brought an end to unemployment.

Aspect 4: Black Americans

- Around 200,000 black Americans gained benefits from the Civilian Conservation Corps and other New Deal agencies.
- Many black Americans benefited from New Deal slum clearance and housing projects.
- Many New Deal agencies discriminated against black people. They either got no work or received worse treatment or lower wages.
- Roosevelt failed to pass laws against the lynching of black Americans. He feared that Democrat senators in the southern states would not support him.

SOURCE 21

Black people queuing for government relief in 1937 in front of a famous government poster.

Aspect 5: Women

- The New Deal saw some women achieve prominent positions. Eleanor Roosevelt became an important campaigner on social issues.
- Mary Macleod Bethune, a black woman, headed the National Youth Administration.
- Frances Perkins was the Secretary of Labor. She removed 59 corrupt officials from the Labor Department and was a key figure in making the Second New Deal work in practice.
- Most of the New Deal programmes were aimed to help male manual workers rather than women (only about 8000 women were involved in the CCC).
- Local governments tried to avoid paying out social security payments to women by introducing special qualifications and conditions.
- Frances Perkins was viciously attacked in the press as a Jew and a Soviet spy. Even her cabinet colleagues tended to ignore her at social gatherings.

Aspect 6: Native Americans

- The Indian Reorganisation Act 1934 provided money to help native Americans to buy and improve land.
- The Indian Reservation Act 1934 helped native Americans to preserve and practise their traditions, laws and culture.
- Native Americans remained a poor and excluded section of society.

SOURCE 22

A UAW leader Walter Reuther with UAW activists Richard Frankensteen and Robert Kanter. On the left are some of Henry Ford's security men.

B Ford's men beating up Richard Frankensteen.

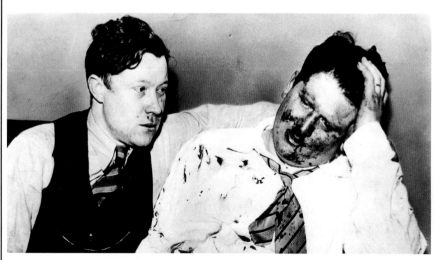

C Reuther and Frankensteen after the attack.

In May 1937 *Detroit News* photographer James Kilpatrick escaped with these pictures only by switching the film he had used with a spare one in his pocket.

SOURCE 23

Many of Roosevelt's experiments were failures, but that is what experimentation entails. He would be satisfied he said if 75 per cent of them produced beneficial results. Experimentation depended on one of his distinctive characteristics: receptivity to new and untried methods and ideas.

Written by historian Samuel Rosemann.

1 Read Source 23. Explain how this source could be used both to praise and to criticise the New Deal.

How successful was the New Deal?

This is a complicated question. You have already spent time thinking about it; now you are going to prepare to write an essay.

First recap some key points:

Roosevelt's aims
1 Look back at page 218. Make a list of Roosevelt's aims for the First New Deal.
2 What new aims did the Second New Deal have?
3 Which of these aims did Roosevelt succeed in? Which did he fail in?

The unemployment problem
4 Explain why unemployment remained high through the 1930s.
5 Does this mean that Roosevelt's New Deal was not a success?

Opposition
6 How far do you think opposition to the New Deal made it hard for the New Deal to work?

Criticisms and achievements
7 Which criticism of the New Deal do you think is the most serious? Why?
8 Which achievement do you think is the most important? Why?
9 Would Roosevelt have agreed with your choice? Why?

Now write your own balanced account of the successes and failures of the New Deal, reaching your own conclusion as to whether it was a success or not. Include:
• the nature and scale of the problem facing Roosevelt
• the action he took through the 1930s
• the impact of the New Deal on Americans
• the reasons for opposition to the New Deal
• your own judgement on its success.
Include evidence to back up your judgements.

The history of the USA is continued in Chapter 13, which covers the years 1941–80 (see page 336).

SECTION 3

Co-operation and conflict 1919–1945

8 The League of Nations

8.1 How successful was the League in the 1920s?

FOCUS

Horrified by the suffering of the First World War, many people in Europe wanted a lasting peace. The League of Nations was supposed to help keep the peace. In the 1920s it had some successes. But by 1937 it had become irrelevant, ignored even by its main members, Britain and France. In 1939, despite the efforts of the League, the world was once again plunged into war.

8.1 covers the League of Nations in the 1920s.

■ **You will investigate some of the League's successes and failures in the 1920s.**
■ **You will look at the organisation of the League and consider whether there were weaknesses in it.**
■ **You will investigate whether the world was a more peaceful and secure place at the end of the 1920s than it had been at the beginning.**

8.2 looks at the League in the 1930s.

■ **You will discover how the worldwide economic depression of the 1930s made the League's work much more difficult.**
■ **You will investigate how two crises, in Manchuria and Abyssinia, contributed to the League's failure in the 1930s.**

1919–1939

The period 1919–1939 is a complex one. The timeline below gives you an overview of the main events of this period that you will be studying in Chapters 8 and 9.

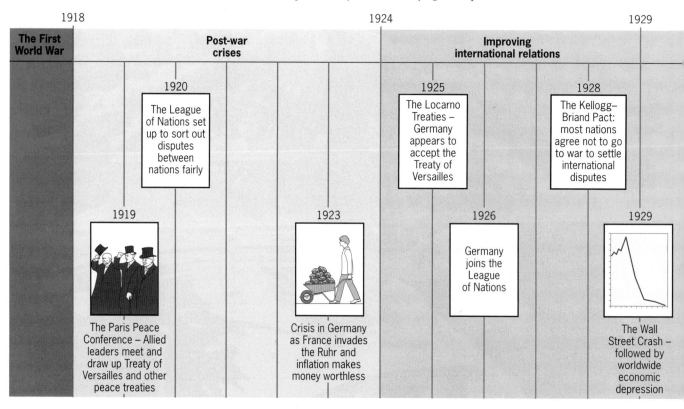

1918

The First World War

Post-war crises

1924

Improving international relations

1929

1920
The League of Nations set up to sort out disputes between nations fairly

1925
The Locarno Treaties – Germany appears to accept the Treaty of Versailles

1928
The Kellogg–Briand Pact: most nations agree not to go to war to settle international disputes

1919
The Paris Peace Conference – Allied leaders meet and draw up Treaty of Versailles and other peace treaties

1923
Crisis in Germany as France invades the Ruhr and inflation makes money worthless

1926
Germany joins the League of Nations

1929
The Wall Street Crash – followed by worldwide economic depression

The birth of the League

SOURCE 1

The front page of the *Daily Express*, 27 December 1918.
Following the Allied victory in the First World War, President Woodrow Wilson was given a rapturous reception by ordinary people wherever he went in Europe.

SOURCE 2

Merely to win the war was not enough. It must be won in such a way as to ensure the future peace of the world.

President Woodrow Wilson, 1918.

1 Which of the three kinds of League proposed by the Allies do you think would be the best at keeping peace?

After the First World War everyone wanted to avoid repeating the mass slaughter of the war that had just ended. They also agreed that a League of Nations – an organisation that could solve international problems without resorting to war – would help achieve this. However, there was disagreement about what kind of organisation it should be.

President Wilson wanted the League of Nations to be like a world parliament where representatives of all nations could meet together regularly to decide on any matters that affected them all. Many British leaders thought the best League would be a simple organisation that would just get together in emergencies. France proposed a strong League with its own army.

1930			1933			1935			1939	
	Worldwide economic depression				**Deteriorating international relations**					**The Second World War**

1931–1933	1933	1933	1935–1936	1937	1939
The Manchurian crisis – Japan begins building a Pacific empire	Japan leaves the League	Germany leaves the League	The Abyssinian crisis – Italy invades Abyssinia	Italy leaves the League	Hitler invades Poland

1933	1933–1935	1936	1938
Hitler becomes leader of Germany	Germany rearms	German troops enter the Rhineland	*Anschluss* Chamberlain's policy of appeasement culminates in the Munich agreement

SOURCE 3

[If the European powers] had dared to discuss their problems for a single fortnight in 1914 the First World War would never have happened. If they had been forced to discuss them for a whole year, war would have been inconceivable.

President Wilson speaking in 1918.

1 From what you have found out about the causes of the First World War (Chapter 1) do you agree with Wilson (Source 3)?

2 Study Source 4. Write a ten-word slogan summarising each reason for opposing the USA's membership of the League.

It was President Wilson who won. He insisted that discussions about a League should be a major part of the peace treaties and in 1919 he took personal charge of drawing up plans for the League. By February he had drafted a very ambitious plan.

All the major nations would join the League. They would disarm. If they had a dispute with another country, they would take it to the League. They promised to accept the decision made by the League. They also promised to protect one another if they were invaded. If any member did break the Covenant (see page 234) and go to war, other members promised to stop trading with it and to send troops if necessary to force it to stop fighting. Wilson's hope was that citizens of all countries would be so much against another conflict that this would prevent their leaders from going to war.

The plan was prepared in a great hurry and critics suggested there was some woolly thinking. Some people were angered by Wilson's arrogant style. He acted as if only he knew the solutions to Europe's problems. Others were worried by his idealism. Under threat of war, would the public really behave in the way he suggested? Would countries really do what the League said? Wilson glossed over what the League would do if they didn't.

Even so, most people in Europe were prepared to give Wilson's plans a try. They hoped that no country would dare invade another if they knew that the USA and other powerful nations of the world would stop trading with them or send their armies to stop them. In 1919 hopes were high that the League, with the United States in the driving seat, could be a powerful peacemaker.

A body blow to the League

Back in the USA, however, Woodrow Wilson had problems. Before the USA could even join the League, let alone take a leading role, he needed the approval of his Congress (see page 183). And in the USA the idea of a League was not at all popular, as you can see from Source 4.

SOURCE 4

Reasons for opposition to the League in the USA.

Why did the USA not join the League of Nations?

You are the American correspondent of the *Daily Express* (see Source 1) in 1921. Write a short report explaining why the USA has not joined the League.

Together, the groups in Source 4 put up powerful opposition to the League. They were joined by Wilson's many political opponents. Wilson's Democratic Party had run the USA for eight troubled years. Its opponents saw the League as an ideal opportunity to defeat him. Wilson toured the USA to put his arguments to the people, but when Congress voted in 1919 he was defeated.

In 1920 Wilson became seriously ill after a stroke. Despite that, he continued to press for the USA to join the League. He took the proposal back to Congress again in March 1920. Source 5 shows you the outcome.

SOURCE 5

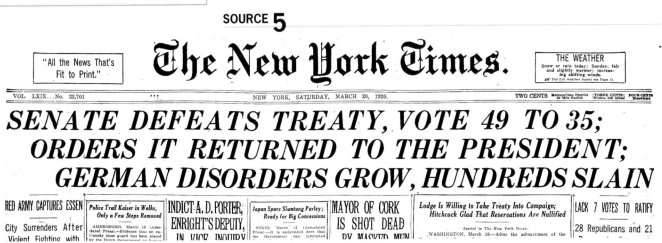

"All the News That's Fit to Print."

The New York Times.

THE WEATHER
Snow or rain today; Sunday, fair and slightly warmer; increasing shifting winds.

VOL. LXIX...No. 22,701   NEW YORK, SATURDAY, MARCH 20, 1920.   TWO CENTS

SENATE DEFEATS TREATY, VOTE 49 TO 35; ORDERS IT RETURNED TO THE PRESIDENT; GERMAN DISORDERS GROW, HUNDREDS SLAIN

RED ARMY CAPTURES ESSEN | *Police Trail Kaiser in Walks, Only a Few Steps Removed* | INDICT A. D. PORTER, ENRIGHT'S DEPUTY, | *Japan Spurs Shantung Parley; Ready for Big Concessions* | MAYOR OF CORK IS SHOT DEAD | *Lodge Is Willing to Take Treaty Into Campaign; Hitchcock Glad That Reservations Are Nullified* | LACK 7 VOTES TO RATIFY

City Surrenders After Violent Fighting with | AMERONGEN, March 19 (Associated Press).—Evidence that an extremely close guard has been placed | IN VICE INQUIRY | TOKIO, March 12 (Associated Press).—It is understood here that the Government has instructed | BY MASKED MEN | Special to The New York Times. WASHINGTON, March 19.—After the adjournment of the | 28 Republicans and 21

The front page of the *New York Times*, 20 March 1920.

SOURCE 6

A

THE OLD ORDER OF THINGS

TO DISARMAMENT AND THE ABOLITION OF WAR

READY TO START.

B

THIS LEAGUE OF NATIONS BRIDGE WAS DESIGNED BY THE PRESIDENT OF THE U.S.A.

Two British cartoons from 1919/1920. The figure in the white top hat represents the USA.

Works in pairs. One of you work with Source 6A and the other with Source 6B.

1 Decide whether your cartoon is optimistic or pessimistic about the League of Nations.
2 Decide whether your cartoon is critical of the United States.
3 Compare your ideas with your partner's. Then write a paragraph summarising the message of the two cartoons.

Still the Democrats did not give up. They were convinced that if the USA did not get involved in international affairs, another world war might follow. In the 1920 election Wilson could not run for President – he was too ill – but his successor made membership of the League a major part of the Democrat campaign. The Republican candidate, on the other hand, campaigned for America to be isolationist. His slogan was to 'return to normalcy', by which he meant life as it was before the war, with the USA isolating itself from European affairs. The Republicans won a landslide victory (see page 183).

So when the League opened for business in January 1920 the American chair was empty. The USA never joined. This was a personal rebuff for Wilson and the Democrats, but it was also a body blow to the League.

How did the League of Nations work?

The aims of the League

A Covenant set out the aims of the League of Nations. These were:

- to discourage aggression from any nation
- to encourage countries to co-operate, especially in business and trade
- to encourage nations to disarm
- to improve the living and working conditions of people in all parts of the world.

1 Design a placard for the rally shown in Source 7. It should summarise the League's aims in ten words or less.

SOURCE 7

A League of Nations Union rally in Hyde Park, London, in 1921.

FACTFILE

The League of Nations

★ The League's home was in Geneva in Switzerland.
★ Despite being the brainchild of the US President, the USA was never a member of the League.
★ The League was based on a Covenant. This was a set of 26 Articles or rules which all members of the League agreed to follow.
★ Probably the most important Article was Article 10. 'The members of the League undertake to preserve against external aggression the territory and existing independence of all members of the League. In case of threat of danger the Council [of the League] shall advise upon the means by which this obligation shall be fulfilled.'
★ Article 10 really meant collective security. By acting together (collectively), the members of the League could prevent war by defending the lands and interests of all nations, large or small.
★ One of the jobs of the League was to uphold and enforce the Treaty of Versailles.
★ Forty-two countries joined the League at the start. By the 1930s it had 59 members.

SOURCE 8

From a menu card for a banquet given by the League of Nations Assembly. It shows the hopes for the League with one of its most influential figures, Briand, as Moses, leading the statesmen of Europe to 'the promised land'.

Membership of the League

In the absence of the USA, Britain and France were the most powerful countries in the League. Italy and Japan were also permanent members of the Council, but throughout the 1920s and 1930s it was Britain and France who usually guided policy. Any action by the League needed their support.

However, both countries were poorly placed to take on this role. Both had been weakened by the First World War. Neither country was quite the major power it had once been. Neither of them had the resources to fill the gap left by the USA. Indeed, some British politicians said that if they had foreseen the American decision, they would not have voted to join the League either. They felt that the Americans were the only nation with the resources or influence to make the League work. In particular, they felt that trade sanctions would only work if the Americans applied them.

For the leaders of Britain and France the League posed a real problem. They were the ones who had to make it work, yet even at the start they doubted how effective it could be.

SOURCE 9

The League of Nations is not set up to deal with a world in chaos, or with any part of the world which is in chaos. The League of Nations may give assistance but it is not, and cannot be, a complete instrument for bringing order out of chaos.

Arthur Balfour, chief British representative at the League of Nations, speaking in 1920.

Both countries had other priorities. British politicians, for example, were more interested in rebuilding British trade and looking after the British Empire than in being an international police force.

France's main concern was still Germany. It was worried that without an army of its own the League was too weak to protect France from its powerful neighbour. It did not think Britain was likely to send an army to help it. This made France quite prepared to bypass the League if necessary in order to strengthen its position against Germany.

SOURCE 10

2 List the strengths and weaknesses of Britain and France as leaders of the League of Nations.
3 France proposed that the League should have an army of its own. Why do you think most people opposed this?
4 Think back to Wilson's ideas for the League. What problems would be caused by the fact that
   a) the USA
   b) Germany
   were not members of the League?

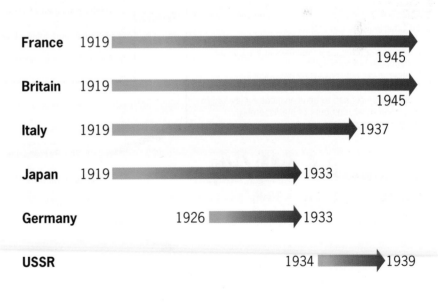

France 1919 — 1945
Britain 1919 — 1945
Italy 1919 — 1937
Japan 1919 — 1933
Germany 1926 — 1933
USSR 1934 — 1939

USA   never joined

Membership of the League of Nations. This chart shows only the most powerful nations. More than 50 other countries were also members.

1 Study Source 12. Which part of the League would deal with the following problems?
   a) An outbreak of a new infectious disease.
   b) A border dispute between two countries.
   c) Accidents caused by dangerous machinery in factories.
   d) Complaints from people in Palestine that the British were not running the mandated territory properly.

The structure of the League of Nations

The Covenant laid out the League's structure and the rules for each of the bodies within it – see Source 12 below.

SOURCE 11

A

B

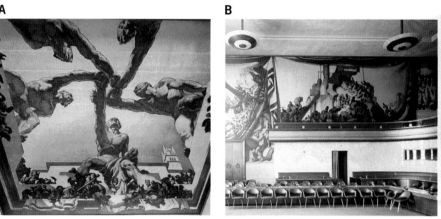

SOURCE 12

The Council
The Council was a smaller group which met more often, usually about five times a year and in case of emergency. It included:
● permanent members. In 1920 these were Britain, France, Italy and Japan.
● temporary members. They were elected by the Assembly for three-year periods. The number of temporary members varied between four and nine at different times in the League's history.
Each of the permanent members of the Council had a VETO. This meant that one permanent member could stop the Council acting even if all other members agreed. The main idea behind the Council was that if any disputes arose between members, the members brought the problem to the Council and it was sorted out through discussion before matters got out of hand. However, if this did not work, the Council could use a range of powers:
● Moral condemnation: they could decide which country was 'the aggressor', i.e. which country was to blame for the trouble. They could condemn the aggressor's action and tell it to stop what it was doing.
● Economic and financial sanctions: members of the League could refuse to trade with the aggressor.
● Military force: the armed forces of member countries could be used against an aggressor.

The Assembly
The Assembly was the League's Parliament. Every country in the League sent a representative to the Assembly. The Assembly could recommend action to the Council and could vote on:
● admitting new members to the League
● appointing temporary members of the Council
● the budget of the League
● other ideas put forward by the Council.
The Assembly only met once a year. Decisions made by the Assembly had to be unanimous – they had to be agreed by all members of the Assembly.

The Secretariat
The Secretariat was a sort of civil service. It kept records of League meetings and prepared reports for the different agencies of the League. The Secretariat had specialist sections covering areas such as health, disarmament and economic matters.

The Permanent Court of International Justice
This was meant to be a key part of the League's job of settling disputes between countries peacefully. The Court was based at the Hague in the Netherlands and was made up of judges from the member countries.
   If it was asked, the Court would give a decision on a border dispute between two countries. It also gave legal advice to the Assembly or Council.
   However, the Court was not like the courts which carried out the law within member countries. It had no way of making sure that countries followed its rulings.

The International Labour Organisation (ILO)
The ILO brought together employers, governments and workers' representatives once a year. Its aim was to improve the conditions of working people throughout the world. It collected statistics and information about working conditions and it tried to persuade member countries to adopt its suggestions.

c

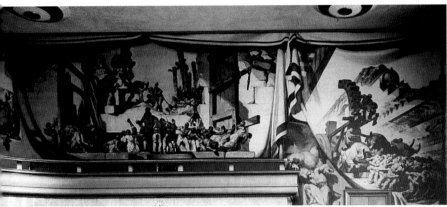

Details of the murals painted on the walls of the Assembly Room of the League of Nations in Geneva by José Maria Sert in the 1930s.

The League of Nations Commissions
As well as dealing with disputes between its members, the League also attempted to tackle other major problems. This was done through commissions or committees such as:

The Mandates Commission
The First World War had led to many former colonies of Germany and her allies ending up as League of Nations mandates ruled by Britain and France on behalf of the League. The Mandates Commission made sure that Britain or France acted in the interests of the people of that territory, not in its own interests.

Peace at last! The League of Nations will keep large and small nations secure

The Refugees Committee
This helped to return refugees to their original homes after the end of the First World War.

The Slavery Commission
This worked to abolish slavery around the world.

I'm not sure. It might look impressive but I think there are weaknesses in the League

The Health Committee
The Health Committee attempted to deal with the problem of dangerous diseases and to educate people about health and sanitation.

Work in pairs.
   Choose one statement each and write out the reasons each diplomat might give for his opinion.
   In your answer make sure you refer to:
• the membership of the League
• what the main bodies within the League can do
• how each body will make decisions
• how the League will enforce its decisions.

The organisation of the League of Nations.

SOURCE 13

The League and border disputes in the 1920s

The treaties signed at the Paris Peace Conference had created some new states and changed the borders of other existing states. However, putting a dotted line on a map was a lot simpler than working out where the boundaries actually lay on the ground. These new boundaries might split a community, putting some people in one state and the rest in another.

It was the job of the League to sort out border disputes. From the start there was so much for the League to do that some disputes were handled by the Conference of Ambassadors. Strictly speaking, this was not a body of the League of Nations. But it had been set up to sort out problems arising from the post-war treaties and was made up of leading politicians from the main members of the League – Britain, France and Italy – so it was very closely linked to the League.

The new Yugoslav–Italian border ran along this river, splitting a village in half. The villagers had to drive their carts through the river to avoid the frontier control.

SOURCE 14

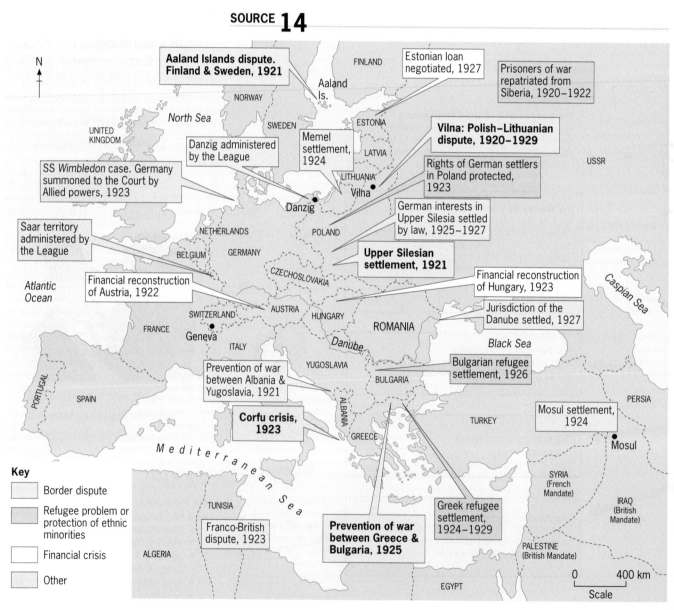

Disputes dealt with by the League of Nations in the 1920s.

Vilna, 1920

Poland and Lithuania were two new states created by the post-war treaties. Vilna (now Vilnius) was made the capital of the new state of Lithuania, but its population was largely Polish. In 1920 a private Polish army simply took control of it.

Lithuania appealed for help. This was a crucial first 'test case' for the League. Both countries were members of the League. Poland was clearly the aggressor, though many people could see its case. The League protested to Poland, but Poland did not withdraw. The League was now stuck. According to the Covenant it could have sent British and French troops to force the Poles out of Vilna. But it did not. The French were not prepared to upset Poland because they saw it as a possible ally against Germany in the future. Britain was not prepared to act alone and send troops right to the other side of Europe.

In the end the League did nothing. The Poles kept Vilna.

Upper Silesia, 1921

Upper Silesia was an industrial region on the border between Germany and Poland. It was inhabited by both German and Polish people. Both Germany and Poland wanted control of it, partly because of its rich iron and steel industry. In 1920 a PLEBISCITE was organised for Silesians to vote on which country they wished to join. French and British troops were sent to keep order at the polling booths.

The industrial areas voted mainly for Germany, the rural areas mainly for Poland. The League therefore divided the region along these lines, but it built in many safeguards to prevent future disputes. It safeguarded rail links between the two countries and made arrangements for water and power supplies from one side of the border to be supplied to the other. Both countries accepted the decision.

Aaland Islands, 1921

Both Sweden and Finland wanted control of the Aaland Islands, which were midway between the two countries. Both countries were threatening to fight for them. They appealed to the League. After studying the matter closely, the League said the islands should go to Finland. Sweden accepted the League's ruling and war was avoided.

Corfu, 1923

One of the boundaries which had to be sorted out after the war was the border between Greece and Albania. The Conference of Ambassadors was given this job and it appointed an Italian general called Tellini to supervise it. On 27 August, while they were surveying the Greek side of the frontier area, Tellini and his team were ambushed and killed.

The Italian leader Mussolini was furious and blamed the Greek government for the murder. On 29 August he demanded that it pay compensation to Italy and execute the murderers. The Greeks, however, had no idea who the murderers were. On 31 August Mussolini bombarded and then occupied the Greek island of Corfu. Fifteen people were killed. Greece appealed to the League for help.

The situation was serious. It seemed very like the events of 1914 which had triggered the First World War. Fortunately, the Council was already in session, so the League acted swiftly. By 7 September it had prepared its judgement. It condemned Mussolini's actions. It also suggested that Greece pay compensation but that the money be held by the League. This money would then be paid to Italy if, and when, Tellini's killers were found.

Officially, Mussolini accepted the League's decision. However, behind the scenes, he got to work on the Conference of Ambassadors and persuaded it to change the League's ruling. The Greeks had to apologise and pay compensation directly to Italy. On 27 September, Mussolini withdrew from Corfu boasting of his triumph.

FOCUS TASK

Five of the problems shown in Source 14 are described on pages 237–38. They are highlighted in bold text on the map on page 236. As you read about each one, score the League's success on a scale of –5 (a total failure) to +5 (a great success).

SOURCE 15

The League had been designed to deal with just such a dangerous problem as this. It had acted promptly and fairly and it had condemned the violence of the Italians. But it had lost the initiative. The result was that a great power had once again got away with using force against a small power.

Historians Gibbons and Morican referring to the Corfu crisis in *The League of Nations and the UNO*, 1970.

SOURCE 16

The settlement of the dispute between Italy and Greece, though not strictly a League victory, upheld the principles on which it was based.

From J and G Stokes, *Europe and the Modern World*, 1973.

1 Sources 15 and 16 are referring to the same event. How do their interpretations differ?
2 Could they both be right? Explain your answer.
3 'The main problem in the Corfu crisis was not the League's organisation but the attitude of its own members.' Explain whether you agree.

The Geneva Protocol

The Corfu incident demonstrated how the League of Nations could be undermined by its own members. Britain and France drew up the Geneva Protocol in 1924, which said that if two members were in dispute they would have to ask the League to sort out the disagreement and they would have to accept the Council's decision. They hoped this would strengthen the League. But before the plan could be put into effect there was a general election in Britain. The new Conservative government refused to sign the Protocol, worried that Britain would be forced to agree to something that was not in its own interests. So the Protocol, which had been meant to strengthen the League, in fact weakened it.

Bulgaria, 1925

Two years after Corfu, the League was tested yet again. In October 1925, Greek troops invaded Bulgaria after an incident on the border in which some Greek soldiers were killed. Bulgaria appealed for help. It also sent instructions to its army (see Source 17).

The League condemned the Greek action. It ordered Greece to pull out and pay compensation to Bulgaria. Faced with the disapproval of the major powers in the League, the Greeks obeyed, although they did complain that there seemed to be one rule for the large states (such as Italy) and another for the smaller ones (such as themselves).

SOURCE 17

Make only slight resistance. Protect the refugees. Prevent the spread of panic. Do not expose the troops to unnecessary losses in view of the fact that the incident has been laid before the Council of the League of Nations, which is expected to stop the invasion.

A telegram from the Bulgarian Ministry of War in Sofia to its army commanders, 22 October 1925.

1 Read Source 17. Why do you think Bulgaria was so optimistic about the League?
2 Look at Source 18. What impression of the League does this cartoon give you?
3 Look back at the Focus Task on page 235. If the diplomats had met up again in 1925, which of the events described on pages 237–38 would each one have used to show that he had been correct?

FOCUS TASK

Can you find evidence to support or challenge each of the following criticisms of the League's organisation?
- That it would be slow to act.
- That members would act in their own interests, not the League's.
- That without the USA it would be powerless.
Use a table like this to record your answers:

Criticism	Evidence for	Evidence against

Focus first on the Bulgarian and Corfu crises. These will be most useful for your exam. Then look for evidence from the other crises.

Keep your table safe. You will need it for a later task.

SOURCE 18

BALKANDUM AND BALKANDEE.
"JUST THEN CAME DOWN A MONSTROUS DOVE
WHOSE FORCE WAS PURELY MORAL,
WHICH TURNED THE HEROES' HEARTS TO LOVE
AND MADE THEM DROP THEIR QUARREL."—LEWIS CARROLL (adapted).

A cartoon about the Bulgarian crisis in *Punch*, 11 November, 1925. The characters are based on Tweedledee and Tweedledum, from the children's book *Alice's Adventures in Wonderland*, who were always squabbling.

How did the League of Nations work for a better world?

The League of Nations had set itself a wider task than simply waiting for disputes to arise and hoping to solve them. Through its commissions or committees (see page 235), the League aimed to fight poverty, disease and injustice all over the world.

SOURCE 19

A

B

Two League of Nations' projects.

• **Refugees** The League did tremendous work in getting refugees and former prisoners of war back to their homelands. It is estimated that in the first few years after the war, about 400,000 prisoners were returned to their homes by the League's agencies.

When a refugee crisis hit Turkey in 1922, hundreds of thousands of people had to be housed in refugee camps. The League acted quickly to stamp out cholera, smallpox and dysentery in the camps.

• **Working conditions** The International Labour Organization was successful in banning poisonous white lead from paint and in limiting the hours that small children were allowed to work. It also campaigned strongly for employers to improve working conditions generally.

It introduced a resolution for a maximum 48-hour week, and an eight-hour day, but only a minority of members adopted it because they thought it would raise industrial costs.

• **Health** The Health Committee, which later became the World Health Organization, worked hard to defeat the dreaded disease leprosy. It started the global campaign to exterminate mosquitoes, which greatly reduced cases of malaria and yellow fever in later decades. Even the USSR, which was otherwise opposed to the League, took Health Committee advice on preventing plague in Siberia.

• **Transport** The League made recommendations on marking shipping lanes and produced an international highway code for road users.

• **Social problems** The League blacklisted four large German, Dutch, French and Swiss companies which were involved in the illegal drug trade. It brought about the freeing of 200,000 slaves in British-owned Sierra Leone. It organised raids against slave owners and traders in Burma. It challenged the use of forced labour to build the Tanganyika railway in Africa, where the death rate among the African workers was a staggering 50 per cent. League pressure brought this down to four per cent, which it said was 'a much more acceptable figure'.

Even in the areas where it could not remove social injustice the League kept careful records of what was going on and provided information on problems such as drug trafficking, prostitution and slavery.

4 Study Sources 19A and 19B. What aspects of the League's work do you think they show?
5 Why do you think the founders of the League wanted it to tackle social problems?
6 The work of the League's commissions affected hundreds of millions of people, yet historians write very little about this side of its work. Why do you think this is?

How did international agreements help the work of the League?

Disarmament in the 1920s

In the 1920s, the League largely failed in bringing about disarmament. At the Washington Conference in 1921 the USA, Japan, Britain and France agreed to limit the size of their navies, but that was as far as disarmament ever got.

In 1923, the League's first attempt at a disarmament treaty was accepted by France and by other nations, but was rejected by Britain because it would tie it to defending other countries.

In 1926, plans were finally made for a disarmament conference, but it took five years even to agree a 'draft convention' for the conference to focus on and in 1933 that was rejected by Germany (see page 248).

The failure of disarmament was particularly damaging to the League's reputation in Germany. Germany had disarmed. It had been forced to. But no other countries had disarmed to the same extent. They were not prepared to give up their own armies and they were certainly not prepared to be the first to disarm.

Even so, in the late 1920s, the League's failure over disarmament did not seem too serious because of a series of international agreements that seemed to promise a more peaceful world (see Factfile). The two most important of these agreements were the Locarno treaties and the Kellogg–Briand Pact.

The Locarno treaties

In October 1925 representatives of France, Britain, Germany, Italy, Belgium, Poland and Czechoslovakia met in Locarno in Switzerland. After many days of hard negotiation they emerged with some important agreements:

• Germany finally accepted the borders with France and Belgium that were laid out in the Treaty of Versailles. Britain and Italy guaranteed to protect France if Germany violated these borders.
• Germany accepted that the Rhineland would remain a demilitarised zone.
• France and Germany agreed to settle any future disputes through the League of Nations.

The Locarno agreements were greeted with terrific enthusiasm, particularly in France. When news of the agreements was announced, church bells were rung, fireworks were set off and celebrations carried on into the night. The agreements seemed to resolve some of the problems left over from the First World War. France felt that at last it was being given some guarantee of border security. Germany had shown more goodwill towards France than ever before.

The agreements paved the way for Germany to join the League of Nations. Germany was granted entry into the League in 1926. Now the Soviet Union was the only major European power not in the League.

SOURCE 20

[At Locarno] a great work of peace has been done, above all because of the spirit in which it was done and the spirit which it had created. It would not have been done unless all the governments had felt the need to start a new and better chapter of international relations.

Austen Chamberlain, British Foreign Secretary, gives his judgement on the Locarno treaties in 1925.

1 Read Source 21. What role had Wilson expected the League to have? You might need to look back at pages 229–30.

2 How did the Locarno treaties help it to fulfil this role?

SOURCE 21

The Locarno agreements gave new hope that the League of Nations might assume the role which Wilson had expected of it and that, in spite of the bitterness of the post-war years, a new international order in Europe might be attainable . . . If one tries to look at the European scene between 1925 and 1929 as it appeared at the time, and without the knowledge of what came after, there seemed to be some grounds for hope.

Written by historian James Joll in 1983.

SOURCE 22

A

A LEAGUE TRIUMPH.

WITH MR. PUNCH'S CONGRATULATIONS TO THE BRITISH COMMISSIONAIRE.

B

British cartoons from 1925. In **A** Fräulein Gretchen stands for Germany.

The Kellogg–Briand Pact, 1928

Three years after Locarno, the Kellogg–Briand Pact marked the high point of international relations in the 1920s. Its terms are set out in Source 23.

There was nothing in the Pact about what would happen if a state broke the terms of the agreement. Nor did the agreement help the League of Nations with disarmament. The states all agreed that they had to keep their armies for 'self-defence'. However, at the time, the Pact was greeted as a turning point in history. If you had asked any observer in 1928 whether the world was a safer place than it had been in the early 1920s, the answer would almost certainly have been yes.

SOURCE 23

3 Look at Sources 22A and B. Are these sources making the same point about Locarno? Explain your answer.

4 Describe fully the contrasting moods shown in the cartoons.

1 The parties . . . condemn war as a means of solving international disputes and reject it as an instrument of policy.

2 The settlement or solution of all disputes . . . shall only be sought by peaceful means.

Terms of the Kellogg–Briand Pact, signed by 65 nations.

How did economic recovery help?

One reason for optimism in 1928 was that, after the difficult days of the early 1920s, the economies of the European countries were once again recovering. The Dawes Plan of 1924 had helped to sort out Germany's economic chaos and had also helped to get the economies of Britain and France moving again (see Source 24). The recovery of trading relationships between these countries helped to reduce tension. That is why one of the aims of the League had been to encourage trading links between the countries. When countries were trading with one another, they were much less likely to go to war with each other. Source 25 also makes this point, but from a negative rather than a positive standpoint.

SOURCE 24

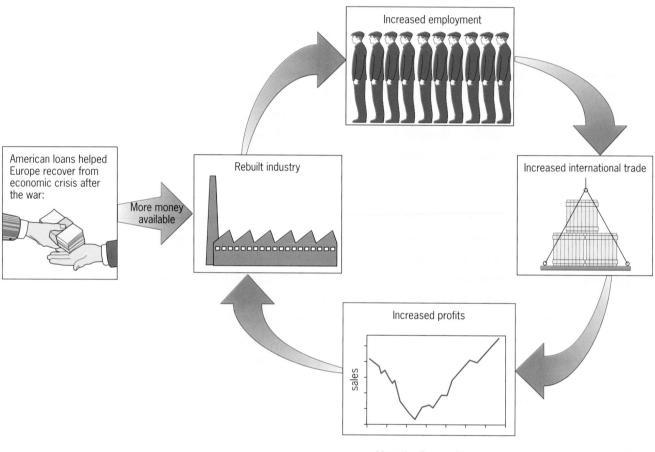

How the Dawes Plan helped economic recovery in Europe.

SOURCE 25

The world still suffers economic anarchy. Every nation pursues its own supposed interest by deliberately beggaring its neighbours. The League of Nations World Economic Conference has begun to cope with this anarchy but it is stopped at every turn by economic nationalism. If nations use tariffs to ruin one another it will not mean much that they have agreed in a treaty to renounce war. The economic struggle may produce war.

Written in 1929 by Gilbert Murray, who was a leading figure in the British League of Nations Union through the 1920s. Abridged from *The Ten Years' Life of the League of Nations.*

1 Read Source 25. What does the writer think of the Kellogg–Briand Pact?

Problems with the agreements

The period 1925–1929 has been called the Locarno Honeymoon. You can probably see why. However, many historians have questioned whether this is an accurate description.

SOURCE 26

Behind the façade of public fellowship the real spirit at Locarno was one of bitter confrontation between a fearful France and a bitter Germany.

Written by historian Sally Marks in 1984.

SOURCE 27

There was a tendency for nations to conduct much of their diplomacy outside the League of Nations and to put their trust in paper treaties. After the USA assisted Europe financially there seemed to be more goodwill which statesmen tried to capture in pacts and treaties. Many of them, however, were of little value. They represented no more than the hopes of decent men.

Written by historian Jack Watson in 1984.

There were other problems raised at the time by the Locarno agreements. Germany agreed to accept its borders in the west, and so Poland and Czechoslovakia wondered whether this meant that Germany might feel free to change its eastern borders in the future. What would the League do then?

SOURCE 28

Very little progress had been made in disarmament. Only in Germany had this happened because Germany had been forced to [disarm]. The countries of Europe still did not trust one another.

From a school textbook written by Christopher Culpin in 1986.

2 Make a list of problems with the international agreements. Use Sources 26–28 and pages 240–41.
3 For each problem on the list, say whether you think it is a serious problem or not, and explain your answer.
4 For each of the agreements mentioned in the Factfile on page 240, say how it helped the League of Nations.
5 Do you think it matters whether or not the League was involved in organising these international agreements?

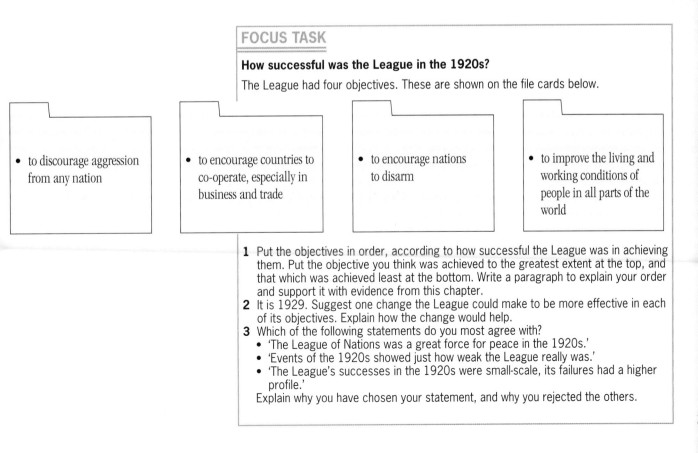

FOCUS TASK

How successful was the League in the 1920s?

The League had four objectives. These are shown on the file cards below.

- to discourage aggression from any nation

- to encourage countries to co-operate, especially in business and trade

- to encourage nations to disarm

- to improve the living and working conditions of people in all parts of the world

1 Put the objectives in order, according to how successful the League was in achieving them. Put the objective you think was achieved to the greatest extent at the top, and that which was achieved least at the bottom. Write a paragraph to explain your order and support it with evidence from this chapter.
2 It is 1929. Suggest one change the League could make to be more effective in each of its objectives. Explain how the change would help.
3 Which of the following statements do you most agree with?
   - 'The League of Nations was a great force for peace in the 1920s.'
   - 'Events of the 1920s showed just how weak the League really was.'
   - 'The League's successes in the 1920s were small-scale, its failures had a higher profile.'
   Explain why you have chosen your statement, and why you rejected the others.

8.2 Why did the League fail in the 1930s?

Historians do not agree about how successful the League of Nations was in the 1920s. However, in contrast, they almost all agree that in the 1930s the League of Nations was a failure. In the second part of this chapter you are going to investigate the factors and events that led to the failure of the League of Nations in the 1930s.

SOURCE 1

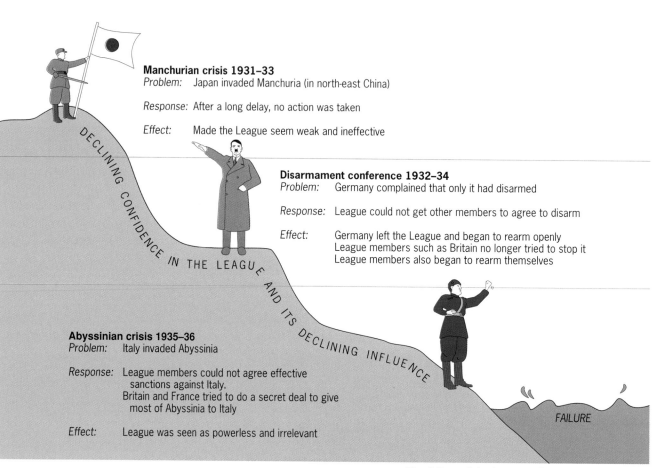

DECLINING CONFIDENCE IN THE LEAGUE AND ITS DECLINING INFLUENCE

Manchurian crisis 1931–33
Problem: Japan invaded Manchuria (in north-east China)

Response: After a long delay, no action was taken

Effect: Made the League seem weak and ineffective

Disarmament conference 1932–34
Problem: Germany complained that only it had disarmed

Response: League could not get other members to agree to disarm

Effect: Germany left the League and began to rearm openly
League members such as Britain no longer tried to stop it
League members also began to rearm themselves

Abyssinian crisis 1935–36
Problem: Italy invaded Abyssinia

Response: League members could not agree effective sanctions against Italy.
Britain and France tried to do a secret deal to give most of Abyssinia to Italy

Effect: League was seen as powerless and irrelevant

FAILURE

The failure of the League of Nations in the 1930s.

How did the economic depression harm the work of the League?

In the late 1920s there had been a boom in world trade. The USA was the richest nation in the world. American business was the engine driving the world economy. Everyone traded with the USA. Most countries also borrowed money from American banks. As a result of this trade, most countries were getting richer. You saw on page 242 how this economic recovery helped to reduce international tension. You also saw in Source 25 how one of the League's leading figures predicted that political disaster might follow if countries did not co-operate economically. The words turned out to be an accurate prediction.

In 1929 economic disaster did strike. In the USA the Wall Street Crash started a long depression that quickly caused economic problems throughout the world (see page 213). It damaged the trade and industry of all countries (see Source 2). It affected relations between countries (see Source 3). It also led to important political changes within countries (see Source 4). Much of the goodwill and the optimism of the late 1920s evaporated.

SOURCE 2

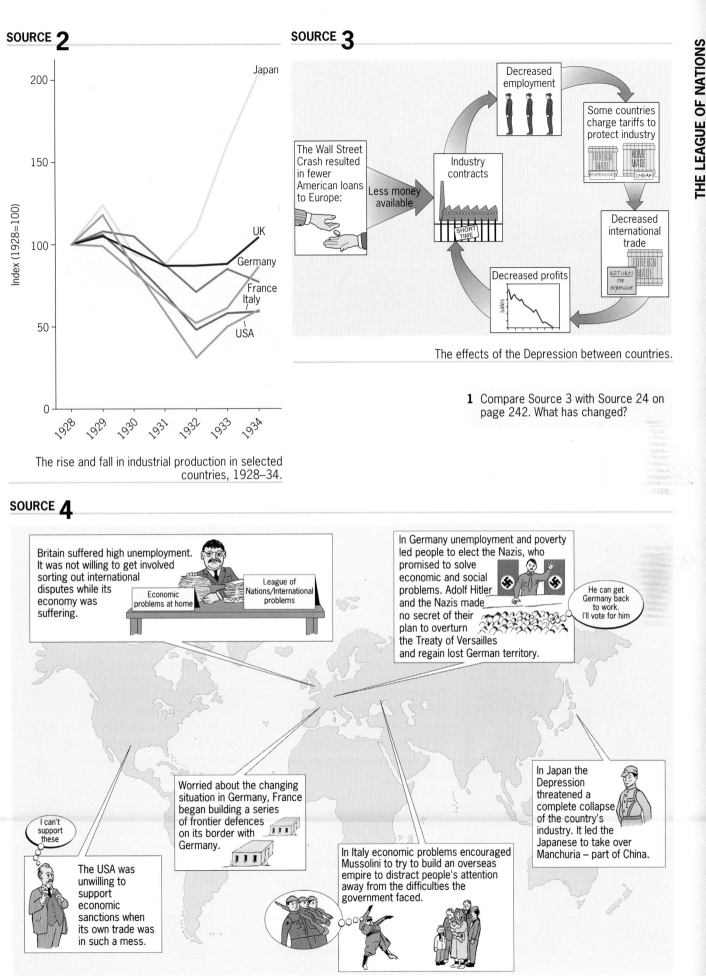

The rise and fall in industrial production in selected countries, 1928–34.

SOURCE 3

The effects of the Depression between countries.

1 Compare Source 3 with Source 24 on page 242. What has changed?

SOURCE 4

The effects of the Depression within various countries.

Why did the Japanese invade Manchuria?

The first major test for the League came when the Japanese invaded Manchuria in 1931.

SOURCE 5

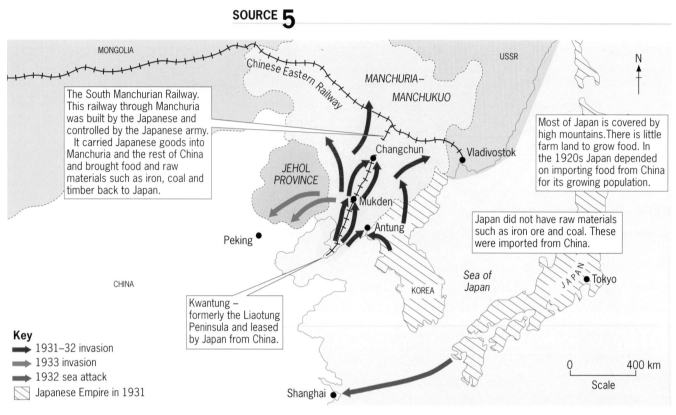

The South Manchurian Railway. This railway through Manchuria was built by the Japanese and controlled by the Japanese army. It carried Japanese goods into Manchuria and the rest of China and brought food and raw materials such as iron, coal and timber back to Japan.

Most of Japan is covered by high mountains. There is little farm land to grow food. In the 1920s Japan depended on importing food from China for its growing population.

Japan did not have raw materials such as iron ore and coal. These were imported from China.

Kwantung – formerly the Liaotung Peninsula and leased by Japan from China.

Key
→ 1931–32 invasion
→ 1933 invasion
→ 1932 sea attack
▨ Japanese Empire in 1931

0   400 km
Scale

The railways and natural resources of Manchuria.

SOURCE 6

Japanese troops in action in Manchuria.

Since 1900 Japan's economy and population had been growing rapidly. By the 1920s Japan was a major power.

- It had a very powerful army and navy – army leaders often dictated government policy.
- It had a strong industry, exporting goods to the USA and China in particular.
- It had a growing empire which included the Korean peninsula (see Source 5).

The Depression hit Japan badly. Both China and the USA put up tariffs (trade barriers) against Japanese goods. The collapse of the American market put the Japanese economy in crisis. Without this trade Japan could not feed its people. Army leaders in Japan were in no doubt about the solution to Japan's problems – they wanted to build up a Japanese empire by force.

In 1931 an incident in Manchuria gave them the opportunity they had been looking for to expand the Japanese Empire. As you can see from Source 5, the Japanese army controlled the South Manchurian Railway. In September 1931 they claimed that Chinese soldiers had sabotaged the railway. In retaliation they overran Manchuria and threw out all Chinese forces. In February 1932 they set up a puppet government in Manchuria – or Manchukuo, as they called it – which did exactly what the Japanese army told it to do. Later in 1932 Japanese aeroplanes and gunships bombed Shanghai. The civilian government in Japan told the Japanese army to withdraw, but its instructions were ignored. It was clear that it was the army and not the government that was in control of Japanese foreign policy.

China appealed to the League. Japan claimed it was not invading as an aggressor, but simply settling a local difficulty. The Japanese argued that China was in such a state of anarchy that they had to invade in self-defence to keep peace in the area. For the League of Nations this was a serious test. Japan was a leading member of the League. It needed careful handling. What should the League do?

1 Why did it take so long for the League to make a decision over Manchuria?
2 Look at Sources 7 and 8. What criticisms are the cartoonists making of:
   a) Japan
   b) the League?
3 Did the League fail in this incident because of the way it worked or because of the attitude of its members?

There was now a long and frustrating delay. The League's officials sailed round the world to assess the situation in Manchuria for themselves. It was September 1932 – a full year after the invasion – before they presented their report. It was detailed and balanced, but the judgement was very clear. Japan had acted unlawfully. Manchuria should be returned to the Chinese.

However, in February 1933, instead of withdrawing from Manchuria the Japanese announced that they intended to invade more of China. They still argued that this was necessary in self-defence. On 24 February 1933 the report from the League's officials was approved by 42 votes to 1 in the Assembly. Only Japan voted against. Smarting at the insult, Japan resigned from the League on 27 March 1933. The next week it invaded Jehol (see Source 5).

The League was powerless. It discussed economic sanctions, but without the USA, Japan's main trading partner, they would be meaningless. Besides, Britain seemed more interested in keeping up good relationships with Japan than in agreeing to sanctions. The League also discussed banning arms sales to Japan, but the member countries could not even agree about that. They were worried that Japan would retaliate and the war would escalate.

There was no prospect at all of Britain and France risking their navies or armies in a war with Japan. Only the USA and the USSR would have had the resources to remove the Japanese from Manchuria by force and they were not even members of the League.

SOURCE 7

A cartoon by David Low, 1933. Low was one of the most famous cartoonists of the 1930s. He regularly criticised both the actions of dictators around the world and the ineffectiveness of the League of Nations.

SOURCE 8

A French poster of 1932.

SOURCE 9

I was sad to find everyone [at the League] so dejected. The Assembly was a dead thing. The Council was without confidence in itself. Beneš [the Czechoslovak leader], who is not given to hysterics, said [about the people at the League] 'They are too frightened. I tell them we are not going to have war now; we have five years before us, perhaps six. We must make the most of them.'

The British elder statesman Sir Austen Chamberlain visited the League of Nations late in 1932 in the middle of the Manchurian crisis. This is an adapted extract from his letters.

All sorts of excuses were offered for the failure of the League. Japan was so far away. Japan was a special case. Japan did have a point when it said that China was itself in the grip of anarchy. However, the significance of the Manchurian crisis was obvious. As many of its critics had predicted, the League was powerless if a strong nation decided to pursue an aggressive policy and invade its neighbours. Japan had committed blatant aggression and got away with it. Back in Europe, both Hitler and Mussolini looked on with interest. Within three years they would both follow Japan's example.

SOURCE 10

To make myself perfectly clear, I would ask: is there anyone within or without Germany who honestly considers the present German regime to be peaceful in its instincts . . . Germany is inhibited from disturbing the peace of Europe solely by its consciousness of its present military inferiority.

Professor William Rappard speaking to the League in 1932.

Why did disarmament fail in the 1930s?

The next big failure of the League of Nations was over disarmament. As you saw on page 240, the League had not had any success in this area in the 1920s either, but at that stage, when the international climate was better, it had not seemed to matter as much. In the 1930s, however, there was increased pressure for the League to do something about disarmament. The Germans had long been angry about the fact that they had been forced to disarm after the First World War while other nations had not done the same. Many countries were actually spending more on their armaments than they had been before the First World War.

In the wake of the Manchurian crisis, the members of the League realised the urgency of the problem. In February 1932 the long-promised Disarmament Conference finally got under way. By July 1932 it had produced resolutions to prohibit bombing of civilian populations, limit the size of artillery, limit the tonnage of tanks, and prohibit chemical warfare. But there was very little in the resolutions to show how these limits would be achieved. For example, the bombing of civilians was to be prohibited, but all attempts to agree to abolish planes capable of bombing were defeated. Even the proposal to ban the manufacture of chemical weapons was defeated.

It was not a promising start. However, there was a bigger problem facing the Conference – what to do about Germany. The Germans had been in the League for six years. Most people now accepted that they should be treated more equally than under the Treaty of Versailles. The big question was whether everyone else should disarm to the level that Germany had been forced to, or whether the Germans should be allowed to rearm to a level closer to that of the other powers. The experience of the 1920s showed that the first option was a non-starter. But there was great reluctance in the League to allow the second option.

This is how events relating to Germany moved over the next 18 months.

SOURCE 11

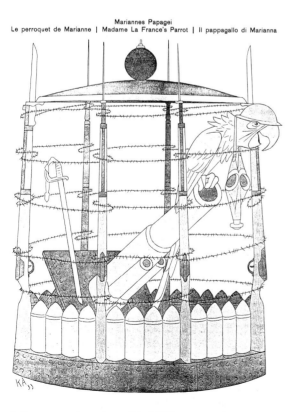

Mariannes Papagei
Le perroquet de Marianne | Madame La France's Parrot | Il pappagallo di Marianna

A German cartoon from July 1933 commenting on France's constant call for more security when it was already well armed.

July 1932
Germany tabled proposals for all countries to disarm down to its level. When the Conference failed to agree the principle of 'equality', the Germans walked out.

September 1932
The British sent the Germans a note that went some way to agreeing equality, but the superior tone of the note angered the Germans still further.

December 1932
An agreement was finally reached to treat Germany equally.

January 1933
Germany announced it was coming back.

February 1933
Hitler became Chancellor of Germany at the end of January. He immediately started to rearm Germany, although secretly.

May 1933
Hitler promised not to rearm Germany if 'in five years all other nations destroyed their arms'.

June 1933
Britain produced an ambitious disarmament plan.

October 1933
Hitler withdrew from the Disarmament Conference, and soon after took Germany out of the League altogether.

By this stage, all the powers knew that Hitler was secretly rearming Germany already. They also began to rebuild their own armaments. Against that background the Disarmament Conference struggled on for another year but in an atmosphere of increasing futility. It finally ended in 1934.

1 Look at Source 12. Explain what Low is saying about:
   a) ordinary people
   b) political leaders.
2 In what ways were each of the following to blame for the failure of the Disarmament Conference:
   a) Germany
   b) Britain
   c) the League itself?

SOURCE 12

David Low's cartoon commenting on the failure of the Disarmament Conference in 1934.

The Conference failed for a number of reasons. Some say it was all doomed from the start. No one was very serious about disarmament anyway. But there were other factors at work.

It did not help that Britain and France were divided on this issue. By 1933 many British people felt that the Treaty of Versailles was unfair. In fact, to the dismay of the French, the British signed an agreement with Germany in 1935 that allowed Germany to build up its navy as long as it stayed under 35 per cent of the size of the British navy. Britain did not consult either its allies or the League about this, although it was in violation of the Treaty of Versailles.

It seemed that each country was looking after itself and ignoring the League.

SOURCE 13

3 Look at Source 13.
   a) Describe the attitude of each country to France's proposals.
   b) Is this cartoon optimistic or pessimistic about peace in Europe? Give reasons.

A cartoon from the *Daily Express*, 19 July 1934, by Sidney Strube. The singer is supposed to be France. France had proposed an alliance with the USSR known as 'Eastern Locarno'.

How did Mussolini's invasion of Abyssinia damage the League?

The fatal blow to the League came when the Italian dictator Mussolini invaded Abyssinia (now Ethiopia) in 1935. There were both similarities with and differences from the Japanese invasion of Manchuria. Like Japan, Italy was a leading member of the League. Like Japan, Italy wanted to expand its empire by invading another country. However, unlike Manchuria, this dispute was on the League's doorstep. Italy was a European power. It even had a border with France. Abyssinia bordered on the Anglo-Egyptian territory of Sudan and the British colonies of Uganda, Kenya and British Somaliland. Unlike events in Manchuria, the League could not claim that this problem was in an inaccessible part of the world. Some argued that Manchuria had been a special case. Would the League do any better in this Abyssinian crisis?

SOURCE 14

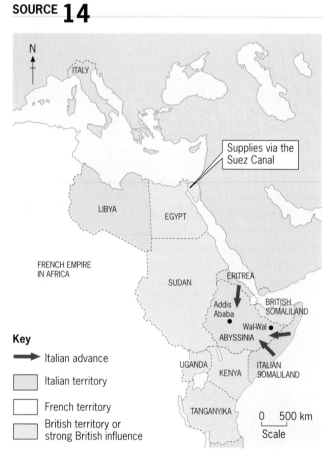

British, French and Italian possessions in eastern Africa.

SOURCE 15

A cartoon from *Punch*, 1935. *Punch* was usually very patriotic towards Britain. It seldom criticised British politicians over foreign policy.

Background

The origins of this crisis lay back in the previous century. In 1896 Italian troops had tried to invade Abyssinia but had been defeated by a poorly equipped army of tribesmen. Mussolini wanted revenge for this humiliating defeat. He also had his eye on the fertile lands and mineral wealth of Abyssinia. However, most importantly, he wanted glory and conquest. His style of leadership needed military victories and he had often talked of restoring the glory of the Roman Empire.

In December 1934 there was a dispute between Italian and Ethiopian soldiers at the Wal-Wal oasis – 80 km inside Abyssinia. Mussolini took this as his cue and claimed this was actually Italian territory. He demanded an apology and began preparing the Italian army for an invasion of Abyssinia. The Abyssinian emperor Haile Selassie appealed to the League for help.

Phase 1 – January 1935 to October 1935: the League plays for time

In this period Mussolini was supposedly negotiating with the League to settle the dispute, while at the same time he was shipping his vast army to Africa and whipping up war fever among the Italian people – he was preparing for a full-scale invasion of Abyssinia.

To start with, the British and the French failed to take the situation seriously. They played for time. They were desperate to keep good relations with Mussolini, who seemed to be their strongest ally against Hitler. They signed an agreement with him early in 1935 known as the Stresa Pact which formalised a protest at German rearmament and a commitment to stand united against Germany. At the meeting to discuss this, they did not even raise the question of Abyssinia. Some historians suggest that Mussolini believed that Britain and France had promised to turn a blind eye to his exploits in Abyssinia in return for his joining them in the Stresa Pact.

However, as the year wore on, there was a public outcry against Italy's behaviour. A ballot was taken by the League of Nations Union in Britain in 1934–35. It showed that a majority of British people supported the use of military force to defend Abyssinia if necessary. Facing an autumn election at home, British politicians now began to 'get tough'. At an assembly of the League, the British Foreign Minister, Hoare, made a grand speech about the value of collective security, to the delight of the League's members and all the smaller nations. There was much talking and negotiating. However, the League never actually did anything to discourage Mussolini.

On 4 September, after eight months' deliberation, a committee reported to the League that neither side could be held responsible for the Wal-Wal incident. The League put forward a plan that would give Mussolini some of Abyssinia. Mussolini rejected it.

Phase 2 – October 1935 to May 1936: sanctions or not?

In October 1935 Mussolini's army was ready. He launched a full-scale invasion of Abyssinia. Despite brave resistance, the Abyssinians were no match for the modern Italian army equipped with tanks, aeroplanes and poison gas.

This was a clear-cut case of a large, powerful state attacking a smaller one. The League was designed for just such disputes and, unlike in the Manchurian crisis, it was ideally placed to act. There was no doubting the seriousness of the issue either. Source 16 shows the view of one cartoonist at the time. The Covenant (see Factfile, page 232) made it clear that sanctions must be introduced against the aggressor. A committee was immediately set up to agree what sanctions to impose.

Sanctions would only work if they were imposed quickly and decisively. Each week a decision was delayed would allow Mussolini to build up his stockpile of raw materials. The League imposed an immediate ban on arms sales to Italy while allowing them to Abyssinia. It banned all loans to Italy. It banned all imports from Italy. It banned the export to Italy of rubber, tin and metals.

However, the League delayed a decision for two months over whether to ban oil exports to Italy. It feared the Americans would not support the sanctions. It also feared that its members' economic interests would be further damaged. In Britain, the Cabinet was informed that 30,000 British coal miners were about to lose their jobs because of the ban on coal exports to Italy.

1 Look at Source 16. What has Mussolini let out?

A cartoon by David Low published in October 1935. The figure taking off the lid is Mussolini.

SOURCE 17

Yes, we know that World War began in Manchuria fifteen years ago. We know that four years later we could easily have stopped Mussolini if we had taken the sanctions against Mussolini that were obviously required, if we had closed the Suez Canal to the aggressor and stopped his oil.

British statesman Philip Noel Baker speaking at the very last session of the League in April 1946.

1 Explain in your own words:
   a) why the Hoare–Laval deal caused such outrage
   b) how it affected attitudes to the League
   c) how the USA undermined the League.
2 Look at Source 18. What event is the cartoonist referring to in 'the matter has been settled elsewhere'?
3 Look back at your chart from page 238. Do a similar analysis for the crises in Manchuria and Abyssinia.

SOURCE 18

A German cartoon from the front cover of the pro-Nazi magazine *Simplicissimus*, 1936. The warrior is delivering a message to the League of Nations: 'I am sorry to disturb your sleep but I just wanted to tell you that you should no longer bother yourselves about this Abyssinian business. The matter has been settled elsewhere.'

More important still, the Suez Canal, which was owned by Britain and France, was not closed to Mussolini's supply ships. The canal was the Italians' main supply route to Abyssinia and closing it could have ended the Abyssinian campaign very quickly. Both Britain and France were afraid that closing the canal could have resulted in war with Italy. This failure was fatal for Abyssinia.

Equally damaging to the League was the secret dealing between the British and the French that was going on behind the scenes. In December 1935, while sanctions discussions were still taking place, the British and French Foreign Ministers, Hoare and Laval, were hatching a plan. This aimed to give Mussolini two-thirds of Abyssinia in return for his calling off his invasion! Laval even proposed to put the plan to Mussolini before they showed it to either the League of Nations or Haile Selassie. Laval told the British that if they did not agree to the plan, then the French would no longer support sanctions against Italy.

However, details of the plan were leaked to the French press. It proved quite disastrous for the League. Haile Selassie demanded an immediate League debate about it. In both Britain and France it was seen as a blatant act of treachery against the League. Hoare and Laval were both sacked. But the real damage was to the sanctions discussions. They lost all momentum. The question about whether to ban oil sales was further delayed. In February 1936 the committee concluded that if they did stop oil sales to Italy, the Italians' supplies would be exhausted in two months, even if the Americans kept on selling oil to them. But by then it was all too late. Mussolini had already taken over large parts of Abyssinia. And the Americans were even more disgusted with the ditherings of the French and the British than they had been before and so blocked a move to support the League's sanctions. American oil producers actually stepped up their exports to Italy.

Mussolini 'obtains' Abyssinia

On 7 March 1936 the fatal blow was delivered. Hitler, timing his move to perfection, marched his troops into the Rhineland, an act prohibited by the Treaty of Versailles (see page 86). If there had been any hope of getting the French to support sanctions against Italy, it was now dead. The French were desperate to gain the support of Italy and were now prepared to pay the price of giving Abyssinia to Mussolini.

Italy continued to defy the League's orders and by May 1936 had taken the capital of Abyssinia, Addis Ababa. On 2 May, Haile Selassie was forced into exile. On 9 May, Mussolini formally annexed the entire country. The League watched helplessly. Collective security had been shown up as an empty promise. The League of Nations had failed.

If the British and French had hoped that their handling of the Abyssinian crisis would help strengthen their position against Hitler, they were soon proved very wrong. In November 1936 Mussolini and Hitler signed an agreement of their own called the Rome–Berlin Axis.

SOURCE 19

Could the League survive the failure of sanctions to rescue Abyssinia? Could it ever impose sanctions again? Probably there had never been such a clear-cut case for sanctions. If the League had failed in this case there could probably be no confidence that it could succeed again in the future.

Anthony Eden, British Foreign Minister, expressing his feelings about the crisis to the British Cabinet in May 1936.

4 From Sources 20–23 make a list of ways in which the Abyssinian crisis damaged the League.

A disaster for the League and for the world

Historians often disagree about how to interpret important events. However, one of the most striking things about the events of 1935 and 1936 is that most historians seem to agree about the Abyssinian crisis: it was a disaster for the League of Nations and had serious consequences for world peace.

SOURCE 20

The crises of 1935–6 were fatal to the League, which was not taken seriously again . . . it was too late to save the League. Instead, it began the emotional preparation among the democracies for the Second World War . . .

Written by historian JR Western in 1971.

SOURCE 21

The implications of the conquest of Abyssinia were not confined to East Africa. Although victory cemented Mussolini's personal prestige at home, Italy gained little or nothing from it in material terms. The damage done, meanwhile, to the prestige of Britain, France and the League of Nations was irreversible. The only winner in the whole sorry episode was Adolf Hitler.

Written by historian TA Morris in 1995.

SOURCE 22

After seeing what happened first in Manchuria and then in Abyssinia, most people drew the conclusion that it was no longer much use placing their hopes in the League . . .

Written by historian James Joll in 1976.

SOURCE 23

The real death of the League was in 1935. One day it was a powerful body imposing sanctions, the next day it was an empty sham, everyone scuttling from it as quickly as possible. Hitler watched.

Written by historian AJP Taylor in 1966.

ACTIVITY

Work in pairs.

Write a caption for one of the two cartoons in Source 24, showing people's feelings about the League after the Abyssinian crisis.

Your teacher can tell you what the original captions were.

SOURCE 24

A

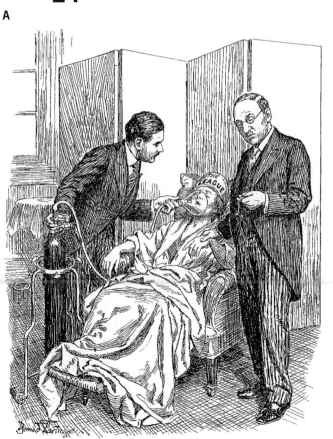

B

Two cartoons from *Punch*, 1938. The doctors in **A** represent Britain and France.

Why did the League of Nations fail in the 1930s?

This diagram summarises the reasons historians give for the failure of the League.

The self-interest of leading members
The League depended on Britain and France to provide firm support in times of crisis. When conflicts occurred, however, neither the British nor the French government was prepared to abandon its own self-interest to support the League.

The USA and other important countries were absent
At any one time important countries were not members. Germany was not a member until 1926 and left in 1933. The USSR did not join until 1934, whilst Japan left in 1933 and Italy left in 1937. Most important, the USA was never a member. Without such major powers the League lacked authority and sanctions were not effective.

Why did the League of Nations fail?

Economic sanctions did not work
Economic sanctions were supposed to be the League's main weapon, but members of the League did not willingly impose them because they worried that without the USA they would not work. When they did impose them they were easily broken. The League therefore lacked the muscle to enforce the decisions of its Assembly and Council.

Lack of troops
If economic sanctions failed, military force was the next option. Yet the League had no armed forces of its own and relied upon the co-operation of its members. Britain and France, however, were not willing to commit troops. At no time did troops ever fight on behalf of the League.

The treaties it had to uphold were seen as unfair
The League was bound to uphold the peace treaties which had created it. In time, however, it became apparent that some of the terms of those peace treaties were harsh and unjust and needed amending. This further undermined the League.

Decisions were slow
When a crisis occurred, the League was supposed to act quickly and with determination. In many cases, however, the League met too infrequently and took too long to make decisions. The need for all members to agree on a course of action undermined the strength of the League.

1 Which of these weaknesses in the League of Nations do you think was the most important factor in:
a) the Manchurian crisis
b) the failure of disarmament
c) the Abyssinian crisis?
2 Explain whether you agree or disagree with this statement: 'The League failed in the 1930s simply because it faced greater challenges than it had faced in the 1920s.'

Causes of the Second World War

9.1 Why did peace collapse in Europe in 1939?

FOCUS

Tension between countries rose dramatically in the 1930s. Hitler was rearming Germany and openly defying the Treaty of Versailles. Dictatorships in other countries became more and more powerful and the democracies seemed either unwilling or unable to stop them. Finally, in 1939 war once again broke out in Europe.

In 9.1 you will investigate why Britain and France declared war on Germany in September 1939. You will make up your own mind as to how far Hitler's own policies were to blame for the war and whether other factors were equally important.

You will consider:

- **whether Britain's policy of appeasing Hitler could be justified**
- **how weaknesses in the First World War peace treaties had long-term consequences for international relations**
- **the consequences of the failure of the League of Nations in the 1930s**
- **how important the Nazi–Soviet Pact was in causing the war.**

In 9.2 you will investigate how the war became a world war.

From foot-soldier to Führer

SOURCE **1**

Adolf Hitler (right) during the First World War.

SOURCE **2**

Adolf Hitler is welcomed by a crowd of Nazi supporters in 1933.

SOURCE **3**

Any account of the origins and course of the Second World War must give Hitler the leading part. Without him a major war in the early 1940s between all the world's great powers was unthinkable.

British historian Professor Richard Overy, writing in 1996.

Less than twenty years separates Sources 1 and 2. Between 1918 and 1933 Adolf Hitler rose from being an obscure and demoralised member of the defeated German army to become the all-powerful Führer, dictator of Germany, with almost unlimited power and an overwhelming ambition to make Germany great once again. His is an astonishing story which you can read about in detail on pages 148–59. Here you will be concentrating on just one intriguing and controversial question: how far was Hitler responsible for the outbreak of the Second World War. Is Source 3 right?

Hitler's plans

Hitler was never secretive about his plans for Germany. As early as 1924 he had laid out in his book *Mein Kampf* what he would do if the Nazis ever achieved power in Germany. His three main aims are described below.

Abolish the Treaty of Versailles!

Like many Germans, Hitler believed that the Treaty of Versailles was unjust.

He hated the Treaty and called the German leaders who had signed it 'The November Criminals'. The Treaty was a constant reminder to Germans of their defeat in the First World War and their humiliation by the Allies. Hitler promised that if he became leader of Germany he would reverse it.

By the time he came to power in Germany, some of the terms had already been changed. For example, Germany had stopped making reparations payments altogether. However, most points were still in place. The table in the Focus Task on page 257 shows the terms of the Treaty that most angered Hitler.

SOURCE 4

We demand equality of rights for the German people in its dealings with other nations, and abolition of the Peace Treaties of Versailles and St Germain.

From Hitler's *Mein Kampf*, 1923–24.

Expand German territory!

The Treaty of Versailles had taken away territory from Germany. Hitler wanted to get that territory back. He wanted Germany to unite with Austria. He wanted German minorities in other countries such as Czechoslovakia to rejoin Germany. But he also wanted to carve out an empire in eastern Europe to give extra *Lebensraum* or 'living space' for Germans.

1 From the evidence of Sources 4 and 5, why might Czechoslovak leaders be concerned about Hitler's plans? You may need to refer to pages 94–95.

SOURCE 5

We turn our eyes towards the lands of the east . . . When we speak of new territory in Europe today, we must principally think of Russia and the border states subject to her. Destiny itself seems to wish to point out the way for us here.

Colonisation of the eastern frontiers is of extreme importance. It will be the duty of Germany's foreign policy to provide large spaces for the nourishment and settlement of the growing population of Germany.

From Hitler's *Mein Kampf*.

Defeat Communism!

A German empire carved out of the Soviet Union would also help Hitler in one of his other objectives – the defeat of Communism or Bolshevism. Hitler was anti-Communist. He believed that Bolsheviks had helped to bring about the defeat of Germany in the First World War. He also believed that the Bolsheviks wanted to take over Germany.

ACTIVITY

It is 1933. Write a briefing paper for the British government on Hitler's plans for Germany. Use Sources 4–6 to help you.

Conclude with your own assessment on whether the government should be worried about Hitler and his plans.

In your conclusion, remember these facts about the British government:
- Britain is a leading member of the League of Nations and is supposed to uphold the Treaty of Versailles, by force if necessary.
- The British government does not trust the Communists and thinks that a strong Germany could help to stop the Communist threat.

SOURCE 6

We must not forget that the Bolsheviks are blood-stained. That they overran a great state [Russia], and in a fury of massacre wiped out millions of their most intelligent fellow-countrymen and now for ten years have been conducting the most tyrannous regime of all time. We must not forget that many of them belong to a race which combines a rare mixture of bestial cruelty and vast skill in lies, and considers itself specially called now to gather the whole world under its bloody oppression.

The menace which Russia suffered under is one which perpetually hangs over Germany. Germany is the next great objective of Bolshevism. All our strength is needed to raise up our nation once more and rescue it from the embrace of the international python . . . The first essential is the expulsion of the Marxist poison from the body of our nation.

From Hitler's *Mein Kampf*.

Hitler's actions

This timeline shows how, between 1933 and 1939, Hitler turned his plans into actions.

DATE	ACTION
1933	Took Germany out of the League of Nations
	Began rearming Germany
1934	Tried to take over Austria but was prevented by Mussolini
1935	Held massive rearmament rally in Germany
1936	Reintroduced conscription in Germany
	Sent German troops into the Rhineland
	Made an anti-Communist alliance with Japan
1937	Tried out Germany's new weapons in the Spanish Civil War
	Made an anti-Communist alliance with Italy
1938	Took over Austria
	Took over the Sudetenland area of Czechoslovakia
1939	Invaded the rest of Czechoslovakia
	Invaded Poland
War	

When you see events leading up to the war laid out this way, it makes it seem as if Hitler planned it all step by step. In fact, this view of events was widely accepted by historians until the 1960s. In the 1960s, however, the British historian AJP Taylor came up with a new interpretation. His view was that Hitler was a gambler rather than a planner. Hitler simply took the logical next step to see what he could get away with. He was bold. He kept his nerve. As other countries gave into him and allowed him to get away with each gamble, so he became bolder and risked more. In Taylor's interpretation it is Britain, the Allies and the League of Nations who are to blame for letting Hitler get away with it – by not standing up to him. As you examine Hitler's actions in more detail, you will see that both interpretations are possible. You can make up your own mind which you agree with.

FOCUS TASK

Hitler and the Treaty of Versailles

1 Draw up a table like this one to show some of the terms of the Treaty of Versailles that affected Germany.
2 As you work through this chapter, fill out the other columns of this 'Versailles chart'.

Terms of the Treaty of Versailles	What Hitler did and when	The reasons he gave for his action	The response from Britain and France
Germany's armed forces to be severely limited			
The Rhineland to be a demilitarised zone			
Germany forbidden to unite with Austria			
The Sudetenland taken into the new state of Czechoslovakia			
The Polish Corridor given to Poland			

SOURCE 7

I am convinced that Hitler does not want war . . . what the Germans are after is a strong army which will enable them to deal with Russia.

British politician Lord Lothian, January 1935.

1 Design a Nazi poster to present the information in Source 10 to the German people.
2 Fill out the first row of your 'Versailles chart' on page 257.
3 What factors allowed Hitler to get away with rearming Germany?

Rearmament

Hitler came to power in Germany in 1933. One of his first steps was to increase Germany's armed forces. Thousands of unemployed workers were drafted into the army. This helped him to reduce unemployment, which was one of the biggest problems he faced in Germany. But it also helped him to deliver on his promise to make Germany strong again and to challenge the terms of the Treaty of Versailles.

Hitler knew that German people supported rearmament. But he also knew it would cause alarm in other countries. He handled it cleverly. Rearmament began in secret at first. He made a great public display of his desire not to rearm Germany – that he was only doing it because other countries refused to disarm (see page 248). He then followed Japan's example and withdrew from the League of Nations.

In 1935 Hitler openly staged a massive military rally celebrating the German armed forces (see Source 8). In 1936 he even reintroduced conscription to the army. He was breaking the terms of the Treaty of Versailles, but he guessed correctly that he would get away with rearmament. Many other countries were using rearmament as a way to fight unemployment. The collapse of the League of Nations Disarmament Conference in 1934 (see pages 248–49) had shown that other nations were not prepared to disarm.

Rearmament was a very popular move in Germany. It boosted Nazi support. Hitler also knew that Britain had some sympathy with Germany on this issue. Britain believed that the limits put on Germany's armed forces by the Treaty of Versailles were too tight. The permitted forces were not enough to defend Germany from attack. Britain also thought that a strong Germany would be a good buffer against Communism.

Britain had already helped to dismantle the Treaty by signing a naval agreement with Hitler in 1935, allowing Germany to increase its navy to up to 35 per cent of the size of the British navy. The French were angry with Britain about this, but there was little they could do.

SOURCE 8

German soldiers and armaments on show at the Proclamation of Freedom to Rearm Rally in 1935.

SOURCE 9

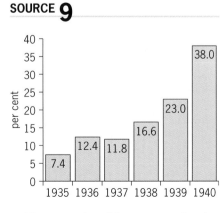

The proportion of German spending that went into armaments, 1935–40.

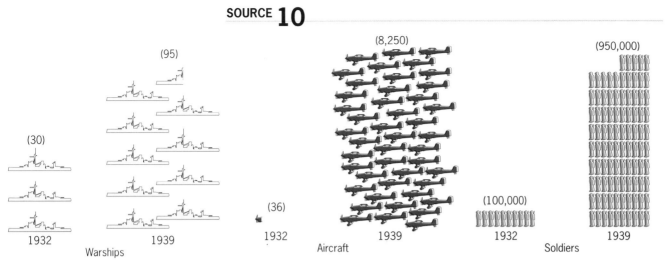

(95)

(30)

1932   1939
Warships

(36)
1932

(8,250)

1939
Aircraft

(950,000)

(100,000)
1932

1939
Soldiers

German armed forces in 1932 and 1939.

The Saar plebiscite

The Saar region of Germany had been run by the League of Nations since 1919 (see page 236). In 1935 the League of Nations held the promised plebiscite for people to vote on whether their region should return to German rule. The vote was an overwhelming success for Hitler. Around 90 per cent of the population voted to return to German rule. This was entirely legal and within the terms of the Treaty. It was also a real morale booster for Hitler.

Following the plebiscite in 1935, people and police express their joy at returning to the German Reich by giving the Nazi salute.

Remilitarisation of the Rhineland

Key

January 1935:
Saar returned
to Germany
after a
plebiscite

March 1936:
German forces
re-enter the
Rhineland

The Rhineland.

In March 1936, Hitler took his first really big risk by moving troops into the Rhineland area of Germany.

The demilitarisation of the Rhineland was one of the terms of the Treaty of Versailles. It had also been accepted by Germany in the Locarno Treaties of 1925 (see page 240). Hitler was taking a huge gamble. If he had been forced to withdraw, he would have faced humiliation and would have lost the support of the German army (many of the generals were unsure about him, anyway). Hitler knew the risks, but he had chosen the time and place well.

France had just signed a treaty with the USSR to protect each other against attack from Germany (see Source 13). Hitler used the agreement to claim that Germany was under threat. He argued that in the face of such a threat he should be allowed to place troops on his own frontier.

Hitler knew that many people in Britain felt that he had a right to station his troops in the Rhineland and he was fairly confident that Britain would not intervene. His gamble was over France. Would France let him get away with it?

1 Does Source 13 support or contradict Hitler's argument that Germany was under threat? Explain your answer.

An American cartoon published in March 1936 showing the encirclement of Germany by France and the USSR.

German troops marching through the city of Cologne in March 1936. This style of marching with high steps was known as goose-stepping.

SOURCE 15

At that time we had no army worth mentioning . . . If the French had taken any action we would have been easily defeated; our resistance would have been over in a few days. And the Air Force we had then was ridiculous – a few Junkers 52s from Lufthansa and not even enough bombs for them . . .

Hitler looks back on his gamble over the Rhineland some years after the event.

SOURCE 16

Hitler has got away with it. France is not marching. No wonder the faces of Göring and Blomberg [Nazi leaders] were all smiles.

Oh, the stupidity (or is it the paralysis?) of the French. I learnt today that the German troops had orders to beat a hasty retreat if the French army opposed them in any way.

Written by William Shirer in 1936. He was an American journalist in Germany during the 1930s. He was a critic of the Nazi regime and had to flee from Germany in 1940.

As the troops moved into the Rhineland, Hitler and his generals sweated nervously. They had orders to pull out if the French acted against them. Despite the rearmament programme, Germany's army was no match for the French army. It lacked essential equipment and air support. In the end, however, Hitler's luck held.

The attention of the League of Nations was on the Abyssinian crisis which was happening at exactly the same time (see pages 250–53). The League condemned Hitler's action but had no power to do anything else. Even the French, who were most directly threatened by the move, were divided over what to do. They were about to hold an election and none of the French leaders was prepared to take responsibility for plunging France into a war. Of course, they did not know how weak the German army was. In the end, France refused to act without British support and so Hitler's big gamble paid off. Maybe next time he would risk more!

SOURCE 17

THE GOOSE-STEP.

"GOOSEY GOOSEY GANDER,
WHITHER DOST THOU WANDER?"
"ONLY THROUGH THE RHINELAND—
PRAY EXCUSE MY BLUNDER!"

A British cartoon about the reoccupation of the Rhineland, 1936. *Pax Germanica* is Latin and means 'Peace, German style'.

2 What do Sources 15 and 16 disagree about? Why might they disagree about it?

3 Fill out row 2 of your 'Versailles chart' on page 257.

4 Would you regard reoccupation of the Rhineland as a success for Hitler or as a failure for the French and the British? Explain your answer by referring to the sources.

5 Why has the cartoonist in Source 17 shown Germany as a goose?

6 Look at the equipment being carried by the goose. What does this tell you about how the cartoonist saw the new Germany?

The Spanish Civil War

These early successes seemed to give Hitler confidence. In 1936 a civil war broke out in Spain between Communists, who were supporters of the Republican government, and right-wing rebels under General Franco. Hitler saw this as an opportunity to fight against Communism and at the same time to try out his new armed forces.

In 1937, as the League of Nations looked on helplessly, German aircraft made devastating bombing raids on civilian populations in various Spanish cities. The destruction at Guernica was terrible. The world looked on in horror at the suffering that modern weapons could cause.

SOURCE 18

A postcard published in France to mark the bombing of Guernica in 1937. The text reads 'The Basque people murdered by German planes. Guernica martyred 26 April 1937'.

The Anti-Comintern Pact, 1936–7

The Italian leader Mussolini was also heavily involved in the Spanish Civil War. Hitler and Mussolini saw that they had much in common also with the military dictatorship in Japan. In 1936, Germany and Japan signed an Anti-Comintern Pact. In 1937, Italy also signed it. Anti-Comintern means 'Anti-Communist International'. The aim of the pact was to limit Communist influence around the world. It was particularly aimed at the USSR. The new alliance was called the Axis alliance.

Anschluss with Austria, 1938

With the successes of 1936 and 1937 to boost him, Hitler turned his attention to his homeland of Austria. The Austrian people were mainly German, and in *Mein Kampf* Hitler had made it clear that he felt that the two states belonged together as one German nation. Many in Austria supported the idea of union with Germany, since their country was so economically weak. Hitler was confident that he could bring them together into a 'greater Germany'. In fact, he had tried to take over Austria in 1934, but on that occasion Mussolini had stopped him. Four years later, in 1938, the situation was different. Hitler and Mussolini were now allies.

There was a strong Nazi Party in Austria. Hitler encouraged the Nazis to stir up trouble for the government. They staged demonstrations calling for union with Germany. They caused riots. Hitler then told the Austrian Chancellor Schuschnigg that only *Anschluss* (political union) could sort out these problems. He pressurised Schuschnigg to agree to *Anschluss*. Schuschnigg asked for help from France and Britain but was refused it. So he called a plebiscite (a referendum), to see what the Austrian people wanted. Hitler was not prepared to risk this – he might lose! He simply sent his troops into Austria in March 1938, supposedly to guarantee a trouble-free plebiscite. Under the watchful eye of the Nazi troops, 99.75 per cent voted for *Anschluss*. *Anschluss* was completed without any military confrontation with France and Britain. Chamberlain, the British Prime Minister, felt that Austrians and Germans had a right to be united and that the Treaty of Versailles was wrong to separate them. Britain's Lord Halifax had even suggested to Hitler before the *Anschluss* that Britain would not resist Germany uniting with Austria.

1 Explain what each of the cartoons in Source 19 is saying about the *Anschluss*.
2 Complete row 3 of your 'Versailles chart' on page 257.

SOURCE 19

GOOD HUNTING

Mussolini. "All right, Adolf—I never heard a shot"

Two cartoons commenting on the *Anschluss*, 1938. **A** is from *Punch*. **B** is a Soviet cartoon showing Hitler catching Austria.

Once again, Hitler's risky but decisive action had reaped a rich reward – Austria's soldiers, weapons and its rich deposits of gold and iron ore were added to Germany's increasingly strong army and industry. Hitler was breaking yet another condition of the Treaty of Versailles, but the pattern was becoming clear. The Treaty itself was seen as suspect. Britain and France were not prepared to go to war to defend a flawed treaty.

Why did Britain and France follow a policy of Appeasement in the 1930s?

Britain signed the naval agreement with Germany in 1935. For the next three years, Britain followed a policy of giving Hitler what he wanted – a policy that became known as APPEASEMENT. Neville Chamberlain is the man most associated with this policy (see Profile, page 267), although he did not become Prime Minister until 1937. Many other British people, including many politicians, were also in favour of this policy. See Source 20 for their reasons.

SOURCE 20

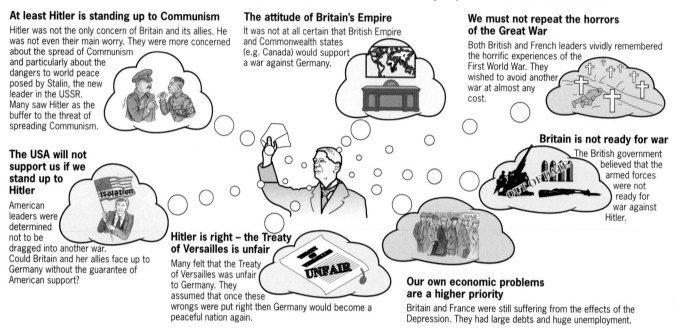

At least Hitler is standing up to Communism
Hitler was not the only concern of Britain and its allies. He was not even their main worry. They were more concerned about the spread of Communism and particularly about the dangers to world peace posed by Stalin, the new leader in the USSR. Many saw Hitler as the buffer to the threat of spreading Communism.

The attitude of Britain's Empire
It was not at all certain that British Empire and Commonwealth states (e.g. Canada) would support a war against Germany.

We must not repeat the horrors of the Great War
Both British and French leaders vividly remembered the horrific experiences of the First World War. They wished to avoid another war at almost any cost.

The USA will not support us if we stand up to Hitler
American leaders were determined not to be dragged into another war. Could Britain and her allies face up to Germany without the guarantee of American support?

Hitler is right – the Treaty of Versailles is unfair
Many felt that the Treaty of Versailles was unfair to Germany. They assumed that once these wrongs were put right then Germany would become a peaceful nation again.

Our own economic problems are a higher priority
Britain and France were still suffering from the effects of the Depression. They had large debts and huge unemployment.

Britain is not ready for war
The British government believed that the armed forces were not ready for war against Hitler.

What was wrong with Appeasement?

Britain's leaders may have felt that they had no option but to appease Hitler, but there were obvious risks to such a policy. Some of these were stated at the time (see Sources 22 –24). Others became obvious with hindsight (Source 21). You will return to these criticisms in the Task on page 274. You may even be able to add to this list from what you have already studied.

SOURCE 21

It encouraged Hitler to be aggressive
With hindsight, you can see that each gamble he got away with encouraged him to take a bigger risk.

It allowed Germany to grow *too* strong
With hindsight, you can see that Germany was not only recovering lost ground: it was also becoming much more powerful than Britain or France.

It put too much trust in Hitler's promises
With hindsight, you can see that Hitler often went back on his promises. Appeasement was based on the mistaken idea that Hitler was trustworthy.

It scared the USSR
With hindsight, you can see how the policy alarmed the USSR. Hitler made no secret of his plans to expand eastwards. Appeasement sent the message to the Soviet Union that Britain and France would not stand in Hitler's way.

1 Look at Source 22. What does the cartoonist think Appeasement will lead to?

2 Most people in Britain supported Appeasement. Write a letter to the London *Evening Standard* justifying Appeasement and pointing out why the cartoonist in Source 22 is mistaken. Use the points given in Source 20.

SOURCE 22

A cartoon by David Low from the London *Evening Standard*, 1936. This was a popular newspaper with a large readership in Britain.

SOURCE 23

THE BLESSINGS OF PEACE
or
MR. EVERYMAN'S IDEAL HOME

A cartoon from *Punch*, November 1937. *Punch* was deeply critical of the British government's policies that allowed Hitler to achieve what he wanted in the 1930s. The magazine was an important influence on public opinion, particularly among educated and influential people. It had a circulation of about 120,000 copies per week during the 1930s.

SOURCE 24

David Low cartoon commenting on the *Anschluss*, 1938.

ACTIVITY

Why Appeasement?

1 Read the explanations in Source 20 of why Britain followed a policy of Appeasement.

2 Make notes under the following headings to summarise why Britain followed a policy of Appeasement:
- Military reasons
- Economic reasons
- Fear
- Public opinion
- Other

3 Use your notes to help you to write a short paragraph to explain in your own words how each of these reasons influenced the policy of Appeasement.

The Sudetenland, 1938

After the Austrian *Anschluss,* Hitler was beginning to feel that he could not put a foot wrong. But his growing confidence was putting the peace of Europe in increasing danger.

SOURCE 25

Central Europe after the *Anschluss.*

SOURCE 26

I give you my word of honour that Czechoslovakia has nothing to fear from the Reich.

Hitler speaking to Chamberlain in 1938.

Unlike the leaders of Britain and France, Edward Beneš, the leader of Czechoslovakia, was horrified by the *Anschluss.* He realised that Czechoslovakia would be the next country on Hitler's list for takeover. It seemed that Britain and France were not prepared to stand up to Hitler. Beneš sought guarantees from the British and French that they would honour their commitment to defend Czechoslovakia if Hitler invaded. The French were bound by a treaty and reluctantly said they would. The British felt bound to support the French. However, Chamberlain asked Hitler whether he had designs on Czechoslovakia and was reassured by Hitler's promise (Source 26).

Despite what he said to Chamberlain, Hitler did have designs on Czechoslovakia. This new state, created by the Treaty of Versailles, included a large number of Germans – former subjects of the Austria-Hungary Empire – in the Sudetenland area (see page 94). Henlein, who was the leader of the Nazis in the Sudetenland, stirred up trouble among the Sudetenland Germans and they demanded to be part of Germany. In May 1938, Hitler made it clear that he intended to fight Czechoslovakia if necessary. Historians disagree as to whether Hitler really meant what he said. There is considerable evidence that the German army was not at all ready for war. Even so the news put Europe on full war alert.

Unlike Austria, Czechoslovakia would be no walk-over for Hitler. Britain, France and the USSR had all promised to support Czechoslovakia if it came to war. The Czechs themselves had a modern army. The Czechoslovak leader, Beneš, was prepared to fight. He knew that without the Sudetenland and its forts, railways and industries, Czechoslovakia would be defenceless.

All through the summer the tension rose in Europe. If there was a war, people expected that it would bring heavy bombing of civilians as had happened in the Spanish Civil War, and in cities around Britain councils began digging air-raid shelters. Magazines carried advertisements for air-raid protection and gas masks.

SOURCE 27

How horrible, fantastic, incredible it is that we should be digging trenches and trying on gas masks here because of a quarrel in a far away country between people of whom we know nothing. I am myself a man of peace to the depths of my soul.

From a radio broadcast by Neville Chamberlain, September 1938.

PROFILE

Neville Chamberlain

★ Born 1869.
★ He was the son of the famous radical politician Joseph Chamberlain.
★ He was a successful businessman in the Midlands before entering politics.
★ During the First World War he served in the Cabinet as Director General of National Service. During this time he saw the full horrors of war.
★ After the war he was Health Minister and then Chancellor. He was noted for his careful work and his attention to detail. However, he was not good at listening to advice.
★ He was part of the government throughout the 1920s and supported the policy of Appeasement towards Hitler. He became Prime Minister in 1937, although he had little experience of foreign affairs.
★ He believed that Germany had real grievances – this was the basis for his policy of Appeasement.
★ He became a national hero after the Munich Conference of 1938 averted war.
★ In 1940 Chamberlain resigned as Prime Minister and Winston Churchill took over.

SOURCE 28

Digging air raid defences in London, September 1938.

In September the problem reached crisis point. In a last-ditch effort to avert war, Chamberlain flew to meet Hitler on 15 September. The meeting appeared to go well. Hitler moderated his demands, saying he was only interested in parts of the Sudetenland – and then only if a plebiscite showed that the Sudeten Germans wanted to join Germany. Chamberlain thought this was reasonable. He felt it was yet another of the terms of the Treaty of Versailles that needed to be addressed. Chamberlain seemed convinced that, if Hitler got what he wanted, he would at last be satisfied.

On 19 September the French and the British put to the Czechs their plans to give Hitler the parts of the Sudetenland that he wanted. However, three days later at a second meeting, Hitler increased his demands. He said he 'regretted' that the previously arranged terms were not enough. He wanted all the Sudetenland.

SOURCE 29

The Sudetenland is the last problem that must be solved and it will be solved. It is the last territorial claim which I have to make in Europe.

The aims of our foreign policy are not unlimited . . . They are grounded on the determination to save the German people alone . . . Ten million Germans found themselves beyond the frontiers of the Reich . . . Germans who wished to return to the Reich as their homeland.

Hitler speaking in Berlin, September 1938.

To justify his demands, he claimed that the Czech government was mistreating the Germans in the Sudetenland and that he intended to 'rescue' them by 1 October. Chamberlain told Hitler that his demands were unreasonable. The British navy was mobilised. War seemed imminent.

With Mussolini's help, a final meeting was held in Munich on 29 September. While Europe held its breath, the leaders of Britain, Germany, France and Italy decided on the fate of Czechoslovakia. On 29 September they decided to give Hitler what he wanted. They announced that Czechoslovakia was to lose the Sudetenland. They did not consult the Czechs, nor did they consult the USSR. This is known as the Munich Agreement. The following morning Chamberlain and Hitler published a joint declaration (Source 31) which Chamberlain said would bring 'peace for our time'.

SOURCE 30

People of Britain, your children are safe. Your husbands and your sons will not march to war. Peace is a victory for all mankind. If we must have a victor, let us choose Chamberlain, for the Prime Minister's conquests are mighty and enduring – millions of happy homes and hearts relieved of their burden.

The *Daily Express* comments on the Munich Agreement, 30 September 1938.

SOURCE 31

We regard the Agreement signed last night . . . as symbolic of the desire of our two peoples never to go to war with one another again. We are resolved that we shall use consultation to deal with any other questions that may concern our two countries, and we are determined to continue our efforts to assure the peace of Europe.

The joint declaration of Chamberlain and Hitler, 30 September 1938.

1 Study Sources 30–36. Sort them into the following categories:
   a) those that support the Munich Agreement
   b) those that criticise the Munich Agreement
2 List the reasons why each source supports or criticises the agreement.

ACTIVITY

Write extracts from the diaries of some of the main parties affected by the Sudetenland crisis, e.g. Chamberlain, Hitler, Beneš or one of the diplomats who was involved in making the agreement, or of an ordinary Briton or an ordinary Czech.

Hitler had gambled that the British would not risk war. He spoke of the Munich Agreement as 'an undreamt-of triumph, so great that you can scarcely imagine it'. The prize of the Sudetenland had been given to him without a shot being fired. On 1 October German troops marched into the Sudetenland. At the same time, Hungary and Poland helped themselves to Czech territory where Hungarians and Poles were living.

The Czechs had been betrayed. Beneš resigned. But the rest of Europe breathed a sigh of relief. Chamberlain received a hero's welcome back in Britain, when he returned with the 'piece of paper' – the Agreement – signed by Hitler (see Profile, page 267).

SOURCE 32

A

"Horrible and Fantastic, that a quarrel in a faraway country between two peoples of whom we know nothing .. ho hum!"

B

Two British cartoons commenting on the Sudetenland crisis of 1938.

A triumph or a sell-out?

What do you think of the Munich Agreement? Was it a good move or a poor one? Most people in Britain were relieved that it had averted war, but many were now openly questioning the whole policy of Appeasement. Even the public relief may have been overstated. Opinion polls in September 1938 show that the British people did not think Appeasement would stop Hitler. It simply delayed a war, rather than preventing it. Even while Chamberlain was signing the Munich Agreement, he was approving a massive increase in arms spending in preparation for war.

A British cartoon from 1938.

SOURCE 33

By repeatedly surrendering to force, Chamberlain has encouraged aggression . . . our central contention, therefore, is that Mr Chamberlain's policy has throughout been based on a fatal misunderstanding of the psychology of dictatorship.

The *Yorkshire Post*, December 1938.

SOURCE 34

We have suffered a total defeat . . . I think you will find that in a period of time Czechoslovakia will be engulfed in the Nazi regime. We have passed an awful milestone in our history. This is only the beginning of the reckoning.

Winston Churchill speaking in October 1938. He felt that Britain should resist the demands of Hitler. However, he was an isolated figure in the 1930s.

ACTIVITY

Write a selection of newspaper headlines for 30 September – the day after the Munich Agreement. Your selection might include headlines for:
- different British newspapers
- a neutral American newspaper
- a German newspaper
- a Czech newspaper
- a Polish newspaper.

For each newspaper decide whether the Agreement would be seen as a triumph or a sell-out.

For one of the headlines write a short article describing the Agreement. You can use quotations from Sources 30, 33 and 34.

3 Complete row 4 of your 'Versailles chart' on page 257.

SOURCE 36

The front page of the *Daily Sketch*, 1 October 1938.

The end of Appeasement

Czechoslovakia, 1939

Although the British people welcomed the Munich Agreement, they did not trust Hitler. In an opinion poll in October 1938, 93 per cent said they did not believe him when he said he had no more territorial ambitions in Europe. In March 1939 they were proved right. On 15 March, with Czechoslovakia in chaos, German troops took over the rest of the country.

SOURCE 37

Key

- October 1938 Teschen taken by Poland
- November 1938 to March 1939 Slovak border areas and Ruthenia taken by Hungary
- October 1938 Sudetenland region given to Germany in the Munich Agreement
- March 1939 Remainder of Czechoslovakia taken under German control
- German border in 1939

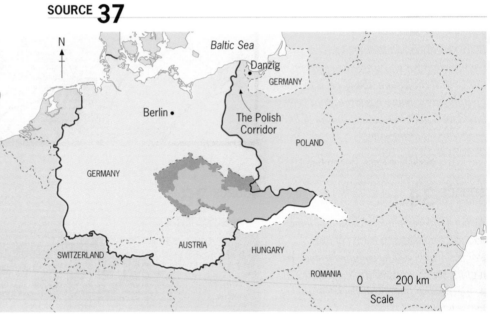

The take-over of Czechoslovakia by 1939.

SOURCE 38

German troops entering Prague, the capital of Czechoslovakia, in March 1939.

1 Choose five words to describe the attitude of the crowd in Source 38.

There was no resistance from the Czechs. Nor did Britain and France do anything about the situation. However, it was now clear that Hitler could not be trusted. For Chamberlain it was a step too far. Unlike the Sudeten Germans, the Czechs were not separated from their homeland by the Treaty of Versailles. This was an invasion. If Hitler continued unchecked, his next target was likely to be Poland. Britain and France told Hitler that if he invaded Poland they would declare war on Germany. The policy of Appeasement was ended. However, after years of Appeasement, Hitler did not actually believe that Britain and France would risk war by resisting him.

The Nazi–Soviet Pact

Look at your 'Versailles chart' from page 257. You should have only one item left. As Hitler was gradually retaking land lost at Versailles, you can see from Source 37 that logically his next target was the strip of former German land in Poland known as the Polish Corridor. He had convinced himself that Britain and France would not risk war over this, but he was less sure about Stalin and the USSR. Let's see why.

Background

Stalin had been very worried about the German threat to the Soviet Union ever since Hitler came to power in 1933. Hitler had openly stated his interest in conquering Russian land. He had denounced Communism and imprisoned and killed Communists in Germany. Even so, Stalin could not reach any kind of lasting agreement with Britain and France in the 1930s. From Stalin's point of view, it was not for want of trying. In 1934 he had joined the League of Nations, hoping the League would guarantee his security against the threat from Germany. However, all he saw at the League was its powerlessness when Mussolini successfully invaded Abyssinia, and when both Mussolini and Hitler intervened in the Spanish Civil War. Politicians in Britain and France had not resisted German rearmament in the 1930s. Indeed, some in Britain seemed even to welcome a stronger Germany as a force to fight Communism, which they saw as a bigger threat to British interests than Hitler (see page 264).

Stalin's fears and suspicions grew in the mid 1930s. He signed a treaty with France in 1935 that said that France would help the USSR if Germany invaded the Soviet Union. But Stalin was not sure he could trust the French to stick to it, particularly when they failed even to stop Hitler moving into the Rhineland, which was right on their own border.

The Munich Agreement in 1938 increased Stalin's concerns. He was not consulted about it. Stalin concluded from the agreement that France and Britain were powerless to stop Hitler or, even worse, that they were happy for Hitler to take over eastern Europe and then the USSR.

SOURCE 39

It will be asked how it was possible that the Soviet government signed a non-aggression pact with so deceitful a nation, with such criminals as Hitler and Ribbentrop . . . We secured peace for our country for eighteen months, which enabled us to make military preparations.

Stalin, in a speech in 1941.

SOURCE 40

THERE'S ANOTHER SIDE TO IT

A British cartoon from 1937. The figures on the left represent Britain and France. The figure on the right is Molotov, the Soviet Foreign Minister.

SOURCE 41

A Soviet cartoon from 1939. CCCP is Russian for USSR. The French and the British are directing Hitler away from western Europe and towards the USSR.

2 What does Source 40 reveal about Soviet attitudes to Britain and France?
3 How might a British politician justify the Munich Agreement to Stalin?

1 Look at Source 44. What point is the cartoonist making about the Nazi–Soviet Pact?
2 Do you agree with his view of the Pact?

SOURCE 42

Hitler regarded the Pact as his master stroke. Although he had promised the Russians eastern Poland, Finland, Estonia and Latvia, he never intended to allow them to keep these territories.

Stalin did not expect Hitler to keep his word either. He was sure he could only gain from a long war in which Britain, France and Germany exhausted themselves. Seldom have two countries entered an alliance so dishonestly.

From *The Modern World since 1870*, a school textbook by LE Snellgrove, published in 1980.

SOURCE 43

Why did Britain and France help Hitler to achieve his aims? By rejecting the idea of a united front proposed by the USSR, they played into the hands of Germany. They hoped to appease Hitler by giving him some Czech territory. They wanted to direct German aggression eastward against the USSR and the disgraceful Munich deal achieved this.

[In 1939] the USSR stood alone in the face of the growing Fascist threat. The USSR had to make a treaty of non-aggression with Germany. Some British historians tried to prove that this treaty helped to start the Second World War. The truth is it gave the USSR time to strengthen its defences.

Soviet historian Kukushkin, writing in 1981.

3 What do Sources 39, 42 and 43 agree about?
4 What do they disagree about?

ACTIVITY

Was the war all Hitler's fault?

Imagine that Hitler is on trial. He is facing the charge that he deliberately planned and started the Second World War.

1 What evidence would the prosecution bring forward?
2 What evidence would be put forward by the defence?

SOURCE 44

A British cartoon from 1939.

Despite his misgivings, Stalin was still prepared to talk with Britain and France about an alliance against Hitler. The three countries met in March 1939, but Chamberlain was reluctant to commit Britain. From Stalin's point of view, France and Britain then made things worse by giving Poland a guarantee that they would defend it if it was invaded. Chamberlain meant the guarantee as a warning to Hitler. Stalin saw it as support for one of the USSR's potential enemies.

Negotiations between Britain, France and the USSR continued through the spring and summer of 1939. However, Stalin also received visits from the Nazi foreign minister Ribbentrop. They discussed a rather different deal, a Nazi–Soviet Pact.

In August, Stalin made his decision. On 24 August 1939, Hitler and Stalin, the two arch enemies, signed the Nazi–Soviet Pact and announced the terms to the world. They agreed not to attack one another. Privately, they also agreed to divide Poland between them.

Why did Stalin sign? It was probably a combination of factors that led to the Pact.

- Stalin was not convinced that Britain and France would be strong and reliable enough as allies against Hitler.
- He also had designs on large sections of eastern Poland and wanted to take over the Baltic states, which had been part of Russia in the Tsar's day.
- He did not believe Hitler would keep his word, but he hoped for time to build up his forces against the attack he knew would come.

War

The Pact was perhaps the pinnacle of Hitler's triumphs. It cleared the way for Germany's invasion of Poland.

On 1 September 1939 the German army invaded Poland from the west. On 17 September Soviet forces invaded Poland from the east. Poland soon fell.

If Hitler was planning ahead at all, then in his mind the next move would surely be an attack against his temporary ally, the USSR. He was certain that Britain and France would not go to war over Poland. But Hitler's triumph was spoilt by a nasty surprise. Britain and France did keep their pledge. On 2 September they declared war on Germany.

Hitler had started a war, but it was not the war he had in mind. It was too soon and against the wrong opponents. Hitler had taken one gamble too many.

Was Appeasement the right policy?

ACTIVITY

Views on Appeasement

- The right policy at the right time.
- The wrong policy, but only with hindsight.
- A betrayal of the people of Czechoslovakia.
- A risky policy that purchased valuable time.

1 Work in pairs or groups. Collect evidence from pages 264–73 to support each of the above views.
2 Choose one viewpoint that you most agree with and write some well argued paragraphs to explain your choice:
   a) what the viewpoint means – in your own words
   b) what evidence there is to support it
   c) what evidence there is against it and why you have rejected that evidence
   d) your conclusion as to why this is a good verdict.

Chamberlain certainly believed in Appeasement. In June 1938 he wrote in a letter to his sister: 'I am completely convinced that the course I am taking is right and therefore cannot be influenced by the attacks of my critics.' He was not a coward or a weakling. When it became obvious that he had no choice but to declare war in 1939 he did.

However, Appeasement was a controversial policy at the time. It is still controversial today. There are two main views:

- **It was the wrong policy because it encouraged Hitler.** Chamberlain's critics say that it simply encouraged Hitler's gambling. They claim that if Britain or France had squared up to him at the start, he would have backed off. Peace would have been secured.
- **It was the right policy because Britain was not ready for war.** Chamberlain's defenders say it was the only policy available to him. They say that to face up to Hitler Chamberlain had to be prepared to take Britain into a war. All the evidence available to Chamberlain told him that Britain was not ready. Public opinion was against it – his own civil service advisers had told him this. Important countries in the empire were against it. The USA was against it. And most importantly, Britain's armed forces were not ready. They were badly equipped and had fallen far behind the Germans.

Did Appeasement buy time for rearmament?

You need to examine this claim in a little more detail. In the 1960s British historian AJP Taylor argued that Chamberlain had an exaggerated view of Germany's strength. Taylor believed that German forces were only 45 per cent of what British intelligence reports said they were.

But Taylor was writing in 1965 – not much help to Chamberlain in the 1930s. Britain had run down its forces in the peaceful years of the 1920s. The government had talked about rearmament since 1935 but Britain only really started rearming when Chamberlain became Prime Minister in 1937. Chamberlain certainly thought that Britain's armed forces were not ready for war. His own military advisers and his intelligence services told him this.

So did appeasement allow Britain the time it needed to rearm? Source 45 will help you to decide.

5 Study carefully graphs A–C in Source 45.
   a) What evidence do they provide to support the view that Britain's armed forces caught up with Germany's between 1938 and 1939?
   b) What evidence do they provide to oppose this view?

SOURCE 45

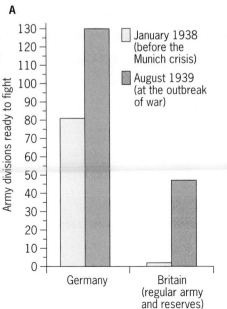

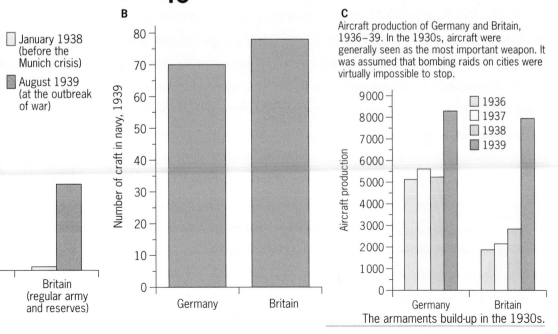

A (Army divisions ready to fight): January 1938 (before the Munich crisis); August 1939 (at the outbreak of war). Germany; Britain (regular army and reserves).

B: Number of craft in navy, 1939. Germany; Britain.

C: Aircraft production of Germany and Britain, 1936–39. In the 1930s, aircraft were generally seen as the most important weapon. It was assumed that bombing raids on cities were virtually impossible to stop. 1936, 1937, 1938, 1939. Germany; Britain.

The armaments build-up in the 1930s.

FOCUS TASK

Why did war break out in Europe in 1939?

Work in groups of five.

1 Each of you take one of the following topics. Write it large at the top of a blank sheet of paper.
   • Hitler's actions
   • The policy of Appeasement
   • The problems caused by the peace treaties
   • The Nazi–Soviet Pact
   • The failures of the League of Nations

2 On your sheet, summarise the ways in which this factor helped lead to war in 1939.

3 Stick the five sheets on to a larger sheet of paper. Draw lines between the causes to show how they are connected to one another.

4 Discuss with your group whether, if you took any of these causes away, there would have been a war.

5 Now, on your own, write an essay on the topic 'Why had international peace collapsed by 1939?' You can use the structure below:

Paragraph 1:
(Explain how and why Hitler was pledged to reverse the Treaty of Versailles and to increase German territory.)

When Hitler came to power in Germany in 1933 . . .

Paragraph 2:
(Explain how the failure of the League of Nations in Manchuria and in Abyssinia made it easier for Hitler to achieve his objectives.)

In the 1930s there were two incidents that really tested the League of Nations . . .

Paragraph 3:
(Explain how the policy of Appeasement allowed Hitler to get away with this. Explain also why Britain and France followed this policy of Appeasement.)

In 1936 Hitler began his policy of reclaiming lost German territory . . .

Paragraph 4:
(Explain how the Nazi–Soviet Pact helped Hitler and Stalin.)

In 1939 Hitler made an agreement with Stalin . . .

Paragraph 5:
(Explain how the invasion of Poland led to war in Europe.)

When Hitler invaded Poland in 1939, Britain and France . . .

Paragraph 6:
(Reach your own conclusion about the importance of the various causes.)

Although it was Hitler's actions which led to war, many other factors were important in making the war happen . . .

9.2 How did the war become a world war?

In its early years, the war in Europe could not have been more different from the First World War. Germany quickly conquered Poland, but there was no fighting in western Europe at all for the first nine months. When Hitler finally invaded France in May 1940 he swept through the Netherlands and Belgium and conquered most of France in two months. It was called Blitzkrieg or 'lightning war' (see page 279). In June 1941 he eventually invaded the USSR.

Meanwhile, on the other side of the world, a separate conflict was developing.

Pearl Harbor

On 7 December 1941, a Sunday, a band was rehearsing on the deck of a warship in the US naval base at Pearl Harbor in Hawaii. A few minutes later, the bandsmen were diving for cover or running to their stations as the first wave of Japanese fighter planes dropped their bombs and torpedoes.

SOURCE 1

The American naval bases at Pearl Harbor, Hawaii and San Diego, California.

SOURCE 2

Part of Pearl Harbor after the attack.

1 Why do you think the Japanese attacked on a Sunday?

By the afternoon of 7 December, Pearl Harbor lay in ruins and the US fleet was a mass of twisted metal. Japan had made its play for domination in the Pacific.

The rivalry begins

Rivalry between Japan and the USA had begun in the 1920s. While the European powers fought out the First World War, Japan was able to take over much of their trading activity in the Far East. By 1921 the rise of Japan was beginning to worry the USA, which also wished to dominate trade in the Pacific. Japan was pressured by the USA into a series of treaties that limited its influence over China and reduced the size of the Japanese navy. The USA and western European countries also placed tariffs on Japanese goods. In response, powerful businessmen and military leaders, such as General Tojo, increasingly called for Japan to build its own empire on the mainland of Asia. When the world trade depression of the 1930s began to hit Japan, these empire builders took their chance and invaded Manchuria in 1931 (see page 246). Six years later, in 1937, Japan launched a full-scale war on China.

SOURCE 3

War is a contagion [an infectious disease] whether it be declared or undeclared. It can engulf states and peoples far from the original scene of hostilities.

We are determined to keep out of war. We are taking measures to minimise our risk of involvement, but we cannot have complete protection in a world of disorder in which confidence and security have broken down.

Roosevelt's 'Quarantine Speech', 1937.

PROFILE

General Tojo

★ Born 1884.
★ Graduated with distinction from military college.
★ Rose quickly to rank of general.
★ He was a leading figure among the militarists in Japan in the 1930s who wanted an aggressive nationalist policy.
★ Served in Manchuria.
★ In 1940 he became War Minister and pulled Japan closer to Germany and Italy.
★ Became Prime Minister in October 1941 and was a key figure in planning the attack on Pearl Harbor.
★ He was removed by Emperor Hirohito in 1944 as the war began to go against Japan.
★ After the war he was tried and hanged as a war criminal.

The USA's concerns grow

These developments were watched with concern in the USA. The American President, Roosevelt, was especially worried when Germany and Japan signed the Anti-Comintern Pact in 1936. Italy signed in 1937, bringing three aggressive regimes together into one alliance. In that same year Japan launched a full-scale invasion of China.

Roosevelt did not want war, but he began to fear that it might be inevitable. American public opinion was still isolationist. Roosevelt knew Americans would not support their country's involvement in foreign war. He began to prepare the American people for the possibility.

By 1941, however, there was a definite shift in the opinions of American politicians and military leaders.

The fall of France in 1940 and the devastating effectiveness of the German army as it swept through western Europe had jolted Americans. They began to take more interest in Europe than at any time since 1918. American spies also informed Roosevelt that there had been top-level meetings between German, Italian and Japanese politicians. On 27 September 1940 these three governments signed another pact (see Source 5). Although the pact did not mention the USA specifically, everyone knew what power it was referring to.

SOURCE 4

German, Japanese and Italian leaders meeting in 1940.

SOURCE 5

[The three powers] will assist one another with all political, economic and military means when one of the three parties is at war with a power at present not involved in the European war or the Chinese–Japanese conflict . . .

The Three-Power Pact signed in 1940 between Germany, Italy and Japan.

Roosevelt and the British war leader, Churchill, kept in touch on this and other matters by letter and by telegram. They developed a close working relationship. Churchill was clearly delighted when Roosevelt was re-elected President in 1940.

SOURCE 6

I prayed for your success and I am truly thankful for it.
Former Naval Person.

Telegram from Churchill to Roosevelt after his re-election in 1940. Whenever Churchill wrote to Roosevelt he used his code name 'Former Naval Person'.

SOURCE 7

Some of our people like to believe that wars in Europe and Asia are no concern of ours. But it is a matter of most vital concern to us that European and Asiatic war-makers should not gain control of the oceans which lead to this hemisphere. If Great Britain goes down, the Axis powers [Japan, Italy and Germany] will control the continents of Europe, Asia, Africa, Australasia and the high seas. All of us would be living at the point of a gun.

From one of Roosevelt's 'Fireside Chats', broadcast in 1940. Roosevelt was the first political leader to use radio regularly to talk directly to his people.

1 Compare Sources 3 and 7. How did Roosevelt's attitude to war change between 1937 and 1940?
2 What factors led to this change?

Although the USA was supposedly neutral, it was clear that Roosevelt supported Britain. He introduced the 'Lend-Lease' scheme to help Britain. It allowed the USA to supply Britain with vital supplies for free. Source 7 gives his response to critics who said this would lead the USA into war.

In addition to the Lend-Lease scheme, US warships harassed German submarines in the north Atlantic in order to 'protect American shipping'. The USA was doing all it could to help the British in the war in Europe – except for fighting with them.

Japan's dilemma

Japan's invasion of China was a spectacular success, but even bigger prizes beckoned once war in Europe broke out. Britain, France and the Netherlands all had large territories in the Far East that they could not possibly defend while they were at war with Germany. President Roosevelt rightly guessed that Japan had designs on these territories and restricted the supply of important materials to Japan from 1940. Roosevelt was worried about American interests in China and in the Pacific, particularly in the Philippines.

This was Japan's dilemma. Japan wanted to carve out an empire in the Far East that would make it self-sufficient in vital materials such as rice, oil, coal and rubber. However, not only was this threatening to the USA, it also threatened Japan's other large and powerful neighbour, the USSR.

SOURCE 8

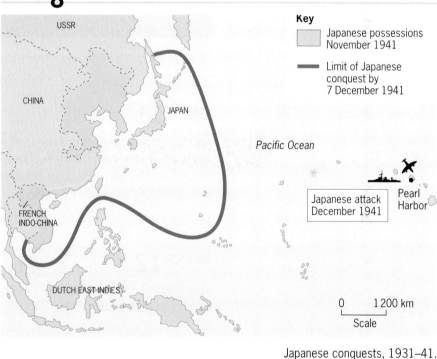

Japanese conquests, 1931–41.

In June 1941, Hitler solved Japan's second problem when he invaded the USSR. Immediately afterwards, in July 1941, Japan took control of French Indo-China and it seemed that Japan had made up its mind to challenge the USA. Roosevelt froze Japanese assets and cut supplies of iron. This made Japan's leaders even more certain that they needed an Asian empire.

The tension grew. While fearsome battles raged between Germany and the USSR, the Japanese made their plans. Japan could not challenge the power of the USA outright, so cunning was needed. Admiral Yamamoto devised a plan to knock out the USA's Pacific fleet in one swift blow. This would give Japan time to create its new empire. By the time the USA had recovered, Japan would be able to draw on the resources of its empire and the USA would be unable to do anything.

SOURCE 9

"I am looking forward to dictating peace to the United States in the White House at Washington"
— ADMIRAL YAMAMOTO

What do YOU say, AMERICA?

An American propaganda poster printed soon after the attack on Pearl Harbor.

1 Look at Source 9. What is the purpose of this poster?

On the morning of 7 December 1941, some 300 planes took off from Japanese aircraft carriers to launch their attack on the US Pacific fleet at Pearl Harbor. The next day, the US Congress declared war on Japan. Three days later, on 11 December, Hitler declared war on the USA.

SOURCE 10

Hitler presents General Oshima (the Japanese ambassador in Berlin) with a medal, December 1941.

SOURCE 11

America is a decayed country. I like an Englishman a thousand times better than an American . . . Everything about the behaviour of American society reveals that it is half Jew and the other half negro. How can one expect a state like that to hold together – a country where everything is built on the dollar.

Hitler writing about the USA before the war began.

SOURCE 12

We can have no choice but to follow the letter of the law in the three-power treaty and declare war on the United States.

From a speech by Goebbels, Hitler's head of propaganda, 9 December 1941.

SOURCE 13

If we do not stand on the side of Japan, the Pact is politically dead. But that is not the main reason. The chief reason is that the United States is already shooting against our ships. They have been a forceful factor in this war, and they have, through their actions, already created a situation which is practically, let's say, a situation of war . . .

From a speech by Hitler, 9 December 1941.

2 Study Sources 11–13. List the reasons they give for Hitler declaring war on the USA.

FOCUS TASK

1 Write a short speech for Roosevelt to give in one of his 'Fireside Chats', explaining to the American people why they are now involved in the war.
2 Write a response to the speech from either Britain or Germany.

10 The world at war 1939–1945

10.1 Why did the Allies win the Second World War?

FOCUS

The Second World War was fought on a larger scale and was even more destructive than the First World War. It was a truly world war with fighting on four continents. It was a high-technology war ending in the first ever use of nuclear weapons. It was a 'TOTAL WAR' where citizens were as much a target as soldiers and where every citizen of the states involved was expected to contribute to the war effort.

- 10.1 provides an overview of the major military campaigns of the Second World War so that you can reach your own conclusions on why the Allies won the war.
- 10.2 examines how Britain was organised to fight the war and how the war changed Britain.

FACTFILE

Axis and Allies

Throughout this chapter, you will see references to the Axis and the Allies.

★ **Axis:** Germany, Japan and Italy (until 1943). These countries signed alliances in the 1930s to form an 'axis of power' against the threat of Communism.
★ **Allies:** The states that opposed the Axis. The main Allied states were Britain and the British Empire; the USA and the USSR (from 1941); France until June 1940 and from September 1944.

1 Write definitions of the following terms in not less than 20 words for each:
 a) Blitzkrieg
 b) 'Phoney War'
 c) the Allies
 d) the BEF.

The war in Europe, 1939–1941

Blitzkrieg

As you have read on page 272, Hitler invaded Poland in September 1939. German forces used tactics that became known as *Blitzkrieg*, or lightning war.

Blitzkrieg used shock tactics. The aim was to paralyse the enemy by a devastating use of the most up-to-date technology and clever military tactics. Motorised vehicles, tanks and air power were co-ordinated by radio communications as they pushed deep into enemy territory. Reinforcements would then follow the advance forces and take secure control of the territory captured.

Hitler used *Blitzkrieg* tactics for two reasons:

- Many people in Germany did not share Hitler's enthusiasm for war. *Blitzkrieg* would deliver quick victories that would get people behind the war effort.
- Germany's economy could not support long-drawn-out campaigns. It lacked important resources such as copper and rubber and, most of all, oil. *Blitzkrieg* allowed the army to seize territory quickly and plunder the resources Germany needed.

The success of *Blitzkrieg* depended on two things: a better use of technology than your enemy and greater mobility. While Hitler had these two advantages, the German army was unbeatable.

The 'Phoney War'

Britain and France had promised to defend Poland. But Hitler was confident that they would not actually do anything to defend it. He was right. Although they declared war on Germany, they did not send troops to defend Poland. It would have been crazy to do so. When Soviet forces attacked Poland on 17 September, Poland quickly collapsed.

Hitler was also confident that he could get Britain and France to agree to a peace deal with him rather than continue the war. So he took no action against them. Britain and France took little action either. Chamberlain ordered soldiers of the British Expeditionary Force (BEF) to France in September. There was even a French attack on the Saar region of Germany in 1939, but it was very cautious and small scale. The period from September 1939 to March 1940 became known as the 'Phoney War'.

Britain gets a new war leader

In April 1940 the war became all too genuine when Hitler invaded Denmark and Norway. Norway was especially important to Hitler, since it would provide naval bases. He was determined that Germany would not be hemmed in by the British navy as it had been in the 1914–18 war. British attempts to help Norway failed and Prime Minister Neville Chamberlain was replaced by a new leader, Winston Churchill.

The BEF in France

In May 1940, the German army turned its power on France. In the interwar years, the French had built a series of huge fortresses called the Maginot Line on the Franco-German border. It was thought that the Germans would never be able to fight their way through this defence system. They didn't even try. The German General von Kleist bypassed the Maginot Line by making a daring advance through the Ardennes region of Belgium. The French had considered it impossible for the Germans to move tanks through the Ardennes forest. The Germans proved them wrong. Once again, German *Blitzkrieg* tactics were devastatingly effective. By the end of May, the Allied forces were surrounded and facing total defeat.

SOURCE 1

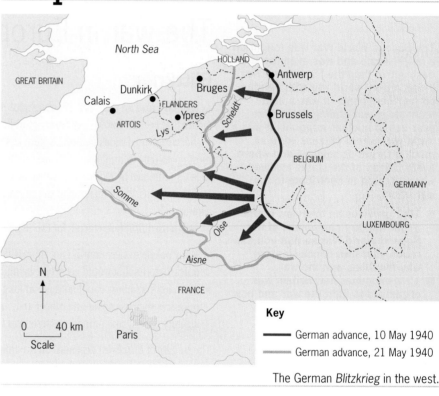

The German *Blitzkrieg* in the west.

Dunkirk

The Allies withdrew to Dunkirk. On the beaches around the port of Dunkirk the situation was very grim indeed. The Allied troops were trapped by the advancing German army. German Stuka dive bombers pounded Allied troops and equipment on the beaches. So did German artillery.

Then, for reasons that are not quite clear, Hitler ordered the advancing German forces to halt. It may be that he lost his nerve, or suspected a trap. He may have been hoping to make an alliance with Britain. It may be that German losses were very severe, especially of tanks. Whatever the reason, the BEF gained the time it needed for a remarkable evacuation that saved a large part of its army. Between 26 May and 4 June, 330,000 British and 10,000 French troops were evacuated by a fleet of large and small boats, many of them crewed by amateur sailors.

Dunkirk was celebrated in Britain as a great achievement. The evacuation certainly was. The Navy organised it superbly. The RAF outfought the Luftwaffe over Dunkirk. The small boats rescued around 80,000 troops. Just as important, the Dunkirk spirit was born. Civilians, government and media came together to create an extremely effective war effort which lasted until 1945. Very little was said about the fact that it was also a bitter and total military defeat. The BEF had been driven out of Europe. The evacuations had begun after only ten days of fighting. Around 300,000 troops were left behind to become prisoners. The French were left to fight the Germans alone. Although most troops had been rescued, the British forces had left most of their equipment behind. *All* of the heavy equipment, such as field guns, anti-aircraft guns, tanks and motor vehicles, was either destroyed or left for the Germans.

SOURCE 2

Dunkirk has been a miracle of deliverance, achieved by valour, by perseverance, by perfect discipline, and resourced by skill and unconquerable fidelity. But we must be very careful not to assign to this deliverance the attributes of a victory. Wars are not won by evacuations …

Winston Churchill, 4 June 1940.

SOURCE 3

At the time, Dunkirk was a military disaster – and one that took the British public by surprise … But almost at once, victory was being plucked from defeat and the newspapers began to manufacture the Dunkirk myth … The Nazi papers taunted the British for abandoning their French allies … But in Britain the Dunkirk spirit had taken root. The government encouraged it to flourish – and allowed nothing to be published which might damage morale. Dunkirk was a military defeat but a propaganda victory.

A BBC media correspondent commenting in 2000 on how the government and media handled Dunkirk.

1 Sources 5 and 6 give different impressions of the events at Dunkirk. Explain how their viewpoints differ.
2 Is it possible that both views are accurate? Explain your answer.
3 Look at Source 4. Explain why Hitler might be so pleased at the defeat of France. You may need to refer back to his own early life (see page 148).

(see page 148)

SOURCE 4

Hitler's victory dance on the French surrender, 1940.

FOCUS TASK

It is June 1940. You were in France and saw the defeat of the BEF and now you have news of the surrender of France. What would you advise the Prime Minister, Winston Churchill, to do now? The choices are to:
• surrender
• fight on
• reach some kind of agreement or alliance with Hitler.

1 Present the pros and cons of each option. You will need to think about:
  • the power of the German army
  • the state of the British army
  • the resources available to Hitler from the territories he has conquered.
2 Now say which option you recommend. Remember you are trying to think about this from the 1940 point of view.
3 Churchill decided to fight on. This was not an easy decision. Several influential politicians and journalists were calling for a deal with Hitler. Churchill could not see ahead to 1945. In 1940 Hitler seemed unstoppable. Discuss with other students in your class: 'How was your decision for question 2 influenced by hindsight?'

SOURCE 5

The Withdrawal from Dunkirk, a painting from June 1940 by the official British war artist Charles Cundall.

SOURCE 6

British and French prisoners are marched away from the beach at Dunkirk in June 1940.

The fall of France

The new British Prime Minister, Winston Churchill, encouraged France to fight on without the BEF. But France had lost 40 per cent of its army at Dunkirk and 80 per cent of its equipment. To make matters worse, on 12 June Italy also declared war on France. The French government surrendered on 21 June 1940.

Considering the scale of the French defeat, the German terms were relatively gentle. The south-east of France became a self-governing region with its capital in Vichy. It was run by Marshal Pétain, who had declared his intention of co-operating with the Nazis. The rest of France was occupied by and run by the German army. Some French leaders who escaped to Britain formed the Free French movement under Charles de Gaulle.

Why did Britain win the Battle of Britain?

1 Work in pairs to complete your own copy of this table. Do two rows each. You will find plenty of examples in the text on pages 282–83.

Factor	How it led to the British victory
Technology	
Weapons	
Tactics	
Leadership	

2 Discuss your completed table. Which factor played the most important role?

SOURCE 7

We were in Normandy, France . . . and from there we flew the Stukas to England. While I was based there we lost 85 planes shot down over England and the Channel. Later on the crews mutinied. They didn't want to fight any more because their planes could not compete with the Hurricanes and Spitfires.

Theodor Plotte was part of the ground crew of a Stuka dive bomber squadron. His main job was to arm the Stukas with bombs.

Why did Britain win the Battle of Britain?

How to deal with Britain was a puzzle for Hitler. For a start, he did not really want war with Britain. He felt that Britain was his natural ally not his enemy. Hitler's main aim was to defeat the USSR and carve out a German empire in the east. However, Britain's new Prime Minister, Winston Churchill, made it clear that he would make no deal with Germany. Britain would fight to the finish.

Another problem for Hitler was that the Blitzkrieg tactics that had worked so well in Poland and France could not work across the Channel. Blitzkrieg was built around rapid and flexible movement of many land troops. To conquer Britain would require a sea and air invasion. Hitler's military advisers made it clear that no invasion could succeed if German forces were being attacked by the RAF and the British navy. The German navy was no match for the British navy. However, the Germans did believe that if the RAF could be wiped out, then the navy's dockyards could be destroyed by bombing. Without the protection of the RAF, British ships would be vulnerable to air attack by German planes.

Operation Sealion (the Germans' code name for the invasion of Britain) had therefore to begin with the destruction of the RAF. German bombers would bomb British air bases and cripple the RAF. On 1 July 1940 the first German aircraft crossed the Channel and the air war that became known as the Battle of Britain had begun.

Could the Luftwaffe succeed? Hermann Goering, head of the Luftwaffe, had every reason to be confident. He had many more high-quality aircraft than the British: the Messerschmitt 109 fighter, and the Heinkel III, the Junkers Ju 88 and the Dornier D.17 bombers. He also had more well trained and experienced pilots. However, the RAF had its strengths and the Luftwaffe also had some weaknesses.

RAF strengths

- The RAF was led by Air Chief Marshal Sir Hugh Dowding. He had been planning Britain's air defence system since 1936 and had brought in many important technical developments (e.g. bullet-proof windscreens for fighter planes). He also introduced command and communication systems which meant that fighters could be quickly and effectively directed to meet enemy attacks.
- Dowding was also a supporter of radar. Radar worked by transmitting radio waves that bounced back off approaching enemy aircraft. Experienced radar operators could accurately estimate the size and speed of approaching aircraft. In previous campaigns the Germans had been able to destroy most of their enemies' aircraft on the ground. Britain's investment in radar in the 1930s meant that RAF planes were not caught on the ground as the Luftwaffe approached.
- The main RAF fighter planes – Spitfires and Hurricanes – were more than a match for the Luftwaffe's aircraft. Only the Messerschmitt 109 could compare with the Spitfire.
- RAF fighters were organised into regions so that they could meet attacks quickly, even if they came from different directions.
- RAF pilots who baled out over Britain could return to duty.

Luftwaffe weaknesses

- Hermann Goering led the Luftwaffe. He was not good at tactics. He did not really understand how modern air warfare worked. He regularly shifted the focus of attacks, causing confusion among pilots.
- The Luftwaffe had a lot of aircraft but not enough of the right type of fighting aircraft. Aircraft like the Stuka dive bomber were geared towards supporting the army in battle, not to gaining air superiority over another air force (see Source 8).
- German fighters only had enough fuel on board to guarantee them 30 minutes' flying time over England.
- Luftwaffe bombers were too small. They did not cause enough damage to their targets to put them completely out of action. There were plans to build big long-range heavy bombers, but they were cancelled. Such bombers could have devastated airfields and aircraft factories.
- German intelligence was poor. The Germans did not realise how important radar was.
- Luftwaffe pilots who baled out over Britain became prisoners of war.

SOURCE 8

	British	German
1–15 Jul	51	108
16–31 Jul	69	117
1–15 Aug	156	259
16–31 Aug	249	332
1–15 Sept	268	323
16–30 Sept	133	213
1–15 Oct	100	147
16–31 Oct	90	161
Totals	**1116**	**1660**

British and German aircraft destroyed,
1 July–31 October 1940.

SOURCE 9

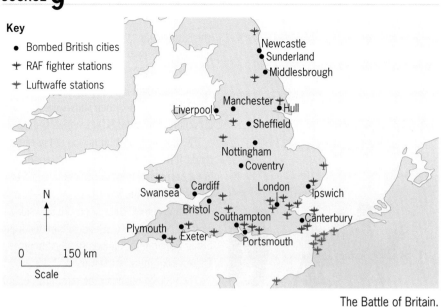

Key
- Bombed British cities
- RAF fighter stations
- Luftwaffe stations

The Battle of Britain.

The Battle of Britain was not a single battle. It was a series of air battles, day after day, that lasted throughout the summer of 1940. Waves of German bombers escorted by fighter aircraft would attack targets in Britain. British fighters were sent to intercept them.

In the air, the RAF was consistently out-shooting the Luftwaffe, as you can see from Source 8. As pilots were killed, hundreds were recruited to fill the gap. As planes were destroyed, more planes were needed. Lord Beaverbrook took over aircraft production and focused on producing only fighter planes (not bombers). From July to September, Britain was making 563 planes per month – out producing the Germans.

The Blitz

In September 1940, the Luftwaffe changed tactics. Instead of attacking the RAF, the Luftwaffe began to bomb London. This gave the RAF breathing space, although it started the most terrifying phase of the war for civilians.

British cities were intensively bombed for the next eight months. This is known as the Blitz – see pages 312–16. The Battle of Britain was effectively over once the Blitz began (although that was not immediately obvious at the time). It gradually became clear that if Hitler had given up on his plan to destroy the RAF, then he must also have given up his plans for invasion. On 19 August, Winston Churchill praised the RAF pilots in one of his most famous speeches, saying 'Never before, in the field of human conflict, has so much been owed, by so many, to so few.'

Was the Battle of Britain a turning point in the war?

YES

- It was Hitler's first real defeat – a morale booster for the Allies.
- Britain's survival was vital to the Allies. Britain was the base for the American and RAF bombing campaigns throughout the war. Britain and Northern Ireland became staging posts for the retaking of western Europe in the D-Day landings of 1944.
- It showed that Germany's armed forces were effective in fast-moving warfare, but could not keep up long-drawn-out confrontations.
- If Britain had been defeated, the USA itself would have been vulnerable to a Nazi-dominated Europe and the might of Japan in Asia.

NO

- Even if the RAF had been defeated, the navy could have held off invasion. That was Britain's real strength.
- Britain only avoided defeat. It was hardly a victory. There was no counter-attack. Hitler was far from beaten.
- Even if Britain had been invaded, the British Empire and Commonwealth would have remained to launch a counter-attack.

The Battle of the Atlantic

The Battle of the Atlantic is the name given to the battle for control of the North Atlantic Ocean. It lasted from 1939 until 1944.

Sources 10–12 give some idea of the scale and nature of the Battle of the Atlantic. Around 50,000 merchant seamen died in the North Atlantic, often in appalling situations. Some were killed instantly when their ships were attacked. Many more were drowned or froze to death in the icy waters of the Atlantic when their ships were sunk.

The Battle of the Atlantic was not as spectacular as the dogfights and roaring engines of the Battle of Britain, but it was just as important. The North Atlantic Ocean was the vital link that brought supplies from Canada and the USA to Britain. Without this lifeline, Britain could not have carried on the war.

Canada entered the war on Britain's side in September 1939. Thousands of Canadian troops crossed the Atlantic to defend Britain and fight in North Africa, Italy and the D-Day landings. Just as importantly, Canada supplied huge quantities of food and raw materials to Britain from the very beginning of the war.

The USA did not enter the war until December 1941, but it played an important role long before that. In November 1940 President Roosevelt introduced the Lend-Lease scheme. This scheme supplied vast amounts of food, fuel and equipment to help the British war effort against Hitler. Once the USA did join the war, it committed equipment and millions of US troops to the war in Europe. However, such military power was worthless if it could not cross the Atlantic to fight against the Axis. It was this which made the Atlantic such an important battleground.

The Germans knew from the start that they had to cut off British supplies from the USA. In the early stages of the Battle of the Atlantic, German submarines were very effective. In 1940 the Germans sank over 1000 ships, a quarter of Britain's merchant fleet. The next two years were even worse for the Allies. In 1941 the Allies lost 1300 ships. In 1942 they lost 1661 ships. Britain was able to import only one-third of what it normally imported in peacetime. In January 1943 the navy had only two months' supply of oil left.

Source 11 explains how German U-boats (submarines) were able to get the upper hand in the early stages of the Battle of the Atlantic.

SOURCE 10

Conditions in the North Atlantic were treacherous. This picture shows sailors on board the British ship HMS *Scylla*, February 1943.

SOURCE 11

The capture of Norway, Denmark, the Netherlands and France in 1940 gave the Germans **secure naval bases** from which their U-boats could operate.

The U-boats laid **mines** around Britain's coasts.

The Germans used converted airliners (Focke-Wulf Condors) as **long-range anti-shipping bombers.** In 1940 alone, these aircraft sank 58,000 tons of shipping.

German intelligence had **cracked** some of **the codes** used by British ships. **Wolf packs** of U-boats were able to lie in wait and **torpedo** the CONVOYS in mid-Atlantic. The U-boats were hard to detect as they deliberately limited the use of their radios to avoid detection.

By attacking from the **surface** and **at night**, the U-boats were able to avoid detection by the British anti-submarine device, ASDIC, which relied on sound waves travelling through water.

When the USA entered the war in 1941, its merchant ships and navy were ill prepared. U-boats torpedoed US ships as they left port because American coastal towns did not black out their lights. The ships were perfectly silhouetted against the lights, making them **easy targets.**

The U-boat menace: how the Germans gained the upper hand.

There is no doubt that in the early years the U-boats had the upper hand. A lot of Allied ships did get through, but it was often more by good luck than tactics. The Allies had no reliable methods for beating the U-boats. Winston Churchill wrote after the war that 'the only thing that ever really frightened me was the U-boat peril'. But these early years also taught Britain some harsh lessons and from 1941 Britain began to be more effective, as you can see from Source 12.

SOURCE 12

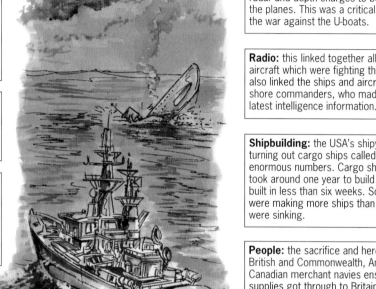

Intelligence: from late 1941 onwards, British code breakers at Bletchley Park got better at decoding German codes. If they **broke the German code**, they knew where the U-boats were and so could guide the convoys away from U-boat wolf packs. Between May 1942 and May 1943, they managed to steer 105 out of 174 convoys across the Atlantic without any interference from U-boats.

New weapons: a specially powerful explosive called Torpex was used in anti-submarine weapons. Another development was the Hedgehog depth charge, which fired clusters of bombs over a wide area.

Naval tactics: training for convoy commanders was improved. Special support groups of destroyers were created, fitted with powerful radar and listening equipment that could pick up radio signals from U-boats. These support groups were supported in turn by specialist aircraft.

Aircraft: long-range bombers were converted to anti-submarine use and fitted with special radar and depth charges to be dropped from the planes. This was a critical development in the war against the U-boats.

Radio: this linked together all of the ships and aircraft which were fighting the U-boats. Radio also linked the ships and aircraft with their on-shore commanders, who made use of the latest intelligence information.

Shipbuilding: the USA's shipyards began turning out cargo ships called Liberty ships in enormous numbers. Cargo ships that once took around one year to build could now be built in less than six weeks. Soon the Allies were making more ships than the Germans were sinking.

People: the sacrifice and heroism of the British and Commonwealth, American and Canadian merchant navies ensured that supplies got through to Britain.

The defeat of the U-boats: how the Allies won the Battle of the Atlantic.

SOURCE 13

The memorial to merchant seamen in Liverpool. There are many such memorials in ports around Britain. Around 50,000 merchant seamen died in the Second World War.

Churchill gave top priority to fighting the U-boat threat. In May 1943 the Allies sank 41 U-boats. In July 1943 over 1600 ships crossed the Atlantic without being attacked. Between June and December 1943 the Allies sank 141 U-boats, losing only 57 ships themselves. U-boats were being sunk at a faster rate than they were sinking enemy ships. In March 1944, Admiral Donitz called off the U-boat campaign. The Battle of the Atlantic had been won.

FOCUS TASK

The Battle of the Atlantic

You have been asked to write questions for this year's history examination paper. You have been asked to include a question on the Battle of the Atlantic. You have two possible questions to choose between:
* *How important* was the Battle of the Atlantic to Britain?
* *Why did the Allies win* the Battle of the Atlantic?

1 Discuss with other students
   a) why each question is a worthwhile question
   b) which you think is harder
   c) which you think is more important.
2 Write a recommendation to the examination board. You should write a few sentences on the strengths of each question and then make your final recommendation of which question it should choose.
3 Draw up a list of key points that you think students should bring up in their answers to your chosen question.
4 Finally, just in case the exam board does not follow your recommendation, do a list of key points that students should bring up in answer to the other question.

Hitler's war against the USSR

Operation Barbarossa, 1941

In Berlin on 4 October 1941 Hitler announced to his people that the Soviet enemy was beaten and would never rise again. This turned out to be one of Hitler's most profound misjudgements. Over the next two years the Soviet Union proved to be the graveyard of the German war effort. Few historians now dispute that the Eastern Front was the critical battleground of the Second World War . . . the Soviet system organised a massive war effort which blunted, and then reversed, the tide of Germany victory.

British historian, Professor Richard Overy, writing in 2000.

Hitler's ultimate dream was to smash the USSR and carve out an empire for his master race of Germans. By the summer of 1941, Hitler felt that the time was right to try to fulfil that dream. On 22 June 1941, Hitler launched Operation Barbarossa. Three million German soldiers in 153 divisions poured across the frontier into the USSR.

There were several disputes about tactics and timing between Hitler and his generals, but the Blitzkrieg against the Red Army had devastating effects. In the first three months of the campaign, the Germans destroyed the USSR's entire air and tank forces (7000 aircraft and 20,000 tanks). The Red Army suffered 4 million casualties (half of them deaths). By September 1941, Leningrad (the second city in the USSR) was under siege. In the south, German forces had control of the Ukraine and had reached as far as the Crimea. In the centre of Russia, the Germans almost reached the capital Moscow, and Stalin seriously considered surrendering.

German advances continued into 1942, but the Red Army had used the winter of 1941–42 to reorganise. In one of the most extraordinary turnabouts in history, the USSR survived and went on to play the key role in the defeat of Hitler. As Winston Churchill said, 'It was the Red Army which tore the heart out of the German army.'

The USSR reorganises

Late in 1941, the German advance was halted by the Russian winter. Stalin and his military leaders used this time to reform the Red Army completely. They copied many of the tactics and ideas that the Germans had used against them and added some of their own ideas as well.

Key

——— German front line, July 1941
——— German advance, December 1941
——— German advance, November 1942

The German invasion of the USSR.

- Officers in the Red Army were given greater freedom and independence to act. Stalin banned Communist Party officials from interfering with military decisions.
- The Red Army created its own specialist tank armies and air forces.
- The USSR developed effective new weapons such as the T34 tank, which could be produced in huge numbers.
- The USSR adopted radio communications and put radios into all tanks and aircraft (mostly supplied by Britain and the USA).
- Specialist units were created to listen in to German radio signals and disrupt them if possible. It is estimated that by 1943 these units were disrupting almost two-thirds of German radio messages.
- Harsh discipline was used, such as Order 227 of July 1942. This was known as 'not a step back'. The Soviet army was ordered to fight and die for every bit of Russian soil. Retreat meant arrest and execution. Thousands were indeed executed.

From 1941 to 1944, 85 per cent of Germany's armed forces were committed to the campaign in the USSR. The Eastern Front was well over 1600 km long. This was a conflict on a vast scale. It was also a conflict conducted with great brutality. The Germans were guilty of savage and inhuman war crimes against the Soviet people, for the normal rules of war did not apply on the Eastern Front. The Germans regarded it as a war of extermination. They believed they were exterminating inferior races and the very notion of Communism.

1 Would you say that the Soviet position in October 1941 (when Soviet records show that Stalin was seriously considering giving up) was worse than Britain's in June 1940? Explain your answer.

ACTIVITY

Many of the new ideas adopted by the Red Army in 1942 were completely different from its previous ways of working.

Put yourself in the position of a Red Army officer in early 1942. Write some notes for a talk in which:
• you explain the changes in organisation and tactics to the men and women under your command
• you reassure them that these changes will help them fight the Germans.

SOURCE **16**

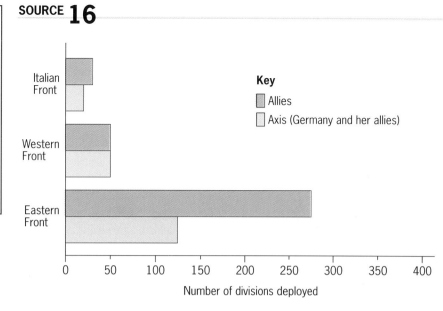

Number of divisions deployed to different fronts in Europe in 1944.

Soviet resistance

The military reforms would not have had much effect if it had not been for the will of the Soviet people to defeat their deadly enemy. The Soviet people rallied to Stalin and to the defence of their country. Like Churchill, Stalin emerged during the war as an outstanding leader who inspired confidence and loyalty in his people. Stalin called upon the people to defend 'Mother Russia' in fighting the 'Great Patriotic War'. (He avoided asking them to fight to defend Communism.) He even allowed the Church (an opponent of Communism) to take a role in the war effort, and it responded by raising 150 million roubles.

The Nazis also helped Stalin. Their brutal treatment of the Soviet population in the areas they controlled increased the will to resist. The Germans completely destroyed over 1700 towns; they murdered thousands and forced thousands more into working as slave labourers.

The Germans found it difficult to make good use of the areas they occupied. As the Red Army retreated, it destroyed everything that could not be transported in a 'scorched earth' policy. It left nothing behind to aid the enemy. Soviet resistance fighters disrupted the German war efforts by blowing up rail links or sabotaging factories in German-held territory. There were an estimated 700,000 resistance fighters operating in 1942.

The Soviet war economy

Even more dramatic was the way in which the Soviet people rebuilt the USSR's economy. The German advances of 1941 captured half of the USSR's food supply, 40 per cent of its electricity generating power and 75 per cent of its supplies of iron, coal and steel. In response, the Soviets dismantled over 2500 major industrial complexes and transported them east by rail to the Urals, Siberia and Kazakhstan – regions safe from the German army. Some 25 million workers were forced to migrate east with these industries.

• Every scrap of raw material and resources went into arms production and nothing else.
• Adults in the USSR received no food unless they worked in some way for the war effort. Soviet citizens survived on one-fifth of the wartime ration in Britain.
• There was much use of slave labour and close control of the population by the secret police.
• The USSR made extensive use of female labour. Half the workforce was female. The Soviet methods were very harsh, but the results were extraordinary. The USSR produced vast quantities of a small range of reliable weapons. The USSR equalled and then passed German war production in 1942. By 1943 the USSR was producing 1.5 times as many aircraft and twice as many tanks as the Germans.

2 Explain how Stalin rallied the Soviet people to fight the Germans.
3 Explain briefly the role of the Soviet people in the USSR's war effort.

Other reasons for Soviet victory

The Germans made many errors in their campaign against the USSR. Hitler often interfered with the way his generals conducted the war. He was overconfident of victory. He expected the war to be over by October 1940, so his soldiers were not equipped for a Russian winter. Hundreds of thousands died from cold and disease. The Germans were not efficient in supplying their troops. They relied heavily on horse-drawn transport for supplies, strangely contrasting with their use of up-to-date technology on the battlefield. German weapons production was not as efficient as the USSR's. The Germans used more raw materials to produce smaller amounts of weapons.

It is also important to remember the contribution of the USSR's allies in the campaign. Britain and the USA supplied vast amounts of food, raw materials and industrial equipment on dangerous shipping routes. The USA provided the USSR with over 500,000 motor vehicles and 1900 locomotives, as well as half of its supply of rubber tyres and copper. Allied bombing also interrupted German arms production.

Mass production of weapons doesn't actually win a war, however. Victory still had to be won on the battlefields. Two battles are generally seen as decisive turning points: Stalingrad and Kursk.

1 Explain how the USSR's allies helped the Soviet war effort.

The Battle of Stalingrad, September 1942–January 1943

Despite all the reforms of the Red Army, 1942 began badly for the USSR. The Germans made further advances, and attempts by the Red Army to push them back led to a further 500,000 casualties. When Hitler decided to strike towards the Caucasus mountains and to capture the USSR's oil fields, the Red Army generals knew they had at all costs to halt the German advance at Stalingrad on the Volga river. Stalingrad was a major industrial and strategic centre. If the Germans seized Stalingrad, they would cut the USSR's links with southern Russia.

The Germans reached the suburbs of Stalingrad despite fierce resistance by the Soviet forces. It became a savage hand-to-hand battle, and in the street fighting the Germans' tanks were of little use. The Germans held on grimly but on 19 November, when the Soviet commander Zhukov counter-attacked in pincer movements north and south of the city, part of the German army was encircled. Outnumbered, the German commander Paulus wanted to retreat and link up with reinforcements, but Hitler ordered him to fight on. Soviet air power gradually cut off his supplies. Soviet artillery, well supplied with shells, pounded the German positions and another new weapon, the Katyusha rocket launcher, rained down explosives on them. By December, the German position was hopeless. Paulus finally surrendered on 31 January 1943, along with 300,000 soldiers.

SOURCE 17

The horses have already been eaten. I would eat a cat, they say its meat is very tasty. The soldiers look like corpses or lunatics, looking for something to put in their mouths. They no longer take cover from Russian shells. They haven't the strength to run or hide.

From the diary of German infantryman William Hoffman, December 1942.

SOURCE 18

Stalingrad is hell on earth. It is Verdun, bloody Verdun, with new weapons. We attack every day. If we capture twenty metres in the morning the Russians throw us back again in the evening.

The comments of a German soldier in a letter home, 1943. (See page 30 for an explanation of 'Verdun'.)

SOURCE 19

Street fighting in Stalingrad. Much of the fighting was hand to hand, with knives and clubs as well as guns.

2 Choose three examples to prove that Stalin was an effective leader in war time.

The Battle of Kursk, July–August 1943

Stalingrad was a defeat for the Germans, but they still held huge amounts of Soviet territory. In July 1943, they launched a huge counter-attack against the Red Army at Kursk. The Germans had planned a surprise attack, but the Red Army had found out about it and prepared itself. In the greatest tank battle in history, the German army was destroyed at Kursk. The Soviets had vast numbers of their highly effective T34 tanks. They had ten times as many aircraft as the Germans. These new aircraft were a match for the Luftwaffe's fighters. They even had ground-attack aircraft which fired anti-tank rockets.

By this time the Soviet factories were geared to maximum production – they were able to replace any tanks and aircraft lost in battle. The Germans, on the other hand, were not able to replace lost tanks and aircraft quickly enough. German production could not increase because of American and British bombing of German factories, and Allied bombing was also destroying rail links between Germany and the USSR. German aircraft had to be diverted from the USSR to help fight off the Allied bombing raids. By August 1943 the Red Army had four times as many tanks as the Germans on the Eastern Front.

Victory

Kursk was the turning point in the war on the Eastern Front. It was the start of the German retreat. The German siege of Leningrad, begun in 1941, was finally lifted in January 1944. By August 1944, the Red Army had reached Poland. The last great battle came in April–May 1945 when the Red Army finally reached Berlin. Hitler committed suicide in his bunker minutes before Soviet troops reached him.

FOCUS TASK

Look at Source 20. It celebrates the Soviet victory over Hitler.

1 Write a explanation of how this victory was achieved. Mention the contribution of:
- the Soviet people
- Soviet technology
- Soviet industry
- the Soviet air force
- Soviet leaders, especially Stalin.

2 Now write two further paragraphs explaining how important you think:
a) German mistakes
and
b) the contribution of the USSR's allies were in the Soviet victory.

SOURCE 20

A 1945 Soviet poster. The USSR is represented by a Soviet flag striking Hitler with a bolt of lightning inside his bunker in Berlin. The caption to the poster is 'Berlin conquered'.

The Allied bombing campaign against Germany

One of the most controversial aspects of the war was the Allied bombing campaign against Germany from 1942 to 1945. There had been RAF bombing raids in 1940 and 1941, but the really intensive bombing of Germany was a policy developed by Sir Arthur Harris, head of RAF Bomber Command from 1942. Harris was committed to strategic bombing because he believed that it would work. Both he and Churchill thought that bombing would demoralise the German population as well as destroy vital industries, rail links and resources such as coal mines.

In 1942 the bombing campaigns were largely directed at targets in France. American B-17s and British Lancasters attacked the ports of Brest and Lorient, where the German submarine pens were. They flattened the towns but left the submarine facilities virtually untouched. When Roosevelt and Churchill met in January 1943, they agreed that their forces would not be ready to attack Europe until 1944. But they were very conscious that Stalin was pressurising them to equal the enormous efforts of the USSR against Germany. They decided that the bombing campaign would be intensified and that it would be focused on targets in Germany. Berlin was bombed regularly from 1943 to 1945. Other German cities were also heavily bombed.

1 Why do you think many people on the Allied side were sceptical about the plan for a major bombing campaign?
2 Choose an example of a technical measure taken by one side and a counter-measure adopted by the other side. Write a short paragraph explaining this process.

SOURCE 21

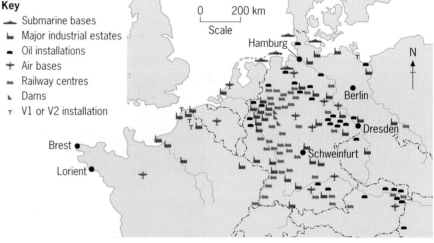

Key
- Submarine bases
- Major industrial estates
- Oil installations
- Air bases
- Railway centres
- Dams
- V1 or V2 installation

The bombing campaign.

Losses among bomber crews were extremely high, but the Allies constantly adapted their tactics and improved their technology to overcome German defences.

SOURCE 22

The effects of Allied bombing on Hamburg, 1943. RAF bombers dropped high explosive and incendiary bombs which caused fires to rage uncontrollably.

- Because bombers were extremely vulnerable to attack from German anti-aircraft guns and fighters, they switched to night raids.
- When the Germans developed a form of radar that enabled their night fighters to find and destroy the Allied bombers, the RAF came up with an ingenious solution. 'Window' consisted of thousands of small strips of metal foil. This produced a blizzard of confusing signals on enemy radar screens, making them virtually useless.
- The RAF developed Oboe – a device that sent out radio beams which bombers followed to help them find their target.
- Harris developed Pathfinder bombers. The Pathfinders used H_2S, a sophisticated ground-sensing radar that could identify targets on the ground even on dark cloudy nights. They then dropped flares to allow the following bombers to hit their targets. This combination of techniques was used to devastating effect against Hamburg in July 1943 (see Sources 22 and 23). In the firestorm, 40,000 people were killed. Almost 75 per cent of the city was destroyed and around 1 million people were made homeless.

SOURCE 23

We found this petrol station. It was situated in the middle of the flattened area but the whole workforce that belonged to it lay dead. We saw thousands of dead bodies, not hundreds but thousands. Some lay in great piles and I took some film and some photographs of these bodies, but I had to stop. I just couldn't take it all in. It was mainly women and children who had been killed in the firestorm, just lying there.

Hans Brunswig, a firefighter in Hamburg in 1943, interviewed for a schools TV programme in 1996.

SOURCE 24

We are outnumbered by about seven to one. The standard of the Americans is extraordinarily high. The day-fighters have lost more than 1000 aircraft during the last four months, among them our best officers. These gaps cannot be filled. We are on the edge of collapse.

Report written by German air force Fighter Commander Adolf Galland, 1944.

Despite these developments, the bombing campaign took a terrible toll on bomber crews. During 1943–44, the RAF lost 10–15 per cent of its planes and crews. The US forces, which flew by day, suffered even higher losses. In October 1943, 300 B-17s attacked the Schweinfurt ball-bearing plant. As soon as their fighter escorts left them, the bombers were attacked by the Luftwaffe, using rockets and bombs dropped from above as well as the usual machine-gun fire. The Americans lost 60 planes, with 138 badly damaged. Losses were so high that the campaign was almost abandoned. However, a simple technical innovation transformed the bombing campaign – escort fighters were fitted with extra fuel tanks. By March 1944, the P-51 Mustang fighters were able to fly with the bombers all the way to Berlin and back. Other fighters soon adopted this innovation and the results for the German people were devastating.

SOURCE 25

Bombing forced Germany to divide the economy between too many competing claims . . . In the air over Germany, or on the fronts in Russia and France, German forces lacked the weapons to finish the job. German forces were denied approximately half their battle front weapons and equipment in 1944. It is difficult not to regard this margin as decisive.

Historian, Professor Richard Overy, writing in 1996.

The controversy over bombing

The bombing campaign had many opponents during and after the war. It also had equally convinced defenders.

The bombing was not justified

- The losses were too high – 140,000 airmen and 21,000 planes.
- The resources that went into bombing could have been used elsewhere.
- Intensive bombing seemed to have little effect on German industrial production (estimated to have fallen by only 10 per cent in 1944).
- The bombing was immoral. The bombing of Dresden has become particularly controversial. Dresden was destroyed by a firestorm from Allied bombing in February 1945. The raid killed 40,000 people. However, Dresden was not a particularly important military or industrial target and at that stage the war was clearly coming to an end.
- Bombing seemed to strengthen the German people's support for the war rather than weakening it.

The bombing was justified

- Although bombing may have only slightly reduced German production, without it production would have expanded massively.
- Bombing absorbed only seven per cent of Britain's war resources.
- Bombing drew off huge numbers of German aircraft from the Russian Front.
- Bombing forced Germany to shift production into anti-aircraft guns rather than tanks.
- In surveys carried out after the war, 91 per cent of Germans said the hardest aspect of civilian life in the war was the bombing.
- Bombing shortened the war and so saved the lives of soldiers and civilians.

FOCUS TASK

Was the bombing justified?

Work in pairs or small groups.

You are preparing for a debate on the above question. Some of you must prepare a speech arguing that:
- *Bombing was effective and therefore it was justified.*
The rest of you have to prepare a speech arguing that:
- *Bombing may have been effective but it cannot be justified.*

The panels above give you the main points for your speech. Add any other points you can think of after reading pages 290–91. How could Sources 21–25 be used in your speech to support your argument? You might also find pages 312–14 useful.

D-Day and the end of the war in Europe

When the Americans entered the war late in 1941, President Roosevelt believed that the American priority was the war against Germany rather than the war against Japan, and so 85 per cent of US resources were targeted at Germany during the war.

SOURCE 26

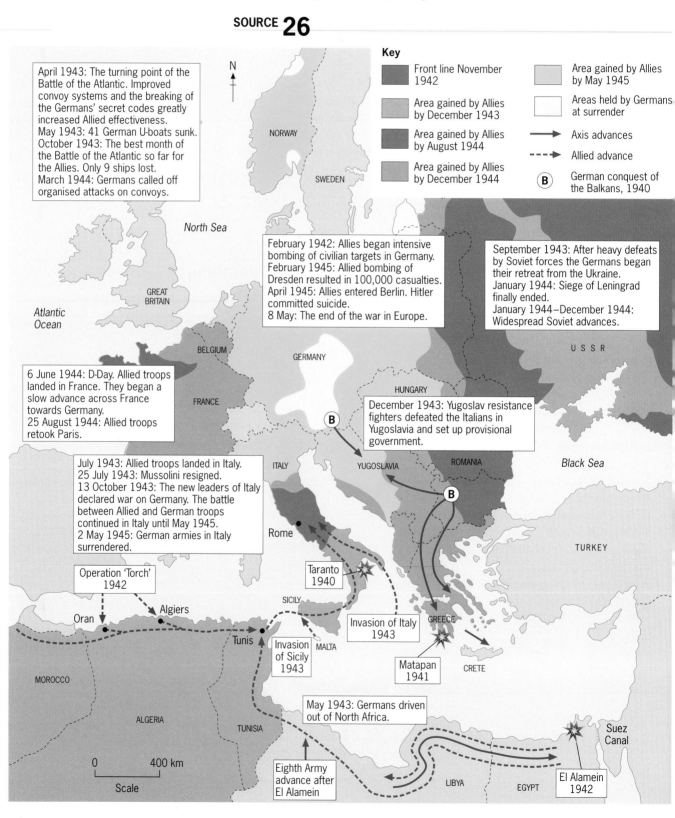

Key

- Front line November 1942
- Area gained by Allies by December 1943
- Area gained by Allies by August 1944
- Area gained by Allies by December 1944
- Area gained by Allies by May 1945
- Areas held by Germans at surrender
- → Axis advances
- - - → Allied advance
- (B) German conquest of the Balkans, 1940

April 1943: The turning point of the Battle of the Atlantic. Improved convoy systems and the breaking of the Germans' secret codes greatly increased Allied effectiveness.
May 1943: 41 German U-boats sunk.
October 1943: The best month of the Battle of the Atlantic so far for the Allies. Only 9 ships lost.
March 1944: Germans called off organised attacks on convoys.

February 1942: Allies began intensive bombing of civilian targets in Germany.
February 1945: Allied bombing of Dresden resulted in 100,000 casualties.
April 1945: Allies entered Berlin. Hitler committed suicide.
8 May: The end of the war in Europe.

September 1943: After heavy defeats by Soviet forces the Germans began their retreat from the Ukraine.
January 1944: Siege of Leningrad finally ended.
January 1944–December 1944: Widespread Soviet advances.

6 June 1944: D-Day. Allied troops landed in France. They began a slow advance across France towards Germany.
25 August 1944: Allied troops retook Paris.

December 1943: Yugoslav resistance fighters defeated the Italians in Yugoslavia and set up provisional government.

July 1943: Allied troops landed in Italy.
25 July 1943: Mussolini resigned.
13 October 1943: The new leaders of Italy declared war on Germany. The battle between Allied and German troops continued in Italy until May 1945.
2 May 1945: German armies in Italy surrendered.

Operation 'Torch' 1942

Taranto 1940

Invasion of Italy 1943

Matapan 1941

Invasion of Sicily 1943

May 1943: Germans driven out of North Africa.

Eighth Army advance after El Alamein

El Alamein 1942

0   400 km

Scale

The war in Europe and North Africa, 1940–45.

A second front?

As early as 1942, the US commander General Eisenhower put together plans for joint US–British attacks on occupied Europe. Stalin was demanding a second front in Europe – that is, for the USA and Britain to attack Hitler from the west, rather than leaving the USSR to bear the brunt of the German onslaught.

Despite these pressures, the British felt that the time was not right. The US army was not sufficienty large or well trained or equipped for such an invasion. Through 1942 and 1943, American forces built up steadily on the British mainland and in Northern Ireland.

North Africa and Italy

Late in 1942 Allied forces, including a large American contingent, began to drive Axis forces out of North Africa in Operation Torch. In 1943 British Empire and US forces invaded Italy from the south. Italy surrendered in September 1943, although the north was then immediately occupied by German forces.

ACTIVITY

In most campaigns in the Second World War victory usually came through a combination of:
• adequate resources
• good technology
• the right tactics.
Explain whether you think this is also true of the D-Day landings.

SOURCE 27

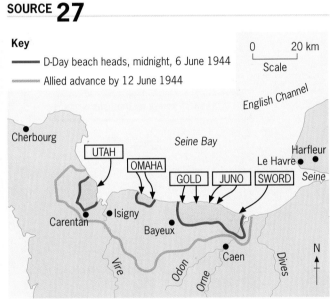

Key
— D-Day beach heads, midnight, 6 June 1944
— Allied advance by 12 June 1944

The D-Day invasion, 1944.

SOURCE 28

One of the Allies' artificial Mulberry harbours off the Normandy coast, June 1944.

Operation Overlord – D-Day

The main objective was still to liberate France. It was a formidable task. The Germans had been in France since 1940. They had strong fortifications. They had well trained and experienced troops led by the very capable Field Marshal Erwin Rommel. It was undoubtedly a high-risk undertaking, but the start of Operation Overlord was nonetheless fixed for 6 June 1944.

Overlord began with a series of air attacks and decoy measures. Some 13,000 Allied aircraft (facing only 400 Luftwaffe aircraft) pounded radar installations, rail links and bridges, and effectively cut off the German defenders in Normandy from reinforcements. About two-thirds of the air attacks were actually away from the invasion area in order to confuse the defenders. Other measures such as false radio messages were also used to convince the Germans that attacks were taking place elsewhere. The invasion took place from several beaches (see Source 27) and was supported by paratroopers dropped from planes or landed in gliders. Casualties were only 11,000 – remarkable in an operation that had brought 130,000 men across the channel by sea and 23,000 by air. But then the Allies had to break out of Normandy before the Germans could recover and trap them. They also needed armour, reinforcements and supplies, which were provided with great ingenuity. Giant floating harbours known as Mulberries were sailed across the Channel and huge floating piers were built. The Allies even built their own oil pipeline called PLUTO (Pipe Line Under The Ocean).

From this point, the Allies used their air superiority to devastating effect against the German forces. Heavy bombers destroyed factories. Fighter bombers such as the American P-47 Thunderbolt and the British Typhoon roamed the countryside attacking German vehicles and trains. Resistance fighters disrupted German communications and destroyed supplies being taken to German forces.

Resistance groups in other occupied territories such as Poland and the Balkans also began to attack the occupying German forces. At the same time, Allied forces were advancing in Italy and the Soviet army was advancing from the east.

Nevertheless, the breakout from Normandy into the rest of France was bloody and costly. Paris was not liberated until 25 August 1944. In December a major German counter-attack in the Ardennes region of Belgium caused tremendous casualties and disrupted the Allied advance.

How about this video?

Have you got anything on D-Day? I need it for a research project, so it must be accurate and reliable.

Victory in Europe

As the Allies advanced, the Germans put some remarkable new weapons into action. The most spectacular of these were the V-1 and V-2 missiles. The V-1 was a flying bomb powered by a rocket engine. It was extremely difficult to shoot down because it travelled so quickly. It flew towards a target area and then came down wherever it ran out of fuel. The V-2 was a genuine guided missile. It flew at supersonic speeds and was impossible to shoot down. Several of these weapons hit London and cities in Belgium and the Netherlands. Jet aircraft were also introduced.

However, none of the new weapons stopped the Allies' advance. There was much hard fighting. One daring Allied attack on the bridges over the Rhine, in the Netherlands in September 1944, was beaten back with heavy losses, but the Allies finally managed to cross the Rhine into Germany in March 1945.

In May 1945 US and British forces met up with Soviet forces and the war in Europe was over.

SOURCE 29

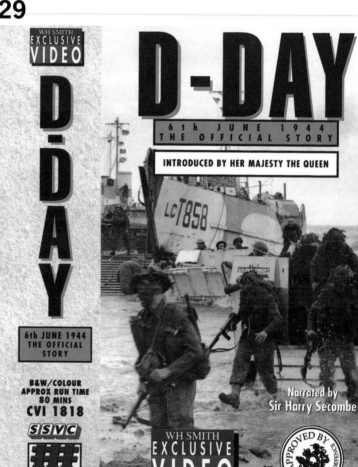

The cover of a video produced in 1994 to commemorate the fiftieth anniversary of D-Day.

1 Analyse the front and back covers of the video in Source 29 and decide whether you will buy it. Make a list of:
 • features on the cover that give you confidence that the video will be useful
 • features that make you wonder whether the video will be a useful resource.
2 You still can't decide. Instead, you note down details of the video and go to the web site of the film maker. Draw up a list of questions you would like to ask about the video before deciding whether or not to buy it.

FOCUS TASK

Produce a display or presentation, using ICT, to explain the reasons for the Allied victory over Germany.

 • You could describe one event or battle which you consider important.
 • You could comment on the roles of:
  – the USSR
  – Britain.
 • You could comment (with examples) on the importance of:
  – resources
  – technology
  – tactics.

Your teacher can give you a sheet to help you.

The war in the Pacific and the Far East

So far in this chapter you have focused mainly on the war in Europe. However, it is important to remember that this was only part of a much wider conflict. In the Far East, Allied troops were fighting the Japanese.

SOURCE **30**

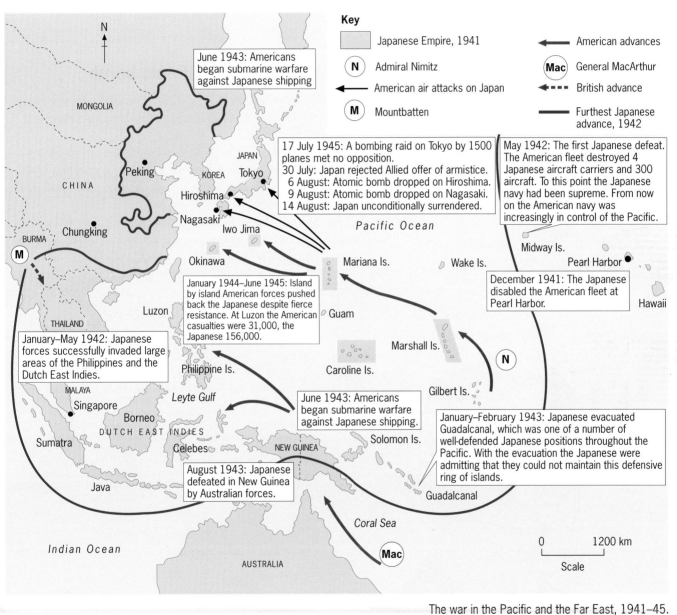

Key

▭ Japanese Empire, 1941	← American advances
Ⓝ Admiral Nimitz	Ⓜ̄ᵃᶜ General MacArthur
← American air attacks on Japan	◄--- British advance
Ⓜ Mountbatten	── Furthest Japanese advance, 1942

June 1943: Americans began submarine warfare against Japanese shipping

17 July 1945: A bombing raid on Tokyo by 1500 planes met no opposition.
30 July: Japan rejected Allied offer of armistice.
6 August: Atomic bomb dropped on Hiroshima.
9 August: Atomic bomb dropped on Nagasaki.
14 August: Japan unconditionally surrendered.

May 1942: The first Japanese defeat. The American fleet destroyed 4 Japanese aircraft carriers and 300 aircraft. To this point the Japanese navy had been supreme. From now on the American navy was increasingly in control of the Pacific.

December 1941: The Japanese disabled the American fleet at Pearl Harbor.

January 1944–June 1945: Island by island American forces pushed back the Japanese despite fierce resistance. At Luzon the American casualties were 31,000, the Japanese 156,000.

January–May 1942: Japanese forces successfully invaded large areas of the Philippines and the Dutch East Indies.

June 1943: Americans began submarine warfare against Japanese shipping.

January–February 1943: Japanese evacuated Guadalcanal, which was one of a number of well-defended Japanese positions throughout the Pacific. With the evacuation the Japanese were admitting that they could not maintain this defensive ring of islands.

August 1943: Japanese defeated in New Guinea by Australian forces.

MONGOLIA · Peking · CHINA · Chungking · BURMA · Ⓜ · THAILAND · MALAYA · Singapore · Sumatra · Java · Borneo · DUTCH EAST INDIES · Celebes · JAPAN · KOREA · Tokyo · Hiroshima · Nagasaki · Iwo Jima · Okinawa · Luzon · Philippine Is. · Leyte Gulf · Mariana Is. · Guam · Caroline Is. · Marshall Is. · Gilbert Is. · Wake Is. · Midway Is. · Pearl Harbor · Hawaii · Ⓝ · Solomon Is. · NEW GUINEA · Guadalcanal · Coral Sea · Ⓜ̄ᵃᶜ · AUSTRALIA · Pacific Ocean · Indian Ocean

0   1200 km
Scale

The war in the Pacific and the Far East, 1941–45.

The conflict between the Allies and Japan was fought over a vast territory and involved millions of American troops as well as troops from Britain, India, Australia and New Zealand. Some 120,000 Africans also fought for the Allies in the Burma campaign. India provided over 2.5 million men and women for the armed forces and spent a staggering 80 per cent of its wealth in 1943–44 on the war effort.

The war in the Pacific changed the way military commanders thought about naval warfare. It also resulted in the first use of nuclear weapons.

Pearl Harbor to Midway

You have seen on pages 275–78 how the Japanese attacked Pearl Harbor in 1941. The only comfort for the US navy was that its aircraft carriers were not in Pearl Harbor at the time of the attack and the Japanese did not hunt down the carriers and destroy them. It was a decisive error.

The US carrier commander, Admiral Halsey, was able to use these carriers throughout 1942, while US shipyards frantically constructed new ships, especially carriers. They also produced huge numbers of superior carrier aircraft, such as the Douglas Dauntless dive bomber and the F-4 Corsair.

The decisive battle came at Midway in May 1942 when the Americans destroyed four Japanese carriers, the very thing the Japanese had failed to do at Pearl Harbor. Without air protection the Japanese navy was hopelessly vulnerable and Japan could not match the output of the USA's shipyards and aircraft factories.

The defeat of Japan and the atomic bomb

Although the Japanese were being pushed back in 1943 and 1944, the Allied losses were huge. The Japanese fought fanatically for each island in the Pacific and each piece of territory in China, Burma and India.

In March 1945, British and US forces took the island of Okinawa. The Allies had to kill or capture every one of the 100,000 Japanese soldiers defending the island – none of them would surrender. Allied ships had also been badly damaged by Japanese kamikaze suicide bombers who crashed themselves deliberately into ships.

By summer 1945, the USA was confident of winning the war eventually. However, the new President, Harry Truman (Roosevelt died in March 1945), was faced with the daunting prospect of a year or more of massive casualties as US troops beat back the Japanese island by island and then had to invade Japan itself. But there was an alternative. An international team of scientists in the USA, working on what was known as the Manhattan Project, had just perfected the world's first nuclear bomb. It was decision time for Truman.

SOURCE 31

US casualties at Okinawa.

SOURCE 32

Decision 1: Should I use nuclear weapons?

One year earlier there would have been no choice for the Allies – to win this war the President would have had to order his forces to press on island by island. In June 1945 there was a choice.

The Manhattan Project had tested the nuclear bomb. All the tests indicated that this was a bomb of such ferocity and power that no country could recover from its impact. Truman met with his military advisers in June. They told him what to expect if they invaded the Japanese mainland. They estimated at least 220,000 casualties in a campaign that would last well into 1946. Truman's mind was made up. He later said that when he came to the decision it was easy.

Yes – use nuclear weapons.

Decision 2: Should I warn the Japanese?

Should he warn the Japanese or maybe even give a demonstration, in the hope it would make them surrender? Most US military advisers opposed this idea. They wanted to see the bomb used as a normal weapon of war and achieve complete surprise. And what if the demonstration bomb failed? Also, in July, Truman received details of secret Japanese signals that showed that the Japanese military were determined to fight to the finish. This convinced him that the bomb had to be used as a 'normal' weapon without a warning.

No – don't warn the Japanese.

1 What factors have affected viewpoints on Truman's decision?
2 Do you think he made the right decision? Give your reasons.

Truman accepted military advice to drop two bombs in quick succession to convince the Japanese that the USA had a large stockpile of the weapons (which it did not). The first bomb was dropped on Hiroshima by a B-29 bomber, the *Enola Gay*, on 6 August 1945. The second was dropped on the city of Nagasaki three days later. Both caused appalling damage and horrific casualties. They also left a legacy of cancer and other radiation-related diseases.

SOURCE 33

The damage caused by the Hiroshima bomb. At least 75,000 people died instantly. Tens of thousands more died from radiation poisoning in the years that followed.

SOURCE 34

JAPAN WAS SEEKING PEACE BEFORE THE FIRST ATOM BOMB WAS DROPPED ON HIROSHIMA, ACCORDING TO DOCUMENTS JUST LEAKED TO THE U.S. PRESS.

"DON'T YOU SEE, THEY HAD TO FIND OUT IF IT WORKED..."

A British cartoon published in the *Evening Standard*, 1960.

FOCUS TASK

How important was technology in the Second World War?

In this chapter you have seen how technology affected the outcome of the Second World War. The side that had the best technology was always likely to win the war. Write a paragraph on the impact of technology on each of the following:
a) Land war (for example, Blitzkrieg on the western or eastern front)
b) The war in the air (for example, the Battle of Britain or the bombing of Germany)
c) The war at sea (for example, the Battle of the Atlantic or the war in the Pacific)
d) The nuclear bombs.

For each key area you should consider:
• how techniques changed or stayed the same compared to the First World War (refer back to Chapter 2)
• the impact of these new technologies on the battlefield or on civilians
• their importance in deciding the outcome of the war.

Did Truman make the right decision?

There were people on the Allied side at the time who felt that the use of these weapons was unnecessary. However, these voices were in the minority. Most were relieved there would be no bloody invasion of Japan. Attitudes towards the Japanese had hardened following the liberation of the Allied prisoner-of-war camps in 1944 and 1945. Accounts of horrific conditions and barbaric treatment by the Japanese guards fed a desire for vengeance against the Japanese.

The Japanese Emperor Hirohito and most of his government told the army to surrender after the Nagasaki bomb, but some of the military leaders attempted to overthrow Hirohito and continue the war. This proved to many people on the Allied side that the decision to use the bombs was right. Hirohito's will prevailed and Japan surrendered on 14 August 1945.

The war was over, but the nuclear age had begun, with far-reaching consequences (see Chapters 11 and 12). Truman's decision has come under intense scrutiny ever since. Some have said the war was already won. The bomb served no military purpose and it was dropped because, as an anti-Communist, Truman wanted to scare the Soviet Union. It is also claimed that army leaders were desperate to test the bomb in real warfare (see Source 34) and this was more important to them than the military need.

Others have argued against this. They say there is little evidence that these considerations affected Truman's judgement and that he dropped the bomb because it would cost fewer lives than a conventional war.

The debate continues.

SOURCE 35

We were captured and forced down the mines . . . The Japanese did not treat the workers like human beings, but like animals. 'Exchange coal with Chinese people's lives' was their slogan. 'There are so many Chinese . . . When you kill one there are always more.' The workers had to drink the stinking water at the bottom of the coal pit. When people became seriously ill they tied their legs and arms, carried them away and kicked them into this hole. Dogs were waiting down there, biting and tearing the bodies to pieces . . .

A Chinese miner remembers his experience of Japanese occupation.

How did the war affect civilians?

The nuclear bombs caused horrific civilian casualties, but that was typical of the Second World War. In this war more civilians died than soldiers. Civilians were in the front line of attack. They were bombed, imprisoned, massacred and starved to death. Sources 35–43 are examples of the war's impact on civilians. In 10.2 you will look in detail at the impact of the war in Britain.

SOURCE 36

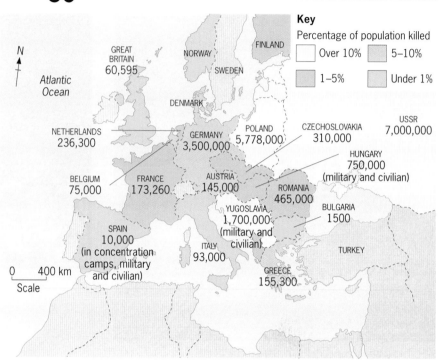

Civilian casualties in Europe.

SOURCE 37

A baby sits in the wreckage of Shanghai railway station after a Japanese bombing raid.

SOURCE 38

In Britain, civilians of German or Austrian origin were rounded up and taken to internment camps. In the USA, Japanese civilians were also interned (see page 369).

SOURCE 39

Inmates of Auschwitz concentration camp, photographed on the camp's liberation by Soviet troops.

SOURCE 40

A German prisoner, captured by civilian resistance fighters in the south of France.

SOURCE 41

Refugees in Russia fleeing from the advancing German army in 1941.

SOURCE 42

Soviet citizens scavenging for food in Stalingrad.

SOURCE 43

I watched my mother and father die. I knew perfectly well that they were starving. But I wanted their bread more than I wanted them to stay alive. And they knew that. That's what I remember about the blockade: that feeling that you wanted your parents to die because you wanted their bread.

A description of life in Leningrad during the long siege by German troops, written by a survivor of the war.

ACTIVITY

It is 1945. You have been asked by the United Nations (see page 319) to make a series of posters with the title 'Never Again' which will remind people for all time of the horrific impact of war on civilians.

Work in groups to draw up a list of ideas for posters. You might think that the posters need to be quite shocking. You might think it better if the posters are subtle and clever.

Each of you should design one of the posters from the list.

How did the war affect politics?

The Second World War also led to important political changes in countries around the world, as you can see from Source 44. These are all changes that had a great impact on international relations after the war. Some of these will be investigated in detail in the following chapters of this book.

SOURCE 44

In many European countries the old pre-war leaders were swept aside, particularly those who were thought to have helped the Germans. In France, Scandinavia and the Balkans the resistance leaders were seen as the natural leaders of the country after the war.

The war gave a real boost to independence movements in colonies owned by European countries. Within three years India had been granted independence from Britain. Twenty years after the war, Britain had lost almost all its empire.

The political impact of the Second World War

The war completely crippled the economies of the European powers. Economic recovery was even more difficult than after the First World War. This actually strengthened the will to co-operate and over the following 20 years led to the setting up of the first stages of the European Union.

The war had shown that the two most powerful countries in the world were the capitalist USA and the Communist USSR. In the war they had been allies against Germany and Japan. The question was whether they would get on after the war. Would the friendship hold? You can find out all about that in Chapters 11 and 12.

The political impact of the Second World War.

10.2 The Home Front 1939–1945: how did the war affect life in Britain?

The outbreak of war in 1939 did not come as a surprise. The British government was far better prepared in 1939 than it had been in 1914. The government quickly took charge of people's lives in ways that would never have been accepted in peacetime. It introduced extensive measures to defend the country from attack by sea and air and to keep popular support. You are going to examine four different measures:

- evacuation – protecting vulnerable citizens by moving them away from the cities that were likely to be bombed
- conscription – ensuring Britain had the soldiers and workers it needed by recruiting civilians
- controlling information – keeping up morale by propaganda and censorship
- rationing – keeping Britain fed and supplied despite the U-boat blockade.

Evacuation

As soon as war was declared in September 1939, around 1.5 million people, mainly school children, were moved from areas at high risk of bombing: big cities, industrial areas, ports and villages and towns near to airfields. The evacuation had been well planned but there were lots of problems, as you would expect with such a huge migration.

- Evacuees were not used to rural life. There was a clash between city and country values. Many evacuees were from poor families in the inner cities. They often found themselves in much wealthier homes and had to cope with different standards of behaviour. They also had to deal with confusing items such as bathrooms and lavatories!
- Evacuees were usually separated from their families. Some evacuee children were badly treated or exploited.
- There was evidence that some people tried to avoid taking evacuees. A report by the Association of Head Masters and Head Mistresses in July 1941 criticised many better-off people for 'shirking their responsibilities'.

SOURCE 1

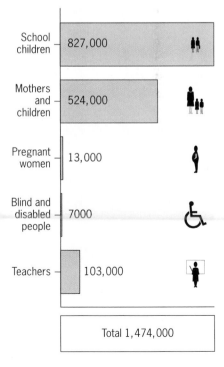

School children	827,000	
Mothers and children	524,000	
Pregnant women	13,000	
Blind and disabled people	7000	
Teachers	103,000	

Total 1,474,000

Numbers of evacuees, September 1939.

SOURCE 2

Evacuees leaving the East End of London, September 1939.

SOURCE 3

[They are] . . . all filthy, the smell of the room is terrible, they refuse all food except tea and bread, the children have made puddles all over the floor . . .

Moya Woodside, a middle-class girl in rural Northern Ireland, describes her experience of evacuees from Belfast. When Belfast was bombed in 1941, 6000 went to Dublin and many thousands more left the dense housing of central Belfast to live in the surrounding countryside.

1 Does Source 4 suggest that the government's evacuation policy was successful? Explain your answer.

There were no air raids during the six months of the 'Phoney War' (see page 279). Many evacuees returned home. But once the Blitz started in 1940 there was a new wave of evacuation and then again in 1944 when Germany was using V-1 flying bombs and V-2 missiles to bomb Britain.

Evacuation saved many lives, but it had other important effects. It freed up many mothers to take on vital war work. Evacuation was also a powerful social force. Youngsters from tough inner city areas saw the countryside, often for the first time. They generally stayed with better-off people, and their eyes were opened to a whole new way of life that they did not know existed. At the same time, many comfortable people outside the cities learnt how bad conditions in the cities were. After the war, they voted for politicians who wanted to stamp out poverty.

SOURCE 4

A 1942 government poster about evacuation.

Conscription

From the start of the war, all men aged 18–41 had to register for war work – either to fight or to work.

Civilian conscription

Most men were eligible for conscription into the armed forces, but they were not all called up. Men in reserved occupations – that is, doing essential jobs where the government needed workers – were not conscripted. Reserved occupations included anything from medical work to coal mining, electronics to demolition (see Source 5).

From 1940, the political parties formed a coalition government under the leadership of Winston Churchill. The Labour Minister Ernest Bevin worked closely with employers and with the trade unions to make Britain's wartime production as efficient as possible. Wages were strictly controlled, but so were prices. Workers could be moved around. For example, when coal stocks fell dangerously low in 1940, some 30,000 miners had to leave the army and return to their old jobs. Coal supplies remained a problem throughout the war. After 1942 men could opt for the mines rather than the army, but few did. Conditions for men and women were often difficult and all workers in essential industries faced long hours – 80-hour weeks were not uncommon. There were strikes, but they were usually short and news about them was strictly censored.

2 What steps did the government take to organise the workforce?

3 Why did so few want to go down the mines?

SOURCE 5

How did the war affect the family?
I spent a lot of hours on my own, because dad went long distance, and I never knew where he was going, when he was coming back.

He worked for the government, didn't he?
Yes, he took bombs and he had to have special passes to get through. He saw a lot more than I did with going to Liverpool. And he went down to London and Fleet Street was blown up so he set to and helped to clear it. Of course it was all round the village, he was missing.

So after that, did he just used to turn up at home?
Yes, he never announced it.

You never knew when he was coming home or anything?
No. It was a very hard life.

Extract from an interview in 1995 with a woman who lived in Hebden Bridge, near Halifax. Her father was a demolition worker who helped to clear bomb damage safely.

Women in the war

By the summer of 1941, over half of the working population was employed by the government or on government schemes. It was not enough, however, and in late 1941 women were conscripted. All women aged 20 or older had to register for war work at a labour exchange. Unless they were ill, pregnant or had small children, they were sent to work in industry or the auxiliary armed forces. Some women were reported as working 80–90 hours per week on aeroplane assembly lines. There were 7.5 million women working in 1939, out of a total population of 40 million. Of these, 260,000 women were working in the munitions industry in 1944. Millions became involved in the war effort in other ways, as air-raid wardens, fire officers, evacuation officers, host families for evacuees, and so on. Large numbers of women joined the armed services and many served overseas.

The novelty of women working in 'men's jobs' wore off much more quickly than during the First World War, because women were doing so in such large numbers. Women workers were taken for granted. Eight times as many women took on war work in the Second World War as in the First. For example, during the First World War the Women's Land Army employed 33,000 women as rural labourers; in 1943, it employed around 2 million.

SOURCE 6

Recruitment poster for the Wrens (Women's Royal Naval Service).

The trade unions accepted women workers much more readily than they had done in the previous war. The TUC campaigned to make sure that women were treated the same as men. For example, the TUC successfully complained against the fact that women were paid 25 per cent less and received lower accident compensation than men in the Rolls-Royce armament factories. Government even began to help women with child care commitments, providing nurseries and encouraging employers to allow women with children to job share.

Despite these changes, there was not exactly a revolution in attitudes to women's role in society. Once the war was over, the government had great trouble persuading women to stay in work. In 1947 around 18 per cent of married women worked, compared to 10 per cent in the 1930s. The government continued to provide help with child care. Discrimination remained an issue – in the mid 1950s women still earned about half as much as men on average.

1 Look at Sources 8 and 9. What impression do you get from these sources of:
   a) the importance of women in the war effort
   b) attitudes to women?
2 Look at Sources 6 and 7. Do they give the same impressions as Sources 8 and 9?
   Explain your answer.

SOURCE 7

British women officers often give orders to men. The men obey smartly and know it is no shame. For British women have proved themselves in this war. They have stuck to their posts near burning ammunition dumps, delivered messages on foot after their motorcycles have been blasted from under them. They have pulled aviators from burning planes . . . There isn't a single record of any British woman in uniformed service quitting her post, or failing in her duty under fire. When you see a girl in uniform with a bit of [medal] ribbon on her tunic, remember she didn't get it for knitting more socks than anyone else in Ipswich.

A War Department booklet for American soldiers coming to Britain in 1942.

ACTIVITY

After the First World War, a leading British politician praised the work of women in the war. He asked: 'How could we have carried on without them?'

Do you think this comment would have been appropriate at the end of the Second World War? Find evidence to support your view.

SOURCE 8

Women's Land Army workers, 1942.

SOURCE 9

Women pilots from the Air Transport Auxiliary Service. Women pilots moved aircraft from one location to another. They were often the first to fly aircraft.

Military conscription

Conscription was introduced in April 1939 – before war had even begun. The government wanted to avoid the mistakes of the last war. Conscription was fairer than in the First World War, in that rich and poor alike were called up. There were few complaints about conscription. In fact, the main complaints were that the pace of conscription was too slow. By the end of 1940, 200,000 men had deferred their call-up for the armed forces because of the importance of their occupation (this was often a result of a request from their employer). However, in the same period, over 1 million men either volunteered for the forces or asked for their call-up to be speeded up.

SOURCE 10

Volunteers for recruitment into the Royal Navy, London 1939.

Military conscription was much more controversial in Northern Ireland. Eire never accepted that Northern Ireland was part of Britain and many Catholics who lived in Northern Ireland felt the same way. The British government in London decided that trying to introduce conscription in Northern Ireland would do more harm than good. Another reason was that Northern Ireland's shipyards, aircraft factories and other industries were doing such important war work that the province was often short of workers. Conscription would have made the problem worse, so it was never introduced.

SOURCE 11

It is extremely doubtful if conscription has the whole-hearted support of either section of the population . . . It will fall more heavily upon the Roman Catholic section than the Protestant because a greater proportion of the latter are in reserved occupations . . . active organisation to resist it will commence at once in every parish . . . Many will cross the Border but from those who remain wide resistance to the enforcement of the Act may be expected . . . conscription will give new life to the IRA . . . It will . . . increase the risk of Protestants adopting the attitude that they go only if the Roman Catholics are taken . . .

The views of Colonel Wickham, head of the Royal Ulster Constabulary (RUC), on conscription in 1941.

FOCUS TASK

Refer back to the Focus Task on page 302.

Note 2

Make a second note about how you will keep essential industries running if so many men are going off to fight.

1 Look at the aims of the government's information policy. Read pages 306–11 and identify one source that is designed to help achieve each aim.

Controlling information

The government used its emergency powers to control information. It aimed to:

- boost morale and support for the war effort
- provide important information and instructions
- make sure the press did not publish and the BBC did not broadcast anything that might be helpful to the enemy.

The press

Newspapers were closely controlled. Journalists had to submit their articles to the censor before they were printed or transmitted. However, most papers happily complied with the regulations, so the censor did not have to force the issue. Most newspapers censored themselves. They reported bad news such as bomb damage or military defeats, but they did so with encouragement not to be downhearted. Victories were celebrated enthusiastically, of course.

Some newspapers were officially censored. For example, the *Daily Worker* was banned in 1941 for claiming that bosses were gaining from the war while workers were making all the sacrifices. But in contrast with Germany, newspaper circulation increased during the war, despite the fact that newspapers became smaller and thinner.

2 Which of Sources 12 and 16 is more useful to historians in finding out how effective propaganda was? Explain your answer.

Radio

The BBC was not controlled by the government. It censored itself and played a key role in informing the public and helping to keep up morale. The transformation of Dunkirk from a military disaster into a morale-boosting triumph was a good example of the BBC's power. By the end of the war, an estimated 25 million people tuned into BBC radio programmes. Most of the great film, radio and stage stars made programmes to boost the morale of civilians and the troops. People took comfort from comedians like Tommy Trinder, who made jokes about wartime hardships but also made fun of Hitler and the Nazis.

Propaganda

The government also produced propaganda, although it was not the same type of propaganda as used by the Nazis. If you had walked around a wartime town, you would have noticed posters encouraging you to conserve food or fuel or to beware of enemy spies. You might also have noticed that many of the film posters showed films relating to the war. Films generally sent a patriotic message, and the newsreels which were shown before the main film also did their bit to boost morale.

Wartime propaganda also made good use of the image of the Prime Minister, Winston Churchill (see Sources 13 and 14). There is no doubt that he was a great wartime leader. However, the way in which newspapers, newsreels and the BBC reported him made him an almost legendary figure.

Observation

The government also monitored the mood of the people by using what became known as Mass Observation reports. Essentially, this involved volunteers (and sometimes police and intelligence agents) listening in on conversations in bars, shops, post offices and other places and then writing up reports of what they had heard. These reports were collected and analysed by the government.

SOURCE 12

YOUR TALK MAY KILL YOUR COMRADES

A wartime poster warning that careless talk can be dangerous.

SOURCE 13

A cartoon produced by the Ministry of Information in 1940.

SOURCE 14

Winston Churchill, in a cartoon from the *Evening Standard*, May 1940.

SOURCE 15

A fake front cover of the *Evening Standard*, 17 February 1940.

SOURCE 16

Tuesday 13 August 1940

The Battle of Britain has begun in earnest. We hear on the news of airmen's experiences during these exciting fights, usually told very calmly, quickly and tersely. Tonight we hear that in fighting round our south-east and south coasts, as well as over Berkshire, Wiltshire and Hampshire, the Germans have lost 57 planes and our losses are nine here and 14 on the Continent. A scrap or two had also taken place between torpedo boats and E-boats [German torpedo boats], with no loss of men to us and only one damaged boat, which got home safely.

Wednesday 14 August 1940

Yesterday's 'bag' of Nazi planes was 78 to 13 of ours. And everybody was tired today because we have all been up the best part of the night. The Nazi planes came over about 11.15 p.m. and so we dressed and went out to the dug-out, taking two rugs and a few oddments in a suitcase.

Extract from *Mrs Milburn's Diaries*. Mrs Clara Milburn was a Warwickshire lady who kept diaries throughout the war.

3 Look carefully at Source 15. Do you think that this article would be accepted or rejected by the government information department? Give your reasons. Your teacher can tell you more about this.

FOCUS TASK

Note 3

Refer back to the Focus Task on page 302.
Make your third note about how you are going to use the media to keep people supporting the war.

SOURCE 17

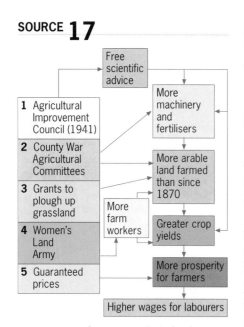

Government help for farmers.

How did Britain feed itself during the war?

Food production

In the First World War, German U-boats tried to cut off Britain's food supplies. In 1917 Britain came within days of running out of food. With this in mind, the government had plans for increased food production from the beginning of the war. It was just as well. As you saw on pages 284–85, the U-boat campaigns against Britain in the Second World War were also very effective.

The more food that could be home-grown, the more space there was in merchant ships for vital war supplies. Throughout the war, the government encouraged people to grow vegetables, and to keep chickens and pigs. Private gardens were also turned over to vegetables. Even window boxes were used to grow lettuces. Playing fields, railway embankments and the grounds of major public buildings were ploughed up. Golf clubs had to plant wheat on their fairways! The number of tractors in use quadrupled during the war. Avoiding waste was essential. Boy scouts and girl guides collected scraps for pigs. Source 17 gives some idea of the measures taken and their success, but even at its most successful Britain only grew 80 per cent of the food it needed.

SOURCE 18

Note: 1 bushel = 8 gallons (36.4 litres)

Increased yields of food, 1935–45.

SOURCE 19

People working on allotments in the moat of the Tower of London.

SOURCE 20

A wartime advertisement for soap. It was common for advertisements to contain useful information like this.

SOURCE 21

'We want your Kitchen Waste': during the war, more than 6900 pig clubs were formed. The government took a share of the pig when it was slaughtered, but the pig keeper kept the rest.

SOURCE 22

Utility clothing.

Rationing and shortages

Much of this good work would have been wasted without rationing. Under Lord Woolton, the Ministry of Food worked out fair rations, gave advice on recipes and looked after the health of the nation. 'Potato Pete' and 'Doctor Carrot' advised on healthy and tasty recipes. Rationing soon went beyond food. Almost every other essential article could only be bought with coupons. In other words, even if you had the money to buy something, you couldn't unless you had the coupons to do so. It was a tremendous force for equality in society, as rich and poor were treated the same. Even the royal family had their own ration books. Since wages rose during the war and prices were controlled, many of Britain's poor got their first glimpse of a better standard of living. For these people, their diet and health actually improved. They were also able to rely on the quality of clothes or other goods, as long as they had the government's utility mark (see Source 22).

SOURCE 23

Meat	1 shilling to two shillings and a pennyworth		Tea	2 oz–4 oz
Bacon	4 oz–8 oz		Sugar	8 oz–16 oz + 2 lbs for jam-making
Cheese	1 oz–8 oz		Sweets	3 oz–4 oz (including chocolate)
Fat	1 oz–8 oz		Dried milk	1 tin
Eggs	1–2		Dried eggs	8th of a packet

The weekly ration allowed during the war per adult. Rations of particular foods changed from month to month depending on the supplies available.

FOCUS TASK

Refer back to the Focus Task on page 302.

Note 4

Make your fourth note about how are you going to keep Britain supplied with food.

SOURCE 24

'Dig for Victory'. This campaign was launched in 1939. By the middle of the war there were 1.4 million allotments in Britain, mostly converted from private gardens or parks.

The effects of rationing and shortages were different in different areas, and even for different families. Very large families with a large number of ration books did not suffer from shortages in the same way as smaller families or families with no children. In rural areas, vegetables were usually relatively easy to come by.

In Northern Ireland, bacon and pork were not rationed. Northern Ireland had enough milk to ship 77,000 litres every day to mainland Britain during the winter of 1940. The abundance of food was one of several reasons why such large numbers of US troops were stationed there from 1942. Some foods were in short supply, however, particularly sugar, tea and fruit from overseas.

Fuel was always desperately short. This affected people in the country more than the towns. Milk roundsmen went back to the horse and cart. Most people walked or cycled. Some people who owned cars never used them for the entire war because it was so hard to get petrol.

Luxury foods and goods such as chocolate and perfume were scarce. Goods such as whisky and tobacco were heavily taxed. Although the government did not like to admit it, there was a flourishing black market. This grew considerably when US troops arrived in Britain bringing these goods with them.

SOURCE 25

A month after rationing began, meat was added, and of all the wielders of power, the butcher became paramount … For the lucky few that he chose to favour, an unknown 'something' in a plain wrapper was surreptitiously slipped into the shopping basket, and not until the customer was well clear of the prying eyes of the queue was the content examined, and oh, the triumph if it was liver!

From *Talking About the War* by Anne Valery, written in 1991.

A wartime poster: 'Britain shall not burn'.

Air Raid Precaution

Apart from invasion, the greatest threat to British people was the air raid. The early fears were as much of poison gas attacks as explosive bombs. Almost from day one of the war, civilians were issued with gas masks and instructions on how to use them. About 1.5 million volunteers worked in various civil defence agencies.

ARP wardens

A new organisation, Air Raid Precaution, was set up. In 1939 it had about 500,000 members. The ARP wardens supervised the black-out. Householders had to make sure no light was visible from their windows after dark and ARP could fine people for showing a light. They also organised patrols during raids to check for incendiary bombs (firebombs). ARP wardens often organised teams of local people, with buckets of sand, to fire-watch for these bombs during raids. Factories and large buildings were especially vulnerable.

The government produced a great deal of advice about air raids. Source 27 gives an idea of how the ideal wartime household might look.

SOURCE 27

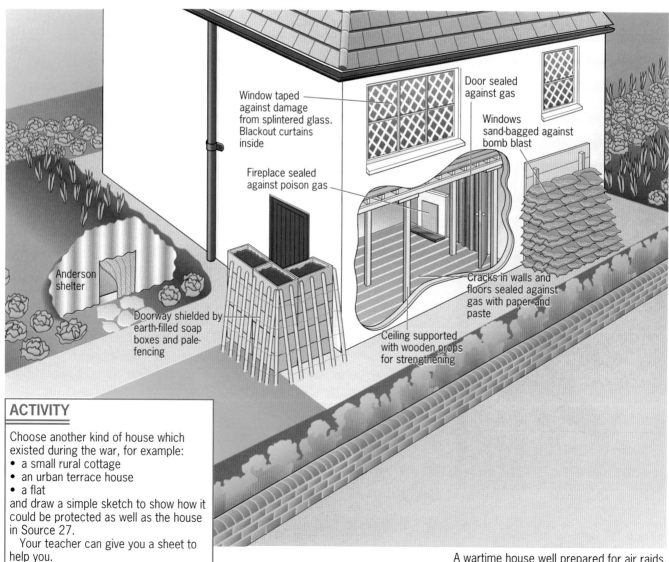

A wartime house well prepared for air raids.

ACTIVITY

Choose another kind of house which existed during the war, for example:
• a small rural cottage
• an urban terrace house
• a flat
and draw a simple sketch to show how it could be protected as well as the house in Source 27.

Your teacher can give you a sheet to help you.

SOURCE 28

Kerbs, trees and even cows were painted so that drivers and pedestrians could see them in the black-out!

1 One of the problems with evidence such as Source 29 is that it is hard to be sure whether the writer's views represent the views of the population as a whole. How would you investigate whether the view was representative?
2 As a general rule, people in Britain resented ARP wardens, but they did not resent rationing. Why do you think this was?

SOURCE 29

Thursday, 7 September 1939

During the week we were called up by the air-raid warden, who found our black-out insufficient, and still more curtains had to be made . . . A very definite black-out was obtained at the bay windows by covering the whole bay . . . with a great black pall . . . The lack of ventilation was stifling in hot weather, but it is wonderful how one can conform to an order when it is absolutely necessary to do so.

From *Mrs Milburn's Diaries.*

FOCUS TASK

Refer back to the Focus Task on page 302.

Note 5

1 Make your final note about how you are going to defend people against air raids.
2 Now it's time for your presentation. Work in pairs.
   a) Think of questions to ask the minister. Write them down.
   b) Run a mock interview – with the minister answering from the presentation cards.
   c) Swap roles so that each person can answer questions on each topic.

Shelters

A major problem was the provision of effective air-raid shelters. The government had provided some public shelters, but not enough of them. Part of the problem was that the government most feared high-explosive bombs and gas attacks (nobody realised that the most destructive weapon would be the incendiary bomb). The government was against deep shelters because of the risk if the shelters were hit. It also feared that the population would simply hide in them and not get on with the war effort. Critics also pointed out that deep shelters were costly, and that the main people to benefit would be the poor in the densely packed areas of the cities (who would not have contributed as much as others to the cost).

Two million Anderson shelters (see Source 27) were provided, along with a government grant to encourage people to build them. The Anderson shelters undoubtedly saved thousands of lives by protecting people from shrapnel and flying glass. However, they had serious weaknesses and were not much protection from falling masonry. In 1939 Stepney Councillor Phil Piratin set up an Anderson shelter outside the War Department in London and got a boxer to punch a hole in the shelter to make his point.

Many poorer people had no gardens in which to build Anderson shelters. The government provided 500,000 Morrison shelters from 1941. These could be set up indoors, usually under the stairs.

Black-out

Another feature of the air-defence measures was the black-out. Homes had to black out, but so did shops, businesses and even trains and cars. The number of road accidents doubled in September 1939, but in time people got used to operating in the black-out.

SOURCE 30

UNTIL YOUR EYES GET USED TO THE DARKNESS, TAKE IT EASY

LOOK OUT IN THE BLACKOUT

A wartime black-out poster.

The Blitz in Britain

What was the Blitz?

'Blitz' means a heavy bombing attack from the air. (The word is a shortened form of the German *Blitzkrieg* – lightning war.) Sometimes people use the word specifically to describe the German air raids on London in 1940, but many other British cities were also blitzed. Even after Hitler had called off his invasion plans, he still thought that Britain could be bombed into submission.

Bombing

★ Bombing was supposedly targeted at military or industrial targets. Civilian areas were often hit by accident. However, there was also terror bombing of civilian populations by both sides.
★ German bombers used three main types of bombs: high explosives (HE), parachute mines and incendiaries.
★ High-explosive bombs exploded on impact or more usually with a timed fuse.
★ Parachute mines floated down by parachute. Designed to tear apart concrete and steel buildings (e.g. workshops), they caused great destruction. The government did not acknowledge that they existed until 1944.
★ Incendiary bombs were a bit like fireworks. They were dropped in huge numbers to start fires.

1 Write your own definition of Blitz.
2 Why did politicians think civilians would give in under attack? Do you think this was a case of lack of experience or lack of respect for their own people?

SOURCE 31

7 Oct 1940
We must continue to attack England on all fronts.
11 Oct 1940
We shall be able to force England to her knees during the next few weeks.
12 Oct 1940
Horrific reports from London. A metropolis on the slide. An international drama without parallel, but we must see it through.
23 Oct 1940
We shall battle on remorselessly to destroy their last hope.
1 Nov 1940
The Führer intends to keep hammering the English until they break.
5 Dec 1940
Things must continue until England falls to her knees and begs for peace.

Extracts from the diary of Joseph Goebbels, one of the most senior Nazis.

In fact, this view was widely held by most politicians. It was thought that civilian populations would not be able to withstand the onslaught of aerial attack and would demand peace. Britain's major cities suffered heavy bombing from the autumn of 1940 to May 1941. Military and industrial centres were usually the targets, but all too often civilians were the victims. As it turned out, theories about civilian bombing proved to be completely wrong in both Britain and Germany. If anything, bombing seemed to increase determination to resist.

The Blitz began on 7 September 1940, with a large raid on London. London suffered far more attacks than any other city. The bombers returned every night until 2 November, and then occasional raids hit London up to June 1941. The target for the first raids was the East End, with its docks and factories. This was also a densely populated area. As the Blitz went on, the rest of London was hit, including Buckingham Palace and St Paul's Cathedral.

London was not the only target. Towns in the south – Bristol, Southampton, Portsmouth – were attacked because of their dockyards. Coventry was devastated in November 1940 and other targets in the midlands were hit. The north-west, and Manchester in particular, was attacked in December 1940. Liverpool was attacked regularly and in May 1941 suffered the biggest single raid on a mainland city. Belfast was also hit, with shattering consequences, in 1941.

The impact of the Blitz

The impact of the Blitz should not be underestimated. In the Blitz, Britain suffered more civilian than military casualties. In each week of September 1940, 40,000 to 50,000 people lost their homes. In November, 4500 people were killed and thousands more injured. In London alone, 12,500 died in December. In Liverpool the biggest raid, on 3 May 1941, involved 500 bombers. Fires burnt out of control because water mains were hit. The city lost some of its finest buildings. A freighter, the SS *Malakand*, carrying 1000 tons of explosives, received a direct hit and the noise was heard over 30 km away. The docks around the ship were devastated, as were the tightly packed terraced homes of the people who lived and worked around the docks.

SOURCE 32

	Killed	Injured
Aug 1940	37	73
Sept	221	357
Oct	106	90
Nov	305	192
Dec	412	382
Jan 1941	43	23
Feb	2	7
Mar	101	99
Apr	36	105
May	1453	1065

Casualties in Liverpool, 1940–41. The city's port, docks and warehouses made it an obvious target for bombs. The nearby chemical factories in Widnes and Runcorn were also attacked.

3 Do the raids appear to have been against civilian or military targets?

4 Why is it difficult to answer question 3?

There were similar stories elsewhere. In September 1940 there was a firestorm in London just as devastating as those that would hit Hamburg, Dresden and other German cities in 1943–45 (see page 290). Coventry was hit by 30,000 incendiary bombs on one November night and the city centre was almost destroyed (see Sources 36–37). People were so terrified that they fled the city each night, sleeping with relatives or in farmers' barns or just camping in open fields. Glasgow and the Clyde shipyard towns were hit hard in the spring of 1941. Belfast was devastated in April and May 1941. At least 1000 people were killed and 150,000 made homeless. Shipbuilding took six months to recover, and German pilots observing the raid described the whole city as a sea of flame.

Other smaller towns and cities were hit in 1941–42 in the so called Baedeker raids. (The targets were chosen by the Germans from the Baedeker tourist guide book.) The cathedral cities of Canterbury and Norwich were among those hit.

There were further air attacks in 1944–45 from the V-1 and V-2 missiles (see page 294). Six thousand V-1 bombs actually reached targets in Britain, causing 20,000 casualties and considerable damage to houses (which were in short supply). The V-2 was a more fearsome weapon than the V-1. Because it was so fast, it could not be shot down or even seen. Around 500 V-2s hit London between September 1944 and March 1945, causing 9000 casualties.

SOURCE 33

Artificial eyes for those who had lost their eyes in the fighting or bombing.

SOURCE 34

A school playground in Catford, London, hit by a bomb.

SOURCE 35

St Paul's Cathedral during the Blitz, December 1940. This is one of the most famous pictures of the war.

5 Why do you think that so many newspapers used Source 35 when covering the London Blitz?

SOURCE 36

Tuesday 14 January

Jack was going to pick up a new battery for the car at the Rover Company, and so I went with him to Coventry. It was not long after reaching the outskirts of the city that we saw evidence of the raiders' visit, and as we drew nearer the damage became greater. We went along Trinity Street and saw the devastated Rex Cinema, bombed twice over, and the other buildings near with all the windows blown out and boarded up. The old stone Grammar School had lost its windows, too, and was pitted and blackened and the Hospital seemed much more damaged than we expected, with its windows all out. St Mark's Church opposite had suffered a good deal. Most decidedly not indiscriminate bombing, but deliberate bombing of non-military objectives guaranteed, as the German brutes think, to cow and terrify the ordinary citizen into fright and subjection.

From *Mrs Milburn's Diaries*, about six weeks after the raid on Coventry.

SOURCE 37

The devastation after the fire-bombing of residential areas in Coventry, November 1940.

SOURCE 38

The centre of Coventry one year after the raid.

1 Explain why Sources 36–38 are more effective as historical evidence when used together than separately.

ACTIVITY

As you read on pages 290–91, Britain pursued its own heavy bombing campaign against Germany from 1942 onwards. Opinion in Britain was divided about the idea.

A Some supported the bombing of Germany because of what had been done to British cities.

B Some opposed it because it might bring German retaliation.

C Others opposed it because they did not want Britain to be responsible for the same suffering as the Germans had caused.

Work in pairs or small groups.

1 Look at Sources 33–39 and decide how far each could be used to support or oppose views A–C.
2 Which sources could be used to support more than one view? Does this make them unreliable?
3 If you had been alive in 1942, which view would you have supported and why?

SOURCE 39

The church was a popular shelter. People felt that nowhere would they be safer than under the protection of the Church – so it was full when the bomb fell. The bomb had burst in the middle of the shelter. The scene resembled a massacre with bodies, limbs, blood and flesh mingled with little hats, coats and shoes. The people were literally blown to pieces. The work of the ARP services was magnificent – by nine o'clock all the casualties were out . . .

After a heavy raid there was the task of piecing the bodies together in preparation for burial. The stench was the worst thing about it – that, and having to realise that these frightful pieces of flesh had once been living, breathing people. It became a grim and ghastly satisfaction when a body was reconstructed – but if one was too lavish in making one body almost whole, then one would have sad gaps. There were always odd limbs which did not fit, and there were too many legs. Unless we kept a very firm grip on ourselves nausea was inevitable.

A first-hand account of the Blitz, by a member of a first-aid post, 14 September 1940.

SOURCE **40**

The presence of a common enemy must have helped Britons feel more united than ever before, but too much emphasis can be put on this. Class distinctions were certainly not totally eradicated: and, as George Orwell once noted, the hardships of rationing were 'to put it mildly, tempered for anyone with over £2000 a year'. He also noted that you could only get an important job if you talked with the right accent. Nor does the image of a united nation take account of the black market that flourished during the war or of looting or of the crime rate, which jumped in 1940 and remained high throughout the war.

Robert Pearce, *Contemporary Britain 1914–79*, published in 1996.

The Spirit of the Blitz

Newspapers and radio broadcasts covered the Blitz in depth. They lost no opportunity to stress the villainous nature of the Nazi attackers. They also talked about a Blitz Spirit. According to the 'Blitz Spirit', everyone was determined to resist Hitler. Everyone was cheerful in the face of adversity. The London Underground was full of jolly singing as people sheltered from the bombs. Everyone trusted the government and everyone was determined to defeat the enemy by continuing to do their bit for the war effort.

Today, we have learned to treat such stories with scepticism. How real was the Spirit of the Blitz? There is not much doubt that industrial production, even in Coventry factories, started again very quickly. In Clydebank, near Glasgow, the munitions factory began work again even though the town was uninhabitable. But how well did morale hold up?

SOURCE **41**

Children sleeping in an Underground shelter. The shelters were often packed. Electricity to the lines was switched off at 10.30p.m. and adults would sleep in the filthy bay between the lines.

SOURCE **43**

Imagine a typical suburban street, which had lived by the golden rule of 'keeping itself to itself', suddenly being plunged into forming warden and first aid posts, savings groups, fire watching teams, make-do-and-mend parties; and, when coal grew scarce, sharing the cooking and evening fires. No wonder that within weeks of continuous raids, communities were forged whose friendship and loyalty was so absolute that they not only survived the worst that the enemy could throw at them, but emerged with a faith in each other that was as unexpected as it was inspiring.

From *Talking About the War* by Anne Valery, 1991.

SOURCE **42**

King George VI and Queen Elizabeth visiting people sheltering in the Underground. When Buckingham Palace was bombed, the Queen said that she was glad: 'It makes me feel that I can look the East End in the face.' The royal family remained in London throughout the Blitz, although many other wealthy families moved out or left Britain altogether.

SOURCE 44

The press versions of life going on normally in the East End are grotesque. There was no bread, no electricity, no milk, no gas, no telephones. There was every excuse for people to be distressed. There was no understanding in the huge buildings of central London for the tiny crumbled streets of densely massed population.

A report from the East End of London, September 1940.

SOURCE 45

Of the Blitz I shall write little. We in 'S' Division were luckier than many London police, but we still had our fill of its cruelty and horror, its sickening destructiveness, its white dusty filth, and its peculiar stink of fresh decay. Just these few words and it begins to depress me again.

From the autobiography of T Clarke, a special constable in the Blitz, published in 1974.

SOURCE 46

[A hotel in Donegal is] almost the last place in Europe where the lights are still alight . . . Last year it was only half-full and those wearing evening dress were in a minority. This year it is crowded out mainly with Belfast's wealthier citizens and about 75 per cent are in evening wear. In fact the display of jewellery and furs is terrific.

From the diary of Moya Woodside, 1941.

SOURCE 47

Will the Right Hon member come with me to the hills and to Divis mountain? Will he go to the barns and sheughs [ditches] throughout Northern Ireland to see the people of Belfast, some of them lying on damp ground? Will he come to Hannahstown and the Falls Road? The Catholics and Protestants are going up there mixed and they are talking to one another. They are sleeping in the same sheugh, below the same tree or in the same barn. They all say the same thing, that the government is no good.

Tommy Henderson, an enormously popular figure and Stormont MP for the Protestant Shankill area of Belfast, criticising the Northern Ireland Prime Minister John Andrews in a debate, 13 May 1941.

FOCUS TASK

SOURCE 48

During the winter and spring of 1940–41 German bombers raided the industrial areas, towns and ports of Britain, day and night, and the awe-struck world wondered for how long the British people could take it. But the nation had something more than its stiff-upper-lip courage to keep it going. Britain had the most inspired war leader this country has ever produced, Winston Churchill. His commanding, bull-dog spirit, his brilliant gift of fiery eloquence and his superb skill in the strategy of war, time and again rallied the people and brought them through the terrifying experiences of this war.

From *History of the World for Young Readers*, 1965.

Source 48 is a classic example of the 'Blitz Spirit' interpretation of the Second World War. You are going to consider how far this view fits the sources you have studied on pages 312–316.

1 On a copy of Source 48 underline or highlight all the words or phrases that
   a) help build an impression of the 'Blitz Spirit'
   b) help explain why spirits remained high.
2 Around the edge of the source summarise any ideas from pages 301–16 which contradict this interpretation.
3 Work in groups to discuss whether each of these statements is true or false:
   • 'Any one version of history is bound to miss out somebody's experience – we can't all have the same experience.'
   • 'The Spirit of the Blitz view is not wrong, just incomplete.'
   • 'Sources that don't support the Blitz Spirit view are just one-offs.'
   Be sure to support your opinions with evidence.

SECTION 4

International relations 1945–1990

The beginnings of the Cold War: 1945–1949

Who was to blame?

FOCUS

In May 1945 American troops entered Berlin from the west, as Russian troops moved in from the east. They met and celebrated victory together. Yet three years later these former allies were arguing over Berlin and war between them seemed a real possibility. What had gone wrong?

In this chapter you will consider:

■ how the wartime alliance between the USA and the USSR broke down
■ how the Soviet Union gained control over eastern Europe and how the USA responded
■ the consequences of the Berlin Blockade in 1948.

Finally, you will make up your own mind as to whether the USA or the USSR was more to blame for the outbreak of the Cold War.

Timeline

This timeline summarises the key events you will be looking at in this chapter. As you study the chapter, add details to your own copy of the timeline.

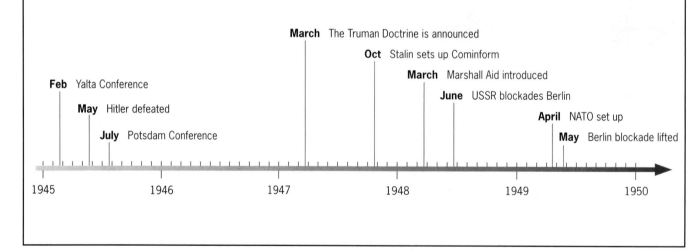

March The Truman Doctrine is announced
Oct Stalin sets up Cominform
March Marshall Aid introduced
June USSR blockades Berlin
Feb Yalta Conference
May Hitler defeated
July Potsdam Conference
April NATO set up
May Berlin blockade lifted

1945　1946　1947　1948　1949　1950

The Yalta Conference, February 1945

In February 1945 it was clear that Germany was losing the European war, so the Allied leaders met at Yalta in the Ukraine to plan what would happen to Europe after Germany's defeat. The Yalta Conference went well. Despite their differences, the Big Three – Stalin, Roosevelt and Churchill – agreed on some important matters.

- Stalin agreed to enter the war against Japan once Germany had surrendered.
- They agreed that Germany would be divided into four zones: American, French, British and Soviet. Since the German capital, Berlin, was deep in the Soviet zone, it was agreed that Berlin itself would also be divided into four zones.

SOURCE 1

The Big Three: Churchill, Roosevelt and Stalin at Yalta, February 1945.

1 Choose two points of agreement from the list and explain why they were significant for the future peace of Europe.

- As Allied soldiers advanced through Germany, they were revealing the horrors of the Nazi concentration camps. The Big Three agreed to hunt down and punish war criminals who were responsible for the genocide.
- They agreed that as countries were liberated from occupation by the German army, they would be allowed to hold free elections to choose the government they wanted.
- The Big Three all agreed to join the new United Nations Organisation, which would aim to keep peace after the war.
- The Soviet Union had suffered terribly in the war. An estimated 20 million Soviet people had died. Stalin was therefore concerned about the future security of the USSR. The Big Three agreed that eastern Europe should be seen as 'a Soviet sphere of influence'.
- The only real disagreement was about Poland. Stalin wanted the border of the USSR to move westwards into Poland (see Source 14 on page 322). Stalin argued that Poland, in turn, could move its border westwards into German territory. Churchill did not approve of Stalin's plans for Poland, but he also knew that there was not very much he could do about it because Stalin's Red Army was in total control of both Poland and eastern Germany. Roosevelt was also unhappy about Stalin's plan, but Churchill persuaded Roosevelt to accept it, as long as the USSR agreed not to interfere in Greece where the British were attempting to prevent the Communists taking over. Stalin accepted this. It seemed that, although they could not all agree, they were still able to negotiate and do business with one another.

SOURCE 2

I want to drink to our alliance, that it should not lose its . . . intimacy, its free expression of views . . . I know of no such close alliance of three Great Powers as this . . . May it be strong and stable, may we be as frank as possible.

Stalin, proposing a toast at a dinner at the Yalta Conference, 1945.

SOURCE 4

In the hallway [at Yalta] we stopped before a map of the world on which the Soviet Union was coloured in red. Stalin waved his hand over the Soviet Union and exclaimed, 'They [Roosevelt and Churchill] will never accept the idea that so great a space should be red, never, never!'

Milovan Djilas writing about Yalta in 1948.

SOURCE 6

The Soviet Union has become a danger to the free world. A new front must be created against her onward sweep. This front should be as far east as possible. A settlement must be reached on all major issues between West and East in Europe before the armies of democracy melt.

Churchill writing to Roosevelt shortly after the Yalta Conference.

SOURCE 8

[At Yalta] Churchill feared that Roosevelt was too pro-Russian. He pressed for a French zone to be added to the other three to add another anti-Russian voice to the armies of occupation.

Written by Christopher Culpin in a school textbook, *The Modern World*, 1984.

FOCUS TASK

What was going on behind the scenes at Yalta?

The war against Hitler had united Roosevelt, Stalin and Churchill and at the Yalta Conference they appeared to get on well. Source 2 illustrates the 'public' face of Yalta. But what was going on behind the scenes? Sources 3–11 will help you decide.

1 Use a table like this to analyse the sources.

Evidence for disagreement	Evidence for agreement	Reasons why the source is reliable or unreliable

SOURCE 3

Perhaps you think that just because we are the allies of the English we have forgotten who they are and who Churchill is. There's nothing they like better than to trick their allies. During the First World War they constantly tricked the Russians and the French. And Churchill? Churchill is the kind of man who will pick your pocket of a kopeck! [A kopeck is a low value Soviet coin.] And Roosevelt? Roosevelt is not like that. He dips in his hand only for bigger coins. But Churchill? He will do it for a kopeck.

Stalin speaking to a fellow Communist, Milovan Djilas, in 1945. Djilas was a supporter of Stalin.

SOURCE 5

Once, Churchill asked Stalin to send him the music of the new Soviet Russian anthem so that it could be broadcast before the summary of the news from the Soviet German front. Stalin sent the words [as well] and expressed the hope that Churchill would set about learning the new tune and whistling it to members of the Conservative Party. While Stalin behaved with relative discretion with Roosevelt, he continually teased Churchill throughout the war.

Written by Soviet historian Sergei Kudryashov after the war.

SOURCE 7

A Soviet cartoon. Churchill is shown with two flags, the first proclaiming that 'Anglo-Saxons must rule the world' and the other threatening an 'iron curtain'.

ACTIVITY

Work in pairs.

One of you produce a press release from the Yalta Conference to be sent to newspapers in Britain. The other produce a confidential note to the government in Britain outlining any problems at Yalta that you think they should know about.

SOURCE 9

One could see that Churchill had left a deep impression on the Soviet leaders as a farsighted and dangerous statesman – although they did not like him.

Milovan Djilas comments, in 1948, on Stalin's assessment of Churchill.

SOURCE 10

[In May 1945] Churchill ordered Montgomery to keep the German arms intact, in case they had to be used against the Russians.

Written by historian Hugh Higgins in *The Cold War*, 1974.

SOURCE 11

One night Stalin stung Churchill when proposing a toast by reminding Churchill of his failures at Gallipoli in the First World War.

Another night Churchill declared (whilst slightly drunk) that he deserved a medal for teaching the Soviet army to fight so well through the intervention at Archangel.

The Soviet Foreign Minister Molotov writing about Yalta. In 1915 Churchill had been responsible for a failed attack at Gallipoli (see page 38). In 1918 Churchill had supported the British decision to send troops to Archangel to help in the fight against the Communists in the Russian Civil War (see page 118).

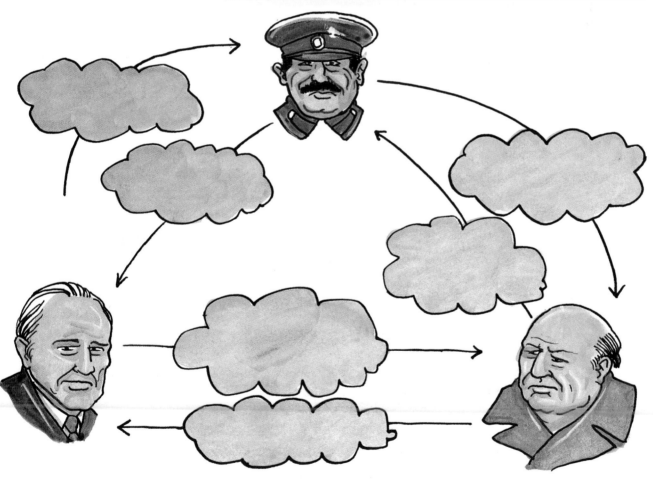

2 Draw a diagram like this and use Sources 2–11 to summarise what each of the leaders thought of the other.
3 Is it possible to tell from these extracts what Stalin and Churchill really felt about each other? Explain your answer.
4 How do Sources 2–11 affect your impression of the Yalta Conference?
5 Write three sentences to sum up the main concerns of each of the Big Three at Yalta. Use the text and Sources 2–11.

The Potsdam Conference, July–August 1945

In May 1945, three months after the Yalta Conference, Allied troops reached Berlin. Hitler committed suicide. Germany surrendered. The war in Europe was won.

1 Source 12 is to be used in a newspaper in April 1945. Write a caption to go with it.

SOURCE 12

American and Soviet soldiers shake hands in April 1945.

SOURCE 13

This war is not as in the past; whoever occupies a territory also imposes on it his own social system. Everyone imposes his own system as far as his army has power to do so. It cannot be otherwise.

Stalin speaking, soon after the end of the Second World War, about the take-over of eastern Europe.

SOURCE 14

Poland has borders with the Soviet Union which is not the case with Great Britain or the USA. I do not know whether a truly representative government has been established in Greece. The Soviet Union was not consulted when this government was being formed, nor did it claim the right to interfere because it realises how important Greece is to the security of Great Britain.

Stalin, replying to Allied leaders about his plans for Poland in April 1945. Britain had helped to prop up an anti-Communist government in Greece (see page 328).

A second conference of the Allied leaders was arranged for July 1945 in the Berlin suburb of Potsdam. However, in the five months since Yalta a number of changes had taken place which would greatly affect relationships between the leaders.

1 Stalin's armies were occupying most of eastern Europe

Soviet troops had liberated country after country in eastern Europe, but instead of withdrawing his troops Stalin had left them there. By July, Stalin's troops effectively controlled the Baltic states, Finland, Poland, Czechoslovakia, Hungary, Bulgaria and Romania, and refugees were fleeing out of these countries fearing a Communist take-over. Stalin had set up a Communist government in Poland, ignoring the wishes of the majority of Poles. Britain and the USA protested, but Stalin defended his action (see Source 14). He insisted that his control of eastern Europe was a defensive measure against possible future attacks (see Source 17).

2 America had a new president

On 12 April 1945, President Roosevelt died. He was replaced by his Vice-President, Harry Truman. Truman was a very different man from Roosevelt. He was much more anti-Communist than Roosevelt and was very suspicious of Stalin. Truman and his advisers saw Soviet actions in eastern Europe as preparations for a Soviet take-over of the rest of Europe.

3 The Allies had tested an atomic bomb

On 16 July 1945 the Americans successfully tested an atomic bomb at a desert site in the USA. At the start of the Potsdam Conference, Truman informed Stalin about it.

2 Read Source 13. At Yalta, Churchill and Roosevelt had agreed with Stalin that eastern Europe would be a Soviet 'sphere of influence'. Do you think Source 13 is what they had in mind?

3 Would they agree with Stalin's views expressed in Sources 13 and 14? Explain your answer.

4 Explain how each of the three developments described in the text might affect relationships at Potsdam.

Disagreements at Potsdam

The Potsdam Conference finally got under way on 17 July 1945. Not surprisingly, it did not go as smoothly as Yalta.

In July there was an election in Britain. Churchill was defeated, so half way through the conference he was replaced by a new Prime Minister, Clement Attlee. In the absence of Churchill, the conference was dominated by rivalry and suspicion between Stalin and Truman. A number of issues arose on which neither side seemed able to appreciate the other's point of view.

- **They disagreed over what to do about Germany.** Stalin wanted to cripple Germany completely to protect the USSR against future threats. Truman did not want to repeat the mistake of the Treaty of Versailles.
- **They disagreed over reparations.** Twenty million Russians had died in the war and the Soviet Union had been devastated. Stalin wanted compensation from Germany. Truman, however, was once again determined not to repeat the mistakes at the end of the First World War and resisted this demand.
- **They disagreed over Soviet policy in eastern Europe.** At Yalta, Stalin had won agreement from the Allies that he could set up pro-Soviet governments in eastern Europe. He said, 'If the Slav [the majority of east European] people are united, no one will dare move a finger against them.' Truman became very unhappy about Russian intentions and soon adopted a 'get tough' attitude towards Stalin.

The 'iron curtain'

The Potsdam Conference ended without complete agreement on these issues. Over the next nine months, Stalin achieved the domination of eastern Europe that he was seeking. By 1946 Poland, Hungary, Romania, Bulgaria and Albania all had Communist governments which owed their loyalty to Stalin. Churchill described the border between Soviet-controlled countries and the West as an iron curtain (see Source 16). The name stuck.

5 How do Sources 16 and 17 differ in their interpretation of Stalin's actions?
6 Explain why they see things so differently.

SOURCE 15

NO ADMITTANCE BY ORDER JOE

EUROPE

A British cartoon commenting on Churchill's 'Iron Curtain' speech, in the *Daily Mail*, 6 March 1946.

SOURCE 16

A shadow has fallen upon the scenes so lately lighted by the Allied victory. From Stettin on the Baltic to Trieste on the Adriatic, an iron curtain has descended. Behind that line lie all the states of central and eastern Europe. The Communist parties have been raised to power far beyond their numbers and are seeking everywhere to obtain totalitarian control. This is certainly not the liberated Europe we fought to build. Nor is it one which allows permanent peace.

Winston Churchill speaking in the USA, in the presence of President Truman, March 1946.

SOURCE 17

The following circumstances should not be forgotten. The Germans made their invasion of the USSR through Finland, Poland and Romania. The Germans were able to make their invasion through these countries because, at the time, governments hostile to the Soviet Union existed in these countries. What can there be surprising about the fact that the Soviet Union, anxious for its future safety, is trying to see to it that governments loyal in their attitude to the Soviet Union should exist in these countries?

Stalin, replying to Churchill's speech (Source 16).

SOURCE 18

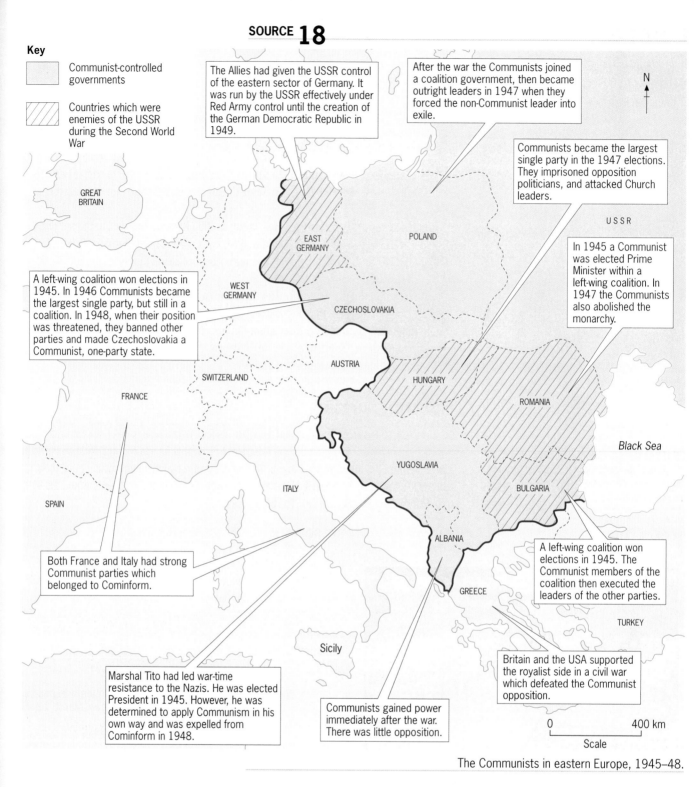

Key

Communist-controlled governments

Countries which were enemies of the USSR during the Second World War

The Allies had given the USSR control of the eastern sector of Germany. It was run by the USSR effectively under Red Army control until the creation of the German Democratic Republic in 1949.

After the war the Communists joined a coalition government, then became outright leaders in 1947 when they forced the non-Communist leader into exile.

Communists became the largest single party in the 1947 elections. They imprisoned opposition politicians, and attacked Church leaders.

In 1945 a Communist was elected Prime Minister within a left-wing coalition. In 1947 the Communists also abolished the monarchy.

A left-wing coalition won elections in 1945. In 1946 Communists became the largest single party, but still in a coalition. In 1948, when their position was threatened, they banned other parties and made Czechoslovakia a Communist, one-party state.

Both France and Italy had strong Communist parties which belonged to Cominform.

A left-wing coalition won elections in 1945. The Communist members of the coalition then executed the leaders of the other parties.

Marshal Tito had led war-time resistance to the Nazis. He was elected President in 1945. However, he was determined to apply Communism in his own way and was expelled from Cominform in 1948.

Communists gained power immediately after the war. There was little opposition.

Britain and the USA supported the royalist side in a civil war which defeated the Communist opposition.

GREAT BRITAIN · EAST GERMANY · POLAND · USSR · WEST GERMANY · CZECHOSLOVAKIA · AUSTRIA · HUNGARY · ROMANIA · SWITZERLAND · FRANCE · YUGOSLAVIA · Black Sea · ITALY · BULGARIA · SPAIN · ALBANIA · GREECE · TURKEY · Sicily

0   400 km

Scale

The Communists in eastern Europe, 1945–48.

Stalin tightens his control

With Communist governments established throughout eastern Europe, Stalin gradually tightened his control in each country. The secret police imprisoned anyone who opposed Communist rule, or might oppose it at a later date.

In October 1947, Stalin set up the Communist Information Bureau, or Cominform, to co-ordinate the work of the Communist Parties of eastern Europe. Cominform regularly brought the leaders of each Communist Party to Moscow to be briefed by Stalin and his ministers. This also allowed Stalin to keep a close eye on them. He spotted independent-minded leaders and replaced them with people who were completely loyal to him. The only Communist leader who escaped this close control was Tito in Yugoslavia. He resented being controlled by Cominform and was expelled for his hostility in 1948.

1 Study Source 18 and make a list of the actions that Communists took to achieve power in eastern Europe.
2 Explain how each factor helped.

The Cold War

SOURCE 19

Unless Russia is faced with an iron fist and strong language another war is in the making. Only one language do they understand – 'how many [army] divisions have you got?' . . . I'm tired of babying the Soviets.

President Truman, writing to his Secretary of State in January 1946.

It was clear by 1946 that the wartime friendship between the Allies had broken down. It had been replaced by suspicion and accusation.

Source 19 was written in a confidential letter. However, the distrust between the USA and the USSR was soon so great that leaders were talking in public about the threat of war between the two countries. Instead of running down arms expenditure after the war, as you would expect them to, the two sides actually increased their stock of weapons.

SOURCE 20

A Soviet cartoon of 1947. The 'ordinary American' is asking the American General Eisenhower why there is so much American military activity focused in an uninhabited area. The General says: 'Can't you see the enormous concentration of enemy forces right here?'

3 Write your own definition of the term 'Cold War' as it might appear in a historical dictionary.
4 Look at Source 21. What point is the cartoonist making about the alliance?

Each side took every opportunity to denounce the policies or the plans of the other. A propaganda war developed. In this atmosphere of tension and recrimination, people began to talk about a Cold War. This Cold War was going to last for 30 years and would dominate relations between the countries for much of that time.

SOURCE 21

A British cartoon from 1941.

Why was the USA so worried about Communism?

Roosevelt and Stalin had got on surprisingly well as individuals, but the wartime alliance of the USSR and the USA had always been an unlikely friendship. It was really only the war that held their alliance together.

The USA and the USSR had little in common as countries and their leaders had different beliefs and ideas. Before the war, they had distrusted each other very greatly. Many Soviets still remembered that US troops had been sent to fight against the Communists in Russia's Civil War, 1918–21 (see page 118). As for the Americans, opinion polls before the war in the USA showed that Americans trusted Communists less than Nazis. The USA had been appalled when Stalin signed his pact with Hitler in 1939. Even during the war the Americans had not really supported Stalin's war effort as he wished. They had not sent troops to help him hold back Hitler in the Soviet Union.

FACTFILE

The USA

★ The USA was a democracy. Its government was chosen in free democratic elections.

★ It was capitalist. Business and property were privately owned.

★ It was the world's wealthiest country. But, as in most capitalist countries, there were extremes – some great wealth and great poverty as well.

★ For Americans, being free of control by the government was more important than everyone being equal.

★ Americans firmly believed that other countries should be run in the American way.

★ Many Americans were bitterly opposed to Communism.

FACTFILE

The USSR

★ The USSR was a Communist state.

★ It was a one-party dictatorship. Elections were held, but all candidates belonged to the Communist Party.

★ It was an economic superpower because its industry had grown rapidly in the 1920s and 1930s, but the general standard of living in the USSR was much lower than in the USA. Even so, unemployment was rare and extreme poverty was rarer than in the USA.

★ For Communists, the rights of individuals were seen as less important than the good of society as a whole. So individuals' lives were tightly controlled.

★ Soviet leaders believed that other countries should be run in the Communist way.

★ Many people in the USSR were bitterly opposed to capitalism.

1 Make your own copies of the diagrams below and then use the Factfiles to make notes around them summarising the two systems.

USSR – COMMUNIST

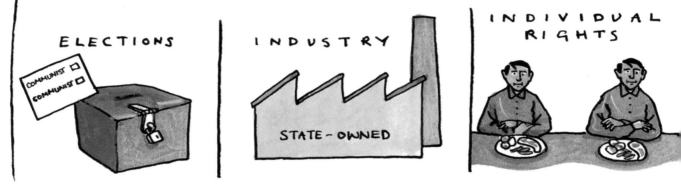

USA – CAPITALIST AND DEMOCRATIC

OURS to fight for...

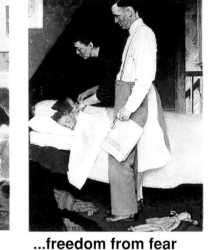

...freedom of speech

...freedom of worship

...freedom from want

...freedom from fear

Reconstruction of an American poster advertising the Four Freedoms.

2 Look at Source 22. Which of these freedoms do you think the Soviet Union would also believe in? Which would it think unimportant?
3 Design an equivalent poster for the USSR advertising its beliefs.

FOCUS TASK

How did the USSR gain control of eastern Europe?

It is 1948. Produce a briefing paper to update President Truman on the situation in eastern Europe. Your report should mention:
• the Communist successes in eastern Europe between 1945 and 1948 and the reasons for them
• Stalin's plan for eastern Europe
• the methods being used by Stalin to control eastern Europe
• whether you think the USA should be worried.

The differing beliefs of the USA and the USSR go some way to explaining why the Cold War developed, but not all the way. After all, they had had these different beliefs in the 1920s and the 1930s and they had not entered into a Cold War. However, there were some important differences between the 1930s and the 1940s.

The USA and the USSR had emerged from the war as the two 'superpowers'. In the 1930s, other countries such as Britain and France had been as important in international affairs. However, the war had finally demoted Britain and France to a second division. They were not big enough, rich enough or strong enough to exercise real international leadership. Only the USA and the USSR were able to do this. They were the superpowers.

The USA was well aware that a responsibility was attached to being a superpower. In the 1930s, the USA had followed a policy of isolation – keeping out of European and world affairs. The Americans might have disapproved of Soviet Communism, but they tried not to get involved. However, by the 1940s the USA had learned a lesson. They did not want to repeat the mistakes they had made before the Second World War. Roosevelt had set the Americans firmly against a policy of isolation. In March 1945 he said to the American Congress that America 'will have to take the responsibility for world collaboration or we shall have to bear the responsibilities for another world conflict'. There would be no more appeasement of dictators. From now on, every Communist action would meet an American reaction.

The reaction of the West

The Western powers were alarmed by Stalin's take-over of eastern Europe. Roosevelt, Churchill and their successors had accepted that Soviet security needed friendly governments in eastern Europe. They had agreed that eastern Europe would be a Soviet 'sphere of influence' and that Stalin would heavily influence this region. However, they had not expected such complete Communist domination. They felt it should have been possible to have governments in eastern Europe that were both democratic and friendly to the USSR. Stalin saw his policy in eastern Europe as making himself secure, but Truman could only see the spread of Communism.

1 Do Sources 23 and 24 have the same message?

SOURCE 23

A French cartoon commenting on Stalin's take-over of eastern Europe. The dancing figure is Stalin.

SOURCE 24

An American cartoon commenting on Stalin's take-over of eastern Europe. The bear represents the USSR.

By 1948, Greece and Czechoslovakia were the only eastern European countries not controlled by Communist governments. It seemed to the Americans that not only Greece and Czechoslovakia but even Italy and France were vulnerable to Communist take-over. Events in two of these countries were to have a decisive effect on America's policy towards Europe.

Greece

When the Germans retreated from Greece in 1944, there were two rival groups – the monarchists and the Communists – who wanted to rule the country. Both had been involved in resistance against the Nazis. The Communists wanted Greece to be a Soviet republic. The monarchists wanted the return of the king of Greece. Churchill sent British troops to Greece in 1945 supposedly to help restore order and supervise free elections. In fact, the British supported the monarchists and the king was returned to power.

In 1946, the USSR protested to the United Nations that British troops were a threat to peace in Greece. The United Nations took no action and so the Communists tried to take control of Greece by force. A civil war quickly developed. The British could not afford the cost of such a war and announced on 24 February 1947 that they were withdrawing their troops. Truman stepped in. Paid for by the Americans, some British troops stayed in Greece. They tried to prop up the king's government. By 1950 the royalists were in control of Greece, although they were a very weak government, always in crisis.

ACTIVITY

Look at Sources 23 and 24. Design or describe a Soviet cartoon or poster commenting on the USSR's actions. It could either:
• attack the attitudes of the West
• justify and explain Soviet actions.

I believe that it must be the policy of the United States to support free peoples who are resisting attempted subjugation by armed minorities or by outside pressures . . . The free peoples of the world look to us for support in maintaining those freedoms. If we falter in our leadership, we may endanger the peace of the world.

President Truman speaking on 12 March 1947, explaining his decision to help Greece.

ACTIVITY

Make a poster summarising the Truman Doctrine in Source 25. Include a short caption.

The Truman Doctrine

American intervention in Greece marked a new era in the USA's attitude to world politics, which became known as 'the Truman Doctrine'.

Under the Truman Doctrine, the USA was prepared to send money, equipment and advice to any country which was, in the American view, threatened by a Communist take-over. Truman accepted that eastern Europe was now Communist. His aim was to stop Communism from spreading any further. This policy became known as CONTAINMENT.

Others thought containment should mean something firmer. They said that it must be made clear to the Soviet Union that expansion beyond a given limit would be met with military force.

Marshall Aid

Truman believed that Communism succeeded when people faced poverty and hardship. He sent the American General George Marshall to assess the economic state of Europe. What he found was a ruined economy. The countries of Europe owed $11.5 billion to the USA. There were extreme shortages of all goods. Most countries were still rationing bread. There was such a coal shortage in the hard winter of 1947 that in Britain all electricity was turned off for a period each day. Churchill described Europe as 'a rubble heap, a breeding ground of hate'.

SOURCE 26

Problems in post-war Europe.

Marshall suggested that about $17 billion would be needed to rebuild Europe's prosperity. 'Our policy', he said, 'is directed against hunger, poverty, desperation and chaos.'

In December 1947, Truman put his plan to Congress. For a short time, the American Congress refused to grant this money. Many Americans were becoming concerned by Truman's involvement in foreign affairs. Besides, $17 billion was a lot of money!

Czechoslovakia

2 Which of the problems shown in Source 26 do you think would be the most urgent for Marshall Aid to tackle? Explain your choice.
3 Explain how events in both Greece and Czechoslovakia affected American policy in Europe.

Americans' attitude changed when the Communists took over the government of Czechoslovakia. Czechoslovakia had been ruled by a coalition government which, although it included Communists, had been trying to pursue policies independent of Moscow. The Communists came down hard in March 1948. Anti-Soviet leaders were purged. One pro-American Minister, Jan Masaryk, was found dead below his open window. The Communists said he had jumped. The Americans suspected he'd been pushed. Immediately, Congress accepted the Marshall Plan and made $17 billion available over a period of four years.

329

1 Draw a diagram to summarise the aims of Marshall Aid. Put political aims on one side and economic aims on the other. Draw arrows and labels to show how the two are connected.

On the one hand, Marshall Aid was an extremely generous act by the American people. On the other hand, it was also motivated by American self-interest. They wanted to create new markets for American goods. The Americans remembered the disastrous effects of the Depression of the 1930s and Truman wanted to do all he could to prevent another worldwide slump.

Stalin viewed Marshall Aid with suspicion. After expressing some initial interest, he refused to have anything more to do with it. He also forbade any of the eastern European states to apply for Marshall Aid. Stalin's view was that the anti-Communist aims behind Marshall Aid would weaken his hold on eastern Europe. He also felt that the USA was trying to dominate as many states as possible by making them dependent on dollars.

SOURCE 27

An American cartoon, 1949.

SOURCE 28

A Soviet cartoon commenting on Marshall Aid. The rope is the 'Marshall Plan' and the lifebelt is 'Aid to Europe'.

2 Do Sources 27–29 support or criticise Marshall Aid?

3 Do you think the sources give a fair impression of Marshall Aid? Explain your answer.

SOURCE 29

A cartoon by David Low, June 1947. The figure on the left is Marshall. The figure nearer to him is Molotov, the Soviet Foreign Minister. Marshall is asking 'Which hand will you have, Comrade?'

FOCUS TASK

How did the USA react to Soviet expansion?

You are an adviser to Stalin. Write a briefing paper on the USA's plans for Europe. Your report should mention:
• President Truman's plans for Europe
• the methods being used by Truman to resist the spread of Communism
• whether you think the USSR should be worried.

Why did the Soviet Union blockade Berlin?

Despite all the threatening talk of the early years of the Cold War, the two sides had never actually fired on one another. But in 1948 they came dangerously close to war.

SOURCE 30

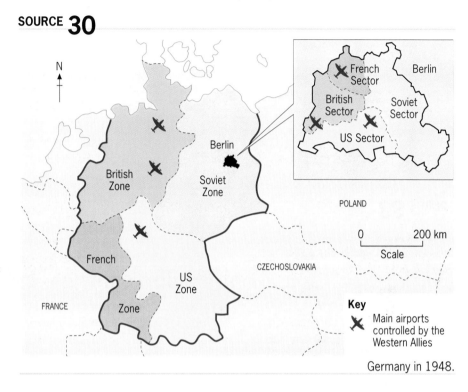

Germany in 1948.

Germany had become a real headache for the Western Allies. After the destruction of war, their zones were in economic chaos. Stalin feared a recovering Germany and wanted to keep it crippled. But it was clear to the Allies that Germany could not feed its people if it was not allowed to rebuild its industries. Although they themselves were wary of rebuilding Germany too quickly, Britain, France and the USA combined their zones in 1946 to form one zone (which became known in 1949 as West Germany; see page 334). In 1948 they reformed the currency and within months there were signs that Germany was recovering.

4 Look at the cartoons in Source 31. Do they make the same point?

SOURCE 31

Two cartoons from 1949. **A** is Soviet and **B** is British. In **A**, the documents on the ground are headed 'Occupation statutes' and 'Bonn constitution'. The caption to **B** is: 'If we don't let him work, who's going to keep him?'

SOURCE 32

On 23 June the Soviet authorities suspended all traffic into Berlin because of alleged technical difficulties . . . They also stopped barge traffic on similar grounds. Shortly before midnight, the Soviet authorities issued orders to . . . disrupt electric power from Soviet power plants to the Western sectors. Shortage of coal was given as a reason for this measure.

US Government report, June 1948.

SOURCE 33

The Berlin air-lift was a considerable achievement but neither side gained anything from the confrontation. The USSR had not gained control of Berlin. The West had no guarantees that land communications would not be cut again. Above all confrontation made both sides even more stubborn.

Historian Jack Watson writing in 1984.

SOURCE 34

The crisis was planned in Washington, behind a smokescreen of anti-Soviet propaganda. In 1948 there was danger of war. The conduct of the Western powers risked bloody incidents. The self-blockade of the Western powers hit the West Berlin population with harshness. The people were freezing and starving. In the Spring of 1949 the USA was forced to yield . . . their war plans had come to nothing, because of the conduct of the USSR.

A Soviet commentary on the crisis, quoted in P Fisher, *The Great Power Conflict*, a textbook published in 1985.

1 Read Source 32. What reasons did the Soviet Union give for cutting off West Berlin?
2 Why do you think the USA did not believe these were genuine reasons?
3 How do Sources 33–35 differ in their interpretation of the blockade?
4 Which do you think is the most useful source for a historian studying the Berlin Blockade?
5 Which source do you think gives the most reliable view of the blockade?

Stalin felt that the USA's handling of western Germany was provocative. He could do nothing about the reorganisation of the western zones, or the new currency, but he felt that he could stamp his authority on Berlin. It was deep in the Soviet zone and was linked to the western zones of Germany by vital roads, railways and canals. In June 1948, Stalin blocked all these supply lines, cutting off the two-million strong population of West Berlin from western help. Stalin believed that this would force the Allies out of Berlin and make Berlin entirely dependent on the USSR.

It was a clever plan. If US tanks did try to ram the road-blocks or railway blocks, Stalin would see it as an act of war. However, the Americans were not prepared to give up. They saw West Berlin as a test case. If they gave in to Stalin on this issue, the western zones of Germany might be next. Truman wanted to show that he was serious about his policy of containment. He wanted Berlin to be a symbol of freedom behind the Iron Curtain.

The only way into Berlin was by air. So in June 1948 the Allies decided to air-lift supplies. As the first planes took off from their bases in west Germany, everyone feared that the Soviets would shoot them down, which would have been an act of war. People waited anxiously as the planes flew over Soviet territory, but no shots were fired. The planes got through and for the next ten months West Berlin was supplied by a constant stream of aeroplanes bringing in everything from food and clothing to oil and building materials, although there were enormous shortages and many Berliners decided to leave the city altogether. By May 1949, however, it was clear that the blockade of Berlin would not make the Western Allies give up Berlin, so Stalin reopened communications.

SOURCE 35

We refused to be forced out of the city of Berlin. We demonstrated to the people of Europe that we would act and act resolutely, when their freedom was threatened. Politically it brought the people of Western Europe closer to us. The Berlin blockade was a move to test our ability and our will to resist.

President Truman, speaking in 1949.

SOURCE 36

Coal being unloaded from a plane at Berlin airport, 1948. For ten months, planes landed every three minutes throughout the day and night.

SOURCE 37

Article 3: To achieve the aims of this Treaty, the Parties will keep up their individual and collective capacity to resist armed attack.
Article 5: The Parties agree that an armed attack against one or more of them in Europe or North America shall be considered an attack against them all.

Extracts from the NATO Charter.

SOURCE 38

The Soviet government did everything it could to prevent the world from being split into two military blocks. The Soviet Union issued a special statement analysing the grave consequences affecting the entire international situation that would follow from the establishment of a military alliance of the Western powers. All these warnings failed, however, and the North Atlantic Alliance came into being.

Stalin commenting on the formation of NATO, 1949.

SOURCE 39

A 1963 Soviet cartoon. The dog's teeth are labelled NATO. He is about to attack the German Democratic Republic (East Germany; see page 334).

Why was NATO set up?

During the Berlin Blockade, war between the USSR and the USA seemed a real possibility. At the height of the crisis, the Western powers met in Washington and signed an agreement to work together. The new organisation they formed in April 1949 was known as NATO (North Atlantic Treaty Organisation).

SOURCE 40

A cartoon by David Low, 1949, entitled 'Your play, Joe'. Western leaders wait to see how Stalin will react to the formation of NATO.

SOURCE 41

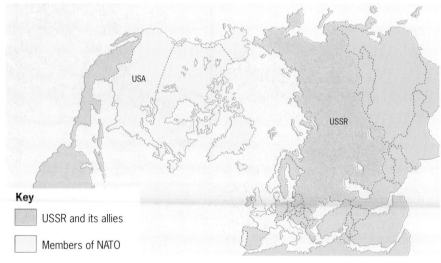

Key

USSR and its allies

Members of NATO

NATO and the Soviet satellites of eastern Europe. With the establishment of NATO, Europe was once again home to two hostile armed camps, just as it had been in 1914.

6 What evidence is there in Sources 37–41 to indicate that NATO was a purely defensive alliance?
7 Read Source 38. What 'grave consequences' do you think Stalin had in mind?

A divided Germany

As a result of the Berlin Blockade, Germany was firmly divided into two nations. In May 1949, the British, French and American zones became the Federal Republic of Germany (known as West Germany). The Communist eastern zone was formed into the German Democratic Republic (or East Germany) in October 1949.

A powerful symbol

Germany would stay a divided country for 41 years. Throughout that time Berlin would remain a powerful symbol of Cold War tensions – from the American point of view, an oasis of democratic freedom in the middle of Communist repression; from the Soviet point of view, an invasive cancer growing in the workers' paradise of East Germany.

SOURCE 42

A 1958 Soviet cartoon. A Soviet doctor is injecting the cancer (the 'Occupation regime' of the Western Allies) with a medicine called 'Free City Status for West Berlin'.

A flashpoint

Berlin was more than a symbol, however. It was also a potential flashpoint. As you study the story of the Cold War, you will find that the USA's and the USSR's worries about what might happen in Berlin affected their policies in other areas of the world. You will pick up the story of Berlin again in Chapter 14.

FOCUS TASK

It is difficult to give an exact date for when the Cold War actually started. Some might say that it was at Yalta, as Stalin, Churchill and Roosevelt argued over Poland, others that it started in 1948 with the Berlin Blockade. There are other possible starting dates as well between 1945 and 1948.

What do you think? As a class, list all the possible candidates you can think of. Then choose three to compare. Whatever your choice, support it with evidence from this chapter.

A pattern for the Cold War

Most importantly, the Berlin Blockade set out a pattern for Cold War confrontations. On the one hand, the two superpowers and their allies had shown how suspicious they were of each other; how they would obstruct each other in almost any way they could; how they would bombard each other with propaganda such as that in Sources 34 and 35. On the other hand, each had shown that it was not willing to go to war with the other. The Berlin Blockade established a sort of tense balance between the superpowers that was to characterise much of the Cold War period.

FOCUS TASK

Who was to blame for the Cold War?

Work in small groups. Five people per group would be ideal.

You are going to investigate who was to blame for the Cold War. The possible verdicts you might reach are:

A The USA was most to blame.
B The USSR was most to blame.
C Both sides were equally to blame.
D No one was to blame. The Cold War was inevitable.

This is our suggested way of working.

1 Start by discussing the verdicts together. Is one more popular than another in your group?
2 **a)** Each member of the group should research how one of the following factors helped to lead to the Cold War.
   • The personal relationships between the various leaders (pages 318–25).
   • The conflicting beliefs of the superpowers (pages 325–27).
   • The war damage suffered by the USSR (pages 319 and 323).
   • Stalin's take-over of eastern Europe (pages 322–24).
   • Marshall Aid for Europe (pages 329–30).
   You can start with the page numbers given. You can introduce your own research from other books or the internet if you wish.
   b) Present your evidence to your group and explain which, if any, of the verdicts A–D your evidence most supports.
3 As a group, discuss which of the verdicts now seems most sensible.
4 Write a balanced essay on who was to blame, explaining why each verdict is a possibility but reaching your own conclusion about which is best.

12 The Cold War 1950–1975

Did the USA manage to contain the spread of Communism?

FOCUS

The USA was strongly opposed to Communism. By 1949, it seemed to the American government that Communism might spread all around the world unless it did something to stop it. From the 1950s to the 1970s, American foreign policy was therefore directed to trying to contain or stop the spread of Communism.

In this chapter:

■ you will explore the different methods of containment used by the United States during the Korean War, the Cuban missile crisis and the Vietnam War
■ you will consider how each of these Cold War crises and the nuclear arms race affected relations between the superpowers
■ you will make up your own mind as to how successful the Americans were in containing the spread of Communism.

The Cold War

This timeline summarises some of the aspects of the Cold War that you will be studying in this chapter and in Chapter 14. In this chapter you will investigate what the USA was doing during the Cold War period. In Chapter 14 you will study what the USSR was doing. As the two chapters overlap in time, you will need to keep a clear overview of the period, so you will be asked to refer to this timeline at a number of stages as you proceed.

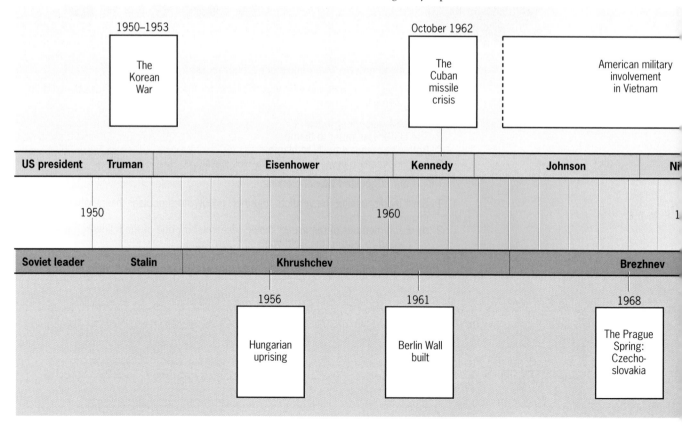

1950–1953		October 1962	
The Korean War		The Cuban missile crisis	American military involvement in Vietnam

US president	Truman	Eisenhower	Kennedy	Johnson	Ni

1950   1960   1

Soviet leader	Stalin	Khrushchev	Brezhnev

1956	1961	1968
Hungarian uprising	Berlin Wall built	The Prague Spring: Czecho-slovakia

Throughout the Cold War the superpowers:

- regularly argued with each other in the United Nations Assembly, where each side openly criticised the actions of the other
- sometimes criticised each other through their television programmes, newspapers, art and films
- sometimes threatened military confrontation with each other, although it never came to war
- commonly sent troops or advisers to help other states or groups to disrupt the aims and plans of their opponents.

The map below summarises some important clashes during the Cold War.

SOURCE 1

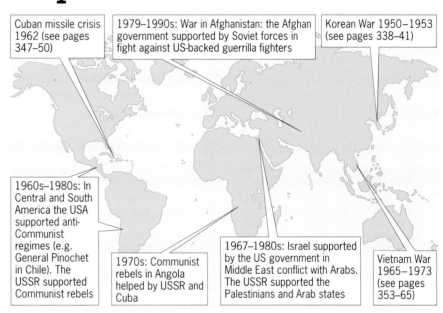

Cuban missile crisis 1962 (see pages 347–50)

1979–1990s: War in Afghanistan: the Afghan government supported by Soviet forces in fight against US-backed guerrilla fighters

Korean War 1950–1953 (see pages 338–41)

1960s–1980s: In Central and South America the USA supported anti-Communist regimes (e.g. General Pinochet in Chile). The USSR supported Communist rebels

1970s: Communist rebels in Angola helped by USSR and Cuba

1967–1980s: Israel supported by the US government in Middle East conflict with Arabs. The USSR supported the Palestinians and Arab states

Vietnam War 1965–1973 (see pages 353–65)

Clashes between the superpowers during the Cold War.

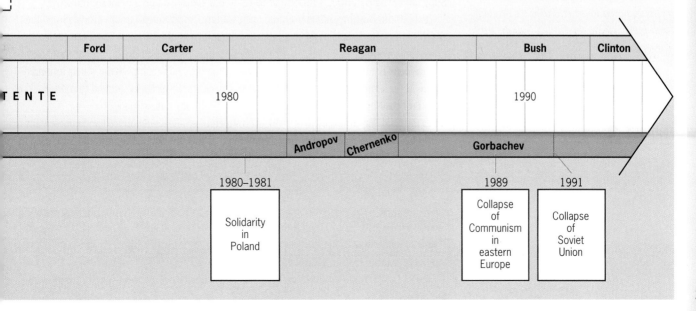

Ford | Carter | Reagan | Bush | Clinton

TENTE   1980   1990

Andropov | Chernenko | Gorbachev

1980–1981
Solidarity in Poland

1989
Collapse of Communism in eastern Europe

1991
Collapse of Soviet Union

Anti-Communism in the USA

As you saw in earlier chapters, there had always been a strong anti-Communist feeling in the USA. After the Second World War this was at its most intense.

Senator Joseph McCarthy heightened the anxiety by alleging that the Soviet Union had a conspiracy to get Communist sympathisers into key positions in American life. He said that Communists had infiltrated American society. He claimed he had discovered 57 Communists in the State Department alone. From 1950 to 1954 he led a 'witch hunt' to find these Communist sympathisers. The government was suspicious of McCarthy, but in the furiously anti-Communist period it didn't want to appear to be resisting him so for four years McCarthy wielded enormous power in the USA. (You can find out a lot more about American anti-Communism in this period on pages 373–75).

Case study 1: the Korean War

McCarthy certainly overstated the influence of Communism in the United States. However, in the 1950s there was plenty of evidence to confirm Americans' belief that Communism was getting stronger around the world.

Soon after the Soviet take-over of eastern Europe, China became Communist in 1949. The Americans had always regarded China as their mainstay in the Far East. Between 1946 and 1949 they pumped $2 billion in aid into China largely to support the Nationalists. Now suddenly a massive new Communist state had appeared on the map.

Furthermore, American spies reported to President Truman that Stalin was using the Cominform to help Communists win power in Malaya, Indonesia, Burma, the Philippines and Korea. Truman and other Americans watched with increasing anxiety. They saw a conspiracy. They thought that Communist countries were acting together to spread Communism. They had visions of the Communists overrunning all of Asia, with country after country being toppled like a row of dominoes. When South Korea was invaded in 1950, it was time for action!

Background

Korea had been ruled by Japan until 1945. At the end of the Second World War the northern half was liberated by Soviet troops and the southern half by Americans (see Source 4). When the war ended, the North remained Communist-controlled, with a Communist leader who had been trained in the USSR, and with a Soviet-style one-party system. The South was anti-Communist. It was not very democratic, but the fact that it was anti-Communist was enough to win it the support of the USA. There was bitter hostility between the North's Communist leader, Kim Il Sung, and Syngman Rhee, President of South Korea. Reunification did not seem likely.

In 1950 this hostility spilled over into open warfare. North Korean troops overwhelmed the South's forces. By September 1950 all except a small corner of south-east Korea was under Communist control.

President Truman immediately sent advisers, supplies and warships to the waters around Korea. At the same time, he put enormous pressure on the UN Security Council to condemn the actions of the North Koreans and to call on them to withdraw their troops.

In the Cold War atmosphere of 1950, each superpower always denounced and opposed any action by the other. So normally, in a dispute such as this, the Soviet Union would have used its right of veto to block the call for action by the UN. However, the USSR was boycotting the UN at this time. When China became Communist in 1949, the USA had blocked its entry to the United Nations, since it regarded the Nationalists (Chiang Kai-shek and his followers) as the rightful government of China. The USSR had walked out of the UN in protest. So when the resolution was passed (see Source 5), the USSR was not even at the meeting to use its veto. The USA was the single biggest contributor to the UN budget and was therefore in a powerful position to influence the UN decision.

The UN was now committed to using member forces to drive North Korean troops out of South Korea.

1 The situation in Korea has sometimes been compared to the situation in Germany in 1945 (which you studied in Chapter 11). Explain:
   a) how these situations were similar
   b) how they were different.
2 Explain how the Communist victory in China helped the USA to get the UN to intervene in North Korea.

SOURCE 2

If the UN is ever going to do anything, this is the time, and if the UN cannot bring the crisis in Korea to an end then we might as well just wash up the United Nations and forget it.

American Senator Tom Connally speaking in 1950. He was a Republican and strongly anti-Communist.

SOURCE 3

Korea is a symbol to the watching world. If we allow Korea to fall within the Soviet orbit, the world will feel we have lost another round in our match with the Soviet Union, and our prestige and the hopes of those who place their faith in us will suffer accordingly.

The US State Department, 1950.

SOURCE 4

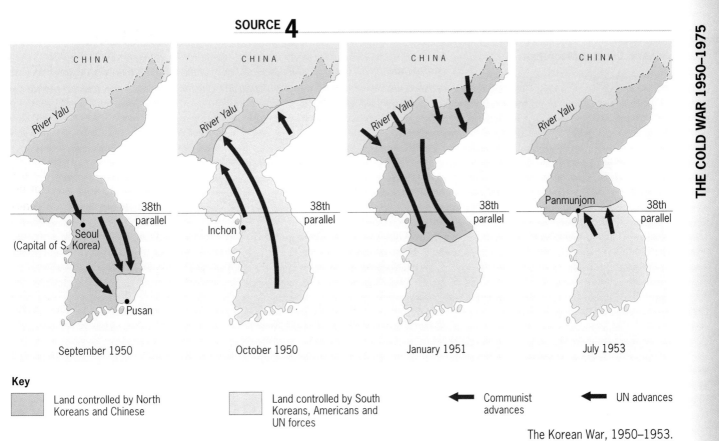

September 1950   October 1950   January 1951   July 1953

Key

Land controlled by North Koreans and Chinese

Land controlled by South Koreans, Americans and UN forces

← Communist advances

← UN advances

The Korean War, 1950–1953.

SOURCE 5

The UN will render such assistance to the republic of Korea as may be necessary to restore international peace and security to the area.

The resolution passed by the United Nations in 1950.

UNO or USA?

Eighteen states (including Britain) provided troops or support of some kind, but the overwhelming part of the UN force that was sent to Korea was American. The commander, General MacArthur, was also an American.

SOURCE 6

IN MEMORY OF THE
LEAGUE OF NATIONS
DIED OF
LACK OF EXERCISE
FACING WANTON AGGRESSION

A cartoon by David Low, 1950.

SOURCE 7

Even the reports to the UN were censored by [American] state and defence departments. I had no connection with the United Nations whatsoever.

From General MacArthur's memoirs.

3 During the Korean War, critics said that the USA simply pulled the strings of the UN like a puppet. How do Sources 6 and 7 support this view?

PROFILE

General Douglas MacArthur

★ Born 1880. His father was a successful army leader.
★ Trained at West Point, the top American military academy.
★ Fought in the First World War. He got 13 medals for bravery. Became the youngest commander in the American army in France.
★ Became chief of staff in the army in 1930.
★ During the Second World War he was the commander of the war against the Japanese. He devised the successful island-hopping strategy that allowed the Americans to drive out the Japanese from their island strongholds.
★ In 1945 he personally accepted the Japanese surrender, and from 1945 to 1951 he virtually controlled Japan, helping the shattered country get back on its feet.
★ His bullying, no-nonsense style enabled him to get things done, but he sometimes annoyed political leaders back in Washington by following his own policies.
★ In 1950, at the age of 70, he was given command of the UN forces in Korea.
★ He was relieved of his duties in Korea in 1951. He tried unsuccessfully to be elected as a presidential candidate in 1952.
★ He died in 1964.

1 Use Source 8 to write an extra sentence for the profile of General MacArthur describing his personality and beliefs.
2 Why did the Americans not support MacArthur in continuing the war and attacking China?

SOURCE 8

I have received your announcement of your appointment of me as United Nations Commander. I can only repeat the pledge of my complete personal loyalty to you as well as an absolute devotion to your monumental struggle for peace and good will throughout the world. I hope I will not fail you.

General MacArthur writing to President Truman in 1950.

United Nations forces stormed ashore at Inchon in September 1950. At the same time, other UN forces and South Korean troops advanced from Pusan. The North Koreans were driven back beyond their original border (the 38th parallel) within weeks. MacArthur had quickly achieved the original UN objective of removing North Korean troops from South Korea. But the Americans did not stop. Despite warnings from China's leader, Mao Tse-tung, that pressing on would mean China's joining the war, the UN approved a plan to advance into North Korea. By October, US forces had reached the Yalu river and the border with China (see Source 4). The nature of the war had now changed. It was clear that MacArthur and Truman were striving for a bigger prize – to remove Communism from Korea entirely.

SOURCE 9

Had they [the Chinese] intervened in the first or second months it would have been decisive, [but] we are no longer fearful of their intervention. Now that we have bases for our Air Force in Korea, there would be the greatest slaughter.

General MacArthur speaking in October 1950.

MacArthur underestimated the power of the Chinese. Late in October 1950, 200,000 Chinese troops (calling themselves 'People's Volunteers') joined the North Koreans. They launched a blistering attack. They had soldiers who were strongly committed to Communism and had been taught by their leader to hate the Americans. They had modern tanks and planes supplied by the Soviet Union. The United Nations forces were pushed back into South Korea. The UN troops then recovered and the fighting finally reached stalemate around the 38th parallel.

At this point, Truman and MacArthur fell out. MacArthur wanted to carry on the war, invading China and even using nuclear weapons if necessary. Truman felt that saving South Korea was good enough. His allies in the UN force convinced him that the risks of attacking China and of starting a war that might bring in the USSR were too great, and so an attack on China was ruled out. However, in March 1951 MacArthur blatantly ignored the UN instruction and openly threatened an attack on China. In April Truman removed MacArthur from his position as commander and brought him back home. He rejected MacArthur's aggressive policy towards Communism. Containment was underlined as the American policy. One of the American army leaders, General Omar Bradley, said that MacArthur's approach would have 'involved America in the wrong war, in the wrong place, at the wrong time, and with the wrong enemy'.

Peace talks between North and South Korea began in June 1951, but bitter fighting continued until 1952 when Truman was replaced by President Eisenhower who wanted to end the war. Stalin's death in March 1953 made the Chinese and North Koreans less confident. An armistice was finally signed in July 1953.

ACTIVITY

Source 8 is MacArthur's letter accepting command of the UN troops. Write a letter from him to Truman, following his removal from that position in April 1951, explaining his actions in the Korean War.

SOURCE 10

Photographs from the Korean War. Conditions were some of the worst the American forces had known, with treacherous cold and blinding snow-storms in the winter of 1950–51. The Chinese forces were more familiar with fighting in the jagged mountains, forested ravines and treacherous swamps – as the landscape was similar to many areas of China. Many civilians suffered as a result of the war and there were also reports of prisoners of war being treated very badly.

SOURCE 11

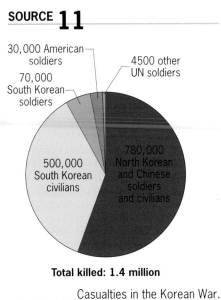

30,000 American soldiers

4500 other UN soldiers

70,000 South Korean soldiers

500,000 South Korean civilians

780,000 North Korean and Chinese soldiers and civilians

Total killed: 1.4 million

Casualties in the Korean War.

FOCUS TASK

Was the Korean War a success for containment?

1 Make your own copy of this chart and fill it out for this case study of Korea.

The issue	What methods did the Americans use?	What problems did they face?	What was the outcome?

2 It is 1952. A new president, Eisenhower, has been elected in the USA. Your task is to write a report for him on what lessons the United States can learn from the war.
   Your report should advise the President on:
   • the USA's aims in Korea
   • how the support of the UN helped
   • how far the USA achieved its aims
   • whether MacArthur should have been allowed to invade North Korea
   • why MacArthur was removed
   • the military and civilian cost of war.
For each point you will need to use the sources and text on pages 338–41 to compile your answer.
   Finally, make up your own mind as to whether, on balance, the policy of containment succeeded and then write up your ideas as a balanced report.

SOURCE 12

We shall never have a secure peace and a happy world so long as Soviet Communism dominates one-third of all the world's people and is in the process of trying to extend its rule to many others. Therefore we must have in mind the liberation of these captive peoples. Now liberation does not mean war. Liberation can be achieved by processes short of war.

A policy which only aims at containing Russia is an unsound policy . . . If our only policy is to stay where we are, we will be driven back.

JF Dulles, US Secretary of State, speaking on his appointment in 1952.

1 Read Source 12. What methods do you think Dulles had in mind to 'liberate captive peoples' without a war?
2 Look at Source 13. Would you agree that the Communist world was encircled?

SOURCE 14

We Communists believe that the ideas of Communism will be victorious throughout the world just as they have been in China and in many states. Many will probably disagree with us. It is their right to think so. We may argue, we may disagree with each other. The main thing is to argue without resort to arms in order to prove that one is right.

Soviet leader Nikita Khrushchev speaking in 1959.

Was containment the right policy?

There was no doubt at all in the USA that Communism had to be resisted. The question was how to do it. Some favoured the aggressive policy proposed by MacArthur. They felt that 'containment' was not enough. They thought that the President had been weak in not going for outright victory in Korea. They wanted the USA to take the fight to the Communists. Even those who did not want war with the Soviet Union still wanted to push back the frontiers of Communism.

Dulles (see Source 12) set up a network of anti-Communist alliances around the world. The South-East Asia Treaty Organisation (SEATO) was formed in 1954. The Central Treaty Organisation (CENTO) was formed in 1955 (see Source 13). The USSR saw these alliances as having a more aggressive purpose. The Soviets felt threatened by them and accused the USA of trying to encircle the Communist world. In 1955, therefore, the Warsaw Treaty Organisation, better known as the Warsaw Pact, was set up between the USSR and all the Communist east European countries except Yugoslavia (see page 401).

SOURCE 13

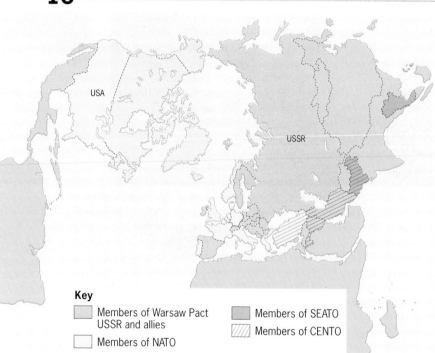

Key
- Members of Warsaw Pact USSR and allies
- Members of NATO
- Members of SEATO
- Members of CENTO

Membership of the organisations allied to the USA and the USSR in 1955.

Co-existence

From 1955, however, the Cold War began to enter a new phase. Stalin had died in 1953. The new Soviet leader was Nikita Khrushchev (see pages 400–401). He seemed keen to ease the tensions with the USA. He talked about peaceful co-existence rather than continuing conflict. After ten years without any meetings between the leaders of the USSR and the USA, he met with Western leaders in 1955 and 1960. The meetings did not achieve anything specific, but the two sides were talking to each other, which was some improvement on the tensions of the early 1950s.

However, not all Western leaders were convinced by Khrushchev. To some, his behaviour in eastern Europe was a constant reminder of the evils of Communism.

- In 1956 there were protests in Poland, sparked off by a rise in food prices. The Red Army moved in to restore order (see page 401).
- Also in 1956 the crushing might of the Red Army put down an anti-Communist rising in Hungary at the cost of some 30,000 Hungarian lives (see pages 402–403).
- In August 1961 the Communists built the Berlin Wall dividing East and West Berlin. The Soviet Union wanted to stop people from leaving East Germany. Border guards shot anyone trying to cross the wall illegally (see pages 407–409).

The arms race

Meanwhile, both the USSR and the USA were engaged in an arms race.

The Americans had developed their first atomic bomb in 1945. They did not share the secret of their bomb with the USSR, even while they were still allies. When the USA dropped the first bombs on Hiroshima and Nagasaki in August 1945, 70,000 people were killed instantly. The awesome power of the explosions and the incredible destruction caused by the bombs made Japan surrender within a week (see pages 295–97). It was clear to both the USA and the USSR that atomic bombs were the weapons of the future.

The timeline below summarises the arms race which followed.

3 Look back at Source 12. Do you think the development of nuclear weapons was what Dulles might have had in mind?

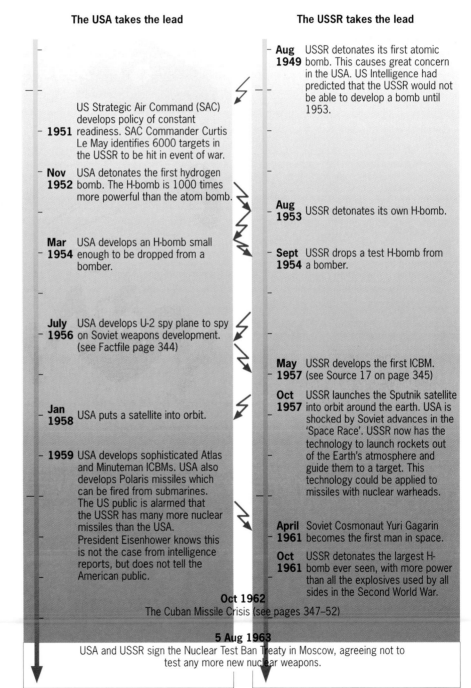

The USA takes the lead

1951 US Strategic Air Command (SAC) develops policy of constant readiness. SAC Commander Curtis Le May identifies 6000 targets in the USSR to be hit in event of war.

Nov 1952 USA detonates the first hydrogen bomb. The H-bomb is 1000 times more powerful than the atom bomb.

Mar 1954 USA develops an H-bomb small enough to be dropped from a bomber.

July 1956 USA develops U-2 spy plane to spy on Soviet weapons development. (see Factfile page 344)

Jan 1958 USA puts a satellite into orbit.

1959 USA develops sophisticated Atlas and Minuteman ICBMs. USA also develops Polaris missiles which can be fired from submarines. The US public is alarmed that the USSR has many more nuclear missiles than the USA. President Eisenhower knows this is not the case from intelligence reports, but does not tell the American public.

The USSR takes the lead

Aug 1949 USSR detonates its first atomic bomb. This causes great concern in the USA. US Intelligence had predicted that the USSR would not be able to develop a bomb until 1953.

Aug 1953 USSR detonates its own H-bomb.

Sept 1954 USSR drops a test H-bomb from a bomber.

May 1957 USSR develops the first ICBM. (see Source 17 on page 345)

Oct 1957 USSR launches the Sputnik satellite into orbit around the earth. USA is shocked by Soviet advances in the 'Space Race'. USSR now has the technology to launch rockets out of the Earth's atmosphere and guide them to a target. This technology could be applied to missiles with nuclear warheads.

April 1961 Soviet Cosmonaut Yuri Gagarin becomes the first man in space.

Oct 1961 USSR detonates the largest H-bomb ever seen, with more power than all the explosives used by all sides in the Second World War.

Oct 1962 The Cuban Missile Crisis (see pages 347–52)

5 Aug 1963 USA and USSR sign the Nuclear Test Ban Treaty in Moscow, agreeing not to test any more new nuclear weapons.

The U-2 crisis, 1960

★ In 1950, without permission from President Truman, US Strategic Air Command began spy flights over the USSR. When he found out, Truman banned them because they violated Soviet air space.

★ In 1956 the flights began again, with the agreement of President Eisenhower. This time they used a brand new spy plane called the U-2. This flew so high it could not be shot down by Soviet fighters or by anti-aircraft missiles, but it carried sophisticated listening devices and such powerful cameras that it could read a newspaper on the ground from 23,000 metres. U-2 spying flights kept the Americans fully informed about Soviet weapons technology through the late 1950s.

★ Soviet missiles improved and in May 1960 one of these new missiles shot down a U-2 piloted by Gary Powers. Powers parachuted to safety but was arrested by Soviet soldiers.

★ The USSR paraded Powers on television and accused the USA of spying. The USA at first denied Powers was on a spying mission, but then admitted he was. However, President Eisenhower refused to apologise or to promise there would be no more flights.

★ The incident caused a dramatic downturn in US–Soviet relations.

★ Gary Powers was sentenced to ten years in a Soviet prison, but was exchanged for a captured Soviet spy (Rudolf Abel) in February 1962.

SOURCE 15

A

B

1 Compare Sources 15A and B. One is from 1949, and the other from 1961. Decide which is which and explain the message of each one.

Two Soviet cartoons. **A** The text on the bomb-shaped balloon reads 'US atomic monopoly'. The balloon is burst by a communiqué from the Soviet news agency TASS on 25 September, announcing that the USSR now has an atomic bomb. **B** The wheels of the train are labelled NATO, SEATO and CENTO. The engine is labelled 'armaments race'. The smoke is labelled 'anti-Communism'.

The arms race: propaganda and intelligence

The arms race developed into a propaganda and intelligence war as well as a forum for technological rivalry. Each side was anxious to show the other to be the one building all the bombs. Their own bombs were purely for protection! Thus the need for propaganda.

At the same time, both sides were keen to find out what the other side was up to. Thus the need for intelligence. The USSR tended to use human spies like Rudolf Abel. He worked in New York until he was arrested in 1957. The USA, on the other hand, preferred hi-tech spying using equipment like the U-2.

SOURCE **16**

2 Look at Source 16. What is the Soviet cartoon saying about the U-2 plane?
3 Read the Factfile on page 344. Explain why the USSR was so angry about the US spy flights.
4 How would the USA justify this violation of Soviet territory?
5 If the USSR had had U-2 planes, do you think it would have used them?

A 1960 Soviet cartoon commenting on the uses of the U-2 spy plane.

SOURCE **17**

6 Look at Source 17. Why do you think the USA had missiles based in Europe?

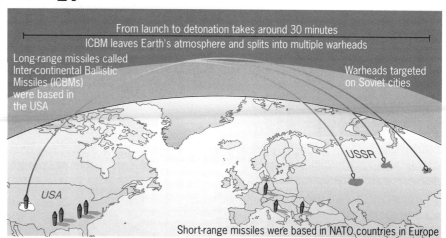

The location of American missiles trained on the USSR. Short-range missiles could hit the USSR in minutes. Long-range ones from the USA would take 30 minutes.

Deterrence and MAD

By 1961, both of the superpowers had hundreds of missiles pointed at each other. The USA had more than the USSR, but the advantage did not really matter because both sides had enough to destroy each other many times over. On each side the theory was that such weapons made them more secure. The enemy would not dare attack first, because it knew that, if it did, the other would strike back before its bombs had even landed and it too would be destroyed. It would be suicidal. So having nuclear weapons deterred the other side from attacking first. This policy also became known as MAD (Mutually Assured Destruction). Surely no side would dare strike first when it knew the attack would destroy itself too!

1 Define the term 'nuclear deterrent' in not more than 20 words.

Did people feel safe?

Leaders might regard their nuclear weapons as a deterrent, but others worried that the world was moving into a very dangerous time. For example, an American B-47 bomber crashed in Norfolk, England, in 1957. The resulting fire came within minutes of setting off two nuclear bombs that would have devastated all of East Anglia. In 1962, a US radar station mistook one of its own satellites for an incoming Soviet missile and was minutes away from triggering a full nuclear 'response' attack on the USSR. Of course, governments did not tell their people about these incidents – both Soviet and US leaders were very secretive about their weapons. But they could not hide the big issue – that the nuclear arms race seemed to have raised the stakes so high that one suicidal leader, one poor decision or (most worryingly of all) one small and innocent mistake could trigger a catastrophe that could destroy Europe, the USA and the Soviet Union within minutes.

It did not help to reassure people when advice such as Source 18 appeared. Fear of 'the bomb' was a common feature of life in 1950s and 1960s USA. The arms race was a topic of everyday conversation. Some people protested against the arms race. Robert Oppenheimer, the man who led the team which developed the atom bomb, opposed the H-bomb. He felt it was wrong to develop a more powerful bomb in peacetime. Others protested at the vast amounts being spent on weapons. But the most common feelings were helplessness and fear. People wondered whether this was the end. Were they the last generation to walk this planet? Would nuclear warfare signal the end of the world?

SOURCE **18**

A nuclear fallout shelter.

SOURCE **19**

Nuclear warfare is an utter folly, even from the narrowest point of view of self-interest. To spread ruin, misery and death throughout one's own country as well as that of the enemy is the act of madmen . . . The question every human being must ask is 'can man survive?'

Bertrand Russell, a leading member of Britain's Campaign for Nuclear Disarmament (CND).

A 1960 Soviet cartoon. The notice held by the US Secretary of State says to Castro in Cuba: 'I forbid you to make friends with the Soviet Union.'

Case study 2: the Cuban missile crisis, 1962

It was against the background of the arms race that Cuba became a major flashpoint of the Cold War.

Background

Cuba is a large island just 160 km from Florida in the southern USA. It had long been an American ally. Americans owned most of the businesses on the island and they had a huge naval base there (see Source 24). Then in 1959, after a three-year GUERRILLA campaign, Fidel Castro overthrew the American-backed dictator Batista. With a new pro-Communist state in what it regarded as its own 'sphere of influence' this was going to be a real test of the USA's policy of containment.

How successful were the early attempts at containment?

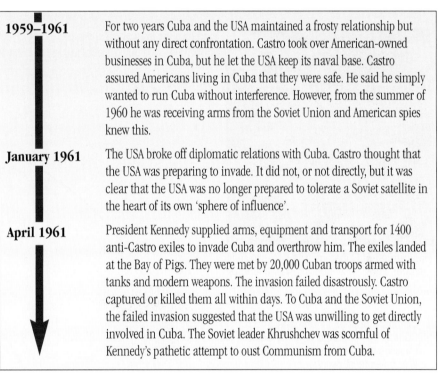

1959–1961	For two years Cuba and the USA maintained a frosty relationship but without any direct confrontation. Castro took over American-owned businesses in Cuba, but he let the USA keep its naval base. Castro assured Americans living in Cuba that they were safe. He said he simply wanted to run Cuba without interference. However, from the summer of 1960 he was receiving arms from the Soviet Union and American spies knew this.
January 1961	The USA broke off diplomatic relations with Cuba. Castro thought that the USA was preparing to invade. It did not, or not directly, but it was clear that the USA was no longer prepared to tolerate a Soviet satellite in the heart of its own 'sphere of influence'.
April 1961	President Kennedy supplied arms, equipment and transport for 1400 anti-Castro exiles to invade Cuba and overthrow him. The exiles landed at the Bay of Pigs. They were met by 20,000 Cuban troops armed with tanks and modern weapons. The invasion failed disastrously. Castro captured or killed them all within days. To Cuba and the Soviet Union, the failed invasion suggested that the USA was unwilling to get directly involved in Cuba. The Soviet leader Khrushchev was scornful of Kennedy's pathetic attempt to oust Communism from Cuba.

Looking back, President Kennedy said he thought that US policy in Cuba – backing the hated dictator Batista – had itself been responsible for the strength of Communism in the first place (see Source 21). Historians too argue that the Bay of Pigs fiasco further encouraged the spread of Communism. On the one hand, it suggested to the USSR that Kennedy was weak. On the other hand, it made Castro and Khrushchev very suspicious of US policy.

2 Why was Cuba so important to the USA?
3 Why do you think the Americans chose to equip Cuban exiles rather than invading themselves?
4 Why did the invasion fail?

I believe there is no country in the world . . . whose economic colonisation, humiliation and exploitation were worse than in Cuba, partly as a consequence of US policy during the Batista regime. I believe that, without being aware of it, we conceived and created the Castro movement, starting from scratch.

President Kennedy speaking in 1963.

5 What do Sources 21 and 22 suggest about the success of the USA's policy of containment?

I think he [Khrushchev] did it because of the Bay of Pigs. He thought that anyone who was so young and inexperienced as to get into that mess could be beaten; and anyone who got into it and didn't see it through had no guts. So he just beat the hell out of me.

If he thinks I'm inexperienced and have no guts, until we remove those ideas we won't get anywhere with him.

Kennedy speaking after a meeting with Khrushchev in 1961. Khrushchev had been very aggressive towards Kennedy.

What was the Soviet Union doing in Cuba?

After the Bay of Pigs fiasco, Soviet arms flooded into Cuba. In May 1962 the Soviet Union announced publicly for the first time that it was supplying Cuba with arms. By July 1962 Cuba had the best-equipped army in Latin America. By September it had thousands of Soviet missiles, plus patrol boats, tanks, radar vans, missile erectors, jet bombers, jet fighters and 5000 Soviet technicians to help to maintain the weapons.

The Americans watched all this with great alarm. They seemed ready to tolerate conventional arms being supplied to Cuba, but the big question was whether the Soviet Union would dare to put nuclear missiles on Cuba. In September Kennedy's own Intelligence Department said that it did not believe the USSR would send nuclear weapons to Cuba. The USSR had not taken this step with any of its satellite states before and the US Intelligence Department believed that the USSR would consider it too risky to do it in Cuba. On 11 September, Kennedy warned the USSR that he would prevent 'by whatever means might be necessary' Cuba's becoming an offensive military base – by which, everyone knew, he meant a nuclear missile base. The same day the USSR assured the USA that it had no need to put nuclear missiles on Cuba and no intention of doing so.

The October crisis

On Sunday, 14 October 1962, an American U-2 spy plane flew over Cuba. It took amazingly detailed photographs of missile sites in Cuba. To the military experts two things were obvious – that these were nuclear missile sites, and that they were being built by the USSR.

SOURCE 23

Photograph of Cuban missile sites taken in October 1962. The labelling was added by the Americans.

1 Compare Source 17 on page 345 with Source 24. Describe how the Soviet missiles on Cuba changed the Cold War balance of power.

SOURCE 25

[Estimates were that the] missiles had an atomic warhead [power] of about half the current missile capacity of the entire Soviet Union. The photographs indicated that missiles were directed at certain American cities. The estimate was that within a few minutes of their being fired 80 million Americans would be dead.

President Kennedy's brother, Robert Kennedy, describing events on Thursday 18 October in the book he wrote about the crisis, *13 Days*.

SOURCE 24

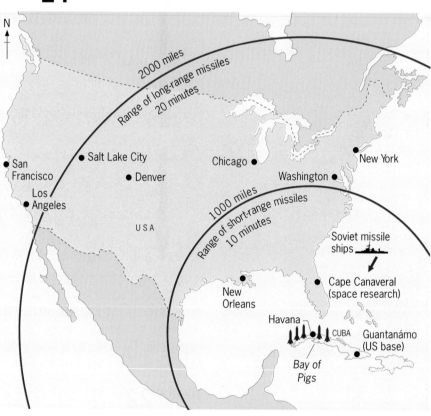

Map showing the location of Cuba and the range of the Cuban missiles.

More photo reconnaissance followed over the next two days. This confirmed that some sites were nearly finished but others were still being built. Some were already supplied with missiles, others were awaiting them. The experts said that the most developed of the sites could be ready to launch missiles in just seven days. American spy planes also reported that 20 Soviet ships were currently on the way to Cuba carrying missiles.

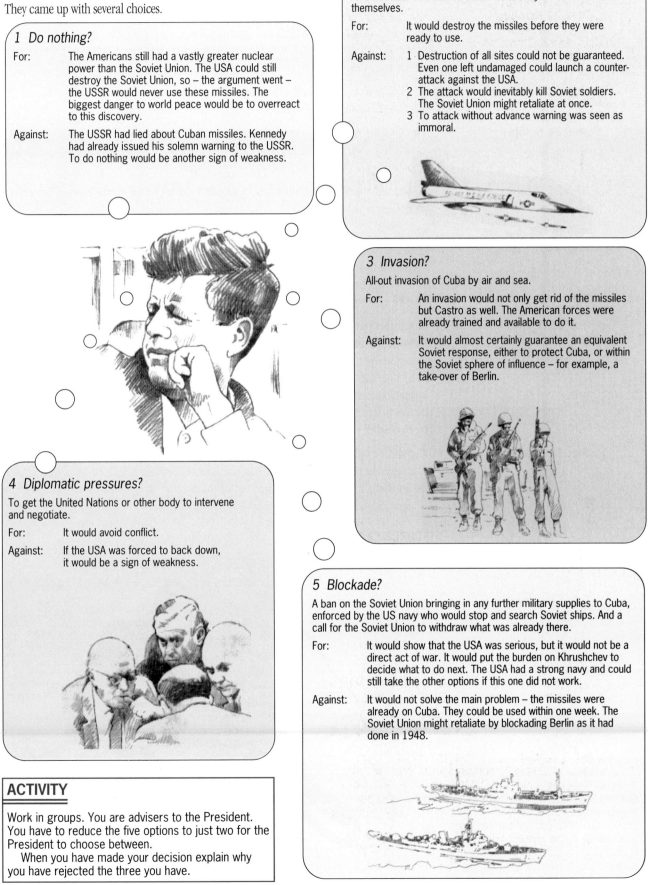

Kennedy's options

On Tuesday 16 October, President Kennedy was informed of the discovery. He formed a special team of advisers called Ex Comm. They came up with several choices.

1 Do nothing?

For: The Americans still had a vastly greater nuclear power than the Soviet Union. The USA could still destroy the Soviet Union, so – the argument went – the USSR would never use these missiles. The biggest danger to world peace would be to overreact to this discovery.

Against: The USSR had lied about Cuban missiles. Kennedy had already issued his solemn warning to the USSR. To do nothing would be another sign of weakness.

2 Surgical air attack?

An immediate selected air attack to destroy the nuclear bases themselves.

For: It would destroy the missiles before they were ready to use.

Against:
1. Destruction of all sites could not be guaranteed. Even one left undamaged could launch a counter-attack against the USA.
2. The attack would inevitably kill Soviet soldiers. The Soviet Union might retaliate at once.
3. To attack without advance warning was seen as immoral.

3 Invasion?

All-out invasion of Cuba by air and sea.

For: An invasion would not only get rid of the missiles but Castro as well. The American forces were already trained and available to do it.

Against: It would almost certainly guarantee an equivalent Soviet response, either to protect Cuba, or within the Soviet sphere of influence – for example, a take-over of Berlin.

4 Diplomatic pressures?

To get the United Nations or other body to intervene and negotiate.

For: It would avoid conflict.

Against: If the USA was forced to back down, it would be a sign of weakness.

5 Blockade?

A ban on the Soviet Union bringing in any further military supplies to Cuba, enforced by the US navy who would stop and search Soviet ships. And a call for the Soviet Union to withdraw what was already there.

For: It would show that the USA was serious, but it would not be a direct act of war. It would put the burden on Khrushchev to decide what to do next. The USA had a strong navy and could still take the other options if this one did not work.

Against: It would not solve the main problem – the missiles were already on Cuba. They could be used within one week. The Soviet Union might retaliate by blockading Berlin as it had done in 1948.

ACTIVITY

Work in groups. You are advisers to the President. You have to reduce the five options to just two for the President to choose between.

When you have made your decision explain why you have rejected the three you have.

What happened next?

Tue 16 October	President Kennedy is informed of the missile build-up. Ex Comm formed.
Sat 20 October	Kennedy decides on a blockade of Cuba.
Mon 22 October	Kennedy announces the blockade and calls on the Soviet Union to withdraw its missiles. 'I call on Chairman Khrushchev to halt and eliminate this reckless and provocative threat to world peace . . . He has the opportunity now to move the world back from the abyss of destruction . . . withdrawing these weapons from Cuba.'
Tue 23 October	Kennedy receives a letter from Khrushchev saying that Soviet ships will not observe the blockade. Khrushchev does not admit the presence of nuclear missiles on Cuba.
Wed 24 October	The blockade begins. The first missile-carrying ships, accompanied by a Soviet submarine, approach the 500-mile (800 km) blockade zone. Then suddenly, at 10.32 a.m., the 20 Soviet ships which are closest to the zone stop or turn around.
Thu 25 October	Despite this, intensive aerial photography reveals that work on the missile bases in Cuba is proceeding rapidly.
Fri 26 October	Kennedy receives a long personal letter from Khrushchev. The letter claims that the missiles on Cuba are purely defensive, but goes on: 'If assurances were given that the USA would not participate in an attack on Cuba and the blockade was lifted, then the question of the removal or the destruction of the missile sites would be an entirely different question.' This is the first time Khrushchev has admitted the presence of the missiles.
Sat 27 October	Khrushchev sends a second letter – revising his proposals – saying that the condition for removing the missiles from Cuba is that the USA withdraw its missiles from Turkey. Kennedy cannot accept this condition. An American U-2 plane is shot down over Cuba. The pilot is killed. The President is advised to launch an immediate reprisal attack on Cuba. Kennedy decides to delay an attack. He also decides to ignore the second Khrushchev letter, but accepts the terms suggested by Khrushchev on 26 October. He says that if the Soviet Union does not withdraw, an attack will follow.
Sun 28 October	Khrushchev replies to Kennedy: 'In order to eliminate as rapidly as possible the conflict which endangers the cause of peace . . . the Soviet Government has given a new order to dismantle the arms which you described as offensive and to crate and return them to the Soviet Union.'

SOURCE 26

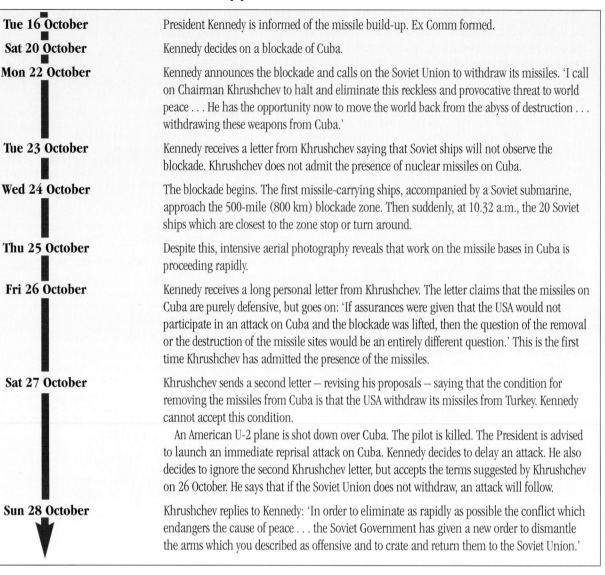

A cartoon published in 1962.

1 Kennedy described Wednesday 24 October and Saturday 27 October as the darkest days of the crisis. Use the information on this page to explain why.

2 Do you think that nuclear war was ever a possibility in this crisis?

3 Is Source 26 a Soviet or an American cartoon? Explain your answer by referring to details in the cartoon.

4 Working with a partner, list any evidence you can find for and against each of the explanations in Source 27.
5 Choose the explanation(s) that you think best fit what you have found out about the crisis. Explain your choice.

Why did the Soviet Union place nuclear missiles on Cuba?

It was an incredibly risky strategy. The USSR must have known that it would cause a crisis. What's more, the USSR made no attempt at all to camouflage the sites, and even allowed the missiles to travel on open deck. This has caused much debate as to what Khrushchev was really doing. Historians have suggested five possible explanations (see Source 27).

SOURCE 27

To bargain with the USA
Khrushchev wanted the missiles as a bargaining counter. If he had missiles on Cuba, he could agree to remove them in return for some American concessions.

To test the USA
In the strained atmosphere of Cold War politics the missiles were designed to see how strong the Americans really were – whether they would back off or face up. The Soviet Union wanted to test out Kennedy.

Why did the Soviet Union put the missiles on Cuba?

To trap the USA
The missiles were a trap. Khrushchev wanted the Americans to find them and be drawn into a nuclear war. He did not even try to hide them.

To get the upper hand in the arms race
Khrushchev was so concerned about the missile gap between the USSR and the USA that he would seize any opportunity he could to close it. With missiles on Cuba it was less likely that the USA would ever launch a 'first strike' against the USSR.

To defend Cuba
The missiles were genuinely meant to defend Cuba.

Some possible explanations for the Soviet decision to place missiles on Cuba.

SOURCE 28

[In 1961] we increased our military aid to Cuba. We were sure the Americans would never agree to the existence of Castro's Cuba. They feared, and we hoped, that a Socialist Cuba might become a magnet that would attract other Latin American countries to socialism. We had to find an effective deterrent to American interference in the Caribbean.

The Caribbean Crisis was a triumph of Soviet foreign policy and a personal triumph in my own career. Today Cuba exists as an independent socialist country right in front of America. Cuba's very existence is good propaganda.

We behaved with dignity and forced the United States to demobilise and to recognise Cuba.

Khrushchev was forced from power in 1964. This extract comes from his memoirs written in 1971.

The outcome

- Cuba stayed Communist and highly armed. However, the nuclear missiles were withdrawn under United Nations supervision.
- Both leaders emerged with something from the crisis. Kennedy came out of the crisis with a greatly improved reputation in his own country and throughout the West. He had stood up to Khrushchev and had made him back down. Khrushchev was also able to claim a personal triumph. Cuba remained a useful ally in 'Uncle Sam's backyard'. The fact that Khrushchev had been forced to back down was quickly forgotten in Soviet circles. Instead, his role as a responsible peacemaker, willing to take the first move towards compromise, was highlighted.
- Historians agree that the Cuban missile crisis helped to thaw Cold War relations between the USA and the USSR. Both leaders had seen how their game of brinkmanship had nearly ended in nuclear war. Now they were more prepared to take steps to reduce the risk of nuclear war. A permanent 'hot line' phone link direct from the White House to the Kremlin was set up. The following year, in 1963, they signed a Nuclear Test Ban Treaty. It did not stop the development of weapons, but it limited tests and was an important step forward.
- Within the USA, the crisis had an effect on anti-Communist opinion. Critics of containment had wanted the USA to invade Cuba – to turn back Communism. However, the Cuban crisis highlighted the weakness of their case. Such intervention was not worth the high risk. A Communist Cuba was an inconvenience to the USA. A nuclear war would be the end of civilisation.

1 How do Sources 28 and 29 differ in their attitudes to the crisis?
2 Who do you think won this battle – Kennedy, Khrushchev or neither? Explain your answer.
3 For each of Sources 28–30 explain why it is useful for historians studying the results of the Cuban missile crisis.

SOURCE 29

Even after it was all over [the President] made no statement attempting to take credit for himself or for his administration for what had occurred. He instructed all [his staff] that no interview should be given, no statement made, which would claim any kind of victory. He respected Khrushchev for properly determining what was in his own country's interests and in the interests of mankind. If it was a triumph, it was a triumph for the next generation and not for any particular government or people.

Written by Robert Kennedy in *13 Days*.

SOURCE 30

President Kennedy will be remembered as the President who helped to bring the thaw in the Cold War. This was always his aim but only after Cuba did he really act. That crisis left its mark on him; he recognised how frightening were the consequences of misunderstandings between East and West.

President Kennedy was shot dead by a gunman in Texas in November 1963. This is from his obituary in the British newspaper, the *Guardian*.

FOCUS TASK

Was the Cuban missile crisis a success for containment?

1 Look back at your chart for the Focus Task on page 341. Make and complete a similar chart for the Cuban missile crisis.
2 In what ways was the Cuban missile crisis a greater test for the USA than the Korean War?
3 Do you regard the Cuban crisis as a success for containment? In your answer refer to:
  - the failure of direct action (the Bay of Pigs)
  - the potential threat of the missiles
  - the options open to Kennedy
  - what Kennedy gained from the crisis.

Key

Communist-controlled areas in the mid 1960s

Ho Chi Minh trail

The location of Vietnam.

Case study 3: the Vietnam War

Although many Americans regarded the Cuban missile crisis as a victory for the USA, it did not reduce their fear of Communism. Very soon they found themselves locked into a costly war in Vietnam which put a massive question mark over the very policy of containment.

The origins of the conflict

Since the late nineteenth century, Vietnam had been ruled by France and it was known as Indochina. French rule was unchallenged except for a rebellion in 1930 which was brutally crushed. The first major blow to French power came in 1940 when France was defeated in the Second World War by Germany. The Japanese (Germany's allies) took control of the main resources of Vietnam (coal, rice, rubber, railways, roads). During the war, a strong anti-Japanese resistance movement (the Viet Minh) emerged under the leadership of Communist Ho Chi Minh. Ho was a remarkable individual. He had lived in the USA, Britain and France. In the 1920s he had studied Communism in the USSR. In 1930 he had founded the Indochinese Communist Party. He inspired the Vietnamese people to fight for an independent Vietnam. When the Second World War ended, the Viet Minh controlled the north of the country and were determined to take control of the whole country. The Viet Minh entered the city of Hanoi in 1945 and declared Vietnamese independence.

The French had other ideas. In 1945 they came back wanting to rule Vietnam again. However, Ho had not fought the Japanese only then to hand over power to the French. In 1946 war broke out between the French and the Viet Minh. Ho Chi Minh cleverly kept quiet about wanting a Communist Vietnam and so countries such as the USA were, if anything, quite sympathetic to him. The struggle was seen as a fight against the colonial rule of France.

However, in 1949 the picture changed. The Communists took over in China and began to give help to Ho Chi Minh. Now the Americans saw the Viet Minh as the puppets of Mao Tse-tung and the Chinese Communists. They feared a Communist plan to dominate all of south-east Asia. The USA poured $500 million a year into the French war effort and helped the French to set up a non-Communist government in the south of the country.

The war dragged on from 1946 to 1954. The French generally controlled the towns, the Viet Minh the countryside. The Viet Minh's guerrilla tactics made them impossible to beat. They tied up 190,000 French troops in hit-and-run raids, causing 90,000 French casualties. French raids against peasant villages simply increased support for the Viet Minh. The decisive event came in 1954 at Dien Bien Phu. A large, well-armed force of French paratroopers was comprehensively defeated. There were several important consequences:

- The French lost 3000 dead in the battle and 8000 more died in captivity.
- The Viet Minh forces had defeated the French in open battle with the help of modern weapons from the USSR and China.
- A small Asian state had defeated a rich European state through a combination of effective leadership, the right tactics and sheer determination (for example, at Dien Bien Phu, the equipment and supplies for the 40,000 Viet Minh soldiers were carried by hand by peasants).
- At the 1954 peace conference held in Geneva, the country was effectively divided into North and South Vietnam until elections could be held to decide its future.

SOURCE **32**

A poor feudal nation had beaten a great colonial power . . . It meant a lot; not just to us but to people all over the world.

Viet Minh commander Vo Nguyen Giap commenting on the victory over France in 1954.

ACTIVITY

It is 1954. The French President must explain to the French media why the modern developed state of France has been forced to pull out of Indochina. You have to prepare some briefing notes for his presentation. Explain, either in paragraphs or bullet points, how each of the following played a part:
- the Second World War
- the French decision to continue ruling in 1945
- Viet Minh attacks, 1946–54
- the support of the Vietnamese people (or lack of it)
- support for the Viet Minh by communist USSR and China.

SOURCE 33

Quang Duc, a 73-year-old Buddhist priest, burns himself to death in protest against the attacks on Buddhist shrines by the government of South Vietnam in 1963.

1 Many neutral observers in Vietnam were critical of US policy. Explain why.
2 Explain how US politicians would have defended their policies.

SOURCE 35

First is the simple fact that South Vietnam, a member of the free world family, is striving to preserve its independence from Communist attack. Second, South East Asia has great significance in the forward defence of the USA. For Hanoi, the immediate object is limited: conquest of the south and national unification. For Peking, however, Hanoi's victory would only be a first step towards eventual Chinese dominance of the two Vietnams and South East Asia and towards exploitation of the new strategy in other parts of the world.

Robert McNamara, US Defence Secretary, explaining in 1964 why he supported the policy of sending US troops to Vietnam.

Why did the USA become increasingly involved in Vietnam?

Under the terms of the cease fire, elections were to be held within two years to reunite the country. You will remember how the USA criticised Stalin for not holding free elections in Soviet-controlled eastern Europe after the war (see page 322). In Vietnam in 1954 the USA applied a different rule. It prevented the elections from taking place because it feared that the Communists would win.

SOURCE 34

It was generally agreed that had an election been held, Ho Chi Minh would have been elected Premier . . . at the time of the fighting, possibly 80 per cent of the population would have voted for the communist Ho Chi Minh as their leader.

President Eisenhower writing after the Vietnam War.

Why did the Americans do this? Their policy was a strange combination of determination and ignorance. President Eisenhower and his Secretary of State JF Dulles were convinced that China and the USSR were planning to spread Communism throughout Asia. The idea was often referred to as the Domino Theory. If Vietnam fell to Communism, then Laos, Cambodia, Thailand, Burma, and possibly even India might also fall – just like a row of dominoes. The Americans were determined to resist the spread of Communism in Vietnam which they saw as the first domino in the row. However, their methods and policies showed their ignorance of the Vietnamese people and the region.

In 1955 the Americans helped Ngo Dinh Diem to set up the Republic of South Vietnam. They supported him because he was bitterly anti-Communist and was prepared to imprison or exile Communists. He belonged to the landlord class, which treated the Vietnamese peasants with contempt. He was a Christian and showed little respect for the Buddhist religion of most Vietnamese peasants (see Source 33). Diem's regime was also extremely corrupt. He appointed members of his family or other supporters to positions of power and refused to hold elections, even for local councils. The Americans were concerned and frustrated by his actions, but as Dulles said, 'We knew of no one better.' The USA supported Diem's regime with around $1.6 billion in the 1950s. Diem was overthrown by his own army leaders in November 1963, but the governments that followed were equally corrupt. Even so, they also received massive US support.

The actions of these anti-Communist governments increased support among the ordinary peasants for the Communist-led National Front for the Liberation of South Vietnam, set up in December 1960. This movement was usually referred to as the Viet Cong. It included South Vietnamese opponents of the government, but also large numbers of Communist North Vietnamese taking their orders from Ho Chi Minh. Peasants who did not support the Viet Cong faced intimidation and violence from them.

The Viet Cong also started a guerilla war against the South Vietnamese government. Using the Ho Chi Minh trail (see Source 31), the Viet Cong sent reinforcements and ferried supplies to guerrilla fighters. These fighters attacked South Vietnamese government forces, officials and buildings, gradually making the countryside unsafe for government forces. They also attacked American air force and supply bases.

By 1962 President Kennedy was sending military personnel (he always called them 'advisers') to fight the Viet Cong (see Source 35). In 1963 and 1964 tension between North and South Vietnam increased and so did American involvement (11,500 troops by the end of 1962; 23,000 by the end of 1964). However, Kennedy said he was determined that the USA would not 'blunder into war, unclear about aims or how to get out again'.

President Kennedy was assassinated in 1963. His successor, Lyndon Johnson, was more prepared than Kennedy to commit the USA to a full-scale conflict in Vietnam to prevent the spread of Communism. His resolve would soon be tested. In August 1964, North Vietnamese patrol boats opened fire on US ships in the Gulf of Tonkin. In a furious reaction, the US Congress passed the Tonkin Gulf Resolution. The Resolution gave Lyndon Johnson the power to 'take all necessary measures to prevent further aggression and achieve peace and security'. It effectively meant that he could take the USA into a full-scale war if he felt it was necessary, and very soon that was the case. On 8 March 1965, 3500 US marines, combat troops rather than advisers, came ashore at Da Nang. America was at war in Vietnam.

What kind of war was the Vietnam War?

If the USA thought that its soldiers would win an easy victory, it was soon proved wrong. American technology and firepower were totally superior, but as time wore on it became clear that the USA needed more than technology to win this kind of war. On the next four pages you will compare Viet Cong and US tactics to see why the US army could not win. Focus Task B will direct your reading.

FOCUS TASK A

Why did the USA get involved in Vietnam?

1 Draw a timeline of the period 1945–1965.
2 Mark on it increasing American involvement using the following headings:
   - No direct American involvement
   - Financial support
   - Political involvement
   - Military involvement.
3 Write annotations to show the date on which each of these phases started and what events triggered the increasing involvement.
4 Choose two events that you think were critical in getting the USA involved in a war in Vietnam. Explain your choice.

FOCUS TASK B

Why was the US army unable to defeat the Communists in Vietnam?

Stage 1: Gathering the evidence

1 Make your own copy of this chart:

Qualities of a successful army	The US army	⟋▲ or ▲⟍	The Viet Cong
Good soldiers			
The right technology			
Good supplies and equipment			
Effective tactics			
Support from the Vietnamese population			
Motivated and committed soldiers			
Other			

2 Using pages 356–61, make notes in columns 2 and 4 to record how far each side had each quality.
3 Add other rows if you wish to.

Stage 2: Thinking it through

4 Next, in each row of column 3, draw some scales to show which way the balance falls for this quality. Did the USA or the Viet Cong have the advantage?
5 Now think about the overall picture – how the strengths and weaknesses work together.
   a) Were the armies finely balanced or was the balance strongly weighted to one side or the other?
   b) Which quality was most important in determining who won the war? Was one feature so important that being ahead in that area meant that other advantages or disadvantages did not matter?

Stage 3: Explaining your conclusions

6 Now write up your answer. You could use this structure:
   a) Describe how the failure of the US army was a combination of its own weaknesses and Viet Cong strengths.
   b) Give balanced examples of US successes and failures.
   c) Give balanced examples of Viet Cong successes and failures.
   d) Choose one American weakness and one Viet Cong strength that you think were absolutely vital in preventing the USA from beating the Viet Cong and explain the significance of the points you have chosen.

Stage 4: Thinking more deeply

Keep your work. You'll be adding to it later, on page 364.

Viet Cong and guerrilla tactics

In early 1965 the Viet Cong had about 170,000 soldiers. They were well supplied with weapons and equipment from China and the USSR, but they were heavily outnumbered and outgunned by the South Vietnamese forces and their US allies. The Communist forces were no match for the US and South Vietnamese forces in open warfare. In November 1965 in the La Dreng Valley, US forces killed 2000 Viet Cong for the loss of 300 troops. This did not daunt Ho Chi Minh. He believed that superior forces could be defeated by guerrilla tactics. He had been in China and seen Mao Tse-tung use guerrilla warfare to achieve a Communist victory there. Ho had also used these guerrilla tactics himself against the Japanese and the French. The principles were simple: retreat when the enemy attacks; raid when the enemy camps; attack when the enemy tires; pursue when the enemy retreats.

Guerrilla warfare was a nightmare for the US army. Guerrillas did not wear uniform. They had no known base camp or headquarters. They worked in small groups with limited weapons. They were hard to tell apart from the peasants in the villages. They attacked and then disappeared into the jungle, into the villages or into their tunnels (see Source 36).

The aim of guerrilla attacks was to wear down the enemy soldiers and wreck their morale. This was very effective. US soldiers lived in constant fear of ambushes or booby traps.

Ho knew how important it was to keep the population on his side. The Viet Cong fighters were expected to be courteous and respectful to the Vietnamese peasants. They often helped the peasants in the fields during busy periods.

However, the Viet Cong could be ruthless – they were quite prepared to kill peasants who opposed them or who co-operated with their enemies. They also conducted a campaign of terror against the police, tax collectors, teachers and any other employees of the South Vietnamese government. Between 1966 and 1971 the Viet Cong killed an estimated 27,000 civilians.

The greatest strength of the Viet Cong fighters was that they simply refused to give in. The Viet Cong depended on supplies from North Vietnam that came along the Ho Chi Minh trail. US and South Vietnamese planes bombed this constantly, but 40,000 Vietnamese worked to keep it open whatever the cost. The total of Viet Cong and North Vietnamese dead in the war has been estimated at 1 million – far higher than US losses. However, this was a price that Ho Chi Minh was prepared to pay. Whatever the casualties, there were replacement troops available.

1 One Viet Cong leader said: 'The people are the water. Our armies are the fish.' What do you think he meant?
2 Choose one piece of evidence to show that the Viet Cong had the support of the Vietnamese people.
3 Choose one piece of evidence that suggests that they did not.

SOURCE 36

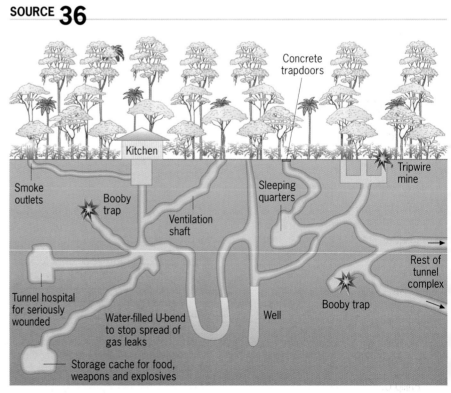

A Viet Cong tunnel complex. To avoid the worst effects of American air power, the Viet Cong built a vast network of underground tunnels, probably around 240 km of them.

SOURCE 37

A Viet Cong poster.

SOURCE 38

U.S. Imperialism, Get Out of South Viet Nam!
L'imperialisme americain hors du Sud-Vietnam!
¡Fuera el imperialismo norteamericano del Sur de Vietnam!

A Chinese poster commenting on the Vietnam War.

SOURCE 39

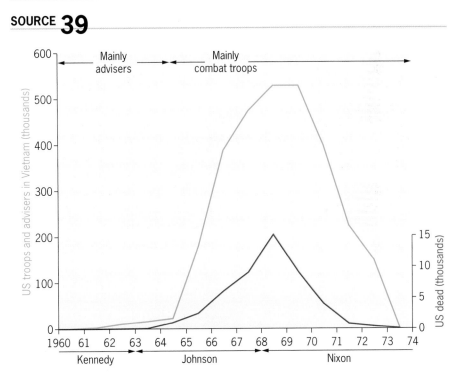

US troops and deaths in Vietnam, 1960–74. US troops were not the only foreign soldiers in the war. About 46,000 Australian and New Zealand troops fought too.

SOURCE 40

I remember sitting at this wretched little outpost one day with a couple of my sergeants. We'd been manning this thing for three weeks and running patrols off it. We were grungy and sore with jungle rot and we'd suffered about nine or ten casualties on a recent patrol. This one sergeant of mine said, 'You know, Lieutenant, I don't see how we're ever going to win this.' And I said, 'Well, Sarge, I'm not supposed to say this to you as your officer – but I don't either.' So there was this sense that we just couldn't see what could be done to defeat these people.

Philip Caputo, a lieutenant in the Marine Corps in Vietnam in 1965–66, speaking in 1997.

FOCUS TASK

Why did the Communists use guerrilla tactics in the Vietnam War?

1 Copy the boxed sentence below. Add bullet points around the central sentence starter to give the Viet Cong's reasons. Use the text and sources on pages 356–57 for ideas. Remember also that the internet has a wealth of material on the Vietnam War that could help you with your research. Your teacher can suggest some sites to help you begin.
2 To each of your bullets, connect a second bullet point giving evidence to support it.

> **The Viet Cong used guerrilla tactics because . . .**

357

US tactics in Vietnam, 1965–1972

Bombing

People in the South Vietnamese city of Hue sort through the wreckage of their homes after a US bombing raid in 1968.

On 7 February 1965 the USA launched Operation Rolling Thunder. Rolling Thunder involved extensive bombing raids on military and industrial targets in North Vietnam. It was the beginning of an air offensive that was to last until 1972. The list of targets was soon expanded to include towns and cities in North and South Vietnam. The list also included sites in Laos and Cambodia along the Ho Chi Minh trail. More bombs were dropped on North Vietnam than were dropped in the whole of the Second World War on Germany and Japan.

To some extent bombing was effective.

- It certainly damaged North Vietnam's war effort and it disrupted supply routes.
- It enabled the USA to strike at Communist forces even when it was reducing US ground forces in Vietnam after 1969.
- From 1970 to 1972, intense bombing campaigns against Hanoi (North Vietnam's capital) and the port of Haiphong forced the North Vietnamese to the negotiating table.

However, US air power could not defeat the Communists – it could only slow them down. The Viet Cong continued to operate its supply lines. Even after major air raids on North Vietnam in 1972, the Communists were still able to launch a major assault on the South.

The cost of the air war was horrendous. The Communists shot down 14,000 US and South Vietnamese aircraft. In 1967 the American *Life* magazine calculated that it cost the USA $400,000 to kill one Viet Cong fighter, a figure that included 75 bombs and 400 artillery shells.

Chemical weapons

The US developed a powerful chemical weapon called Agent Orange. It was a sort of highly toxic 'weedkiller'. It was used to destroy the jungle where the Viet Cong hid. The Americans used 82 million litres of Agent Orange to spray thousands of square kilometres of jungle. Napalm was another widely-used chemical weapon. It destroyed jungles where guerrillas might hide. It also burned through skin to the bone. Many civilians and soldiers were also killed by these chemical weapons.

A ten-year-old Vietnamese girl runs naked after tearing her burning clothes from her body following a napalm attack. This photograph became one of the most enduring images of the war.

THE COLD WAR 1950-1975

1 'Mixed results.' Is this a fair summary of the effectiveness of bombing in the Vietnam War? Explain your answer.
2 Would you say the US ground forces in Vietnam were more or less effective than the air forces? Explain your answer.

Search and destroy

Bombing could not defeat a guerrilla army. The US commander General Westmoreland developed a policy of search and destroy. He established secure and heavily defended US bases in the south of the country and near to the coasts. From here, US and South Vietnamese forces launched search-and-destroy raids from helicopters. They would descend on a village and destroy any Viet Cong forces they found. Soldiers had to send back reports of body counts.

Search-and-destroy missions did kill Viet Cong soldiers, but there were problems.

- The raids were often based on inadequate information.
- Inexperienced US troops often walked into traps.
- Innocent villages were mistaken for Viet Cong strongholds.
- Civilian casualties were extremely high in these raids. For every Viet Cong weapon captured by search-and-destroy, there was a body count of six. Many of these were innocent civilians.
- Search-and-destroy tactics made the US and South Vietnamese forces very unpopular with the peasants. It pushed them towards supporting the Viet Cong.

SOURCE 43

An increasing number of recruits scored so low on the standardised intelligence tests that they would have been excluded from the normal peacetime army. The tour of duty in Vietnam was one year. Soldiers were most likely to die in their first month. The large majority of deaths took place in the first six months. Just as a soldier began gaining experience, he was sent home. A rookie army which constantly rotated inexperienced men was pitted against experienced guerrillas on their home ground.

From *Four Hours in My Lai* by Michael Bilton, 1992. The average age of US combat troops in Vietnam was only 19. Many recruits had just left school. This was their first experience of war.

SOURCE 44

US troops on a search-and-destroy mission in Vietnam.

The Tet Offensive, 1968 – a turning point

In 1968 the Communists launched a major offensive. During the Tet New Year holiday, Viet Cong fighters attacked over 100 cities and other military targets. One Viet Cong commando unit tried to capture the US embassy in Saigon. US forces had to fight to regain control room by room. Around 4500 fighters tied down a much larger US and South Vietnamese force in Saigon for two days.

In many ways the Tet Offensive was a disaster for the Communists. They hoped that the people of South Vietnam would rise up and join them. They didn't. The Viet Cong lost around 10,000 experienced fighters and were badly weakened by it.

However, the Tet Offensive proved to be a turning point in the war because it raised hard questions about the war in the USA.

- There were nearly 500,000 troops in Vietnam and the USA was spending $20 billion a year on the war. So why had the Communists been able to launch a major offensive that took US forces completely by surprise?
- US and South Vietnamese forces quickly retook the towns captured in the offensive, but in the process they used enormous amounts of artillery and air power. Many civilians were killed. The ancient city of Hue was destroyed (see Source 41). Was this right?

3 Why was the Tet Offensive a turning point? Explain your answer.

The Peace Movement in the USA

SOURCE 45

Vietnam is thousands of miles from the USA . . . Contrary to the 1954 Geneva conference, the USA has ceaselessly intervened in Vietnam. The US government has committed war crimes . . . Half a million US troops have resorted to inhuman weapons . . . Napalm, toxic chemicals and gases have been used to massacre our people, destroy our crops and raze our villages to the ground . . . US aircraft have dropped thousands of bombs destroying towns, villages, hospitals, schools. We will never submit to force; never accept talks under threat of bombs.

Ho Chi Minh speaking in 1967.

SOURCE 46

One does not use napalm on villages and hamlets sheltering civilians if one is attempting to persuade these people of the rightness of one's cause. One does not defoliate [destroy the vegetation of] the country and deform its people with chemicals if one is attempting to persuade them of the foe's evil nature.

An American comments on US policy failure in Vietnam.

For a war on such a scale the USA had to have the support of the American public, but it was increasingly difficult to keep it. Public opinion in the USA was turning against the war even before the Tet Offensive. After it, the war became very unpopular. Many Americans felt deeply uncomfortable with what was going on in Vietnam.

The Vietnam War was a media war. Thousands of television, radio and newspaper reporters, and a vast army of photographers sent back to the USA and Europe reports and pictures of the fighting. Television showed prisoners being tortured or executed (see Source 47), or women and children watching with horror as their house was set on fire.

SOURCE 47

A Viet Cong suspect is executed in the street by a South Vietnamese policeman in February 1968. Televisions beamed this scene into the living rooms of the USA. It deeply shocked the American people.

SOURCE 48

The Quang Ngai area of Vietnam.

The media showed crying children burned by American napalm bombs. Was this why 900,000 young Americans had been drafted? Instead of Vietnam being a symbol of a US crusade against Communism, it had become a symbol of defeat and confusion. There were anti-war protests all over the country. Students taunted the American President Lyndon B Johnson with the chant 'Hey, Hey LBJ, how many kids did you kill today?' Thousands began to 'draft dodge' – refusing to serve in Vietnam when they were called up. There were hundreds of demonstrations in universities across the USA (see page 387). At the most infamous, at Kent State University in Ohio, the National Guard broke up the demonstration, killing four students. The public was horrified. The Vietnam War seemed to be making the USA unstable.

Against this background one event had a particularly devastating effect on American and international support for the war – the My Lai Massacre.

The My Lai massacre

In March 1968, a unit of young American soldiers called Charlie Company started a search-and-destroy mission in the Quang Ngai region of South Vietnam. They had been told that in the My Lai area there was a Viet Cong headquarters, and 200 Viet Cong guerrillas. The soldiers had been ordered to destroy all houses, dwellings and livestock. They had been told that all the villagers would have left for market because it was a Saturday. Most of them were under the impression that they had been ordered to kill everyone they found in the village.

Early in the morning of 16 March, Charlie Company arrived in My Lai. In the next four hours, between 300 and 400 civilians were killed. They were mostly women, children and old men. Some were killed while they worked in their fields. Many of them were mown down by machine-gun fire as they were herded into an irrigation ditch. Others were shot in their homes. No Viet Cong were found in the village. Only three weapons were recovered.

At the time, the army treated the operation as a success. The commanding officer's report said that 20 non-combatants had been killed by accident in the attack, but the rest of the dead were recorded as being Viet Cong. The officers and men involved were praised. The event passed into army folklore. All the soldiers knew that it had taken place, but they just took it to be a normal and inevitable part of the war.

However, 12 months later, a letter arrived in the offices of 30 leading politicians and government officials in Washington. It was written by Ronald Ridenhour, an American soldier who had served in Vietnam and who personally knew many of the soldiers who took part in the massacre. He had evidence, he said, of 'something rather dark and bloody' that had occurred in My Lai – or Pinkville as the American soldiers called it. He recounted in detail all the stories he had been told about what had taken place and asked Congress to investigate.

Soon after, *Life* magazine, one of the most influential magazines in the USA, published photographs of the massacre at My Lai that had been taken by an official army photographer.

This triggered an investigation that ended in the trial for mass murder of Lieutenant William Calley. He was an officer in Charlie Company. He had personally shot many of the people in the irrigation ditch at My Lai. In September 1969 he was formally charged with murdering 109 people. Ten other members of the company and the commanding officers were also charged. The charges were too much for the army. They placed all responsibility on Calley. They denied that Calley was acting under orders. His senior officers were acquitted. After a long court case surrounded by massive media attention and publicity, in March 1971 Calley was found guilty of the murder of 22 civilians. In August he was sentenced to 20 years' hard labour. In November 1974 he was released.

The revelations about My Lai deeply shocked the American public. It was the clearest evidence that the war had gone wrong. In November 1969, almost 700,000 anti-war protesters demonstrated in Washington DC. It was the largest political protest in American history.

SOURCE 49

In the end anybody who was still in that country was the enemy. The same village you'd gone in to give them medical treatment . . . you could go through that village later and get shot at by a sniper. Go back in and you would not find anybody. Nobody knew anything. We were trying to work with these people, they were basically doing a number on us. You didn't trust them anymore. You didn't trust anybody.

Fred Widmer, an American soldier, speaking in 1969.

SOURCE 50

A photograph taken at My Lai on 16 March 1968.

1 Are Sources 51 and 52 making the same point?
2 Why do you think it took 12 months for anyone to do anything about the massacre?
3 Why was the massacre so shocking to the American public?

FOCUS TASK

Work in pairs.

You are opponents of American involvement in Vietnam. Use the evidence in this chapter to make a poster or a leaflet putting forward your views.

You can include stories and images from pages 353–61. However, you must also include an explanation that will convince the supporters of containment that the policy is not working in Vietnam.

SOURCE 51

Most of the soldiers had never been away from home before they went into service. And they end up in Vietnam going there many of them because they thought they were going to do something courageous on behalf of their country, something which they thought was in the American ideal.

But it didn't mean slaughtering whole villages of women and children. One of my friends, when he told me about it, said: 'You know it was a Nazi kind of thing.' We didn't go there to be Nazis. At least none of the people I knew went there to be Nazis.

Written by Ronald Ridenhour.

SOURCE 52

We were not in My Lai to kill human beings, really. We were there to kill ideology that is carried by – I don't know – pawns. Blobs. Pieces of flesh. And I wasn't in My Lai to destroy intelligent men. I was there to destroy an intangible idea. To destroy Communism.

From Lieutenant Calley's account of the event, *Body Count*, published in 1970.

Ending the war in Vietnam

After the Tet Offensive President Johnson concluded that the war could not be won militarily. He reduced the bombing campaign against North Vietnam and instructed his officials to begin negotiating for peace with the Communists. In March 1968 a peace conference began in Paris.

Johnson also announced that he would not be seeking re-election as President. It was an admission of failure. In the election campaign both Republican and Democrat candidates campaigned to end US involvement in Vietnam. The anti-Vietnam feeling was so strong that if they had supported continuing the war they would have had no chance of being elected anyway. It was no longer a question of 'could the USA win the war?' – now it was 'how can the USA get out of Vietnam without it looking like a defeat?'

In November 1968 Richard Nixon was elected President. From 1969 to 1973 he and his National Security Adviser Henry Kissinger worked tirelessly to end US involvement in Vietnam. This was not easy because the bigger question of how to contain world Communism – the one that had got the USA into Vietnam in the first place – had not gone away. They did not want to appear simply to hand Vietnam to the Communists. They used a range of strategies.

SOURCE 53

Pressure on the USSR and China
In 1969 the USSR and China fell out. Indeed, late in 1969, it seemed possible that there would even be a war between these two powerful Communist countries. As a result, both the USSR and China tried to improve relations with the USA.

- In 1970 Nixon began Strategic Arms Limitation Talks (SALT) with the USSR to limit nuclear weapons. He asked Moscow to encourage North Vietnam to end the war.
- Nixon also started to improve relations with China. In February 1972 Nixon was invited to China. As with the USSR, he asked China to pressure North Vietnam to end the war.

Peace negotiations with North Vietnam
From early 1969, Kissinger had regular meetings with the chief Vietnamese peace negotiator, Le Duc Tho.

'Vietnamisation' of the war effort
In Vietnam Nixon began the process of Vietnamisation – building up South Vietnamese forces and withdrawing US troops. Between April 1969 and the end of 1971 almost 400,000 US troops left Vietnam.

Bombing
Nixon increased bombing campaigns against North Vietnam to show he was not weak. He also invaded Viet Cong bases in Cambodia, causing outrage across the world, and even in the USA.

US strategies to extricate US troops from involvement in Vietnam.

SOURCE 54

1 *Immediate cease-fire.*
2 *Release of all prisoners of war within 60 days.*
3 *Withdrawal of all US forces and bases.*
4 *Full accounting of missing in action.*
5 *Self-determination for South Vietnam.*

The main points of the peace agreement of January 1973.

In 1972, the North Vietnamese launched a major offensive but were unable to conquer South Vietnam. In Paris in January 1973, Le Duc Tho, Nixon and the South Vietnamese President Thieu signed a peace agreement (see Source 54). Nixon was jubilant. He described the agreement as 'peace with honour'. Others disagreed (see Source 56), but the door was now open for Nixon to pull out all US troops. By 29 March 1973, the last American forces had left Vietnam.

SOURCE 55

WHO LOST VIET NAM?

"NOT I," SAID IKE. "I JUST SENT MONEY."

"NOT I," SAID JACK. "I JUST SENT ADVISORS."

"NOT I," SAID LYNDON. "I JUST FOLLOWED JACK."

"NOT I," SAID DICK. "I JUST HONORED JACK AND LYNDON'S COMMITMENTS."

"NOT I," SAID JERRY. "WHAT WAS THE QUESTION?"

"YOU LOST VIETNAM," SAID HENRY, "BECAUSE YOU DIDN'T TRUST YOUR LEADERS."

A 1975 American cartoon commenting on the end of the Vietnam War.

SOURCE 56

FOR WHOM THE BELL TOLLS

. . . the nation began at last to extricate itself from a quicksandy war that had plagued four Presidents and driven one from office, that had sundered the country more deeply than any event since the Civil War, that in the end came to be seen by a great majority of Americans as having been a tragic mistake.

. . . but its more grievous toll was paid at home – a wound to the spirit so sore that news of peace stirred only the relief that comes with an end to pain. A war that produced no famous victories, no national heroes and no strong patriotic songs, produced no memorable armistice day celebrations either. America was too exhausted by the war and too chary of peace to celebrate.

Reaction to the agreement of January 1973 in the American magazine *Newsweek*, 5 February 1973.

1 Describe the attitude of Sources 55 and 56 to the agreement of January 1973.

ACTIVITY

Why isn't the USA celebrating the end of the Vietnam War?

It is 1973. Peace has been secured in Vietnam and the final US troops have left. You have to write an article for a British newspaper explaining why the USA is not celebrating. You are trying to convey the mood of the American people. Use the evidence on pages 354–63.

Remember that you are writing for a British audience. They will know about the Vietnam War. However, they will not be clear on how it has affected Americans.

The fall of South Vietnam, 1973–75

It is not clear whether Nixon really believed he had secured a lasting peace settlement. But within two years it was meaningless and South Vietnam had fallen to the Communists.

Nixon had promised continuing financial aid and military support to Vietnam, but Congress refused to allow it. They did not want to waste American money. The evidence was that the South Vietnamese regime was corrupt and lacked the support of the majority of the population. Even more important, Nixon himself was in big political trouble with the Watergate Scandal (see pages 394–95). In 1974 Nixon was forced to resign over Watergate, but the new President, Gerald Ford, also failed to get the backing of Congress over Vietnam.

Without US air power or military back-up and without the support of the majority of the population, the South Vietnamese government could not survive for long. In December 1974 the North Vietnamese launched a major military offensive against South Vietnam. The capital, Saigon, fell to Communist forces in April 1975.

One of the bleakest symbols of American failure in Vietnam was the televised news images of desperate Vietnamese men, women and children trying to clamber aboard American helicopters taking off from the US embassy. All around them Communist forces swarmed through Saigon. After 30 years of constant conflict, the struggle for control of Vietnam had finally been settled and the Communists had won.

FOCUS TASK A

Why did the USA lose the Vietnam War?

Look back at your answers to Focus Task B on page 355. You will find them very useful for this summary activity.

The Americans did not lose purely for military reasons. There were other factors as well.

1 In the centre of a large sheet of paper put the question: Why did the USA lose the Vietnam War?
2 Around the question, draw six boxes. In five boxes write an explanation or paste a source which shows the importance of the following factors:
   • US military tactics in Vietnam
   • the unpopularity of the South Vietnamese regime
   • the experience of the Viet Cong and the inexperience of the American soldiers
   • opposition to the war in the USA
   • Chinese and Soviet support for the Viet Cong.
3 In the sixth box write: 'But did they really lose?' and summarise the argument put forward in Source 57, and your view on it.
4 Add other boxes if you think there are factors you should consider.
5 Add lines to connect the factors and write an explanation of the connection.

SOURCE 57

The American military was not defeated in Vietnam –
The American military did not lose a battle of any consequence. From a military standpoint, it was almost an unprecedented performance. This included Tet 68, which was a major military defeat for the VC and NVA.

The United States did not lose the war in Vietnam, the South Vietnamese did –
The fall of Saigon happened 30 April 1975, two years AFTER the American military left Vietnam. The last American troops departed in their entirety 29 March 1973. How could we lose a war we had already stopped fighting? We fought to an agreed stalemate.

The Fall of Saigon –
The 140,000 evacuees in April 1975 during the fall of Saigon consisted almost entirely of civilians and Vietnamese military, NOT American military running for their lives.

There were almost twice as many casualties in Southeast Asia (primarily Cambodia) the first two years after the fall of Saigon in 1975 than there were during the ten years the US was involved in Vietnam.

An extract from a website, 'Vietnam War Statistics', by an American ex-serviceman.

FOCUS TASK B

How successful was the USA's policy of containment?

1 Look back at your chart from page 341. Make and complete a similar chart for the Vietnam War.
2 You have now looked at three very different case studies of the USA's attempts to contain Communism. Using the work you have done for the tasks on pages 341, 352 and this page, explain:
   • how successful you feel the American policy was
   • what the main reasons were for its success or failure.

How did the Vietnam War affect the policy of containment?

The American policy of containment was in tatters.

It had failed militarily. The war had shown that even the USA's vast military strength could not stem the spread of Communism.

It had also failed politically. Not only did the USA fail to stop South Vietnam going Communist, but the heavy bombing of Vietnam's neighbours, Laos and Cambodia, actually helped the Communist forces in those countries to win support. By 1975 both Laos and Cambodia had Communist governments. Instead of slowing it down, American policies actually speeded up the domino effect in the region.

It was also a propaganda disaster. The Americans had always presented their campaign against Communism as a moral crusade. But atrocities committed by American soldiers and the use of chemical weapons damaged the USA's reputation. The whole campaign was shown to be flawed. The Americans were propping up a government that did not have the support of its own people.

The failure greatly affected the USA's policies towards Communist states. After the war, the Americans tried to improve their relations with China. They ended their block on China's membership of the UN, and the President made visits to China. They entered into a period of greater understanding with the Soviet Union. In fact, during the 1970s both the Soviet Union and China got on better with the USA than they did with each other. The Americans became very suspicious of involving their troops in any other conflict which they could not easily and overwhelmingly win. This was an attitude that continued to affect American foreign policy into the twenty-first century.

What were the consequences of the Vietnam War?

Thirty years of war leaves its mark on a country. War is not a game. After a war you don't just pack up your kit, have a shower and get on with life. The diagram below summarises some of the consequences of the war on Vietnam and the USA.

FOCUS TASK

1 Study this diagram.
2 Are there other consequences that you have studied on pages 353–64 which should be added to it?
3 Compare the impact of this war with the impact of another conflict you have studied. Do you think it was lesser or greater? Give your reasons.

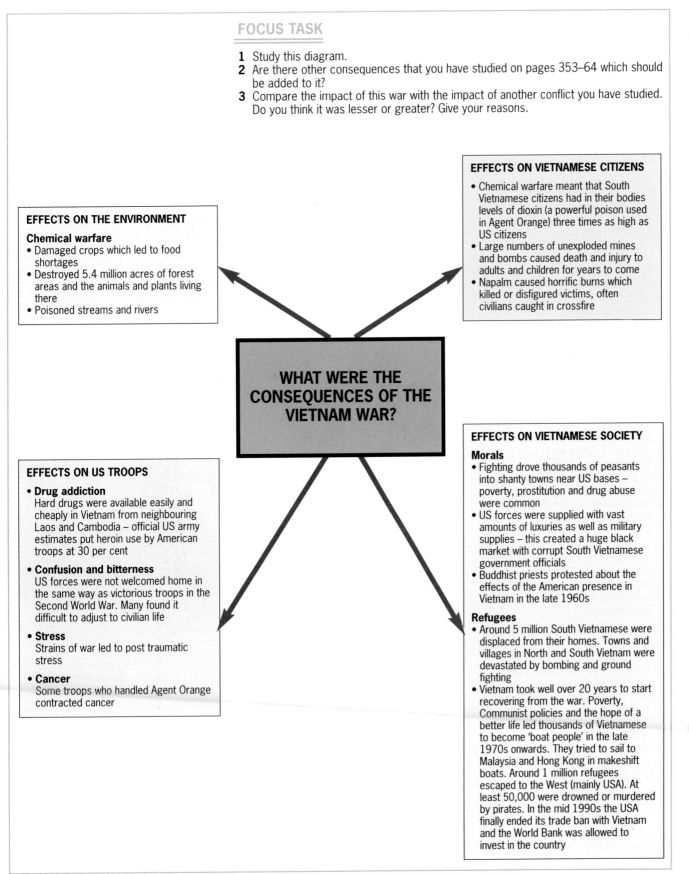

EFFECTS ON THE ENVIRONMENT

Chemical warfare
- Damaged crops which led to food shortages
- Destroyed 5.4 million acres of forest areas and the animals and plants living there
- Poisoned streams and rivers

EFFECTS ON VIETNAMESE CITIZENS
- Chemical warfare meant that South Vietnamese citizens had in their bodies levels of dioxin (a powerful poison used in Agent Orange) three times as high as US citizens
- Large numbers of unexploded mines and bombs caused death and injury to adults and children for years to come
- Napalm caused horrific burns which killed or disfigured victims, often civilians caught in crossfire

WHAT WERE THE CONSEQUENCES OF THE VIETNAM WAR?

EFFECTS ON US TROOPS

- **Drug addiction**
  Hard drugs were available easily and cheaply in Vietnam from neighbouring Laos and Cambodia – official US army estimates put heroin use by American troops at 30 per cent

- **Confusion and bitterness**
  US forces were not welcomed home in the same way as victorious troops in the Second World War. Many found it difficult to adjust to civilian life

- **Stress**
  Strains of war led to post traumatic stress

- **Cancer**
  Some troops who handled Agent Orange contracted cancer

EFFECTS ON VIETNAMESE SOCIETY

Morals
- Fighting drove thousands of peasants into shanty towns near US bases – poverty, prostitution and drug abuse were common
- US forces were supplied with vast amounts of luxuries as well as military supplies – this created a huge black market with corrupt South Vietnamese government officials
- Buddhist priests protested about the effects of the American presence in Vietnam in the late 1960s

Refugees
- Around 5 million South Vietnamese were displaced from their homes. Towns and villages in North and South Vietnam were devastated by bombing and ground fighting
- Vietnam took well over 20 years to start recovering from the war. Poverty, Communist policies and the hope of a better life led thousands of Vietnamese to become 'boat people' in the late 1970s onwards. They tried to sail to Malaysia and Hong Kong in makeshift boats. Around 1 million refugees escaped to the West (mainly USA). At least 50,000 were drowned or murdered by pirates. In the mid 1990s the USA finally ended its trade ban with Vietnam and the World Bank was allowed to invest in the country

13

The USA 1941–1980

FOCUS

The USA dominated the history of the twentieth century. Its economic and military power made it the most important country in the world.

In Chapters 11 and 12, you studied how the USA abandoned its isolationist stance and tried to get involved in sorting out other countries' problems – with mixed results. In this chapter, you now turn your attention to what was going on within the USA. How well did the US government tackle the problems it faced at home from the 1940s to the 1980s? You will:

■ examine the impact of the Second World War on the US economy and society
■ analyse the reasons for McCarthyism and the anti-Communist Red Scare of the 1950s
■ investigate the civil rights movement of the 1950s and 1960s and see how far the campaign to win equal rights for black Americans succeeded
■ find out why the 1960s saw so many other protest movements
■ compare the achievements of Presidents Kennedy and Johnson and make up your own mind how far their reputations are deserved
■ consider why the Watergate scandal in the 1970s was so damaging to President Nixon's reputation and to the American government.

Some people would say that in this period the USA's troubled domestic history shows it to be more the 'divided' states than the 'united' states. In this chapter you can decide whether this is justified.

ACTIVITY

Look closely at Source 1 and explain what picture the mural paints of the USA at war. You could present your views as a paragraph of text, as a set of bullet points or by annotating your own copy of the mural.

Keep your work – you are going to need it again on page 370.

A divided union?

The USA at war

Source 1 shows you how the US government, during the Second World War, wanted people to see the war effort. But does this view fit with the evidence? You will come back to this question on page 370.

SOURCE 1

New York's Grand Central Station in 1942. The entire east wall was covered by a gigantic mural promoting war bonds. Ordinary people bought war bonds which helped to pay for the war effort.

SOURCE 2

B-26 bombers being produced in the Martin factory in Baltimore, April, 1941

SOURCE 3

A poster produced by the Studebaker motor company in 1944.

Wartime production

The achievements of the American war economy were staggering. In a summit meeting Soviet leader Stalin proposed a toast: 'To American production, without which this war would have been lost.'

The USA shifted from peacetime to wartime production amazingly quickly. Between 1941 and 1945, American factories produced 250,000 aircraft, 90,000 tanks, 350 naval destroyers, 200 submarines and 5600 merchant ships. By 1944, the USA was producing almost half of the weapons being made in the world – more than twice the production of Germany and Japan combined. American industry was also providing food, clothing, vehicles, rubber tyres, engines and engine parts, tools and countless other items for not only its own huge forces but also those of its Allies. How was this done?

Willing industrialists

In January 1942, President Roosevelt set up the War Production Board under the industrialist William Knusden. Knusden believed it would be impossible for the USA to get the goods it wanted without the willing co-operation of factory bosses. He called in the USA's leading industrialists. He asked their advice about how to meet war production needs rather than setting them targets. He even let them decide which companies would produce particular goods. For example:

- General Motors produced heavy machine guns and thousands of other war products.
- The Chrysler Corporation produced anti-aircraft guns.
- General Electric increased its production of turbines by 300 times in 1942.

Around 80 per cent of American contracts went to only 100 firms, although the work ended up with thousands of smaller firms which were subcontracted to supply tools, materials and equipment. These large firms wanted to help the war effort, but they also stood to make a lot of money out of it.

One of the most important industrialists in the USA's war effort was Henry J Kaiser. He had been a major force in the Tennessee Valley Authority during the New Deal programme (see page 219). Kaiser developed the USA's metal and shipbuilding industries. He designed and built the Liberty ships, turning out one of these large cargo ships every 42 days by 1943.

SOURCE 4

If you are going to try to go to war . . . in a capitalist country you've got to let business make money out of the process or business won't work.

From the diary of Henry Stimson, the US Secretary for War, written in 1941.

---

1 What is the aim of Source 3?
2 Look at Source 4. Is it right that businesses should make money out of war? What do you think?

Extra workers

Around 16 million American men and women served in the US armed forces, so on the home front they needed many more workers. Fourteen million worked in the factories. General Motors alone took on an extra 0.75 million workers during the war. Most of the manufacturing jobs were in the industrial north or on the Pacific coast. Around 4 million workers migrated from the rural south to these areas. This included a very significant number of black Americans. Nearly 0.75 million black Americans found work in the war industries. (You can find out how they fared on pages 370–71). California saw an influx of 1.5 million new workers.

All available women

Before the war, there were already 12 million working women. During the war, 300,000 women joined the armed forces and another 7 million joined the workforce. Women's air service pilots (WASPs) flew every type of American warplane in tests and delivery runs from the factories to the airfields where they were stationed. One in three aircraft workers were women. Women were often given difficult welding jobs in awkward parts of aircraft bodies because they were smaller and more agile. In the munitions and electronics industries, one in two workers was a woman. Most fuses were made by women, because they generally had nimbler fingers. In a government survey, 60 per cent of American plant managers said that the women were their best workers. The media created a poster campaign featuring Rosie the Riveter (see Source 5). Hollywood even made a movie about Rosie.

However, it was not all positive for women. Women workers were not always welcomed by their male colleagues or by trade unionists who felt that women were a threat to jobs and to pay levels – women earned up to 60 per cent less than men for the same work. Factories made little or no effort to provide child-care facilities. Congress resisted President Roosevelt's plans to ensure equal pay for men and women in the armed forces.

After the war, women simply left their wartime jobs – they had to, since they had been doing 'men's jobs'. But many did not give up paid work completely. They may not have been riveters any more, but they found other work as secretaries, clerks and shop assistants. One result of wartime employment was a big shift in work patterns over the next 20 years (see page 384).

1 Why are Sources 5 and 6 more useful to historians when studied together than separately?
2 Were changes for US women revolutionary? Explain your answer.

SOURCE 5

A poster from wartime USA featuring Rosie the Riveter.

SOURCE 6

Women at work riveting an aircraft.

SOURCE 7

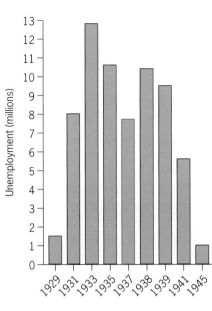

Unemployment in the USA, 1929–45.

War and prosperity

Of all the countries involved in fighting the Second World War, the USA was the only one that emerged economically stronger as a result.

- More than half a million new businesses started up during the war. Many became rich as a result of war contracts. Coca-Cola set up plants to follow the troops around the world (in the process, making Coca-Cola the most successful soft drink in the world). Wrigley took on the role of packaging rations for US forces (adding Wrigley's chewing gum to the rations, of course).
- The war effort ended unemployment – something that Roosevelt's New Deal had failed to do (see page 218).
- Even American farmers, after almost 20 years of depressed prices and economic crisis, began to enjoy better times as the USA exported food to help its allies.
- Ordinary Americans invested their income in bonds. They effectively lent money to the government by buying war bonds, with a promise that the bonds would be paid back *with interest* at the end of the war. In the course of the war, Americans contributed $129 billion to the war effort by buying bonds.

The Americans suffered hardships, of course. There was rationing, but shortages were not on the scale that Europe and Japan were enduring. American companies even turned the shortages to their advantage. They ran adverts explaining to customers who could not get their favourite chocolate or soap that the shortages were because their goods were being sent to the forces, boosting the image of their products in the process!

Internment of Japanese Americans

The USA had a large Japanese immigrant population – particularly on the Pacific coast. The Japanese attack on Pearl Harbor in December 1941 (see page 275) created a wave of anti-Japanese feeling in much of the USA. On the West Coast, however, most residents were sympathetic to the Japanese Americans to start with. They did not blame them for Japanese aggression. However, official propaganda whipped up hysteria against the Japanese Americans. Under General John De Witt, US security forces rounded up 120,000 Japanese Americans in California, Washington State, Arizona and Oregon in 1942. It was a brutal policy:

- They were transported to bleak internment camps in remote areas of the USA and most were kept there until 1945.
- Many of them lost most of their property, or were forced to sell it at very low prices.
- No account was taken of whether the people were Issei (immigrants actually born in Japan) or Nisei (children of immigrants and therefore born in the USA).
- In other US states, Japanese people were subjected to vandalism, abuse and even murder.

With hindsight, it is easy to see that this policy owed more to racism than to security. No German or Italian Americans were interned, although the USA was also at war with those countries. Chinese Americans were mistakenly attacked simply because they looked Japanese. On the other hand, the US state of Hawaii did not intern Japanese Americans (and it suffered no sabotage).

The interned Japanese Americans themselves amazed the guards in the camps with their dignity and patriotism. They raised the Stars and Stripes flag each morning. In January 1943, Congress allowed Japanese Americans to serve in the armed forces and 33,000 immediately volunteered, including thousands who were in the internment camps. The all-Nisei infantry units in the US army were among the most highly decorated for bravery in the war.

Not all Americans supported the internment policy. Many lawyers argued that it was a contravention of the US Constitution. As early as 1944, a US Supreme Court judge called the policy 'government racism'. In 1988 the US Congress voted an apology for the policy and paid $20,000 compensation each to all surviving internees.

ACTIVITY

Imagine you are a journalist in the USA in 1942. You have just found out about the internment of the Japanese. Explain:

1 How you could write a very controversial article, and what you could put in it.
2 Why you probably won't do this.

Black Americans

For black Americans the war effort was full of contradictions.

In the armed forces

US forces were fighting against Nazi Germany, a state that was openly racist. Black Americans rallied to the cause. Over 1 million black Americans joined the armed forces.

However, their wartime experience highlighted the extent of racism and discrimination in the USA itself. In the army, black soldiers usually served in black-only units with white officers. It was not until 1944 that the US marines allowed black soldiers into combat. Up to that point, they had only been used for transporting supplies, or as cooks and labourers (they were often referred to as mules). Many black women served in the armed forces as nurses, but they were only allowed to tend black soldiers. In one incident in the American south, a rail company restaurant refused to serve US black soldiers who were guarding German prisoners of war on a train, yet they were prepared to serve the white German prisoners.

From 1944, black soldiers were fighting in combat units and there were hundreds of black officers in the army and marines. Black units distinguished themselves in Europe at the Battle of the Bulge (1944) and in the Pacific in the Battle of Iwo Jima (1945). There were also fighter squadrons of black pilots, such as the 332nd Fighter Group commanded by Captain Benjamin Davis.

By 1945 there were many integrated units in the army. US Supreme Commander General Eisenhower strongly supported integrated combat units.

Discrimination was worst in the navy. By the end of the war, only 58 black sailors had risen to officer rank. It was exclusively black sailors who were assigned to the dangerous job of loading ammunition on to ships bound for the war zones. In July 1944 a horrific accident killed 323 people, most of them black sailors (see Source 9). The government ordered the navy to end all racial discrimination by February 1946.

In the workplace

Over 400,000 black Americans migrated from the south to the USA's industrial centres. On average, they doubled their wages to about $1000 per year.

However, they faced prejudice and discrimination. Black workers generally earned half what white workers earned. Black leaders led by Philip Randolph threatened a mass march of 50,000 people to Washington to end discrimination at work. In June 1941, Roosevelt signed Executive Order 8802 which ordered employers on defence work to end discrimination. But it took more than executive orders to change attitudes. In 1942, at the Packard electronics company, 3000 white workers walked out when three black workers had their jobs upgraded as a result of the order (and the management walked out too).

During the war, poor workers (both blacks and whites) created racial tension. There were race riots in 47 cities during the war, the worst of which was in Detroit during June–July 1943.

The war highlighted racial tensions, but it also sowed the seeds for the successes of the civil rights movement in the 1950s and 1960s – you will return to that story on page 376.

1 Do you think the example of the black fighter squadron is a positive or negative aspect of attitudes to black servicemen?
2 Make a list of improvements for black people brought about by the war.

FOCUS TASK

Was wartime USA united or divided?

Look back at Source 1 on page 366. This mural is promoting war bonds, but is also presenting an interpretation of the USA at war. Is that picture a complete picture?

1 Look carefully at the mural. Make a list of all the ways in which it shows the USA united behind the war effort.
2 Now use the rest of your work from this section to write a second paragraph or a second list of bullet points, adding features of wartime USA that do not appear on the mural.
3 All governments control information and put their own 'spin' on events, especially during wartime. Do you think the government could have made this mural more representative, yet still achieved its objective of uniting people behind the war effort? Discuss your view with others in your class.

SOURCE INVESTIGATION

Black Americans in the Second World War

Study Sources 8–12 below.

1 What does Source 8 suggest about black American attitudes to the war?
2 What evidence is there that this attitude is either typical or exceptional?
3 Why do you think that the pamphlet in Source 9 was so effective in stirring up public opinion?
4 Look at Sources 10–12. Which of these three sources do you think most accurately sums up the experience of black people in wartime USA? Explain your answer.
5 Sources 8–12 show positive and negative aspects of the experience of black Americans during the war. Write a paragraph explaining whether you think the balance of positive and negative aspects is too far one way or the other, or is about right. You will need to mention some of these points:
   • how far the positive sources are reliable (backed up by other sources or information) and typical (representative of people's experiences)
   • how far the negative sources are reliable and typical
   • whether there should be more or fewer sources of one type or the other (with an explanation of your reasons).

SOURCE 8

There may be a lot wrong in America, but there is nothing Hitler can fix.

World heavyweight boxing champion Joe Louis, a black American who served in the US army during the war.

SOURCE 9

The wreckage that resulted along the Port Chicago waterfront after two ammunition ships blew up in the harbour. Almost 300 black men died in the blast as they loaded ammunition onto the ships; no whites had been ordered to help with the loading.

SOURCE 10

Soldiers receiving Good Conduct Medals in 1943. No black soldier received the Congressional Medal of Honour (the USA's highest award) in the Second World War.

SOURCE 11

A sign erected to prevent black people moving into a government housing project, Detroit, 1942.

SOURCE 12

Dear Yank
My plane was in Los Angeles at the height of the so-called zoot suit riots. I saw several of them and was ashamed of the servicemen I saw. It must be understood, and no amount of baloney can hide it, that the zoot suit riots were really race riots, directed mainly against the Mexican, and to some extent the Negro citizens of Los Angeles. It's about time a certain element in the armed forces be told that a man can be a good American citizen regardless of the colour of his skin, and has all the rights of a good citizen. To those servicemen who took part in the riots I'd like to ask a question: What the hell uniform do you think you're wearing, American or Nazi?

A letter from Crew Chief Patterson Field to the US army weekly magazine, *Yank*, in 1943. Zoot suits were fashionable suits of the 1940s, first worn by Mexican Americans.

How did the US economy perform, 1945–1980?

Key ideas: a) The richest country

The USA emerged from the war with a strong economy. It continued to stay strong. There were uneven years but, as you can see from Source 13, the nation's wealth grew each year – sometimes very quickly indeed. From 1945 to 1980 the USA was the richest country in the world.

SOURCE 13

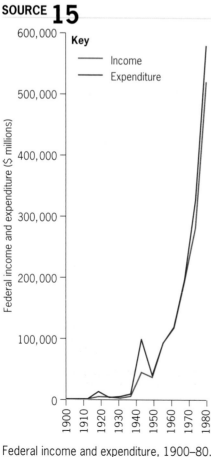

US economic growth, 1940–80.

SOURCE 14

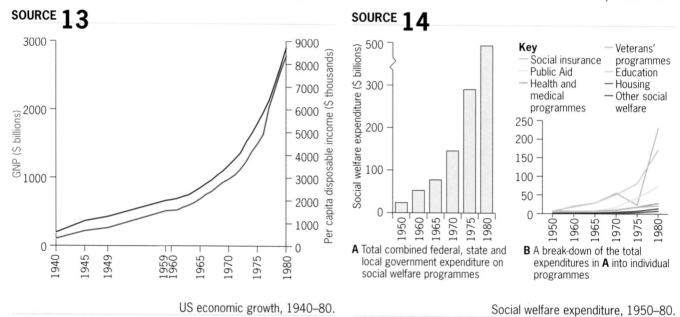

A Total combined federal, state and local government expenditure on social welfare programmes

B A break-down of the total expenditures in **A** into individual programmes

Social welfare expenditure, 1950–80.

SOURCE 15

Federal income and expenditure, 1900–80.

b) ... but what should be done with all that money?

Such wealth was quite a responsibility. On the one hand, the president was judged by whether he (they have all been men) kept the economy growing. The president had to keep American business happy.

On the other hand, such wealth gave the government enough money to do almost anything it wanted to do – whether that be a prestige project such as putting a man on the moon before the USSR did, a massive military project such as fighting a war in far-away Vietnam or a social project such as improving health care for children from poor families in the USA's inner cities.

c) Congress versus President

In election campaigns, each president made bold promises about how he would use the government's income. Usually, he then had a long tussle with Congress as to whether it would let him do this – and very often Congress won.

d) Government help or self-help?

This conflict will lie behind much of what you study in the rest of this chapter. There were those who argued very convincingly that in such a rich country there should be no poor people. They also argued that all American citizens should have equal rights and opportunities in terms of laws, voting and jobs. But there were others who argued just as convincingly that it was not government's role to help poor people – it was up to them to work hard and improve themselves. They also argued that radical new laws or rapid social changes could destabilise the country and lead to violence.

McCarthyism and the Red Scare

What do you think of Communists? It's probably a question that no one has ever asked you before. You may think it is totally unimportant. In 1950s USA, however, it could not have been more different. How you answered that question could affect your whole life – your career and your future. The USA was in the grip of extreme anti-Communism. And if you thought Communism was good, you might be 'blacklisted', sacked or even attacked.

Why had this happened?

As you saw from pages 325–27, there had always been much anti-Communist feeling in the USA. Now there were some obvious factors making that feeling worse. Relations between the capitalist USA and the Communist USSR had turned sour; the Cold War had started; both sides were developing powerful new weapons. US agents were spying on the USSR – so it was reasonable for Americans to suppose that the USSR was doing the same. It was naturally a time of suspicion.

Against this background, however, various individuals and events helped to stir up this natural suspicion to the point of hysteria in what became known as the Red Scare.

1 Write a sentence for each of the following, explaining its role in the Red Scare:
   • Federal Employee Loyalty Program
   • HUAC
   • Hiss case
   • Rosenbergs
   • McCarran Act.

The Federal Bureau of Investigation

The Federal Bureau of Investigation (FBI) had a strongly anti-Communist director, J Edgar Hoover. He had been a driving force behind the Red Scare after the First World War (see page 199). In 1947 President Truman let him set up the Federal Employee Loyalty Program. This allowed Hoover's FBI loyalty boards to investigate government employees to see if they were current or former members of the Communist Party. From 1947 to 1950, around 3 million were investigated. Nobody was charged with spying. But 212 staff were said to be security risks (that is, Communist sympathisers) and were forced out of their jobs.

The House Un-American Activities Committee

From the 1930s, the US Congress had a House Un-American Activities Committee (HUAC). It had the right to investigate anyone who was suspected of doing anything un-American. Un-American mostly meant Communist! To start with, the committee was hardly noticed. But in 1947 it became big news.

The FBI had evidence that a number of prominent Hollywood writers, producers and directors were members of the Communist Party. HUAC called them to be questioned by the committee. They were not government employees. It was not illegal to be a Communist in a free democratic country such as the USA. So when the Hollywood Ten, as they became known, appeared before the committee, they refused to answer any questions. Every time they were asked the standard question: 'Are you now or have you ever been a member of the Communist Party?', they pleaded the First Amendment of the US Constitution (which guaranteed all Americans freedom to believe what they wanted) and said that the HUAC did not even have the right to ask the question.

They were each jailed for one year for contempt of court because they refused to answer questions. Hollywood studios 'blacklisted' the ten, and most of them never worked again in Hollywood. Because the film industry was the highest profile industry in the country, HUAC was suddenly catapulted into front-page news. Now everyone had heard of it.

The Hiss case

In 1948 a man called Whittaker Chambers faced the HUAC. He admitted to having been a Communist in the 1930s. He also said that Alger Hiss had been a member of his group. Hiss was a high-ranking member of the US State Department. Hiss accused Chambers of lying and Truman dismissed the case. However, a young politician called Richard Nixon (a member of the HUAC) decided to pursue the case. He found convincing evidence that Hiss did know Chambers, and debatable evidence that Hiss had passed information to the USSR during the war. Hiss was never tried for spying, but he was convicted of perjury in 1950 and spent nearly five years in prison.

It is still not known whether Hiss was guilty of passing secrets or not.

The Rosenbergs

The Soviet Union developed its own atomic bomb in 1949. This was much sooner than expected. The USA had been sure it would take Soviet scientists four more years. The US government strongly suspected that spies had passed its atomic secrets to the USSR. In 1950 a German-born British physicist, Klaus Fuchs, was convicted of passing US and British atomic secrets to the USSR.

The investigation into Fuchs also led to suspicions against Julius Rosenberg and his wife Ethel. At their trial in March 1951 they denied all the charges against them. But they were found guilty and sentenced to death. They were executed in June 1953.

The evidence that convicted the Rosenbergs appeared to be flimsy. However, historians today believe that the Rosenbergs were guilty. They now know of coded telegrams between the Rosenbergs and Soviet agents that began in 1944. The telegrams were eventually published in 1995.

The McCarran Act

The Hiss and Rosenberg cases helped to lead to the McCarran Act, passed by Congress against President Truman's wishes.

• All Communist organisations had to be registered with the US government.
• No Communist could carry a US passport or work in the defence industries.

SOURCE 16

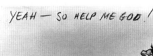

YEAH — SO HELP ME GOD !

LOYALTY OATH

An American cartoon from the early 1950s.

1 After Democrat Adlai Stevenson had made a speech in the 1952 presidential election campaign, a woman praised him: 'You have captured the vote of every thinking person in America.' Stevenson is said to have replied, 'Thank you, Ma'am, but we need a majority!' What do you think he meant by this?

2 Compare Sources 16 and 17. Which was made by supporters of the HUAC and which by its opponents? Explain your choice carefully.

Hysteria

How did the people of the USA react to this Red Scare? Most of the evidence suggests that they lapped it up. Some were hysterically anti-Communist themselves and welcomed every exposé as another victory for American values. Even those who were not violently anti-Communist got caught up in the drama of it all. Interrogations were filmed and photographed. Just to appear before HUAC could ruin a career. 'Suspects' were asked to 'name names'. If they did not tell, they were suspected of being a Communist. If they did, then those they named were, in turn, investigated.

Politicians on both sides could also see the vote winning potential of it all. To win elections they must be seen to be tough on Communism. Into this steaming atmosphere stepped a ruthless and ambitious young Republican Senator called Joseph McCarthy.

McCarthyism

In 1950 McCarthy was in search of a headline. He got it! He claimed that he had a list of over 200 Communists in the State Department. He had not found these Communists himself. His 200 Communists were from the official report from the FBI's loyalty board investigations. He claimed there were 57 card-carrying Communists in the government. This was also based on FBI reports. In fact, 35 of the 57 had been cleared and the other 22 were still being investigated.

McCarthy confessed that he was amazed by the amount of publicity his comments generated, but he was determined to use his new-found prominence. Democrat Senator Millard Tydings declared that the charges lacked foundation. McCarthy simply attacked Tydings for being un-American.

With elections just around the corner, Republican senators backed McCarthy and in the 1952 US Senate elections the Republicans reaped the benefits. They won many seats. Tydings himself lost his seat to a McCarthy supporter.

McCarthy was on a roll. After the election, President Eisenhower appointed him as head of a White House committee to investigate Communist activists in the government. Throughout 1952 and 1953, McCarthy extended his own investigations and turned his committee into a weapon to increase his own personal power and terrify others. His methods mainly involved false accusations and bullying. He targeted high-profile figures and accused anyone who criticised him of being a Communist.

SOURCE 17

'Investigate *them*? Heck, that's mah possee' – a cartoon by Bill Mauldin from 1946. A posse is a group of men gathered together to hunt down a criminal. To find out about the KKK see page 201. Mauldin had served as a GI during the war and had been wounded. This cartoon was kept in an FBI file as evidence of un-American attitudes.

SOURCE 18

Senator McCarthy gives a press conference.

SOURCE 19

A hearing of the House Un-American Activities Committee in 1952.

McCarthy said that General George Marshall (the American general most admired by Winston Churchill and the author of the Marshall Plan which gave US economic aid to Europe after the Second World War – see pages 329–30) was at the centre of a gigantic conspiracy against the USA. President Eisenhower did virtually nothing to protect his great friend Marshall from these accusations because he did not want to clash with McCarthy.

Thousands of others found their lives and careers ruined by the witch hunt. False accusations led to their being 'blacklisted' which meant that they could not work. Over 100 university lecturers were fired as universities came under pressure from McCarthy. The HUAC 'blacklisted' 324 Hollywood personalities. Studio bosses such as Walt Disney, Jack Warner and Louis Mayer supported the HUAC and refused to employ anyone who was suspected of having Communist sympathies. They also did their bit to raise the temperature further by producing science-fiction films such as *Invasion of the Body Snatchers*, which fed the hysteria by introducing the threat of alien invaders – which was clearly supposed to represent the Communist threat to the USA.

3 Do you think McCarthy created anti-Communist hysteria in the USA or simply exploited it? Explain your answer.
4 Is it fair to say that McCarthy was helped by inaction from people who might have opposed him?

FOCUS TASK

What was the Red Scare?

1 You are going to draw your own cloud diagram for the Red Scare. Write 'The Red Scare' like this in a cloud in the middle of your page:

The Red Scare

2 Now draw four clouds around the central cloud:
   • Fear of Communist spies
   • Rivalry between the political parties
   • Politicians trying to raise their own profile
   • American public hysteria.
3 Now add another ring of clouds with examples of each of these factors.
4 Write a short paragraph explaining how each of the four clouds contributed to the Red Scare.
5 Now add one last section explaining whether all Americans were taken in by McCarthyism.

The end of McCarthyism

Not everybody approved of McCarthy. In fact, public opinion polls showed that McCarthy never achieved more than a 50 per cent popular approval rating at any time between 1950 and 1954.

• Many senators spoke up against him, including the Republican Senator Ralph Flanders from Vermont.
• Some of Hollywood's biggest stars protested against McCarthy's actions.
• Quality newspapers such as the *Washington Post, New York Times* and *Milwaukee Journal* produced sensible and balanced reporting that damaged McCarthy's credibility.
• TV journalist Ed Murrow produced a devastating programme on the *See It Now* series in 1954 that mainly consisted of film of McCarthy's own statements.

But it was four years before McCarthy finally ran out of steam. In 1954 he turned his attacks on the army. By this time, his accusations seemed ridiculous. He had become an alcoholic. In televised hearings McCarthy was steadily humiliated by the lawyer representing the army, Joseph Welch. At one point, the court burst into applause for Welch when he accused McCarthy of having no decency. McCarthy lost all credibility and was finished as a political force. He died three years later, in 1957.

Conservatives versus radicals

After McCarthy's death anti-Communism was more muted, but it did not disappear. The battle between conservatives and radicals continued in other forms, as you will see through the rest of this chapter. McCarthy's popularity also empowered other conservative right-wingers – including the young Senator Richard Nixon, waiting in the wings, whom you will meet again later in this chapter, and a young researcher, Phyllis Schlafly, who later led the campaign against equal rights for women (see page 386).

The Red Scare was part of a much more widespread yearning for the USA to return to the traditional values that had been disrupted by the chaos of the 1920s and 1930s and then by the trauma of the war years. In the 1950s, a McCarthy supporter would not only dislike Communism, he or she would also be likely to support calls for women to stay in the home and not to work; for rock-and-roll music to be banned or controlled; for black people to be content with their lowly place in American society.

In the 1940s and early 1950s, conservative USA was on top. But, as so often in history, the pendulum swings and on pages 376–96 you will see how quickly and completely it swung over the next two decades.

The story of how the radicals gained the upper hand in the USA begins with the story of black civil rights, which you are now going to study in detail.

How far did black Americans achieve equality in civil rights in the 1950s and 1960s?

In the 1920s and 1930s, vicious racial prejudice had been common in American life (see pages 201–203). During the Second World War, significant steps were taken to prevent racial discrimination in the army and in employment (see page 370). This encouraged those trying to win equality for black people. However, in the 1950s racism was still an everyday experience for black people, particularly in the southern states of the USA.

- Seventeen states fully enforced the 'Jim Crow' laws (see Source 20), which segregated everyday facilities such as parks, buses and schools.
- Black Americans had officially been given the right to vote early in the century, but various practices were used to prevent them from voting — most commonly, the threat of violence. In Mississippi, for example, black people who tried to register to vote faced intimidation or even lynching. Only five per cent of the black population in Mississippi was registered to vote.
- Law officers (police) not only failed to stop attacks on black people, they frequently took part in them. White juries almost always acquitted whites accused of killing blacks.
- Black Americans faced official and legal discrimination in areas such as employment and education. In the south, white teachers earned 30 per cent more than black teachers.
- The best universities were closed to blacks. In 1958, a black teacher called Clemson King was committed to a mental asylum for applying to the University of Mississippi.

The civil rights movement

In a fair country, every citizen should have equal civil rights. The US Constitution was supposed to guarantee that all people were treated equally. It was clearly failing its black citizens.

There were many campaigners working to win equal civil rights for black Americans, but there was also a powerful minority resisting them. Some whites believed that giving civil rights to black people was a grave danger to their way of life. They would fight it every inch of the way.

SOURCE 20

The 'Jim Crow' states (coloured orange) in the 1950s, and the sites of some civil rights protests, 1950–70.

ACTIVITY

Design a leaflet to be sent to the government setting out the grievances of black people in the southern states of the USA.

FOCUS TASK

On pages 376–83 you are going to study the main events in the civil rights campaign. You will see that campaigners used a range of methods and tackled a wide range of issues. Make your own copy of this chart and complete it as you work through the chapter.

Method of campaigning	Example	Score out of 5 and/or comment
1 Court case/ legal challenge		
2 Non-violent direct action		
3 Empowering ordinary people		
4 Marches and demonstrations		
5 Violent protest		

SOURCE 21

Confrontation at Little Rock Central High School, Arkansas, September 1957.

SOURCE 22

One of the black students at Little Rock, 15-year-old Elizabeth Eckford, trying to ignore the abuse of the 1000-strong crowd. Forty years later the woman yelling at Eckford publicly apologised for her actions.

The struggle for equal education: a legal challenge

For decades, it had been legal in the USA for states to have separate schools for black and white children. Schools for black children were almost always less well equipped. The National Association for the Advancement of Colored People (NAACP) and the black civil rights lawyer Thurgood Marshall brought a series of complaints about segregated schools in the late 1940s that eventually came before the Supreme Court in 1950. Judge Julius Waring ruled that states had to provide equal education for black and white students. However, he did not say that they had to provide integrated schools open to both black and white children.

Brown v Board of Education of Topeka, 1954

Many states still did nothing to bring black schools up to the standard of white schools. Campaigners believed that the only way to secure equal education was to get blacks into white schools.

In September 1952 the NAACP brought a court case against the Board of Education in Topeka, Kansas. The case was about a girl called Linda Brown who had to travel several kilometres and cross a dangerous rail track to get to school, rather than attend a whites-only school nearby. This was a test case to see whether the Supreme Court would allow states to continue to segregate schools.

In May 1954 Chief Justice Earl Warren finally announced in favour of Brown and the NAACP. Warren stated that segregated education could not be equal. It created a feeling of inferiority for black students and that meant that all segregated school systems were unequal ones. He ordered the southern states to set up integrated schools 'with all deliberate speed'.

The case demonstrated a pattern that was going to work well in the civil rights campaign that was to follow. The campaigners would pick up an individual story of discrimination and take it to the Supreme Court to see if it would declare the practice illegal. If the Supreme Court said that something was illegal or against the Constitution, then the states had to do something about it.

Little Rock, Arkansas

Integration was introduced quickly and effectively in some states, but met with bitter resistance in others. Arkansas had still not integrated three years later. In 1957 the Supreme Court ordered the Governor, Orval Faubus, to let nine black students attend a white school in Little Rock. Faubus ordered out state troops to prevent the black students from attending school. He claimed that this was because he could not guarantee their safety. Faubus only backed down when President Eisenhower sent federal troops to protect the students and make sure that they could join the school. The troops stayed for six weeks.

Once the troops withdrew there were no further major racial incidents at the school. But Faubus' actions gained him widespread popularity and he was re-elected for a total of six terms.

1 Why was the *Brown v Board of Education of Topeka* case significant?

The great glory of American democracy is the right to protest for right. There will be no crosses burned at any bus stops in Montgomery. There will be no white persons pulled out of their homes and taken out on some distant road and murdered. There will be nobody among us who will stand up and defy the constitution of the Nation.

From Martin Luther King's speech at Montgomery, Alabama, in 1955.

A law may not make a man love me, but it can stop him from lynching me. It can also stop him from refusing to serve me in a restaurant.

King writing to President Eisenhower in 1957 after the President expressed his view that laws cannot make people behave in a moral way.

1 Why was the Montgomery incident so important? Was it because of the victory won or the way in which it was achieved?
2 What evidence is there that civil rights actions increased racial tensions? Is this an argument against them?

The Montgomery bus boycott: non-violent direct action

What we now call the civil rights movement is often said to have started with the actions of Rosa Parks from Montgomery, Alabama, in December 1955.

Montgomery had a local law that black people were only allowed to sit in the back seats of a bus and they had to give up those seats if white people wanted them. Rosa Parks was a civil rights activist and she decided to make a stand against Montgomery's racially segregated bus service. She refused to give up her seat to a white man. She was promptly arrested and convicted of breaking the bus laws.

The civil rights movement helped the black people of Montgomery to form the Montgomery Improvement Association (MIA). The MIA decided that the best way to protest and to generate publicity was to boycott the buses. On the first day of the boycott, the buses were empty and 10,000–15,000 people turned out to hear a speech from the newly elected MIA president, Martin Luther King (see Profile opposite).

The boycott was a great success. The bus company lost 65 per cent of its income. The black community organised a car pool which carried about two-thirds of the passengers that the buses would have carried (the rest walked). It was the first major example of the power of non-violent direct action – that is, challenging discrimination by refusing to co-operate with it. It showed how powerful black people working together could be.

At the same time, civil rights lawyers fought Rosa Parks' case in court. In December 1956, the Supreme Court declared Montgomery's bus laws to be illegal. This meant that all other such bus services were illegal and by implication that all segregation of public services was illegal.

Throughout the boycott, its leaders were subjected to massive intimidation. King was arrested twice. Local judges passed an injunction declaring the car pool to be illegal. Churches and homes were set on fire and racially integrated buses were shot at by snipers (seven bombers and snipers were charged, but all were acquitted).

Direct action gathers pace

After the success in Montgomery, the civil rights campaign took off in the late 1950s and early 1960s. A number of different groups began to organise similar direct action.

King formed the Southern Christian Leadership Conference (SCLC). It ran conferences and trained civil rights activists in techniques of non-violent protest and how to handle the police, the law and the media.

Black and white American students were deeply moved by the civil rights movement and played a major role in it. They set up the Student Nonviolent Coordinating Committee (SNCC). Another civil rights activist, James Farmer, formed the Congress of Racial Equality (CORE). Together these groups staged many different protests. For example:

- In Greensboro, North Carolina, SNCC students began a campaign to end segregation of restaurants in the town in 1960. Within a week, 400 black and white students were organising sit-ins at lunch counters in the town.
- In February 1960 in Nashville, Tennessee, 500 students organised sit-ins in restaurants, libraries and churches. Their college expelled them, but then backed down when 400 teachers threatened to resign. The students were attacked and abused, but eventually Mayor Ben West was convinced by their actions. By May 1960 the town had been desegregated.
- In May 1961 CORE activists began a form of protest called 'freedom rides'. Many states were not obeying the order to desegregate bus services after the Montgomery ruling. The freedom riders deliberately rode on buses in the city of Birmingham, Alabama, to highlight this. They faced some of the worst violence of the civil rights campaigns. The SNCC then took up the freedom rides, with the same violent reaction as a result. Two hundred freedom riders were arrested and spent 40 days in jail. The Governor of Alabama, John Patterson, did little to protect the riders, although credit should go to Alabama's Director of Public Safety, Floyd Mann, whose actions probably saved several lives. Patterson eventually caved in to tremendous pressure from the new US President, John F Kennedy, to protect freedom riders.

PROFILE

Martin Luther King

Many black Americans played an important role in the 1950s and 1960s civil rights movements. One leader emerged above all of the others, Dr Martin Luther King.

★ He was a Baptist minister and leader of the civil rights movement.
★ He was a mesmerising speaker whose speech in Source 30 has become one of the most famous speeches of the twentieth century.
★ He believed passionately in non-violent protest. He favoured actions such as the bus boycott and the sit-in.
★ In December 1964 he was awarded the Nobel Peace Prize.
★ He was certainly not afraid to face confrontation and was subject to considerable violence himself.
★ Not all civil rights activists agreed with his methods.
★ He was assassinated in 1968 by Earl Ray. There have been many theories that Ray was simply a hired killer, and that he was employed to murder King by King's opponents.

3 Use the text and sources on pages 378–83 to add five more bullet points to this Profile.

SOURCE 25

Black and white SNCC protesters in a sit-in at a segregated restaurant in Jackson, Mississippi, June 1963.

How had the civil rights situation improved by 1961?

The events of a single day – 11 June 1961 – summed up both the hope and the despair of civil rights activists in the USA. On the one hand, it was a night of great excitement because the new President, John F Kennedy, committed himself to a wide ranging civil rights programme of laws and regulations. On the other hand at the same time as Kennedy was speaking, the leading black activist in the state of Mississippi, Medgar Evers, was murdered by a known racist. In the past, such murders of black people by white people were not even investigated by the police (who were all white). In this case, the police did find the killer and brought him to court but, true to form, the court acquitted him.

ACTIVITY

You are a member of the SNCC in the early 1960s. Someone asks you why you are part of the movement, suggesting that all that you and the other civil rights groups have achieved is a bus ride, getting beaten up and being arrested. Give an answer (either written or verbally) to this criticism. You could mention:
• the practical advances made since the late 1950s (for example, desegregation)
• the moral importance of these advances
• why you believe non-violence is the right tactic
• where you think your protests might go from here.

SOURCE 26

Instead of submitting to surreptitious cruelty in thousands of dark jail cells and on countless shadowed streets, we are forcing our oppressor to commit his brutality openly – in the light of day – with the rest of the world looking on. To condemn peaceful protesters on the grounds that they provoke violence is like condemning a robbed man because his possession of money caused the robbery.

Martin Luther King commenting on his tactics in Birmingham, Alabama, in 1963. Critics had accused him of deliberately stirring up violence.

The voting rights campaign: empowering ordinary people

The next phase of the campaign was dominated by two issues: the proposed civil rights bill and voting rights.

Kennedy was sworn in as President in January 1961. His speech at his inauguration (see page 390) caught a positive mood of change and expectation. Civil rights activists wanted Kennedy to introduce a civil rights bill that would enshrine black civil rights in law. Kennedy and his brother Robert (the Attorney General) said they first wanted to concentrate on the issue of voting rights. They thought that if enough black people registered to vote then they would have great power over the decisions that politicians made.

The NAACP and other civil rights movements were happy to take protest in this direction. They organised courses for black Americans in voting procedures and how to register to vote. It is worth remembering that this took great courage. Black people who registered faced threats, intimidation and even murder. As Source 27 shows, the numbers registering rose steadily.

The voting rights campaign was helped greatly by the fact that the civil rights movement was now becoming a major national issue and had built up great momentum.

Birmingham and Washington: civil rights marches and rallies

In April 1963 King organised a march on Birmingham, Alabama. Six years after the Montgomery decision, this city had still not desegregated. Its police force was notoriously racist. It had links to the Ku Klux Klan (see page 201).

The aim of the march was to turn media attention on Birmingham to expose its policies to national attention. Police chief Bull Connor obliged. In the full glare of media publicity, police and fire officers turned dogs and fire hoses on the peaceful protesters. The police arrested over 1000 protesters (including King, see Source 29) and put many in jail.

In May 1963 President Kennedy intervened. He pressured Governor George Wallace to force the police to release all the protesters and to give more jobs to black Americans and allow them to be promoted. Birmingham was desegregated, but it remained a bitterly divided place. In September 1963 a Ku Klux Klan bomb killed four black children in a Birmingham church.

SOURCE 27

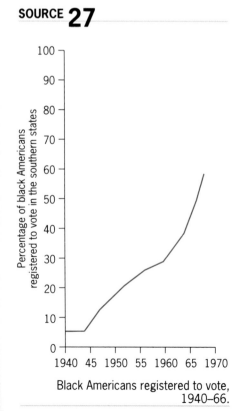

Black Americans registered to vote, 1940–66.

SOURCE 28

Fire hoses being used against protesters in Birmingham, Alabama, in 1963. The water pressure was so powerful that it could knock bricks out of walls.

SOURCE 29

But when you have seen vicious mobs lynch your mothers and fathers at will and drown your brothers and sisters at whim; when you have seen hate-filled policemen curse, kick and even kill your black brothers and sisters; when you see the vast majority of your twenty million Negro brothers smothering in an airtight cage of poverty in the midst of an affluent society; when you are harried by day and haunted by night by the fact that you are a Negro . . . when you are forever fighting a degenerating sense of nobodiness; then you will understand why we find it difficult to wait.

Extract from Martin Luther King's letter from Birmingham jail, Alabama, in 1963.

SOURCE 30

I have a dream that one day this nation will rise up and live out the true meaning of its creed: We hold these truths to be self-evident, that all men are created equal.

I have a dream that one day on the red hills of Georgia the sons of former slaves and the sons of former slave owners will be able to sit together at the table of brotherhood.

I have a dream that one day even the state of Mississippi, a state sweltering with the heat of injustice . . . and oppression will be transformed into an oasis of freedom and justice. I have a dream that my four little children will one day live in a nation where they will not be judged by the colour of their skin but the content of their character.

From Martin Luther King's most famous speech, August 1963.

1 How much progress had been made in achieving civil rights by the end of 1963?
2 How much progress was made in civil rights between 1963 and 1968?

In August 1963, King staged his most high-profile event. Over 200,000 blacks and 50,000 whites marched together to the federal capital Washington. Their aim was to pressure President Kennedy to introduce a civil rights bill. There was no trouble at the march, not even any litter. At the rally, King gave his famous 'I have a dream' speech (Source 30). The event had a tremendous impact on American public opinion.

The Civil Rights Act and 'freedom summer', 1964

By 1963 civil rights was a key national issue. Almost everyone in the USA had a view on it.

In November 1963, President Kennedy was assassinated. Kennedy's successor, Lyndon Johnson, proved to be just as committed to the ideal of civil rights. On 2 July 1964 he signed the Civil Rights Act. The Act made it illegal for local government to discriminate in areas such as housing and employment.

The summer of 1964 has been called the 'freedom summer'. With the momentum from the Civil Rights Act, King and the SCLC continued to encourage black Americans to register to vote. They were helped by young white people from the northern states who came south in great numbers to help. In the 20 months that followed the Civil Rights Act, 430,000 black Americans registered to vote.

SOURCE 31

President Johnson signs the Civil Rights Act in 1964.

Selma and voting rights

King deliberately targeted areas where discrimination was worst. In early 1965 he organised a march through Selma, Alabama. Only 2.4 per cent of Selma's blacks were registered to vote and the town was notorious for its brutally racist sheriff, Jim Clark. The authorities banned the planned march. However, on 7 March, about 600 people went ahead with the march (without King). They were brutally attacked. The media called it 'Bloody Sunday'. King tried to keep the pressure on and rearranged the march. However, he compromised on 11 March by leading a token march. It turned back after a short distance.

King's compromise avoided more violence. It annoyed the more radical black activists but King's restraint probably helped President Johnson to push through a Voting Rights Bill in 1965. This was finally passed by Congress and became law in 1968.

The Act allowed government agents to inspect voting procedures to make sure that they were taking place properly. It also ended the literacy tests that voters had previously had to complete before they voted. These discriminated against poor blacks in particular. After 1965 five major cities, including Detroit, Atlanta and Cleveland, all had black mayors. In Selma, blacks began to register to vote and in the next election Jim Clark lost his job.

Black nationalism and black power: violent protest

As the campaign for voting rights was taking place, there were other developments within the black communities of the USA as well. Black nationalism was one.

Most black nationalists rejected the non-violence of the civil rights movement. They felt that force was justified in order to achieve equality for black Americans. Others did not want equality so much as complete separation.

One movement that attracted many disillusioned black Americans was the Nation of Islam, headed by Elijah Muhammad. The Nation of Islam attracted figures such as boxer Cassius Clay (who changed his name to Muhammad Ali), who was an outspoken critic of racial discrimination. Another follower of the Nation of Islam was Malcolm Little, better known as Malcolm X. He was bitterly critical of Martin Luther King's methods, and believed that the civil rights movement held back black people. He wanted to see black Americans rise up and create their own separate black state in the USA, by force if necessary (see Source 32). He was assassinated in 1965.

The SNCC became more radical when the black student Stokely Carmichael was elected chairman in 1966. He talked in terms of 'black power'. He set out a radical view of 'black power' and in the process he was critical of Martin Luther King. Typical comments were: 'This nation [the USA] is racist from top to bottom, and does not function by morality, love and non-violence, but by power.'

Even more radical than Carmichael were the Black Panthers. They had around 2000 members and were a political party but also a small private army. They believed black Americans should arm themselves and force the whites to give them equal rights. They clashed many times with the police forces, killing nine police officers between 1967 and 1969.

SOURCE 32

a) *The white man has taught the black people in this country to hate themselves as inferior, to hate each other, to be divided against each other. The brainwashed black man can never learn to stand on his own two feet until he is on his own. We must learn to become our own producers, manufacturers and traders; we must have industry of our own, to employ our own. The white man resists this because he wants to keep the black man under his thumb and jurisdiction in white society. He wants to keep the black man always dependent and begging – for jobs, food, clothes, shelter, education. The white man doesn't want to lose somebody to be supreme over.*

b) *I am for violence if non-violence means we continue postponing a solution to the American black man's problems. If we must use violence to get the black man his human rights in this country then I am for violence.*

Comments of Malcolm X in the 1960s.

SOURCE 33

Members of the Black Panther Party protest against the arrest of one of their leaders, Huey Newton, in 1967.

1 Write a sentence to describe each of the following:
 • Malcolm X
 • black power
 • Black Panthers.
2 Look at Source 33. How would the Black Panthers affect public opinion in the USA?

Race riots

From 1965 to 1967 American cities suffered a wave of race riots. The cause in most cases was poor relations between the police and black people. Most of the USA's cities were divided along race lines. Most of the police forces were white. Many black working-class people who lived in the inner cities felt that they did not get the same protection from crime as whites. They distrusted the police.

Many black rioters were influenced by the radical black nationalists. Others simply joined the riots as an expression of their frustration about the way they were treated in the USA.

Major riots took place in most of the USA's cities, but the most serious were in the Watts area of Los Angeles in August 1965 and in Detroit in July 1967. President Johnson asked the Governor of Illinois to investigate the riots and his conclusion was that racism was the cause. He talked of two USAs, one black and one white.

SOURCE 34

A highway patrolman stands guard over protesters after the Watts riots, Los Angeles, 1965. There were an estimated 30,000 rioters in this incident and 34 deaths.

The assassination of Martin Luther King, 1968

In 1968 Martin Luther King was assassinated, probably by a hired killer, although it has never been proved which of King's enemies employed the assassin. King's death marked the end of an era for the civil rights movement. During his life, King had helped to transform the movement from a southern sideshow to a national movement. Major battles had been fought and won. Segregation was now illegal; the Civil Rights Act had enshrined black civil rights in law; black people in the south now held real political power.

But, at the same time, there was a feeling of insecurity among many people who had watched the escalating violence since 1964. The law might have changed, but had attitudes changed with it? What did the future hold?

The women's movement

The campaign for black civil rights was a major achievement in its own right. But it also gave many people a feeling that other faults in American society could be put right if enough people wanted to do so. In this way, the black civil rights movement helped to give birth to other protest movements. It is no coincidence that the decade of 'I have a dream' was also a decade of protest about other issues.

One of the most important protest movements was the women's movement, which aimed to win equal rights for women. Since the Second World War women's role had been changing. This change was resisted by conservative Americans, who thought it was women's role to make a home and bring up a happy family, and men's role to work. But by the 1960s that view no longer fitted the real world.

1 How did each of the following factors help create the women's movement?
a) the Second World War
b) the struggle for black civil rights
c) individuals
d) education and work

Trend 1: more women workers

The Second World War had increased the number of working women (see page 368). That trend continued after the war.

- In 1940 women made up 19 per cent of the workforce.
- In 1950 women made up 28.8 per cent of the workforce.
- In 1960 women made up almost half of the workforce.

In 1960, Eleanor Roosevelt, the widow of President Roosevelt, pressured President Kennedy to set up a commission on the status of women and particularly on their status at work. It reported in 1963. Women were almost half of the workforce, yet:

- 95 per cent of company managers were men.
- 88 per cent of technical workers were men.
- Only 4 per cent of lawyers and 7 per cent of doctors were women.
- Women earned around 50–60 per cent of the wages of men, even for the same work.
- Work for women was overwhelmingly low paid, part time and low level with no responsibility.
- Women could still be dismissed when they married.

SOURCE 35

You are asking that a stewardess be young, attractive and single. What are you running, an airline or a whorehouse?

Congresswoman Martha Griffiths asked the directors of National Airlines about its policy on air stewardesses, who were fired when they married or reached the age of 32.

Trend 2: changed expectations

After the Second World War, there had been a mass rush by women to get married and have babies.

Fifteen years later, many of these women were extremely disillusioned. In 1963 Betty Friedan described the problem in her influential million-copy best-seller, *The Feminine Mystique*. The 'feminine mystique' was her term for the set of ideas that said that women's happiness came from total involvement in their role as wives and mothers.

Friedan said that married women must be helped to continue in paid employment, if they were not to get bored, frustrated and deskilled.

Friedan asked hundreds of college-educated women what they wished they had done differently since graduating in the 1940s. She found a generation of educated and capable women who felt like domestic servants – there simply to meet the needs of their families, with little chance to develop their own careers or expand their horizons. They felt undervalued and depressed.

SOURCE 36

As the American woman made beds, shopped for groceries, matched slipcover material, ate peanut butter sandwiches with her children, chauffered Cub Scouts and Brownies, lay beside her husband at night, she was afraid to ask even of herself the question: 'Is this all?'

From *The Feminine Mystique*, by Betty Friedan, 1963.

Friedan called women's deep sense of dissatisfaction with their traditional role 'the problem that had no name'.

The women's movement

These trends led to what was called the women's movement. It was not a single organisation. There were thousands of different groups, all with different angles but with similar aims – to raise the status of women and end discrimination against women in all areas of life.

Following the Status Commission's report in 1963, the government passed the Equal Pay Act. Equally important was the Civil Rights Act in 1964 which outlawed discrimination against women.

However, women's groups felt these Acts were not being fully implemented, so Betty Friedan founded the National Organisation for Women (NOW) in 1966.

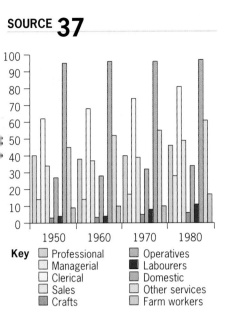

Proportion of women in the workforce of selected occupations in the USA, 1950–80.

By the early 1970s NOW had 40,000 members. It co-operated with a wide range of other women's movements, such as the National Women's Caucus, the Women's Campaign Fund, the North American Indian Women's Association and the National Black Feminist Organisation.

NOW learned some tactics from the civil rights movement and organised demonstrations in the streets of American cities. They also challenged discrimination in the courts. In a series of cases between 1966 and 1971, NOW secured $30 million in back pay owed to women who had not been paid wages equal to those of men. In 1972 the Supreme Court ruled that the US Constitution did give men and women equal rights.

'Women's Lib'

NOW was at one end of a broad spectrum of women's movements. Friedan, for example, was a feminist but she still believed in traditional family values and marriage. NOW used conventional methods, such as political pressure and court cases.

At the other end of the spectrum were younger feminists with more radical objectives and different methods to achieve them. They became known as the Women's Liberation Movement (or Women's Lib).

Feminists ran 'consciousness-raising' groups, where women could talk about their lives in depth and discuss how to challenge discrimination in their lives. They said that 'the personal was political' – everything you did in your personal life could affect the way people treated all women. For example, it was an act of protest against male supremacy to go out without make-up. It was like saying, 'Look at me – I don't care if you think I am pretty or not.' Some of the most radical members of Women's Lib were lesbians who regarded men as surplus to requirements. One saying went: 'A woman without a man is like a fish without a bicycle.'

Some groups hit the headlines with their bra-burning protests. Bras were burned as a symbol of male domination – women only wore them to look pretty for men. In 1968 radical women picketed the Miss World Beauty contest in Atlantic City. They said that the contest treated women like objects not people. To make their point, they crowned a sheep as Miss World. Demonstrations such as this raised the profile of the feminist movement – the media loved them – but some critics felt they did not help their cause because the protests were not taken seriously.

Roe v. Wade – the right to abortion

One of the most important campaigns for radical feminists was the campaign to legalise abortion. Abortion was illegal in the USA but feminists believed this law discriminated against women. They said they should not be forced to bear a child they did not want. They said that a woman had the right to choose what happened to her body and so should have the right to have an abortion if she wished to.

The struggle over abortion began in the early 1960s. A young medical technician, Estelle Griswold, challenged the anti-abortion laws in her home state of Connecticut. In Connecticut not only abortion but contraceptive devices, too, were illegal. Even giving information about contraception was illegal. Griswold's lawyers challenged Connecticut's laws. They handled their case cleverly. They did not argue directly against the abortion laws. They argued that these laws were an illegal restriction on the privacy of ordinary Americans. The right to privacy was contained in the Fourteenth Amendment of the US Constitution. The case went all the way to the Supreme Court. In 1965 the Supreme Court judges ruled 7–2 in favour of Griswold.

This victory gave power to the lawyers in an even more important case in 1970. This was the *Roe v. Wade* case, which lasted from 1970 to 1973. Jane Roe was the legal name given to Norma McCorvey to protect her anonymity. McCorvey was a troubled teenager who had been raised in a reform school. When she got married she was beaten by her husband. She already had three children – all of whom had been taken away from her because she couldn't care for them. She was pregnant again and wanted an abortion. She came to Sarah Weddington, a feminist lawyer, who saw this as the ideal test case to get the courts to allow abortion. She took the case through the courts and won McCorvey the right to have an abortion. That victory established a precedent that led to abortion becoming freely available.

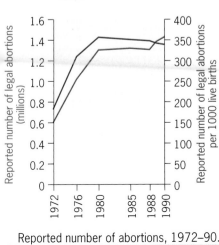

Reported number of abortions, 1972–90.

SOURCE 39

The Positive Woman starts with the assumption that the world is her oyster. She rejoices in the creative capability within her body and the power potential of her mind and spirit. She understands that men and women are different and that those differences provide the key to her success as a person and fulfilment as a woman.

Phyllis Schlafly, *The Power of the Positive Woman*, 1977.

FOCUS TASK

1 Prepare a presentation entitled 'The mixed success of the women's movement in the 1960s and 1970s'. You can get a planning sheet from your teacher.

2 Below are the methods of campaigning used by black civil rights activists:
   - court case/legal challenge
   - non-violent direct action
   - empowering ordinary people
   - marches and demonstrations
   - violent protest.
   a) Which of these were also used by feminists? Give examples.
   b) Which do you think was most important for the Women's Liberation Movement?

Opposition

At a time when attacking Communists had gone out of fashion, many right-wingers enjoyed attacking the extremes of feminism. This may help to explain the success of some of the anti-feminist movements. The most high profile was STOP ERA led by Phyllis Schlafly.

ERA stood for the Equal Rights Amendment, which was a proposal to amend the US Constitution specifically to outlaw sex discrimination. In the reforming climate of the 1960s, Congress was in favour of ERA, and so were 63 per cent of the population. However, Phyllis Schlafly led a successful campaign to prevent its becoming law.

She argued that feminists devalued the woman's role by making it equal with a man's and that they denied the rights of the unborn child by their support for abortion. She compared the feminist woman's complaints to the 'positive' woman's approach (see Source 39).

The Equal Rights Amendment became bogged down in Congress as a result of Schlafly's campaigning. The measure was finally defeated by three votes in 1982.

Schlafly was helped by the fact that by 1980 the pendulum was swinging away from radicalism once again. The anti-abortion movement was growing stronger. Economic problems for poor women were getting worse not better – feminism did not seem to be relevant to their lives. Even mainstream feminists were prepared to accept that women had their own values and that equal rights might be a false objective.

SOURCE 40

"And now, our guest speaker–Phyllis Schlafly, Harvard grad, TV star and radio commentator, whose distinguished career has taken her all over the country during the past three years fighting for the need for women to stay put in the home where they belong!"

A 1975 cartoon by Paul Szep, attacking Phyllis Schlafly, in the *Boston Globe*.

There is a time when the operation of the machine becomes so odious, makes you so sick at heart, that you can't take part; you can't even passively take part and you've got to put your bodies upon the gears and upon the wheels, upon the levers, upon all the apparatus and you've got to make it stop.

Mario Savio, a Berkeley student radical in the 1960s. Berkeley University, California, was one of the centres of student radicalism.

SOURCE 42

Student protesters stage a sit-in at Columbia University, New York, April 1968.

SOURCE 43

The Kent State University demonstrations in Ohio, 4 May 1970.

The student movement

Maybe you have had enough of protest movements. Many people in the USA had. Black people were protesting; women were protesting. Then along came the students!

Getting involved – student radicalism

There were many different groups involved in student protests. One of the main organisations was Students for a Democratic Society. It was set up in 1959. To start with, its aim was to obtain for students more say in how their courses and universities were run. Soon there were 150 colleges involved. This number rose to 400 with 100,000 members by the end of the 1960s.

The student movements were not isolated from the other protest movements. Students were deeply involved in the black civil rights campaign and also the women's movement. The civil rights movement was particularly influential. Idealistic young students had been appalled at the injustices experienced by black people. They had also been strengthened by discovering the influence they could have.

In 1964 radical students in many different universities organised rallies and marches to support the civil rights campaign. They tried to expose racism in their own colleges. Some universities tried to ban these protests. Students responded with a 'free speech' campaign to demand the right to protest. This was not a small minority of students. Up to half of Berkeley's 27,500 students were engaged in the Free Speech Movement.

Across the USA there were demonstrations on campuses. The students were rejecting the values and the society that their parents had created. Society was often referred to as 'the system' or the machine (see Source 41). Any individual or group whom students saw as victims of the machine could count on the support of student groups and could expect to see demonstrations in their support. Student groups backed campaigns for nuclear disarmament and criticised US involvement in South America. They supported the black civil rights movement, taking part in marches and freedom rides (see page 378).

The Vietnam War

Critics said that students simply adopted any radical cause without really understanding it. However, one issue above all others united student protest – the Vietnam War. Half a million young Americans were fighting in a war that was very unpopular with students. The anti-war protests reached their height during 1968 to 1970 (see page 360). In the first half of 1968, there were over 100 demonstrations against the Vietnam War involving 40,000 students. Frequently, the protest would involve burning the American flag – a criminal offence in the USA and a powerful symbol of the students' rejection of American values.

Anti-war demonstrations often ended in violent clashes with the police. At Berkeley, Yale and Stanford universities, bombs were set off. The worst incident by far came in 1970. At Kent State University in Ohio, students organised a demonstration against President Nixon's decision to invade Vietnam's neighbour, Cambodia. Panicked National Guard troopers opened fire on the demonstrators. Four students were killed and 11 others were injured. The press in the USA and abroad were horrified. Some 400 colleges were closed as 2 million students went on strike in protest at the action.

The wider picture

Student radicalism was not confined to the USA. Similar protests were taking place in Europe. In Northern Ireland, student protests in the late 1960s to secure civil rights for Catholics set off a chain reaction of events that resulted in the Troubles. Student demonstrations in France in 1968 caused enormous damage to cities all over the country.

1 Explain why the violence at Kent State was such an important event.

SOURCE 44

*Come mothers and fathers throughout the
  land
And don't criticize what you can't
  understand
Your sons and your daughters are beyond
  your command
Your old road is rapidly aging
Please get out of the new one if you can't
  lend a hand
For the times they are a-changin'*

From the song 'The Times They Are A-changin'' by Bob Dylan, written in 1963.

Dropping out – the hippy movement

Some young people took up an entirely different kind of protest. They 'dropped out' and became hippies. They opted out of the society their parents had created. They decided not to work or to study. They grew their hair long. They travelled around the country in buses and vans, which they decorated with flowers or psychedelic designs. They talked about peace and love. They experimented with sex and drugs and went to huge open-air concerts to listen to musicians like Bob Dylan (see Source 44).

You may think this is nothing to get worked up about, but to many Americans this was a more deeply disturbing form of protest than student radicalism. The parents of these hippies were ordinary middle-class American families. They had been brought up to believe in the virtues of working hard in school and then working hard at a career to earn more money, buy a bigger house, car, etc. They were also the generation that had fought to preserve American ideals of democracy in the Second World War and the Korean War. Now their children were rejecting their lifestyles. They were refusing to join the army and fight in Vietnam. In many ways, people thought that the USA was in crisis.

SOURCE 45

*And it's one, two, three, what are we fighting for?
Don't ask me I don't give a damn. Next stop is Vietnam
And it's five, six, seven, open up the pearly gates
Well I ain't got time to wonder why. We all gonna die*

Country Jo and the Fish singing at the Woodstock Festival in 1968.

SOURCE 46

Hippies at the Woodstock Festival in 1968. Woodstock, in New York state, attracted half a million young Americans. It was a rock festival, but it was also a celebration of an 'alternative' drop-out lifestyle mixed with a strong element of anti-war protest.

Links

It is all too easy to see history in isolated patches because it is easiest to study it that way. However, movements in history are often linked to one another. The protest movements of the 1960s are a good example. People were not members of just one group. A radical young student might at different times have taken part in:

- the civil rights freedom rides (see page 378)
- a feminist consciousness-raising group (see page 385)
- a free speech sit-in (see page 387)
- an anti-Vietnam march (see page 387)
- the Woodstock Festival.

FOCUS TASK

In 1966 one right-wing politician described the student protest movement as all about 'sex, drugs and treason'. Write your own phrase to sum up the student movement. It should be no more than five words long, but you should be able to explain fully why you think your phrase effectively sums up the movement.

Two presidents

While black Americans worked to gain their civil rights, women campaigned for equality and students protested against the Vietnam War, you might wonder what the US presidents of the time were doing.

The protest movements of the 1960s and 1970s were only one part of the challenge they faced. You are going to compare the achievements and the reputations of two presidents: John F. Kennedy and Lyndon Johnson.

FOCUS TASK

Use the text on pages 390–93 to add five more points to each of the profiles below so that they tell a fuller story.
a) You could work in pairs and take one profile each.
b) You should include a definition of:
 • Kennedy's New Frontier
 • Johnson's Great Society.
c) Make sure you include points about each president's successes *and* his failures.
d) You should look back to pages 347–52 (about the Cuban Missile Crisis) and 353–65 (about the Vietnam War) to include bullet points about each president's foreign policy successes and failures.

PROFILE

Lyndon B Johnson, President 1963–1969

★ Nickname LBJ.
★ Born 27 August 1908 in Texas.
★ He saw poverty around him as he grew up and as a teacher he came into contact with many poor immigrant children, which gave him a commitment to social reform.
★ He was elected to Congress as a Democrat in 1937 and was a strong supporter of President Roosevelt's New Deal (see pages 218–26).
★ He served with the US navy in the Pacific during the Second World War.
★ Johnson became a senator in 1948. He led the Democrats in the Senate from 1953.
★ In the 1960 election campaign he was chosen to be JFK's vice-presidential candidate. As a mature, respected, skilful congressman he was seen as the ideal balance for Kennedy's youthful idealism. It was thought that he would know how to handle Congress.
★ He became president when Kennedy was assassinated in 1963 and he successfully carried through Kennedy's planned measures, cutting taxes and introducing a new civil rights bill.
★ Johnson was elected president again in his own right in 1964 with the widest margin of victory ever achieved in a presidential election.
★ Johnson pushed through a huge range of radical measures on medical care, education, conservation, and help for economically depressed areas.
★ He was a keen supporter of space technology. In December 1968 three US astronauts orbited the moon.
★ His domestic achievements were overshadowed by the USA's involvement in the war in Vietnam.
★ In 1968 Johnson announced he would not seek re-election for the presidency. Instead he would concentrate on trying to end the war in Vietnam.
★ He died of a heart attack in January 1973.

PROFILE

John F Kennedy, President 1961–1963

★ Nickname JFK.
★ Born 29 May 1917 into a wealthy Massachusetts family of Irish descent.
★ The Kennedy family was influential. JFK's father was an adviser to President Roosevelt and ambassador to Britain at the beginning of the Second World War.
★ While still at Harvard University, JFK wrote a best-selling book, examining how (in his view) Britain had allowed Hitler to start the war.
★ During the Second World War he commanded a torpedo boat in the South Pacific. He was shipwrecked, badly wounded and decorated for bravery.
★ After the war, he became a Democratic congressman in 1947, then in 1952 he was elected to the US Senate.
★ In 1953 he wrote an award-winning book called *Profiles in Courage* about American politicians who risked their careers to stand up for things they believed in.
★ In 1960 the Democrats chose him to run for president, with Lyndon Johnson as his vice-president.
★ Kennedy narrowly defeated Republican Richard Nixon and was sworn in as president in January 1961.
★ Kennedy's short time as president was dominated by Cold War tensions with the USSR (see pages 347–52).
★ He was assassinated in November 1963, while driving in an open car through Dallas, Texas. It has never been proved who was responsible for his murder.

John F Kennedy and the New Frontier

Kennedy was one of the great 'what ifs' of world history. He narrowly beat Republican Richard Nixon in the election of November 1960. He was the youngest ever US president. He put the emphasis on youth and idealism. He talked of the USA's being at the edge of a New Frontier. He wanted to make the USA a better, fairer place for all Americans. He wanted the USA to carry its ideals and messages around the world. He asked Americans to join him in being 'new frontiersmen'. In his inaugural speech, he urged Americans to 'ask not what your country can do for you, ask what you can do for your country'. He also asked the nations of the world to join together to fight what he called 'the common enemies of man: tyranny, poverty, disease, and war itself'. The great 'what if' in Kennedy's case is whether he would have achieved these aims if he had not been assassinated in November 1963.

What was the New Frontier?

Kennedy's New Frontier might sound like just a political slogan – and to start with the 'new frontier' was more an idea than a programme. Kennedy needed a powerful 'big idea' to unite the American people behind him after a desperately close election. He wanted them to sense they were on the edge of something new and exciting.

The most controversial aspects of his New Frontier were social reforms to help poor Americans (see Source 48). Kennedy hoped to make the USA a fairer society by giving equal civil rights to all blacks, and by helping people to better themselves. He knew many Americans were against these reforms, so his talk of a 'new frontier' was meant to make Americans feel excited about helping other Americans so that they would give his proposed social legislation a smoother ride!

As part of his New Frontier he created the 'peace corps'. This was an organisation which sent young American volunteers to less economically developed countries to work as doctors, teachers, technical experts, etc. This greatly appealed to idealistic young Americans.

1 Source 47 is due to appear in an American magazine. Write two possible captions: one which uses the photo to praise Kennedy; one which uses it to criticise him.

SOURCE 47

The Kennedys preparing to entertain guests at a White House reception, 8 February 1961.

The Brains Trust

As a politician, Kennedy seemed to be a breath of fresh air. He gathered together the brightest young experts from the USA's universities. His team of advisers became known as the Brains Trust. The best known was Secretary of Defence Robert McNamara. Most of these advisers had never worked for the government before. Kennedy liked that idea because he believed they would come up with new solutions to old problems.

However, behind the scenes Kennedy's advisers and even his own Vice-President, Lyndon Johnson, worried about the Brains Trust. They asked what these whizz-kids knew about politics. One adviser said to Johnson, 'they may be every bit as intelligent as you say but I'd feel a whole lot better about them if just one of them had run for sheriff once.'

The 'Camelot' factor

Kennedy's personal style was also a change. He was young, good looking and charming. His wife Jackie was an equally glamorous celebrity. Jackie filled the White House with the most beautiful art, and held parties and concerts with the very best performers of the day. The pair were almost like film stars and they spent a lot of time with celebrities such as Frank Sinatra and Marilyn Monroe.

However, behind the scenes the Kennedys were not a happy family. President Kennedy was regularly unfaithful. He had affairs with both Marilyn Monroe and the girlfriend of a Mafia boss. There were even suspicions that the Mafia blackmailed Kennedy over this and so prevented him taking action against organised crime in the USA.

Civil Rights

Aim: to achieve equality for black Americans
- in September 1962 Kennedy made a major speech on nationwide TV committing himself to the cause of black civil rights
- he made high level black appointments: the first black US circuit judge and the first black senior government official
- he stood up to the governors of the southern states and tried to force them to defend the freedom riders (see page 378)
- in October 1962 he sent 23,000 government troops to ensure that just one black student, James Meredith, could study at the University of Mississippi without being hounded out by racists

... but
- he frustrated civil rights campaigners who said he was not doing enough or moving quickly enough
- he worried congressmen from the southern states who said he was moving too quickly. They blocked many of his measures.

Economy

Aim: to keep the US economy the strongest in the world
- Kennedy cut income taxes to give people more spending money
- he gave grants to companies to invest in high-tech equipment and train their workers
- he made $900 million available to businesses to create new jobs
- he increased spending on defence. In areas like Seattle, with lots of defence companies, one in four workers depended on government contracts
- he massively increased spending on space technology
- he promised that the USA would put a man on the moon by the end of the decade (which they did – although he did not live to see it)
- the economy grew quickly (see Source 13 on page 372). For those who had a secure job this was a good time ...

... but
- technology did not help unemployment in traditional industries – in fact, less workers were needed because of increased technology
- the rate of black unemployment was twice that of white unemployment
- corporations made big profits but the extra money did not trickle down to all Americans
- critics said it was dangerous that the boom depended on government spending. What happens when a new President comes in who decides to cut spending.

Poverty

Aim: to tackle deprivation and ensure poor Americans had the opportunity to help themselves
- Kennedy increased the minimum wage
- under his Area Redevelopment Act, poor communities could get loans, grants or advice from the government to start new businesses or build infrastructure (like roads, telephone lines, etc.)
- under his Housing Act, people in run-down inner city areas could get loans to improve their housing; or local authorities could get money to clear slums
- under his Social Security Act, more money was available for payments to the elderly and unemployed
- his Manpower Development and Training Act retrained the unemployed

... but
- the minimum wage only helped those who already had a job
- the housing loans did not help the poorest people since they could not afford to take out loans
- slum clearance led to housing shortages in the inner cities
- many poor black families from the south moved to northern cities looking for work, where they experienced poverty and racial tension.

Kennedy's successes and failures, 1961–63.

The nation mourns

In 1963 Kennedy was shot dead while visiting Dallas, Texas, in an open car. The assassination shocked Americans and the world. There is no doubt that by November 1963 Kennedy had achieved only a small part of what he had set out to do. It was left to his vice-president, Lyndon Johnson, to take up the challenge.

ACTIVITY

It is said that everyone who was alive on the day that Kennedy died can remember where they were when they heard the news. Do some research among your own relatives to see if the theory is correct and, if so, why it was such a shock.

An American cartoon of November 23, 1963. The statue of the most celebrated US president, Abraham Lincoln, weeps for the death of John F. Kennedy.

1 Sources 50 and 51 show the same man. Describe the different impression they give of Johnson.
2 Use your knowledge from this section and other parts of your course to discuss possible reasons for the difference.

SOURCE 50

Johnson with his long-time friend and adviser, Abe Fortas in 1965. Johnson had a very 'direct' approach when dealing with people, friends and rivals alike.

SOURCE 51

Johnson at home playing dominoes with dinner guests during a crisis in the Vietman War.

Lyndon Johnson and the 'great society'

Lyndon Johnson became president when Kennedy was assassinated in 1963. One year later, he had to seek election in his own right. He won a sweeping victory, partly because of the American public's sympathy after the assassination of Kennedy. When he came to power, he wanted to take Kennedy's work much further. In his first speech as president, he talked in terms of a 'great society', a place where the meaning of man's life matches the marvels of man's labour'. He declared 'unconditional war on poverty' and called for 'an immediate end to racial injustice'. However, unlike Kennedy, Johnson does not have a reputation as being a great president. Conservatives in Congress attacked him for spending too much on welfare reform. Liberals think badly of him because he escalated American involvement in the Vietnam War and this did much damage to the USA. His 'great society' is largely forgotten. See if you think this is fair.

The Johnson style

Johnson was not a showman like Kennedy. While Kennedy was all youthful vision, Johnson was more the seasoned politician. However, he was extremely good at politics. He was much more successful than Kennedy had been in getting measures passed by Congress – in fact, more successful than almost any other president. The vast majority of the measures he put to Congress were passed. In fact, Johnson had so much influence over Congress that he managed to persuade them to grant him enormous personal power during the Vietnam War, which enabled him to take decisions without consulting them.

To start with, Johnson kept Kennedy's cabinet but he did not work well with the whizz-kid advisers, as you can see from Source 52.

SOURCE 52

An American cartoon of 1972 commenting on the difference in style between Kennedy and Johnson. The eggs are Kennedy's 'egghead' (clever) advisers!

What was Johnson's 'great society'?

Johnson's style might have been different from Kennedy's but the policies were not. Johnson is often contrasted to Kennedy but he believed just as strongly in social justice and tackling poverty. His 'great society' tried to bring about radical social change. It was less moral and theoretical than the New Frontier, and more practical. Johnson tackled areas that Kennedy had not been able to touch; for example 'medicare', which provided free medical care for the poor.

ACTIVITY

On page 391 we presented Kennedy's policies in chart form. Using the text on these pages, create your own chart to summarise Johnson's achievements and failures in the area of civil rights, the economy and poverty. You can get a sheet from your teacher to help you.

SOURCE 53

An American cartoon of March 1968 after Johnson announced he would not be seeking re-election.

3 Spending on welfare rose steadily during Johnson's presidency. Is this evidence of the success or the failure of his policies?

FOCUS TASK

Here are some factors which have affected the reputations of Kennedy and Johnson:
- social policy
- the Civil Rights movement
- leadership style
- speeches
- the nature of their deaths
- the Vietnam War.

1 For each factor explain, with examples, how this has affected the presidents' reputations, positively or negatively.
2 Which do you think is the biggest factor in making or breaking their reputations?
3 Out of a possible score of ten what would you give to each of the Presidents? Write a paragraph to explain your scores and to explain how far you think each President deserves his reputation.

Civil rights

You have already read about Johnson's Civil Rights Act (1964) on page 381. Johnson also appointed the first ever black Americans to the White House cabinet and the Supreme Court. He also passed the Voting Rights Act (see page 381). The Immigration Act (1965) ended the system of racial quotas for immigrants into the USA. Decisions on whether to allow immigrants to enter the USA were based purely on the merits of the case. However, the period also saw growing racial tensions, with serious rioting and many deaths in several cities in summer 1968.

The economy

Johnson cut taxes, which helped the better off. He improved transport links such as railways and highways. These benefited middle-class commuters most. He increased funding for universities which also helped the middle classes, who generally sent their children to university.

Johnson also introduced a range of consumer laws. These meant that manufacturers and shops had to label goods fairly and clearly. They also gave consumers the right to return faulty goods and exchange them without a complicated legal battle.

On the down side, unemployment and inflation continued to rise. Critics blamed Johnson's welfare policies, but most historians now say that the huge cost of the Vietnam War was the real reason. Either way, Johnson was responsible.

One other problem was that during the 1960s major US companies increasingly invested their profits abroad. By the early 1970s, US companies were earning 40 per cent of their profits from factories outside the USA. This did nothing to reduce unemployment at home.

Poverty

Johnson's war on poverty involved a range of measures.

- The Medical Care Act (1965) put federal funding into health care along the lines of Britain's National Health Service, but it was not as comprehensive. It funded health care for elderly people and for families on low incomes.
- Johnson increased the minimum wage from $1.25 to $1.40 per hour.
- He increased the funding to the Aid of Families with Dependent Children (AFDC) scheme. This gave financial help to 745,000 families on low incomes.
- Poorer families also received food stamps to buy groceries.
- The VISTA programme tried to create work in poor inner city areas.
- The Head Start and Upward Bound programmes tried to persuade inner city populations of the importance of education.
- The Elementary and Secondary Education Act (1965) put federal funding into improving education in poorer areas. Until this time, the USA's education system had been locally funded. This meant that poorer areas found it harder to raise enough money for good schooling than wealthier areas. This was a major innovation in government policy, designed to back up the Head Start and similar programmes.
- There was a Job Corps to help school dropouts to find work.
- The Neighbourhood Youth Corps did a similar job, encouraging local youngsters to do work such as clearing graffiti or keeping parks clean.
- The Model Cities Act (1966) linked to the other inner city employment programmes. It improved inner city environments by clearing slums or providing parks or sports facilities. It also gave top-up payments to people on low incomes to help to pay their rents.

The nation celebrates

Johnson decided not to run for president again in 1968. It was an admission of defeat – almost an act of political suicide (see Source 53). With race riots; high inflation and high unemployment; government spending out of control; and the anti-Vietnam War movement at its peak, it is doubtful whether Johnson would have won the election if he had decided to run. He did not and the nation was very glad.

In the 1968 election the Democrats lost by a landslide, and the nation gave its verdict on the eight years of Democrat Presidency. How far this was a rejection of the radical social reforms and how far it was a reaction to the Vietnam War is a matter of debate, but a combination of the two spelt the end for Johnson

A 1974 cartoon commenting on allegations that Nixon doctored tapes that were submitted to Congress as evidence.

1 What were:
  a) CREEP
  b) dirty tricks
  c) the Watergate building?

2 Explain why the Senate investigation was set up.

3 Why were the tapes so important?

The Watergate Scandal

How many times have you heard of a scandal of any kind being called 'something-gate'? The reason why '-gate' is always used goes back to the Watergate Scandal which rocked the USA in the early 1970s and was seen as the single greatest threat to the US Constitution in its history. The scandal started with a small revelation but gradually snowballed into a constitutional crisis.

Phase 1: CREEP comes under suspicion

On 17 June 1972 five 'burglars' were arrested in the offices of the Democratic Party in the Watergate Building, Washington DC and these burglars turned out to be rather unusual.

- They were not stealing from the offices. They were planting electronic bugging devices.
- One burglar turned out to be a former member of the CIA (the government's secret service).
- All five turned out to be connected to the Committee for the Re-election of the President (CREEP) set up by President Nixon.

CREEP was now under scrutiny. The FBI (Federal Bureau of Investigation) gradually uncovered a massive campaign of spying on Nixon's opponents, as well as attempts to disrupt their political campaigning. It emerged that CREEP had raised $60 million for the President's re-election campaign. Much of this money had been raised from corporations working on government contracts. They had been pressured to donate money through fear that they might lose their contract. What is more, some of the money was specifically allocated to John Mitchell, the director of the campaign and a former US Attorney General, to pursue actions (known as 'dirty tricks') against the President's Democratic Party opponents. Two reporters from the *Washington Post*, Carl Bernstein and Bob Woodward, pursued their own investigations. However, despite press reports to the contrary, Nixon denied that he or his immediate advisors were involved. In the presidential elections of 1972 he won a landslide victory. He felt confident that he could forget Watergate and get on with running the USA. He was wrong.

Phase 2: Did the President know?

In January 1973 the Watergate burglars went on trial. All were convicted. In March, when they were sentenced, one of the defendants claimed in court that the White House was covering up its involvement in the break-in and that witnesses had lied during the trial. Nixon himself was not named, but senior figures in the administration were.

Nixon still denied all knowledge of the break-in or of attempts to cover it up. He announced an investigation and appointed Archibald Cox as special Watergate prosecutor.

The Senate decided to hold its own investigation, headed by Senator Sam Ervin. The Senate Watergate Committee heard evidence between May and November 1973. In the televised public hearing it became clear that very senior White House officials were involved. Three of Nixon's leading advisers resigned. One of them told the investigation that he had discussed the Watergate burglary at least 35 times with Nixon. Nixon still denied any involvement.

Phase 3: The battle for the tapes

One of the most significant facts to emerge from the Senate investigation was that since 1971 Nixon had secretly taped conversations in his office in the White House. Both the Senate Committee and Cox wanted these tapes. Nixon refused.

On 20 October 1973, Nixon tried to undermine the investigation by getting the Attorney General to sack Cox. Cox was indeed sacked but the Attorney General himself also resigned.

It did Nixon little good. The new special prosecutor, Leon Jaworski, also demanded the tapes. In December Nixon released some tapes, but one had an unexplained gap of 18½ minutes.

The arguments continued. In April 1974 Nixon gave the investigation 1200 pages of transcripts of the tapes, but they were heavily edited. Jaworski appealed to the Supreme Court and it ordered all the White House tapes be handed over.

ACTIVITY

What was the impact of Watergate on Americans?

1 Study Sources 54–56. Which do you think makes each of the following points?
   a) Nixon is a liar
   b) America is in crisis
   c) Don't trust politicians.
2 You are planning a newspaper feature on the impact of Watergate. You can include just one of the cartoons. Which will you choose and why? Write a paragraph to explain your choice.

Phase 4: The end

Finally, the Supreme Court ordered Nixon to hand over the tapes. He did. They revealed conclusively that:

• Nixon had been involved in the initial campaign of dirty tricks
• throughout the investigation he had repeatedly tried to cover up the truth.

On 27 July, Congress's House Judiciary Committee voted to impeach the President (put him on trial) for obstructing justice. An opinion poll showed that 66 per cent of the American public were in favour of this. To avoid being impeached, Nixon resigned on 8 August 1974. Nixon could then have been tried as a criminal, but Jaworski decided not to prosecute him. He was pardoned by President Ford, his successor, a month later, but 31 of his officials went to prison for various offences relating to Watergate.

The aftermath

Congress passed a series of measures that aimed to prevent similar things happening again.

• The Privacy Act (1974) allowed American citizens to inspect government files held on them.
• The Budget Act (1974) meant that the president had to account for all the money spent (Nixon was suspected of spending millions of dollars of government money on his own personal properties and of evading $400,000 in tax).
• The Election Campaign Act limited the amount of money parties could raise for elections, and banned foreign contributions.

The scandal utterly destroyed Nixon's reputation. He was seen as corrupt and untrustworthy. People called him Tricky Dicky. Any achievements of his presidency seemed insignificant.

However, the deeper damage of Watergate was that it undermined confidence in politics. It seemed as if political leadership had been replaced by cynical manipulation. Some people could not believe that these events were taking place in the USA. The question was whether Nixon was a corrupt one-off or whether this kind of behaviour was an inevitable part of the political system. People feared that the problem ran deep. Stirring up and uncovering scandal became a preoccupation of the press. The confidence and idealism of the 1960s were replaced by doubt and cynicism.

SOURCE 55

A 1973 American cartoon.

SOURCE 56

A cartoon from the Los Angeles Times, published in 1973.

PROFILE

Richard Nixon, President 1969–1974

★ Born in California in 1913.
★ Established a reputation as a brilliant scholar and lawyer.
★ Served as a navy lieutenant commander in the Pacific during the Second World War.
★ Elected to Congress from his California district after the war. In 1950, he won a seat in the Senate. He helped in the McCarthy anti-Communist witch hunts.
★ In 1952 he became Eisenhower's running mate for the presidential elections, and was vice-president 1953–1961.
★ Was the Republican candidate in the 1960 election and was narrowly defeated by John F Kennedy.
★ Stood again in 1968 and was elected president.
★ He was re-elected president in 1972. However, controversy over the Watergate Affair plagued him. He was about to be impeached when he resigned in 1974.
★ He died in 1994.

1 Add five more bullet points to Nixon's profile, so that it tells a fuller story.

FOCUS TASK

Verdicts on Nixon

Imagine you are reading about Nixon's resignation. In pairs or small groups, discuss how people might have reacted after they had finished reading. You could role play your conversation or you could write down your ideas. You could assign at least one person in the group to defend Nixon, to ensure that his side of the story is heard.

What else did Nixon do?

The Watergate scandal overshadows everything else in the Nixon presidency. But some people believe that, in some ways, he was an extremely successful and effective president.

During his presidency, Nixon was overwhelmingly concerned with foreign affairs. He worked hard to improve relations between the USA and China in the early 1970s and succeeded. He also had considerable success in agreeing with the USSR to reduce stocks of nuclear weapons. He tried hard to bring peace to the Middle East, with some success.

At his election, Nixon had promised to get the USA out of the Vietnam War. He was looking for what he called 'peace with dignity'. He did get the USA out of the war and he ended the draft (compulsory military call up). Whether the peace deal was a worthwhile achievement is a matter of debate (see pages 362–363).

Nixon's presidency saw important advances in social issues. More black Americans went to college (over 400,000 by 1970), more registered to vote, more entered politics (there were 13 black congressmen and 81 black mayors by 1971). However, although these things happened during Nixon's presidency, he was not the cause. In fact, he did not see his role as being one of an engineer of social change. He annoyed Congress by saying 'I've always thought this country could run itself domestically without a president.'

Nixon's economic policies were confused. He inherited a big problem from Johnson – high inflation. To reduce demand for goods and slow down inflation he tried to control credit and lending. However, he failed to control wage rises, so his policies had a limited effect on inflation. People did not need to borrow money to spend because they were getting large pay rises! The main effect of credit control was to stop businesses from expanding. This caused increased unemployment. By 1971 inflation was rising and unemployment was rising too.

Nixon's other main economic policy was to cut taxes. Republican presidents nearly always did this. Unfortunately, this also fed inflation.

SOURCE 57

A newspaper reporting Nixon's resignation in 1974.

Eastern Europe and the Cold War 1948–1989

14.1 How secure was Soviet control of eastern Europe 1948–1968?

How did Stalin control eastern Europe?

As you saw in Chapter 11, after the Second World War the Communists quickly gained control of eastern Europe. The chaotic situation in many of the countries helped them.

- After the war there was a political vacuum in many countries in eastern Europe. The Soviet leader Stalin helped the Communist parties in them to win power. Through Cominform (see Factfile on page 398) he made sure that these eastern European countries followed the same policies as the Soviet Union. They became one-party states. The Communist Party was the only legal party. Secret police arrested the Communists' opponents.
- There was also a need to restore law and order. This provided a good excuse to station Soviet troops in each country.
- The economies of eastern Europe were shattered. To rebuild them, the governments followed the economic policies of the Soviet Union. They took over all industry. Workers and farmers were told what to produce. Through Comecon (see Factfile on page 398) Stalin made sure that the countries of eastern Europe traded with the USSR. He promised aid to countries that co-operated with the Soviet Union.
- When Soviet control was threatened, the Soviet Union was prepared to use its tanks to crush opposition (see Source 1).

SOURCE 1

"WHO'S NEXT TO BE LIBERATED FROM FREEDOM, COMRADE?"

David Low comments on Stalin's control of eastern Europe, 2 March 1948.

FACTFILE

Cominform

★ Cominform stands for the Communist Information Bureau.

★ Stalin set up the Cominform in 1947 as an organisation to co-ordinate the various Communist governments in eastern Europe.

★ The office was originally based in Belgrade in Yugoslavia but moved to Bucharest in Romania in 1948 after Yugoslavia was expelled by Stalin because it would not do what the Soviet Union told it to do.

★ Cominform ran meetings and sent out instructions to Communist governments about what the Soviet Union wanted them to do.

FACTFILE

Comecon

★ Comecon stands for the Council for Mutual Economic Assistance.

★ It was set up in 1949 to co-ordinate the industries and trade of the eastern European countries.

★ The idea was that members of Comecon traded mostly with one another rather than trading with the West.

★ Comecon favoured the USSR far more than any of its other members. It provided the USSR with a market to sell its goods. It also guaranteed it a cheap supply of raw materials. For example, Poland was forced to sell its coal to the USSR at one-tenth of the price that it could have got selling it on the open market.

★ It set up a bank for socialist countries in 1964.

SOURCE 2

Key

- Territory taken over by USSR at end of Second World War
- Soviet-dominated Communist governments
- Other Communist governments

Eastern Europe, 1948–56.

What did ordinary people in eastern Europe think of Soviet control?

For some people of eastern Europe the Communists brought hope. The Soviet Union had achieved amazing industrial growth before the Second World War. Maybe, by following Soviet methods, they could do the same. Soviet-style Communism also offered them stable government and security because they were backed by one of the world's superpowers. Faced by shortages and poverty after the war, many people hoped for great things from Communism (see Source 3).

However, the reality of Soviet control of eastern Europe was very different from what people had hoped for. Countries that had a long tradition of free speech and democratic government suddenly lost the right to criticise the government. Newspapers were censored. Non-Communists were put in prison for criticising the government. People were forbidden to travel to countries in western Europe.

Between 1945 and 1955 eastern European economies did recover. But the factories did not produce what ordinary people wanted. They actually produced what the Soviet Union wanted. Wages in eastern Europe fell behind the wages in other countries. They even fell behind the wages in the Soviet Union. Eastern Europe was forbidden by Stalin to apply for Marshall Aid from the USA (see pages 329–30) which could have helped it in its economic recovery.

Long after economic recovery had ended the wartime shortages in western Europe, people in eastern Europe were short of coal to heat their houses, short of milk and meat. Clothing and shoes were very expensive. People could not get consumer goods like radios, electric kettles or televisions which were becoming common in the West.

In addition, they had little chance to protest. In June 1953 there were huge demonstrations across East Germany protesting about Communist policies. Soviet tanks rolled in and Soviet troops killed 40 protesters and wounded over 400. Thousands were arrested and the protests were crushed. Similar protests in Czechoslovakia, Hungary and Romania were dealt with in the same way.

SOURCE 3

Twenty years ago we jumped head first into politics as though we were jumping into uncharted waters . . . There was a lot of enthusiasm . . . You're like this when you are young and we had an opportunity, which had long been denied, to be there while something new was being created.

Jiři Ruml, a Czech Communist, writing in 1968.

SOURCE 4

A 1949 Soviet cartoon. Marshal Tito, leader of Yugoslavia, is shown accepting money from the Americans. His cloak is labelled 'Judas' – 'the betrayer'. Yugoslavia was the only Communist state to resist domination by Stalin. The Soviet Union kept up a propaganda battle against Tito. Despite the Cold War, there were more cartoons in the official Communist newspapers attacking Tito than cartoons criticising the USA.

2 Study Source 4. Why do you think Tito wished to remain independent of the Soviet Union?

3 Why do you think the Soviet Union was worried about Tito's independence?

4 Look at Source 2. Does this help to explain why the Soviet Union allowed Tito to remain independent?

FOCUS TASK

It is 1953. Stalin has died. Write an obituary for him explaining how he gained control of eastern Europe.

The rise of Khrushchev

Stalin was a hero to millions of people in the USSR. He had defeated Hitler and given the USSR an empire in eastern Europe. He made the USSR a nuclear superpower. When he died in 1953, amid the grief and mourning, many minds turned to the question of who would succeed Stalin as Soviet leader. The man who emerged by 1955 was Nikita Khrushchev. He seemed very different from Stalin. He ended the USSR's long feuds with China and with Yugoslavia. He talked of peaceful co-existence with the West. He made plans to reduce expenditure on arms. He attended the first post-war summit between the USSR, the USA, France and Britain in July 1955. He also said he wanted to improve the living standards of ordinary Soviet citizens and those of eastern Europe.

Khrushchev even relaxed the iron control of the Soviet Union. He closed down Cominform. He released thousands of political prisoners. He agreed to pull Soviet troops out of Austria (they had been posted there since the end of the Second World War). He seemed to be signalling to the countries of eastern Europe that they would be allowed much greater independence to control their own affairs.

ACTIVITY

Look at Source 5.

1 Make a list of the features of the cartoon which show Khruschev as a new type of leader.
2 Explain:
   a) why he is shown destroying the snowman, and
   b) what this is supposed to suggest about his attitude to the Cold War.
3 Design another cartoon which shows him relaxing the Soviet grip on Eastern Europe. Think about:
   • how you would show Khruschev
   • how you would represent the states of Eastern Europe (as maps? as people?)
   • how you would represent Soviet control (as a rope? getting looser? tighter?).
You could either draw the cartoon or write instructions for an artist to do so.

SOURCE 5

ПО-ШАХТЕРСКИ

A 1959 Soviet cartoon. The writing on the snowman's hat reads 'cold war'. Khrushchev is drilling through the cold war using what the caption calls 'miners' methods'.

SOURCE 6

We must produce more grain. The more grain there is, the more meat, lard and fruit there will be. Our tables will be better covered. Marxist theory helped us win power and consolidate it. Having done this we must help the people eat well, dress well and live well. If after forty years of Communism, a person cannot have a glass of milk or a pair of shoes, he will not believe Communism is a good thing, whatever you tell him.

Nikita Khrushchev speaking in 1955.

Nikita Khrushchev

★ Born 1894, the son of a coal miner.
★ Fought in the Red Army during the Civil War, 1922–1923.
★ Afterwards worked for the Communist Party in Moscow. Was awarded the Order of Lenin for his work building the Moscow underground railway.
★ In 1949 he was appointed by the Communist Party to run Soviet agriculture.
★ There was a power struggle after Stalin's death over who would succeed him. Khrushchev had come out on top by 1955 and by 1956 he felt secure enough in his position to attack Stalin's reputation.
★ Became Prime Minister in 1958.
★ Took his country close to nuclear war with the USA during the Cuban missile crisis in 1962 (see pages 347–352).
★ Was forced into retirement in 1964.
★ Died in 1971.

ACTIVITY

Write your own definition of 'de-Stalinisation'. Make sure you include:
• at least two examples
• an explanation of why it was radical.

De-Stalinisation

At the Communist Party International in 1956, Khrushchev made an astonishing attack on Stalin. He dredged up the gory evidence of Stalin's purges (see page 134) and denounced him as a wicked tyrant who was an enemy of the people and kept all power to himself. Khrushchev went on to say much worse things about Stalin and began a programme of 'de-Stalinisation':

• He released more political prisoners.
• He closed down Cominform as part of his policy of reconciliation with Yugoslavia.
• He invited Marshal Tito to Moscow.
• He dismissed Stalin's former Foreign Minister, Molotov.

Those in eastern Europe who wanted greater freedom from the Soviet Union saw hopeful times ahead.

SOURCE 7

Stalin used extreme methods and mass repressions at a time when the revolution was already victorious . . . Stalin showed in a whole series of cases his intolerance, his brutality and his abuse of power . . . He often chose the path of repression and physical annihilation, not only against actual enemies, but also against individuals who had not committed any crimes against the Party and the Soviet government.

Khrushchev denounces Stalin in 1956. For citizens of eastern Europe who had been bombarded with propaganda praising Stalin, this was a shocking change of direction.

The Warsaw Pact

One aspect of Stalin's policy did not change, however. His aim in eastern Europe had always been to create a buffer against attack from the West. Khrushchev continued this policy. In 1955 he created the Warsaw Pact. This was a military alliance similar to NATO (see page 333). The members would defend each other if one was attacked. The Warsaw Pact included all the Communist countries of eastern Europe except Yugoslavia, but it was dominated by the Soviet Union (see Source 13, page 342).

How did the USSR deal with opposition in eastern Europe?

Khrushchev's criticism of Stalin sent a strong signal to opposition groups in eastern Europe that they could now press for changes. The question was: how far would Khrushchev let them go? The first opposition Khrushchev had to deal with as leader was in Poland.

In the summer of 1956 demonstrators attacked the Polish police, protesting about the fact that the government had increased food prices but not wages. Fifty-three workers were killed by the Polish army in riots in Poznan. The Polish government itself was unable to control the demonstrators. Alarmed, Khrushchev moved troops to the Polish border.

By October 1956 Poland was becoming more stabilised. A new leader, Wladyslaw Gomulka, took charge on 20 October. During the Nazi occupation Gomulka had been a popular leader of the Communist resistance (not the main underground army, the AK). However, he was also a nationalist. He had not seen eye to eye with many Polish Communists, who were totally loyal to Stalin. Khrushchev accepted Gomulka's appointment – a popular move in Poland for the next couple of years.

There was also an agreement that the Communists would stop persecuting members of the Catholic Church. The Red Army withdrew to the Polish border and left the Polish army and government to sort things out.

Case study 1: Hungary, 1956

Khrushchev was soon put to the test again in Hungary in October 1956.

Why was there opposition in Hungary?

Hungary was led by a hard-line Communist called Mátyás Rákosi. Hungarians hated the restrictions which Rákosi's Communism imposed on them. Most Hungarians felt bitter about losing their freedom of speech. They lived in fear of the secret police. They resented the presence of thousands of Soviet troops and officials in their country. Some areas of Hungary even had Russian street signs, Russian schools and shops. Worst of all, Hungarians had to pay for Soviet forces to be in Hungary.

SOURCE 8

Living standards were declining and yet the papers and radio kept saying that we had never had it so good. Why? Why these lies? Everybody knew the state was spending the money on armaments. Why could they not admit that we were worse off because of the war effort and the need to build new factories? . . . I finally arrived at the realisation that the system was wrong and stupid.

A Hungarian student describes the mood in 1953.

SOURCE 9

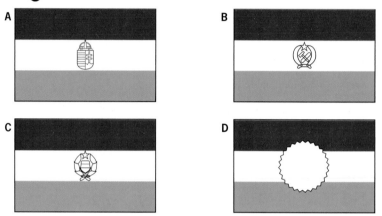

Flags representing different stages of Hungary's position, 1949–89.

In June 1956 a group within the Communist Party in Hungary opposed Rákosi. He appealed to Moscow for help. He wanted to arrest 400 leading opponents. Moscow would not back him. Rákosi's assistant said sarcastically: 'Might I suggest that mass arrests are not reconcilable with our new brand of socialist legality.' The Kremlin ordered Rákosi to be retired 'for health reasons'.

However, the new leader, Ernö Gerö, was no more acceptable to the Hungarian people. Discontent came to a head with a huge student demonstration on 23 October, when the giant statue of Stalin in Budapest was pulled down. The USSR allowed a new government to be formed under the well-respected Imre Nagy. Soviet troops and tanks stationed in Hungary since the war began to withdraw. Hungarians created thousands of local councils to replace Soviet power. Several thousand Hungarian soldiers defected from the army to the rebel cause, taking their weapons with them.

Nagy's government began to make plans. It would hold free elections, create impartial courts, restore farmland to private ownership. It wanted the total withdrawal of the Soviet army from Hungary. It also planned to leave the Warsaw Pact and declare Hungary neutral in the Cold War struggle between East and West. There was widespread optimism that the new American President Eisenhower, who had been the wartime supreme commander of all Allied Forces in western Europe, would support the new independent Hungary.

SOURCE 10

Wearing western clothes was considered dangerous. To cite a small example: my colleague John showed up at lectures one day in a new suit, a striped shirt and necktie from the United States. His shoes were smooth suede and would have cost one month's wages in Hungary. After classes John was summoned by the party officer. He received a tongue-lashing and was expelled.

Written by László Beke, a student who helped lead the Hungarian uprising in 1956.

How did the Soviet Union respond?

Khrushchev at first seemed ready to accept some of the reforms. However, he could not accept Hungary's leaving the Warsaw Pact. In November 1956 thousands of Soviet troops and tanks moved into Budapest. Unlike in Poland, the Hungarians did not give in. Two weeks of bitter fighting followed. Some estimates put the number of Hungarians killed at 30,000. However, the latest research suggests about 3000 Hungarians and 7000–8000 Russians were killed. Another 200,000 Hungarians fled across the border into Austria to escape the Communist forces. Imre Nagy and his fellow leaders were imprisoned and then executed.

1 Use the text and Sources 8 and 10 to give reasons why the Hungarians disliked Communist control.
2 Which of their demands do you think would be most threatening to the USSR?

SOURCE 11

In Hungary thousands of people have obtained arms by disarming soldiers and militia men . . . Soldiers have been making friends with the embittered and dissatisfied masses . . . The authorities are paralysed, unable to stop the bloody events.

From a report in a Yugoslav newspaper. Yugoslavia, although Communist, did not approve of Soviet policies.

SOURCE 12

We have almost no weapons, no heavy guns of any kind. People are running up to the tanks, throwing in hand grenades and closing the drivers' windows. The Hungarian people are not afraid of death. It is only a pity that we cannot last longer. Now the firing is starting again. The tanks are coming nearer and nearer. You can't let people attack tanks with their bare hands. What is the United Nations doing?

A telex message sent by the Hungarian rebels fighting the Communists. Quoted in George Mikes, *The Hungarian Revolution,* 1957.

3 How do Sources 11 and 12 differ in the impression they give of the Hungarian uprising?

4 Why do you think they differ?

5 Do the photos in Source 14 give the same impression as either Source 11 or Source 12?

6 Write a paragraph explaining the nature of the fighting in Budapest using Sources 11–14.

FOCUS TASK

Explain which of these statements you most agree with:

- 'The severity of the Red Army in dealing with Hungary in 1956 shows how fragile the Soviet hold on Hungary really was.'
- 'The speed at which the Red Army crushed resistance in Hungary shows how completely the Soviet Union controlled Hungary.'

7 Look back at Source 2. Why do you think Hungary's membership of the Warsaw Pact was so important to the Soviet Union?

8 Why do you think the Hungarians received no support from the West?

SOURCE 13

October 27, 1956. On my way home I saw a little girl propped up against the doorway of a building with a machine gun clutched in her hands. When I tried to move her, I saw she was dead. She could not have been more than eleven or twelve years old. There was a neatly folded note in her pocket she had evidently meant to pass on to her parents. In childish scrawl it read: 'Dear Mama, Brother is dead. He asked me to take care of his gun. I am all right, and I'm going with friends now. I kiss you. Kati.'

Written by László Beke, a Hungarian student.

SOURCE 14

A

B

The effects of the uprising in Budapest. **A** shows the scene of destruction outside the Kilian Barracks, where heavy fighting was experienced. **B** shows an armed fifteen-year-old girl.

The Hungarian resistance was crushed in two weeks. The Western powers protested to the USSR but sent no help; they were too preoccupied with the Suez crisis in the Middle East.

Khrushchev put János Kádár in place as leader. Kádár took several months to crush all resistance. Around 35,000 anti-Communist activists were arrested and 300 were executed. Kádár cautiously introduced some of the reforms being demanded by the Hungarian people. However, he did not waver on the central issue – membership of the Warsaw Pact.

SOURCE 15

In Czechoslovakia the people who were trusted [by the Communist government] were the obedient ones, those who did not cause any trouble, who didn't ask questions. It was the mediocre man who came off best.

In twenty years not one human problem has been solved in our country, from primary needs like flats, schools, to the more subtle needs such as fulfilling oneself . . . the need for people to trust one another . . . development of education.

I feel that our Republic has lost its good reputation.

From a speech given by Ludvik Vaculik, a leading figure in the reform movement, in March 1968.

SOURCE 16

The Director told them they would produce 400 locomotives a year. They are making seventy.

And go look at the scrapyard, at all the work that has been thrown out. They built a railway and then took it down again. Who's responsible for all this? The Communist Party set up the system.

We were robbed of our output, our wages . . . How can I believe that in five years' time it won't be worse?

Ludvik Vaculik quotes from an interview he had with the workers in a locomotive factory run by the Communists.

Case study 2: Czechoslovakia and the Prague Spring, 1968

Twelve years after the brutal suppression of the Hungarians, Czechoslovakia posed a similar challenge to Soviet domination of eastern Europe. Khrushchev had by now been ousted from power in the USSR. A new leader, Leonid Brezhnev, had replaced him.

Why was there opposition in Czechoslovakia?

In the 1960s a new mood developed in Czechoslovakia. People examined what had been happening in 20 years of Communist control and they did not like what they saw. In 1967 the old Stalinist leader was forced to resign. Alexander Dubček became the leader of the Czech Communist Party. He proposed a policy of 'socialism with a human face': less censorship, more freedom of speech and a reduction in the activities of the secret police. Dubček was a committed Communist, but he believed that Communism did not have to be as restrictive as it had been before he came to power. He had learned the lessons of the Hungarian uprising and reassured Brezhnev that Czechoslovakia had no plans to pull out of the Warsaw Pact or Comecon.

The Czech opposition was led by intellectuals who felt that the Communists had failed to lead the country forward. As censorship had been eased, they were able to launch attacks on the Communist leadership, pointing out how corrupt and useless they were. Communist government ministers were 'grilled' on live television and radio about how they were running the country and about events before 1968. This period became known as 'The Prague Spring' because of all the new ideas that seemed to be appearing everywhere.

By the summer even more radical ideas were emerging. There was even talk of allowing another political party, the Social Democratic Party, to be set up as a rival to the Communist Party.

SOURCE 17

All the different kinds of state in which the Communist Party has taken power have gone through rigged trials . . . There must be a fault other than just the wrong people were chosen. There must be a fault in the theory [of Communism] itself.

Written by Luboš Dubrovsky, a Czech writer, in May 1968.

How did the Soviet Union respond?

The Soviet Union was very suspicious of the changes taking place in Czechoslovakia. Czechoslovakia was one of the most important countries in the Warsaw Pact. It was centrally placed, and had the strongest industry. The Soviets were worried that the new ideas in Czechoslovakia might spread to other countries in eastern Europe. Brezhnev came under pressure from the East German leader, Walter Ulbricht, and the Polish leader, Gomulka, to restrain reform in Czechoslovakia.

The USSR tried various methods in response. To start with, it tried to slow Dubček down. It argued with him. Soviet, Polish and East German troops performed very public training exercises right on the Czech border. It thought about imposing economic sanctions – for example, cancelling wheat exports to Czechoslovakia – but didn't because it thought that the Czechs would ask for help from the West.

In July the USSR had a summit conference with the Czechs. Dubček agreed not to allow a new Social Democratic Party. However, he insisted on keeping most of his reforms. The tension seemed to ease. Early in August, a conference of all the other Warsaw Pact countries produced a vague declaration simply calling on Czechoslovakia to maintain political stability.

Then 17 days later, on 20 August 1968, to the stunned amazement of the Czechs and the outside world, Soviet tanks moved into Czechoslovakia.

1 According to Sources 15–17, what are the worries of the Czech people?
2 How are they similar to and different from the concerns of the Hungarian rebels (see Sources 8 and 10)?

SOURCE 18

Czechs burning Soviet tanks in Prague, August 1968.

3 Explain how and why Sources 19 and 21 differ in their interpretation of the Soviet intervention.

SOURCE 19

Yesterday troops from the Soviet Union, Poland, East Germany, Hungary and Bulgaria crossed the frontier of Czechoslovakia . . . The Czechoslovak Communist Party Central Committee regard this act as contrary to the basic principles of good relations between socialist states.

A Prague radio report, 21 August 1968.

SOURCE 21

The party and government leaders of the Czechoslovak Socialist Republic have asked the Soviet Union and other allies to give the Czechoslovak people urgent assistance, including assistance with armed forces. This request was brought about . . . by the threat from counter revolutionary forces . . . working with foreign forces hostile to socialism.

A Soviet news agency report, 21 August 1968.

SOURCE 20

A street cartoon in Prague.

There was little violent resistance, although many Czechs refused to co-operate with the Soviet troops. Dubček was removed from power. His experiment in socialism with a human face had not failed; it had simply proved unacceptable to the other Communist countries.

Dubček always expressed loyalty to Communism and the Warsaw Pact, but Brezhnev was very worried that the new ideas coming out of Czechoslovakia would spread. He was under pressure from the leaders of other Communist countries in eastern Europe, particularly Ulbricht in East Germany. These leaders feared that their own people would demand the same freedom that Dubček had allowed in Czechoslovakia. Indeed, in 1968 Albania resigned from the Warsaw Pact because it thought that the Soviet Union itself had become too liberal since Stalin had died! Brezhnev made no attempt to force Albania back into the Pact because he did not consider it an important country.

When internal and external forces hostile to socialism attempt to turn the development of any socialist country in the direction of the capitalist system, when a threat arises to the cause of socialism in that country, a threat to the socialist commonwealth as a whole – it becomes not only a problem for the people of that country but also a general problem, the concern of all socialist countries.

The Brezhnev Doctrine.

Brezhnev Doctrine

The Czechoslovak episode gave rise to the Brezhnev Doctrine. The essentials of Communism were defined as

- a one-party system
- to remain a member of the Warsaw Pact.

Unlike Nagy in Hungary, Dubček was not executed. But he was gradually downgraded. First he was sent to be ambassador to Turkey, then expelled from the Communist Party altogether. Photographs showing him as leader were 'censored'.

SOURCE **23**

A

B

These two photographs show the same scene. In **A**, Dubček is shown by the arrow. How has he been dealt with in photograph **B**?

FOCUS TASK

You are going to compare the two rebellions in Hungary in 1956 and Czechoslovakia in 1968.
For each rebellion consider:
- the aims of the rebels
- attitude towards Communism
- attitude towards democracy
- attitude to the USSR
- attitude to the West
- why the Soviet Union intervened
- how each state responded to Soviet intervention.

Before the Soviet invasion, Czechoslovakia's mood had been one of optimism. After, it was despair. A country that had been pro-Soviet now became resentful of the Soviet connection. Ideas that could have reformed Communism were silenced.

Twenty years later, Mikhail Gorbachev, the leader of the USSR, questioned the invasion, and was himself spreading the ideas of the Prague Spring that the Soviet Union had crushed in 1968.

Why was the Berlin Wall built?

You have already seen how important Berlin was as a battleground of the Cold War (see pages 331–32). In 1961 it also became the focus of the Soviet Union's latest attempt to maintain control of its east European satellites.

The crushing of the Hungarian uprising had confirmed for many people in eastern Europe that it was impossible to fight the Communists. For many, it seemed that the only way of escaping the repression was to leave altogether. Some wished to leave eastern Europe for political reasons – they hated the Communists – while many more wished to leave for economic reasons. As standards of living in eastern Europe fell further and further behind the West, the attraction of going to live in a capitalist state was very great.

The contrast was particularly great in the divided city of Berlin. Living standards were tolerable in the East, but just a few hundred metres away in West Berlin, East Germans could see some of the prize exhibits of capitalist West Germany – shops full of goods, great freedom, great wealth and great variety. This had been deliberately done by the Western powers. They had poured massive investment into Berlin. East Germans could also watch West German television.

SOURCE 24

A 1959 Soviet cartoon – the caption was: 'The socialist stallion far outclasses the capitalist donkey'.

1 Look at Source 24. What is the aim of this cartoon?
2 Why might someone living in a Communist country like it or dislike it?

SOURCE 26

West Berlin . . . has many roles. It is more than a showcase of liberty, an island of freedom in a Communist sea. It is more than a link with the free world, a beacon of hope behind the iron curtain, an escape hatch for refugees. Above all, it has become the resting place of Western courage and will . . . We cannot and will not permit the Communists to drive us out of Berlin.

President Kennedy speaking in 1960, before he became President.

3 Which photograph in Source 25 do you think shows East Berlin and which shows West Berlin? Explain your choice and write a detailed description of the differences between the two areas based on the sources and the text.

SOURCE 25

A

B

Berlin in the 1950s.

In the 1950s East Germans were still able to travel freely into West Berlin (see Source 27). From there they could travel on into West Germany. It was very tempting to leave East Germany, with its harsh communist regime and its hardline leader, Walter Ulbricht. By the late 1950s thousands were leaving and never coming back.

SOURCE 27

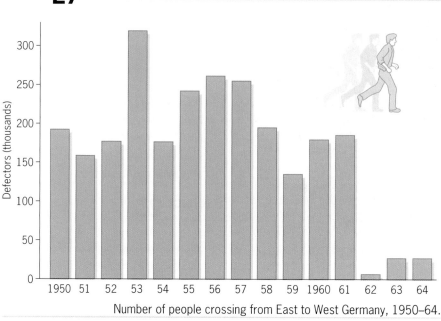

Number of people crossing from East to West Germany, 1950–64.

SOURCE 28

A

Those who were defecting were very often highly skilled workers or well-qualified managers. The Communist government could not afford to lose these high-quality people. More importantly, from Khrushchev's point of view, the sight of thousands of Germans fleeing Communist rule for a better life under capitalism undermined Communism generally.

In 1961 the USA had a new President, the young and inexperienced John F Kennedy. Khrushchev thought he could bully Kennedy and chose to pick a fight over Berlin. He insisted that Kennedy withdraw US troops from the city. He was certain that Kennedy would back down. Kennedy refused. However, all eyes were now on Berlin. What would happen next?

At two o'clock in the morning on Sunday 13 August 1961, East German soldiers erected a barbed-wire barrier along the entire frontier between East and West Berlin, ending all free movement from East to West. It was quickly replaced by a concrete wall. All the crossing points from East to West Berlin were sealed, except for one. This became known as Checkpoint Charlie.

Families were divided. Berliners were unable to go to work, chaos and confusion followed. Border guards kept a constant look-out for anyone trying to cross the wall. They had orders to shoot people trying to defect. Hundreds were killed over the next three decades.

B

C

Stages in the building of the Berlin Wall. On the sign in **B**, Ulbricht assures the world that 'no one has any intention of building a wall'.

SOURCE 29

East German security guards recover the body of a man shot attempting to cross the wall in 1962.

SOURCE 30

The Western powers in Berlin use it as a centre of subversive activity against the GDR [the initial letters of the German name for East Germany]. In no other part of the world are so many espionage centres to be found. These centres smuggle their agents into the GDR for all kinds of subversion: recruiting spies; sabotage; provoking disturbances.

The government presents all working people of the GDR with a proposal that will securely block subversive activity so that reliable safeguards and effective control will be established around West Berlin, including its border with democratic Berlin.

A Soviet explanation for the building of the wall, 1961.

The West's reaction to the Berlin Wall

For a while, the wall created a major crisis. Access to East Berlin had been guaranteed to the Allies since 1945. In October 1961 US diplomats and troops crossed regularly into East Berlin to find out how the Soviets would react.

On 27 October Soviet tanks pulled up to Checkpoint Charlie and refused to allow any further access to the East. All day, US and Soviet tanks, fully armed, faced each other in a tense stand-off. Then, after 18 hours, one by one, five metres at a time, the tanks pulled back. Another crisis, another retreat.

The international reaction was relief. Khrushchev ordered Ulbricht to avoid any actions that would increase tension. Kennedy said, 'It's not a very nice solution, but a wall is a hell of a lot better than a war.' So the wall stayed, and over the following years became the symbol of division – the division of Germany, the division of Europe, the division of Communist East and democratic West. The Communists presented the wall as a protective shell around East Berlin. The West presented it as a prison wall.

SOURCE 31

There are some who say, in Europe and elsewhere, we can work with the Communists. Let them come to Berlin.

President Kennedy speaking in 1963 after the building of the Berlin Wall.

FOCUS TASK

Why was the Berlin Wall built in 1961?

Work in pairs.

Make a poster or notice to be stuck on the Berlin Wall explaining the purpose of the wall. One of you do a poster for the East German side and the other do a poster for the West German side. You can use pictures and quotations from the sources in this chapter or use your own research.

Make sure you explain in your poster the reasons why the wall was built and what the results of building the wall will be.

SOURCE 32

A Soviet cartoon from the 1960s. The sign reads: 'The border of the GDR (East Germany) is closed to all enemies.' Notice the shape of the dog's tail.

Why did Soviet control of eastern Europe collapse in 1989?

Why did the Cold War thaw in the 1970s?

Détente means a relaxing of tension. For much of the 1970s, superpower tensions eased. Arms control and human rights were discussed openly. The fact that the superpowers were in contact at all was seen as a major achievement. Here are some of the high points of détente.

Worries about the arms race (i) Nuclear testing damaged the environment, cost a fortune and was seen by many as immoral. There were anti-nuclear movements in the West that supported détente.

The end of the Vietnam War improved relations between the USA, USSR and China (see page 364).

Détente in the 1970s

Worries about the arms race (ii) The space programmes of the USA and USSR had helped them to develop extremely complex missiles that could carry many nuclear warheads.
Another new and deadly weapon was the submarine-launched missile. These were virtually impossible to detect and yet carried enough firepower to wipe out several cities.
The arms race was very costly. Both superpowers saw this as money that could be spent more wisely on foreign aid to poor countries or improving the conditions of their own people at home.

High hand shake! American astronauts and Soviet cosmonauts met up and shook hands in space. This was quite literally the high point of détente.

Helsinki conference, August 1975. All countries recognised the borders set out after the Second World War, including the division of Germany. They agreed to respect human rights – e.g. freedom of speech, freedom to move from one country to another.

Worries about the arms race (iii) The leaders held summit meetings. Brezhnev visited Washington and Nixon went to Moscow twice – the first American president to do so. The nuclear arms limitation treaty, SALT 1, was signed in 1972 and great progress was made towards a possible SALT 2.

Why did the Cold War freeze again in the 1980s?

From the late 1970s there was increasing distrust and hostility between the superpowers.

Revolution in Iran

The Shah of Iran was overthrown in 1979. The USA had supported the Shah because it needed Iran's oil. The new government was strongly anti-American but also strongly anti-Communist. It wanted a society based on Islamic values. The Iranian revolution changed the balance of power in the Middle East and increased tension between the superpowers, who were worried about how each other would react.

Civil wars in Nicaragua and El Salvador and in Angola

Communist rebels (supported by Cuban and Soviet money and expertise) tried to overthrow the governments of these states in South America and Africa. The USA funded the governments against the rebels. In Angola, the USA and the USSR helped to fund a long-running civil war.

Human rights

Jimmy Carter (US President, 1977–81) openly criticised the USSR's suppression of dissidents – people who spoke out against the government in both the USSR and eastern Europe.

New nuclear weapons

In 1977 the USSR began replacing out-of-date missiles in eastern Europe with new SS-20 nuclear missiles. The West saw these missiles as a new type of battlefield weapon that could be used in a limited nuclear war confined only to Europe. In response, President Carter allowed the US military to develop the Cruise missile. By 1979 the USA had stationed Pershing missiles in western Europe as an answer to the SS-20s.

Collapse of SALT 2

The main terms of the SALT 2 agreement had been set out as early as 1974. It was not until June 1979 that SALT 2 was finally signed. By that time, relations between the USA and the USSR had deteriorated so much that the US Congress refused to ratify SALT 2.

Afghanistan

In 1979 the pro-Soviet regime in Afghanistan was under serious threat from its Muslim opponents, the Mujahideen. To protect the regime, Soviet forces entered Afghanistan on 25 December 1979. Western powers were alarmed that the USSR could get so close to the West's oil supplies in the Middle East. President Carter described the Soviet action as 'the most serious threat to peace since the Second World War'.

The USA secretly began to send very large shipments of money, arms and equipment to Pakistan and from there to the USSR's Mujahideen opponents. The campaign became the Soviet Union's equivalent of the Vietnam War. It was a nightmare campaign, virtually unwinnable for the Soviet forces, although they remained there until the early 1990s.

The Moscow and Los Angeles Olympics

In protest at Soviet involvement in the Afghan War, the USA boycotted the 1980 Olympic games held in Moscow. In retaliation, the USSR and eastern European teams boycotted the Los Angeles Olympics held four years later.

Ronald Reagan

In 1981, the USA elected the former Hollywood film actor Ronald Reagan as President. Reagan made no secret of his dislike of Communism and the USSR, calling it the Evil Empire. He supported anti-Communist forces in Afghanistan and Nicaragua. Reagan was helped by the fact that many of Europe's leaders at this time (including Britain's Prime Minister, Margaret Thatcher) supported his tough line against the USSR.

His boldest plan was to escalate the arms race in order to end it. He increased US defence spending by $32.6 billion. In 1982, he gave the go-ahead for the Strategic Defense Initiative (popularly known as Star Wars). This was a multi-billion dollar project to create a system using satellites and lasers that could destroy missiles before they hit their targets. Clearly, a weapon such as this could change the whole nature of nuclear war.

FOCUS TASK

Superpower relations, 1970–85

1 Make your own copy of this graph.
2 Mark on the graph:
   • three developments that improved superpower relations in this period
   • three developments that harmed superpower relations in this period.
3 Compare your graph with those of other people in your class.

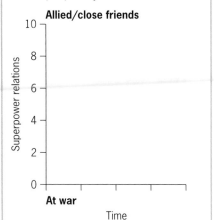

How significant was Solidarity?

Throughout the years of Communist control of Poland there were regular protests. However, unlike the protests in both Hungary and Czechoslovakia, they tended to be about wages or food prices. In 1956, then again in 1970, such protests earned Polish workers increased wages, reduced prices or both. In these protests they did not try to get rid of the government or challenge the Soviet Union. They simply wanted to improve their standard of living. The workers were keenly aware that they lagged behind workers in the West. The government for its part seemed aware that it would only survive if it could satisfy the Poles' demands for consumer goods.

During the first half of the 1970s Polish industry performed well. Most Poles were becoming better off and were finding it easier to buy what they wanted. In a survey in 1975, 60 per cent expected their standard of living to rise still further in future years. They were generally optimistic and seemed happy with the kind of Communist state that had evolved in Poland.

But in the late 1970s the Polish economy hit a crisis: 1976 was a bad year and 1979 was the worst year for Polish industry since Communism had been introduced. The government seemed to have no new ideas about how to solve Poland's problems – just more propaganda. Workers' patience was sorely tried by the government's propaganda, telling them how well Poland was performing when it clearly wasn't.

As in most Communist countries, there were official trade unions, but they were ineffective. In the late 1970s Polish workers became involved in setting up small, independent trade unions. In the summer of 1980 strikes broke out all over the country. Over the next six months Solidarity, a new trade union, went from strength to strength.

SOURCE 1

Is it any wonder that people are in despair? They must begin queuing outside the butcher's early in the morning and they may still find there is no meat to buy.

We want to achieve a free trade union movement which will allow workers to manage the economy through joint control with the government.

Lech Walesa, leader of Solidarity, speaking in 1980.

SOURCE 2

- *More pay*
- *End to censorship*
- *Same welfare benefits as police and party workers*
- *Broadcasting of Catholic church services*
- *Election of factory managers.*

Some of the 21 points.

July 1980	The government announced increases in the price of meat. Strikes followed.
August 1980	Workers at the Gdansk shipyard, led by Lech Walesa, put forward 21 demands to the government, including free trade unions and the right to strike (see Source 2). They also started a free trade union called Solidarity.
30 August 1980	The government agreed to all 21 of Solidarity's demands.
September 1980	Solidarity's membership grew to 3.5 million.
October 1980	Solidarity's membership was 7 million. Solidarity was officially recognised by the government.
January 1981	Membership of Solidarity reached its peak at 9.4 million – more than a third of all the workers in Poland.

SOURCE 3

Solidarity members giving the 'V for victory' sign outside Warsaw cathedral, as Polish farmers celebrate the first anniversary of Rural Solidarity (see page 414).

PROFILE

Lech Walesa

★ Born 1943. His father was a farmer.
★ Like many of his fellow pupils at school he went to work in the shipyards at Gdansk. He became an electrician.
★ In 1970 he led shipyard workers who joined the strike against price rises.
★ In 1976 he was sacked from the shipyard for making 'malicious' statements about the organisation and working climate.
★ In 1978 he helped organise a union at another factory. He was dismissed – officially because of the recession, unofficially because of pressure from above.
★ In 1979 he worked for Eltromontage. He was said to be the best automotive electrician in the business. He was sacked.
★ He led strikes in Gdansk shipyard in the summer of 1980.
★ With others, he set up Solidarity in August 1980 and became its leader soon after.
★ He was a committed Catholic and had massive support from the Polish people and from overseas.
★ He was imprisoned by the Polish government in 1982.
★ In prison, he became a symbol of eastern Europe's struggle against Communist repression. He won the Nobel Peace Prize in 1983.
★ In 1989 he became the leader of Poland's first non-Communist government since the Second World War.

1 Look at Source 4. Make a list of the complaints that appear in this extract.
2 What are the strengths and weaknesses of this source as evidence of attitudes to the Communist Party in Poland?

Why did the Polish government agree to Solidarity's demands in 1980?

In the light of all you know about the Communist rule of eastern Europe, you might be surprised that the government gave in to Solidarity in 1980. There are many different reasons for this.

- The union was strongest in those industries that were most important to the government – shipbuilding and heavy industry. Membership was particularly high among skilled workers and foremen. A general strike in these industries would have devastated Poland's economy.

- In the early stages the union was not seen by its members as an alternative to the Communist Party. More than one million members (30 per cent) of the Communist Party joined Solidarity. People joined Solidarity simply because they thought it would 'make things better' in Poland. In one survey of members in 1981 almost 40 per cent gave this as their reason for joining Solidarity, whereas only 5 per cent said that they joined because Solidarity had a better programme than the government.

- Lech Walesa was very careful in his negotiations with the government. He tried to avoid provoking a dispute that might bring in the Soviet Union. Behind the scenes he worked with the Communist leader Kania to control the radicals, because they both feared that the USSR would send in the tanks if the extremists went too far.

- The union was immensely popular. Almost half of all workers belonged. Lech Walesa was a kind of folk hero, and the movement which he led was seen as very trustworthy. In a survey in 1981, 95 per cent of Poles said they trusted Solidarity.

- Solidarity had the support of the Catholic Church. In principle, Communism was anti-religious. Elsewhere in eastern Europe, Communist governments had tried to crush the Christian churches. In Poland, however, the strength of the Catholic religion meant that the government always had to compromise with the Church. Almost all Poles were Catholics. Catholicism was part of the glue that held Poland together. The Pope – the head of the whole Catholic Church – was Polish and had recently made a very influential visit home to Poland. The Communist government and the Catholic Church had settled into a pattern – if you don't interfere with us, we won't interfere with you. So the Catholic Church's backing for Solidarity was very significant. The government dared not confront the Catholic Church.

- The government was playing for time. As early as 25 August 1980 the government drew up plans to introduce martial law (rule by the army) if the situation got out of hand. But to start with, it decided to play for time. It hoped that Solidarity would split into factions just as previous protest movements had – then its job would be easy.

- Finally, the Soviet Union had half an eye on the West. Solidarity had gained support in the West in a way that neither the Hungarian nor the Czech rising had. Walesa was regularly interviewed and photographed for the Western media. Solidarity logos were bought in their millions as posters, postcards and even car stickers throughout the capitalist world. The scale of the movement and the charismatic appeal of Lech Walesa ensured that the Soviet Union treated the Polish crisis cautiously.

SOURCE 4

Inequality and injustice are everywhere. There are hospitals that are so poorly supplied that they do not even have cotton, and our relatives die in the corridors; but other hospitals are equipped with private rooms and full medical care for each room. We pay fines for traffic violations, but some people commit highway manslaughter while drunk and are let off . . . In some places there are better shops and superior vacation houses, with huge fenced-in grounds that ordinary people cannot enter.

Extract from 'Experience and the Future', a report drawn up in 1981 by Polish writers and thinkers who were not members of the Communist Party. They are describing the inequality in Poland between Communist Party members and ordinary people.

1 What do you think 'preventive and cautionary talks' might mean?
2 How can you tell that the writer of Source 6 is critical of Jaruzelski's actions?
3 The text describes four problems which led to the government clamp down. Which of these problems do you think would most worry the government?
4 Between August 1980 and December 1981, Solidarity went through some rapid changes. Choose two moments in this period that you think were particularly important in the rise and fall of Solidarity and explain why they were important.

SOURCE 5

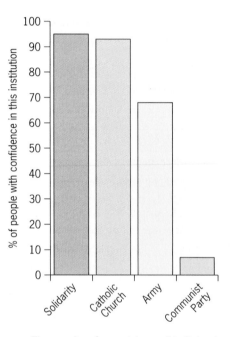

The results of an opinion poll in Poland, November 1981. The people polled were asked whether they had confidence in key institutions in Poland. It is known that 11 per cent of those polled were Communist Party members.

SOURCE 6

Thousands of people were dragged from their beds and ferried through the freezing night to prisons and concentration camps, while tanks patrolled the snow-covered streets and stormtroopers were deployed in trouble spots. Communications were cut and a 'State of War' declared.

Adam Zamoyski describes the events of December 1981 in *The Polish Way*, 1981.

Clampdown

In February 1981 the civilian Prime Minister 'resigned' and the leader of the army, General Jaruzelski, took over. From the moment he took office, people in Poland, and observers outside Poland, expected the Soviet Union to 'send in the tanks' at any time.

February 1981	General Jaruzelski, leader of the army, became head of the Communist Party and Prime Minister of Poland.
March 1981	After negotiations with Jaruzelski, Walesa called off a strike at Bydgoszcz. Many Solidarity members were unhappy about this.
May 1981	'Rural Solidarity' was set up as a farmers' union.
September 1981	Lech Walesa was elected chairman of Solidarity. The Solidarity Congress produced an 'open letter' to workers of eastern Europe saying that they were campaigning not only for their own rights but for the rights of workers throughout the communist bloc.
November 1981	Negotiations between Walesa and Jaruzelski to form a government of 'National Understanding' broke down. Poland was at the edge of chaos. The government was very unstable.

Finally, in December, after nine months of tense relationships, the Communist government acted. Brezhnev ordered the Red Army to carry out 'training manoeuvres' on the Polish border. Jaruzelski introduced martial law (rule by the army). He put Walesa and almost 10,000 other Solidarity leaders in prison. He suspended Solidarity.

The workers were unprepared for this sudden change of policy. There was little resistance. At the mines in Silesia workers staged a long sit-in, but it ended in tragedy when the army opened fire. During December a total of 150,000 Solidarity members were taken into custody for 'preventive and cautionary talks'.

Why did the Polish government clamp down on Solidarity in December 1981?

There were a number of factors that caused the government to change its policy towards Solidarity.

- There were increasing signs that Solidarity was acting as a political party. The government said it had secret tapes of a Solidarity meeting at which leaders talked of Solidarity setting up a new provisional government – without the Communist Party. The tapes may well have been forgeries, but even so they were treated as a serious challenge to Communist authority. Solidarity formed a direct challenge to the Soviet plan for eastern Europe. Brezhnev would not have a Communist Party within the Soviet bloc dictated to by an independent union.
- Poland was sinking into chaos. Meat and fish supplies were down by 25 per cent. Almost all Poles felt the impact of food shortages. Rationing had been introduced in April 1981. National income had fallen by 13 per cent in a year, industrial production by 11 per cent and foreign trade by 20 per cent. Wages had increased by less than inflation. Unemployment was rising. Strikes were continuing long after the Solidarity leadership had ordered them to stop.
- Solidarity itself was also tumbling into chaos. There were many different factions. Some felt that the only way to make progress was to push the Communists harder until they cracked under the pressure. Against the advice and better judgement of Walesa, a motion was passed at the October 1981 Congress to 'issue a statement of sympathy and support for all the downtrodden peoples of the Soviet bloc and to all the nations of the Soviet Union'. It proclaimed that the Poles were fighting 'For Your Freedom and for Ours'. Walesa was well aware how dangerous a course this was, but by then the different factions in Solidarity were threatening to pull the organisation apart and Walesa could no longer stop them.

- Underlying all these points was the attitude of the Soviet Union. It thought the situation in Poland had gone too far. If Poland's leaders would not restore Communist control in Poland, then it would. This was something the Polish leaders wanted to avoid.

In December 1981, looking back on the past 18 months, two things were obvious:

- The Polish people no longer trusted the Communists. Supporting Solidarity was the best way that Polish people could show that they simply did not accept the leadership of the Communist Party any longer. They respected Solidarity. They respected the Church. They would rather trust their future to their hands. Any claims by the Communist Party that it represented the majority of working people in the country seemed hollow and empty.
- The only thing that kept the Communists in power was force or the threat of force. When Jaruzelski finally decided to use force, Solidarity was easily crushed. But while they waited and while they wavered, Poland had been on the edge. The lesson was clear. If military force was not used, then Communist control seemed very shaky indeed.

The aftermath

Over the next 12 months Jaruzelski tried to normalise the situation. He declared Solidarity illegal in 1982. In place of Solidarity he pressurised people to join the Patriotic Movement for National Regeneration – if they did not, they might lose their jobs!

From early 1983 he began releasing jailed Solidarity leaders. However, the friends of Solidarity in other countries were not impressed. The released Solidarity leaders were harassed. Some were murdered. Others were hounded from their jobs. In 1983 Jaruzelski even started a campaign against the Catholic Church. A number of priests were beaten up by the army and some were murdered, including a popular priest called Father Jerzy Popieluszko, who was battered to death by the secret police in 1984. After the détente of the 1970s the USA was once again becoming suspicious of the Soviet Union. The USA and other Western nations imposed trade sanctions on Poland. Economic chaos followed. The currency was devalued twice. Inflation hit 70 per cent.

Despite being outlawed, Solidarity was once again reasserting its influence. It never again became a mass organisation, but it was operating almost openly. It threatened to call a nationwide strike against price rises in 1986 and the government backed down. Solidarity co-operated closely with the Catholic Church. It openly broadcast Radio Solidarity from 1986, spreading its views about the government. It organised a boycott of Polish elections in 1988. Officials from foreign governments visited Lech Walesa almost as if he were the leader of a government-in-waiting and consulted him on whether to ease sanctions against Poland.

But in 1986 the focus of international attention was drawn away from Solidarity on to a new threat to Soviet domination of eastern Europe. This time it came from within the Soviet Union itself – it was Mikhail Gorbachev, the new supreme leader of the Soviet Union.

President Walesa

Ideally, you should now read pages 416–18 and then come back to this page later on because, from 1986 onwards, developments in the Soviet Union had as much impact on Poland as events in Poland itself.

In March 1989 Mikhail Gorbachev, the new leader of the Soviet Union, told the Communist leaders of eastern Europe that they must listen to their peoples and that the USSR would no longer send in troops to prop up unpopular Communist regimes.

From that moment, the days of the Communist government in Poland were numbered. Solidarity had long been demanding open elections. In June 1989 it got them. Solidarity won nearly all the seats it contested. A Solidarity leader, Tadeusz Mazowiecki, became Prime Minister. In 1990 Lech Walesa became the first non-Communist President of Poland since before the Second World War.

FOCUS TASK

How important was Solidarity?

Why on earth does Solidarity get four pages to itself in this book? It was just a trade union, it only lasted two years and it failed to achieve anything. It just doesn't deserve this much space.

1 Do you agree with this view on Solidarity? Discuss it with a partner and come up with two lists of points that
   a) support
   b) oppose
   this view.
2 Put yourself in the position of the author of this book. Use your points to write a letter or prepare a presentation explaining the significance of Solidarity. You should mention:
   - how Solidarity influenced attitudes to the Communist Party
   - the influence of Solidarity in the West
   - the links between Solidarity and the Catholic Church.

How did Gorbachev change eastern Europe?

ACTIVITY

Work in groups.

Sources 7–15 are all from letters sent to Mikhail Gorbachev in the late 1980s. From the letters alone, work out as much as you can about Gorbachev.

You could split the work up like this, each person or pair working on one topic:

- What kind of person was Gorbachev?
- What changes did he introduce to the Soviet Union?
- What was his policy on eastern Europe?
- What was his attitude to nuclear disarmament?
- What did he think about human rights?

SOURCE 7

Dear Mr Gorbachev

I hope you are feeling well after your journey to Rome to meet Our Leader, Pope John Paul II, with your lovely lady, Raisa. It was indeed a historical and memorable occasion. I want to thank you for all you have done. It is marvellous that . . . the people in Eastern Europe have been granted freedom. It is unbelievable how fast all these wonderful things are happening. We were delighted when the news reached our ears that the people in Russia now have the freedom to practise their faith.

Rosalee (aged 4), John (aged 9), Mary-Lucia (aged 11), Thérèse (aged 12), Majella (aged 13), Patricia (aged 15) and Patrick Furlong (aged 16). Enniscorthy, Co. Wexford, Ireland, December 1989.

SOURCE 8

Dear Mr Gorbachev

. . . I have been deeply moved by the events that have taken place in this country since 9 November 1989 . . .

Dear Mr Gorbachev, I would like to express my deeply felt thanks for this, for, in the final analysis, it was you, with your policy of perestroika who set the heavy stone of politics in motion.

You can have no idea how many people in Germany revere you and consider you to be one of the greatest politicians of the present age. On that day when the people of East Berlin and of East Germany were able to come to us freely, thousands of people shouted out your name 'Gorbi, Gorbi, Gorbi . . .'

The people fell into each other's arms and wept for joy, because at last they were free after forty-five years of suppression and authoritarian rule under a communist–Stalinist system. This dreadful wall and border, which was now being opened up and carried away stone by stone, cost many people their life, and was a source of bitter suffering for many families.

Roman von Kalckreuth, Berlin, West Germany, 14 February 1990.

SOURCE 9

My dear Mikhail Gorbaciov

. . . This is the first time in my life I have ever written to a politician . . . You wonder why I am writing to you? It's hard to explain. I'm writing to remind you that someone said fairy tales never come true. You, Mikhail Gorbaciov, have shown this to be false. I have to tell you this, for love of the truth. You are the most beautiful fairy tale come true. All my life I have been observing your wonderful country, and loving it. I love its history, its culture, its magnificence. For me, Mother Russia had only one defect.

The only thing that was lacking was you, Mikhail Gorbaciov! You, the new man . . . You have broken barriers, crossed mountains, hurled down taboos with the force of a mythical giant! Nothing could stop you!

Flora Pinto d'Albavilla Capaldo, Naples, Italy, 6 October 1988.

SOURCE 10

Dear Gorbaciov and Reagan

We are nine-year-old Italian children, pupils at the Pero elementary school in the province of Milan.

We saw on television and read in the papers about your meeting, during which you came to an important decision: to begin to destroy a small part of your nuclear weapons. We want you to know that we all heaved a sigh of relief, because we think that all the weapons are dangerous, useless, damaging and producers of violence, death, fear and destruction and that their only purpose is to do evil.

We want you to know that we are happy about your initiative, but we also want to tell you that is not enough. For there to be true peace all arms must be destroyed.

Children from Pero (Milan), Italy, 16 December 1987.

SOURCE 11

Respected Sir

I, a citizen of India, very heartily congratulate you on the giant step you have initiated towards a more human and presidential form of government.

I have already read a lot about glasnost and other policies you have been introducing from time to time in your country . . .

Your sincerity, straightforwardness, foresight, capabilities, fearless nature, and eye for minute details will set a shining example for centuries to come and you will go down in the golden annals of history. You are a shining star on the horizon. The sapling which you have sown will become a tree for others to climb.

Naren R Bhuta, Bombay, India,
1 July 1988.

SOURCE 12

Dear General Secretary Gorbachev

I followed the events of the recent Soviet–American summit with a mixture of uneasy feelings. My one clear feeling was admiration of you – of your intellectual energy, personal strength, and dignity.

Hearing our President's well-intended but often condescending lectures to the Soviet Union's people and political leadership, I was embarrassed for my country . . .

Your term of office, General Secretary Gorbachev, has been marked by a straightforward commitment to address the world we really live in, and to improve it. I admire your combination of pragmatism and idealism, which permits you to work for progress while dealing practically with the regressive elements present in any large political system . . .

It seems to me that you face internal obstacles greater than any American leader does, but perhaps the Soviet system has provided more groundwork for perestroika than is clear to Americans.

The 'tightrope' that you yourself are walking, balanced between certain difficult traditions of your society on one side and Western pressures on the other side, seems a great and exhausting challenge. But I ask you to remain strong, and to remember that you are not walking it for yourself alone.

David Bittinger, Wisconsin, USA, 6 June 1988.

SOURCE 13

Dear Mr Gorbachev

May I offer a few comments on your speech of 2 November, in which you reviewed the history of the Soviet Union? Naturally, I found the discourse of very great interest, and hope that I have understood its significance . . .

May I suggest that in your recasting of the view of Soviet history, there are at least two important things which would make that effort more credible for those people outside of the Soviet Union who have some understanding of that history. One would be to more frankly admit the monstrosity of the tyranny of Stalin – for example, the fact that he killed more communists than anyone else in history. The other would be to give recognition to Leon Trotsky as the person who organised the Red Army and led it to victory in the 1918–21 Civil War.

Professor Robert Alexander, Rutgers University, New Brunswick, New Jersey, USA, 5 November 1987.

SOURCE 14

Dear Mr Gorbachev

I would like to express my appreciation for your efforts to promote peace and understanding between our two countries. As a token of that appreciation, I am enclosing a copy of my book, The Human Rights Movement, *which seeks to promote dialogue between the US and the USSR on human rights . . .*

I agree with you that each country needs to learn more about the other's concepts of human rights – that is we need a lot more listening and a lot less confrontation. This is the basic argument of my book.

Warren Holleman, Baylor College of Medicine, Houston, Texas, USA, 16 June 1988.

SOURCE 15

Sr D Mijail Gorbachov

. . . When I see you on television, your face shining with justice, good nature, firmness and good intentions, I see . . . that you are giving the whole world a masterly lesson on how to eliminate the horrors of war.

All human beings love peace, although I do perhaps more strongly, because at the end of the Spanish Civil War, my father, mother and brother were sentenced to death by Military Court for having socialist ideals. My mother and brother's sentences were commuted, but my father's was not and he was shot.

I am asking you, with all respect and feeling, to continue along that path and struggle for peace and justice for the whole world.

(Name withheld), Madrid, Spain, 28 April 1988.

The time is ripe for abandoning views on foreign policy which are influenced by an imperial standpoint. Neither the Soviet Union nor the USA is able to force its will on others. It is possible to suppress, compel, bribe, break or blast, but only for a certain period. From the point of view of long-term big time politics, no one will be able to subordinate others. That is why only one thing – relations of equality – remains. All of us must realise this . . . This also obliges us to respect one another and everybody.

Gorbachev speaking in 1987.

ACTIVITY

Design a poster promoting one of Gorbachev's reforms. Your poster should include an explanation of why the reform is needed.

PROFILE

Mikhail Gorbachev

★ Born 1931. One grandfather was a kulak – a landowning peasant – who had been sent to a prison camp by Stalin because he resisted Stalin's policy of collectivisation. The other grandfather was a loyal Communist Party member.
★ His elder brother was killed in the Second World War.
★ Studied law at Moscow University in the 1950s. Became a persuasive speaker.
★ Worked as a local Communist Party official in his home area. By 1978 he was a member of the Central Committee of the party and in charge of agriculture.
★ In 1980 he joined the Politburo.
★ He was a close friend of Andropov, who became Soviet leader in 1983. He shared many of Andropov's ideas about reforming the USSR. When Andropov was leader, he was effectively second in command.
★ In 1985 he became leader of the USSR.
★ In October 1990 he was awarded the Nobel Peace Prize.

Why did Gorbachev try to change the Soviet Union?

Gorbachev became leader of the Soviet Union in 1985. It was in crisis. Its economy was very weak. It was spending far too much money on the arms race. It was locked into a costly and unwinnable war in Afghanistan. There had been almost no new thinking about how to run the Soviet economy since the days of Stalin. Each leader had followed the same policies and had ignored the warning signals that things were going wrong.

Gorbachev was different. He was very concerned about the attitude of Soviet people to work. The Soviet system protected them against economic problems – it guaranteed them a job and a home – but it also gave them no incentive to work harder or better. Work standards were slipping. In the days of Stalin, people had worked out of loyalty or fear, but they had worked hard. Those days were long gone and had been replaced by cynicism. Many Soviet citizens had no loyalty to the government, did not believe what the government said, but even worse they did not care.

Gorbachev had a particular worry about alcoholism, which was reaching epidemic proportions in the USSR. Life expectancy of Soviet men had actually declined from 67 in 1964 to 62 in 1980, largely as a result of chronic alcoholism. He brought in advisers who told him that alcoholism was one reason for the decline in Soviet industry.

Gorbachev was worried that Soviet goods didn't seem to work properly. He complained that while Soviet scientists could send a pin-point accurate space probe to investigate a comet, Soviet refrigerators were shoddy. The standards of building work in the USSR had also declined.

He knew that to solve these problems Communist slogans were not enough. Some cherished party policies had failed. The economy was being run by remote bureaucrats on a 'trial and error' basis. What the Soviet Union needed was a rethink.

He had to be cautious, because he faced great opposition from hardliners in his own government, but gradually he declared his policies.

The two key ideas were glasnost (openness) and perestroika (restructuring). He called for open debate on government policy and honesty in facing up to problems.

In 1987 his perestroika programme allowed market forces to be introduced into the Soviet economy. For the first time in 60 years it was no longer illegal to buy and sell for profit.

He began to cut spending on defence. After almost 50 years on a constant war footing, the Red Army began to shrink. The arms race was an enormous drain on the Soviet economy at a time when it was in trouble anyway. Gorbachev was realistic enough to recognise that his country could never hope to outspend the USA on nuclear weapons. He took the initiative. He announced cuts in armament expenditure. Two years later, the USA and the USSR signed a treaty to remove most of their missiles from Europe.

At the same time, Gorbachev brought a new attitude to the USSR's relations with the wider world. He withdrew Soviet troops from Afghanistan, which had become the USSR's Vietnam, consuming lives and resources. In speech after speech, he talked about international trust and co-operation as the way forward for the USSR, rather than confrontation. He also announced a new policy on eastern Europe (see Source 16).

US President Reagan and Mikhail Gorbachev at their first summit meeting in Geneva, November 1985. They went on to meet in Reykjavik (October 1986), Washington (December 1987) and Moscow (June 1988).

Why did Soviet control of eastern Europe collapse?

Gorbachev was popular but his policies were not successful – or not in the way he intended. After two years of perestroika, it was clear that the economy could not be modernised as quickly as people wanted.

SOURCE 18

a) *There are three kinds of person in the Soviet Union:*

The optimists – they believe in what Gorbachev says;
The pessimists – they are learning English and planning to emigrate;
The realists – they are taking rifle lessons and getting ready for civil war.

b) *There are two ways of resolving the crisis of the Soviet economy:*

The realistic way – aliens from outer space will land and straighten out the mess.
The fantastic way – the Soviet people will sort it out for themselves.

Two jokes circulating in the USSR in 1989.

1 Why do you think these jokes are useful as historical evidence about attitudes to Gorbachev?

By 1989 it seemed that Gorbachev himself had no real idea which way to go. Was it wise, Soviet people asked, to entrust the aircraft (the Soviet state) to a pilot (Gorbachev) who did not know where he was going and didn't have any charts? Of course, there was no one else who did have charts – the Soviet Union was entering uncharted territory. What was clear was that it could not turn back. Gorbachev's reforms had released a pent-up longing for freedom across all of the Communist world.

In eastern Europe, the leaders of other countries in the Communist bloc looked on in confusion. Twenty years earlier, the Soviets had sent tanks into Czechoslovakia to crush the development of the very ideas that Gorbachev was now proposing.

In March 1989 Gorbachev made it clear to them that they would no longer be propped up by the Red Army and that they would have to listen to their peoples. The following months saw an extraordinary turn-about, as you can see from Source 20 on page 420, which led to the collapse of Communism in eastern Europe.

SOURCE 19

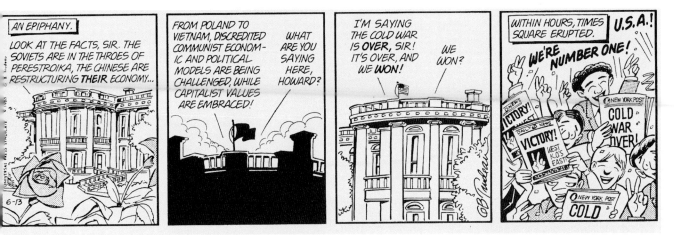

A cartoon by Doonesbury which appeared in the *Guardian* on 13 June 1988.

SOURCE 20

START HERE

May 1989
Hungarians begin dismantling the barbed-wire fence between Hungary and non-Communist Austria.

June
In Poland, free elections are held for the first time since the Second World War. Solidarity wins almost all the seats it contests. Eastern Europe gets its first non-Communist leader.

The cracks in the Soviet domination of eastern Europe begin to appear and the complete collapse of the Red Empire begins with the people of East Germany.

March 1990
Latvia leads the Baltic republics in declaring independence from the USSR.

December
In Romania there is a short but very bloody revolution that ends with the execution of the Communist dictator Nicolae Ceausescu.

The Communist Party in Hungary renames itself the Socialist Party and declares that free elections will be held in 1990. In Bulgaria, there are huge demonstrations against the Communist government.

November
There are huge demonstrations in Czechoslovakia. The Czech government opens its borders with the West, and allows the formation of other parties.

September
Thousands of East Germans on holiday in Hungary and Czechoslovakia refuse to go home. They escape through Austria into West Germany.

October
There are enormous demonstrations in East German cities when Gorbachev visits the country. He tells the East German leader Erich Honecker to reform. Honecker orders troops to fire on demonstrators but they refuse.

Gorbachev makes it clear that Soviet tanks will not move in to 'restore order'.

November
East Germans march in their thousands to the checkpoints at the Berlin Wall. The guards throw down their weapons and join the crowds. The Berlin Wall is dismantled.

Key

Territory taken over by USSR at end of Second World War

Soviet-dominated Communist governments

Other Communist governments

0   200 km
Scale

ACTIVITY

On your own copy of this map, add labels to summarise in your own words how Communism collapsed in each country of eastern Europe.

The collapse of Communism in eastern Europe

A demonstrator pounds away at the Berlin Wall as East German border guards look on from above, 4 November 1989. The wall was dismantled five days later.

For most west Europeans now alive, the world has always ended at the East German border and the Wall; beyond lay darkness . . . The opening of the frontiers declares that the world has no edge any more. Europe is becoming once more round and whole.

The *Independent*, November 1989.

FOCUS TASK

How far was Gorbachev responsible for the collapse of Soviet control over eastern Europe?

You are making a documentary film to explain 'The Collapse of the Red Empire in eastern Europe'. The film will be 90 minutes long.

1 Decide what proportion of this time should concentrate on:
 • Solidarity in Poland
 • Gorbachev
 • actions of people in eastern Europe
 • actions of governments in eastern Europe
 • other factors.
2 Choose one of these aspects and summarise the important points, stories, pictures or sources that your film should cover under that heading.
 You may be able to use presentation software to organise and present your ideas.

Reunification of Germany

With the Berlin Wall down, West German Chancellor Helmut Kohl proposed a speedy reunification of Germany. Germans in both countries embraced the idea enthusiastically.

Despite his idealism, Gorbachev was less enthusiastic. He expected that a new united Germany would be more friendly to the West than to the East. But after many months of hard negotiations, not all of them friendly, Gorbachev accepted German reunification and even accepted that the new Germany could become a member of NATO. This was no small thing for Gorbachev to accept. Like all Russians, he lived with the memory that it was German aggression in the Second World War that had cost the lives of 20 million Soviet citizens.

On 3 October 1990, Germany became a united country once again.

The collapse of the USSR

Even more dramatic events were to follow in the Soviet Union itself.

Early in 1990, Gorbachev visited the Baltic state of Lithuania – part of the Soviet Union. Its leaders put their views to him. They were very clear. They wanted independence. They did not want to be part of the USSR. Gorbachev was for once uncompromising. He would not allow this. But in March they did it anyway.

Almost as soon as he returned to Moscow from Lithuania, Gorbachev received a similar demand from the Muslim Soviet Republic of Azerbaijan.

What should Gorbachev do now? He sent troops to Azerbaijan to end rioting there. He sent troops to Lithuania. But as the summer approached, the crisis situation got worse.

Reformers within the USSR itself demanded an end to the Communist Party's domination of government.

In May the Russian Republic, the largest within the USSR, elected Boris Yeltsin as its President. Yeltsin made it clear that he saw no future in a Soviet Union. He said that the many republics that made up the USSR should become independent states.

In July the Ukraine declared its independence. Other republics followed. By the end of 1990 nobody was quite sure what the USSR meant any longer.

In January 1991 events in Lithuania turned to bloodshed as Soviet troops fired on protesters. In April the Republic of Georgia declared its independence.

The USSR was disintegrating. Gorbachev was struggling to hold it together, but members of the Communist elite had had enough. In August 1991 hardline Communist Party members and leading military officers attempted a coup to take over the USSR. The plotters included Gorbachev's Prime Minister, Pavlov, and the head of the armed forces, Dimitry Yazov. They held Gorbachev prisoner in his holiday home in the Crimea. They sent tanks and troops on to the streets of Moscow. This was the old Soviet way to keep control. Would it work this time?

Huge crowds gathered in Moscow. They strongly opposed this military coup. The Russian President, Boris Yeltsin, emerged as the leader of the popular opposition. Faced by this resistance, the conspirators lost faith in themselves and the coup collapsed.

This last-ditch attempt by the Communist Party to save the USSR had failed. A few days later, Gorbachev returned to Moscow. He might have survived the coup, but it had not strengthened his position as Soviet leader. He had to admit that the USSR was finished and he with it.

In a televised speech on 25 December 1991, Gorbachev announced the end of the Soviet Union.

SOURCE 23

Russian President Boris Yeltsin addressing supporters from the top of a tank after the attempted coup of August 1991.

ACTIVITY

1 Draw a horizontal timeline for 1990–91, marking on each month.
2 Annotate the timeline to show the events that led to the break-up of the USSR. Put Gorbachev's actions above the line; other people's actions below the line.
3 Who do you think bears most responsibility for the collapse of the USSR: Gorbachev or other people? Write a paragraph to explain your point of view, supporting it with evidence from your timeline.

SOURCE 24

Mikhail Gorbachev after receiving the Nobel Peace Prize, 15 October 1990.

SOURCE 25

A sense of failure and regret came through his [Gorbachev's] Christmas Day abdication speech – especially in his sorrow over his people 'ceasing to be citizens of a great power'. Certainly, if man-in-the-street interviews can be believed, the former Soviet peoples consider him a failure.

History will be kinder. The Nobel Prize he received for ending the Cold War was well deserved. Every man, woman and child in this country should be eternally grateful.

His statue should stand in the centre of every east European capital; for it was Gorbachev who allowed them their independence. The same is true for the newly independent countries further east and in Central Asia. No Russian has done more to free his people from bondage since Alexander II who freed the serfs.

From a report on Gorbachev's speech, 25 December 1991, in the US newspaper the *Boston Globe*.

FOCUS TASK

Mikhail Gorbachev – hero or villain?

Read Source 25 carefully. Here are three statements from the source.
- *'the former Soviet peoples consider him a failure'*
- *'History will be kinder'.*
- *'His statue should stand in the centre of every east European capital'.*

Do you agree or disagree with each statement? For each statement, write a short paragraph to
a) explain what it means, and
b) express your own view on it.

Glossary

alliance   an agreement where each member country promises to help the other members if they are attacked

Anschluss   the political union of Austria and Germany in 1938

Appeasement   the name given to the policy of attempting to avoid war by making concessions. It is particularly associated with British policy towards Hitler in the 1930s

April Theses   a document by Lenin which he read out to his supporters in Petrograd in April 1917. In it he insisted that Russia should leave the war and continue on the path of revolution by de-recognising the Provisional Government, transferring all power to the soviets and confiscating private land

aristocracy   a nobility or privileged class

autocracy   a system where one person has the power to rule absolutely (without any restrictions), as in Tsarist Russia

blockade   cutting a place off by surrounding it with troops or ships

Bolsheviks   members of the larger group (*see also* Menshevics), led by Lenin, which was formed after the split of the Social Democratic Party in 1903. They believed that Russia was ready for violent revolution

bureaucracy   the officials who are appointed to run a political system

capitalists   the owners of the means of creating wealth, for example landowners

colony   a country which is administered by the government of another country. Officials and many inhabitants often come from the 'mother country' which exploits the colony for its own benefit

conscription   a law requiring all men of a certain age (and sometimes women) to join the armed forces and be available if called to fight at any time

containment   the actions of the US government which, having accepted that eastern Europe was Communist, wanted to prevent Communism from spreading to any other countries

convoy   warships travelling with merchant vessels to protect them

Freikorps   group of anti-Communist ex-soldiers in Germany who joined with the government to fight the Spartacists (revolutionary Communists)

general strike   strike of workers in all or most trades

ghetto   an area where members of a particular racial group are forced or choose to live

guerrilla warfare   the strategy of fighting by small committed groups harassing the enemy, rather than a large army

home rule   the government of a country or region by its own citizens

hunger strike   the refusal of food as a form of protest

isolationist   (believing in) withdrawing from international politics, used especially in relation to American policy towards Europe

mandates   countries governed by another country, appointed to do so by the League of Nations in 1919

Mensheviks   members of the smaller group (*see also* Bolsheviks) which was formed after the split of the Social Democratic Party in Russia in 1903. They believed that Russia was not yet ready for revolution

munitions   military weapons and ammunition

Orthodox   the Christian Church in Russia

plebiscite   a referendum or direct vote on one issue by the population of a country or a region

prohibition   the forbidding by law of the manufacture or sale of alcoholic drinks

reparations   money that Germany was ordered to pay as compensation to the Allies by the Treaty of Versailles in 1919

Siberia   a vast region of the USSR stretching from the Ural Mountains to the Pacific and from the Arctic Ocean to the borders with China and Mongolia

Spartacists   Communist party in Germany who wanted a revolution similar to that which had taken place in Russia

stalemate   a deadlock in a battle situation where neither side makes any progress

tariff   a charge imposed on imports into a country. This makes it more expensive for other nations to export goods into that country, so the prices of their goods are less competitive than home-produced goods

total war   war with no restraints, using every weapon at the combatants' disposal, so affecting civilians rather than just soldiers

tribunal   a body appointed to adjudicate in some disputed matter

veto   the right to block a decision made by others. In the United Nations, any one of the five permanent members of the Security Council can block a decision

Zeppelins   German airships used as observation decks and then bombers in the First World War

Index